W9-BSD-591

Handbook of Counseling *and* Psychotherapy *With* Lesbian, Gay, Bisexual, *and* Transgender Clients

SECOND EDITION

EDITED BY

Kathleen J. Bieschke

Ruperto M. Perez

Kurt A. DeBord

AMERICAN PSYCHOLOGICAL ASSOCIATION • WASHINGTON, DC

Copyright © 2007 by the American Psychological Association. All rights reserved. Except as permitted under the United States Copyright Act of 1976, no part of this publication may be reproduced or distributed in any form or by any means, including, but not limited to, the process of scanning and digitization, or stored in a database or retrieval system, without the prior written permission of the publisher.

Second Printing, June 2007
Third Printing, December 2010

Published by
American Psychological Association
750 First Street, NE
Washington, DC 20002
www.apa.org

To order
APA Order Department
P.O. Box 92984
Washington, DC 20090-2984
Tel: (800) 374-2721; Direct: (202) 336-5510
Fax: (202) 336-5502; TDD/TTY: (202) 336-6123
Online: www.apa.org/books/
E-mail: order@apa.org

In the U.K., Europe, Africa, and the Middle East, copies may be ordered from
American Psychological Association
3 Henrietta Street
Covent Garden, London
WC2E 8LU England

Typeset in Goudy by Apex Publishing LLC, Madison, WI

Printer: Edwards Brothers, Inc., Ann Arbor, MI
Cover Designer: Berg Design, Albany, NY
Project Manager: Apex Publishing LLC, Madison, WI

The opinions and statements published are the responsibility of the authors, and such opinions and statements do not necessarily represent the policies of the American Psychological Association.

Library of Congress Cataloging-in-Publication Data
Handbook of counseling and psychotherapy with lesbian, gay, bisexual, and transgender clients / edited by Kathleen J. Bieschke, Ruperto M. Perez, and Kurt A. DeBord.—2nd ed.
        p.   cm.
    Includes bibliographical references and index.
    ISBN 13: 978–1–59147–421–0
    ISBN 10: 1–59147–421–3
    1. Counseling.   2. Psychotherapy.   3. Lesbians—Counseling of.   4. Gays—Counseling of.   5. Bisexuals—Counseling of.   I. Bieschke, Kathleen J.   II. Perez, Ruperto M.   III. DeBord, Kurt A.
    BF637.C6H3125   2007
    158'.30866—dc22   2006009704

British Library Cataloguing-in-Publication Data
A CIP record is available from the British Library.

Printed in the United States of America
Second Edition

CONTENTS

CONTRIBUTORS

Mary Z. Anderson, PhD, Western Michigan University, Kalamazoo
Julie R. Arseneau, MA, University of Maryland, College Park
Lee Beckstead, PhD, University of Utah, Salt Lake City
Kathleen J. Bieschke, PhD, Pennsylvania State University, State College
Kelly A. Blasko, MA, Pennsylvania State University, State College
James M. Croteau, PhD, Western Michigan University, Kalamazoo
Julie M. Davis, MA, Western Michigan University, Kalamazoo
Kurt A. DeBord, PhD, Lincoln University, Jefferson City, MI
Ruth E. Fassinger, PhD, University of Maryland, College Park
Beth A. Firestein, PhD, Inner Source Psychotherapy and
   Gender Solutions Consulting, Loveland, CO
Ann R. Fischer, PhD, Southern Illinois University, Carbondale
Beverly Greene, PhD, St. John's University, Queens, NY
Douglas C. Haldeman, PhD, University of Washington, Seattle
Stephen C. Halpert, PsyD, Berkeley, CA
Tania Israel, PhD, University of California, Santa Barbara
Shannon Chavez Korell, MA, Pennsylvania State University, University
   Park
Arlene Istar Lev, LCSW, CASAC, Choices Counseling and Consulting,
   Albany, NY
Melissa A. Lidderdale, MA, Western Michigan University, Kalamazoo
Becky J. Liddle, PhD, Ontario Institute for Studies in Education
   of the University of Toronto, Ontario, Canada
Peggy Lorah, DEd, Pennsylvania State University, University Park
Connie R. Matthews, PhD, Pennsylvania State University, University
   Park
Charlotte J. Patterson, PhD, University of Virginia, Charlottesville
Parrish L. Paul, MEd, Pennsylvania State University, State College

Daniel J. Potoczniak, MSEd, University of Florida, Gainesville
Brian Reinhardt, PhD, California State University, East Bay, Hayward
Michael R. Stevenson, PhD, Miami University, Oxford, OH
Michael J. Toohey, PsyD, New Leaf: Services for Our Community,
   San Francisco, CA
Darrick Tovar-Murray, PhD, Illinois State University, Normal

FOREWORD:
THE "COMING OF AGE" OF LESBIAN, GAY, BISEXUAL, AND TRANSGENDER-AFFIRMATIVE PSYCHOLOGY

LINDA GARNETS

In sitting down to write this foreword, I was flooded with memories of my own graduate education. My time in graduate school, from 1971 to 1979, coincided with the years of my coming out as a lesbian. How I wish that there had been a resource like this one to guide my professors, my supervisors, and my therapists in addressing lesbian, gay male, bisexual, and transgender (LGBT) concerns. But I came out when few psychologists questioned the dominant belief that homosexuality was a sign of mental illness.

In my first year of graduate school in 1971, after I had just come out to close friends, my professor in a psychopathology course invited two gay men and two lesbians to talk about their lives. After they left the room, the professor spent the rest of the class pointing out each person's pathology and tying it to his or her gayness. This sent me a powerful message that being lesbian was sick and something I should hide.

Soon after I became involved with my first female partner, I went to see a therapist. He persistently tried to change my sexual orientation. He actively encouraged me to seek out heterosexual relationships, informed me that everything I did with my homosexual lover was "foreplay" and not "real" or "mature" sexuality, told me that I was "developmentally immature" because I was a lesbian, and continually pointed out that all of the problems with my female partner were happening because I was in a lesbian relationship. Now, it is true that there were difficulties in my relationship with Laurie, but because he attributed them all to my being gay, he and I were never able to discuss those problems. Ultimately, when it came down to choosing between my therapist and my lesbian partner—I chose my lover. The net effect of therapy was detrimental. It contributed to my feeling bad about myself, interfered with my being able to reduce my internalized homophobia and come to terms with being a lesbian, and deprived me of support I needed to develop my relational capacities at an important developmental stage in my life.

While in graduate school, I also witnessed the beginning of major paradigm shifts in how professional psychology understood and treated LGB individuals. A significant change occurred in 1973. As a result of political activism and the accumulating empirical evidence that failed to link homosexuality with mental illness or emotional instability, the American Psychiatric Association voted to remove homosexuality per se from its list of mental disorders. I remember the feeling I had when I learned of this vote. I went to bed sick and woke up healthy! It was the quickest cure. The American Psychological Association supported this change and in 1975 adopted a resolution that urged psychologists "to take the lead in removing the stigma of mental illness that has long been associated with homosexual orientations."

So, by the time I graduated in the late 1970s, an affirmative perspective had emerged within psychology to guide research and practice. This model focused on helping LGB people to cope adaptively with the impact of stigma, minority status, and difference from the heterosexual mainstream. This approach assisted LGB individuals in understanding and accepting their sexual orientation as a natural part of themselves, helped them develop strategies for coping and forming a positive sense of identity, and taught them the effect of negative social attitudes, prejudice, and discrimination on psychological functioning.

This book, in contrast to my graduate school experience, represents organized psychology's continued commitment to ensuring that we in the field take the lead in removing the stigma of mental illness and practice ethically and competently. The editors approach this second edition from the perspective of three main themes: (a) the definition and practice of affirmative psychotherapy with LGBT clients, (b) the role of a diverse LGBT community in identity development and social connection, and (c) the growing sociopolitical clout of the LGBT community. I explore each of these themes here by reviewing the major paradigm shifts that have taken place in each of these areas.

DEFINITION AND PRACTICE OF AFFIRMATIVE PSYCHOTHERAPY WITH LGBT CLIENTS

Over the past 30 years, great strides have been made to identify the specific knowledge, skills, and sensitivities necessary to treat LGBT individuals affirmatively and appropriately. Let me highlight some of the critical advances.

The definition and conceptualization of sexual orientation have changed. Professionals increasingly see homosexuality as a natural variant in the development and expression of erotic attractions and commitment. Reliance on a dichotomous model of heterosexual versus homosexual has been replaced by a multidimensional approach that captures the complex nature of men's and women's sexualities and sexual orientations. This has resulted in a greater recognition of bisexuality as a distinct sexual identity and of transgender experience as a distinct gender identity. The editors use this new paradigm by recognizing the great diversity of men's and women's erotic experiences and by emphasizing the many sociocultural factors that shape men's and women's sexuality and sexual orientation across the life span.

Clinical practice with LGB clients has also changed. I cochaired the American Psychological Association task force that surveyed a large and diverse sample of psychologists in 1986. The results suggested that psychologists vary widely in their adherence to a standard of unbiased practices with gay men and lesbians. The research showed that a wide range of negative biases and misinformation about homosexuality persisted that could affect therapy practice.

In September 1991, a special issue of the *American Psychologist* provided affirmative approaches to research, practice, and public policy with LGB clients. More recently, guidelines for psychotherapy with LGB clients were adopted by the American Psychological Association Council of Representatives (2000). In response to the resurgence of conversion therapy, the American Psychological Association Council adopted the Policy of Appropriate Therapeutic Responses to Sexual Orientation (1998) that stressed the need to assess psychological and social contexts in which questioning or discomfort occur.

A new minority stress model has now emerged to understand psychological well-being among LGBT individuals. This model posits that LGBT people may be at increased risk for mental distress due to exposure to stressors related to negative social attitudes. There also has been increased attention to understanding psychological resilience and the ways in which persons successfully cope with stress and stigma.

Although the earlier edition of this handbook laid the groundwork for defining affirmative psychotherapy, the second edition provides specific tools for practitioners. The book articulates the core conditions for affirmative therapy by specifying the attitudes, knowledge, and skill components necessary for counselor competence with LGBT clients. Moreover, the second edition expands the provision of affirmative approaches into the arenas of supervision, work and career counseling, and public policy. It also provides a comprehensive discussion of assessment and treatment issues in working with transgender clients.

In addition to reminding the readers of general principles of ethical practice with this population, the authors present guidelines for addressing sexual orientation conversion therapy. They emphasize a centrally important ethical issue: "Does the valuative framework of conversion therapy proponents cause harm?" They conclude that it does.

This handbook also provides an excellent articulation of best practices in negotiating and clarifying complex ethical dilemmas among those who self-identify in multiple and diverse ways. The editors strived to address how to "be affirmative of sexual and gender orientation while simultaneously honoring other aspects of diversity." The book offers valuable recommendations to help religious LGB clients from various cultural backgrounds to explore their sexual and religious identities, to evaluate their conflicts, and to come to individual resolutions and choices about managing them.

ROLE OF A DIVERSE LGBT COMMUNITY IN IDENTITY DEVELOPMENT AND SOCIAL CONNECTION

A new model of sexual orientation is developing based on multiplicity, not sameness, that examines the overlapping identities and statuses of culture, gender, age, race, ethnicity, class, religion, disability, and sexuality. A central principle of this model is that no single element of identity, be it class, race, gender, or sexual orientation, can truly be understood except in relation to the others. When individuals are forced to separate these aspects of themselves from one another, they experience a sense of alienation. The challenge is to integrate multiple identities, each of which can be disparaged and can work in social disadvantage. The editors, relying on this model, aim to "promote understanding of the multidimensional identities of LGBT persons." Their goal was to be inclusive of issues of diversity within each chapter and to ensure a thoughtful and complex appreciation of context throughout the handbook.

A growing body of research on gender and sexuality has contributed to new perspectives on sexual and gender orientations. For example, there is growing scientific evidence that the nature and development of sexuality and sexual orientation are different for women and men. Girls and women tend to have a relational or partner-centered orientation to sexuality, whereas boys and men tend to have a recreation or body-centered orientation. Recognizing these gender differences, the editors organized the chapters to separately examine the experiences of sexual minority women and men.

Recent research has also questioned the role that gender plays in partner choice. In particular, data about bisexual men and women challenge the old view that gender is the primary criterion for selecting a sexual or romantic partner. The findings suggest that bisexuals seem to be less restricted by gender in their sexual and affectional attraction than heterosexuals, gay men, or lesbians. They appear to attend more to characteristics of the person than to his or her gender. The chapters on bisexual experience point out well the implication of these findings for identity and community development.

The problems inherent in narrow and rigid societal dichotomous definitions of gender have led to a new conceptualization that recognizes that an understanding of sexual orientations needs a better framework for thinking about gender itself. By implication, a perplexing issue is raised—what does it mean to be a "man" or to be a "woman"? Some people view their own gender as potentially changeable and as defying bimodal categories of male versus female and of masculine versus feminine. ~~Transgender~~ is a broad term used to describe the ~~continuum of individuals whose gender identity and expression, to varying degrees, does not correspond with their biological sex~~. There has been a shift in perspective about transgender individuals away from notions of gender pathologies to ones of gender "nonconformity."

The editors recognize the emergence of the transgender community as a political force and recognize how the transgender community is meaningfully connected to the LGB community. Authors emphasize the complexities of sexuality and gender, including the conflating of homosexuality and gender variance in the process of the medicalization of sex and gender. Complex ethical dilemmas are described, dilemmas raised by many mental health providers' dual roles of "counselor" and "evaluator."

GROWING SOCIOPOLITICAL CLOUT OF THE LGBT COMMUNITY

A gay and lesbian rights movement was launched in the United States in 1969 on the heels of the powerful civil rights and feminist movements. Overall, this movement has helped to identify sources of bias against sexual minorities, worked to change social institutions that maintain the marginality of LGBT people, and fostered a collective identity among LGBT individuals as members of a minority group.

In addition to actual civil rights gains, the involvement of members of the LGBT community has facilitated decreased stigma and increased empowerment and self-esteem. On balance, the struggle for nondiscrimination laws and against right-wing views of so-called traditional marriage and family values has been positive in terms of mental health and personal growth of LGBT individuals. The movement has identified the problem—it is not sexual orientation; it is bigotry, hatred, and prejudice. This handbook weaves the role of community into the identity models that are presented, stressing how community building enhances resiliency, psychological empowerment, and well-being.

The editors stress that affirmation for LGBT clients "extends beyond the therapy hour." They remind all of us that we as psychologists and as members of professional associations can continue to contribute to social progress for LGBT people by playing multiple roles. LGBT affirmation must be present in the training and supervision of students and in social advocacy activities. The editors offer a rationale and description of possible roles in advocating for the LGBT community—content experts, role models, and witnesses. Each of these roles may help to maintain the mental health of LGBT clients. In these ways, psychologists can continue the tradition of empowerment started by members of LGBT communities and by organized psychology.

This invaluable resource strongly encourages that greater attention be placed on ensuring that LGBT-affirmative concepts are fully integrated into current personality theories and therapy approaches; that education, training, ethical and professional guidelines, and research are used to reduce bias in theories and practice; and that the promotion and dissemination of empirical testing of LGBT-affirmative models and theories continue.

ACKNOWLEDGMENTS

The ink on the first edition of the *Handbook of Counseling and Psychotherapy With Lesbian, Gay, and Bisexual Clients* was barely dry when we began to discuss the possibility of a second edition. After initiating a readership survey of those who had read and used the first edition of this handbook, we spent an entire year discussing a new structure, only to abandon it during one of our highly interactive weekly phone conferences. To truly capture what we believed to be the most important contemporary issues for lesbian, gay, bisexual, and transgender (LGBT) psychology, we returned to the drawing board. After much brainstorming, we created the current structure and focus for this edition. The second edition of the handbook reflects our collective vision of LGBT-affirmative psychotherapy—contextual, developmental, culturally sensitive, and infused with the thoughtful application of skills and attention to social advocacy concerns. Simply identifying the factors that account for our collective vision reminds us of how frequently we discuss the underlying themes of the book and how fortunate we are to have the opportunity to work on this project. Although the work has been, to say the least, demanding, what we have gained has been invaluable.

Our authors are truly exceptional. Without a doubt, we have learned something from each one, and we are profoundly grateful. We believe that as a group of contributors, they would describe us as demanding and maybe even unrelenting. In light of that, we very much appreciate their willingness to persevere. More so, we admire their dedication to this work. These contributions reflect the expertise and commitment of the authors to the provision of LGBT-affirmative counseling and psychotherapy.

We also wish to express our appreciation to the Books Department of the American Psychological Association, particularly Susan Reynolds and Ed Meidenbauer. As an editing team, the three of us can be a force of nature (that's what happens after 10 years of working together), and both Susan and Ed weathered the storm nicely. Susan was appropriately patient with us as we struggled to finish the book on time; her encouragement resulted in a far better initial manuscript. Ed (along with two reviewers) provided us with excellent feedback about the first draft of the book. The subsequent revision is very much a reflection of Ed's thoughtful distillation of reviewers' comments as well as his own. Most specifically, we owe the inclusion of "transgender" in the title of the book to Ed; we were split on whether to include it in the title (see the Introduction for a detailed description of this decision), and Ed's objective assessment tipped the scales in favor of inclusion.

Two of us worked closely with a research team throughout this process, and these teams' editorial comments and perspectives were invaluable. Many thanks to Kelly Blasko, Jodi Boita, Parrish Paul, and Shanti Pepper from Penn State University and to Tiffany Graham, Melinda Goodman, Brian Mistler, Daniel Potoczniak, and Jacob van den Berg from the University of Florida for their assistance in reviewing early chapter drafts and providing thoughtful and helpful feedback. Thanks to colleagues at the University of Florida Counseling Center for their support in the development of this edition. Also, thanks to the University of Missouri Counseling Center staff for providing valuable insights and opportunities for discussions regarding the development of this book.

In addition, we are grateful to those people in our lives who are a constant source of support. In particular, Kathy Bieschke would like to thank Daryl Gregory, Kelly Blasko, and Parrish Paul for their steadfast support, ability to discuss a topic from an infinite number of perspectives, and patient acceptance of what at times seemed to be an unending process. Kurt DeBord would like to thank Wayne Mayfield, Mara Aruguete, and Walter Cal Johnson for their support and willingness to discuss this project for 5 years. Toti Perez would like to thank Bella Perez, Stephen Cook, Steve Brown, Kitty Uzes, Lynne Reeder, Martha White, Diana Tomlinson, Steven Kaye, Kip Matthews, Jill Barber, and Angela Londoño-McConnell for their constant support and encouragement.

Finally, we are all grateful we have had this opportunity to work with one another. We agree that our working relationship is unique, given the depth of our conversations, the extent to which we challenge one another, and the ways in which we share the workload. Not only are our weekly conversations sources of professional development and engagement, but we also have seen each other through the twists and turns of each of our lives. Few professional relationships have been as deeply satisfying and meaningful as this one.

Handbook of Counseling *and* Psychotherapy
With Lesbian, Gay, Bisexual, *and* Transgender Clients

INTRODUCTION: THE CHALLENGE OF PROVIDING AFFIRMATIVE PSYCHOTHERAPY WHILE HONORING DIVERSE CONTEXTS

KATHLEEN J. BIESCHKE, RUPERTO M. PEREZ, AND KURT A. DeBORD

What does it mean to be affirmative of lesbian, gay, bisexual, and transgender (LGBT) clients? And how can therapists and scholars engage in counseling and research practice that reflects these clients' affirmation? At first glance the answers to these questions may appear to be straightforward. The American Psychological Association (APA) and other mental health organizations (the American Psychiatric Association and the American Counseling Association) have supported the provision of affirmative interventions and have issued resolutions (e.g., DeLeon, 1998) and guidelines (e.g., APA, Division 44/Committee on Lesbian, Gay, and Bisexual Concerns Joint Task Force, 2000) encouraging such affirmation. Yet there is some indication (see Bieschke, Croteau, Lark, & Vandiver, 2004) that the level of affirmation of LGBT individuals and clients is shallow, oversimplified, and noninclusive. In other words, even though many counselors and psychologists profess that "it's okay to be gay," knowledge regarding how to meaningfully integrate that understanding into work with clients is lacking. We believe that responding to the question of how to infuse LGBT affirmation into the provision of mental health services deserves a complex answer, and the second edition of the *Handbook of Counseling and Psychotherapy With Lesbian, Gay, Bisexual, and Transgender Clients* represents an attempt to do just that.

In many ways, the goals of this edition of the handbook are similar to those of the first edition (Perez, DeBord, & Bieschke, 2000). In the first edition, we attempted to provide readers with contextual information relative to social, historical, and developmental factors for LGB clients. We focused on the provision of services to LGB clients, and we provided information about emerging content areas of particular relevance to providers of mental health services. We sought to base our recommendations on the very best science available, and we encouraged authors to incorporate empirical data whenever possible. Our hope was that both practitioners and scholars would find the handbook useful.

Yet for those familiar with the first edition of the handbook, even a cursory appraisal of the current edition will lead to the conclusion that this is a very different book. The impetus for the change in organizational structure and scope of content was initially due to what seemed to be an explosion of empirical literature and scholarly thought focused on LGBT individuals (Goldfried, 2001; Perez, chap. 17, this volume). As we began to discuss the implications for the book of the existing literature, we became aware that the American sociopolitical climate for LGBT individuals was shifting, often in ways we could not predict. For example, we were struck by how the political visibility of LGB people had increased in tandem with increased oppression (see Patterson, chap. 15, this volume; Stevenson, chap. 16, this volume, for further detail about this phenomenon). In addition, we were becoming increasingly aware of the transgender community as a political force and of how the transgender community was meaningfully connected to the LGB community. After a full year of discussion, we recognized that this changing landscape might be best addressed by emphasizing and fostering an understanding of the LGBT population within the context of community while also addressing the specific issues for LGBT clients in counseling and psychotherapy. Our goal is to promote understanding of the multidimensional identities of LGBT persons. This goal is most evident in the book's first section, which explicitly emphasizes an understanding of the LGBT population as a whole as well as an understanding of the subpopulations within (e.g., bisexual men, bisexual women, lesbians, gay men, and transgender individuals). Yet all of our authors in the other two sections also incorporate thoughtful and complex appreciation of context into their approaches to their chapters.

Further, this edition of the handbook reflects our recognition that psychotherapists and counselors may vary widely in regard to their levels of affirmation of LGBT clients, because of personal characteristics, training backgrounds, and professional role models. Although we maintain, however, that all psychologists must develop the capacity to provide effective and affirmative counseling or psychotherapy to all clients, we also believe that simply giving psychologists and counselors a mandate to be affirmative is ineffective. This edition of the handbook attempts to provide readers, including those who identify as LGBT, with the tools to develop their affirmation for LGBT individuals and clients in complex and meaningful ways. We believe that the path to affirmation begins with the realization that as members of a heterosexist society, all of us, regardless of sexual orientation, bring our heterosexual biases into our work as counselors and therapists.

Finally, this edition of the handbook also reflects our belief that affirmation for LGBT clients extends beyond the therapy hour. LGBT affirmation is not a piece of clothing one can take on and off at will. Rather, we contend that affirmation for LGBT individuals must be present during each and every therapy hour, not only when counselors or psychotherapists are seeing an LGBT client. Further, LGBT affirmation must also be present when such professionals are training students or engaging in social advocacy activities. Manifestation of LGBT affirmation will not look the same for everyone. This edition of the handbook is intended to provide readers with the opportunity to meaningfully explore how it will look for them.

We determined that some aspects of the first handbook should be present in the second. As in the first edition, we strive here to represent a spectrum of unique perspectives that come together thematically. We adopted a structure in which a variety of authors could voice their perspectives while the overall book maintained a comprehensive and unified feel. We wanted to be inclusive of issues of diversity within each chapter, which includes paying attention to the social and political issues that influence LGBT clients and their communities (e.g., the intersection of religion and sexual orientation). Finally, though LGBT psychology continues to develop, it is still a relatively young field. Therefore, empirical findings are often scarce. We urged authors to incorporate empirical evidence into their chapters whenever possible. As a result, each chapter reflects dedicated effort and thoughtful scholarship as well as patience with a demanding editorial team. Our hope is that both practitioners and scholars will find this book useful.

THE INCLUSION OF TRANSGENDER CLIENTS

One of the aspects that we discussed the most was how best to include in the book issues of importance to transgender individuals. To us it seemed clear that understanding transgender individuals is essential to understanding the LGB community. We had all noticed the frequency with which transgender individuals were being included, at least nominally, in references to the LGB population via the acronym LGBT. We were in agreement that we wanted to explain to our readers (and to ourselves) how transgender individuals functioned as part of and in relation to the LGB community. Finally, we wanted to foster understanding about how mental health services might be best provided, thus reducing the bias these individuals encounter from mental health professionals.

We began this edition of the handbook with varying levels of knowledge regarding the transgender population, and we were concerned about our ability to effectively edit chapters focused on this population. Similarly, we wondered whether our authors would be capable of meaningfully including content pertaining to the transgender population, given limitations regarding expertise as well as page constraints. Considering that sexual orientation and gender identity are not interchangeable constructs, we debated whether it was even possible to achieve such integration. Further, we were fearful that superficial inclusion would maintain rather than reduce the marginalization of transgender individuals. So we initially agreed to proceed with inclusion of content about transgender individuals, but we stopped short of including the term *transgender* in the title of the book or mandating inclusion in each chapter. We agreed that though the content we planned to include (see Fassinger & Arseneau, chap. 1, this volume; Korell & Lorah, chap. 11, this volume; Lev, chap. 6, this volume) was substantive, there was simply not enough of it to justify the inclusion of the term *transgender* in the title, particularly given the handbook function of this volume.

As work on the book progressed, we revisited this decision several times. We recognized that by not choosing to include transgender in the title, we would be masking the contents of the book to potential readers interested in learning about this population. We became painfully aware that we had not debated the decision to include the term *bisexual* in the first issue of the handbook, despite having relatively little content devoted to either bisexual women or bisexual men. This prompted us to examine how our own biases were evident in the construction of this volume. We also struggled with how this decision limited our ability to act as advocates for this population. Inclusion in the title would provide transgender individuals with some measure of recognition and legitimacy within the psychological community. Simultaneously, our initial misgivings continued about the lack of content present in the book. Although matters pertaining to the transgender community are meaningfully included in this volume, we were well aware that the information contained in the book was not sufficient for working with or applicable to all transgender clients, and we were concerned that lack of more meaningful inclusion might be perceived as marginalization of this population.

As is evident, we ultimately decided to include the term transgender in the title of the book. We very much appreciate the extremely useful consultation we received from staff at APA, our chapter authors, and members of the transgender community. Although some aspects of this decision will no doubt be criticized, we are in agreement that inclusion is consistent with our goals for this edition of the handbook. Our only regret is that we did not make this decision at the outset so that we could provide our authors with the opportunity to meaningfully include this population in their chapters. Regardless, we are hopeful that the content provided will prompt readers to pursue more training in how to best work with the transgender population.

THE CHALLENGE OF AFFIRMATION WITHIN THE CONTEXT OF DIVERSITY

Part of the challenge of providing LGBT-affirmative counseling and psychotherapy begins with gaining a deeper understanding of what LGBT-affirmative therapy is and how it may manifest with clients. Existing definitions tend to reflect more of an attitude than a set of behaviors or specific instructions (e.g., Chernin & Johnson, 2003; Tozer & McClanahan, 1999). For example, Tozer and McClanahan (1999) stated that an affirmative therapist "celebrates and advocates the authenticity and integrity of lesbian, gay, and bisexual persons and their relationships" (p. 736). Recently, however, Israel and her colleagues (Israel, Ketz, Detrie, Burke, & Shulman, 2003) have identified, via a modified Delphi technique, a comprehensive list of attitudes, knowledge, and skill components that collectively constitute counselor competence with LGB clients. This effort reflects an important shift in LGB-affirmative psychotherapy, one that entails increasing specificity and complexity.

As stated earlier, this book is our effort to define LGBT-affirmative psychotherapy. Our collective vision of LGBT-affirmative psychotherapy is that it is contextual, developmental, and culturally sensitive. Further, only with a deep appreciation of this context can therapists effectively work with clients. LGBT-affirmative psychotherapy is not solely focused on understanding the client, however. Engaging in such work necessitates meaningful self-exploration on the part of therapists (regardless of sexual orientation) to determine how heterosexist biases may manifest in their work with clients as well as in other professional activities.

We also want to emphasize that the act of celebrating all aspects of a client's identity may at times feel less like a party and more like a wake. In other words, striving to be affirmative of sexual and gender orientation while simultaneously honoring other aspects of diversity can be challenging, difficult, and heartbreaking. We think it is important to acknowledge the conflicts that clients and psychologists might encounter. Further, we think accepting the ambiguity inherent in these conflicts is important because wrestling with apparent value conflicts that sometimes arise can often lead to more honest dialogues and the generation of creative solutions. Though we have attempted to instill each chapter with this perspective, three chapters address this challenge directly (Beckstead & Israel, chap. 9, this volume; Bieschke, Paul, & Blasko, chap. 12, this volume; Fischer & DeBord, chap. 13, this volume). All of these chapters highlight the complex issues faced by individuals whose identities are in conflict. After analyzing these chapters, readers will likely come to the conclusion that these challenges seem to be most present when issues of religious identity conflict with issues of sexual orientation. The authors of these chapters provide perspectives that are at least thought-provoking and perhaps even revolutionary at times.

Consistent with our emphasis on context, the first section is intended to provide readers with an understanding of the social, political, and historical cultural contexts within which LGBT individuals develop. The second section moves to a more specific focus on the delivery of services to this population. The final section highlights emerging issues pertinent to the LGBT population that, though not explicitly related to service delivery, have the potential to facilitate equitable and affirmative treatment of LGBT individuals. Although it is not necessary to read the chapters in order, doing so will facilitate a comprehensive understanding of delivering services to LGBT individuals.

Part I: Essential Considerations of Cultural Contexts in Working With Lesbian, Gay, Bisexual, and Transgender Clients

As reflected in the title, the purpose of this section is to provide readers with a context for understanding the LGBT population. In the first chapter, Fassinger and Arseneau provide the foundation for this section, and indeed the entire book. Their purpose is to provide a framework for understanding the differences and similarities that exist among LGBT individuals through focus on contextual conditions (i.e., temporal influences and gender, sexual, and cultural orientations) and developmental arenas (i.e., personal, interpersonal, social, sociopolitical). Fassinger and Arseneau discuss the LGBT community as a whole, but we are convinced that knowing something about each specific community can help counselors understand the values, resources, and influences that shape LGBT lives. The remaining five chapters in this section focus on some of the subpopulations contained within the LGBT population: lesbian women (Liddle, chap. 2, this volume), gay men (Haldeman, chap. 3, this volume), bisexual women (Firestein, chap. 4, this volume), bisexual men (Potoczniak, chap. 5, this volume), and transgender individuals (Lev, chap. 6, this volume). Each of these chapters addresses historical influences on the development of these communities and highlights the themes of resilience and defiance threaded throughout the community as a whole. One need not read the first section of the book prior to reading chapters contained within the other sections. We believe, however, that doing so will provide readers with a foundation that will foster a deeper understanding of the material presented in subsequent chapters.

Part II: Affirmative Counseling and Psychotherapy With Lesbian, Gay, Bisexual, and Transgender Clients

In this section, readers are provided with a broad overview of how best to provide affirmative counseling and psychotherapy to LGBT individuals. Each of the authors attends to the role of context within the process of counseling and psychotherapy. Issues specific to transgender clients are not integrated throughout this section. Readers will undoubtedly notice that these chapters are not population-specific (with the exception of the chapter focused on transgender clients); we have chosen instead to focus our attention on issues that are likely to manifest themselves when therapists work with all LGBT clients.

The first three chapters in this section focus on the wide range of possibilities psychotherapists may encounter when working with LGB clients. Ethical concerns often associated with contextual issues (e.g., heterosexism, multiple identities, conversion therapy) are discussed in Greene's chapter (chap. 7, this volume). Her thoughtful examination of these issues provides readers a perspective that they may wish to incorporate into their approach to working with LGB clients. Matthews's chapter (chap. 8, this volume) emphasizes the importance of being affirmative with all clients, even those who may not currently identify or present as lesbian, gay, or bisexual. Matthews goes on to discuss how to work with clients who may best be described as having a normative coming out experience or who have already come to accept their sexual orientation. Beckstead and Israel (chap. 9, this volume) focus on how psychotherapists may work with clients who are in conflict regarding sexual orientation issues, typically as to the relation to religious or racial identity. Attending to workplace issues is a concern for the vast majority of LGBT clients, and Lidderdale, Croteau, Anderson, Tovar-Murray, and Davis (chap. 10, this volume) provide a comprehensive theoretical model intended to guide theory and interventions regarding sexual identity management in the workplace. This section concludes with a chapter by Korell and Lorah (chap. 11, this volume), who provide a comprehensive overview of counseling and psychotherapy with transgender individuals.

Part III: Emerging Issues in Counseling and Psychotherapy

The third section focuses on those topics of interest to counselors and psychologists that may inform their approach to working with LGB clients. Transgender clients are addressed only intermittently throughout this section. Further, and though this was not our initial intention, the authors of these chapters all devote some portion of their chapters to issues of social advocacy.

As in the first edition of the handbook, Bieschke, Paul, and Blasko (chap. 12, this volume) begin this section with a critical examination of the empirical literature focused on the provision of counseling and psychotherapy to LGB clients. These authors were surprised to find that a significant proportion of the research was focused on conversion therapy. Their chapter attempts to provide a critical and unbiased critique of these findings as well as recommendations for practice based on this review. Similarly, Patterson's chapter on family concerns (chap. 15, this volume) and Stevenson's chapter on public policy (chap. 16, this volume) are influenced by what seems to be a bewildering array of changes in the LGB political landscape; both of these chapters are informative and highlight the importance of staying abreast of the ever-changing context in which LGBT individuals live. Fischer and DeBord's chapter (chap. 13, this volume) tackles what may appear to be an insurmountable challenge of affirming both religious and sexual orientation diversity. Their application of a feminist, ethical decision-making model to this conflict provides the reader with guidance for considering this issue as a trainer and as a therapist. Halpert, Reinhardt, and Toohey's chapter (chap. 14, this volume) focuses explicitly on training. Specifically, these authors synthesize current supervision theory into an accessible and useful model of affirmative clinical supervision. Finally, Perez concludes this section by providing an informed perspective on the state of LGB scholarship. Further, he addresses the themes that emerge from the book as a whole as he discusses the implications of these themes for research, training, and practice.

CONCLUSION

With the second edition of this handbook, our goal was to go beyond the scope of information and topics presented in the first edition. Our hope is that this book will promote practice and scholarship that attend to the contexts within which affirmation occurs in the counseling and psychotherapy process. Authentic engagement in affirmation necessitates acknowledgment of the multiple realities and identities that LGBT clients experience as well as careful consideration of how counselors and psychotherapists function as part of the context. Although the process of understanding and engaging in affirmation is not easy, we believe that a deeper understanding and appreciation of what it means to be an LGBT individual can only result in these clients' receiving the competent, ethical, and affirmative services they deserve.

REFERENCES

American Psychological Association, Division 44/Committee on Lesbian, Gay, and Bisexual Concerns Joint Task Force on Guildelines for Psychotherapy With Lesbian, Gay, and Bisexual Clients. (2000). Guidelines for psychotherapy with lesbian, gay, and bisexual clients. *American Psychologist, 55,* 1440–1451.

Bieschke, K. J., Croteau, J. M., Lark, J. S., & Vandiver, B. J. (2004). Toward a discourse of sexual orientation equity in the counseling professions. In J. M. Croteau, J. S. Lark, M. Lidderdale, & Y. B. Chung (Eds.), *Deconstructing heterosexism in the counseling professions: Multicultural narrative voices* (pp. 189–210). Thousand Oaks, CA: Sage.

Chernin, J. N., & Johnson, M. R. (2003). *Affirmative psychotherapy and counseling for lesbians and gay men.* Thousand Oaks, CA: Sage.

DeLeon, P. H. (1998). Proceedings of the American Psychological Association, Incorporated, for the legislative year 1997: Minutes of the Annual Meeting of the Council of Representatives, August 14 and 17, Chicago, Illinois; and June, August, and December 1997 meetings of the Board of Directors. *American Psychologist, 53,* 882–939.

Goldfried, M. R. (2001). Integrating gay, lesbian, bisexual issues into mainstream psychology. *American Psychologist, 56,* 977–988.

Israel, T., Ketz, K., Detrie, P. M., Burke, M. C., & Shulman, J. L. (2003). Identifying counselor competencies for working with lesbian, gay, and bisexual clients. *Journal of Gay & Lesbian Psychotherapy, 7,* 3–21.

Perez, R. M., Debord, K. A., Bieschke, K. J. (Eds.). (2000). *Handbook of counseling and psychotherapy with lesbian, gay, and bisexual clients.* Washington, DC: American Psychological Association.

Tozer, E., & McClanahan, M. (1999). Treating the purple menace: Ethical considerations of conversion therapy and affirmative alternatives. *The Counseling Psychologist, 27,* 722–742.

I

ESSENTIAL CONSIDERATIONS OF CULTURAL CONTEXTS IN WORKING WITH LESBIAN, GAY, BISEXUAL, AND TRANSGENDER CLIENTS

INTRODUCTION: ESSENTIAL CONSIDERATIONS OF CULTURAL CONTEXTS IN WORKING WITH LESBIAN, GAY, BISEXUAL, AND TRANSGENDER CLIENTS

Communities are critical to identity. McCarn and Fassinger (1996) underscored the fundamental relationship between community and identity when they proposed a model for lesbian identity development. This model recognized identification with one's group as one of the two basic processes in overall personal development. In our work with clients, trainees, and the public, we have been struck repeatedly by the validity of McCarn and Fassinger's model. In fact, whenever we are asked to provide a referral for a lesbian, gay, bisexual, or transgender (LGBT) client, one specific question usually follows: "Does the counselor know anything about the LGBT or LGB community?" Why does this question so consistently follow the request for a referral? It is because community is critically important in providing the support and challenges that make LGBT identity formation possible. The chapters in this section explore and support this assertion with great detail. The authors in this section insightfully articulate the commonalities and unique qualities that define the lesbian, gay, bisexual female, bisexual male, and transgender communities.

In chapter 1, Fassinger and Arseneau introduce a conceptual model that effectively allows researchers and practitioners to simultaneously consider how LGBT similarities and differences in "identity enactment" occur over time in four major developmental arenas. Their model provides a tool with which to form provocative questions and shape potential responses with regard to gender, sexual orientation, and culture. Although the authors are careful and thoughtful in their consideration of the complexities that separate lesbian, gay, bisexual, and transgender communities, they are daringly bold and exacting in their claim that "all LGBT people are 'gender transgressive sexual minorities'" (Fassinger & Arseneau, chap. 1, this volume).

Readers of this chapter will undoubtedly be challenged to reconsider their conceptions of how and why LGBT communities fit together.

Chapter 2 is the first of five chapters to delve deeply and specifically into one specific part of the LGBT community. Liddle examines the lives of lesbian women and the factors that influence their community ties and identity formation, including race, age, disability, spirituality, and family choices. Liddle includes in her chapter a combination of empirical evidence and illustrative examples to reveal the complexities of lesbian lives in a way that facilitates the development of more multifaceted, and therefore more accurate, working models for practitioners who serve this population.

Haldeman begins chapter 3 on gay male communities with a list of criteria describing what defines a community. After identifying how gay men have affiliated in ways that meet these criteria, Haldeman outlines the evolution of gay male communities during the past few decades in the United States. Haldeman's chronological approach incorporates discussion of the diversity that has characterized, enriched, and transformed the gay male community to this day. He ends with thought-provoking discussions about the future of the gay male community and about the costs and benefits of assimilation into "mainstream" American culture.

Bisexual members of the LGBT community, by their very existence, challenge simplistic notions of sexual orientation, identity development, and what it means to forge connections with communities of support. In chapter 4, which focuses on bisexual women, Firestein elaborates upon how bisexual women creatively, and often fluidly, define themselves in ways that allow for positive mental health and relationships that crisscross diverse community boundaries. Firestein provides extensive treatment of the therapeutic implications of the empirical work she reviews.

Chapter 5 is devoted to the exploration of bisexual men's psychosocial and historical contexts. First, Potoczniak briefly reviews the role that bisexual men have played in the history of the sexual minority sociopolitical movement. He then articulates how biphobia, present in both the straight and the gay communities, negatively affects the psychological well-being of bisexual men, with an emphasis on the destructive consequences of internalization of biphobia. Subsequently, Potoczniak reviews four models of bisexual-identity development and describes the models' relation to psychotherapeutic interventions.

The final chapter in this section, "Transgender Communities: Developing Identity Through Connection," by Arlene Istar Lev, identifies how and why transgender people, their issues, and their communities are of fundamental relevance to LGB communities. Lev explicates basic terminology for those who are unfamiliar with the transgender community. She also sketches the history of transgender people in the United States, making clear the astounding psychological resilience transgender people have evinced in light of the complicated and tense political dynamics that surround gender, sexual orientation, and personal identity in the medical community and the society at large. Lev concludes with a consideration of the current state of transgender communities and how their progress can be enhanced by the erasure of prejudice and misunderstandings and by the further establishment of online virtual communities.

When counselors, psychologists, or mental health providers sit down with an LGBT client, they should know something about the social, political, and historical context from which the client is coming. Alternately, if an LGBT client is unaffiliated with an LGBT community, counselors should be prepared to intelligently discuss the community resources that are available to said client. These chapters provide the foundations for just such work.

REFERENCE

McCarn, S. R., & Fassinger, R. E. (1996). Revisioning sexual minority identity formation: A new model of lesbian identity and its implications. *Counseling Psychologist, 24,* 508–534.

1

"I'D RATHER GET WET THAN BE UNDER THAT UMBRELLA": DIFFERENTIATING THE EXPERIENCES AND IDENTITIES OF LESBIAN, GAY, BISEXUAL, AND TRANSGENDER PEOPLE

RUTH E. FASSINGER AND JULIE R. ARSENEAU

Sexual minorities—typically classified into the four categories of lesbian, gay, bisexual, and transgender (LGBT) people—face common struggles with societal oppression related to their sexual minority status, and they therefore face similar difficulties in developing positive individual identities and healthy communities within that context of oppression. The increasingly frequent addition of "T" to "LGB" speaks to the public—and professional—conflation of all sexual minority concerns under a shared umbrella of invisibility, isolation, and discrimination. However, there are particular dimensions of experience that differentiate these four sexual minority groups in important ways, shaping group-specific trajectories for the development and enactment of identity (for the purposes of this discussion, we refer to these as between-group differences). Moreover, the sociocultural context for sexual minority identity-related experiences is complicated by diverse demographic locations related to such factors as gender, race and ethnicity, social class, religion, disability, and age, further particularizing individual experiences even within groups characterized by the same sexual minority status (thus referred to as within-group differences). This chapter addresses differences between and within LGBT groups of people, with the ultimate aim of focusing practice (e.g., counseling and therapy, education, training, advocacy) more sharply. For example, psychotherapy with a female same-sex couple in which one woman labels as lesbian and the other as bisexual will be most effective if the therapist understands and addresses possible differences in the experiences and self-perceptions of the two clients. Similarly, professional training in advocacy regarding sexual minority issues can be enhanced by increasing trainee awareness of the marginalization of transgender people in existing legal and policy initiatives.

We begin, however, with a caveat about discussing sexual minority population groupings as if they were distinguishable, homogeneous entities with an indisputable sociosexual identity existing across time and place. A core issue in the discussion of both gender and sexual orientation is the extent to which they are viewed as "essential" aspects of humanness (i.e., possessing some irrefutable essence based on biological, physiological, genetic, or evolutionary reality, and thus manifested across cultures and historical time) or as "socially constructed" (i.e., formed out of collective societal assumptions, beliefs, and expectations regarding gendered and sexual preferences and behaviors, and thus constituting cultural and historical artifacts; see Fassinger, 2000). Using sexual orientation as an example, most contemporary scholars acknowledge the possibility of some genetic, biological, and physiological influences on the development of sexual orientation (e.g., see Diamond's [2004] claim regarding hormonal links to gender differences in sexual orientation), supporting at least quasi-essentialist interpretations of this human characteristic. However, the social construction of sexual orientation as an identity is difficult to ignore, given that the articulation of an identity attached to widespread cross-cultural, cross-historical same-sex behavior is a largely Euro-American phenomenon of the past 150 years (Greenberg, 1988; Whelehan, 2001). Moreover, the debate over essentialist versus social-constructionist views of sexual orientation is not merely linguistic quibbling, but is embedded in a sociopolitical reality in which essentialist causation theories are invoked in legal and political actions aimed at challenging oppression based on these identity statuses (i.e., using "protected class" arguments in civil rights legislation and hate-crimes legislation; D'Augelli, 1994). The opposing perspectives also probably represent fundamental differences in individual core values and worldviews, manifested in both the ferocity of the debate and its linkage to moral judgments; Wren (2002), for example, found that parental belief in biological causes of transgenderism (an essentialist attribution) was associated with parents' more benign view of their adolescent child, implying greater support for deviant behavior that was perceived as beyond the control of the person exhibiting the behavior.

Even if the essentialist-versus-constructivist debate could be resolved, the grouping of identities related to gender and sexuality into four (and only four) categories is itself problematic (Bohan, 1996; Fassinger, 2000). Contemporary scholars believe human sexuality to be characterized by a continuum rather than by discrete categories, a continuum in which biological, physiological, and genetic contributions combine to determine an individual's ascribed or claimed sex, whereas gender expression, sexuality, and sexual behavior constitute fluid, dynamic processes in which that individual engages (e.g., Fausto-Sterling, 1998). Aspects of sexual identity can include affectional and intimate preferences and attachments, gender identity, social sex roles, sexual behaviors, erotic fantasies, sexual and emotional arousal patterns, self-identification, lifestyle, community, disclosure, political commitments, social preferences, and consistency or change over time (e.g., Gonsiorek, 1995; Klein, 1993; Peplau & Garnets, 2000; Rothblum, 1994, 2000a; Stearns, 1995). The complex interactions of these factors are unlikely to sort into narrow, rigid categorizations. Thus, our discussion of between- and within-group differences in LGBT populations necessitates surrender to an inadequate, limiting classification system, and we devote much of this chapter to interrogating and deconstructing these categories even as we attempt to describe them. For the purposes of this chapter, we acknowledge the following delimited but commonly accepted LGBT group definitions (borrowed, in part, from Bohan).

1. Lesbians—Women whose primary emotional, erotic, and relational preferences are same-sex (homophilic) and for whom some aspect of their self-labeling acknowledges these same-sex attachments; designation as lesbian refers to the sex of one's (actual or imagined) intimate partner choices, not gender expression, which may take a variety of forms.

2. Gay men—Men whose primary emotional, erotic, and relational preferences are same-sex (homophilic) and for whom some aspect of their self-labeling acknowledges these same-sex attachments; designation as gay refers to the sex of one's (actual or imagined) intimate partner choices, not gender expression, which may take a variety of forms.

3. Bisexual women and men—Individuals whose emotional, erotic, and relational preferences are toward both same- and other-sex individuals, either serially or simultaneously, and for whom some aspect of their self-labeling acknowledges the same-sex attachments; designation as bisexual refers to the sex(es) of one's (actual or imagined) intimate partner choices, not gender expression, which may take a variety of forms.

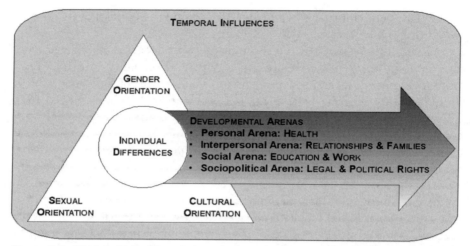

Figure 1.1. Model of identity enactment of gender-transgressive sexual minorities.

4. ~~Transgender people~~—Individuals who are gender-variant or gender-"transgressive,"[1] that is, expressing their gender in ways not considered socially "appropriate" based on their (perceived) biological sex; also referred to as "gender-bending/ blending," gender transgression can range from matters of dress and mannerisms to hormone treatments and reconstructive surgery aimed at changing one's genitalia or secondary sex characteristics to fit one's own sense of one's gender. Designation as transgender (or any of its variants) refers to gender expression, not the sex of one's (actual or imagined) intimate partner choices; transgender people may identify as lesbian, gay, bisexual, or heterosexual, and self-labeling may change over time.

The inadequacy of these group definitions (and any other socially imposed terminology) is revealed by the complexities of self-labeling regarding gender expression and sexual orientation. For example, a woman who is in her first relationship with a woman may self-label strongly as a lesbian even though all of her previous partners have been men; she also may self-label as "stone butch" if she is highly traditionally masculinized in her gender expression. Her current female partner may self-label as bisexual even if she previously has had relationships with women only; she also may self-label as "femme" if she is quite conventionally feminine in her gender

---

[1] We deliberately use the word *transgressive* here to denote the conscious defiance of societal norms that are often cloaked in a rhetoric of morality and sin and to connote the strength required for such deviance. We also note our choice of *transgender* as the most inclusive term to describe the full range of gender-variant identifications (including those who undergo surgery to change gender and technically are transsexual).

expression. A man whose sexual partners are exclusively male and whose gender expression is extremely stereotypically masculine may not self-label as gay; in fact, much contemporary safe-sex education uses labels such as "men who have sex with men" (MSM) in order to target men whose same-sex sexual behavior does not necessarily result in self-labeling as gay. Lesbians, gay men, and bisexual men and women all may casually use the term "wife" to refer to an intimate partner, regardless of the biological sex or gender expression of either partner. Bisexual men and women who reject a dichotomous view of gender as either male or female may prefer the alternative terms "pansexual" or "omnisexual." These labels highlight a belief in a more fluid gender orientation and attraction to individuals across the gender spectrum.

The plethora of terms used to denote gender transgression (e.g., transgenders, transvestites, transsexuals, androgynes, bigendered people, butch lesbians, drag queens) speaks to the complexity of self-labeling as well. Cromwell (1999, cited in Lev, 2004, p. 73), for example, noted the difficulty in distinguishing between (female-to-male transgender individuals transmen) and butch lesbians—not all of whom may self-label as transgender—and suggested the use of "female-bodied men," highlighting the difficulties in labeling identity manifestations that exist along a continuum. For some transgender individuals, the terms MTF (male-to-female) and FTM (female-to-male) are used to acknowledge a transition from one (perceived) gender to another. However, other transgender individuals prefer to self-label as MTM (male-to-male) or FTF (female-to-female) to highlight a permanent sense of identity beyond the existence of specific genitalia. For example, an individual born genitally and genetically female may never have self-identified as a woman, such that the claiming of a self-concept that is strongly male is less a gender transition (i.e., FTM) than a consistent sense of a gendered self over time (i.e., MTM); this individual additionally may self-label as gay if he prefers male intimate partners. Self-labeling of sexual orientation also may change over time for transgender people; a heterosexually identified individual born biologically male who later claims a female identity and does not change partner preferences may come to self-label as a lesbian woman.

Finally, it should be noted that many sexual minority people do not identify with *any* of the labels discussed here and use instead the self-label "queer" because they prefer a pan-descriptive term that embodies defiance of existing norms about gender and sexuality rather than a term claiming membership in a particular category. The complicated nature of attitudes toward reference group and self-labeling is captured quite pointedly in the objections to a "transgendered" label by one of Lev's (2004, p. 6) gender-variant clients, who declared, "I'd rather get wet than be under that umbrella." The defiance implicit in this statement offered an irresistible title for this chapter!

For the individual living out a unique and complex identity, it can be assumed that this identity will be shaped by several sets of interacting influences related to one's reference group (creating between-group differences), sociocultural context (highlighting within-group differences), and personal preferences, characteristics, and styles (commonly viewed as individual differences variables). Although in reality these influences intersect in complex ways, for the purpose of easing our discussion of differences, we present a simple model, represented in Figure 1.1. In this model, identity enactment occurs within an overall contextual layer of temporal influences in which identity is shaped by the interactive influence of experiences of gender and gender expression (here termed "gender orientation"), sexuality and sexual expression (here termed "sexual orientation"), and cultural variables such as race, ethnicity, social class, disability, and religion (here termed "cultural orientation"). These three types of influences act upon the individual who brings to the identity process a host of individual differences variables (e.g., personality, abilities and capacities, attributional styles, coping habits, and resilience). The individual moves along a developmental trajectory in which issues are negotiated in four broad arenas: the personal health arena (including both mental and physical health); the interpersonal arena of relationships and families; the social arena of education and work; and the sociopolitical arena of legal and political rights.

This chapter is structured according to our model, using a mere sampling of issues for illustrative purposes rather than providing comprehensive coverage of any single topic. After a brief discussion of temporal influences, we outline the effects of gender orientation, sexual orientation, and cultural orientation, all of which result in important within-group differences. Although our assumption is that these contextual influences are filtered through individual characteristics (e.g., resilience, personality), the latter variables are so highly unique to each person that even the briefest review is beyond the scope of this chapter. Hence, our discussion of contextual determinants is followed by a consideration of the shared, unique experiences of each reference group within the health, relationships, education and work, and legal or political arenas, thus highlighting between-group differences in these domains. We end the chapter with a brief conclusion.

We note by way of caution that the scholarly foundation on which the information in this chapter rests is highly uneven. Studies of lesbians have lagged behind studies of gay men, and bisexuals often have been dismissed entirely or included sloppily in LG studies, without clear attention given to bisexuals' unique characteristics and issues. Until recently, much of the existing research on sexual orientation has focused on White, educated, (temporarily) able-bodied people, and what we know about transgender populations comes predominantly from research done outside the United States. The relative paucity of research on sexual minorities is disheartening, given that Evelyn Hooker's pioneering studies occurred in the late 1950s and 1960s, the American Psychological Association (APA) declared homosexuality a viable lifestyle in 1975, and APA issued "Guidelines for Psychotherapy With Lesbian, Gay, and Bisexual Clients" in 2000. Continuing stigmatization of sexual minorities (and the people who study them) probably contributes to the problem, as do the issues of populations that are difficult to access, instrumentation that is questionable at best, and theories that are deeply entrenched in heterosexist and patriarchal (i.e., heteropatriarchal) assumptions that largely dismiss or ignore same-sex and female experiences (e.g., the literatures on couples, families, and sexuality). Combined with the caveats we noted earlier regarding the historical and cultural confines of sexual identity conceptualizations and the constraints of categorizing human sexuality, this chapter must be read with healthy skepticism.

CONTEXTUAL CONDITIONS

In the following sections, we discuss general issues regarding each of the domains of contextual influence (temporal influences, gender orientation, sexual orientation, and cultural orientation) under consideration. It is our assertion that these domains of contextual influence create within-group differences across all four (LGBT) populations in predictable, describable ways (e.g., the experience of being wealthy confers certain privileges whether one identifies as L, G, B, or T, and thus differentiates a wealthy LGBT person from poorer people who might share that person's LGBT identity—hence, a within-group difference). For the sake of brevity, in each section we focus primarily on one or two of the four (LGBT) groups for illustrative purposes, and we include briefer mention of the other groups as relevant.

Temporal Influences

Two kinds of temporal influences provide the context for and permeate the process of identity development: cohort experiences and age experiences. A cohort is a group of people who share similar experiences, typically based on similar age during particular historical periods. Cohort influences thus are broad historical conditions that shape the social, legal, and interpersonal context at any given point in time, and they act both at the societal level and within particular sexual minority communities.

When cohort effects on LGBT populations are examined, examples of within-group differences are readily apparent, particularly regarding LGB people, about whom some examination of historical influences already has occurred (Duberman, Vicinus, & Chauncy, 1989; Greenberg, 1988; Rothblum, 2000b). Current older LGB populations, for example, are likely to have "come out" (i.e., come to terms with a sexual minority identity) in a historical context of pervasive stigma and discrimination; therefore, older LGB individuals may be more likely than younger people to remain isolated and closeted (even in long-term relationships) and may have internalized relatively high degrees of homophobia (Barón & Cramer, 2000; Reid, 1995).

Younger cohorts, by contrast, are more likely than their aging counterparts to have had exposure to sexual minority issues through the media and also may have greater access to electronic information and resources, even if isolated geographically (Hershberger & D'Augelli, 2000), all of which may hasten the coming out process. Fox (1995) noted as positive the fact that contemporary bisexual people are coming out earlier than their older counterparts, but D'Augelli (1998) pointed out dangers in earlier acknowledgment and acceptance of sexual minority status on the part of LGB youth, given that coming out brings greater exposure to physical and psychological risk at ever more vulnerable ages. As another example of cohort effects, the decimation of older gay and bisexual male cohorts by HIV/AIDS, in addition to creating a historical context permeated by fear, trauma, and profound loss, has contributed to decreased social and romantic networks and has exacerbated isolation for many individuals (Haldeman, chap. 3, this volume; Paul, Hays, & Coates, 1995; Reid, 1995). Members of younger male cohorts, on the other hand, who have had a vastly different experience of the HIV/AIDS epidemic, may be less conscious of health threats and more apt to engage in sexual risk behavior; circuit parties, for example, attended primarily by younger men, have been linked to recreational drug use and high-risk sexual behavior (Mansergh et al., 2001; Ross, Mattison, & Franklin, 2003).

The second temporal cause of within-group differences involves the actual age of an LGBT person at any given point in time. LGBT youth, for example, probably have limited access to age-appropriate communities and may not be welcomed into adult communities. Furthermore, as minors who lack autonomy and are subject to adult authority, they face limited choices within families and educational and religious institutions. Older LGBT individuals also may face limited access to communities on the other end of the age spectrum, particularly retirement communities and other resources for dealing with aging. Older sexual minority men, in particular, may experience unique difficulties related to aging, particularly isolation due to the combined effects of "accelerated" aging (i.e., perceptions about what age is old[er] are skewed toward younger actual chronological age in a subculture that prizes youthfulness and physical prowess), fewer children or extensive friendship networks, greater age bias in partner selection, and shorter life spans (Barón & Cramer, 2000; Reid, 1995).

D'Augelli (1994) pointed out that basic developmental processes are presumed to lead to increased individual variability and plasticity over time due the interplay of age and historical effects. The implication is that younger members of sexual minority populations are likely to be more similar to one another than they are to older members and than older members are among themselves and that one's experience within one's own cohort will change with age. This suggests the subtle and complex interaction of individual age and cohort influences. The experience of being an African American lesbian in a relationship with a White bisexual woman, for example, would be different in 2006 than it would have been in 1946; moreover, a cross-racial relationship offers different challenges to a couple in their teens than to a middle-aged couple, whatever the cohort and historical context. As another example, for older LGBT individuals, who probably encounter more frequent interactions with medical care providers (an age effect), the likely concealment of identity (a cohort effect) may result in compromised health care; further, if these older LGBT individuals are in same-sex relationships, the illness or death of one's partner may force reluctant self-disclosure. In either case, the complex interaction of age and cohort influences creates contextual challenges for the LGBT individual.

A final point to be made in regard to cohort and age influences is that most of the existing models of sexual minority identity development that guide research and form the basis for LGB-affirmative practice were developed in the 1970s and 1980s, based largely on the experiences of White gay male (and to a lesser degree, lesbian) adults. These models therefore are based on the coming out processes engaged in by LG individuals during the 1930s through the 1970s. Although these models supposedly articulate a common process of recognizing and coming to terms with a stigmatized sexual identity, their shortcomings in describing the experiences of bisexual and transgender people are obvious, and they may not even accurately capture the experiences of LG people coming out under contemporary conditions. Research regarding identity formation is temporally bound and must be updated continually in order to be useful in practice.

Gender Orientation

The term *gender orientation* as we use it here refers to the constellation of affective, cognitive, and behavioral characteristics that constitute an individual's sense of self as male or female and masculine or feminine; factors include social expectations and roles, self-presentation and self-labeling, cognitive schemas and beliefs, feelings and values, and behavioral expression. Gender is critically important as an overarching organizer of social and interpersonal experience. There is evidence that people categorize others according to gender before making any other demographic distinctions (e.g., race, class, age, or other variables) and that gender beliefs and attitudes interact strongly with these other variables (Kite, 2001). LGBT people share in common their participation in gender transgression, whether intentional or not and whether enduring or not. Individuals who conspicuously break from accepted gender norms (e.g., by dressing in clothing appropriate to or usually worn by the "opposite" sex or by assuming behaviors highly stereotypic of the opposite sex) are obvious gender transgressors. However, because socially prescribed norms and expectations about gendered behavior include implicit assumptions about the sex of one's intimate partner choices (i.e., "opposite" sex only), same-sex partner choices also become a form of gender transgression in their defiance of acceptable gender-related practices regarding intimate relationships. It is within this expanded conceptualization of gender transgression that the increasingly common inclusion of transgender people with LGBs as "sexual minorities" (even though many transgender people self-label as heterosexual) makes sense—broadly defined, ~~all LGBT people are *gender-transgressive sexual minorities*~~ in that ~~they together compose a subpopulation of individuals who challenge~~ (deliberately and persistently or not) ~~prevailing social conventions regarding the expression of gender and sexuality.~~

Transgender people reveal the restrictive, proscriptive nature of socially constructed gender-role ideologies and highlight the hidden (and erroneous) conflation of sex and gender in society, given that ~~for some, if not all, of the individuals in this population, biologically determined sex is hardly synonymous with gender expression~~. Whether they are modifying some aspect of their physiology to feel more psychologically congruent or making choices about how to dress or behave, transgender individuals exhibit a profound gender consciousness that acknowledges that people "do" (rather than "have") gender—that people enact and reinforce internalized beliefs about men and women constantly, dynamically, and largely unconsciously (Fassinger, 2000; Gilbert & Scher, 1999). It is only when people are confronted by clear transgressions of behavioral and role assumptions that those assumptions become obvious to them. It is a sad irony that despite (or perhaps because of) the critical role that transgender people play in dismantling the fetters of constrictive gender ideologies, they remain largely isolated and invisible in contemporary society.

Transgender people also exemplify dramatic within-group differences related to gender orientation and thus serve a useful illustrative purpose here. Some transgender individuals may demonstrate fluidity in gender expression, others may modify their gender in a physiological way, others may aspire to gender neutrality or androgyny, and still others may experience themselves as bi- or pan-gender (Lev, chap. 6, this volume). Because of these varied approaches to gender expression, it becomes exceedingly difficult to build and maintain a coherent community rooted in transgenderism. Many transsexual people, for example, do not want to be identified as transsexual for the rest of their lives; their goal is to "pass," that is, to be as clearly gender-categorized as possible (Lev, 2004). Therefore, their gender transgression, though radical, is time-limited and not necessarily conducive to a strong or lasting alliance with the transgender community. They may not be interested in challenging the very foundations of gender, but rather may desire to fit into existing categories both internally and in the perceptions of others (Kessler & McKenna, 2000). Other transgender individuals reject community pressure to "pass" precisely because it replicates the larger social emphasis on "either/or" rather than "both/neither" in terms of gender expression (Roen, 2002).

Unlike transgender people, not all LGB individuals challenge ascribed gender roles directly; however, the wide range in gender orientation among LGB people, from decidedly gender-stereotypic to extremely gender nontraditional, highlights the significance of within-group differences in the gender domain. Perhaps the most obvious within-group gender differences for LGB people exist among bisexuals, in that some are women and some are men; however, the commonly used group label of "bisexual" does not differentiate between maleness and femaleness (as do the terms "lesbians" and "gay men"). Although underscoring similarities in sexual orientation, this single label is problematic because bisexual women experience the same gender socialization that characterizes women more generally, rendering them far more similar to women of any sexual orientation than to their male bisexual counterparts (Firestein, chap. 4, this volume; Potoczniak, chap. 5, this volume). Failing to distinguish bisexual women from bisexual men ignores some of the unique issues they face as women. For example, identity development processes of bisexual women are more similar to those of lesbians than to those of bisexual men (Rust, 2000), whose experiences, in turn, are more likely to mirror those of other men (Fox, 1995).

In addition to the problematic conflation of sex and gender, there also exists the widespread misconception that gender expression and sexual orientation are inexorably linked—that is, the parallel yet contradictory assertions that gender transgressions are indicative of same-sex sexual preferences (the incorrect assumption that transgender people "really" are all LG) and that lesbians and gay men want to be men and women, respectively (the misconception that LGs "really" want to be the other gender). There is evidence that the strong prejudice against LGBT people is based, at least in part, on "gender fundamentalism" (Lombardi, 2001, p. 91) and antipathy toward gender-role deviance, manifested most egregiously in the form of hate crimes and violence (Kite, 1994; Lombardi, Wilchins, Priesting, & Malouf, 2002). Franklin (2001) asserted that the high levels of victimization of transgender people constitute a form of "gender terrorism" designed to punish gender nonconformity, also noting that the similarities between violence directed at gender nonconformists and violence toward lesbians and gay men obscure the motivational distinctions between various kinds of hate crimes; moreover, the structure of the justice system (because it handles hate crimes within very specific categories) virtually ensures that "the aspect of anti-homosexual violence that is based on cultural ideas about masculinity and femininity is rendered largely invisible" (p. 574). It seems clear that massive social education is needed to neutralize the presumed threat posed by the lack of understanding of and the animosity toward nonconformist gender expression, a challenging invitation to psychologists to assume advocacy roles in the gender-orientation domain.

Sexual Orientation

The term *sexual orientation* as we use it here refers to the constellation of affective, cognitive, and behavioral characteristics that constitute an individual's sense of self as a sexual and intimately relational being. These include such factors as self-labeling, beliefs and schemas, feelings and preferences, behavioral expression, and societal and sexual minority community expectations and roles. The term "sexual orientation" typically is used to distinguish among lesbian, gay, bisexual, and heterosexual people and thus is grounded conceptually only in the sex of one's intimate partner choices; this is problematic because the concept focuses on the sex or gender of the sexual object but ignores the ways in which one is "sexually oriented" (i.e., tending toward particular intimate-partner preferences) based on other social categories, such as age, body type, race and ethnicity, personality, religion, social class, and other non-gender-related variables (Stearns, 1995). An elaborated deconstruction of the entire concept of sexual orientation is beyond the scope of this chapter, but even a broadened conceptualization that simply moves beyond a partner's sex or gender to encompass myriad sexual and relational aspects of partner bonding can serve to highlight important differences within sexual minority populations.

Transgender people provide the most obvious example of enduring within-group differences in the sexual orientation domain because some claim lesbian, gay, or bisexual identities, and some claim heterosexual preferences (the possible shifts in their own past and present self-identified gender notwithstanding). Bisexual individuals also provide a clear exemplar of within-group differences because they may report a bisexual identity but exclusively heterosexual or same-sex relationships at any given point in time, and they thus explicitly challenge a dichotomous view of sexual orientation as "gay/lesbian" or "straight" (Fox, 1995). Perhaps because they so overtly defy categorization, bisexuals are "caught in an unstable gap of disidentification" (Bower, Gurevich, & Mathieson, 2002, p. 23) and face a great deal of discrimination both within and outside of sexual minority communities (Firestein, chap. 4, this volume; Herek, 2002; Mulick & Wright, 2002; Peplau & Beals, 2001; Potoczniak, chap. 5, this volume). Fox noted prevailing negative myths about bisexuality—that bisexuality is a transition on the way to exclusive same-sex orientation, that bisexual individuals are in denial about their sexual orientation, and that bisexuals deliberately avoid self-labeling their same-sex preference in order to reap the benefits of heterosexual privilege—and D'Augelli and Garnets (1995) pointed out the profound lack of community for bisexuals; both biphobia and lack of community highlight the risks of refusing to subscribe to narrow categories of self-identification.

Although transgender and bisexual people offer the most apparent example of within-group differences in sexual orientation, lesbians also provide a useful exemplar because the fluidity and relationality of their sexual orientation development and expression produce great variability (for detailed discussion, see Brown, 1995, 2000; Diamond, 2004; Liddle, chap. 2, this volume; Peplau, 2003; Peplau & Garnets, 2000; Rothblum, 1994, 2000a; Rust, 1997, 2000; Tolman & Diamond, 2001). For women, the linkages among sexual behavior, sexual desire, and sexual identity or orientation may be weak or inconsistent, with very small percentages of lesbians reporting congruence across these areas at any given time. Moreover, for lesbians, sexuality may change across contexts or time, as evidenced by arousal patterns that include males as well as females and by ongoing connections with or possibility of male partners. Acknowledging the fluidity in lesbian partner preferences over time is critical to providing viable models of identity development for women. Tolman and Diamond have noted that most research on sexual orientation tends to focus on continuity rather than discontinuity and change; thus, the gay-affirmative messages that are implicit in identity models for sexual minorities may inadvertently reinforce an image of development that is more clear and uncomplicated than the development that many women actually experience.

Lesbians also demonstrate a wide range of behaviors and feelings in their definitions and practices of the erotic, including some practices that may appear "unconventional" based on prevailing social expectations (e.g., passionate friendships [Diamond, 2000] and Boston marriages [Rothblum & Brehony, 1993], both of which involve intimate couple relationships that are not explicitly sexual). The flexibility in erotic expression exhibited by lesbians highlights the inadequacy of conceptualizations of sexual orientation that privilege "sex" over other kinds of intimacy while also highlighting the inadequacy of the heteropatriarchal definitions of sexual expression prizing genital contact, frequency, and orgasm. Moreover, the invisibility of the range of lesbian erotic activity contributes to the myth of lesbian "bed death" (the widespread belief, even among lesbians themselves, that lesbians give up relating sexually to their intimate partners over time), serving to shore up prevailing stereotypes of women as nonsexual beings. Finally, heteropatriarchal conceptualizations ignore the emotional, interpersonal, social, and even political motivations that drive sexual "orientation" (including partner preferences) for many lesbians.

Brown (2000) noted that lesbians make obvious the reality of women's sexuality because the very act of claiming a lesbian identity implies the importance of a sexual life and clear erotic preferences. This argument can be extended by returning to bisexual women. It might be presumed that bisexual women present even greater challenge to the societal status quo; not only are they declaring that they are sexual beings (and, in the viewpoint of many, aberrantly so), but they also represent a constant dismissal of the assumption that only men can fulfill the sexual needs of women—even women who choose men as intimate partners. Moreover, Berenson (2002) found "a distinct lack of rules for membership and a resistance to policing the boundaries of their identity category" (p. 9) in bisexual women, again highlighting the within-group variability in this population and providing a cogent reminder that "sexual orientation" is a construct that defies neat categories of "sexual" behavior and intimate partner "orientation."

Cultural Orientation

The term *cultural orientation* as we use it here refers to a constellation of influences on LGBT identity trajectories that are rooted in people's locations along various demographic dimensions cited frequently in multicultural psychological literature; these include such factors as religion, disability, geographic location, race and ethnicity, and socioeconomic status and social class (though neither of these latter pairs of terms is synonymous, both represent pairs of variables with similar influence often discussed jointly). These cultural variables interact and serve to differentiate among members within each of the LGBT reference groups because each individual's particular pattern of influences is highly specific and creates a unique context for identity development and expression. Each of these factors merits comprehensive discussion, and their myriad combinations result in countless distinct cultural locations for sexual minority individuals. We offer here a few examples to underscore the differential effects of culture within sexual minority groups.

Race and ethnicity not only shape the experience of LGBT people, but also may dictate specific rules for membership in particular groups or offer unique self-labels. For example, among men in some cultures (e.g., Mediterranean and Latin American) only anally receptive partners traditionally self-label as gay (Fox, 2000; Potoczniak, chap. 5, this volume), whereas other men involved in sexual or affectional relationships with men may self-label as bisexual or heterosexual. In Native American communities, bigender, bisexual "two-spirit" individuals are often highly respected (Garrett & Barret, 2003; Tafoya, 1997). Higher levels of homophobia in certain racial and ethnic communities that force sexual minority individuals to choose between disjunctive communities of support have been tied to a belief that lesbian or gay identity is a manifestation of undesirable assimilation into the dominant (White) culture (Greene, 2000). It also is worth noting that within-group differences often ascribed to racial or ethnic group membership sometimes might be understood more accurately as resulting from differences in socioeconomic status or social class, which are linked to racial and ethnic stratification in the United States (Greene, 1997, 2000).

Finally, the cultural orientation of an individual L, G, B, or T person inevitably interacts with the cultural orientation of that person's romantic or sexual partner(s). There is evidence to suggest that interracial and intercultural couples and families are more prevalent in gay and lesbian communities than in heterosexual communities (Greene, 2000). Although Peplau and

Beals (2001) noted that same-sex interracial couples demonstrate levels of relationship satisfaction similar to those of interracial couples more generally, it is reasonable to presume that differential experiences related to race or ethnicity (particularly as linked to social class) produce unique circumstances and add distinctive complexity to interracial relationships (Greene, 1997). Considering also the increasing numbers of racially blended families through transracial adoption (Lee, 2003), it becomes increasingly critical to consider the effects of race and ethnicity in LGBT families.

Race and ethnicity also often interact with the cultural variable of religion, with religious beliefs and activities serving as an important component of some racial and ethnic communities (e.g., Catholicism in Latin communities, fundamentalist Christianities in African American or Black communities; Davidson, 2000). Much has been written regarding the myriad ways in which religion-based homonegativity, both societal and internalized, compromises the identity development and mental health of some sexual minority individuals. For example, two thirds of the LGB respondents in Schuck and Liddle's (2001) study reported religious conflicts resulting in reactions such as shame, depression, and suicidal ideation, and these conflicts were associated with greater difficulty in coming out and greater diversity in age at coming out. Moreover, most of the current therapeutic attempts to eliminate homosexual feelings and behaviors (so-called corrective, or reparative, therapies) are founded in religious—particularly Christian—communities (see Haldeman, 2000; Morrow & Beckstead, 2004). However, LGBT-affirmative faith communities appear to be increasing in visibility and may function, at least in part, to support positive identity development and maintenance (e.g., faith-based essentialist benevolence and religious consecration of same-sex relationships even in the absence of legal recognition). Thus, the extent to which individuals have been exposed to or embrace homonegative religious beliefs creates a clear continuum for the manifestation of within-group differences in LGBT populations.

Matters of ability, disability, and geographic location are additional cultural variables that differentially affect LGBT people and can function similarly to restrict access to similar others and supportive communities. For example, access to a sexual minority community may be denied to disabled people who depend on caretakers or family members for care if those others do not accept the disabled individuals' sexual orientation or if those caregivers deny the individuals' sexuality altogether (Greene, 2000). Physical disabilities also may restrict opportunities to recognize or meet other LGBT people. For example, visual impairments may interfere with "gaydar," the reputed and empirically supported (Shelp, 2002) ability of sexual minority individuals to identify one another in mixed groups (Asch, 1988, cited in Greene, 2000). In addition, the impact of disability is affected profoundly by social class because assistive technologies that enhance sensory or mobility functioning may be quite costly. Given that depressed earnings and underemployment are realities for most people with disabilities (see Fassinger & Gallor, 2006), it is highly likely that many LGBT people with disabilities will lack the assistive supports necessary for accessing LGBT communities.

Isolation in rural geographic areas is another factor that may limit opportunities for sexual minority individuals to develop positive identities and viable same-sex relationships; although the Internet may help contemporary rural LGBT people to connect virtually, socioeconomic and cohort factors may limit the availability of electronic resources. It is worth noting that geographic isolation poses greater danger than mere inconvenience; there is evidence that men who have sex with other men and who live outside urban "gay ghettos" are less likely to identify as gay, have access to gay media information, or be tested for HIV (Mills et al., 2001), suggesting that communities play a critical role in promoting mental and physical health.

Finally, it must be remembered that the interaction of the various factors comprising an individual's cultural orientation is embedded within the broader interplay among one's cultural orientation, gender orientation, and sexual orientation, producing complex outcomes that defy neat categorization according to any one of these variables. For example, Battle and Lemelle (2002) found that African American women exhibit more positive attitudes toward gay men than do African American men, suggesting that the effects of racial group membership (an aspect of cultural orientation) are influenced by gender orientation. The researchers further found that although the temporal and cultural variables of age, religious attendance, education, and income all were significantly related to homophobic attitudes independently, when these effects were held constant, the gender gap in homophobic attitudes widened, again highlighting the complicated interrelationships among temporal context and gender, sexual, and cultural orientations.

DEVELOPMENTAL ARENAS

Individual developmental trajectories for LGBT people are enacted within a broad array of arenas in which reference-group membership (whether acknowledged and embraced or not) presents a shared, unique set of tasks that need to be negotiated for optimal development to proceed; because these issues are specific to each group, they create between-group differences. Here we offer brief examples of issues unique to each group in the personal arena of health, the interpersonal arena of relationships and families, the social arena of education and work, and the sociopolitical arena of legal issues. Unfortunately, the presentation of issues group by group serves to highlight the paucity of information about bisexual and (especially) transgender people, and much of the existing research reflects dominant stereotypes regarding each of the four groups. Nonetheless, differences are evident even given the nascent and biased status of research.

Personal Arena: Health

This handbook contains extensive coverage of mental health issues, so we confine our observations here to physical health. In the health arena, LGBT people share the similar experiences of persistent institutionalized discrimination that sanctions inadequate or biased provision or outright refusal of proper services to sexual minority patients and of the concomitant underutilization of health services by those patients. However, the particulars vary according to each group. For example, for LGB individuals (particularly older people), the historical classification of homosexuality as a mental disorder in the *Diagnostic and Statistical Manual of Mental Disorders (DSM)* has, understandably, left many reluctant to seek appropriate care, although this may be expected to change due to the more recent removal of homosexuality from the *DSM*. For transgender individuals, however, the continued inclusion of transvestic fetishism and gender identity disorder in the *DSM*, along with health services frequently provided and divided according to genetic or genital sex rather than gender orientation, persists in alienating many, regardless of sexual orientation.

A primary focus of the research on gay men in the health arena is sexual risk behavior and HIV/AIDS, perhaps not surprising given the widespread fear and disapproval of sex between men. Public-health messages targeting the gay community in the first waves of the AIDS pandemic have been criticized retrospectively for failing to acknowledge the sexual activity of MSMs who do not self-label as gay (Meyer, 2001). Although the highest HIV-infection rates are currently found in heterosexual women (Landrine & Klonoff, 2001), the impact of HIV and AIDS on the population of gay men cannot be understated. And though there are important within-group differences among gay men in the experience of HIV/AIDS (e.g., African American and Latino men are disproportionately affected in comparison to White, Asian, and Native American men, and those from lower socioeconomic backgrounds are more likely to face inadequate health insurance and disease progression; Wolitski, Valdiserri, Denning, & Levine, 2001), it bears remembering that HIV/AIDS has devastated the gay male community in ways not experienced by other sexual minority groups (Haldeman, chap. 3, this volume; Paul, Hays, & Coates, 1995). Moreover, because bereavement can impair the immune functioning of a surviving infected partner (Peplau & Beals, 2001) and death of loved ones is associated with temporary compromised mental health for any individual, it can be assumed that the profound losses experienced in gay male communities continue to exert unique effects on the people in these communities over time.

In terms of health issues for lesbians, the focus of research often has been on comparisons to heterosexual women regarding behaviors that defy stereotypes of "feminine" behavior (e.g., harmful habits, poor self-care). For example, studies have shown that lesbian women use alcohol and cigarettes at higher than normative rates for women (Aaron et al., 2001; Gruskin, Hart, Gordon, & Ackerson, 2001). Lesbians also are less likely than heterosexual women to be covered under health insurance (Cochran et al., 2001), and up to 60% of lesbians fail to seek preventative care (Landrine & Klonoff, 2001). Lesbian women, for example, are less likely than heterosexual women to have routine pelvic exams (Marrazzo, Koutsky, Kiviat, Kuypers, & Stine, 2001), a discrepancy that has been attributed to a possible misapprehension that such exams are necessary only for those with male sexual partners; however, lack of health coverage and bias in service provision probably contribute to this problem. Indeed, Landrine and Klonoff noted widespread bias in health insurance, health care, and prescribing of drugs, both in who is covered (men more than women) and what is covered (diseases common to men).

Health research related to transgender individuals often focuses narrowly on the experiences of transsexuals who elect hormonal or surgical procedures, concordant with the misperception that transgenderism and transsexualism are synonymous, beliefs that transsexuals unilaterally choose surgery, and a general preoccupation with secondary sex characteristics. For those who do undertake sex reassignment surgery (SRS)—alternatively termed gender reorientation surgery (GRS; Blanchard, Clemmensen, & Steiner, 1983)—studies have indicated high levels of satisfaction (Lawrence, 2003), although more for surgical procedures than for psychosocial factors (Ettner, 1999). Most other health-related issues within the transgender community have been ignored in research, though there is evidence that levels of HIV infection are high among transgender women (Lombardi, 2001) and that preoperative and nonoperative transgender individuals face unique difficulties navigating health services that often are separated by biological sex (Korell & Lorah, chap. 11, this volume).

Little is known about the specific health issues of bisexual men and women, although it is reasonable to presume that gender-related health care disparities are as likely to apply to bisexuals as to lesbians and gay men. However, a recent study enumerated a host of unique negative experiences with health care providers for bisexual people, including not receiving information about safer sex with men and women, being told that they must be either straight or gay, and an assumption on the part of providers that bisexuality is equated with having multiple partners (Ontario Public Health Association, 2003–2004). (This demonstrates the negative impact of biphobia within the health care system, emphasizing another important between-group difference in the health arena.)

Interpersonal Arena: Relationships and Families

Despite some commonalities in experiences of stigmatization, isolation, and invisibility, there are unique issues faced by each of the four (LGBT) populations in the arena of interpersonal relationships. Same-sex couples and families, for example (regardless of whether the same-sex partners self-identify as lesbian, gay, or bisexual), face all of the same issues as heterosexual couples and families, but they have to negotiate these relationships within a context of oppression (Patterson, chap. 15, this volume) that gives rise to a host of common difficulties, including the following: lack of legal and fiscal supports for the relationship; lack of support from families-of-origin, schools, and religious and other communities; persistent denial of the relationship by others regardless of commitment or longevity (or presence of children); lack of exposure to role models for same-sex relationships, intimacy, and parenting; forced definition of the relationship in sexual terms because other avenues (e.g., legal and religious) often are closed; and dealing with the daily stresses of identity development and management. These relationship challenges are buttressed by pervasive legal discrimination (Stevenson, chap. 16, this volume): at this writing, only one state (Massachusetts) issues marriage licenses to same-sex couples, and 44 states specifically prohibit this practice (either through direct legislation modeled after the 1996 federal Defense of Marriage Act or amendments to state constitutions). Barriers to adoption, social security benefits, domestic partner benefits, medical decisions, and other basic relationship and family rights are part of everyday life for most same-sex couples (see Fassinger & Gallor, 2006).

Moreover, due to gender socialization and the effects of living in a gendered society, there are a multitude of between-group differences related to male same-sex relationships and female same-sex relationships (Kurdek, 2003; Matthews & Lease, 2000; Ossana, 2000; Peplau & Beals, 2001; Rose, 2000). For example, depressed earnings for females relative to males means that lesbians or bisexual women in same-sex couples and families are more likely to be living in situations of financial hardship or difficulty than gay male couples; this economic strain may be exacerbated by the presence of dependent children (or elders) in the home, a situation more common for lesbians than gay men. Women also are more likely than men to have experienced past events, such as sexual violence, that complicate intimacy, particularly erotic intimacy. In addition, since women tend to be the most intimate friends of both men and women, lesbians have the additional complication (and potential threat) of negotiating these friendships within the context of the primary relationship, and the friendship networks of lesbian women are more likely to include ex-partners or ex-lovers (Liddle, chap. 2, this volume).

There also is evidence that lesbians and gay men "do" relationships differently (for detailed discussion, see Brown, 2000; Kurdek, 2003; Ossana,

2000; Peplau & Beals, 2001; Rose, 2000). For example, a higher percentage of lesbians than gay men report being in committed relationships, and lesbians are more likely to desire and strive for egalitarian relationships while experiencing levels of autonomy similar to those in gay male relationships. Lesbian women also are more likely to report intimacy in their relationships than gay men, have more positive beliefs and attitudes about relationships, and describe higher levels of relationship satisfaction. Because gender-role socialization for men values autonomy over intimacy and connection, it may be more difficult for gay men to achieve the level of intimacy that they might prefer in their relationships. Moreover, lesbian couples tend to match their partners on demographic variables such as age, income, and education; the larger discrepancies in demographic match between gay male partners may create particular strains in their relationships.

In terms of sexual intimacy, lesbian and gay couples tend to report similar levels of sexual satisfaction, though lesbian couples generally report less sexual frequency. However, these reported and widely cited stats about sexual frequency are founded in heteropatriarchal definitions of sexual activity that render much of lesbian erotic life irrelevant, invisible, or dysfunctional (Brown, 2000). For example, the dominant model of sexuality privileges genital contact, penile penetration, male pleasure, female passivity, monogamy, and reproduction. In this model of sexuality, frequency is prized over duration, orgasm over emotional intimacy. Reports by lesbian women of high levels of sexual satisfaction despite relatively low levels of sexual frequency suggest that this traditional model of sexuality is incompatible with the experiences of many lesbian women.

The invisibility of lesbian sexuality confers a paradoxical benefit from which gay men are unable to profit, given that gay male sexuality is both more highly visible and more highly vilified. The result is greater oppression of gay men than lesbians and well-documented higher levels of homonegativity directed at gay men. For example, the higher rates of nonmonogamy among gay men relative to lesbians (Peplau & Beals, 2001) often are viewed as unhealthy or immoral; however, nonmonogamy could be viewed just as legitimately as a behavioral choice that simply needs to be negotiated within the context of one's primary relationship. Similarly, a constrictive model of sexuality that prizes heterosexual monogamy also focuses on reproduction in ways that are particularly detrimental to gay men. Fatherhood is not seen as an appropriate role for gay men, and homonegativity in its most egregious forms leads to views of gay men as unsafe for children, resulting in greater difficulty for gay men than lesbians in adopting or maintaining custody of children or navigating public institutions, such as hospitals or schools (Patterson, chap. 15, this volume). For obvious reasons of biology, gay men face more obstacles to having biological children than do lesbian couples.

A heteropatriarchal model of sexuality also produces unique relationship difficulties for bisexual people. A primary challenge in discussing bisexual relationships and families (about which little empirical research exists; Peplau & Beals, 2001) is the wide variety of relationship configurations in which bisexual people might engage. For bisexuals in monogamous other-sex relationships (appearing, for all intents and purposes, to be heterosexual relationships), the issues noted previously are not likely to occur. However, for bisexual individuals in monogamous same-sex relationships, any of the previously noted issues may be very salient. For bisexual men and women in any kind of polyamorous or nonmonogamous relationship arrangement, problems related to nonmonogamy are likely to be encountered, such as harmful stereotypes of bisexual people as promiscuous, rooted in the cultural idealization of monogamy, which bisexual men and women do not always observe (Firestein, chap. 4, this volume; Potoczniak, chap. 5, this volume; Rust, 2003). Researchers have suggested that bisexual men and women who are married and in polyamorous relationships are able to engage in fulfilling relationships with their spouses (Edser, 2002; Reinhardt, 2002), suggesting that polyamory can be a viable relationship option for some. We would be remiss not to note, however, that these studies reinforce heteronormative assumptions and stereotypes of bisexuals by focusing on those who engage in polyamory and on the quality of the primary spousal (i.e., heterosexual) relationship. Radically new approaches to research on bisexual relationships and families clearly are needed.

What little empirical work exists on the experiences of transgender individuals tends to focus solely on the relationships of postoperative transsexual individuals, not unexpected given the proscriptive nature of heteropatriarchal assumptions regarding sexuality and the preoccupation with genitalia. For example, Lief and Hubschman (1993) noted that sexual frequency increased 100% in postoperative FTMs and that phalloplasty did not appear to be a critical factor in orgasm or in sexual satisfaction, but the authors' implicit narrow definitions of sexual functioning are clear: "[it] seems possible to change one's body image and sexual identity and be sexually satisfied *despite inadequate* sexual functioning" (p. 145, italics added). It is reasonable to presume that societal preoccupations with genital sexual activity suggest that transgender people, whether heterosexual or LGB identified, are likely to experience difficulty finding partners who will accept their gender orientation or reorientation and the level of gender transgression that it represents. Finally, in terms of families, the pervasive and pernicious pathologizing of gender transgression virtually ensures that transgender people will experience difficulties (e.g., legal, social) in maintaining relationships with children (see Lev, 2004).

Social Arena: Education and Work

In workplaces and educational institutions, LGBT people share common experiences of discrimination, marginalization, and even threats to personal safety (e.g., Lidderdale, Croteau, Anderson, Tovar-Murray, & Davis, chap. 10, this volume). However, because there are pronounced disadvantages in schools and workplaces related to gender, it can be presumed that the educational and work experiences of lesbians (as well as bisexual and transgender women) generally will be more negative than those of gay men. We already have noted the depressed earnings of women relative to men, but there are well-documented barriers to women's participation and success in the education system and the workplace that extend far beyond wage discrimination. Some of these barriers include occupational stereotyping and segregation; educational discrimination (including classroom climate, pedagogical practices, exclusion, lack of support, and lack of opportunity); oppressive workplace climates; lack of mentors and exclusion from professional networks; double standards for achievement and behavior; inequities in the distribution of resources (e.g., benefits, "perks"); discriminatory evaluation practices; burdensome "shadow jobs"; harassment and violence; tokenism, norms, and policies that render the home–work interface exceedingly difficult and produce multiple-role conflict; and internalized oppression resulting in poor self-efficacy and low outcome expectations (see Fassinger, 2002, for a detailed discussion).

For women in same-sex relationships, the impact of discriminatory workplace environments is magnified, given that the likelihood of at least one partner facing difficulties is increased. In addition, the exclusion from equitable distribution of workplace resources (e.g., access to health benefits, social security, retirement funds) faced by any sexual minority in a same-sex relationship is especially problematic for women because (as we noted previously) they are more likely to be caring for children and elders, to face depressed earnings, and to be coping with compromised health care. The current battles being waged over domestic partner benefits and same-sex marriage nationwide thus are especially salient to the economic survival of lesbians, bisexual women, and transgender women (indeed, a MTF acquaintance of the first author once commented that the biggest disappointment of transitioning had been her reclassification at her job and a subsequent drop in earnings and benefits).

Regrettably, there are more questions than answers about the unique situation of bisexual women and men in educational and work environments. Some of the research in this domain explores the experiences of bisexual women and lesbians, or bisexual and gay men, jointly, without examining possible differences among them. However, although we have noted the importance of gender-related between-group differences for these populations (e.g., economic and educational overprivileging of men), it also is reasonable to presume that bisexual people may encounter distinct difficulties in these contexts. For example, in workplaces where same-sex relationships receive few or none of the benefits assigned to heterosexual relationships, the relative status of a bisexual person may fluctuate according to partner choice. Likewise, identity management in the workplace, a commonly negotiated problem for all sexual minorities, can become much more complicated for bisexual people whose partner gender changes over time.

Transgender people also face unique problems in educational institutions and workplaces. Indeed, limited data indicate that transgender people are at high risk for employment discrimination, denial, and loss, as well as underemployment (Prentiss & McAnulty, 2002). Transsexual individuals in particular may be more vulnerable to discrimination in occupational settings because the process of transitioning effectively requires disclosure to supervisors and administrators, even in workplaces suspected or known to be hostile. Thus, though being forced to remain closeted in homonegative educational and work settings hardly can be considered positive for LGB people, remaining closeted is rarely even an option for transgender people. It is not atypical for transgender people who transition to seek new employment because of difficulties in negotiating changed-identity statuses in their workplaces (Korell & Lorah, chap. 11, this volume; Lev, chap. 6, this volume). However, for many this is impossible for financial reasons; they cannot risk termination of health benefits, for example, or cannot be without employment even temporarily because of the high costs involved in transitioning (e.g., hormone treatments, wardrobe replacement, psychotherapy, and the like; Prentiss & McAnulty, 2002). The complicated nature of their identity status calls for clear legal protections for transgender people in educational institutions and workplaces; unfortunately, these protections are uncommon.

Sociopolitical Arena: Legal and Political Rights

As noted at the outset of this chapter, LGBT people are united under a shared history of oppression, rendering legal and policy issues salient for each of these four reference groups. There are a number of relevant but constantly changing legal and policy concerns for these populations, including issues related to basic personal and civil rights, workplace discrimination, safety for LGBT youth in schools, and protection of nonheterosexual (nonmarried) couples and their families. Outlining the intricacies of current legislative efforts is well beyond the scope of this chapter (however, see Fassinger & Gallor, 2006). Thus, we focus here on one important between-group difference that is also embedded in every other arena we have discussed—that is, the estrangement of the legal and policy concerns of transgender people from legislative efforts pertaining to larger sexual minority (LGB) communities.

The interests of transgender people may be served well by many legislative initiatives concerning LGB individuals, couples, and families (e.g., prohibitions against housing discrimination based on marital status). However, the transgender community often is eliminated from pending legislation if the community's inclusion threatens the success of those legislative initiatives. As a result, transgender individuals occupy a much more precarious position in the legal and policy arena than do lesbians, gay men, or bisexual people (the latter of whom, though rarely addressed explicitly in legal or political initiatives, typically benefit from any protections conferred upon lesbians and gay men).

For example, patterns in hate-crimes regulations indicate far less protection for the basic civil rights and safety of transgender people. At this writing, 31 states and the District of Columbia (DC) have laws that address hate or bias crimes based on sexual orientation, but only 10 states and DC include gender identity or expression in their hate- or bias-crime laws. In workplaces, the absence of federally mandated prohibitions against discrimination renders the protection of LGBT workers dependent on an uneven patchwork of state, municipal, and local laws as well as individual organizational commitments; protections based on gender identity or expression are rarely included with protections based on sexual orientation (Fassinger & Gallor, 2006). At this writing, for example, 16 states, as well as 173 counties, cities, and government organizations, have workplace antidiscrimination laws explicitly naming sexual orientation (an additional 10 states extend protection in their own public workforces). However, only three states and 203 public and private employers prohibit discrimination based on gender identity or expression. Studies of large companies such as the Fortune 500 indicate that most (72%–95%) have instituted antidiscrimination policies related to sexual orientation, but only about 11% have included gender identity or expression in their policies. Similarly, in educational institutions, eight states and DC currently have laws banning discrimination or harassment of students based on sexual orientation (three additional states have adopted protective regulations based on sexual orientation), but only three states and DC prohibit discrimination or harassment based on gender identity or expression.

In terms of legal and policy issues for couples and families, the complications for transgender people who are married are magnified when SRS or GRS is involved because legal prohibitions against same-sex marriage become binding after transitioning has occurred. Moreover, because medical personnel wish to be protected from lawsuits brought by angry spouses, many current treatment practices require proof of divorce before surgical intervention is permitted (Lev, 2004). Transgender people also face another difficulty in the legal arena related to surgery. In order to change sex or gender indicated on legal documents in most states, they must be able to demonstrate having undergone sex reassignment surgery. Thus, the requirements for the benefits associated with congruence between one's individual gender orientation and one's "legal" or "institutional" sex effectively force surgical procedures for many transgender individuals who would not otherwise seek such interventions to address gender-identity issues (Lombardi, 2001), an important demonstration of the intrusion of legal issues into matters of personal health.

Finally, we note that movement in the legislative arena presents a conundrum for those fighting for the civil rights of LGBT people. Civil rights legislation largely is based on arguments regarding protected-class status of minority groups. Thus (as noted previously), political advocacy requires essentialist definitions of sexuality, which, in turn, negate the fluidity and flexibility of psychological and psychosexual identity development for many sexual minority people. For those who regard identity to be a function of choices proscribed by socially constructed categories, rights granted in response to essentialist arguments represent a double-edged sword, one that often cleaves communities trying to fight collectively for those rights.

CONCLUSION

Although common experiences of invisibility, oppression, isolation, and marginalization are faced by all or most LGBT people, these populations also encounter issues that are shared uniquely by their reference groups, as well as influences that are particular to their own individual constellation of contextual effects on identity development and enactment. These between- and within-group differences call for a highly refined and sensitive approach to practice with these populations, in which views of important reference-group characteristics are tempered by awareness of the diverse manifestations of distinctiveness within and between these reference groups. In short, one must both suspend and sustain disbelief simultaneously in order to work effectively with the complex issues of identity embodied in these populations.

Herdt (2001) asserted that recent social change reflects a growing resistance to heteronormative beliefs and practices, and he suggested that more alternatives for identities related to gender and sexuality are emerging. Presumably, this can lead to a wider range of variability in sexual behaviors and gender expression and to greater opportunities for individuals to locate and articulate their own unique ways of being. Psychologists have knowledge and power that can be used in teaching and training about sexual minority people, in developing interventions to prevent and ameliorate the harmful effects of stigma and discrimination, and in advocating for a socially just world in which sexual minority people are appreciated and understood in all their diversity. It is our hope that practice in the LGBT arena does not become stymied by monolithic assumptions about these reference groups, but instead maintains full recognition of the myriad gendered, sexual expressions of the self.

REFERENCES

Aaron, D. J., Markovic, N., Danielson, M. E., Honnold, J. A., Janosky, J. E., & Schmidt, N. J. (2001). Behavioral risk factors for disease and preventative health practices among lesbians. *American Journal of Public Health, 91,* 972–975.

Asch, A. (1998). Disability: Its place in the curriculum. In P. A. Bronstein & K. Quina (Eds.), *Teaching a psychology of people: Resources for gender and sociocultural awareness* (pp. 156–167). Washington, DC: American Psychological Association.

Barón, A., & Cramer, D. W. (2000). Potential counseling concerns of aging lesbian, gay, and bisexual clients. In R. M. Perez, K. A. DeBord, & K. J. Bieschke (Eds.), *Handbook of counseling and psychotherapy with lesbian, gay, and bisexual clients* (pp. 207–224). Washington, DC: American Psychological Association.

Battle, J., & Lemelle, A. J., Jr. (2002). Gender differences in African American attitudes toward gay males. *Western Journal of Black Studies, 26,* 134–139.

Berenson, C. (2002). What's in a name? Bisexual women define their terms. *Journal of Bisexuality, 2*(2–3), 9–21.

Blanchard, R., Clemmensen, L. H., & Steiner, B. W. (1983). Gender reorientation and psychosocial adjustment in male-to-female transsexuals. *Archives of Sexual Behavior, 12,* 503–509.

Bohan, J. S. (1996). *Psychology and sexual orientation: Coming to terms.* New York: Routledge.

Bower, J., Gurevich, M., & Mathieson, C. (2002). (Con)tested identities: Bisexual women reorient sexuality. *Journal of Bisexuality, 2*(2–3), 23–52.

Brown, L. S. (1995). Lesbian identities: Concepts and issues. In A. R. D'Augelli & C. J. Patterson (Eds.), *Lesbian, gay, and bisexual identities over the lifespan: Psychological perspectives* (pp. 3–23). New York: Oxford University Press.

Brown, L. S. (2000). Dangerousness, impotence, silence, and invisibility: Heterosexism in the construction of women's sexuality. In C. B. Travis & J. W. White (Eds.), *Sexuality, society and feminism* (pp. 273–298). Washington, DC: American Psychological Association.

Cochran, S. D., Mays, V. M., Bowen, D., Gage, S., Bybee, D., Roberts, S. J., et al. (2001). Cancer-related risk indicators and preventive screening behaviors among lesbians and bisexual women. *American Journal of Public Health, 91,* 591–597.

Cromwell, J. (1999). *Transmen and FTMs: Identities, bodies, genders, and sexualities.* Champaign: University of Illinois Press.

D'Augelli, A. R. (1994). Lesbian and gay male development: Steps toward an analysis of lesbians' and gay men's lives. In B. Greene & G. M. Herek (Eds.), *Lesbian and gay psychology: Theory, research, and clinical applications* (pp. 118–132). Thousand Oaks, CA: Sage.

D'Augelli, A. R. (1998). Developmental implications of victimization of lesbian, gay, and bisexual youths. In G. M. Herek (Ed.), *Stigma and sexual orientation: Understanding prejudice against lesbians, gay men, and bisexuals* (pp. 187–210). Thousand Oaks, CA: Sage.

D'Augelli, A. R., & Garnets, L. D. (1995). Lesbian, gay, and bisexual communities. In A. R. D'Augelli & C. J. Patterson (Eds.), *Lesbian, gay, and bisexual identities over the lifespan: Psychological perspectives* (pp. 293–320). New York: Oxford University Press.

Davidson, M. G. (2000). Religion and spirituality. In R. M. Perez, K. A. DeBord, & K. J. Bieschke (Eds.), *Handbook of counseling and psychotherapy with lesbian, gay, and bisexual clients* (pp. 409–434). Washington, DC: American Psychological Association.

Diamond, L. M. (2000). Passionate friendships among adolescent sexual-minority women. *Journal of Research on Adolescence, 10*(2), 191–209.

Diamond, L. M. (2004). Emerging perspectives on distinction between romantic love and sexual desire. *Current Directions in Psychological Science, 13,* 116–119.

Duberman, M. B., Vicinus, M., & Chauncey, G., Jr. (Eds.). (1989). *Hidden from history: Reclaiming the gay & lesbian past.* New York: New American Library.

Edser, S. J., & Shea, J. D. (2002). An exploratory investigation of bisexual men in monogamous, heterosexual marriages. *Journal of Bisexuality, 2*(4), 5–29.

Ehrenberg, M. (1996). Aging and mental health: Issues in the gay and lesbian community. In C. Alexander (Ed.), *Gay and lesbian mental health: A sourcebook for practitioners* (pp. 189–209). New York: Harrington Park Press.

Ettner, R. (1999). *Gender-loving care: A guide to counseling gender-variant clients.* New York: Norton.

Fassinger, R. E. (2000). Gender and sexuality in human development: Implications for prevention and advocacy in counseling psychology. In S. Brown & R. Lent (Eds.), *Handbook of counseling psychology* (3rd ed., pp. 346–378). New York: Wiley.

Fassinger, R. E. (2002). Hitting the ceiling: Gendered barriers to occupational entry, advancement, and achievement. In L. Diamant & J. Lee (Eds.), *The psychology of sex, gender, and jobs: Issues and solutions* (pp. 21–46). Westport, CT: Greenwood Press.

Fassinger, R. E., & Gallor, S. M. (2006). Tools for remodeling the master's house: Advocacy and social justice in education and work. In R. Toporek, L. Gerstein, N. Fouad, G. Roysircar, & T. Israel (Eds.), *Handbook for social justice in counseling psychology: Leadership, vision, and action* (pp. 256–275). Thousand Oaks, CA: Sage.

Fausto-Sterling, A. (1998). The five sexes: Why male and female are not enough. In D. L. Anselmi & A. L. Law (Eds.), *Questions of gender: Perspectives & paradoxes* (pp. 24–28). Boston: McGraw-Hill.

Fox, R. C. (1995). Bisexual identities. In A. R. D'Augelli & C. J. Patterson (Eds.), *Lesbian, gay, and bisexual identities over the lifespan: Psychological perspectives* (pp. 48–86). New York: Oxford University Press.

Fox, R. C. (2000). Bisexuality in perspective: A review of theory and research. In B. Greene & G. L. Croom (Eds.), *Education, research, and practice in lesbian, gay, bisexual, and transgendered psychology: A resource manual* (pp. 161–206). Thousand Oaks, CA: Sage.

Franklin, K. (2001). Hate crimes. In J. Worrell (Ed.), *Encyclopedia of women and gender: Sex similarities and differences and the impact of society on gender* (pp. 571–576). San Diego, CA: Academic Press.

Garrett, M. T., & Barret, B. (2003). Two spirits: Counseling Native American gay, lesbian, and bisexual people. *Journal of Multicultural Counseling and Development, 31*(2), 131–142.

Gilbert, L. A., & Scher, M. (1999). *Gender and sex in counseling and psychotherapy.* Boston: Allyn Bacon.

Gonsiorek, J. C. (1995). Gay male identities: Concepts and issues. In A. R. D'Augelli & C. J. Patterson (Eds.), *Lesbian, gay, and bisexual identities over the lifespan: Psychological perspectives* (pp. 24–47). New York: Oxford University Press.

Greenberg, D. F. (1988). *The construction of homosexuality.* Chicago: University of Chicago Press.

Greene, B. (1997). Ethnic minority lesbians and gay men: Mental health and treatment issues. In B. Greene (Ed.), *Ethnic and cultural diversity among lesbians and gay men* (pp. 216–239). Thousand Oaks, CA: Sage.

Greene, B. (2000). Beyond heterosexism and across the cultural divide: Developing an inclusive lesbian, gay, and bisexual psychology: A look to the future. In B. Greene & G. L. Croom (Eds.), *Education, research, and practice in lesbian, gay, bisexual, and transgendered psychology: A resource manual* (pp. 1–45). Thousand Oaks, CA: Sage.

Gruskin, E. P., Hart, S., Gordon, N., & Ackerson, L. (2001). Patterns of cigarette smoking and alcohol use among lesbians and bisexual women enrolled in a large health maintenance organization. *American Journal of Public Health, 91,* 976–979.

Haldeman, D. C. (2000). Therapeutic responses to sexual orientation: Psychology's evolution. In B. Greene & G. L. Croom (Eds.), *Education, research, and practice in lesbian, gay, bisexual, and transgendered psychology: A resource manual* (pp. 244–262). Thousand Oaks, CA: Sage.

Herdt, G. (2001). Social change, sexual diversity, and tolerance for bisexuality in the United States. In A. R. D'Augelli & C. J. Patterson (Eds.), *Lesbian, gay, and bisexual identities and youth: Psychological perspectives* (pp. 267–283). New York: Oxford University Press.

Herek, G. M. (2002). Heterosexuals' attitudes toward bisexual men and women in the United States. *Journal of Sex Research, 39,* 264–274.

Hershberger, S. L., & D'Augelli, A. R. (2000). Issues in counseling lesbian, gay, and bisexual adolescents. In R. M. Perez, K. A. DeBord, & K. J. Bieschke (Eds.), *Handbook of counseling and psychotherapy with lesbian, gay, and bisexual clients* (pp. 225–248). Washington, DC: American Psychological Association.

Kessler, S., & McKenna, W. (2000). Who put the "trans" in transgender? Gender theory and everyday life. *International Journal of Transgenderism, 4*(3).

Kite, M. (2001). Gender stereotypes. In J. Worrell (Ed.), *Encyclopedia of women and gender: Sex similarities and differences and the impact of society on gender* (pp. 561–570). San Diego, CA: Academic Press.

Kite, M. E. (1994). When perception meets reality: Individual differences in reactions to lesbians and gay men. In B. Greene & H. M. Herek (Eds.), *Lesbian and gay psychology: Theory, research, and clinical applications* (pp. 25–53). Thousand Oaks, CA: Sage.

Klein, F. (1993). *The bisexual option* (2nd ed.). New York: Harrington Park Press.

Kurdek, L. A. (2003). Differences between gay and lesbian cohabiting couples. *Journal of Social & Personal Relationships, 20*(4), 411–436.

Landrine, H., & Klonoff, E. A. (2001). Health and health care: How gender makes women sick. In J. Worrell (Ed.), *Encyclopedia of women and gender: Sex similarities and differences and the impact of society on gender* (pp. 577–592). San Diego, CA: Academic Press.

Lawrence, A. A. (2003). Factors associated with satisfaction or regret following male-to-female sex reassignment surgery. *Archives of Sexual Behavior, 32,* 299–315.

Lee, R. M. (2003). The transracial adoption paradox: History, research, and counseling implications of cultural socialization. *The Counseling Psychologist, 31,* 711–744.

Lev, A. I. (2004). *Transgender emergence: Therapeutic guidelines for working with gender-variant people and their families.* Binghamton, NY: The Haworth Clinical Practice Press.

Lief, H. I., & Hubschman, L. (1993). Orgasm in the postoperative transsexual. *Archives of Sexual Behavior, 22,* 145–155.

Lombardi, E. (2001). Enhancing transgender health care. *American Journal of Public Health, 91,* 859–872.

Lombardi, E. L., Wilchins, R. A., Priesting, D., & Malouf, D. (2002). Gender violence: Transgender experiences with violence and discrimination. *Journal of Homosexuality, 42*(1), 89–101.

Mansergh, G., Colfax, G. N., Marks, G., Rader, M., Guzman, R., & Buchbinder, S. (2001). The circuit party and men's health survey: Findings and implications for gay and bisexual men. *American Journal of Public Health, 91,* 953–958.

Marrazzo, J. M., Koutsky, L. A., Kiviat, N. B., Kuypers, J. M., & Stine, K. (2001). Papanicolaou test screening and prevalence of genital human papillomavirus among women who have sex with women. *American Journal of Public Health, 91,* 947–952.

Matthews, C. R., & Lease, S. H. (2000). Focus on lesbian, gay, and bisexual families. In R. M. Perez, K. A. DeBord, & K. J. Bieschke (Eds.), *Handbook of counseling and psychotherapy with lesbian, gay, and bisexual clients* (pp. 249–274). Washington, DC: American Psychological Association.

Meyer, I. H. (2001). Why lesbian, gay, bisexual, and transgender public health? *American Journal of Public Health, 91,* 856–859.

Mills, T. C., Stall, R., Pollack, L., Paul, J. P., Binson, D., Canchola, J., & Catania, J. A. (2001). *American Journal of Public Health, 91,* 55–58.

Morrow, S. L., & Beckstead, A. L. (2004). Conversion therapies for same-sex attracted clients in religious conflict: Context, predisposing factors, experiences, and implications for therapy. *The Counseling Psychologist, 32,* 641–650.

Mulick, P. S., & Wright, L. W., Jr. (2002). Examining the existence of biphobia in the heterosexual and homosexual populations. *Journal of Bisexuality, 2*(4), 45–64.

Ontario Public Health Association. (2003–2004). *Improving the access and quality of public health services for bisexuals.* Retrieved April 7, 2006, from http://www.opha.on.ca/ppres/2003–04_pp.pdf

Ossana, S. M. (2000). Relationship and couples counseling. In R. M. Perez, K. A. DeBord, & K. J. Bieschke (Eds.), *Handbook of counseling and psychotherapy with lesbian, gay, and bisexual clients* (pp. 275–302). Washington, DC: American Psychological Association.

Paul, J. P., Hays, R. B., & Coates, T. J. (1995). The impact of the HIV epidemic on U.S. gay male communities. In A. R. D'Augelli & C. J. Patterson (Eds.), *Lesbian, gay, and bisexual identities over the lifespan: Psychological perspectives* (pp. 347–397). New York: Oxford University Press.

Peplau, L. A. (2003). Human sexuality: How do men and women differ? *Current Directions in Psychological Science, 12*(2), 37–40.

Peplau, L. A., & Beals, K. P. (2001). Lesbians, gay men, and bisexuals in relationships. In J. Worrell (Ed.), *Encyclopedia of women and gender: Sex similarities and differences and the impact of society on gender* (pp. 657–666). San Diego, CA: Academic Press.

Peplau, L. A., & Garnets, L. D. (2000). A new paradigm for understanding women's sexuality and sexual orientation. *Journal of Social Issues, 56*(2), 329–350.

Prentiss, C., & McAnulty, R. (2002). Gender identity disorder in the workplace. In L. Diamant & J. Lee (Eds.), *The psychology of sex, gender, and jobs: Issues and solutions* (pp. 171–184). Westport, CT: Praeger.

Reid, J. D. (1995). Development in late life: Older lesbian and gay lives. In A. R. D'Augelli & C. J. Patterson (Eds.), *Lesbian, gay, and bisexual identities over the lifespan: Psychological perspectives* (pp. 215–242). New York: Oxford University Press.

Reinhardt, R. (2002). Bisexual women in heterosexual relationship. *Journal of Bisexuality, 2*(2–3), 163–171.

Roen, K. (2002). "Either/or" and "both/neither": Discursive tensions in transgender politics. *Signs, 27,* 501–522.

Rose, S. (2000). Heterosexism and the study of women's romantic and friend relationships. *Journal of Social Issues, 56*(2), 315–328.

Ross, M. W., Mattison, A. M., & Franklin, D. R., Jr. (2003). Club drugs and sex on drugs are associated with different motivations for gay circuit party attendance in men. *Substance Use & Misuse, 38,* 1173–1183.

Rothblum, E. D. (1994). Transforming lesbian sexuality. *Psychology of Women Quarterly, 18,* 627–641.

Rothblum, E. D. (2000a). Sexual orientation and sex in women's lives: Conceptual and methodological issues. *Journal of Social Issues, 56*(2), 193–204.

Rothblum, E. D. (2000b). "Somewhere in Des Moines or San Antonio": Historical perspectives on lesbian, gay, and bisexual mental health. In R. M. Perez, K. A. DeBord, &

K. J. Bieschke (Eds.), *Handbook of counseling and psychotherapy with lesbian, gay, and bisexual clients* (pp. 57–80). Washington, DC: American Psychological Association.

Rothblum, E. D., & Brehony, K. A. (Eds.). (1993). *Boston marriages: Romantic but asexual relationships among contemporary lesbians.* Amherst: University of Massachusetts Press.

Rust, P. C. R. (1997). "Comin out" in the age of social constructionism: Sexual identity formation among lesbian and bisexual women. *Journal of Lesbian Studies, 1*(1), 25–54.

Rust, P. C. R. (2000). Bisexuality: A contemporary paradox for women. *Journal of Social Issues, 56*(2), 205–222.

Rust, P. C. R. (2003). Monogamy and polyamory: Relationship issues for bisexuals. In L. D. Garnets & D. C. Kimmel (Eds.), *Psychological perspectives on lesbian, gay, and bisexual experiences* (pp. 475–496). New York: Columbia University Press.

Schuck, K. D., & Liddle, B. J. (2001). Religious conflicts experienced by lesbian, gay, and bisexual individuals. *Journal of Gay & Lesbian Psychotherapy, 5*(2), 63–82.

Shelp, S. G. (2002). Gaydar: Visual detection of sexual orientation among gay and straight men. *Journal of Homosexuality, 44*(1), 1–14.

Stearns, D. C. (1995). Gendered sexuality: The privileging of sex and gender in sexual orientation. *NWSA Journal, 7*(1), 8–29.

Tafoya, T. (1997). Native gay and lesbian issues: The two-spirited. In B. Greene (Ed.), *Ethnic and cultural diversity among lesbians and gay men* (pp. 1–10). Thousand Oaks, CA: Sage.

Tolman, D. L., & Diamond, L. M. (2001). Sexuality and sexual desire. In J. Worrell (Ed.), *Encyclopedia of women and gender: Sex similarities and differences and the impact of society on gender* (pp. 1005–1022). San Diego, CA: Academic Press.

Whelehan, P. (2001). Cross-cultural sexual practices. In J. Worrell (Ed.), *Encyclopedia of women and gender: Sex similarities and differences and the impact of society on gender* (pp. 291–302). San Diego, CA: Academic Press.

Wolitski, R. J., Valdiserri, R. O., Denning, P. H., & Levine, W. C. (2001). Are we headed for a resurgence of the HIV epidemic among men who have sex with men? *American Journal of Public Health, 91*, 883–888.

Wren, B. (2002). "I can accept my child is transsexual but if I ever see him in a dress I'll hit him": Dilemmas in parenting a transgendered adolescent. *Clinical Child Psychology and Psychiatry, 7*, 377–397.

2

MUTUAL BONDS: LESBIAN WOMEN'S LIVES AND COMMUNITIES

BECKY J. LIDDLE

The need to belong or feel a part of a particular group is a deeply human urge. For lesbians, it has special importance, for a sense of community helps to establish and maintain lesbian identity, gives one a sense of belonging somewhere, and provides the affirmation and acceptance that is missing in the larger culture.

(Pearlman, 1987, p. 313)

Models of lesbian identity development have become progressively more complex as researchers have learned more about lesbians' lives, but finding an affirming community is part of nearly every model of the coming out process (Ritter & Terndrup, 2002; Rust, 2003). The task of finding community must be repeated each time a lesbian relocates and is complicated by the hidden or informal nature of some communities. This chapter addresses the identity development process for lesbians, emphasizing the variety of possible developmental paths. I consider the role of identity disclosure (coming out) within this context, along with the importance of finding community. Finally, I address special issues related to the role of community in the lives of lesbians of various ethnicities, ages, religions, and locations. Therapists will find relevant recommendations for practice throughout the chapter.

Gratitude is expressed to Kathy Liddle who provided feedback on an earlier draft of this chapter.

THE IDENTITY DEVELOPMENT PROCESS

Early gay and lesbian identity development models (e.g., Cass, 1979; Coleman, 1982; McDonald, 1982) proposed a fairly standard sequence of events, typically moving from lack of awareness of sexual orientation through a dawning of awareness (often accompanied by negative feelings) to self-affirmation, immersion in the gay or lesbian community, and disclosure of sexual orientation. McCarn and Fassinger (1996) pointed out that community affiliation may not occur at predictable times with reference to the self-awareness tasks of identity development. They proposed two processes: one related to self-discovery and self-labeling (individual identity), and the other involving affiliation (e.g., finding a lesbian community). Rosario, Hunter, Maguen, Gwadz, and Smith (2001) went a step further, suggesting that identity development is multidimensional, encompassing sexual identity, attitudes toward homosexuality, comfort with homosexuality, self-disclosure, and involvement in gay and lesbian activities. Separating aspects of identity development in these ways creates more flexible models that can better encompass the variety of lesbian experiences. However, the simplicity of early identity development models may still provide practitioners with a convenient framework for discussing common issues encountered in the identity development process. What follows is a brief summary of lesbian identity development, based loosely on classic development models, but including more recent research demonstrating the variety and complexity of this process.

LESBIAN IDENTITY DEVELOPMENT

Typically, models of identity development begin with an assumption of heterosexuality, such as when a girl assumes that she will someday marry a man. This is followed by the dawning awareness that she is different in some way; she may not be boy-crazy during adolescence, for example. A client entering therapy before she has consciously acknowledged her sexual orientation may nonetheless have related presenting concerns; for example, she may display hurt feelings when a crush on another girl is not reciprocated. At some point, she will begin to consider applying the label of gay, lesbian, or bisexual to herself. Although for men, self-labeling is typically a result of sexual attraction, research suggests that for women it is more commonly spurred by emotional attraction (Markowe, 2002; Savin-Williams & Diamond, 2000). Markowe's interviewees typically reported "falling in love with or having crushes on other girls or women as their first lesbian feelings, whether or not these were labeled as such at the time" (p. 70).

Self-labeling as lesbian may (or may not) be accompanied by a crisis, provoked by fears or strong feelings of not wanting to be different from the norm in this way. Many clients enter therapy at this point because they are confused, upset, or isolated, and they need a safe place to sort out their feelings. Negative feelings or fears, if present, may arise from social stigma (e.g., fears of rejection by parents or friends or of loss of job or social standing), religious teachings, or the grieving of personal-life fantasies that included the classic model of marriage and family.

During this period, lesbians may need to grieve the loss of assumed life paths, as well as the loss of societal approval granted to heterosexuals. Although some losses (e.g., equal rights) are still fairly universal, lesbians in the coming out process may need to only readjust, rather than completely abandon, some life plans. For example, parenthood is quite common in the lesbian community, sometimes from previous marriages, but also through donor insemination, adoption, and coparenting arrangements. Rostosky and Riggle (2002) found that more than a third of their gay and lesbian sample reported having children living with them. Thus, clients who are mourning lost dreams of family and children may need to examine whether those dreams must be abandoned, or whether these life goals may merely become more complex to achieve. A full discussion of the special issues and challenges of lesbian parenting is beyond the scope of this chapter. However, with the exception of the additional challenges of social and legal legitimacy of the nonbiological mother (Bos, van Balen, & van den Boom, 2004; Hequembourg & Farrell, 1999), somewhat less contact with the extended family of the nonbiological mother (Patterson, Hurt, & Mason, 1998), and occasional reports of homophobia among child-care or health care providers, teachers, or peers (Gartrell et al., 1999, 2000), lesbian mothers and their children are doing at least as well as heterosexual parents and children in a broad range of psychosocial variables, such as the child's social competence and emotional well-being, and parents' competence and level of stress. (See Bos et al., 2004, and Litovich & Langhout, 2004, for recent summaries of this literature.)

The developmental task of moving from negative feelings about being a lesbian to a positive sense of identity, although not by any means universal, is still relevant for many individuals, and therapists must be prepared to facilitate this process. Books, organizations, and Web sites that target the source of negative feelings can be important resources in this process. For example, an Asian lesbian who lacks lesbian role models in her local community may strengthen or reinforce her sense of identification with other Asian lesbians by reading relevant books or visiting Web sites of organizations for lesbians or lesbian, gay, bisexual, and transgender (LGBT) people of Asian heritage. Similarly, fundamentalist Christians may benefit from books that present alternative Biblical interpretations or services at a local MCC[1] church. Therapists who are knowledgeable about such resources have been shown to be more effective with their gay and lesbian clients (Liddle, 1996). Methods for identifying specific resources include consulting with LGBT colleagues, posing a query on the

---

[1] The Metropolitan Community Church is a denomination for LGBT Christians with congregations in most major U.S. cities.

electronic mailing list of the American Psychological Association's Division 44 (Society for the Psychological Study of Lesbian, Gay, and Bisexual Issues), consulting local resources (e.g., feminist bookstores, LGBT bookstores, "gay yellow pages," LGBT newspapers, and university LGBT offices), or searching the Internet. Because clients early in the identity development process may feel overwhelmed or especially vulnerable, it may be important for therapists to do this research rather than assign the task to the client.

Once the client begins to self-label as lesbian or bisexual (or some other term of her choice), all models acknowledge the importance for her of finding other members of that community. Finding and getting involved in a community helps the client feel less isolated and provides reassurance that she isn't the only one. It also exposes her to role models who can help her form a positive lesbian identity. Seeing other lesbians who are successful and happy goes far in allaying fears of the future of misery and isolation that some lesbians first envision.

As a client begins to form a more positive identity, she may become angry that society's ignorance and bigotry initially caused her to feel upset or to postpone living a fulfilling life as a lesbian. Some models (e.g., Cass, 1979) suggest that this anger may fuel a stage of gay pride or activism, during which the woman's lesbian identity is particularly central to her definition of self. Cass then suggests a waning of this centrality and anger, as the lesbian identity becomes integrated into the self as simply one of many sources of self-definition (e.g., a woman's simultaneous identities as a teacher, an African American, and a Christian).

LIMITATIONS OF IDENTITY DEVELOPMENT MODELS

The identity development models summarized here do not describe a universal experience, but rather summarize a series of events experienced by a number of lesbians, during a particular historical period. Rust (2003) pointed out that most models were created during the 1970s and 1980s, when most lesbians experienced distress about their sexual orientation before becoming self-accepting. Now that societal attitudes and exposure to positive role models are improving, there is a great deal of variety in individual affective experience. Some lesbians may feel little or no threat in discovering their sexual orientation and may, in fact, experience joy in finding a community of women like themselves. Reactions to coming out may also vary according to such demographic variables as ethnicity, locale, and age, which will be discussed later.

Rust (2003) noted that although most models of lesbian identity assume an end point of stable lesbian identity, recent research suggests that sexual orientation, especially among women, may change over time. Thus an "end point" of identity development in which a woman sees herself as 100% and permanently lesbian may be unrealistic. Rust (1992) found that only one third of self-identified lesbians claimed to be 100% attracted to women; the remainder said they were 5% to 50% attracted to men. Rust also found that 43% of self-identified lesbians reported having had a romantic relationship with a man since coming out as a lesbian. These findings suggest a few possibilities: that a large proportion of self-identified lesbians are actually (to some degree) bisexual, that emotional attractions can "trump" sexual orientation, or that sexual orientation for these women changes over time. Regardless of the interpretation, such shifts in the objects of one's affections can be confusing for women who self-identify as lesbian and previously believed they were established in their sexual orientation or were finished with their identity development process (Rust, 2003). Having relationships with men after identifying as a lesbian can also interfere with a woman's friendships and community involvement, due to biphobia in the lesbian community or due to perceptions of such relationships as betrayals or conversions to heterosexuality. Readers are referred to Firestein (chap. 4, this volume) for a discussion of these issues.

Two final cautions about identity development relate to research on average ages of various life events. Research that reports average ages of events (such as first same-sex attraction, self-identification as lesbian, or coming out to others) is sometimes misinterpreted as indicating "typical" ages (e.g., Barrett & Logan, 2002, p. 117) or as indicative of a universal order of events. On the contrary, the women in Rust's (2003) study reported age of first realization that they were not heterosexual ranging from earliest memory to age 54, and order of events (e.g., whether they identified as lesbian before their first relationship with a woman) also varied. Women come out at every age and stage of life, from childhood to middle age and beyond, and therapists must be prepared to help with this transition, regardless of the age of their clientele or order of events.

DISCLOSURE OF SEXUAL ORIENTATION

Empirical findings consistently indicate a correlation between concealment of one's sexual orientation and negative health outcomes (reviewed in Herek, 2003). Thus, it is tempting to assume all clients should be open about their sexual orientation. However, these findings are merely correlations: It may be that the negative health outcomes, rather than being a result of the concealment itself, are a result of living in a hostile environment in which concealment is actually necessary. Although early models of identity development conflated outness and political activity with more advanced identity development (McCarn & Fassinger, 1996), research shows that level of outness seems to be influenced by a variety of situational and social factors (e.g., occupation, income, and location) unrelated to stage of identity development (Harry, 1993).

Forming a positive identity *without* coming out to family or at work is possible and may be especially common among particular ethnic, regional, or religious groups. For example, a national poll in 1989 found that the percentage of respondents not out to their families of origin varied dramatically by region, ranging from 23% to 40% (as cited in Herek, 2003). Bradford, Ryan, and Rothblum (1994) found outness varied by age, and that White lesbians were out more often than Latina or African American women. Likewise, numerous authors have pointed out that gay and lesbian members of the African American and Latino communities tend to be well tolerated and integrated into the community (despite overt cultural homophobia), as long as sexual orientation is not explicitly stated (e.g., Espin, 1987; Greene, 1997; Morales, 1992). Similar findings have been reported for rural White lesbians in the Midwest (Oswald & Culton, 2003). Thus, therapists must be aware that the end point in the coming out process will vary by community. Members of some communities may live their lives fairly openly, while conforming to cultural rules against naming their sexual identity or labeling their partner as such; straight members of these communities are expected to reciprocate by not asking about the nature of the relationship (Smith, 1997). Smith states that in some ethnic communities, one has successfully come out when one's family treats one's lesbian partner just as they would treat a spouse, even though the romantic nature of the relationship is not explicitly stated. In my experience, White Southerners often take a similar approach.

In addition to cultural expectations, employment discrimination is another factor affecting decisions about disclosure of sexual orientation. Reports of discrimination are positively correlated with outness at work (Ragins & Cornwell, 2001). Because discrimination based on sexual orientation is currently illegal in only 17 U.S. states (Human Rights Campaign, 2006), most who suffer discrimination have no legal recourse.

Because different social and cultural environments, careers, and life circumstances greatly impact the social, familial, and financial costs of coming out, it is important that therapists (no matter how well-intentioned) not hold values about a "right answer" regarding how out their clients should be. Decisions may change over time and with life circumstances. Therapists must be unbiased as they help clients weigh the risks and benefits of coming out. Young women, especially, should consider whether they are safe and financially independent if there is any risk of severe negative reaction from parents. High school students are sometimes thrown out of their homes, and many college students have had college funding from their parents terminated after coming out to their families. Pilkington and D'Augelli (1995) reported that 10% of their sample of LGB youth (ages 15–21) had, because of their sexual orientation, even been physically attacked by a family member. Thus, sometimes disclosure to birth family, if it happens at all, must be delayed for reasons of safety or practicality.

Finally, therapists should be aware that varying levels of outness are a common source of friction in lesbian couples because one member's openness may implicitly disclose the other's sexual orientation. Thus, one woman may feel constrained by her partner's closet while the other is frightened by her partner's outness. (See Rostosky & Riggle, 2002, for a review and discussion of partner outness.) Although conflicts about outness occur in many relationships, they may be ~~particularly common in interracial couples because of differing cultural norms regarding disclosure of sexual orientation~~ (Smith, 1997).

LESBIAN COMMUNITIES

Many authors have discussed the role of community involvement as a buffer against minority stress (e.g., Meyer, 2003). Although all individuals experience stress, minority stress refers to the additional stress experienced by minority individuals due to stigma and discrimination. Active involvement in the lesbian or LGBT community may help buffer lesbians against this additional stress in a variety of ways, providing, among other things, opportunities for social interaction in an environment free of this stress, role models and other resources for development of a positive identity, a sense of group solidarity, and general social support. Meyer (2003) reviewed the literature on minority stress in LGB people's lives, including the role of community involvement in buffering against minority stress. What follows here is a discussion of the literature specific to lesbian communities and the important roles these communities play in lesbian lives.

Although other aspects of identity development models have been criticized, the ~~importance of finding community—of finding friends and role models who share one's sexual orientation~~—is not an aspect that has been questioned. Membership in a lesbian community "~~provides definition, acceptance, and inclusion~~; it ~~offers sources for social life, political activity, friendships, lovers, places to go, and other types of assistance~~" (Pearlman, 1987, p. 314). For lesbians who are just coming out, finding a community of lesbians is likely to be an important task to be addressed in therapy.

Visible LGBT organizations are key to helping newly out (or newly relocated) lesbians to find the community and its associated opportunities for friendships and social activities. Such institutions include bars, women's centers, feminist bookstores, self-help groups, hotlines, concert and theater groups, political organizations, and LGBT newspapers (Lockard, 1986). A large city is likely to have a variety of organizations available. For example, among musical organizations alone, Atlanta's LGBT community boasts three choruses (men's, women's, and mixed) and a marching band. Thus, in large metropolitan areas, finding community may be as simple as sampling interest groups until finding one that feels comfortable.

In the 1970s and 1980s, lesbians and gay men flocked to the cities in search of such community resources, in what Weston (1995) called "the Great

Gay Migration." In addition to providing a visible community, such ~~migration may allow some lesbians to come out in relative privacy, at a distance from their families of origin~~. Although the migration to cities has slowed somewhat as gay and lesbian people have been able to find community and acceptance in smaller cities and towns, it is still a common phenomenon. Indeed, the vast majority of the respondents to the National Lesbian Health Care Survey lived in or near metropolitan areas and reported a host of lesbian organizations available to them: Most reported "that their community had lesbian support groups (70%), lesbian cultural events (70%), lesbian sports teams (68%), a lesbian bar or night-club (67%), lesbian or gay religious groups (66%), lesbian or feminist bookstores (60%), lesbian hotline or information center (55%), and lesbian social clubs (51%)" (Bradford et al., 1994, p. 236). Those who have access to lesbian institutions and friendship networks typically make good use of them. Nearly two thirds of lesbians reported attending lesbian events at least once a month, and about two-thirds also reported that most of their women friends were lesbians (Bradford et al., 1994). Thus, lesbian community plays an important role in these women's lives.

In contrast, the lack of visible lesbian institutions in most small cities and towns makes it difficult for newcomers to find community. A survey of 527 nonmetropolitan LGBT people in Illinois, for example, found respondents frequently complaining that bars were the only visible local community resources and that bars did not meet their social needs (Oswald & Culton, 2003). The LGBT community was often described as "too small, too hidden, too fragmented, and/or too lacking in resources" (Oswald & Culton, 2003, p. 75). On the other hand, rural living was also seen as offering a positive quality of life by many respondents, and many lived near enough to larger cities to occasionally access the more varied community institutions available there. Occasional trips to larger cities or to one-time events (e.g., women's music festivals or a gay-rights march) provide opportunities to be immersed temporarily in a community of lesbians. This need to be surrounded, even temporarily, by "people like us" may be difficult for majority therapists to understand. But it is lesbian community that provides safety and comfort in a hostile world: it is a place to relax and be all of oneself without censoring; a place to find affirmation and to feel at home.

In small cities, lesbian communities are typically made up of friendship circles (Oswald & Culton, 2003), in which lesbian or LGBT people get together for dinners, parties, and other social events. Informal communities are difficult for newcomers (whether just coming out or relocating) to find. A therapist who can provide even a single contact point can have a tremendously beneficial impact on a client's ability to locate community. If there are no public institutions available, therapists should try to have a contact in the local lesbian community who can orient newcomers to the community. I should note that although I have been making reference to lesbian communities, in many locales, gay, lesbian, and bisexual communities and friend networks are interwoven.

Whatever forms lesbian communities take, whether formal or informal, they are typically very important to the members of the community. Oswald (2000) found that community provided young lesbians with safety, support, information, and a sense of belonging. Kurdek and Schmidt (1987) found that lesbians listed friends as sources of social support three times more often than they listed family. Lesbian community may also provide concrete support in times of need. For example, Aronsona (1998) documented three (separate) networks of caregivers, all in the context of lesbian community, banding together to care for women in the last stages of breast cancer. Such studies provide concrete examples of how lesbian communities may buffer lesbians not only against minority stress, but against other life stresses as well.

LESBIANS OF COLOR

Cochran and Mays (as cited in Ritter & Terndrup, 2002) found that, in contrast to White lesbians, who often depend heavily on the lesbian community for support, Black lesbians who need instrumental help (from small favors to help in financial crisis) turn first to heterosexual members of the African American community, rather than to White lesbians. Thus, for lesbians of color, any chance of estrangement from the ethnic community is especially risky since the ethnic community serves as a buffer against societal racism (Greene, 1994a) and typically serves as both a social and an instrumental support system. Indeed, a study of Black lesbians who were mostly out in the straight Black community found that most of these women also felt some isolation from that ethnic community (Jackson & Brown, 1996). Therapists must therefore not downplay ethnic minority clients' concerns about the possible risks in coming out within the ethnic community. The perceived risk may be even greater for immigrants of color, who rely heavily on their ethnic or language communities for support and belonging. Immigrant lesbians are particularly likely to remain very closeted and isolated from the American lesbian community (Greene, 1994b).

Although some identity development models (e.g., Cass, 1979) include an "integration" stage, in which various identities (e.g., cultural, professional, and spiritual identities) are intertwined, Fukuyama and Ferguson (2000) assert that identity development models that do not recognize concurrent multiple identities are inadequate for lesbians of color, who may maintain a sexual orientation identity quite separate from other identities. Lesbians of color are less likely than White lesbians to report being out to family of origin (Bradford et al., 1994) and typically report conflicts in allegiances to the ethnic and sexual orientation groups to which they belong (e.g., Chan, 1997; Greene, 1994a; Loiacano, 1989; Walters, 1997).

In addition, conflicts between the cultural values of communities may hinder a synthesis of the two identities. For example, the American Indian, Asian, and Latina cultural values of collective identity and keeping peace within the group may conflict with the common (White) gay and lesbian community value on coming out publicly to family and friends (Chan, 1997; Greene, 1997; Walters, 1997). Even within communities and families that might be tolerant of same-sex sexual behavior, there may be a strong cultural demand not to name the identity explicitly (Greene, 1997). Chan (1989) suggested that coming out among Asian lesbians may be particularly difficult because a child coming out may be seen as a failure of the parents and a rejection of family and culture. Chan's respondents frequently reported fears of parental rejection, and although most had disclosed their identity to friends and some family (most often a sister), only 26% of those surveyed had come out to a parent. Therapists familiar with the historical place of two-spirit people among pre-European American Indians[2] should not assume that this history makes coming out easier for this ethnic group. Much of this acceptance was lost after colonization of North America by homophobic Europeans, and most American Indians currently report that they feel no special role in their ethnic community as a result of being gay or lesbian (Jacobs & Brown, 1997).

One response to the lack of acceptance of a lesbian identity within an ethnic community is to form an ethnic identity and a lesbian identity that function independently of each other. Fygetakis (1997), for example, found that her sample of lesbian Greek Americans remained involved but closeted in the Greek American community while also being very involved and politically active in the nonethnic lesbian community. Others, however, may choose to socialize in only one community. Chan's (1989) Asian gay and lesbian respondents (recruited from Asian gay and lesbian events) typically self-identified with both identities, but 75% socialized exclusively in the mainstream LGB community. (Only 26% reported socializing in both the LGB and the Asian communities.)

The contrast between White lesbians' experiences and those of lesbians of color was apparent among Weston's (1997) interviewees: "Whites without a strong ethnic identification often described coming out as a transition from no community *into* community, whereas people of color were more likely to focus on conflicts *between* different identities instead of expressing a sense of relief and arrival" (p. 134). Many authors have discussed the phenomenon of same-sex orientation being perceived in ethnic communities

---

[2] "Two-spirit people" is one translation of the many terms Native American tribes traditionally had for those whose gender expression or sexuality did not correspond to typical behaviors of those of their anatomical sex. Two-spirit people were typically respected and often ascribed with special powers or ceremonial functions (Brown, 1997).

as a White thing (e.g., Chan, 1989; Espin, 1987; Greene, 1997; Tremble, Schneider, & Appathurai, 1989), and heterosexual members of ethnic communities may see members of their community coming out as lesbian as a betrayal of the ethnic community (Chan, 1989; Greene, 1994a, 1997; Rust, 2003). Such attitudes make it especially difficult for lesbians of color to be out in their ethnic communities. Garnets and Kimmel (1991) reviewed relevant literature and concluded that lesbians of color tend to be more identified with their ethnic community, but feel more comfortable when among lesbians. Greater comfort should not, however, be confused with *complete* comfort in the lesbian and gay community. For example, a survey of lesbian and gay Asian Americans found that although 74% socialized exclusively within the lesbian and gay community, 86% reported not feeling acknowledged and accepted within that community (Chan, 1989). Thus, for those forced to choose between socializing in the ethnic community and socializing in the (predominantly White) gay and lesbian community, there is no place of complete comfort (Greene, 1997).

One common solution to this lack of a comfort zone (and one approach to synthesizing multiple identities) is to find communities that share both ethnicity and sexual orientation (Loiacano, 1989; Weston, 1997). For example, 26% of Chan's (1989) respondents reported socializing primarily within an Asian American lesbian and gay community. For lesbians of color living in larger cities, ethnic lesbian communities may be fairly easy to find. There are often local affiliates of national organizations such as Llegó (for LGBT Latinos and Latinas) or local organizations (such as Zami in Atlanta or Affinity in Chicago, both for African American lesbians). Local gay publications or a search of the Internet can identify such groups. However, outside of major cities, such groups are typically not available locally (Tremble et al., 1989). Where such groups are not available, lesbians of color may find each other through the Internet or may simply find an informal social network of other lesbians who share their ethnicity (Jackson & Brown, 1996). Rust (2003, p. 235) has assembled a list of books that may be particularly helpful to lesbians of color, as well as a list of articles for therapists working to help clients of color through the lesbian identity development process.

AGE DIFFERENCES

Young lesbians, especially those still in high school or living at home, face particular barriers to finding community. Gay bars may not be accessible to those under the age of 21, and many small cities lack other public gathering places for LGBT people (Oswald & Culton, 2003). Harassment and violence are very realistic concerns for LGB youth. Pilkington and D'Augelli (1995) found that among LGB youth ages from 15 to 21, 80% had been verbally insulted, 44% threatened with violence, 17% physically assaulted, and 22%

sexually assaulted as a result of their sexual orientation. Various studies have found that one third to one half of LGB junior high and high school students have experienced some form of victimization because of their sexual orientation (see D'Augelli, 1998, for a review). Because of realistic fears of harassment, coming out enough to find community is particularly dangerous for school-age students, making isolation common. For this reason, gay-straight alliances (pro-gay student organizations attended by gay-affirmative straight students as well as LGBT students) may be particularly valuable because one need not publicly self-identify as gay or lesbian in order to attend. School counselors or other school personnel working at high schools that do not yet have such an organization might consider starting one. Another essential role for school counselors is providing anti-homophobia and antiviolence education in the schools. In addition to any positive impact this has in making the school a safer place for LGBT students, the resulting visibility identifies the counselor as an ally whom LGBT students can safely consult. Sears (1991) found that 94% of Southern lesbian and gay adults surveyed said they would have liked to have known an "understanding adult" they could have talked to during high school. LGBT counselors and teachers typically cannot be visible advocates for fear of losing their jobs. Thus, it falls to heterosexual allies to be the visible resources for LGBT youth.

Lesbians coming out later, in young adulthood, face particular issues of their own. They may have to integrate their lesbian identity into other existing identities. For example, they may have already chosen a career (such as public school teaching) that is hostile to lesbians and have to decide whether to remain closeted, change careers, or relocate to one of the few states where discrimination based on sexual orientation is illegal. It is not uncommon for women to marry and have children before coming to identify as lesbian. Thus, adult women working through the coming out process may be dealing with child-custody battles, where discrimination based on sexual orientation is often a realistic concern.

Finally, older lesbians face unique issues, due both to aging and to cohort differences. Because societal attitudes have become more accepting over the last several decades, the era during which a woman formed her lesbian identity may influence her identity and associated values (such as whether she values coming out publicly and whether she is comfortable with the larger gay community and politics). For example, lesbians over the age of 55 are less likely to be out to their families of origin than are younger lesbians (Bradford et al., 1994). Perhaps because of differences in style, norms, and values, lesbians in many communities have formed groups for older women (e.g., "over 40" groups) so that members can socialize with others with whom they feel they have more in common. In addition to cohort differences, there are some age-related issues of special interest to older lesbians, such as finding gay-friendly retirement communities or dealing with health-related issues, such as hospital visitation rights for partners or rights of survivorship (Barón & Cramer, 2000). As with other subsets of the lesbian community, there are also national organizations for older lesbians that can provide resources or social contacts (Barón & Cramer, 2000).

COMMUNITY NORMS

It is very important for lesbians (and their therapists) to understand that lesbian community norms are important variables in lesbians' lives. Various lesbian communities hold different normative behaviors and values. Differences between individuals' own values and behaviors and the perceived norms of the local lesbian community can prevent absorption of that lesbian into the community in at least two ways. First, a lesbian who does not conform to the normative values of the community may be excluded by that community for not conforming. For example, one of Oswald and Culton's (2003) respondents reported being shunned in a rural LGB community for being too out. Second, when community norms are perceived to be at odds with an individual's values, she may avoid the community (Krieger, 1982). Schroeder & Shidlo (2003), for example, found that many of those who sought out religion-based conversion therapy in an attempt to change an LGB orientation reported doing so because of a "profound sense of alienation and failure to connect with either the LGB or heterosexual communities" (p. 5) and reported that "they viewed a homosexual orientation as an intrinsic obstacle to creating a sense of community" (p. 5). Thus, the perceived need for conversion to heterosexuality was, for some, an outgrowth of a failure to find a community of LGB people with whom they could identify.

However, even when the values of the dominant LGB community conflict with a client's values, it is often possible to locate subcommunities where individual lesbians feel more at home. Helping clients understand that there are many lesbian communities or friendship circles, rather than just one, in a given city or region can help clients understand that their decision may not be about whether to become active in *the* lesbian community, but rather may be about seeking *a* community of lesbians (or LGBT people) within which they will feel most at home. Finally, in some cases, isolated lesbians may need to consider relocating to a larger city or to a town where lesbian community is more available. Anecdotally, it is not uncommon (or unreasonable) for lesbians to carefully consider the presence of visible and accessible lesbian community when making decisions about jobs or relocations.

SPIRITUAL COMMUNITIES

Lesbians in some spiritual communities may experience some of the same conflicts between communities as do lesbians of color. Dworkin (1997) described the triple jeopardy of lesbian Jews, who often face homophobia in mainstream synagogues, sexism in gay and lesbian synagogues, and anti-Semitism in the lesbian community. The cultural expectation that a woman meet her social needs within the Jewish community can also make involvement in the broader lesbian community feel like a betrayal of her Jewish community (Dworkin, 1997). Greek lesbians face similar issues in a culture in which the Greek Orthodox Church serves as the center of the ethnic community (Fygetakis, 1997).

Many religious lesbians experience conflicts between religious teachings and their sexual orientation as they are coming out, and they report dealing with these perceived conflicts in a variety of ways. (See Schuck & Liddle, 2001, for a summary of successful approaches and resources that facilitated these resolutions.) Therapists should be prepared to help clients find more affirming denominations or congregations or find books and Web sites that reinterpret problematic Biblical passages. Therapists should also be aware that every major U.S. denomination has a corresponding LGB organization, which can easily be found on the Internet. These organizations may provide a good starting point for many religious clients experiencing conflict.

LESBIANS WITH DISABILITIES

Access to lesbian communities may be particularly challenging for lesbians with disabilities. For those with mobility impairments who depend on family members to transport them to events, accessing lesbian events may be difficult (Greene, 2003). Although the lesbian community has historically been ahead of the mainstream community in trying to make events accessible to those with disabilities (e.g., by providing sign language interpreters or asking attendees to avoid wearing fragrances that make others ill), accessibility remains an issue for lesbians with disabilities. Assertiveness (e.g., asking organizations of interest to meet in accessible locations or frequently reminding attendees of a no-scent policy) may be essential in allowing disabled women to remain connected to the larger community.

FAMILIES OF CHOICE

For some lesbians, certain friends take on a status of "family of choice" or "gay family" (Weston, 1997). Gartrell et al. (1999) found that 38% of lesbian couples who had had a baby together had incorporated close friends as aunts and uncles to create an extended family network. For lesbians estranged from blood family, chosen family may take the place of family of origin for support, serving as emotional support systems, providing support in caring for children, and even providing a safe landing place when a member of the chosen family is sick or hungry or homeless. For others, blood family remains intact, but chosen family fulfills a different role, providing a lifetime of emotional support from people who understand them in a way that straight family never will (Weston, 1997).

For lesbians, ex-lovers are often a part of this chosen family. Weston's (1997) interviews revealed that remaining emotionally intimate with (selected) ex-lovers is not uncommon in the lesbian community. Although maintaining close contact with one's ex is far from universal, ex-lovers who have managed to make the transition from lover to chosen family have reported tremendous value in these relationships (Weston, 1997), and therapists for whom such a relationship seems strange must not pathologize this cultural difference.

TREATMENT ISSUES AS THEY RELATE TO COMMUNITIES

Because of the high value of lesbian communities in lesbians' lives, therapists should consider the value, where possible, of providing mental health treatment in the context of lesbian communities. Although few cities have clinics specifically dedicated to serving the LGB community, many cities do have groups such as lesbian support groups, a lesbian incest survivor group, or an LGB Alcoholics Anonymous (AA) meeting. Lesbian clients may be more willing to attend such groups because they won't fear homophobia-based rejection, and such groups may help integrate isolated lesbians into the community. Local lesbian therapists may know of or provide support groups, and most large cities have LGB or LGB-friendly AA meetings.

CONCLUSION

Lesbian clients may come to therapy at any point in the identity development process. Sometimes their presenting concerns are directly related to their sexual orientation (e.g., when they need help coming to terms with a lesbian identity or deciding whether to come out to parents). At other times, their presenting concerns will be primarily unrelated to sexual orientation (e.g., when choosing a career or dealing with health problems). But even when it is not a central topic, sexual orientation may complicate client concerns because of issues such as discrimination or social support. Thus, even when sexual orientation issues are not paramount, lesbians' lives and communities form a backdrop that therapists must understand to be effective in their work with these clients. Understanding identity development and disclosure, the importance of lesbian community, and the special issues of lesbians of various backgrounds—the themes addressed in this chapter—should help therapists begin building an understanding of the complex social environment in which their lesbian clients live. This understanding, sometimes central to the therapeutic work, and sometimes only residing in the background, will always be important to therapeutic effectiveness.

REFERENCES

Aronsona, J. (1998). Lesbians giving and receiving care: Stretching conceptualizations of caring and community. *Women's Studies International Forum, 21*, 505–519.

Barón, A., & Cramer, D. W. (2000). Potential counseling concerns of aging lesbian, gay, and bisexual clients. In R. M. Perez, K. A. DeBord, & K. J. Bieschke (Eds.), *Handbook of counseling and psychotherapy with lesbian, gay, and bisexual clients* (pp. 207–223). Washington, DC: American Psychological Association.

Barret, B., & Logan, C. (2002). *Counseling gay men and lesbians: A practice primer.* Pacific Grove, CA: Brooks/Cole.

Bos, H. M. W, van Balen, F., & van den Boom, D. C. (2004). Experience of parenthood, couple relationship, social support, and child-rearing goals in planned lesbian mother families. *Journal of Child Psychology and Psychiatry, 45*, 755–764.

Bradford, J., Ryan, C., & Rothblum, E. D. (1994). National lesbian health care survey: Implications for mental health care. *Journal of Consulting and Clinical Psychology, 62*, 228–242.

Brown, L. B. (Ed.). (1997). *Two spirit people: American Indian lesbian women and gay men.* Binghamton, NY: Haworth Press.

Cass, V. C. (1979). Homosexual identity formation: A theoretical model. *Journal of Homosexuality, 4*(3), 219–235.

Chan, C. S. (1989). Issues of identity development among Asian-American lesbians and gay men. *Journal of Counseling and Development, 68*, 16–21.

Chan, C. S. (1997). Don't ask, don't tell, don't know: The formation of a homosexual identity and sexual expression among Asian American lesbians. In B. Greene (Ed.), *Psychological perspectives on lesbian and gay issues: Vol. 3. Ethnic and cultural diversity among lesbians and gay men* (pp. 240–248). Thousand Oaks, CA: Sage.

Coleman, E. (1982). Developmental stages of the coming-out process. *Journal of Homosexuality, 7*(2/3), 31–43.

D'Augelli, A. R. (1998). Developmental implications of victimization of lesbian, gay, and bisexual youths. In G. M. Herek (Ed.), *Psychological perspectives on lesbian and gay issues: Vol. 4. Stigma and sexual orientation: Understanding prejudice against lesbians, gay men, and bisexuals* (pp. 187–210). Thousand Oaks, CA: Sage.

Dworkin, S. H. (1997). Female, lesbian, and Jewish: Complex and invisible. In B. Greene (Ed.), *Psychological perspectives on lesbian and gay issues: Vol. 3. Ethnic and cultural diversity among lesbians and gay men* (pp. 63–87). Thousand Oaks, CA: Sage.

Espin, O. (1987). Issues of identity in the psychology of Latina lesbians. In Boston Lesbian Psychologist Collective (Eds.), *Lesbian psychologies: Explorations and challenges* (pp. 35–51). Urbana: University of Illinois.

Fukuyama, M. A., & Ferguson, A. D. (2000). Lesbian, gay, and bisexual people of color: Understanding cultural complexity and managing multiple oppressions. In R. M. Perez, K. A. DeBord, & K. J. Bieschke (Eds.), *Handbook of counseling and psychotherapy with lesbian, gay, and bisexual clients* (pp. 81–105). Washington, DC: American Psychological Association.

Fygetakis, L. M. (1997). Greek American lesbians: Identity odysseys of honorable good girls. In B. Greene (Ed.), *Psychological perspectives on lesbian and gay issues:*

Vol. 3. Ethnic and cultural diversity among lesbians and gay men (pp. 152–190). Thousand Oaks, CA: Sage.

Garnets, L., & Kimmel, D. (1991). Lesbian and gay male dimensions in the psychological study of human diversity. In J. D. Goodchilds (Ed.), *Psychological perspectives on human diversity in America* (pp. 137–192). Washington, DC: American Psychological Association.

Gartrell, N., Banks, A., Hamilton, J., Reed, N., Bishop, H., & Rodas, C. (1999). The National Lesbian Family Study: 2. Interviews with mothers of toddlers. *American Journal of Orthopsychiatry, 69,* 362–369.

Gartrell, N., Banks, A., Reed, N., Hamilton, J., Rodas, C., & Deck, A. (2000). The National Lesbian Family Study: 3. Interviews with mothers of five-year-olds. *American Journal of Orthopsychiatry, 70,* 542–548.

Greene, B. (1994a). Ethnic-minority lesbians and gay men: Mental health and treatment issues. *Journal of Consulting and Clinical Psychology, 62,* 243–251.

Greene, B. (1994b). Lesbian women of color: Triple jeopardy. In L. Comas-Diaz & B. Greene (Eds.), *Women of color: Integrating ethnic and gender identities in psychotherapy* (pp. 389–427). New York: Guilford.

Greene, B. (1997). Ethnic minority lesbians and gay men: Mental health and treatment issues. In B. Greene (Ed.), *Psychological perspectives on lesbian and gay issues: Vol. 3. Ethnic and cultural diversity among lesbians and gay men* (pp. 216–239). Thousand Oaks, CA: Sage.

Greene, B. (2003). Beyond heterosexism and across the cultural divide—Developing an inclusive lesbian, gay, and bisexual psychology: A look to the future. In L. D. Garnets & D. C. Kimmel (Eds.), *Psychological perspectives on lesbian, gay, and bisexual experiences* (2nd ed., pp. 357–400). New York: Columbia University Press.

Harry, J. (1993). Being out: A general model. *Journal of Homosexuality, 26,* 25–39.

Hequembourg, A. L., & Farrell, M. P. (1999). Lesbian motherhood: Negotiating marginal-mainstream identities. *Gender & Society, 13,* 540–557.

Herek, G. M. (2003). Why tell if you're not asked? Self-disclosure, intergroup contact, and heterosexuals' attitudes toward lesbians and gay men. In L. D. Garnets & D. C. Kimmel (Eds.), *Psychological perspectives on lesbian, gay, and bisexual experiences* (2nd ed., pp. 270–298). New York: Columbia University Press.

Human Rights Campaign. (2006). *Statewide anti-discrimination laws & policies.* Retrieved March 2006, from http://www.hrc.org/Template.cfm?Section=Your_Community&Template=/ContentManagement/ContentDisplay.cfm&ContentID=14821

Jackson, K., & Brown, L. B. (1996). Lesbians of African heritage: Coming out in the straight community. *Journal of Gay & Lesbian Social Services, 5*(4), 53–67.

Jacobs, M. A., & Brown, L. B. (1997). American Indian lesbians and gays: An exploratory study. In L. B. Brown (Ed.), *Two spirit people: American Indian lesbian women and gay men* (pp. 29–41). Binghamton, NY: Haworth. (Simultaneously published as *Journal of Gay & Lesbian Social Services, 6*(2), 29–41)

Krieger, S. (1982). Lesbian identity and community: Recent social science literature. *Signs, 8,* 91–108.

Kurdek, L. A., & Schmidt, J. P. (1987). Perceived emotional support from family and friends in members of homosexual, married, and heterosexual cohabiting couples. *Journal of Homosexuality, 14,* 57–68.

Liddle, B. J. (1996). Therapist sexual orientation, gender, and counseling practices as they relate to ratings of helpfulness by gay and lesbian clients. *Journal of Counseling Psychology, 43,* 394–401.

Litovich, M. L., & Langhout, R. D. (2004). Framing heterosexism in lesbian families: A preliminary examination of resilient coping. *Journal of Community & Applied Social Psychology, 14,* 411–435.

Lockard, D. (1986). The lesbian community: An anthropological approach. *Journal of Homosexuality, 11*(3–4), 83–95.

Loiacano, D. K. (1989). Gay identity issues among black Americans: Racism, homophobia, and the need for validation. *Journal of Counseling and Development, 68,* 21–25.

Markowe, L. A. (2002). Coming out as lesbian. In A. Coyle & C. Kitzinger (Eds.), *Lesbian and gay psychology: New perspectives* (pp. 63–80). Oxford, England: Blackwell.

McCarn, S. R., & Fassinger, R. E. (1996). Revisioning sexual minority identity formation: A new model of lesbian identity and its implications for counseling and research. *The Counseling Psychologist, 24,* 508–534.

McDonald, G. J. (1982). Individual differences in the coming-out process for gay men: Implications for theoretical models. *Journal of Homosexuality, 8*(1), 47–60.

Meyer, I. H. (2003). Prejudice, social stress, and mental health in lesbian, gay, and bisexual populations: Conceptual issues and research evidence. *Psychological Bulletin, 129,* 674–697.

Morales, E. S. (1992). Counseling Latino gays and Latina lesbians. In S. H. Dworkin & F. Gutierrez (Eds.), *Counseling gay men and lesbians: Journey to the end of the rainbow* (pp. 125–139). Alexandria, VA: American Association for Counseling and Development.

Oswald, R. F. (2000). Family and friendship relationships after young women come out as bisexual or lesbian. *Journal of Homosexuality, 38*(3), 65–83.

Oswald, R. F., & Culton, L. S. (2003). Under the rainbow: Rural gay life and its relevance for family providers. *Family Relations: Journal of Applied Family & Child Studies, 52,* 72–81.

Patterson, C. J., Hurt, S., & Mason, C. D. (1998). Families of the lesbian baby boom: Children's contact with grandparents and other adults. *American Journal of Orthopsychiatry, 68,* 390–399.

Pearlman, S. F. (1987). The saga of continuing clash in lesbian community, or Will an army of ex-lovers fail? In Boston Lesbian Psychologies Collective (Eds.), *Lesbian psychologies: Explorations and challenges* (pp. 313–326). Chicago: University of Illinois.

Pilkington, N. W., & D'Augelli, A. R. (1995). Victimization of lesbian, gay, and bisexual youth in community settings. *Journal of Community Psychology, 23,* 34–56.

Ragins, B. R., & Cornwell, J. M. (2001). Pink triangles: Antecedents and consequences of perceived workplace discrimination against gay and lesbian employees. *Journal of Applied Psychology, 86,* 1244–1261.

Ritter, K. Y., & Terndrup, A. I. (2002). *Handbook of affirmative psychotherapy with lesbians and gay men*. New York: Guilford.

Rosario, M., Hunter, J., Maguen, S., Gwadz, M., & Smith, R. (2001). The coming-out process and its adaptational and health-related associations among gay, lesbian, and bisexual youths: Stipulations and exploration of a model. *American Journal of Community Psychology, 29*, 133–160.

Rostosky, S. S., & Riggle, E. D. B. (2002). "Out" at work: The relation of actor and partner workplace policy and internalized homophobia to disclosure status. *Journal of Counseling Psychology, 49*, 411–419.

Rust, P. C. (1992). The politics of sexual identity: Sexual attraction and behavior among lesbian and bisexual women. *Social Problems, 39*, 366–386.

Rust, P. C. (2003). Finding a sexual identity and community: Therapeutic implications and cultural assumptions in scientific models of coming out. In L. D. Garnets & D. C. Kimmel (Eds.), *Psychological perspectives on lesbian, gay, and bisexual experiences* (2nd ed., pp. 227–269). New York: Columbia Univeristy Press.

Savin-Williams, R. C., & Diamond, L. M. (2000). Sexual identity trajectories among sexual-minority youths: Gender comparisons. *Archives of Sexual Behavior, 29*, 607–627.

Schroeder, M., & Shidlo, A. (2003). Religiously based conversion therapy: The need to belong. *Division 44 Newsletter, 19*(1), 5.

Schuck, K. D., & Liddle, B. J. (2001). Religious conflicts experienced by lesbian, gay, and bisexual individuals. *Journal of Gay & Lesbian Psychotherapy, 5*, 63–82.

Sears, J. T. (1991). Research methods, methodological issues, and participant data. In J. T. Sears (Ed.), *Growing up gay in the South: Race, gender, and journeys of the spirit* (pp. 431–464). New York: Harrington Park Press.

Smith, A. (1997). Cultural diversity and the coming-out process: Implications for clinical practice. In B. Greene (Ed.), *Psychological perspectives on lesbian and gay issues: Vol. 3. Ethnic and cultural diversity among lesbians and gay men* (pp. 279–300). Thousand Oaks, CA: Sage.

Tremble, B., Schneider, M., & Appathurai, C. (1989). Growing up gay or lesbian in a multicultural context. *Journal of Homosexuality, 17*, 253–267.

Walters, K. L. (1997). Urban lesbian and gay American Indian identity: Implications for mental health service delivery. In L. B. Brown (Ed.), *Two spirit people: American Indian lesbian women and gay men* (pp. 43–65). Binghamton, NY: Haworth. (Simultaneously published as *Journal of Gay & Lesbian Social Services, 6*(2), 43–65)

Weston, K. (1995). Get thee to a big city: Sexual imaginary and the Great Gay Migration. *GLQ, 2*, 253–277.

Weston, K. (1997). *Families we choose: Lesbians, gays, kinship*. New York: Columbia University Press.

3

THE VILLAGE PEOPLE: IDENTITY AND DEVELOPMENT IN THE GAY MALE COMMUNITY

DOUGLAS C. HALDEMAN

The presumption of heterosexuality as the only normal sexual identity and behavior, or *heterocentrism*, was institutionalized in postwar American culture. Lesbian, gay male, bisexual, and transgender (LGBT) individuals in the 1950s and 1960s were cast under a shroud of perversion and illness. The normative response to this stigma on the part of most LGBT individuals was closetedness; the resulting effect was a near-total lack of social support. American society was largely unaware of its LGBT members—the vast majority of whom were living secret lives.

The Stonewall era ushered in a movement of social change that continues to the present day. LGBT individuals now have communities in which to connect socially, develop communication networks, establish an economic and political power base, and create cultural institutions and traditions. Given the daily presence of lesbian and gay characters on television programs, as well as the prominence of gay-related issues in the news media, it is no longer possible for the dominant culture to be unaware of LGBT individuals and their concerns. This exposure has resulted in a significant shift in the mainstream public's attitudes toward LGBT individuals and in increased support for those individuals' civil rights (Seidman, 2002). Conversely, not all LGBT individuals support assimilation into the dominant culture, and some warn against the loss of sociocultural uniqueness that is the hallmark of gay culture (Harris, 1997), pointing out that ~~gay assimilation does not revoke heterosexual privilege~~.

This chapter examines the LGBT community's evolution and function from a developmental perspective, with a particular focus on institutions created and used by gay men. The institutions of the present-day gay community, the issues of diversity therein, and the benefits—and risks—of membership in the gay community are examined, as is the role of the gay community in an individual's gay identity development. The relevance of these issues for clinicians working with gay men is discussed throughout the chapter. Finally, some observations about the gay communities of the future, as well as about the evolving relationship between the gay community and the dominant culture, concludes the chapter.

For purposes of terminology, the term *gay* is used in reference to men who endorse a primary erotic and affiliative attraction to other men, who have so identified, and who are, at least to some degree, "out"—in the gay male community or in the mainstream culture. Men who engage in homosexual activity, either regularly or episodically, but who do not identify as gay, are referred to, for the purposes of this discussion, as *same-sex attracted* (SSA). LGB (lesbian, gay, and bisexual) is used when the reference is intended to include lesbian women and bisexual men and bisexual women along with gay men. Transgender members of the larger LGBT community are referenced when appropriate. It should also be noted that the function of gay male communities—on personal as well as social, economic, and political levels—is under-researched. As a result, most of the work in this area is theoretical or sociographic in nature.

The term *gay community*, as it is used in this chapter, refers to the sociocultural world of gay men. Clearly, there is a great deal of overlap between the cultural organizations and institutions of gay men, lesbians, and bisexuals. Furthermore, maximum solidarity among various elements of the LGBT communities is desirable for a variety of political and economic reasons. Nevertheless, the history and function of lesbian-community institutions are distinct from those of gay men's community institutions and are chronicled by Liddle (chap. 2, this volume). Similarly, although there is considerable continuity between the gay male and bisexual communities, the bisexual community is a distinct group with its own institutions. For a cogent discussion of the relationship between bisexual identity development and the bisexual and lesbian and gay communities, the reader is referred to Firestein (chap. 4, this volume), Potoczniak (chap. 5, this volume), and Rust (1996).

An awareness of the gay community and its institutions and traditions is an asset for any clinician working with gay male clients. The community has been viewed as a significant attachment element in the gay man's life during the coming out process (Gonsiorek & Rudolph, 1991). Furthermore, it is an important resource for social activity as well as for any number of creative, political, or athletic organizations that may be of interest to the gay male client. The experience of LGBT identity can initially be quite isolating. It is connection with the community that heals the wounds internalized by LGBT people from a heterocentric and sometimes-unwelcoming dominant culture.

"IT TAKES A VILLAGE"

The gay community is most often associated with large urban centers, although many smaller cities and towns now offer opportunities for LGB individuals to connect socially with one another and are developing their own community institutions (Miller, 1989; Seidman, 2002). Personal connections in the community may be facilitated by social venues and institutions or by any of a number of LGB groups organized around cultural, political, athletic, aesthetic, religious, or professional interests. It is clear that the gay community, since its inception post-Stonewall, has expanded from a few urban centers and diversified tremendously. The Internet creates opportunities for connection that have redefined the ways in which we socialize and exchange information, and the communities in most urban areas now feature subcultures for those with particular eroto-social orientations, such as leather men and "bears," or subcultures with specific aesthetic and gender-focused elements, such as the drag court.

Murray (1996) identified two characteristics of community: (a) territory and (b) solidarity and collective action. In terms of territory, Murray's review of San Francisco census data revealed that a number of neighborhoods in that city have a substantial or majority gay male population. Many urban centers have areas with a visible gay presence, in terms of both residential and entrepreneurial elements. Not all who identify as members of the gay community reside in these neighborhoods or work in these businesses or areas. However, the presence of institutions is critical to the definition of community. Murray found, "The existence of distinctive institutions is more salient to the identification of a community—both for insiders and for outsiders—than is residential segregation or concentration" (1996, p. 190). The first, and still most prominent, such institution was the gay bar. In addition to being a social venue, the bar is historically regarded as a safe place to exchange information, develop informal support networks, and engage in community organizing. In this regard, the gay bar ironically resembles religious groups and institutions of oppressed ethnic minorities.

The second community criterion identified by Murray is solidarity and collective action. The proliferation of groups and organizations in the gay community has generated a concomitant increase in the number and kind of activities that are available for gay men wishing to become involved in the community. The gay community in urban areas provides a base from which the gay man is able to socialize, perform service work, participate in cultural and athletic events, pursue hobbies with other gay men, engage in political activity, and patronize gay-owned businesses. The gay and mainstream media facilitate these activities by providing local and national coverage of initiatives that are important to the lives of gay men and their families.

These concepts are salient for the clinician who works with gay male clients. The concept of territory is key to the felt sense of safety that is important to gay men. Recently, traveling across the country with our dogs, my partner and I encountered homophobic taunting—in, of all places, Laramie, Wyoming: the very town where Matthew Shepard was murdered in 1998. Despite being middle-aged and having come out in the 1970s, this incident shook me to the core. It reminded me that whatever our stage in life, and whether we are urban or rural LGBT people, we need a sense of safety in order to function optimally—a sense that is still inconsistent in many places in our country.

On the other hand, solidarity and collective action are important for the joy and energy that they have the potential to create. Participating in the gay community's groups and traditions offers many a chance to grow socially and emotionally, while also offering a place for LGBT individuals to bond together and to contribute to the social well-being of the entire community. It is important for clinicians working with gay men to understand that the LGBT community holds potential for personal identity development as well as potential for social and existential growth. It may not be realistic for non-LGBT clinicians to have an in-depth knowledge of the LGBT community, especially in a large urban area where the community may be quite diverse. Nonetheless, it would be helpful for the clinician to have at least a passing knowledge of the resources available and traditions that are commonly practiced in the local LGBT community. Not only is this relevant from the practical standpoint of being able to offer information to the gay client, but this also can have a positive effect on the therapeutic relationship between the gay client and the non-LGBT or non-identified therapist. A therapist's knowing, for example, when the local Gay Pride celebration takes place may be beneficial to the LGBT client and the therapeutic relationship itself.

How do LGBT communities differ from other cultural groups? In contrast to ethnolingusitically distinct communities, for example, not being able to speak the language of the dominant culture does not oblige gay men to associate. Many gay men are able to "pass" as heterosexual in the dominant culture and may move—with varying degrees of ease—back and forth between jobs in the mainstream and residences or social outlets in the gay community. In fact, in some urban areas, antidiscrimination protection and prevailing social attitudes have rendered "passing" obsolete. Gay men choose to participate in community based on the common denominator of sexual and affiliative orientation. Unlike members of some ethnolinguistic communities, however, the gay man may come to his community with a weak sense of social continuity or history. Therefore, to Murray's list of community criteria, I would add the concept of *traditions and cultural values*. The gay community is made up of individuals who may not be legally or biologically related. This highlights the importance of common values and cultural traditions as a factor to enhance solidarity in the community. Another important solidifying factor is the physical and psychological sense of security offered by the community in a heterocentric dominant culture.

Given the preceding attributes of the gay community, or "village," we turn to the question of who its inhabitants—or, "village people," if you will—are. Murray's survey of San Francisco gay men (1996) identified three factors as significant in determining whether or not an individual belonged to the gay community: identifying as gay, residing in a gay neighborhood, and socializing with other gay friends. His research showed that by far, the most important variable was identifying as gay, which was seen as significantly more important than either geographic residence or choice of friends.

Conventional wisdom about LGBT communities validates Murray's findings. An unknown number of same-sex attracted (SSA) individuals, so defined by their homoerotic behaviors, engage in sexual activity on the physical margins of the gay community (in restrooms or parks). These men may be married to women, or they may be single; typically, they live in a world that views them as heterosexual. They may interact with gay-identified men who seek sexual variety in the aforementioned venues, but they themselves are not part of the gay community.

Other gay men may live and work outside the geographic boundaries of the gay community or may reside in a place that has no gay community per se. Nevertheless, they are members of the community if they so identify. Socializing with other gay men and participating in community events such as concerts, sporting events, or the annual Pride parade indicate a connection to the community. Participating in any of the community's myriad groups and organizations, engaging in service work, even making a point of shopping at the local gay bookstore—these are all activities that can foster a bond between the individual and his community, the potential developmental and therapeutic import of which has been previously noted.

Sexual orientation is a variable that cuts across all races, cultures, age groups, and ability statuses. The LGBT community therefore reflects this diversity, although its embrace of some of these attributes may vary. Gay men of color, for instance, may experience the same racism in the gay community that is present in the dominant culture (Seidman, 2002). This marginalization may be compounded by the fact that they have experienced homophobic attitudes and behaviors from their families or communities of color. In some areas, the most visible members of the gay community, and its norms for interpersonal relating, are Euro-American. In other cities, especially in large urban areas, the visible representation is more ethnically diverse. Other cultures may have different norms for interpreting sexual behavior and identity, which further distances the gay community from some of its members of color. Rust (1996) emphasized the importance of access to culturally relevant resources for people of color in gay communities. Seidman (2002) pointed out that in some cases, connection with an ethnic minority subculture within the gay community may be the most satisfactory way for a gay person of color to truly feel a sense of belonging in his community.

Historically, the gay community has been characterized as youth- and looks-focused. Although this is becoming less true over time, given the general aging of the gay population, many gay men over 40 still experience social exclusion in the community. This issue is compounded for differently abled gay men, who report feeling invisible in the context of gay society (American Psychological Association [APA], Division 44/Committee on Lesbian, Gay, and Bisexual Concerns Joint Task Force, 2000). Most gay communities now offer a variety of resources for gay men over 40, and some offer groups and workshops on intergenerational friendships. Nevertheless, issues of loneliness and isolation are shown to be a significant concern for the aging gay population (Grossman, D'Augelli, & O'Connell, 2003) and hence for clinicians working with men in that population.

EVOLUTION OF THE COMMUNITY

"Without a shared sense of historical and cultural experience, lesbians and gay men must often recreate their communities" (Garnets & D'Augelli, 1995, p. 305). These authors pointed out that the modern LGBT communities are founded on a rich history that, although relatively recent, is unknown by many LGBT individuals. Gay historian Eric Marcus has offered a detailed, in-depth examination of the pioneers of gay history, as well as anecdotal accounts of the recent past (2002). Psychologists will be particularly interested in the work of Rothblum (2000), whose work chronicles gay history from the standpoint of LGB mental health. Kaiser's publication (1997), in a contextual discussion of gay social history and the development of the gay community's institutions, frames the community's establishment as a successful coping strategy for a poisonous social environment. The cultural and aesthetic history of the gay community, including an in-depth examination of camp and the pantheon of gay icons, has been presented by McCourt (2004).

Rothblum (2000) noted that although the stage was set for the creation of gay and lesbian communities by the post–World War II migration of lesbian and gay service personnel to urban centers, it was the Stonewall uprisings of 1969 that are usually seen as the point of departure for the modern-day gay rights movement and the LGBT community. These pivotal events are chronicled in Martin Duberman's 1993 book, *Stonewall*. If a psychologist working with gay clients is unfamiliar with the Stonewall rebellion, he or she may find Duberman's account of interest. After New York City police had been harassing gay bars and their patrons for years, the Stonewall Inn was the first site where LGBT people fought back against this organized oppression. An actual fight ensued between patrons and police in June of 1969, and paradoxically, for all of its socioaesthetic emphasis on the value of hypermasculinity, the Stonewall rebellion was led by a group of exasperated drag queens. Prior to Stonewall, of course, gay bars had existed in many urban areas, but in secret. Doors leading to gay clubs were generally unmarked; there were no windows. What Stonewall changed was the collective consciousness of shame and submission on the part of gay people. As the custom of hiding social venues behind solid doors without signs began to change, gay culture became more open, and a visible community was born. Further information about the Stonewall rebellion is available in Duberman (1993) and Rothblum (2000).

Garnets and D'Augelli (1995) observed that the Stonewall era ushered in "the development of visible subcultures, the formation of lesbian/gay-identified settings and institutions, and intensified political mobilization" (p. 296). They further pointed out, "The philosophy guiding the post-Stonewall gay liberation movement of the early 1970's was that invisibility maintained social oppression by fueling stereotypes and allowing myths to remain unchanged" (pp. 296–297). As a result, the importance of coming out was paramount; disclosure was seen as central to advancing the cause of gay liberation. Clinically speaking, this concept is still true today on a personal level. Psychologists are encouraged to remember that optimal mental health for LGB individuals is associated with individuals' acceptance of their sexual orientation (APA, Division 44/Committee on Lesbian, Gay, and Bisexual Concerns Joint Task Force, 2000).

During the 1970s, social institutions of the gay community began to develop and expand. The dark hideaways of the 1950s and 1960s gave way to bright, glitzy discos with a visible location in the community as a whole. The gay liberation era was in its infancy, and babe that it was, the community reveled in its narcissistic glory. For the first time, gay men claimed an entitlement to openness about their sexual expression. This sense of openness was reflected in the music, attire, and behavior of the time. Heteromimetic, monogamous models for relationships were for the most part rejected by gay men in favor of sexual variety. For gay men, liberation equaled sexual freedom, and gay cultural institutions of the time were a mirror for an era of unparalleled sexual permissiveness.

It was at this time that the diversity inherent in the gay community began to surface. The Castro Street–inspired "clone" style—a hypermasculine form of attire and body type—became enthroned as the gay male ideal, in sharp contrast to the acceptance of "nelly," feminized presentations in the 1950s and 1960s. Sexual tastes were codified in color handkerchiefs, and these were worn in the back pocket of Levis, depending on one's preference for passive or dominant sexual roles. Generally speaking, if it was about sex, it was visible; an entire generation of baby-boomer gay men who had suffered in silence through adolescence was suddenly catapulted into an arena where their deepest, darkest secrets were not just permitted—they were encouraged. The result was exhilarating, and on the foundation of free sexual expression was built a network of businesses and agencies aimed at creating a gay economy and culture.

This increased visibility, predictably, generated a cultural backlash. In 1977, former entertainer Anita Bryant started the "Save Our Children" campaign (or as it was later known, "Protect Our Children"), in fear that the recognition of LGB people as legitimate citizens would empower their "recruitment" efforts toward the nation's children, many of whom would be hypnotically drawn to this glamorous lifestyle. Her political activism, however, was no joke: When Bryant engineered a recall of Miami/Dade County's antidiscrimination ordinance in housing and employment to lesbians and gay men, the gay community knew it was facing a civil rights fight, a civil rights battle that continues, in some form, to the present day. Bryant's initiative sparked similar efforts in St. Paul, Minnesota, and Wichita, Kansas.

These initiatives, however, generated a transition in the gay community from a previously social culture to one solidified around political and economic interests. Bryant had been employed as a spokesperson by the Florida Orange Growers' Commission. After an aggressive boycott of Florida orange juice by the LGB community, her contract was terminated. This success fueled a mobilization of political organizing to successfully turn back initiatives in Seattle that opposed civil rights for the LGB community. A particularly vicious ballot initiative to ban gay men and lesbians from teaching in California's public schools was soundly defeated in late 1978. After years spent in the bars and gyms, the gay community was finding—and flexing—its political muscle.

The winds of change were in the air at the end of the decade, however. Two weeks after the victory for gay teachers in California, San Francisco's Mayor, George Moscone, and one of the nation's first openly gay elected officials, Supervisor Harvey Milk, were assassinated at City Hall. Many gay and lesbian individuals later described this event as their "Kennedy assassination," and it served to signal to the community that some had responded to the community's visibility with unimaginable hatred. Little did anyone know at the time that these events would serve as a bridge from the 1970s, the gay community's carefree childhood, into the most sobering of adolescent experiences imaginable in the 1980s.

Fortunately, there had been 10 years' worth of community network building in place prior to the advent of the health crisis in the early

1980s. The mood, and focus, of the gay community shifted radically from pleasure-seeking to caregiving. The free sexual expression that had heretofore been so highly valued became associated with debilitating illness and premature death. The community was suddenly called upon to create networks for health care and social support in the face of a lethal illness whose cause was poorly understood and upon which the government turned a deaf ear. It was at this time that the community's resolve was most sorely tested. Community and philanthropic groups sprang up quickly to provide support for those living with AIDS/HIV and for their support networks. One positive byproduct of this catastrophe seemed to be a deeper sense of connection among many in the community, as well as with the lesbian sisters who had been disaffected some years before by many gay men's patriarchal attitudes. Furthermore, responses to the health crisis laid the groundwork for an enhanced relationship between the gay community and its heterosexual allies.

The political mobilization generated by the health crisis was useful when, in the 1990s, the gay community was confronted with religious political extremists intent on excluding lesbians and gay men from civil rights and protection against discrimination. With the distorted but catchy sound bite "no special rights" (for lesbians and gay men) resounding in rhetoric, the nation was swept with a host of local and state ballot initiatives designed to establish lesbians and gay individuals as members of a group who had "freely chosen" their "lifestyles" and were thus undeserving of "special" protection from discrimination in housing and employment. Combating these initiatives required considerable resources of time and funding but also provided the indirect benefit of an again-strengthened community. It was not until the U.S. Supreme Court overturned Colorado's Amendment 2, which would have excluded lesbians and gay men from state antidiscrimination statutes, that these initiatives were stopped for being unconstitutional. Conservative Christianity's political activists require polarities. The righteous cannot be elevated without identifying sinners; "good" cannot be conceptualized in this dichotomous religious system without targeting "evil." Lesbians and gay men are the last remaining social target of many fundamentalists armed with scriptural justification (Herman, 1997). Psychologists should consider the potentially stigmatizing effect of this kind of political activity on the individual (APA, Division 44/Committee on Lesbian, Gay, and Bisexual Concerns Joint Task Force, 2000), considering that many LGBT people report significant emotional trauma when their civil rights are up for a vote.

The gay community started as a mechanism for social connection and has evolved to include political activism, cultural development, and caregiving. The community is diverse in terms of race and ethnicity and in terms of generational differences. The ongoing demands of the AIDS epidemic and the need for education require that the community maintain its focus on health-related concerns. The social issues most prominent for lesbians and gay men at present are those associated with family. As more lesbians and gay men have or adopt children, protection of custodial and adoptive parental rights becomes an issue of paramount importance. Same-sex marriage has emerged as a prominent civil rights issue. With LGB individuals existing more in the dominant culture's awareness, the question of how much social "assimilation" is desirable is prominent in the gay community's life. We examine this question from an assimilationist and a liberationist perspective later in the chapter.

GAY IDENTITY DEVELOPMENT AND THE COMMUNITY

Reynolds and Hanjorgiris (2000) have noted that identification with the gay community has been associated with the adoption of a positive gay identity. They quoted Berger and Mallon (1993; cited in Reynolds & Hanjorgiris, p. 42):

> Gay men look to the gay community for support in the broadest sense: to provide an alternative, non-stigmatizing definition of their status, and to provide role models and a "career path," as well as a range of social and sexual opportunities. (Berger & Mallon, 1993, p. 156)

Whether we are gay or not, we are all socialized in a heterocentric culture that requires extra work on the part of the lesbian or gay man to create a positive identity (Gonsiorek & Rudolph, 1991). The phenomenon that Rust referred to as the "default heterosexual identity" (1996, p. 87) characterizes the individual's journey from "presumed straight" to the coming out process, which leads the LGB individual to integration of an appropriate identity. The various models of coming out and gay identity development are considered here to the extent that the gay community is involved in them as an agent for change and development. Readers interested in a more comprehensive discussion of these models are referred to Reynolds and Hanjorgiris (2000). Psychologists working with LGBT clients are encouraged to learn about the wide range of pathways LGBT individuals may take in developing and solidifying an identity.

Most models of LGB identity development and coming out make either direct or indirect reference to the evolving relationship between the individual and the gay community. The first such model was developed by Cass (1979), in which the gay community is an indirect player, insofar as it serves as a source of gay and lesbian individuals to which the person coming out may draw comparisons and contrasts. A subsequent model, developed by Coleman (1982), relies more heavily on other persons in the individual's world, to whom disclosures of sexual orientation are made. Coleman's model also extends the process beyond coming out to an exploration of social and romantic relationships with other gay people, including norms and interpersonal skills specific to the gay community. McCarn and Fassinger (1996) developed a model of lesbian identity development that separates the process into two parallel tracks: an internal sexual identity process and a group-membership–identity process. These two tracks exert catalytic influence on one another, but they do not presuppose an outcome that is consistent for all, given the tremendous variation in other factors such as race and ethnicity, age, geographical location, ability, status, and so on.

The theory of gay identity development in which the gay community has the most central role is that of Gonsiorek and Rudolph (1991). In their model, which is an adaptation of Heinz Kohut's self-psychology theory, the individual's community and social support network function as an attachment object in and of itself. Through the process of identity development, the wounds acquired from living in a heterocentric society are healed by the individual's internalizing of a variety of positive factors offered by the community. The community serves a surrogate parental function by instilling values and personal confidence in the newly out LGB individual.

For the gay man coming out of a heterocentric culture, community serves essential corrective and replacement functions. It is useful for a therapist to recognize that some heterosocial patterns of relating that many gay men will have attempted to master will have no place in their lives as out gay men. Additionally, clinicians may wish to consider what shame or discomfort is associated with a client's inability to meet heterosocial expectations. Positive social contacts in the gay community afford him the opportunity to identify with like-minded others, and in so doing, neutralize the guilt and self-negation that LGBT individuals sometimes feel. Furthermore, LGBT individuals need to be "schooled" in the ways of their respective tribes. Not having previously been exposed to LGBT people or their normative patterns of sociosexual relating, the newly out person relies on friends from the support network to serve valuable mentoring functions. These are all restorative functions for which the LGBT individual looks to the community for guidance. This appears to be true whether an individual comes out in his 20s or sometime later in life.

MEMBERSHIP IN THE COMMUNITY

Not all gay or SSA men choose to identify with the community. Still others are inhibited or prevented from participating by a variety of factors, including difficulties in coming out, heterosexism, and a number of what Garnets and D'Augelli (1995) have referred to as "identification barriers," such as invisibility, lack of group awareness, or an absent sense of lesbian and gay history (p. 304). Like all communities, the gay community has much to offer its members—as well as some liabilities.

The most visible attribute of the gay community, at least in most urban areas, is its rich array of social resources. Moon (1996) observed that availability of places to meet "like-minded others" is of central interest to most gay men. The presence of generic institutions, such as bars, coffeehouses, bookstores, and community centers, is a given in most cities; a cursory glance through the gay newspaper of most American urban areas reveals dozens of interest groups and organizations through which individuals with similar interests can connect socially. For gay men, some of these are eroto-social in nature: If one identifies as a "bear," or is interested in the leather subculture, there are likely groups meeting in one's geographic area. For the athletic, there are hiking, running, rowing, bowling, swimming, softball, and skiing groups. Nearly every religious denomination has gay-affirmative support groups, and many of those groups host services. Almost any unique hobby or interest—from classic automobiles to opera—is the focus of a gay social group that people may attend, with meeting others as either a primary or a secondary objective. Gay musical and dance performance groups are among the most respected of many cities' arts organizations. Furthermore, the gay community offers groups that serve allies and family members. Most notable of these is PFLAG (Parents, Families, and Friends of Lesbians and Gays), which offers social support and education for family members and loved ones of LGB individuals.

Geography presents a challenge, however, in that the socially developed gay community is still mostly a phenomenon of urban areas. The gay inhabitant of a rural area is more likely to have access to an occasional bar, or a public place for "cruising," than to have access to the variety of social and interest groups described previously. The Internet notwithstanding, this lack of community and resources can increase the sense of social isolation for rural gay men. This, coupled with the possibility of heightened anxiety, given the greater potential for isolation and antigay violence in rural areas (Kimmel, 2003), can make some rural areas daunting places for gay men to live. Some rural gay men may be more likely to be closeted in some fashion, whether this involves a "double life" with periodic forays to nearby cities or some other coping strategy.

Another counterpoint to the mentioned plethora of gay community organizations is the difficulty many report in navigating the sometimes-challenging waters of gay society. The gay bar, which has been mentioned as one of the fundamental community institutions, is relatively accessible. But gay bars are also uncomfortable social environments for those whose physical appearance or age does not conform to the high standards of gay beauty. Bars can also be challenging for an introvert or even for a person who might be socially facile elsewhere. The annual Pride festival, which is a major event in essentially every LGBT community across the country, can be a great source of togetherness—or serious infighting. The Internet has emerged as a popular source of social and romantic connection for LGBT individuals, but it too holds challenges—especially for the recently out. It behooves all clinicians working with recently out LGBT individuals to be attentive to their developing patterns of social and sexual relating.

Since the 1970s, the gay community has been creating a political and economic power base far beyond its social institutions. Openly gay candidates run for public office; for the first time, the media has featured comment on the "gay vote" in every national election since 1992; and gay men and lesbians are sought after by all manner of advertisers eager for gay disposable income. All of these developments have the added effect of further normalizing gay life experiences for the dominant culture, and images of lesbians and gay men in the media are represented in greater proportion than ever. Although many of these images are based upon stereotype (*Queer Eye for the Straight Guy*), hypersexuality (*Queer as Folk*), or lack of sexuality (*Will and Grace*), they create a new pathway for dominant-culture identification. The popular show *Queer Eye for the Straight Guy*, for instance, is controversial among gay men for its stereotypy. At the same time, it is the first show to demonstrate a friendly relationship between openly gay and heterosexual men. Moreover, it is the first program in which gay men are valued and in a position of influence over their straight counterparts. Whether it is light television fare such as this, or a life-insurance commercial featuring two lesbians, these images reinforce the notion that lesbians and gay men are humans struggling with some of the same issues as the mainstream—all in the unique context of heterosexist bias.

Heterosexuals do not fear maltreatment based upon sexual orientation, but LGBT individuals do, and higher visibility of LGBT individuals is thought to be a contributing factor in an increase in violent crime against the community. Most gay men, for instance, report having had at least one experience of harassment, threat of violence, or actual violence in their lives. This fosters heterophobia, or a generalized fear of heterosexual men, particularly in groups (Haldeman, 2001), and leads to a cultural attitude of suspicion and counter-hostility against heterosexuals. This phenomenon affects the ways in which gay men interact with heterosexual men and the entire dominant culture and may even have a negative impact on the relationships that gay men have with each other (Haldeman, 2001). Psychologists should strive to understand not only the normatively internalized homophobia of their clients (APA, Division 44/Committtee on Lesbian, Gay, and Bisexual Concerns Joint Task Force, 2000), but also their clients' heterophobia (Haldeman, 2001). Given that some of the worst serial gay-bashings have taken place in or near gay neighborhoods, the community itself clearly cannot always protect gay men from violence or harassment. Still, most gay men feel generally safer and freer in the geographic confines of the gay community.

LGBT communities offer the only opportunity to celebrate and acknowledge traditions that have become a part of gay life since Stonewall. The most visible of these are local gay communities' annual Pride celebrations, which commemorate the Stonewall rebellion. Pride festivals now take place the world over, from late spring into the autumn. They provide local communities an opportunity to showcase everything from the gay "Chamber of Commerce" to performing arts groups. In most locales, the local Pride parade is also on the list of all but the most conservative politicians seeking the gay vote. Given the diversity of the gay community, the annual Pride celebration may be the only time during the year that the entire LGBT community assembles in one place. Ironically, it is the planning of the annual Pride celebration itself that highlights, in many cities, the factionalism within the LGBT communities. The communities' diversity does not confer a common vision, and at no time are differences in perspective, social class, and values more apparent than during organization of the Pride celebration, when inevitable conflicts arise.

The rainbow flag itself, designed for San Francisco's Pride celebration, is a universal symbol of gay pride. The six stripes of the flag appear as stickers affixed to everything from automobiles to businesses to denote owners' gay-friendliness. Other community events include National Coming Out Day (in October), and other community organizations include lobbying groups (e.g., the Human Rights Campaign) and organizations combating stigma, such as the Gay and Lesbian Alliance Against Defamation, the Safe Schools Project, the Gay and Lesbian Public Awareness Project, and the New York City Campaign to End Gay Violence.

GAY COMMUNITIES IN THE NEW MILLENNIUM

The function of the gay community—from both a practical and a psychological standpoint—is an area that is underresearched. The few extant studies are nearly all based on White, economically advantaged gay men, and almost all studies are outside the domain of psychology. A better, empirical understanding of the importance of the gay community should be a research priority. How to maximize the community's organizational effectiveness, what the community means in terms of gay life-span development, and what the impact is of domestic partner benefits are examples of potential topics for investigation.

The gay community, like the rest of the world, has become smaller through the Internet. Individuals who found it difficult to navigate the social terrain in a gay bar or club now make connections with others online. Time that might have previously been invested in the laborious process of meeting and getting to know someone is now bypassed because profiles and biographies can be reviewed in minutes. A range of interpersonal connections, from quick sex to long-term relationships, has been made possible by the technology that now permeates most of our lives. The use of technology to facilitate personal interaction can benefit a community whose members have sometimes been challenged in finding each other due to social constraints. The main concern is that reliance on Internet communication does not come to subvert what lesbian and gay individuals have worked so long and hard to achieve: the mechanisms to meet and develop personal relationships with one another.

There are new institutions that the community needs to create and existing ones that should be expanded to meet the needs of the gay population. Owing to the mobility of our society, it is not just LGBT people who face the prospect of declining health in advanced age without obvious resources—such as adult children—to function as caregivers. The gay community will need to care for its aging population—and perhaps would already be doing so had not so many of the resources of the baby-boom generation been devoted to the health crisis and were not so many of the baby-boom generation's members already now deceased. In any case, the gay communities of the future will need to create space for living and socializing, in addition to focusing on health care. The recent trend toward the establishment of gay community centers is a positive step toward ensuring that the isolation so many gay people faced earlier in life is not replicated at the end of it.

TO ASSIMILATE OR LIBERATE?

Sitcoms and style shows on television with gay characters, extensive media coverage of same-sex marriage, openly gay bishops—this is an unprecedented level of cultural visibility. Since the inception of gay-rights advocacy organizations in the early 1950s, many LGB individuals have hoped to advance the cause for civil rights in part by realistic depiction of their lives in films and on television. Historically, it has been observed that personal contact is the primary variable in reducing antigay prejudice (Herek, 2000), and the advent of gay characters in the mainstream media serves to further familiarize the dominant culture with LGB people and their lives. "Going mainstream" has normalized the life experiences of LGB individuals, and several prominent gay-culture assimilationists (Bawer, 1993; Sullivan, 1996) predict that this trend can only benefit the advancement of gay civil rights issues—for despite the current wave of visible progress (increase in corporations and municipalities offering domestic-partner benefits, sodomy laws struck down, gay marriage legal in one state), federal statutes still prohibit open disclosure of homosexuality among service personnel, and there is an undeniable sociopolitical backlash developing relative to same-sex marriage. Nonetheless, the assimilationist perspective views social integration and acceptance as LGB culture's primary—and, given the relatively rapid social change over the past 35 years, a realistic—goal.

In regard to same-sex marriage, the American Psychological Association has gone on record in support of it, noting that there are more than 1,000 benefits associated with marital status that should be available to same-sex partners (Paige, 2005). Assimilationist LGB individuals are divided between pursuit of full marital rights and the "compromise" position of civil-union status. Civil unions are not legally recognized in the same way as are marriages. Therefore, some view civil unions as ascribing second-class status to gay relationships, whereas others view them as an intermediate step toward full marriage that is currently more palatable for a society that is favorable toward equal rights, but reluctant to view same-sex relationships as "marriages." Still others view marriage as a heterocentric, proprietary institution that is both inappropriate and irrelevant for LGB individuals.

Not all LGB individuals, however, would endorse sociocultural assimilation as an important goal. The Stonewall era marked the beginning of another—sometimes parallel, sometimes divergent—track within the struggle for gay rights: the liberation movement. In contrast to the assimilationist perspective, the liberation movement focuses on the unique cultural attributes and specific needs of the gay community and LGB people in general. This movement has served and does serve the important function of establishing a separate "turf" on which to fight for equality. Its most recent visible effort was the "ACT-UP" AIDS advocacy groups of the 1980s and early 1990s. At present, those supporting a strictly separatist or liberationist agenda appear to be somewhat marginalized in the gay community. Although both assimilationist and liberationist perspectives share the goal of blowing the doors off the collective gay closet, liberationists find the full inclusion in the social mainstream so desired by the assimilationists to be restrictive and inappropriate for gay norms of sociosexual relating.

There are other concerns pertinent to the assimilation-versus-liberation debate. In *The Rise and Fall of Gay Culture*, Harris (1997) lamented the fact that in rushing to integrate into a "media and business-driven" mainstream culture, there is a very real risk of losing the cultural and aesthetic uniqueness that is particular to gay culture. Sacrificing the gay aesthetic is a loss for the dominant culture as well. McCourt (2004) chronicled the cultural contributions of gay aestheticians in detail, highlighting the connection between the gay artistic spirit and the status as socially marginalized. Would gay art culture thrive—or even continue to exist—without antigay oppression?

Furthermore, assimilation does not challenge heterosexual privilege. The inclusion of LGB individuals in mainstream society, in and of itself, does not confer true equality (Vaid, 1996) or deconstruct society's heterocentric base. Seidman (2002) noted that antigay social values and heterosexual dominance were formed in the postwar period by a process he calls *homosexual pollution*. This process of vilification that was—and to some extent, continues to be—supported by organized religion, sociocultural norms, and the media rendered the closet the only reasonable place for most LGB people in the 1950s and 1960s. The advent of the gay community has had a significant role in changing the dominant culture's view of LGB people, but still, as Seidman (2002) pointed out, "Heterosexuals enjoy a privileged, superior social status that is secured by the state, social institutions, and popular culture. Gay life today is defined by a contradiction: *"Many individuals can choose to live beyond the closet but they must still live and participate in a world where most institutions maintain heterosexual domination"* (p. 6).

Ultimately, ~~if the primary function of the gay community is to provide a cultural base from which gay people can create social, economic, and political networks,~~ what is the community's future if gay people are assimilated into the dominant culture? Already it has been suggested that the exodus of LGB people to major urban areas has slowed because of greater overall cultural acceptance (Seidman, 2002). Does the need for the kinds of community institutions described here diminish over time? Ultimately, does the community vanish altogether? Conversely, does the community resist further integration with a dominant culture in which it will never gain true equality? The answer may lie somewhere between the two extremes: The ~~gay community, with its cultural values and positive attributes intact, becomes a distinct and valued segment of a diverse American society.~~ Having survived cultural oppression and epidemic with its sense of style and humor intact, the gay community has a great deal to offer the dominant culture and the world. It must be preserved and nurtured, however, in such a way that allows it to keep offering its best features of inclusion and solidarity to its own people.

CONCLUSION

The LGBT community serves a multiplicity of functions in the development and establishment of gay identity, and it is useful for the clinician to have some understanding of these processes. Most LGBT people cannot come out in a vacuum; the existence of a vibrant, diverse gay community serves as a resource, to be sure, but also as an attachment figure in and of itself. As has been noted, most LGB developmental theorists involve the gay community in some way relative to identity evolution, and it is wise for the clinician to have some understanding in this area.

The LGBT community has a relatively short history in terms of years—but it is rich with the astounding variety associated with diversity and intense with the passion associated with a lifelong struggle against oppression and misunderstanding. The struggle continues, even as we enter an age of increased visibility and opportunity to assimilate into the dominant culture. Anyone working with LGBT clients should be aware that there is a wide spectrum of possible relationships to the gay community—from quite detached to deeply involved. There is, of course, no prescription for how LGBT individuals should respond to their community. Simply, it is important to be aware that the LGBT community exists as a resource for many—and can have a powerful impact on the lives and development of its very diverse members.

REFERENCES

American Psychological Association, Division 44/Committee on Lesbian, Gay, and Bisexual Concerns Joint Task Force on Guidelines for Psychotherapy With Lesbian, Gay, and Bisexual Clients. (2000). Guidelines for psychotherapy with lesbian, gay, and bisexual clients. *American Psychologist, 55,* 1440–1451.

Bawer, B. (1993). *A place at the table: The gay individual in American society.* New York: Simon & Schuster.

Cass, V. (1979). Homosexual identity formation: A theoretical model. *Journal of Homosexuality, 4,* 219–236.

Coleman, E. (1982). Developmental stages of the coming-out process. In J. Gonsiorek (Ed.), *Homosexuality and psychotherapy: A practitioner's handbook of affirmative models* (pp. 31–44). New York: Haworth Press.

Duberman, M. (1993). *Stonewall.* New York: Penguin Press.

Garnets, L., & D'Augelli, A. (1995). Lesbian, gay and bisexual communities. In A. D'Augelli & C. Patterson (Eds.), *Lesbian, gay and bisexual identities over the lifespan* (pp. 293–320). New York: Oxford University Press.

Gonsiorek, J., & Rudolph, J. (1991). Homosexual identity: Coming out and other developmental events. In J. Gonsiorek & J. Weinrich (Eds.), *Homosexuality: Research implications for public policy* (pp. 161–176). Newbury Park, CA: Sage.

Grossman, A., D'Augelli, A., & O'Connell, T. (2003). Being lesbian, gay, bisexual and sixty or older in North America. In L. Garnets & D. Kimmel (Eds.), *Psychological perspectives on lesbian, gay and bisexual experiences* (pp. 629–653). New York: Columbia University Press.

Haldeman, D. (2001). Don't come any closer: How heterophobia contaminates intimate relationships between gay men. *Newsletter of the Society for the Psychological Study of Men and Masculinity, 4*(1), 1–4.

Harris, D. (1997). *The rise and fall of gay culture.* New York: Ballantine Books.

Herek, G. (2000). The psychology of sexual prejudice. *Current Directions in Psychological Science, 9,* 19–22.

Herman, D. (1997). *The anti-gay agenda.* Chicago: University of Chicago Press.

Kaiser, C. (1997). *The gay metropolis: A history of gay life in America since World War II.* New York: Harcourt Brace.

Kimmel, D. (2003). Identifying and addressing health issues of gay, lesbian, bisexual, transgender (GLBT) populations in rural communities: Psychological perspectives. In L. Garnets & D. Kimmel (Eds.), *Psychological perspectives on lesbian, gay and bisexual experiences* (pp. 435–448). New York: Columbia University Press.

Marcus, E. (2002). *Making gay history.* New York: HarperCollins.

McCarn, S., & Fassinger, R. (1996). Revisioning sexual minority identity formation: A new model of lesbian identity and its implications for counseling and research. *The Counseling Psychologist, 24,* 508–534.

McCourt, F. (2004). *Queer street: The rise and fall of an American culture, 1947–1985.* New York: Norton.

Miller, N. (1989). *In search of gay America*. New York: Harper & Row.

Moon, L. (1996). Working with single people. In D. Davies & C. Neal (Eds.), *Pink therapy: A guide for counselors and therapists working with lesbian, gay and bisexual clients* (pp. 89–100). Buckingham, England: Open University Press.

Murray, S. (1996). *American gay*. Chicago: University of Chicago Press.

Paige, R.U. (2005). Proceedings of the American Psychological Association, Incorporated, for the legislative year 2004: Minutes of the Annual Meeting of the Council of Representatives, July 28 & 30, 2004, Honolulu, Hawaii. Retrieved November, 2004, from http://www.apa.org/governance/.

Reynolds, A., & Hanjorgiris, W. (2000). Coming out: Lesbian, gay and bisexual identity development. In R. Perez, K. DeBord, & K. Bieschke (Eds.), *Handbook of counseling and psychotherapy with lesbian, gay and bisexual clients* (pp. 35–55). Washington, DC: American Psychological Association.

Rothblum, E. (2000). "Somewhere in Des Moines or San Antonio": Historical perspectives on lesbian, gay, and bisexual mental health. In R. Perez, K. DeBord, & K. Bieschke (Eds.), *Handbook of counseling and psychotherapy with lesbian, gay and bisexual clients* (pp. 57–79). Washington, DC: American Psychological Association.

Rust, P. (1996). Managing multiple identities: Diversity among bisexual women and men. In B. Firestein (Ed.), *Bisexuality: The psychology and politics of an invisible minority* (pp. 53–83). Newbury Park, CA: Sage.

Seidman, S. (2002). *Beyond the closet: The transformaton of gay and lesbian life*. New York: Routledge.

Sullivan, A. (1996). *Virtually normal: An argument about homosexuality*. New York: Vintage Press.

Vaid, U. (1996). *Virtually equal: The mainstreaming of gay and lesbian liberation*. New York: Doubleday.

4

CULTURAL AND RELATIONAL CONTEXTS OF BISEXUAL WOMEN: IMPLICATIONS FOR THERAPY

BETH A. FIRESTEIN

Women who are bisexual in their behavior, emotional bonding, attractions, and self-identification frequently seek therapy, yet are underrepresented in the professional literature on counseling (Israel, 2003a; Martin & Meezan, 2003; Pachankis & Goldfried, 2004). The cultural, relational, and community contexts of bisexual women shape these women, their identities, and their life experiences (Bradford, 1997; Hutchins, 1996; Rust, 1996a, 1996b), and bisexual women live as both "insiders" and "outsiders" within mainstream heterosexual and lesbian communities (Bradford, 1997; Ochs, 1996). It is therefore critical to understand bisexual women in these contexts in order to offer effective psychotherapy to this population (Firestein, 1996c). This chapter highlights several areas of theoretical, empirical, and clinical importance related to counseling bisexual women.

The cultural contexts of bisexual women overlap significantly with those of heterosexual women and lesbians, yet embody certain complexities unique to bisexual women's sexual identity and orientation (Falco, 1996; Israel, 2003a). The relational contexts of bisexual women also vary tremendously (Rust, 1996b). Bisexual women may maintain relationship involvements with lesbians, heterosexual men, bisexual men, bisexual women, and with people who are diverse with respect to gender identity (transgendered or transsexual) or gender expression (butch or femme) (Alexander & Yescavage, 2004). Clinicians and counselors need to be prepared to assist bisexual women within a variety of life contexts, including bisexual women in monogamous relationships; women maintaining honest, consensual relationships with more than one person; and women who may affiliate with alternative sexual communities (Hutchins, 2001, 2002; Lenius, 2001; Queen, 1996a, 1996b; Rust, 1996b). Bisexual women are frequently invisible when embedded in heterosexual relationships and stigmatized or rendered invisible when engaged in same-sex relationships and living within queer communities (Bradford, 1997; Hutchins, 1996). Relational issues and issues of community affiliation frequently overlap in complicated ways for bisexual women; for example, these women face a variety of difficulties when attempting to form relationships within lesbian social and political communities (Esterberg, 1997; Ochs, 1996; Rust, 1995).

There is presently a small but growing body of professional literature addressing issues of bisexuality and mental health, including both qualitative and quantitative empirical research. This research is beginning to explore several of the mental health and lifestyle concerns of bisexual women and men (Firestein, 1996a, 1996c; Jorm, Korten, Rodgers, Jacomb, & Christensen, 2002; Ketz & Israel, 2002; Mathy, Lehmann, & Kerr, 2004; Page, 2004) and bisexual adolescents (Robin et al., 2002; Russell & Joyner, 2001; Russell & Seif, 2002).

I begin this chapter by discussing the challenges and positive aspects of identifying as bisexual and by exploring the gender, racial, and community contexts that affect bisexual women. Next, I discuss the community contexts embracing bisexual women as they interface with lesbian culture and with heterosexual society and discuss the question of whether a bisexual women's community really exists. The next section explores bisexual women's experiences in several different relational contexts. Bisexual women's relationships with lesbians, relationships with men, and relationships with bisexual women and bisexual men are discussed in some detail.

In the final section of the chapter, I turn to the empirical research on bisexual women, including mental health and service utilization, empirical research addressing other areas of importance to bisexual women, and implications of the research literature for counseling bisexual women. Finally, I turn to a discussion of affirmative approaches to conducting therapy with bisexual women and propose that counseling bisexual women is, in fact, a multicultural competency requiring significant shifts in the attitudes and skills sets of counselors seeking to work in effective and culturally sensitive ways with this population. I conclude by discussing the larger shift occurring in the field of psychology—toward a lesbian, gay, bisexual, and transgender

(LGBT)-affirmative paradigm for understanding sexual behavior and working with sexual minorities across a variety of disciplines.

CHALLENGES AND POSITIVE ASPECTS OF BISEXUAL IDENTIFICATION

Falco (1996) noted that women who love women experience several common identifiable stressors, such as the continual nature of choices about whether to disclose or "pass" with respect to one's sexual minority identification, absence of social support for loving another woman, internalized homophobia/biphobia, and the absence of visible role models and cultural history. Bisexual women often face stressors that are unique to them as a group, including pressure to adopt a nonbisexual identity based on the gender of one's partner and bisexual women's own resistance to self-identifying or adopting the label "bisexual" (Bower, Gurevich, & Mathieson, 2002). These stressors frequently compel many bisexual women to confront their own intellectual and emotional confusion because of the conflicts inherent within many of society's demands.

For example, there is considerable pressure on women who are in a current relationship with a woman to identify as lesbian, for women in current relationships with men to pass as heterosexual, and for women involved with more than one gender to "make a choice" (Rust, 2003). Rust's (1995) careful analysis of lesbians' relationships to bisexuality and bisexual women revealed that lesbians frequently consider bisexuality "politically irrelevant or nonexistent, placing bisexually-identified women in continual positions of invalidation and political exclusion relative to a significant portion of other women-loving-women" (p. 200).

Bisexual individuals also face the challenge of self-acceptance (A. Fox, 1991), the challenge of choosing relational forms and structures that fit with their identity (Rust, 1996b), and the challenge of finding a sense of community to which one's "whole self" can belong (Esterberg, 1997; Hutchins, 1996; Ochs, 1996). Bisexual identity has been conceptualized as multidimensional, involving elements of attraction, fantasy, behavior, social preference, emotional preference, sexual identity, and lifestyle, or community affiliation (Klein, 1990; Klein, Sepekoff, & Wolf, 1985). Incongruence among these dimensions and the experience of confusion are natural sequelae for bisexuals living in a culture that "permits" only gay and heterosexual identities.

There are both negative consequences and psychological benefits to embracing a bisexual identity. A disproportionate amount of attention has been given to the negative consequences of embracing a bisexual identity, but there are a number of psychological benefits to identifying as bisexual as well. The positive aspects of identifying as bisexual include the sense of freedom to define oneself, the satisfaction of having the ability to function as a bridge between straight and gay worlds, and the richness of being able to develop intimate relationships with either sex (Oxley & Lucius, 2000).

Empirical evidence supports the notion that adopting a bisexual identity can accompany positive psychological outcomes. For example, it has been shown that bisexual individuals may be more flexible in their relationship roles (Matteson, 1996), more resilient (Zinik, 1984), and have life satisfaction and self-esteem equivalent to that found in their gay, lesbian, and heterosexual counterparts (Fox, 1995; Jorm et al., 2002). Bradford's (1997) research participants reported that their bisexuality affected their self-concepts in three major ways: increased self-reliance, openness to others who are "different," and personal or spiritual enrichment (p. 167). The benefits of acknowledging one's bisexuality and embracing a bisexual identity exist in a delicate and dynamic balance with the difficulties of doing so. I encourage counselors working with bisexual women to attend carefully to the balance of supportive and challenging influences in their clients' lives and to actively assist clients to focus on the positive aspects of identity in order to counteract the damaging effects of the culture's negative messages about being bisexual.

Clearly, there are factors unique to bisexual women's struggle to establish a positive identity, and these challenges pose unique and sometimes ongoing trials for women living these identities and experiences. But bisexual women's identity development, mental health, and emotional well-being are also strongly influenced by sexism, heterosexism, homophobia, racism, and other cultural factors (Greene, 2003).

GENDER, RACIAL, AND COMMUNITY CONTEXTS OF BISEXUAL WOMEN

Sexism and Heterosexism

Bisexual women, like all women, live in a culture pervaded by sexism, racism, classism, heterosexism, and homophobia (Balsam, 2003; Pharr, 1988; Rothblum & Bond, 1996). In particular, bisexual women face issues of discrimination that include many of those faced by women with exclusive same-sex orientations, with the addition of elements unique to the bisexual experience (Nichols, 1994; Ochs, 1996). For example, lesbians, heterosexual women, and bisexual women all are vulnerable to the effects of institutionalized sexist and heterosexist bias and may have similar histories with respect to violence and traumatic victimization (Balsam, 2003; Nichols, 1994).

The sexism that pervades heterosexual society operates in powerful and unquestioned ways. Blackwood and Wieringa (2003) noted that "because sexualities are informed by and embedded in gender hierarchies and gender ideologies that impose different constraints on women and men, sexual roles, behaviors, meanings and desires are different for women and men" (p. 419). Bisexual women and lesbians may experience a layering of the negative effects of oppression because of their dual status as women and sexual minorities (Balsam, 2003). Race, culture of origin, religion, and immigrant status also have dramatic influences on the sexual identity development of these women (Greene, 1994, 1997).

Racial and Ethnic Minority Status as Cultural Factors Affecting Bisexuals

The past 25 years have witnessed substantial growth in published writing in the areas of understanding the experiences of ethnic and racial minority LGB individuals living in European American and North American cultures (Chan, 1992; Comas-Diaz & Greene, 1994; Greene, 1994, 2003; Morales, 1989). Within the past 10 to 15 years, such writing has begun to take seriously the issues of bisexual people of color (Diamond & Savin-Williams, 2003; Hutchins & Ka'ahumanu, 1991; Rust, 1996a, 2000, 2003). Critiques of sexual identity development models have begun to address both the White, Eurocentric focus of such models as well as the limitations of such models predicated on dichotomous conceptions of sexual identity (Fox, 1996; Rust, 2000) and teleological, linear notions of sexual identity development (Diamond & Savin-Williams, 2003; Rust, 2003).

Although a complete review of this literature is beyond the scope of the present chapter, it is valuable to highlight some of the recurring themes emerging out of the more recently published literature. First, LGB ethnic minority individuals are likely to encounter marginalization in multiple ways (Rust, 2000), facing both the dominant culture's racism and their own ethnic or racial group's heterocentrism and homophobia/biphobia (Greene, 1994, 2003; Pachankis & Goldfried, 2004; Rust, 2000). Second, models of coming out and sexual identity development tend to be Eurocentric, with little or no acknowledgment as to the extent and the ways that expressions of sexuality vary culturally (Rust, 1996a, 2000, 2003). Counselors need to be mindful of the ways that sexual identity labels and sexual terms differ across cultural, racial, and ethnic groups (Rust, 1996a). Finally, although within-group variations are notable, the differences that exist among racial, ethnic, and cultural groups in regard to LGB affirmation and acceptance have important implications for counseling LGB clients (Rust, 2000, 2003). This is especially significant for counselors who are assisting LGB clients who are contemplating coming out to their families and social support networks. For example, counselors must be prepared to intervene differently with clients depending on the recency of their immigration to the United States, their degree of acculturation to U.S. sexual norms, and whether they are currently living with other members of their family. It is sometimes unwise to strongly urge unacculturated clients or those who are financial dependent upon their families to come out to their families without first carefully exploring the client's options for economic and emotional independence.

Recently, research and theoretical work has begun to explore the challenging and positive elements associated with biracial identities.

Further, this work has examined the potential value of comparing models of biracial identity development and models of bisexual identity development (Collins, 2000; Gillem & Thompson, 2004; Israel, 2004; Rust, 2000; Stanley, 2004). Both biracial and bisexual individuals (and particularly women who are both biracial and bisexual) must learn to balance living in multiple, simultaneous cultural contexts. Many bisexual women, for example, must learn to live successfully in both lesbian culture and heterosexual society. Biracial and multiracial women must balance loyalties to multiple heritages, families, and communities. This is complicated by the fact that neither the heterosexual culture nor the predominantly Euro-American LGB culture is immune to the effects of racial and ethnic discrimination, stereotyping, and prejudice (Greene, 1994; Rust, 2000, 2003).

On a positive note, achieving a personal sense of empowerment with respect to racial or multiracial heritage may allow ethnic and sexual minority women to develop many of the coping skills needed to successfully negotiate their sexual minority identity within a predominantly heterosexual culture (Matteson, 1996; Rust, 1996a, 2000). Skills developed to cope with racial or ethnic marginalization may assist bisexual women in handling their sexual marginalization (Rust, 1996a, 2000). Biracial sexual minority women face challenges that reflect significant similarity to the challenges bisexual women of all racial and ethnic backgrounds face when intimately involved in predominantly lesbian women's communities. It is to the issue of bisexual women and lesbian culture that we now turn.

Bisexual Women and Lesbian Culture

Several authors have written about the cultural issues and challenges that arise when bisexual women affiliate with lesbian communities (Bower et al., 2002; Ochs, 1996; Rust, 1992, 1993a, 1993b, 1995). Rust (2000) noted, "Bisexuality is particularly controversial in lesbian communities" (p. 413). In support of her assertion, Rust (2000) provided an excellent overview of the research on relations between bisexual women and lesbians. Counselors need to understand the complicated histories of feminism, lesbianism, and bisexual women and how these histories have influenced one another (Rust, 1995) in order to serve their female bisexual (and lesbian) clients in optimal ways. An extensive explanation of this history is beyond the scope of this chapter, but here I highlight the primary themes discussed in Rust's review.

The literature in this area has focused on three primary topics: the content of the negative attitudes lesbians hold with respect to bisexual women, the sociopolitical and historical roots of this antipathy, and the social, political, and psychological explanations for the tension between lesbians and bisexual women. In her sample of 346 lesbian participants, Rust (1993b) found that a majority of her participants endorsed the beliefs that bisexual women were "in transition" or in denial of a "true" lesbian identity, that bisexual women are "not as committed to other women as lesbians are" (p. 485), and that bisexuals want to pass as heterosexual more than lesbians want to pass as heterosexual. Obviously, Rust's work provides evidence for the existence of some lesbians' negative beliefs about bisexual women.

The sociopolitical and historical roots of the antipathy between some lesbians and bisexual women are complex, but most authors have discussed this tension as having some basis in the emergence of identity-based politics in the 1970s and 1980s and the subsequent development of lesbian-feminist political perspectives that assigned lesbians a "higher moral status" than bisexual women (Rust, 1992, 1995, 2000, 2003). Although many lesbians are supportive of bisexual women and bisexuality, some lesbian communities have historically reduced the "threat" posed by inclusion of bisexual women in the larger lesbian or queer community by dismissing bisexuals as "confused individuals" (Rust, 1993b). By depoliticizing bisexual identity, these groups have effectively denied bisexual women's unique perspectives and political concerns (Rust, 1993b). These issues differ significantly between women who are coming out as bisexual after identifying as heterosexual and women who are coming out as bisexual after identifying as lesbian (Esterberg, 1997; Matteson, 1996).

Women who are in the initial stages of exploring their attractions toward other women and who are emerging from heterosexual identities and cultural contexts often find that lesbian or queer communities provide gathering places and cultural events where they are likely to meet other women-loving women, most of whom identify as lesbian. Many women with established bisexual identities and some women who are in relationships or marriages with men also find that participation in women's communities, whether feminist, lesbian, or queer, meets important social and emotional needs (Hutchins & Ka'ahumanu, 1991; Weise, 1992). Many bisexual women find that only a part of their identity can be reflected and supported within the lesbian community, yet being a part of this community is extremely important to them (Esterberg, 1997). Counselors need to assist bisexual women in realistically evaluating the potential for support or hostility in their local lesbian community and assist them in making decisions that take this into account. Bisexual women experience different issues when interacting primarily with the dominant heterosexual culture.

Bisexual Women and Heterosexual Society

Whether monoracial, biracial, Caucasian, or minority in ethnic identification, all sexual minorities in the United States exist within the structures of the western, American culture that declares heterosexuality to be "normative" and all other sexual identities "aberrant" or otherwise suspect. This has led several writers to discuss heterosexism and heteronormative culture as major factors influencing the identity development and lived experiences of all sexual minority individuals, regardless of their race or gender (Blumenfeld & Raymond, 1988; Herek, 2003).

Heterosexism refers to the "system by which heterosexuality is assumed to be the only acceptable and viable life option" (Blumenfeld & Raymond, 1988, p. 226). The term *heteronormative culture* refers to the fact that society is structured to reflect the unquestioned and largely unconscious assumption that everyone living in the culture is heterosexual — or should be heterosexual (Pharr, 1988; Rothblum & Bond, 1996). Any person who is not heterosexual is perceived as abnormal, unnatural, and in some cases, sinful and morally corrupt (Herek, 2003; Pharr, 1988). Society's laws and structures, such as the institution of marriage and the definition of family, reflect these assumptions (Herek, 2003; Rothblum & Bond, 1996).

Within heteronormative society, LGBT people are considered undeserving of equal access to heteronormative structures such as marriage, family, inheritance laws, or adoption privileges; these are the unquestioned rights and privileges of the heterosexual majority. The effects of heterosexism are pervasive. As Greene (2003) explained, "Heterosexism is not a singular or isolated experience or event. As such, heterosexism cannot be disconnected from the broader context of an individual's development or existence any more than sexism, for example, can be understood apart from the context of a woman's ethnicity, socioeconomic class, religion, or other significant aspects of her life" (p. 358).

Recently, "gay marriage" has become a major issue for the culture at large and is currently being actively contested in legislatures and courts across the United States. Bisexuals are in a unique position with respect to the institution of marriage. Bisexual men and women are allowed to marry complementary sex partners but not same-sex partners (Solot & Miller, 2001). Therefore, bisexuals have the right to marry to the extent that they are heterosexually involved and choose to remain invisible with respect to their bisexuality, but they face barriers identical to those confronted by gays and lesbians when involved in committed same-sex partnerships. Therefore, the issue of concern to society is actually "same-sex marriage" rather than "gay marriage," since gay men, lesbians, and bisexual people routinely marry other-gender partners.

The privileging of heterosexual desire and lifestyle choices are perceived by some lesbians as influencing bisexual women to choose heterosexual relationships over relationships with women (Ochs, 1996; Rust, 1995). However, Adrienne Rich (1980) asserted that even heterosexual women are without meaningful "choice" because of the heterosexual imperatives that pervade the culture. Providing some evidence for this, Bradford (1997) noted that 11 out of the 20 bisexual women and men she interviewed indicated first thinking that they were heterosexual before coming to a realization of their bisexuality. Many of her participants cited societal reinforcement of heterosexuality as a factor in their assumption that they were straight, in spite of the fact that these men and women had same-sex attractions and experiences. Interestingly, approximately 30% of Bradford's (1997) interviewees reported coming out as lesbian or gay prior to identifying as bisexual, which might be taken to provide evidence of the power of same-sex attraction in the face of pervasive heterosexism and the pressure to conform.

Counselors must be careful not to underestimate the complexity of certain decisions, such as the decision to marry a man, in a heterosexist, biphobic, and homophobic culture. Some bisexual women find the decision to marry to be one involving a great deal of ambivalence and concern, particularly insofar as a bisexual woman may see such a decision as having a potentially negative impact upon her standing vis-à-vis the lesbian and queer women's communities.

IS THERE A BISEXUAL WOMEN'S COMMUNITY?

Community is a major issue in the lives of bisexual women. Bisexual women face the difficult reality that there are very few heterosexual or gay and lesbian communities in which they can feel a sense of full belonging and acceptance, although this is an important need for women who are seeking to develop positive bisexual identities (A. Fox, 1991). These difficulties exist regardless of whether bisexual women choose to affiliate primarily within the dominant heterosexual culture (a necessity for all sexual minority individuals) or to affiliate primarily within lesbian and gay communities (Ochs, 1996), though the challenges within these cultural contexts differ.

So, are there bisexual communities, and if so, what do these communities have to offer? Bisexual women seek and sometimes find a sense of community with other bisexual women and with bisexual men (Bradford, 1997, 2004). Much of this community occurs via the Internet, at local, regional, national, and international bisexual gatherings, or in the few large, urban centers that have some sort of organized bisexual community. Therefore, the organized bisexual community, insofar as it exists at all, has two components: physical communities and virtual communities.

Physical bisexual communities exist in some larger, urban areas, such as Boston, San Francisco, Chicago, Seattle, New York City, Minneapolis and St. Paul, and Los Angeles. These bi communities are often fluid in structure and participation levels and may be difficult to locate relative to gay and lesbian resources in a given community (Bradford, 1997). Physical bisexual communities generally consist of some combination of the following: support groups; the proactive inclusion of bisexuals in PFLAG (Parents, Families, and Friends of Lesbians and Gays) and other lesbian, gay, and queer organizations; bisexual events and conferences; and bisexual political organizations (such as BiNet chapters). Some urban centers also contain communities (such as polyamory, kink, and BDSM communities) whose membership may be pansexual or include substantial numbers of openly bisexual individuals. To my knowledge, there are no bisexual bookstores, coffee houses, or theaters or other gathering places specifically catering to bisexuals, though the Twin Cities of Minneapolis and St. Paul have a local television program, "Bi Cities," that is produced by and for the bisexual community. Some bisexual women may choose to establish their own support groups or special interest groups within women's centers, gay and lesbian community centers, or queer youth groups (Bradford, 1997).

These physical community resources are supplemented by a large number of "virtual" community resources for bisexuals. If one is able to weed through the enormous number of sex-specific ads and services that cater to people of all sexual orientations who are titillated by notions of "bisexual women," there are a number of excellent online resources to be found. These include bisexual-specific educational sites (e.g., http://www.bisexual.org), online discussion groups or forums, and social and sexual networks for meeting same and other-gender partners (e.g., http://www.lovingmore.com). Any attempt to comprehensively list such virtual resources is likely to be outdated quickly, given the ever-changing nature of online resources and communities. Suffice it to say that such resources perform vital functions, particularly for LGB and gender-variant individuals in more rural geographic locations. Robyn Ochs's (2001) *International Directory of Bisexual Groups* provides the most comprehensive list of active bisexual organizations and support groups worldwide. Fortunately, it is updated every few years.

In summary, bisexual communities have several dimensions. Such communities have both a physical component and a virtual component, which perform different but equally vital functions for bisexual women in search of community. In actuality, bisexual communities consist of a fluctuating, dynamic, loosely connected network of distinct organizations, groups, and events. Physical communities tend to be event-oriented, time-limited, and located in larger urban areas. This limits bisexual women's access to bisexual communities to those women who are aware, electronically "connected," socioeconomically advantaged (able to attend events), or located in the few urban areas housing substantial populations of bisexually identified activists willing and able to organize activities for the bi community. Counselors need to understand these various dimensions and limitations of bisexual communities and be familiar with how to assist clients in locating and becoming involved with such communities. Although it is critical to understand the cultural contexts permeating the lives and experiences of bisexual women, it is equally vital to understand the variety of relational contexts of bisexual women.

RELATIONAL CONTEXTS OF BISEXUAL WOMEN

Bisexual Women in Lesbian Relationships

Many bisexual women find themselves in relationships with women who self-identify as lesbian. Some of these lesbian partners have had past heterosexual involvement or marriages, and others have had only female lovers. Women with histories of past sexual involvement with men and who currently identify as lesbian may have identified as bisexual or heterosexual in the past (Abbott & Farmer, 1995; Dixon, 1984, 1985; Strock, 1998) and may have a variety of positive and negative feelings about their past identities and relational involvements. Some lesbian women believe bisexual women are really lesbians who have simply failed to complete the coming out process (Esterberg, 1997; Fox, 1996), and many lesbians express reluctance to become involved with bisexual women (Rust, 1995).

A bisexual woman in a committed relationship with a woman may adopt a lesbian identity for the duration of her primary involvement with a woman (Esterberg, 1997). Other bisexual women in same-sex relationships choose to retain a bisexual identity, whereas still others reject identity labels altogether. Counselors are frequently asked to assist bisexual women in deciding when and how to come out to their lesbian-identified partners or to women they are just beginning to date. A bisexual woman whose attractions to women are substantially stronger than her attractions to men may be willing to let go of her bisexual identity in order to accommodate her partner's need to perceive her as lesbian (Ochs, in press). If these women choose to maintain a monogamous relationship, this may make the bisexual partner's identity less problematic for her lesbian partner, even when the bisexual partner maintains her private awareness of her bisexual identity.

It is clear that bisexual women in same-sex relationships face a variety of issues, including unique pressures around self-identification, social affiliation, and negotiation of intimacy issues within their woman-to-woman relationships. As is the case with bisexual women involved with men, bisexual women may choose to be monogamous or may negotiate agreements that allow for the expression of attractions and feelings for opposite- or other-gendered people within the context of their primary relationship with a woman (Rust, 1996b). Bisexual women who identify as polyamorous are likely to conduct these negotiations openly with their partner, whereas women who are unfamiliar with ethical nonmonogamy may not feel comfortable doing so.

Bisexual Women in Relationships With Men

Many women have long histories of heterosexual involvement, including marriage and children, before discovering or accepting their lesbian or bisexual orientations (Abbott & Farmer, 1995; Dixon, 1984, 1985; Strock,

1998). There is no single trajectory characterizing the life paths of bisexual women. Bisexual women who are presently involved in relationships with men frequently struggle with issues of invisibility, lack of validation of their women-loving feelings, and an absence of community and opportunities for self-expression. In addition, bisexual women are frequently fetishized and hyper-eroticized by mainstream heterosexual culture and sometimes by their male partners. This can create conflict and confusion for a bisexual woman, especially for one whose first introduction to bisexuality may occur in the context of her heterosexual partner's attraction to lesbian sexuality.

Bisexual women have used a variety of approaches to living in relationships with men once they have discovered their bisexual orientation. Some women make a continued commitment to monogamous sexual involvement with their male partner. Other bisexual women negotiate "exceptions" to monogamy for the expression of their bisexuality, with clear, well-thought-out guidelines for protecting a primary relationship (see Anapol, 1997; Easton & Liszt, 1997; and Nearing, 1992, for practical manuals on negotiating these agreements in a respectful and consensual manner).

Counselors need to be prepared to assist these women in finding creative, workable strategies that support both the individual woman and her primary relationship partner or partners. Therapists need to let women and couples know that these options exist—that there are people living them successfully—and refer their clients to appropriate resources and community supports (Weitzman, in press). Finally, it is important that the counselor or psychotherapist listen nonjudgmentally to the needs of all partners in the relationship to ascertain areas of acceptable expression and issues of common concern within the framework of that couple's or expanded family's ethics, values, and aspirations, which may be nontraditional relative to the conventional structures governing most committed, heterosexual relationships.

Bisexual Women Involved With Bisexual Women and Men

Unless a woman lives in a fairly large, urban center in the United States, she is unlikely to have access to an organized bisexual community. This diminishes the likelihood that she will have the experience of being involved with another self-identified bisexual woman or man or with an individual who is transgendered. Special joys and challenges are associated with being involved in a same-orientation relationship, and a number of writers have noted that the gender of one's partner influences the specific "flavor" of that relational involvement (see Hutchins & Ka'ahumanu, 1991).

For example, it seems apparent that a bisexual woman's involvement with a bisexual woman who is predominantly lesbian in orientation will be quite different from her involvement with a bisexual man who is predominantly heterosexual. Her involvement with a male who cross-dresses will bring up different issues for her than will her relationship with a preoperative transgender person. These issues will differ yet again from those posed by an involvement with a queer-identified, femme bisexual woman. When these issues are considered along with the diversity of demographic factors (e.g., race, age, social class, education) that can influence one's identity and perspective on relationships, it is clear why counselors must be exceptionally open to the variety of relationship styles they are likely to encounter when working with bisexual women.

Consider an example of a same-sex relationship between two bisexual women. The two women may share similarities in the balance of their attractions and their relationship preferences around issues of monogamy and polyamory, yet one woman may be extremely "out" to her family whereas the other woman may be entirely closeted. This would likely set up dynamics of tension that would need to be addressed, possibly in couple therapy.

In relationships with other self-identified bisexuals, women may feel an increased sense of permission to name and express all elements of their attractions and desires and to discuss their full histories without the fear of homophobic or heterophobic responses that may be more likely to occur in relationships with a monosexual partner. Counselors may wish to support their bisexual female clients in actively thinking about the possibility of romantic involvement with other bisexually identified partners, given that many clients may never have considered this to be a viable option. The client's responses to such a discussion may provide the clinician with a useful understanding of the projected meanings and internalized dimensions of biphobia yet to be addressed within the individual client. When the individual's projections about what it would be like to be involved with other bisexual people are brought forward, internalized myths, fears, and stereotypes can be effectively explored in the emotional safety of the consulting room.

Let us turn now to an examination of what empirical research tells us about bisexual mental health, particularly the mental and psychological health issues affecting bisexual women.

EMPIRICAL RESEARCH ON BISEXUAL WOMEN

Mental Health Research and Service Utilization

Research on sexual minority women (SMW) and mental health includes research on lesbians, bisexual women, and women who have past or current female sexual partners. It may also include some women who are diverse with respect to gender identity or presentation. Silverschanz (2004) described SMW as "women who have had (or wish to have) conscious and meaningful sexual contact with other women, regardless of how they name that desire" (p. 38). Most studies on SMW focus on lesbians or fail to differentiate between lesbians and bisexual women (Horowitz, Weis, & Laflin, 2003), collapsing data on all women who have sex with women, thereby obscuring differences between these groups of women. Until recently, there has been relatively little empirical research specifically targeting bisexual mental health or the therapy experiences of bisexual women and men (Martin & Meezan, 2003).

Research differentiating between lesbian and bisexual women or gay and bisexual men or comparing lesbian, gay, bisexual, and heterosexual participants across a variety of dimensions of lifestyle and psychological functioning has increased greatly in the past 5 to 10 years, giving us a much richer understanding of between-group differences and similarities. The past five years witnessed the emergence of a refereed journal specifically on bisexual issues, entitled *Journal of Bisexuality*, which publishes a wide variety of articles, including many on bisexual health and mental health. This refereed professional publication provides a much-needed focal point for gathering and disseminating high quality, up-to-date research on bisexuality and the psychological and physical health of bisexual people.

To date, studies examining bisexuality and mental health have produced results that have been somewhat inconsistent (Horowitz et al., 2003). I briefly review several key studies in this area.

Utilizing data from the National Opinion Research Center (NORC) that resulted from a longitudinal, large-scale population study covering an 8-year period (1988–1996; Davis & Smith, 1996), Horowitz et al. (2003) examined quality of life, lifestyle, and health indicators from 11,563 interviews with LGB and heterosexual individuals. These authors reported "no significant differences among [sexual orientation] groups for happiness, job satisfaction, perceived health, drinks too much, used illegal drugs, tried to quit smoking, or hours of TV watched" (p. 24). Echoing these results, one recent study (Ketz & Israel, 2002) discovered no differences in perceived wellness between women who report having sex with both women and men and identify as "bisexual" and women who report having sex with both women and men and identify as "lesbian." Similarly, Bronn (2001) found that bisexual participants did not have substantially lower scores than other participants on self-reflective "quality of life" scales. Finally, on an optimistic note, Bradford (2004) found that forming and maintaining a bisexual identity had positive effects on her participants' self-concept, including enhanced self-reliance, openness to others who are also "different," and life enrichment (such as a deepened ability to love and increased opportunities for personal growth).

In contrast, Silverschanz's (2004) review of the literature found that bisexual participants, when they could be distinctly identified within the study populations, frequently manifested higher levels of psychological distress and greater mental health difficulties relative to gay, lesbian, and heterosexual respondents (Jorm et al., 2002; Rothblum & Factor, 2001; Saphira &

Glover, 2000). More specifically, Jorm et al. (2002) found significant differences among Australian bisexual, homosexual, and heterosexual survey respondents, with bisexual participants reporting higher levels on all measures of anxiety, depression, alcohol misuse, and negative affect. Mathy et al. (2004) found that bisexual females and transgendered individuals reported significantly higher rates of suicidal intent, mental health difficulties, and psychological-service utilization than bisexual males. Unfortunately, bisexual females also appear to be at higher risk for physical assault than are their female heterosexual counterparts (Horowitz et al., 2003).

An even more recent review by Dodge and Sandfort (in press) reaches similar conclusions about the health and mental health risks associated with a bisexual orientation. To make matters more confusing, one of the studies mentioned previously that found no differences among sexual orientation groups in measures of overall quality of life (Bronn, 2001) did find that female and male bisexual respondents reported slightly lower scores on measures of self-esteem and general well-being.

Cultural factors—such as contemporary economic and political conditions within the United States and abroad; characteristics of urban, suburban, and rural environments; and the specific racial, ethnic, and cultural communities within which bisexual individuals are living—are also likely to have an impact on findings related to the psychological adjustment and mental health of the bisexual individuals studied (Bradford, 2004). Mathy et al. (2004) interpreted their finding of substantial psychological risk factors among their bisexual participants as suggestive of the fact that sexism and heterosexism (particularly affecting both bisexual females and transgendered individuals) have an interactive effect that "compounds the social weight of oppression and increases risks for overwhelming sexual minorities' adaptive functioning" (p. 104).

Given the data just described, perhaps one of the most important areas of recent research on bisexual women is on their use of mental health services. Silverschanz (2004) found that SMW utilize psychological services at rates considerably higher than utilization rates reported in general population studies, although some studies indicate that the reasons bisexual people seek therapy are often for clinical issues unrelated to their sexual orientation per se (Page, 2004). Rogers, Emanuel, and Bradford (2003) found considerable support for previous findings indicating high levels of utilization by bisexual and lesbian women relative to their heterosexual counterparts. Page (2004) found that approximately three-fourths of the participants in her sample were utilizing mental health services at the time of her survey.

One recent review reported on two studies that found mental health providers directed greater degrees of heterosexual bias toward bisexual participants than they directed at lesbian and gay participants (Lucksted, 1996; Moss, 1994, cited in Page, 2004). Page (2004) also completed an investigation that constituted a major step in defining what constitutes deficient practice and exemplary practice in conducting psychotherapy with bisexual women and men. In considering her participants' substantive responses, Page (2004) found that the key ingredients to affirmative therapy with a bisexual woman included the counselor's validation of the client's bisexuality, support for her bisexual identity and its expression, thoughtful and discerning feedback for her around issues of relationship and community, and finally, a proactive and celebratory stance toward her capacity to love people of more than one gender.

To summarize, the state of empirical research on bisexual women is still in a very early stage of development. Research that differentiates between lesbian and bisexual women and between gay and bisexual men or that compares participants of varying sexual orientations across a variety of dimensions of psychological functioning is increasing, but there has not been enough replication of studies using reliable and valid instrumentation to conclusively determine the risk factors and individual or cultural benefits associated with bisexual identification.

Clearly, however, cultural factors and the specific racial and ethnic communities within which bisexual individuals are living have an impact on the psychological adjustment and mental health of the bisexual individuals studied (Bradford, 2004), and the issue of heterosexual bias directed toward bisexual individuals by therapists needs further study and clarification. Future research will refine our understanding of what constitutes deficient and exemplary psychotherapy practice with bisexual women and men. Fortunately, research on bisexual women is beginning to branch out in new directions, as described next.

Empirical Evidence in Additional Areas Critical to Bisexual Women

A number of recent studies have explored areas that are of paramount importance to the provision of mental health services to bisexual women. These studies have addressed such topics as the psychological adjustment of bisexual women in marriages with heterosexual and bisexual male partners (Buxton, 2004; Pallotta-Chiarolli & Lubowitz, 2003); factors in the success of mixed-orientation marriages after husbands or wives come out as bisexual or lesbian (Buxton, 2004; Edser & Shea, 2002); and the impact of heterosexism and biphobia on bisexual mental health (Israel & Mohr, 2004; Mulick & Wright, 2002).

There has also been recent empirical research on the interacting effects of biracial identity, bicultural identification, religious identity, and politics on bisexual women's identity development (Dworkin, 2002); the impact of feminism and women's communities on the physical appearance and attire that bisexual women choose when interfacing with various (lesbian and straight) communities (Taub, 2003); and unique factors impacting bisexual women's friendships with heterosexual women (Galupo, Sailer, & St. John, 2004). Every new study increases understanding of the intrapsychic, social, and cultural-community dimensions of bisexual women's lives, and all of these studies are essential for charting directions for effective and ethical counseling and psychotherapy with this population of women. I strongly encourage counselors seeking to serve this population to familiarize themselves with the recent, published literature. The *Journal of Bisexuality* provides one excellent resource in this regard, and a number of other professional journals are also publishing work in this area.

Implications of Empirical Research for Counseling Bisexual Women

Bisexual female clients may seek counseling for a variety of presenting concerns. These concerns include confusion about their sexuality; awareness of bisexuality, but discomfort with accepting it; internalized biphobia; working through others' reactions to their bisexuality; feelings of rejection or isolation related to being bisexual; the desire to expand an existing stable relationship to include another partner or partners; and prior unsatisfying experiences with therapists who were unable to embrace or affirm a bisexual identity (Oxley & Lucius, 2000).

Recent empirical research suggests that bisexual individuals may suffer from the effects of oppression or "double discrimination" by both heterosexuals and some members of the lesbian and gay community (Ochs, 1996; Rust, 2000) and may manifest psychological difficulties at rates exceeding those of lesbian, gay, and heterosexual people (Jorm et al., 2002). Therefore, it is crucial that counselors be attentive to the presence of psychological manifestations of distress (e.g., depression, anxiety, panic, substance abuse, suicidality) and be prepared to identify and assist clients with these profound sources of personal suffering. This remains important regardless of whether the origins of these difficulties are external (e.g., societal oppression, biphobia, sexism, racism, or homophobia) or internal (e.g., internalization of these forces of oppression within the individual, predispositions to suffering grounded in the genetic heritage of the client, or early developmental trauma). Working with clients that have multiply layered and internally complex identities "raises the bar" with respect to practice standards for practitioners working with these individuals and families.

When bisexuality is a primary therapeutic issue, counselors play crucial roles in validating women in their bisexuality (Page, 2004) and in assisting them in exploring their own personal feelings for other women, apart from influences of partner(s) or culture (Bradford, 2004). Clients benefit from working with counselors who are knowledgeable about negotiating nonmonogamy in intimate relationships (McLean, 2004) and about successful paradigms for maintaining mixed-orientation marriages when one or both partners are bisexual (Buxton, 2004; Edser & Shea, 2002; Pallotta-Chiarolli & Lubowitz, 2003). Additionally, therapists can assist bisexual women in confronting myths and shame-based conceptions of bisexuality, providing these women with support and information and assisting them in placing their experiences in a larger cultural perspective.

Empirical research on bisexuality and mental health is still relatively young, but the past 10 years have witnessed a substantial increase in the number of quantitative and qualitative studies conducted that pertain to bisexual women. Early research on sexual identity formation and on the existence of bisexual behavior among populations who self-identify with a variety of labels is now being enhanced by studies on numerous topics related to bisexuality. Research focusing on the individual is being expanded to include the cultural, relational, ethnic, and community contexts of bisexual women and their psychological, sociological, and political implications. In the next section, I explore what I believe to be the essential elements for developing an affirmative approach to counseling women dealing with bisexuality.

AFFIRMATIVE COUNSELING AND PSYCHOTHERAPY WITH BISEXUAL WOMEN

Diversity and complexity characterize the lives of women whose hearts and souls embody bisexuality in any of its multiple expressions. Women who experience themselves as capable of multiply gendered forms of love and attraction come in every shape, size, color, socioeconomic status, and religious or spiritual orientation. The unique and varied cultural, relational, and community contexts of bisexual women raise a number of important considerations for therapists working with these women. In this section, I create a "frame" for providing therapeutic assistance to bisexual women, explore LGB counseling as a form of multicultural competence, and discuss the necessary shifts in perspective that lead us toward effective, culturally sensitive clinical practice with bisexual women.

Creating the Frame

Bisexuality disrupts some of our most fundamental assumptions about gender and about the nature of sexual attraction, and in so doing, it challenges some of our most deeply held convictions about the nature of love, intimacy, and committed partnership. As noted in one of my previous publications, bisexuality functions as a lens through which a more fluid, continuous understanding of sexual and gender identity and expression become visible (Firestein, 1996b). But that which becomes visible can also be profoundly disturbing. The acknowledgment of bisexual reality shines a light on the frequency with which inconsistencies occur among behavior, attraction, and self-identity, ultimately challenging some of our most cherished concepts in regard to sexual orientation. Bisexuality challenges essentialist notions of sexual identity; the "achievement" of sexual identity stability as a marker of psychological health; and the use of biological, ethnic, and assimilationist approaches to achieve social acceptance and civil rights for gay, lesbian, bisexual, and transgender people within the dominant culture.

Counselors and psychotherapists need to acknowledge the reality and existence of identity fluidity and change, just as we have acknowledged the existence of change and fluidity in clients' careers, relationships, and other areas of life functioning. Understanding the cultural, relational, and community contexts of women who embody bisexual feelings and desire is an important step toward ethical, effective, and affirmative practice with bisexual, lesbian, transgender, and gay clients, their partners, and their families.

Therapy With Bisexual Clients: A Multicultural Competency

Effective psychotherapy and counseling with bisexual women is not an uncomplicated extension of affirmative counseling for gays and lesbians, but is clearly related to these approaches. Counseling bisexual women overlaps considerably with the multicultural counseling competency necessary to effectively work with ethnic and racial minority clients and biracial clients. In an innovative contribution to the training and psychotherapy literature, Tania Israel and Mary Selvidge (2003) have brought the two fields of counseling together by outlining multicultural counseling's contributions to three areas of counselor competence with LGB clients: conceptualization of competence, counselor education and training, and assessment of counselor competence.

Israel and Selvidge (2003) note the similarities in the identity development process, shared experiences of stereotyping by the culture, and histories of stigmatization within the field of psychology common to these two groups, while acknowledging that the cultural and social realities of LGB individuals differ in significant ways from those of ethnic minorities. The research applies models of counselor competence that address knowledge, attitudes, and skills needed for multicultural counseling and extends application of these concepts to work with LGB clients. Israel (2003b) has recommended using guidelines for counseling women and LGB individuals as adjuncts to existing multicultural counseling competencies. Encouraging our counseling-related disciplines to move in this direction would be of particular benefit to ensuring effective training in counseling bisexual clients, especially bisexual women of color and biracial or multiracial bisexual women. These considerations add up to a rather complex challenge for practitioners: the challenge to continually expand and integrate more facets of identity and culture into practitioners' understanding and their work with individual clients and clients' families.

IMPLICATIONS FOR THERAPISTS AND DIRECTIONS
FOR FURTHER EXPLORATION

Counselors' interactions with bisexual women bring into sharp relief the uncomfortable truth of difference; difference not simply of degree but of "kind." For many of our clients, it is profoundly challenging to embrace an identity that so powerfully undermines their own unconscious assumptions about identity and intimacy. It can be profoundly uncomfortable simply to be a bisexual person in this society, much less trying to discover ways to live out this identity while achieving a sense of belonging within one's family and community. Furthermore, I believe that many therapists feel uncomfortable with their bisexual clients, particularly those who are exploring polyamory. In addition, few identities are as politicized as bisexual identities are across both lesbian and heterosexual cultures. What does all of this mean for practitioners?

It is clear that clinicians cannot afford to ignore the sociological and political dimensions of bisexual identity or dismiss the strength of their own internalized, frequently unconscious investment in dichotomous models of sexual orientation or gender. Practitioners who wish to effectively serve clients of all sexual orientations and gender identities must be willing to reexamine a number of traditional notions about psychological health and maturity, love, committed partnership, monogamy, and marriage.

Specifically, counselors and therapists need to explore their own monosexual assumptions, acknowledge the possibility that committed relationships may involve the simultaneous expression of love and intimacy with more than one partner of more than one gender, embrace the possibility that these forms of loving can occur in psychologically and emotionally healthy ways, and cultivate the skills and perspectives necessary to distinguish individual differences from pathology in psychologically meaningful ways. This ultimately requires the development of new models of sexual identity development that take into account experiences of sexual fluidity and identity change across the life span.

I am intrigued with several questions at the present time. For example, What constitutes a healthy developmental trajectory for a bisexual woman, man, or transgendered person coming of age in a culture that is still largely dichotomous with respect to gender identity and sexual orientation? How might a bisexual young person be encouraged to constructively explore his or her authentic interests in bisexual expression, polyamory, or alternative sexuality? What constitutes optimal psychological and social functioning for a polyamorous bisexual woman? For single bisexual women? For older, African American bisexual women in a racist society? For a bisexual woman coming out in a biphobic lesbian community? Or for a transgendered individual who is recently discovering her or his bisexual desires? This is an exciting time to be studying and serving bisexual people. There are far more questions than there are answers. But at least we are now able to begin framing the questions.

Affirmative practice is ethical practice, and enough is now known about bisexuality to allow counselors who wish to work with this population to become adequately informed. Specific psychotherapy training in working effectively with bisexual clients is seldom, if ever, formally available through current graduate training programs for therapists. However, the American Psychological Association, Division 44/Committee on Lesbian, Gay, and Bisexual Concerns Joint Task Force (2000) and the ethical standards of several counseling associations pertaining to the provision of services to LGBT individuals and families provide valuable guidance to counselors seeking support in this area of practice.

CONCLUSION

There is considerable evidence of the emergence of the LGBT-affirmative paradigm I first discussed in the paradigm-shift chapter of my first book, *Bisexuality: The Psychology and Politics of an Invisible Minority* (Firestein, 1996b). LGBT-affirmative psychotherapy goes beyond tolerance, even beyond acceptance, to the level of affirmation and celebration of our incredibly rich and diverse sexualities. As we in the field of psychology transform our paradigms of research, our paradigms of practice must change to reflect this transformation.

Providing cultural and therapeutic space for women to explore, express, and validate their bisexuality also provides more psychological, social, and cultural space for the expression of lesbian, gay, and transgender identities (Firestein, 1996b). This context of permission and validation also provides support for individuals who may move through and among a variety of sexual or gender identity categories across their life span. Embracing this new understanding of the ethnic, cultural, and relational contexts of bisexual women, we move powerfully to create truly affirmative LGBT approaches to counseling and psychotherapy that embrace diversity and, in so doing, give bisexual women a place of belonging, acceptance, and inclusion—a place to call "home."

REFERENCES

Abbott, D., & Farmer, E. (Eds.). (1995). *From wedded wife to lesbian life: Stories of transformation*. Freedom, CA: The Crossing Press.

Alexander, J., & Yescavage, J. (Eds.). (2004). *InterSEXions of the others: Bisexuality and transgenderism*. Binghamton, NY: Haworth Press.

American Psychological Association, Division 44/Committee on Lesbian, Gay, and Bisexual Concerns Joint Task Force on Guidelines for Psychotherapy With Lesbian, Gay, and Bisexual Clients. (2000). Guidelines for psychotherapy with lesbian, gay, and bisexual clients. *American Psychologist, 55,* 1440–1451.

Anapol, D. (1997). *Polyamory: The new love without limits*. San Rafael, CA: IntiNet Resource Center.

Balsam, K. (2003). Traumatic victimization in the lives of lesbian and bisexual women: A contextual approach. *Journal of Lesbian Studies, 7*(1), 1–14.

Blackwood, E., & Wieringa, S. E. (2003). Sapphic shadows: Challenging the silence in the study of sexuality. In L. D. Garnets & D. C. Kimmel (Eds.), *Psychological perspectives on lesbian, gay and bisexual experiences* (2nd rev. ed., pp. 410–434). New York: Columbia University Press.

Blumenfeld, W., & Raymond, D. (1988). *Looking at gay and lesbian life*. New York: Philosophical Library.

Bower, J., Gurevich, M., & Mathieson, C. (2002). (Con)Tested identities: Bisexual women reorient sexuality. In D. Atkins (Ed.), *Bisexual women in the twenty-first century* (pp. 23–52). New York: Harrington Park Press.

Bradford, M. (1997). *The bisexual experience: Living in a dichotomous culture*. Unpublished doctoral dissertation, Fielding Institute, Santa Barbara, CA.

Bradford, M. (2004). The bisexual experience: Living in a dichotomous culture. *Journal of Bisexuality, 4*(1/2), 7–23.

Bronn, C. D. (2001). Attitudes and self-images of male and female bisexuals. *Journal of Bisexuality, 1*(4), 5–29.

Buxton, A. P. (2004). Works in progress: How mixed-orientation couples maintain their marriages after the wives come out. *Journal of Bisexuality, 4*(1/2), 57–82.

Chan, C. S. (1992). Cultural considerations in counseling Asian-American lesbians and gay men. In S. Dworkin & F. Gutierrez (Eds.), *Counseling gay men and lesbians: Journey to the end of the rainbow* (pp. 115–124). Alexandria, VA: American Association for Counseling and Development.

Collins, J. F. (2000). Biracial-bisexual individuals: Identity coming of age. *International Journal of Sexuality and Gender Studies, 3*, 221–253.

Comas-Diaz, L., & Green, B. (Eds.). (1994). *Women of color: Integrating ethnic and gender identities in psychotherapy*. New York: Guilford.

Davis, J. A., & Smith, T. W. (1996). *General social surveys, 1972–1996: Cumulative codebook*. Chicago: National Opinion Research Center.

Diamond, L., & Savin-Williams, R. C. (2003). Explaining diversity in the development of same-sex sexuality among young women. In L. D. Garnets & D. C. Kimmel (Eds.), *Psychological perspectives on lesbian, gay and bisexual experiences* (2nd rev. ed., pp. 130–148). New York: Columbia University Press.

Dixon, J. K. (1984). The commencement of bisexual activity in swinging married women over age thirty. *Journal of Sex Research, 20*(1), 71–90. (Reprinted from *Bisexuality in the United States: A social science reader*, pp. 203–216, by P. Rodríguez Rust, Ed., 2000, New York: Columbia University Press)

Dixon, J. K. (1985). Sexuality and relationship changes in married females following the commencement of bisexual activity. *Journal of Homosexuality, 11*(1/2), 155–134. (Reprinted from *Two lives to lead: Bisexuality in men and women*, pp. 115–113, by F. Klein & T. J. Wolf, Eds., 1985, New York: Harrington Park Press)

Dodge, B., & Sandfort, T. (in press). Mental health research on bisexual individuals: A critical review. In B. A. Firestein (Ed.), *Becoming visible: Counseling bisexuals across the life span*. New York: Columbia University Press.

Dworkin, S. H. (2002). Biracial, bicultural, bisexual: Bisexuality and multiple identities. *Journal of Bisexuality, 2*(4), 93–107.

Easton, D., & Liszt, C. A. (1997). *The ethical slut: A guide to infinite sexual possibilities*. San Francisco: Greenery Press.

Edser, S. J., & Shea, J. D. (2002). An exploratory investigation of bisexual men in monogamous heterosexual marriages. *Journal of Bisexuality, 2*(4), 5–43.

Esterberg, K. G. (1997). *Lesbian and bisexual identities: Constructing communities, constructing selves*. Philadelphia: Temple University Press.

Falco, K. (1996). Psychotherapy with women who love women. In R. P. Cabaj & T. S. Stein (Eds.), *Textbook of homosexuality and mental health* (pp. 397–412). Washington, DC: American Psychiatric Press.

Firestein, B. A. (1996a). Bisexuality as paradigm shift: Transforming our disciplines. In B. A. Firestein (Ed.), *Bisexuality: The psychology and politics of an invisible minority* (pp. 263–291). Thousand Oaks, CA: Sage.

Firestein, B. A. (1996b). *Bisexuality: The psychology and politics of an invisible minority*. Thousand Oaks, CA: Sage.

Firestein, B. A. (1996c). Introduction. In B. A. Firestein (Ed.), *Bisexuality: The psychology and politics of an invisible minority* (pp. xix–xxvii). Thousand Oaks, CA: Sage.

Fox, A. (1991). Development of a bisexual identity: Understanding the process. In L. Hutchins & L. Ka'ahumanu (Eds.), *Bi any other name: Bisexual people speak out*. Boston: Alyson.

Fox, R. C. (1995). Bisexual identities. In A. R. D'Augelli & C. J. Patterson (Eds.), *Lesbian, gay and bisexual identities over the lifespan* (pp. 48–86). New York: Oxford University Press.

Fox, R. C. (1996). Bisexuality in perspective: A review of theory and research. In B. A. Firestein (Ed.), *Bisexuality: The psychology and politics of an invisible minority* (pp. 3–50). Thousand Oaks, CA: Sage.

Galupo, M. P., Sailer, C. A., & St. John, S. C. (2004). Friendship across sexual orientations: Experiences of bisexual women in early adulthood. *Journal of Bisexuality, 4*(1/2), 37–53.

Gillem, A. R., & Thompson, C. A. (2004). *Biracial women in therapy: Between the rock of gender and the hard place of race*. New York: Haworth Press.

Greene, B. (1994). Ethnic-minority lesbians and gay men: Mental health and treatment issues. *Journal of Consulting and Clinical Psychology, 62*, 243–251.

Greene, B. (1997). *Ethnic and cultural diversity among lesbians and gay men*. Thousand Oaks, CA: Sage.

Greene, B. (2003). Beyond heterosexism and across the cultural divide: Developing an inclusive lesbian, gay, and bisexual psychology: A look to the future. In L. D. Garnets & D. C. Kimmel (Eds.), *Psychological perspectives on lesbian, gay and bisexual experiences* (2nd rev. ed., pp. 357–400). New York: Columbia University Press.

Herek, G. M. (2003). Why tell if you're not asked? Self-disclosure, intergroup contact, and heterosexuals' attitudes toward lesbians and gay men. In L. D. Garnets & D. C. Kimmel (Eds.), *Psychological perspectives on lesbian, gay and bisexual experiences* (2nd rev. ed., pp. 270–298). New York: Columbia University Press.

Horowitz, S. M., Weis, D. L., & Laflin, M. T. (2003). Bisexuality, quality of lifestyle and health indicators. *Journal of Bisexuality, 3*(2), 5–28.

Hutchins, L. (1996). Bisexuality: Politics and community. In B. Firestein (Ed.), *Bisexuality: The psychology and politics of an invisible minority* (pp. 242–259). Thousand Oaks, CA: Sage.

Hutchins, L. (2001). *Erotic rites: A cultural analysis of contemporary U.S. sacred sexuality traditions and trends.* Unpublished doctoral dissertation, Union Institute Graduate College.

Hutchins, L. (2002). Bisexual women as emblematic sexual healers and the problematics of the embodied sacred whore. In D. Atkins (Ed.), *Bisexual women in the twenty-first century* (pp. 205–226). New York: Harrington Park Press.

Hutchins, L., & Ka'ahumanu, L. (Eds.). (1991). *Bi any other name: Bisexual people speak out.* Boston: Alyson.

Israel, T. (2003a). What counselors need to know about working with sexual minority clients. In D. R. Atkinson & G. Hackett (Eds.), *Counseling diverse populations* (pp. 347–364). Boston: McGraw-Hill.

Israel, T. (2003b). Integrating gender and sexual orientation into multicultural counseling competencies. In G. Roysircar, P. Arredondo, J. N. Fuertes, J. G. Ponterotto, & R. L. Toporek (Eds.), *Multicultural counseling competencies 2003: Association for Multicultural Counseling and Development* (pp. 69–77). Alexandria, VA: Association for Multicultural Counseling and Development.

Israel, T. (2004). Conversations, not categories: The intersection of biracial and bisexual identities. In A. R. Gillem & C. A. Thompson (Eds.), *Biracial women in therapy: Between the rock of gender and the hard place of race* (pp. 173–184). New York: Haworth Press.

Israel, T., & Mohr, J. J. (2004). Attitudes toward bisexual women and men: Current research, future directions. *Journal of Bisexuality, 4*(1/2), 117–134.

Israel, T., & Selvidge, M. M. D. (2003). Contributions of multicultural counseling to counselor competence with lesbian, gay and bisexual clients. *Journal of Multicultural Counseling and Development, 31,* 84–97.

Jorm, A. F., Korten, A. E., Rodgers, B., Jacomb, P. A., & Christensen, H. (2002). Sexual orientation and mental health: Results from a community survey of young and middle-aged. *British Journal of Psychiatry, 188,* 423–427.

Ketz, K., & Israel, T. (2002). The relationship between women's sexual identity and perceived wellness. In D. Atkins (Ed.), *Bisexual women in the twenty-first century* (pp. 227–242). New York: Harrington Park Press.

Klein, F. (1990). The need to view sexual orientation as a multi-variable dynamic process: A theoretical perspective. In D. P. McWhirter, S. A. Sanders, & J. M. Reinisch

(Eds.), *Homosexuality/heterosexuality: Concepts of sexual orientation* (pp. 277–282). New York: Oxford University Press.

Klein, F., Sepekoff, B., & Wolf, T. J. (1985). Sexual orientation: A multi-variable dynamic process. In F. K. Klein & T. J. Wolf (Eds.), *Two lives to lead: Bisexuality in men and women* (pp. 35–49). New York: Harrington Park Press.

Lenius, S. (2001). Bisexuals and BDSM: Bisexual people in a pansexual community. *Journal of Bisexuality, 1*(4), 71–78.

Lucksted, A. (1996, March). *Lesbian and bisexual women who are mental health care consumers: Experiences in the mental health system.* Paper presented at the Annual Conference of the Association for Women in Psychology, Portland, OR.

Martin, J., & Meezan, W. (2003). Applying ethical standards to research and evaluations involving lesbian, gay, bisexual, and transgender populations. *Journal of Gay and Lesbian Social Services, 15*(1/2), 181–201.

Mathy, R. M., Lehmann, B. A., & Kerr, D. (2004). Bisexual and transgender identities in a nonclinical sample of North Americans: Suicidal intent, behavioral difficulties, and mental health treatment. In J. Alexander & J. Yescavage (Eds.), *Bisexuality and transgenderism: InterSEXions of the others* (pp. 93–109). Binghamton, NY: Haworth Press.

Matteson, D. (1996). Counseling and psychotherapy with bisexual and exploring clients. In B. Firestein (Ed.), *Bisexuality: The psychology and politics of an invisible minority* (pp. 185–213). Thousand Oaks, CA: Sage.

McLean, K. (2004). Negotiating (non)monogamy: Bisexuality and intimate relationships. *Journal of Bisexuality, 4*(1/2), 83–97.

Morales, E. S. (1989). Ethnic minority families and minority gays and lesbians. *Marriage and Family Review, 14*, 217–239.

Moss, J. F. (1994). The heterosexual bias inventory (HBI): Gay, lesbian and bisexual clients' perceptions of heterosexual bias in psychotherapy (Doctoral dissertation, Michigan State University, 1994). *Dissertation Abstracts International, 55*(12), 5571B.

Mulick, P. S., & Wright, L. W., Jr. (2002). Examining the existence of biphobia in the heterosexual and homosexual populations. *Journal of Bisexuality, 2*(4), 45–64.

Nearing, R. (1992). *The polyfidelity primer* (3rd ed.). Captain Cook, HI: PEP.

Nichols, M. (1994). Bisexuality in women: Myths, realities, and implications for therapy. In E. Cole & E. Rothblum (Eds.), *Women and sex therapy: Closing the circle of sexual knowledge* (pp. 235–252). New York: Harrington Park Press.

Ochs, R. (1996). Biphobia: It goes more than two ways. In B. Firestein (Ed.), *Bisexuality: The psychology and politics of an invisible minority* (pp. 217–239). Thousand Oaks, CA: Sage.

Ochs, R. (Ed.). (2001). *The international directory of bisexual groups.* Cambridge, MA: Bisexual Resource Center.

Ochs, R. (in press). What's in a name? Why women embrace or resist a bisexual identity. In B. A. Firestein (Ed.), *Becoming visible: Counseling bisexuals across the life span.* New York: Columbia University Press.

Oxley, E., & Lucius, C. A. (2000). Looking both ways: Bisexuality and therapy. In C. Neal & D. Davies (Eds.), *Issues in therapy with lesbian, gay, bisexual and transgender clients*. Buckingham, England: Open University Press.

Pachankis, J. E., & Goldfried, M. R. (2004). Clinical issues in working with lesbian, gay, and bisexual clients. *Psychotherapy: Theory, Research, Practice, Training, 41*, 227–246.

Page, E. (2004). Mental health services experiences of bisexual women and bisexual men: An empirical study. *Journal of Bisexuality, 4*(1/2) 137–160.

Pallotta-Chiarolli, M., & Lubowitz, S. (2003). "Outside Belonging": Multi-sexual relationships as border existence. *Journal of Bisexuality, 3*(1), 53–85.

Pharr, S. (1988). *Homophobia: A weapon of sexism*. Inverness, CA: Chardon Press.

Queen, C. (1996a). Sexual diversity, bisexuality and the sex positive perspective. In B. A. Firestein (Ed.), *Bisexuality: The psychology and politics of an invisible minority*, (p. 103–124). Thousand Oaks, CA: Sage Publications.

Queen, C. (1996b). Women, S/M, and therapy. *Women and Therapy, 19*(4), 65–73.

Rich, A. (1980). Compulsory heterosexuality and lesbian existence. *Signs: Journal of Women in Culture and Society, 5*, 631–660.

Robin, L., Brener, N. D., Donahue, S. F., Hack, T., Hale, K., & Goodenow, C. (2002). Associations between health risk behaviors and opposite-, same-, and both-sex sexual partners in representative samples of Vermont and Massachusetts high school students. *Archives of Pediatrics & Adolescent Medicine, 156*, 349–355.

Rogers, T. L., Emanuel, K., & Bradford, J. (2003). Sexual minorities seeking services: A retrospective study of mental health concerns of lesbian and bisexual women. In T. L. Hughes, C. Smith, & A. Dan (Eds.), *Mental health issues for sexual minority women: Redefining women's mental health* (pp. 127–146). New York: Harrington Park Press.

Rothblum, E. D., & Bond, L. (Eds.). (1996). *Preventing heterosexism and homophobia* (pp. 36–58). Thousand Oaks, CA: Sage Publications.

Rothblum, E. D., & Factor, R. (2001). Lesbians and their sisters as a control group: Demographic and mental health factors. *Psychological Science, 12*, 63–69.

Russell, S. T., & Joyner, K. (2001). Adolescent sexual orientation and suicide risk: Evidence from a national study. *American Journal of Public Health, 91*, 573–578.

Russell, S. T., & Seif, H. (2002). Bisexual female adolescents: A critical analysis of past research and results from a national survey. In D. Atkins (Ed.), *Bisexual women in the twenty-first century* (pp. 73–94). New York: Harrington Park Press.

Rust, P. C. (1992). The politics of sexual identity: Sexual attraction and behavior among lesbian and bisexual women. *Social Problems, 39*, 366–386.

Rust, P. C. (1993a). "Coming out" in the age of social constructionism: Sexual identity formation among lesbian and bisexual women. *Gender and Society, 7*, 50–77.

Rust, P. C. (1993b). Neutralizing the political threat of the marginal woman: Lesbians' beliefs about bisexual women. *Journal of Sex Research, 30*, 214–228.

Rust, P. (1995). *Bisexuality and the challenge to lesbian politics: Sex, loyalty, and revolution*. New York: New York University Press.

Rust, P. (1996a). Managing multiple identities: Diversity among bisexual women and men. In B. A. Firestein (Ed.), *Bisexuality: The psychology and politics of an invisible minority* (pp. 53–83). Thousand Oaks, CA: Sage.

Rust, P. (1996b). Monogamy and polyamory: Relationship issues for bisexuals. In B. A. Firestein (Ed.), *Bisexuality: The psychology and politics of an invisible minority* (pp. 127–148). Thousand Oaks, CA: Sage.

Rust, P. R. (2000). Heterosexual gays, homosexual straights. In P. R. Rust (Ed.), *Bisexuality in the United States: A social science reader* (pp. 279–306). New York: Columbia University Press.

Rust, P. C. (2003). Finding a sexual identity and community: Therapeutic implications and cultural assumptions in scientific models of coming out. In L. D. Garnets & D. C. Kimmel (Eds.), *Psychological perspectives on lesbian, gay and bisexual experiences* (2nd rev. ed., pp. 227–269). New York: Columbia University Press.

Saphira, M., & Glover, M. (2000). New Zealand national lesbian health survey. *Journal of the Gay and Lesbian Medical Association, 4*(2), 49–56.

Silverschanz, P. (2004). *Sexual minority women and mental health: A review of the research 1992–2002.* Unpublished manuscript.

Solot, D., & Miller, M. (2001). Unmarried bisexuals: Distinct voices on marriage and family. *Journal of Bisexuality, 1*(4), 81–90.

Stanley, J. L. (2004). Biracial lesbian and bisexual women: Understanding the unique aspects and interactional processes of multiple minority identities. In A. R. Gillem & C. A. Thompson (Eds.), *Biracial women in therapy: Between the rock of gender and the hard place of race* (pp. 159–172). New York: Haworth Press.

Strock, C. (1998). *Married women who love women.* New York: Doubleday.

Taub, J. (2003). What should I wear? A qualitative look at the impact of feminism and women's communities on bisexual women's appearance. *Journal of Bisexuality, 3*(1), 9–22.

Weise, E. R. (1992). *Closer to home: Bisexuality and feminism.* Seattle, WA: Seal.

Weitzman, G. (in press). Counseling bisexuals in polyamorous relationships. In B. A. Firestein (Ed.), *Becoming visible: Counseling bisexuals across the life span.* New York: Columbia University Press.

Zinik, G. A. (1984). The relationship between sexual orientation and eroticism, cognitive flexibility, and negative affect (Doctoral dissertation, University of California, Santa Barbara, 1983). *Dissertation Abstracts International, 45*(8), 2707B.

5

DEVELOPMENT OF BISEXUAL MEN'S IDENTITIES AND RELATIONSHIPS

DANIEL J. POTOCZNIAK

In recent years, the label of "LGBT" (lesbian, gay, bisexual, and transgender) has come to encompass all people of nontraditional sexual or gender orientation. Despite the appearance of unity, however, there are significant differences among the groups that have come to compose the acronym (Weiss, 2003). This chapter explores one of the least discussed and least understood components of the LGBT community, the bisexual male community. I discuss bisexual men's role in history, and in that context, biphobia directed toward bisexual men is addressed. Further consideration is given to bisexual men's identity development, with a focus on how this identity may be influenced by issues of culture, race, and ethnicity. For greater clarity and to promote greater ease in research and clinical work, a descriptive model is presented to clarify the four extant models of identity. When possible, recognizing the nascent state of empirical research on bisexual individuals, I provide empirical support to lend greater specificity to particular ideas or suggestions. Finally, in light of these topics, I propose future directions for research, clinical practice, and community building with the bisexual male community.

OVERVIEW OF THE BISEXUAL MALE COMMUNITY

A particularly salient difference between contemporary and early 20th-century sexual cultures in the United States is the latter's lack of any particular label for men who had sex with men (Chauncey, 1994). Also, men of that earlier period who did engage in same-sex sexual behavior would not typically have considered themselves abnormal or pathological (Chauncey, 1994) with respect to their individual identities. A stereotypically "masculine" man, perhaps described as "trade" in the lingo of the era, might have looked to boys or to more effeminate men for sexual activity without questioning his status as anything but average or ordinary. Some men might have alternated between partners of either gender without believing that interest in one was exclusive of interest in the other, and this sexual fluidity would not have been described as reflecting any essential, dispositional difference (Chauncey, 1994). The difference between these men and men in the later 20th century's sociosexual milieu was the former's lack of a "heterosexual *versus* homosexual" axis of sexuality (Chauncey, 1994). Regardless of this dichotomy's absence in the past, it is currently alive and very strongly set in contemporary European American culture. Unfortunately, when sexuality is dichotomously viewed as heterosexual *versus* homosexual, it ignores individuals who fail to fit neatly into either category; indeed, many people do not fit such a bipolar model (Blumstein & Schwartz, 1976; Fox, 1996; Kinsey, Pomeroy, & Martin, 1948; Klein, 1993; Lever, Kanouse, Rogers, Carson, & Hertz, 1992; Ochs, 1996; Steinman & Beemyn, 2001; Weinberg, Williams, & Pryor, 1994; Wolff, 1977).

Bisexuality in men may be regarded in four ways: (a) as having sexual attractions to both men and women (bisexual attraction); (b) as having sexual relations with both men and women (behavioral bisexuality); (c) as having romantic feelings for both men and women (romantic bisexuality); and (d) as identifying oneself or one's sexual orientation as bisexual (identity-based bisexuality; Weinberg et al., 1994). In terms of behavioral bisexuality, bisexual men are often obscured in studies on sexuality by being labeled in the same way as gay men, thus rendering them undistinguishable or invisible (Fox, 1996; Lever et al., 1992; MacDonald, 1983). Regarding identity-based bisexuality, previous theories of gay male sexual identity (e.g., Cass, 1979) have classified bisexuality as a "phase" or a transitional period some men experience en route to a gay identity. In contemplating a man's attractions, romantic feelings, behavior, or identity, it is important to note that inclusion in one type of bisexuality does not mandate membership in any of the others.

Reported estimates of the total number of men who have had same-sex sexual experiences vary widely, depending on the study in question. They include estimates that 20.3% of men have ever had a same-sex experience, that 9.1% have had such experiences since puberty, and that 4.9% to 6.7% have had such experiences since age 18 or age 20 (Rust, 2000c). However, although the above numbers of men have had same-sex sexual experiences, ~~less than one percent of men self-identify as bisexual in the U.S. population~~ (Rust, 2000c). This unwillingness to label oneself as bisexual should come as little surprise, considering the stigma placed on men who do not fit into a traditional, dichotomous paradigm (Eliason, 2001).

Bisexual male invisibility also extends to scholarly circles. Historically, the literature on bisexuality has been largely feminist in content and predominantly female in authorship (Hemmings, 2002; Steinman, 2001). Between 1991 and 2001, five bisexual analytical and personal anthologies were published (Firestein, 1996a; Hutchins & Kaahumanu, 1991; Rust, 2000a; Tucker, 1995; Weise, 1992). All five were individually or collectively edited by women. The focus of one of the volumes was feminism and bisexuality, consisting of work composed exclusively by female contributors. Another two contained work mostly from female writers: 51 women to 25 men in one, and 27 to 6 in the other (Steinman, 2001). Outside of the United States, a women's bisexual anthology was published by a group of Canadian women (Bisexual Anthology Collective et al., 1995). Additionally, a recent anthology from the United Kingdom included 34 female and 22 male contributors (Rose, Stevens, & the Off Pink Collective, 1996). The exception to the rule is one compilation that consists of selected e-mails from an Internet discussion group dedicated to bisexual and gay men who are married to women (Klein & Schwartz, 2001). Clearly, in scholarly circles, bisexual men's identities and communities have only begun to receive attention.

Popular culture and entertainment also tend to ignore male bisexuality. In 1991, the film *Together Alone* was released and won the "Audience Award" at the San Francisco International Lesbian & Gay Film Festival and the "Best Film" Award at the Los Angeles Gay & Lesbian Film Festival. The entire film consists of dialogue between two men who have just had sex, one of whom blatantly states that he is a bisexual man with a wife and children. In the *Los Angeles Times*, critics described the film as "one of the most honest, realistic and intimate conversations between two gay men to appear on screen" (Thomas, 1993, p. A15). Eadie (2002) reported that the British Film Institute's CD-ROM Film Index described the film as concerning "a young gay man who feels insecure because of the AIDS epidemic, and his relationship with a man with whom he spends the night." Neither commentary used the word "bisexual" to describe the contents of the film, despite the obvious bisexual material. Although the LGBT community is often described as an "invisible minority," it appears that in popular media and scholarly work, the bisexual male community may be the least visible of all.

The Bisexual Movement in the Recent History of Sexual Minorities

The phenomenon of men having sexual encounters with both males and females is not new. Contemporary European American culture tends to view the phenomenon, though, in terms of a more recently developed sexual dichotomy: a man is either heterosexual or gay, with any instance of same-sex intimacy suggesting that the man in question must be gay (or, at least on the way to "becoming" gay). Because of heterosexual and LG people's tendency to view sexuality dichotomously (Firestein, 1996b), male bisexuality traditionally has been marginalized or ignored by most of society.

The modern bisexual-rights movement has its roots in the lesbian and gay movement, which began the fight for equal rights based on differences in sexual identity (Udis-Kessler, 1996). Activists in the gay rights movement included not only men who may have been exclusively gay, but also men who may have been bisexual in behavior, if not identity. From the beginning of the movement, the Chicago Society for Human Rights, the first U.S. homophile organization that existed briefly in the 1920s, explicitly excluded bisexual men (Beemyn, 2002; Loughery, 1998). Some years later, bisexual men were not explicitly excluded by the Mattachine Society (a gay rights organization incorporated in 1961), but they were frequently marginalized, and their right to be included was often debated (Loughery, 1998). The group's newsletter, *The Mattachine Review,* ran just one article about bisexuality during more than a decade of publishing (Marotta, 1981). Only two other articles from the newsletter even acknowledged the existence of people who were attracted to both men and women. Despite the lack of printed material, bisexuality was discussed within the Mattachine Society, and heated debates sometimes arose. For example, when the findings of Kinsey et al.'s (1948) research—suggesting that many people have sexual experiences with both women and men over the course of their lives—were raised in a 1968 meeting, the leader of Mattachine Society–Washington responded that "people are always either one or the other" and that "those who engage in sexual acts with men and women both are simply 'closet queens' who use their heterosexual acts as a façade to hide their homosexual behavior" (Marotta, 1981, p. 60). In response, the president of the Mattachine Society–New York argued that bisexual individuals were a primary constituency of the group, calling attention to the scientific literature and the number of behaviorally bisexual men who sought help from Mattachine (Marotta, 1981). Thus, since the earliest moments of the gay rights movement, bisexuality has never held a politically stable position, despite bisexual men consistently populating its ranks. This pressure to identify as "gay" and to obscure any opposite-sex attraction ensured that bisexual men remained mostly invisible.

In light of these factors, it may be affirming for many bisexual men to realize that the men at the Stonewall riots of 1969, who made a profound contribution to bisexual and gay liberation, may have identified as bisexual *or* gay. Historical accounts of the riots typically refer to the drag queens and gay men who helped provoke the riots (Carter, 2004; Kaiser, 1997). Regardless of the typical omission of bisexual men, the documentation of the riots and those who started it draws attention to the fluidity of sex and gender roles as well as the same-sex attractions that provided a basis for the Stonewall Inn's existence. This emphasis on sexual fluidity and multidimensionality would strongly influence bisexual persons over the next 20 years, albeit in different ways depending on one's sex. Women of the Stonewall and post-Stonewall era often focused on visibility through activism for LG civil rights, whereas many gay and bisexual men of the post-Stonewall 1970s found themselves possessed with new fervor around sexuality and sexual pleasure-seeking (North, 1990; Steinman, 2001; Udis-Kessler, 1996). For these men, "promiscuity was seen as a form of personal liberation and social revolt and a vehicle for change" (Steinman, 2001, p. 33). Expectations for openly stating one's sexual identity were thus different for men and for women: activism that was common among women often necessitated disclosure, but anonymous sexual encounters more typical among men were by definition just that— anonymous (Udis-Kessler, 1996).

If sexuality defined and confirmed the identity of bisexual men in the 1960s and 1970s, then the onset of the AIDS epidemic in the 1980s meant that these men suddenly had to reevaluate what once was identity affirming. The most common view of this time period for bisexual men, as well as for bisexual women, was that "the days of sexual freedom were over" (Weinberg et al., 1994, p. 211). The celebration of sexuality as a liberating force that was so pervasive in the 1970s and early 1980s was all but completely absent by the end of that latter decade. This was especially true for bisexual men who became known as sexual pariahs due to being a possible "bridge" for HIV between gay communities and the general population. This viewpoint was due in no small part to announcements from the Centers for Disease Control to this effect, as well as articles in popular magazines and newspapers echoing the sentiment (Gelman, 1987; Hutchins, 1996, p. 245; Miller, 2002; Nordheimer, 1987; North, 1990; Weinberg et al., 1994). Many bisexual men began to participate exclusively in opposite-sex relationships due to fears of getting sick, dying, and being labeled as a stigmatized sexual minority during the incipient AIDS crisis. Alternately, some other bisexual men began to feel more strongly aligned with gay men because of admiration for and identification with the community's strength through the crisis or because of the fact that bisexual men were often viewed as less attractive partners to women. Some men also decided to become monogamous, which was not an easy adaptation since bisexual men often engaged in anonymous sexual encounters through "swing parties" and gay bathhouses. Despite these difficulties, bisexual activism for both men and women increased in the late 1970s and 1980s (Hutchins, 1996). This activism varied in appearance and level of publicity, ranging from small community groups that met in campus dorm lounges or community centers to larger women's and men's bisexual groups that became active in large cities such as Boston and Seattle. Most publicly, at least one bisexual candidate ran for public office in San Francisco (Hutchins, 1996).

The 1990s began on a positive note for bisexual men. In 1990, the New York Area Bisexual Network mobilized a successful national writing campaign against the Hetrick-Martin Institute (which founded the Harvey Milk High School for lesbian, gay, bisexual, transgender, and questioning [LGBTQ] adolescents). This campaign successfully persuaded the Institute to remove a workshop entitled "Bisexual Men: Fact or Fiction?"—the presence of which illustrated that biphobia directed toward bisexual men was indeed a presence in the lesbian and gay communities (Hutchins & Ka'ahumanu, 1991a). The period of the 1990s was also a positive and prolific period for bisexual literature, with Eliason going so far as to call the late 1990s the "bisexual moment of fame" (Eliason, 2001, p. 139). During this heyday of bisexuality, women continued to hold the majority of leadership roles and achieved greater authority and visibility in the bisexual community than they had in the 1970s (Steinman, 2001; Udis-Kessler, 1996). Steinman (2001) stated that bisexual men's invisibility during this period reflected an unspoken but significant tolerance of their orientation within the gay male community because that community has traditionally been more erotically than politically focused. Somewhat similarly, Udis-Kessler (1996) presented the belief that bisexual men's invisibility has been due almost entirely to the absence of the bisexual male community in political activism. Whatever the case, bisexual men remain in the shadows of an otherwise progressive movement. As in so many cases, that which is unknown or unseen is frequently feared or hated. Bisexual men constitute no exception.

Biphobia

Biphobia has been defined by Hutchins and Ka'ahumanu (1991) as "the fear of intimacy and closeness to people who don't identify with either the hetero- or homosexual orientation, [with the fear manifesting] as homophobia in the heterosexual community and heterophobia in the homosexual community" (p. 369). As the previously discussed history reveals, bisexual people have been a relatively invisible population, with bisexual men remaining more out of view and generally more stigmatized than bisexual women (Eliason, 2001; Steinman, 2001). This stigma is depicted in empirical findings from Eliason (2001), who conducted survey-based research regarding college students' opinions about sexual minorities. Data collected from a sample of 229 self-identified heterosexual college students (170 females, 59 males) indicate that 26% found bisexual men as a group "very unacceptable," as compared to 21% for gay men, 14% for lesbians, and 12% for bisexual women (no tests for statistically significant differences were indicated). Perhaps even more isolating for the bisexual male community than this stigmatization is the fact that biphobia seems as present in the gay male community as it is in the heterosexual community (Matteson, 1996; Ochs, 1996; Paul, 1985; Weinberg et al., 1994). The present discussion of biphobia aims to explore biphobia's historical roots as they exist in both gay and heterosexual communities. Additionally, internalized biphobia is addressed as a possible negative influence on bisexual men's mental health (Bronn, 2001; Page, 2004).

Although biphobia and homophobia are closely related, an extensive review of fear and negativity toward same-sex intimacy is beyond the scope of this chapter. For a discussion of homophobia that is male-specific, the reader is referred to Lock and Kleis (1998). In considering biphobia toward men in contemporary times, keeping the previous history of bisexual men in mind proves useful, particularly Udis-Kessler's (1991) point that oppression of racial minorities is similar to oppression of LGB individuals. In Udis-Kessler's model, sexual orientation is akin to skin color, complete with all its implications: it is inborn, immutable, and essential to a person's identity.

Many of the men who identified as gay in the early part of the gay rights movement experienced sexual attraction strictly toward men. Accordingly, being exclusively homosexual in one's intimate relationships was also assumed to be indicative of one's commitment to the gay community. This assumption placed the person who was not exclusively homosexual—the bisexual male—at a disadvantage: If one found himself attracted to both men *and* women, choosing to keep one's social and romantic relationships restricted to men was viewed by the gay community as morally superior and politically purer (Blumstein & Schwartz, 1977; Paul, 1985).

By and large, the gay male community continues to hold tenaciously to the dichotomous, monosexual, and essentialist nature of sexual orientation. One may conjecture that behind gay men's biphobia is a competition for recognition, a competition that has existed since the earliest moment of the gay rights movement. The biphobia of the gay community that states, "You don't exist" can be interpreted as translating to the gay community's proclamation "I do exist" (Udis-Kessler, 1991, p. 356). Apart from the fact that this dichotomously viewed sexuality may represent a lived truth for many men, the gay community's rejection of bisexual people may alternately be seen as a necessary defense that affirms a "pure" and "unchosen" group identity. Further, gay men's biphobia may result from a fear of losing the popular and political clout gained by the gay rights movement (Ochs, 2001). This fear may be grounded in bisexual men's declared ability to partner with either men or women, making sexuality appear to be a preference or choice rather than an immutable orientation. As such, gay men may fear that their rights gained on the basis of a dichotomous, nonfluid, and inborn sexual orientation could be jeopardized. Yet another view on biphobia among gay men is that although many men who identify as gay may be attracted only to men, other gay-identified men may actually experience more fluid sexual attractions. The truth of this statement could bring some men to realize that they, too, have attractions to both genders, thus necessitating a second (and probably unpleasant) "coming out" (Ochs, 1996). Last, gay men may view bisexual men as possessing a degree of heterosexual privilege due to their ability to "pass" in a heterosexual setting. Whatever the cause of the gay community's biphobia, none of these proposed explanations ameliorate the dually stigmatized experience of men who identify as bisexual. As Ochs (1996) explains, if a bisexual man is physically assaulted for being with a same-sex partner, he cannot plead with his assailant that he is "bisexual, not gay, so please only beat [me] up on one side" (p. 222).

Biphobia toward bisexual men also comes from the heterosexual community. The previously discussed arguments concerning an essential, dichotomous sexuality are still relevant, as is society's general negativity toward same-sex relations. It is important to recognize that in addition to the bi- and same-sex negativity that bisexual men have had to confront, bisexual men have often been viewed as conduits of HIV from the gay community to the heterosexual community since the AIDS crisis began. Bisexual men in the 1990s were frequently portrayed in the popular media such as *Newsweek* and the *New York Times* as a primary risk group in the transmission of HIV (Miller, 2002; North, 1990). This may have been the case in some instances, but research generally suggests that there is no correlation between sexual identity per se and high-risk sexual behavior (e.g., unprotected anal or vaginal sex; Taywaditep & Stokes, 1998). Taywaditep and Stokes's (1998) study used cluster analysis[1] to analyze data from 535 men (52% African American and 48% Caucasian, with a mean age of 25 years) who, despite self-identifying as "gay," "straight," or "bisexual," all had had sexual experience with both men and women in the previous three years. The resulting clusters revealed that there was notable and significant ($p < .01$) within-group variance according to the participants' self-reported sexual orientations and sexual risk behavior. In other words, in considering AIDS/HIV and sexual orientation, it is more useful to focus on a man's sexual risk-taking behavior than on that man's possible identity, bisexual or otherwise. Conflation of the two factors—sexual identity and sexual risk-taking behavior—in considering HIV transmission may prove problematic for men who are exploring attractions to both sexes. Inappropriate focus on sexual identity itself as a risk-factor may transform the dominant culture's fear-based accusations into a facet of internalized biphobia (Levya, 1991; Steinman & Beemyn, 2001).

---

[1] Cluster analysis involves statistical processes that are used to group individuals together who are highly similar to each other according to the variables in the study. For example, in the Taywaditep and Stokes (1998) study, the analysis was able to group men into eight clusters, with two clusters including men who were having sex predominantly with other men, two clusters of men who were having sex predominantly with women, and four clusters made up of men who were having sex with more equal amounts of men and women. There is more than one group for each category of behavior due to differences and similarities regarding other variables apart from the gender of sexual partner(s).

INTERNALIZED BIPHOBIA

Lesbians and gay men may sometimes introject society's condemnation and stereotypes about same-sex affection and intimacy, resulting in what is popularly termed "internalized homophobia" (Rowen & Malcolm, 2002; Szymanski & Chung, 2003). For bisexual people, internalized biphobia is equally problematic. Beliefs that may contribute to this phenomenon include the assumption that bisexual individuals are confused about their sexuality; that they are really lesbian or gay people who haven't come "all the way" out; that bisexual individuals are overly promiscuous, obsessed with sex, and unable to commit to one person; that bisexual persons always have more than one partner at a time; and that bisexual persons are mostly responsible for spreading HIV to heterosexuals (Eliason, 2001).

These damaging beliefs are often quite pervasive. For example, in arguing against the Employment Non-Discrimination Act (ENDA), one critic claimed that "ENDA is bad legislation because it . . . puts the federal government officially in support of promiscuity since bisexuals by definition have sex with more than one person" (Knight, 1996, p. A15). Rust (1996a) eloquently dismissed the prominent stereotype of bisexual promiscuity through an analogy using eye color: "Imagine concluding that a person who finds both blue and brown eyes attractive would require two lovers, one with each eye color, instead of concluding that this person would be happy with either a blue-eyed or a brown-eyed lover" (p. 128). In a more empirically based dismissal of bisexual male promiscuity, Matteson (1996) stated that polyamory or multiple concurrent relationships may be attractive only to a minority of bisexual men, with less than 20% of bisexual respondents in several studies engaging in simultaneous relationships with both men and women at the time of the studies. As for the negative stereotype of bisexual men having an "obsession" with sex, this assertion is also empirically groundless. In one study that used a national randomized sample of 11,536 men and women from various backgrounds, behaviorally heterosexual and bisexual men were compared on the basis of sexual frequency. Behaviorally heterosexual men reported significantly more sexual activity than behaviorally bisexual men during the previous 12 months and also since the age of 18 (Horowitz, Weis, & Laflin, 2003). The difference according to sexual orientation explained 9% of the variance for sexual frequency ($p < .0001$).

Part of the psychological growth process for a bisexual man that is especially relevant for clinical consideration is overcoming feelings of shame regarding sexual orientation (Ochs, 1996), feelings that may lead to continued concealment of sexual orientation. Such concealment has negative effects on men's mental health (Coleman, 1985), including depression, sexual compulsivity, "workaholism," and alcohol abuse. Empirical research by Bronn (2001), using a sample of 112 geographically diverse Internet-recruited participants (64 male and 48 female, with most under 35 years of age), found that bisexual women scored "somewhat higher" (p. 21) on questions regarding general well-being ($p < .05$) than did bisexual men. Page's (2004) study on the mental health of bisexual individuals provides somewhat similar findings, using data from a sample of 217 self-identified bisexual women (71%) and men (29%). Although women tended to report more serious overall clinical issues than men (33% vs. 17%), men reported more extreme levels of stress regarding a bisexual identity. Specifically, though 66.7% of women and 50.0% of men reported "minor" or "some" stress around a bisexual identity, 27.5% of women and 46.8% of men reported that a bisexual identity was either "quite difficult" or "the hardest thing in life." These differences were statistically significant chi ($X^2 = 8.775$, $df = 4$, $p < .01$). Especially relevant for mental health practitioners is the additional finding that 34.9% of bisexual male respondents, compared with 14.3% of bisexual female respondents, reported bisexual issues as "the only or main" reason for seeking therapy ($X^2 = 13.52$, $df = 4$, $p < .01$). These findings suggest that relative to bisexual women, bisexual men tend to experience lower levels of well-being and greater degrees of stress regarding a bisexual identity.

For mental health professionals, understanding the causes, maintenance, and effects of internalized biphobia may be the first step in helping this population. One important factor in causing and maintaining biphobia is the dearth of role models for bisexual individuals, leaving many in this community with a sense of isolation (Ochs, 1996). Another factor influencing internalized biphobia is that bisexual individuals spend a majority of their time in the community that corresponds with the sex of their current romantic partner. Though practically and emotionally convenient, this may lead to a sense of shame around the "other" part of oneself and a sense of discontinuity in one's shifting from one community to another (Ochs, 1996). To avoid conflict and condemnation by one community or another (heterosexual or gay male), bisexual men may label as "straight" or "gay," feeling horror at the prospect of going without the support of the relevant community. Having to choose one type of desire instead of another likely leads to a sense of existing in two separate worlds without fully fitting into either. On a personal level, this internal conflict of having to favor one community over another could also apply to the support received from a particular romantic partner. Some bisexual individuals may stay in a relationship without "coming out" as bisexual, fearing they would lose the partner and the support she or he provides (Ochs, 1996). The resulting shame and secrecy can play a detrimental role in a man's developing a positive bisexual identity (Blumstein & Schwartz, 1976; Weinberg et al., 1994).

Bisexual Men's Identity Development

In discussing a "bisexual man's identity," one runs the risk of suggesting a conclusive, set, or essential state of being. In fact, there are many different types of bisexual men, and no bisexual identity should be seen as definitive (Rust, 1996b). In the study described earlier, Taywaditep and Stokes (1998) found that their sample was most efficiently grouped into eight separate categories, each grouped according to contrasting personal characteristics and behaviors. Given that this reductionistic methodology managed to find a variety of types of bisexual men (all of whom were under 30 years of age, leaving one to wonder about groupings of a larger age range), it is senseless to conclude that there is one single bisexual male identity. Rather, there appear to be at least eight possible types of bisexual identities that are multifaceted, multidimensional, dynamic, and individualized. One facet of bisexual men's identity and relationships that does appear somewhat consistent is that bisexual men tend to be more opposite-sex rather than same-sex oriented in their preferences for sexual encounters and intimate relationships (Bronn, 2001; Edser & Shea, 2002; Lever et al., 1992; Weinberg et al., 1994). However, there are obvious exceptions even to this relative consistency (Wolf, 1985).

Bearing in mind the bisexual male community's diversity and multidimensionality, models of bisexual identity development that attempt to provide a universal developmental framework do exist. Weinberg et al. (1994) devised the first model of bisexual identity development, followed by Brown (2002) and Bradford (2004). Although Weinberg et al.'s (1994) and Bradford's (2004) models are similar, one significant difference between them is Bradford's focus on bisexual community building and the transformation of stigmatization into social action. Also, Bradford accommodates the fact that many bisexual people begin the identity development process with a heterosexual identity, rather than initially identifying as gay or lesbian. This potentiality is especially relevant for bisexual men (Fox, 1995).

Brown's (2002) model also has a number of similarities to Weinberg et al.'s (1994), but is unique in its consideration of developmental differences based in gender. Brown (2002) states that with regard to identity development in general, (a) men often experience same-sex attraction as more difficult and stressful than women do and (b) men are more likely to experience sexuality as independent from social context. For these reasons, developing an identity that incorporates attraction to both men and women may be difficult and confusing for many men. The first stage of both of these theories is appropriately named *initial confusion* (Brown, 2002; Weinberg et al., 1994), with Bradford's (2004) similar stage named *questioning reality*. In this stage, men experience internal conflict between their accustomed gender role and their "new" (same-sex or opposite-sex) sexual feelings. They likely experience anxiety around this conflict. Beliefs about traditional, dichotomous sexuality and concerns over rejection by others may generate distress (Brown, 2002). In a monosexual culture that considers sexuality as heterosexual-or-gay, a man's attraction to another man often equates with the latter option. Thus, discovering one's attraction to both sexes could prove a source of confusion.

The second stage in both Brown's (2002) and Weinberg et al.'s (1994) models is *finding and applying the label*. A man must first understand that the "bisexual" label exists and must feel that it applies to aspects of his feelings and behaviors in order to identify as such. Bradford (2004) alternately calls this stage *inventing reality*, suggesting that rather than finding an identity, one may invent it in a constructivist fashion. Although bisexuality has been considered "trendy" or "chic" from time to time in recent history (Rust, 2000b), the label is not generally embraced in the heterosexual community (Eliason, 2001) or the LG community. In addition to being the object of stigmatization in these monosexual cultures, a man's adopting the bisexual label may also stimulate anxiety about the stability and social acceptance of one's gender and sex roles. It is important during this second stage of development not only that the person find and apply the appropriate label, but also that he do so in a social context of identity affirmation. Finding this support may be a challenge for many bisexual men.

During this second stage of identity development, it is possible that men, in contrast to women, may experience the identity as an "essential" part of themselves (Brown, 2002). This assertion is based on findings from self-labeled gay men who generally report the experience of owning one's same-sex attractions as sudden and involving essential, personal characteristics (Brown, 2002). Such an "essentialist" suggestion is logical to postulate in a model of men's sexual identity, but is contrary to much of the bisexual literature mentioned in this chapter. Because of this theoretical contradiction, the assertion should be taken cautiously, pending future empirical support. Brown's (2002) model also suggests that just as gay men experience more psychological distress than do women concerning sexual activity as they progress through the stages of identity development, bisexual men may be at increased risk for similar levels of heightened distress (Brown, 2002). The previously mentioned studies regarding bisexual individuals and mental health (Bronn, 2004; Page, 2004) suggest that this gender-based disparity in distress is a reality for many men.

Weinberg et al. (1994) and Brown (2002) titled their third stage identically, *settling into the identity*. It is important for a bisexual man at this developmental stage to have a supportive social network. Such support will be crucial as he sets out to develop more relationships and as he begins to define his bisexuality as stable or transitional (Brown, 2002). An important difference between being heterosexual or gay and being bisexual at this stage of development is the latter's lack of access to a community of similar others (see Firestein, chap. 4, this volume). Certain geographic areas of the United States (e.g., Boston) may be more amenable than others to hosting a bisexual community (Hoburg, Konik, Williams, & Crawford, 2004), with urban centers generally offering greater opportunities for social support for sexual minorities. Even for those who do not live in an area that is hospitable to differences in sexual identity or behavior, Internet-based virtual communities, such as BiNet USA (http://www.binetusa.org), may offer support where there would otherwise be none. Bradford's (2004) third developmental stage, *maintaining identity*, appears more relevant to the consideration of such supportive environments because it involves discussion of the strengthening of a bisexual community and the formation of a strong bisexual identity in the face of marginalization.

Also relevant, a man who is "settling in" to a bisexual identity within a supportive community has an ability to explore his identity as an individual. Brown (2002) noted that men may have more opportunities than women have to explore and maintain attractions to both sexes since they are more likely than women to be sexual partners of both (Weinberg et al., 1994). Just as gay men who explore and act on their same-sex attractions appear to begin their gay identity development earlier than men who do not act on these attractions, bisexual men who act upon their same-sex attractions earlier in life may develop a bisexual identity more rapidly than those who don't (Brown, 2002). This conjecture is supported by research (Lever et al., 1992) that found that a nonheterosexual identity is more than seven times more likely for men with adolescent same-sex sexual experience. Among those men with bisexual adult experience, the odds of adopting a bisexual identity are four times higher for those with frequent versus no adolescent same-sex experience. Even more specifically, the percentage of men who identify as bisexual increases approximately fourfold from 15.6 to 33.1 to 63.5, depending on whether reported adolescent same-sex experience occurred "no more than once," "a few times," or "frequently," in that order (Lever et al., 1992). In this light, though not a definitive factor, adolescent same-sex experience appears to have lasting effects on "settling into" one's identity.

Weinberg et al. (1994) named their fourth stage *continued uncertainty*, reflecting their finding that some bisexual people may experience confusion as they navigate relationships with both women and men throughout their lives. Brown (2002) entitled this stage *identity maintenance*, asserting that this phraseology accurately reflects the findings of research on bisexual identity development. Some bisexual men and women tend to retain an identity at least through midlife, regardless of the gender of one's partner, contact with the bisexual community, or the salience of one's bisexual identity (Weinberg, Williams, & Pryor, 2001). Occasional cognitive or emotional uncertainty is a normal aspect of this last stage, but does not necessarily affect the stability of a bisexual identity. The difference between Brown's (2002) and Weinberg et al.'s (1994) last developmental stages appears to rest not so much in the theoretical content, but in the focus of that content. More specifically, Brown (2002) stressed that a natural, inherent, and paradoxically stable aspect of maintaining a bisexual identity actually is the occasional uncertainty of the identity, and as such, Brown's model has a focus on the *process* of maintaining identity. In contrast, although Weinberg et al.'s (1994) concept is similar, these authors placed greater focus on an individual's uncertainty in searching for an identity; as such, their model's last stage is more *outcome*-focused (Brown, 2002). Interestingly, Bradford's (2004) model of identity development makes no mention of uncertainty in identity and, rather, names the fourth stage *transforming adversity*. For Bradford (2004), the final stage of development involves not the occasional questioning of identity, but transforming experiences of adversity and marginalization into motivation for community leadership and social action.

In summary, these described models of bisexual identity development all attempt to provide a series of stages through which bisexual men may progress in their process of self-definition. The models all include an initial period in which the bisexual man experiences confusion and a time in which he becomes aware of a label for his experience. Descriptions of advanced stages typically include further exploration and acceptance of a bisexual identity, gaining social support from others, possible questioning and exploration of the identity throughout the life span, and the transformation of bisexuality's stigma into community leadership and activism. As with any developmental framework, especially one designed to model such a multifaceted and poorly understood community, the stages must be viewed as containing some fluidity.

It is crucial to recognize that Weinberg et al.'s (1994) and Brown's (2002) models were grounded in popular conceptions of bisexuality that existed in San Francisco in the 1980s. San Francisco is arguably the most sexually liberal city in the United States. Thus, opportunities for exploration and for finding social support were more likely to be available for sexual minorities in this city at that time than in other cities. Additionally, the sample used for the foundational Weinberg et al. (1994) model was 95% Caucasian. Therefore, it may not be representative of those who identify as ethnic or racial minorities (Brown, 2002). For this reason, the following section will discuss various cultures' views of bisexual men, as well as a model of identity development that may more accurately describe racial- and ethnic-minority men's experiences.

Multicultural Views of Bisexual Men's Identities

The models of bisexual identity development discussed in the previous section (Bradford, 2004; Brown, 2002; Weinberg et al., 1994) suggest possible ways in which a bisexual individual may develop a sense of self. The current section presents a model of biracial and bisexual identity development that may better describe such development for bisexual people from minority racial or ethnic backgrounds. Also, culture-specific attitudes toward some behavioral aspects of bisexuality are considered.

Bisexuality exists in many cultures throughout the world, such as indigenous African, Australian, Mediterranean, Latino, Native American, and Indian cultures, and it has various purposes and functions in each

(Fox, 1996; Rust, 1996a; Stokes, Miller, & Mundhenk, 1998; Udis-Kessler, 1991). Different cultural norms naturally affect how people from these cultures view their own sexuality and whether they view their individual identities as influenced by issues of sexuality. For example, a Native American or Latino American man may engage in same-sex behavior without in any way associating himself with Western conceptions of bisexual or gay identity (Udis-Kessler, 1991). Understanding this, when one considers a possible bisexual identity in a man who is grounded partially or fully in a non–European American culture, it is important to assess his level of acculturation to European American culture as well as his level of comfort in balancing sexuality across cultures (Stokes, Taywaditep, Vanable, & McKirnan, 1996). A fully acculturated client may find European American concepts of sexuality intrinsically meaningful, whereas a less acculturated client may find the concepts lacking in meaning and personal applicability (Rust, 1996a).

Collins (2000) proposed a model of biracial and bisexual identity development that was developed through research with people of dual ethnicities. The model's genesis involved a sample of 15 Japanese Americans from the San Francisco area, which, given that other cultures apart from Japanese American culture were not represented, may limit the model's generalizability. Collins (2000) stated that bisexual individuals appear to experience a similar course of identity development as biracial individuals do, though it should be noted that Collins's sample was relatively small and racially homogeneous. Regardless, the model is worth considering for its alternate presentation of identity development.

Collins's (2000) first phase, titled *questioning/confusion*, states that people with two identities initially face confusion regarding how to self-identify. The awareness of being different may be more intense for people with dual-community affiliations. A person in this situation may feel a lack of complete identification with one community or the other. It is during this first stage that one begins to ask, "What am I?" (Collins, 2000, p. 244) and begins to feel the impact of being a "dual minority" (Matteson, 1996). The second phase, *refusal/suppression*, brings the individual to select one identity over the other. In doing so, he typically represses the identity that has been rejected. This stage reflects research findings indicating that many bisexual men often identify initially as gay or as heterosexual (Fox, 1995; Weinberg et al., 1994). For a man who is developing a bisexual identity, issues of being a nonheterosexual man may be especially prominent at this stage, especially the question of what it means to be a "straight" versus a "gay" man.

Most of the extant bisexual communities are predominantly White. As such, bisexual men of color may feel particularly torn in their allegiances when choosing which "half" of themselves to explore at this second stage. Exploring a predominantly "White" bisexual or nonheterosexual community is difficult for many people of color because of the racism they experience in such settings (Hutchins & Ka'ahumanu, 1991; Stokes et al., 1998). Also, such exploration may result in a loss of support from family or from one's racial or ethnic community (Stokes et al., 1998). Black men, particularly, who integrate themselves in a bisexual, White community may be accused of "selling out" (Frieden, 2002) and feel torn between their racial minority identity (with its concomitant community affiliations) and the bisexual "part" of themselves. Asian American bisexual men may experience a similar internal conflict around their sexuality because Asian American cultures typically place great importance on fulfilling family roles (e.g., marrying, producing a son, continuing the family name; Matteson, 1997). Despite or perhaps because of the cultural norm of denying gay or bisexual men's existence (Chan, 1989), Asian American bisexual or gay men tend to prioritize their sexual identities over their racial or ethnic identities (Chan, 1989; Matteson, 1997).

Some Latino cultures may implicitly condone bisexual activity on the part of men, provided that the man has a primary heterosexual relationship or marriage and is always in the active (*activo*) or insertive role in sexual activity (Fox, 1996; Leyva, 1991; Rust, 1996a). For this reason, exploring same-sex attractions may sometimes be less stressful in a Latino culture. If, however, the man wishes to explore a sexual or intimate role in which he is a "passive" or receptive partner (*pasivo* or *joto*), this role does not fall within culturally sanctioned heterosexual norms and bears a harsh stigma (Fox, 1996; Leyva, 1991; Rust, 1996a). A Latino man's level of acculturation into European American culture is crucial to consider in relation to issues of bisexual identity, with less acculturated individuals possibly holding traditional dominant-culture norms with some tenacity. For these less acculturated individuals, the Latino dichotomy of sexuality may be understood as "*joto*" versus "*macho*," with little room for a bisexual man between the two (Leyva, 1991).

Collins's (2000) third stage of identity development, *infusion/exploration*, states that the early choice of prioritizing one identity over another can lead to further confusion about the "neglected half" of the individual. A bisexual man at this stage may begin to reach out for support, beginning to integrate previously rejected aspects of his identity. This stage can take many different appearances. Consider the example of a bisexual man who has chosen to marry a woman without disclosing his bisexual attractions. In the marriage, he continues to long for intimate contact with another man (many such cases are apparent in Klein & Schwartz, 2001). For men of any race or ethnicity who are in a committed relationship or marriage, simultaneously exploring previously rejected same- or other-sex attractions within the context of the primary relationship will likely be a strain on the relationship. Although a seemingly risky situation in terms of relationship stability, this exploration may eventually strengthen the primary relationship if it is carried out in a caring and honest way (Brownfain, 1985; Buxton, 1994; Coleman, 1985; Edser & Shea, 2002; Gochros, 1989; Matteson, 1985; Wolf, 1985). A complete discussion of this topic is not possible in the current chapter, because of space constraints. There are, however, a few points that do appear consistent regarding infusion of one's bisexuality in a significant relationship or marriage. One important concept is that of keeping the primary relationship just that—primary. Relationships that attempt an integration of the male partner's bisexual explorations often benefit from certain rules or agreements that allow the primary partner to continue to feel valued, and indeed, primary. This demonstration of the primary relationship's importance often involves a healthy, ongoing sexual relationship with the primary partner. Another important, although perhaps obvious, point is the importance of open communication between partners regarding the nature of the male's exploration of his bisexuality. This communication may or may not have limits. For instance, it is probable that the bisexual male's partner will want to discuss his exploration, but both partners will likely benefit from agreeing on that conversation's degree of depth and detail.

This third stage of identity development also applies to a recent phenomenon in the Black community that has become publicized more in popular than academic literature, called the "Down Low," or "DL" (Harris, Roberts, & Bandele, 2004; King, 2004; Mays, Cochran, & Zamudio, 2004; Smith, 2004). A common "DL" scenario may include a socially upstanding man in the Black community who attends church regularly and is a committed husband or father, but who secretly has same-sex encounters outside of the marital relationship with other men as a way to explore his same-sex attractions. Maintaining one's manhood and traditional view of masculinity (as being attracted solely to women) in the Black community is necessary at almost all costs in order to avoid any association with the label "bisexual" or "gay." To be perceived as anything other than masculine may bring to mind stigmatized images of flamboyant, feminine Black men such as RuPaul, Sylvester, or the "Men on Film" in the 1990s television sitcom *In Living Color* (King, 2004). Black bisexual men's mental health and racial and sexual identity development are obviously important issues here, but equally momentous is the possibility that secretive and unsafe DL sex could be one of the main reasons that Black women's rate of HIV infection has risen dramatically since the beginning of the epidemic (Smith, 2004). Exploration of the DL phenomenon is too recent to state anything about it with empirical certainty, but the issue is critically important and merits further research.

The last developmental stage for Collins (2000), *resolution/acceptance*, is "the most exhilarating phase" (Collins, 2000, p. 245) in which the bisexual person can state, "I am who I am" (p. 245). At this point the individual is able to acknowledge the two parts of his identity and to consider each of them equally valid. How this resolution evolves in an individual man may ④ differ from culture to culture. Regardless of the culture, social support of like-minded or empathic others can be a tremendous psychological resource at any point of identity development for ethnic and sexual minorities (Rust, 1996a).

TABLE 5.1 Theories of Bisexual Identity Development

Stage number and common theme	Weinberg et al. (1994)	Collins (2000)	Brown (2002)	Bradford (2004)
1. Confusion and questioning one's identity	Initial confusion. *Conflict arises between one's initial gender/sex role in a monosexual context and "new" sexual feelings; same-sex attraction may be difficult to accept, especially for men.*	Questioning/Confusion. *External challenges (e.g., stigma) and internal challenges (e.g., an extant but insufficient self-definition) are encountered; "What are you?" and "What am I?" are relevant questions.*	Initial confusion. *Conflict arises between one's initial gender/sex role in a monosexual context and "new" sexual feelings; same-sex attraction may be difficult to accept, especially for men.*	Questioning reality. *This stage involves questioning one's same- and other-sex experiences and attractions, because of the pressure of a monosexual culture.*
2. Finding, choosing, or creating an identity	Finding and applying the label. *One finds that the label "bisexual" applies to his experience, but also continues to experience intermittent self-doubt and confusion.*	Refusal/Suppression. *Self-identification in a monosexual context likely leads to acceptance of one so-called half of a bisexual identity and to suppression of the other "half"; confusion and/or guilt may result because of this suppression.*	Finding and applying the label. *One finds that the label "bisexual" applies to his experience; however, men may reject the label because of anxiety and stigma. Also, men may be more likely to experience their sexual identity as an essential, nonchosen aspect of identity.*	Inventing reality. *With an ability to affirm the reality of same- and other-sex attractions, one structures reality and gives it meaning by creating a personal definition for it.*

	Theory 1	Theory 2	Theory 3	Theory 4
3. Accepting and integrating one's whole identity	Settling into the identity *Greater comfort with one's sexuality is experienced, frequently through social support; questions about its permanent or transitional nature arise.*	Infusion/Exploration *One reaches out to others in an attempt to infuse and explore the previously rejected identity; one might ask, "What about my other half?"*	Settling into the identity *Greater comfort and acceptance of a bisexual identity are supported by a strong social network; especially for men, increased sexual activity may occur.*	Maintaining identity *Having come to terms with who one is, a person must work to maintain that identity in the face of stigma in a monosexual culture; also, one must establish a sense of community with other bisexual individuals.*
4. Resolution, affirmation, and maintenance of identity	Continued uncertainty *Despite comfort with one's own bisexuality, questioning and confusion about this sexual identity continue.*	Resolution/Acceptance *After periods of self-devaluation, struggle, and identity confusion, one can say, "I am who I am." This stage involves a self-based inward focus on an integrated sense of identity, compared with previous stages' external focus.*	Identity maintenance *Occasional questioning and uncertainty appear to be intrinsic to maintaining a stable bisexual identity.*	Transforming adversity *One begins to transform monosexual stigma and adversity into social action, identity strengthening, and bisexual community leadership.*

Note. Summary of four theories of bisexual identity development by general theme, including points specific to each theory.

In comparison to other models of bisexual identity development (see Table 5.1), Collins's (2000) model shares some of the same shortcomings of previous models, such as being based on a limited geographic sample. Nonetheless, because of its focus on a racial or ethnic minority during its inception, the model expands our conceptions of possible developmental paths of bisexual identity. Future models might consider and specify multiple races and ethnicities. Clinicians should approach application of the models with some caution, given that knowledge about bisexual identity development, especially that of males, is still in its incipient stages. As with other issues relevant to bisexual men and their community, further theorizing and research is necessary to determine a clearer picture of these men's development, especially regarding how issues of mental health may influence developmental progression.

Future Directions for Research, Clinical Work, and Community Building

Affirming the existence of bisexuality in men requires extending our awareness of sexual diversity and broadening of dichotomous and narrow views of male sexuality. In order to understand bisexual men, one must be able to accept and affirm all the variations of sexual identity expression, with such variations possibly occurring in sexual behavior or fantasy, in interpersonal relations, in sexual identity, and perhaps in an overall lifestyle that includes nonsexual elements. Sexuality is a fundamental aspect of any person's identity, but it is not the only factor that contributes to one's individuality (Paul, 1985). It is also not the only factor that galvanizes or defines communities.

For heterosexual and gay men, there are many nonerotic components that define significant portions of identity. Although extensive consideration of these components is beyond the scope of this chapter, some of the more salient components may include heterosexual family traditions and activities, gay notions of spirituality (Thompson, 1995), and gay conceptions of culture (Fellows, 2004). This is not to suggest that bisexual men should mimic gay or heterosexual men's communities or follow their models of identity. However, researchers and community builders may discover heretofore unrecognized strengths in the bisexual male community if they attempt to discover what constitutes bisexual male identity apart from issues of sexual attraction. An unchanging, static view of the bisexual male community identity is likely inadequate. Instead, what is called for is an understanding that sexual identity and any group identity may be fluid, multidimensional, and constantly in flux (Paul, 1985). Just as the ethnic and racial minority communities discussed in this chapter have changed drastically over the past two decades, so may bisexual men and their community's ideals shift and settle, and shift again.

Despite much of sexual minorities' past being regarded as "gay history," bisexual men may want to empower themselves and their communities by reclaiming the history of bisexual men who have gone before them (see Klein, 1993, and Hutchins & Ka'ahumanu, 1991, for a discussion of both male and female bisexual figures in art and history). Additionally, the topic of bisexual spirituality is hinted at both in Native American traditions through "two-spirited" men (Garrett & Barret, 2003; Rios, 1991; Thompson, 1995) and in some Western bisexual male traditions (Hutchins, 1991). Future researchers and active communities of bisexual men may serve to expand views of spirituality by further exploring and documenting bisexual men's spiritual journeys. Similarly, in terms of clinical issues, bisexual men may well share much in common with other sexual minorities and their mental health issues. However, there are unique and significant differences to consider in working with bisexual individuals (Dworkin, 2001). Clinicians and their clients will benefit from exploring the uniqueness of bisexuality and what it means to be a male striving to develop a positive bisexual identity.

For example, in light of the developmental models described in this chapter, it appears that confusion about one's identity is an experience that spans all four models. A supportive clinician would understand that this confusion likely stems from a variety of marginalizing and biphobic sources, not excluding a client's own internalized biphobia. A supportive, validating, and nonjudgmental environment may be the first opportunity for some clients to recognize a bisexual identity as healthy, legitimate, and perhaps not transitional. Uncertainty and confusion may apply not only to one's identity, but also to one's intimate and familial relationships. Becoming familiar with literature regarding men's bisexuality in intimate relationships and regarding how relationships may healthfully function with the inclusion of a bisexual identity would be an important step (this topic is complex and merits referral to more exhaustive discussions, such as Brownfain, 1985; Buxton, 1994; Coleman, 1985; Edser & Shea, 2002; Gochros, 1989; Klein & Schwartz, 2001; and Wolf, 1985). Equally important is the idea that just as bisexual men's identities can be unique and multidimensional, so may their relationships be. Whereas one man may desire a monogamous relationship with a woman, another may be content with a polyamorous relationship that entails varying types and degrees of commitment. A last important factor to remember is that just as heterosexual individuals incur stress on a daily basis that is not due to their sexual orientation, not all bisexual men will present with stress that is related to their bisexuality.

However exploration of bisexual men's lives occurs for mental health professionals, it is clear that more empirical work, both quantitative and qualitative, is needed in order for researchers, therapists, and community builders to understand this community more accurately. It is important to recognize that the political and religious climate of a particular geographical region may affect the available resources for bisexual men's community services and research. For example, recent U.S. historical events and movements (including Joseph McCarthy's persecution of sexual minorities, Anita Bryant's *Save Our Children* crusade [later renamed *Protect America's Children*], and the Defense of Marriage Act) illustrate some of the oppressive zeitgeist prevalent in both politics and religion aimed at restricting the rights of sexual minorities. Various states and countries hold disparate views on same-sex relationships and their social acceptability. These different standards will likely continue to affect the mental health climate for bisexual men, their communities, and the research meant to enhance understanding of the two.

CONCLUSION

In summary, bisexual men are one of the least visible of sexual minorities. Beyond scant research exploring bisexual men's communities and identities, little is known. The question yet to be explored by the literature is, "Apart from questions of romantic and sexual attraction, what constitutes a bisexual male identity?" Since bisexual men often feel marginalized by heterosexual and gay communities, it is important to approach community building, clinical work, and research with an open mind and with an affirming stance toward bisexual men's development. As one participant in Weinberg et al.'s (1994) study explained, "It's been a hell of a time for being recognized as bisexual, that bisexuality is an option" (p. 215). It should be clear at this point that bisexuality is an option for some men, and for these men, the traditional dichotomous view of sexuality is not sufficient. With the mental health profession's attempts to understand bisexual men's lives and sexualities, the bisexual male community holds the potential to help reformulate concepts of current sexuality in a nondichotomous, multidimensional, and fluid way.

REFERENCES

Beemyn, B. (2002). "To say yes to life": Sexual and gender fluidity in James Baldwin's *Giovanni's room* and *Another country*. In B. Beemyn & E. Steinman (Eds.), *Bisexual men in culture and society* (pp. 55–72). New York: Harrington Park Press.

Bisexual Anthology Collective, Chater, N., Falconer, D., Lewis, S., McLennan, L., Nosov, S., & Acharya, L. (Eds.). (1995). *Plural desires: Writing bisexual women's realities*. Toronto, Ontario, Canada: Sister Vision Press.

Blumstein, P. W., & Schwartz, P. (1976). Bisexuality in men. *Urban Life, 5*(3), 339–358.

Blumstein, P. W., & Schwartz, P. (1977). Bisexuality: Some social psychological issues. *Journal of Social Issues, 33*(2), 30–45.

Bradford, M. (2004). The bisexual experience: Living in a dichotomous culture. *Journal of Bisexuality, 4*(1/2), 7–23.

Bronn, C. D. (2001). Attitudes and self-images of male and female bisexuals. *Journal of Bisexuality, 1*(4), 5–29.

Brown, T. (2002). A proposed model of bisexual identity development that elaborates on experiential differences of women and men. *Journal of Bisexuality, 2*(4), 67–91.

Brownfain, J. J. (1985). A study of the married bisexual male: Paradox and resolution. In F. K. Klein & T. Wolf (Eds.), *Two lives to lead: Bisexuality in men and women* (pp. 173–188). New York: Haworth Press.

Buxton, A. P. (1994). *The other side of the closet: The coming-out crisis for straight spouses and families.* New York: Wiley.

Carter, D. (2004). *Stonewall: The riots that sparked the gay revolution.* New York: St. Martin's Press.

Cass, V. C. (1979). Homosexual identity formation: A theoretical model. *Journal of Homosexuality, 4,* 219–235.

Chan, C. S. (1989). Issues of identity development among Asian-American lesbians and gay men. *Journal of Counseling and Development, 68*(1), 16–20.

Chauncey, G. (1994). *Gay New York: Gender, urban culture, and the making of the gay male world, 1890–1940.* New York: Basic Books.

Coleman, E. (1985). Integration of male bisexuality and marriage. In F. K. Klein & T. Wolf (Eds.), *Two lives to lead: Bisexuality in men and women* (pp. 189–207). New York: Haworth Press.

Collins, J. F. (2000). Biracial-bisexual individuals: Identity coming of age. *International Journal of Sexuality and Gender Studies, 5,* 221–253.

Dworkin, S. H. (2001). Treating the bisexual client. [Special issue] *Journal of Clinical Psychology: In Session, 57,* 671–680.

Eadie, J. (2002). In dialogue: Problems and opportunities in "Together Alone's" visions of queer masculinity. In B. Beemyn & E. Steinman (Eds.), *Bisexual men in culture and society* (pp. 9–35). Binghamton, NY: Harrington Park Press.

Edser, S. J., & Shea, J. D. (2002). An exploratory investigation of bisexual men in monogamous, heterosexual marriages. *Journal of Bisexuality, 2*(4), 5–43.

Eliason, M. (2001). Bi negativity: The stigma facing bisexual men. *Journal of Bisexuality, 1*(2/3), 137–154.

Fellows, W. (2004). *A passion to preserve: Gay men as keepers of culture.* Madison: University of Wisconsin Press.

Firestein, B. A. (Ed.). (1996a). *Bisexuality: The psychology and politics of an invisible minority.* Thousand Oaks, CA: Sage.

Firestein, B. A. (1996b). Bisexuality as paradigm shift: Transforming our disciplines. In B. A. Firestein (Ed.), *Bisexuality: The psychology and politics of an invisible minority* (pp. 263–291). Thousand Oaks, CA: Sage.

Fox, R. C. (1995). Coming out bisexual: Identity, behavior, and sexual orientation self-disclosure (Doctoral dissertation, California Institute of Integral Studies, 1993). *Dissertation Abstracts International, 55*(12), 5565.

Fox, R. C. (1996). Bisexuality in perspective: A review of theory and research. In B. A. Firestein (Ed.), *Bisexuality: The psychology and politics of an invisible minority* (pp. 3–50). Thousand Oaks, CA: Sage.

Frieden, L. (2002). Invisible lives: Addressing black male bisexuality in the novels of E. Lynn Harris. In B. Beemyn & E. Steinman (Eds.), *Bisexual men in culture and society* (pp. 73–90). Binghamton, NY: Harrington Park Press.

Garrett, M. T., & Barret, B. (2003). Two spirit: Counseling Native American gay, lesbian, and bisexual people. *Journal of Multicultural Counseling and Development, 31*, 131–142.

Gelman, D. (1987, July 13). A perilous double life. *Newsweek, 110*(3), 44–46.

Gochros, J. S. (1989). *When husbands come out of the closet.* New York: Haworth Press.

Harris, E. L., Roberts, T., & Bandele, A. (2004). Passing for straight. *Essence, 35*(3), 156–163.

Hemmings, C. (2002). *Bisexual spaces.* New York: Routledge Press.

Hoburg, R., Konik, J., Williams, M., & Crawford, M. (2004). Bisexuality among self-identified heterosexual college students. *Journal of Bisexuality, 4*(1/2), 25–36.

Horowitz, S. M., Weis, D. L., & Laflin, M. T. (2003). Bisexuality, quality of life, lifestyle, and health indicators. *Journal of Bisexuality, 3*(2), 5–28.

Hutchins, L. (1991). Letting go: An interview with John Horne. In L. Hutchins & L. Ka'ahumanu (Eds.), *Bi any other name: Bisexual people speak out* (pp. 112–116). Los Angeles: Alyson Books.

Hutchins, L. (1996). Bisexuality: Politics and community. In B. A. Firestein (Ed.), *Bisexuality: The psychology and politics of an invisible minority* (pp. 241–259). Thousand Oaks, CA: Sage.

Hutchins, L., & Ka'ahumanu, L. (Eds.). (1991). *Bi any other name: Bisexual people speak out.* Los Angeles: Alyson Books.

Kaiser, C. (1997). *The gay metropolis: 1940–1996.* Boston: Houghton Mifflin.

King, J. L. (2004). *On the down low: A journey into the lives of "straight" black men who sleep with men.* New York: Broadway Books.

Kinsey, A. C., Pomeroy, W. B., & Martin, C. E. (1948). *Sexual behavior in the human male.* Philadelphia: W. B. Saunders.

Klein, F. (1993). *The bisexual option* (2nd ed.). New York: Haworth Press.

Klein, F., & Schwartz, T. (Eds.). (2001). *Bisexual and gay husbands.* New York: Harrington Park Press.

Knight, R. (1996, August 22). Prelude to sexual legal anarchy? *The Washington Times,* p. A15.

Lever, J., Kanouse, D. E., Rogers, W. H., Carson, S., & Hertz, R. (1992). Behavior patterns and sexual identity of bisexual males. *Journal of Sex Research, 29*, 141–167.

Leyva, O. (1991). ¿Que es un bisexual? In L. Hutchins & L. Kaahumanu (Eds.), *Bi any other name: Bisexual people speak out* (pp. 201–202). Los Angeles: Alyson Books.

Lock, J., & Kleis, B. (1998). Origins of homophobia in males: Psychosexual vulnerabilities and defense development. *American Journal of Psychotherapy, 52,* 425–536.

Loughery, J. (1998). *The other side of silence.* New York: Holt.

MacDonald, A. P., Jr. (1983). A little bit of lavender goes a long way: A critique of research on sexual orientation. *Journal of Sex Research, 19,* 94–100.

Marotta, T. (1981). *The politics of homosexuality.* Boston: Houghton Mifflin.

Matteson, D. R. (1985). Bisexual men in marriage: Is a positive homosexual identity and stable marriage possible? In F. K. Klein & T. Wolf (Eds.), *Two lives to lead: Bisexuality in men and women* (pp. 149–171). New York: Haworth Press.

Matteson, D. R. (1996). Counseling and psychotherapy with bisexual and exploring clients. In B. A. Firestein (Ed.), *Bisexuality: The psychology and politics of an invisible minority* (pp. 185–213). Thousand Oaks, CA: Sage.

Matteson, D. R. (1997). Bisexual and homosexual behavior and HIV risk among Chinese-, Filipino-, & Korean-American men. *Journal of Sex Research, 34,* 93–104.

Mays, V. M., Cochran, S. D., & Zamudio, A. (2004). HIV prevention research: Are we meeting the needs of African American men who have sex with men? *Journal of Black Psychology, 30,* 78–105.

Miller, M. (2002). "Ethically Questionable?": Popular media reports on bisexual men and AIDS. In B. Beemyn & E. Steinman (Eds.), *Bisexual men in culture and society* (pp. 93–112). New York: Harrington Park Press.

Nordheimer, J. (1987, April 3). AIDS specter for women: The bisexual man. *The New York Times,* p. A1.

North, G. (1990). Where the boys aren't: The shortage of men in the bi movement— An interview with Robyn Ochs. In T. Geller (Ed.), *Bisexuality: A reader and sourcebook* (pp. 40–46). Ojai, CA: Times Change Press.

Ochs, R. (1996). Biphobia: It goes more than two ways. In B. A. Firestein (Ed.), *Bisexuality: The psychology and politics of an invisible minority* (pp. 217–239). Thousand Oaks, CA: Sage.

Ochs, R. (2001). Biphobia. In R. Ochs (Ed.), *Bisexual resource guide* (4th ed., pp. 45–51). Boston: Bisexual Resource Center.

Page, E. H. (2004). Mental health services experiences of bisexual women and bisexual men: An empirical study. *Journal of Bisexuality, 4*(1/2), 137–160.

Paul, J. P. (1985). Bisexuality: Reassessing our paradigms of sexuality. *Journal of Homosexuality, 11*(1/2), 21–34.

Rios, J. (1991). What do Indians think about? In L. Hutchins & L. Kaahumanu (Eds.), *Bi any other name: Bisexual people speak out* (pp. 37–39). Los Angeles: Alyson Books.

Rose, S., Stevens, O., & the Off Pink Collective (Eds.). (1996). *Bisexual horizons: Politics, histories, lives.* London: Lawrence & Wishart.

Rowen, C. J., & Malcolm, J. P. (2002). Correlates of internalized homophobia and homosexual identity formation in a sample of gay men. *Journal of Homosexuality, 43*(2), 77–92.

Rust, P. C. (1996a). Managing multiple identities: Diversity among bisexual women and men. In B. A. Firestein (Ed.), *Bisexuality: The psychology and politics of an invisible minority* (pp. 53–83). Thousand Oaks, CA: Sage.

Rust, P. C. (1996b). Sexual identity and bisexual identities: The struggle for self-description in a changing sexual landscape. In B. Beemyn & M. Eliason (Eds.), *Queer studies: A lesbian, gay, bisexual and transgender anthology* (pp. 64–86). New York: New York University Press.

Rust, P. C. R. (Ed.). (2000a). *Bisexual in the United States: A social science reader*. New York: Columbia University Press.

Rust, P. C. R. (2000b). Popular images and the growth of bisexual community and visibility. In P. C. R. Rust (Ed.), *Bisexual in the United States: A social science reader* (pp. 537–553). New York: Columbia University Press.

Rust, P. C. R. (2000c). Review of statistical findings about bisexual behavior, feelings, and identities. In P. C. R. Rust (Ed.), *Bisexual in the United States: A social science reader* (pp. 129–184). New York: Columbia University Press.

Smith, T. (2004). Deadly deception. *Essence, 35*, 148–152.

Steinman, E., & Beemyn, B. (2001). Introduction. *Journal of Bisexuality, 1*(2/3), 1–14.

Stokes, J. P., Miller, R. L., & Mundhenk, R. (1998). Toward an understanding of behaviourally bisexual men: The influence of context and culture. *The Canadian Journal of Human Sexuality, 7*, 101–113.

Stokes, J. P., Taywaditep, K., Vanable, P., & McKirnan, D. J. (1996). Bisexual men, sexual behavior, and HIV/AIDS. In B. A. Firestein (Ed.), *Bisexuality: The psychology and politics of an invisible minority* (pp. 149–168). Thousand Oaks, CA: Sage.

Szymanski, D. M., & Chung, B. Y. (2003). Internalized biphobia in lesbians. *Journal of Lesbian Studies, 7*(1), 15–25.

Taywaditep, K. J., & Stokes, J. P. (1998). Male bisexualities: A cluster analysis of men with bisexual experience. *Journal of Psychology & Human Sexuality, 10*(1), 15–41.

Thomas, K. (1993, May 6). "Together Alone": A tête-à-tête among strangers. *Los Angeles Times*, p. A15.

Thompson, M. (1995). *Gay soul: Finding the heart of gay spirit and nature*. New York: HarperCollins.

Tucker, N. (Ed.). (1995). *Bisexual politics: Theories, queries, and visions*. Binghamton, NY: Harrington Park Press.

Udis-Kessler, A. (1991). Present tense: Biphobia as a crisis of meaning. In L. Hutchins & L. Ka'ahumanu (Eds.), *Bi any other name: Bisexual people speak out* (pp. 350–357). Los Angeles: Alyson Books.

Udis-Kessler, A. (1996). Identity/politics: Historical sources of the bisexual movement. In B. Beemyn & M. Eliason (Eds.), *Queer studies: A lesbian, gay, bisexual and transgender anthology* (pp. 52–63). New York: New York University Press.

Weinberg, M. S., Williams, C. J., & Pryor, D. W. (1994). *Dual attraction: Understanding bisexuality*. New York: Oxford University Press.

Weinberg, M. S., Williams, C. J., & Pryor, D. W. (2001). Bisexuals at midlife: Commitment, salience, and identity. *Journal of Contemporary Ethnography, 30*, 180–208.

Weise, E. R. (Ed.). (1992). *Closer to home: Bisexuality and feminism*. Seattle, WA: Seal.

Weiss, J. T. (2003). GL vs. BT: The archaeology of biphobia and transphobia within the U.S. gay and lesbian community. *Journal of Bisexuality, 3*(3/4), 25–55.

Wolf, T. J. (1985). Marriages of bisexual men. In F. K. Klein & T. Wolf (Eds.), *Two lives to lead: Bisexuality in men and women* (pp. 135–148). New York: Haworth Press.

Wolff, C. (1977). *Bisexuality: A study*. New York: Quartet Books.

6

TRANSGENDER COMMUNITIES: DEVELOPING IDENTITY THROUGH CONNECTION

ARLENE ISTAR LEV

> We know the rules of community; we know the healing effect of community. . . . It is our task—our essential, central, crucial task—to transform ourselves from mere social creatures into community creatures. It is the only way that human evolution will be able to proceed.
>
> (Peck, 1998, p. 165)

Gender-variant people, those known today as transsexual and transgender, have always existed throughout human history and transculturally across all nations and ethnic groups (Bullough & Bullough, 1993). Long before the advent of modern synthetic hormones and surgical reassignment, individuals were living cross-gendered from the biological sex in which they were born and outside of the social restrictions of their assigned sex. Today, transsexualism is viewed typically through a medical lens, where it is often assumed that a transgender person is interested in hormonal treatments and surgical sex-change. However, there have always been people who choose to live their lives within the social parameters often attributed to the opposite sex with medical interventions (Hausman, 1995; Meyerowitz, 2002). This means they present themselves, through mannerism and appearance, as members of the other sex, adopting new names. If they are able to pass (i.e., not be recognized as members of their natal sex), they are often able to work and live out their lives within their chosen sex. Historically, many cultures allowed for these sex transpositions without any disruption of communal life.

It is only in the last two decades, however, that public communities and activist organizations have developed that foster social identities for gender-variant people *as* a transgender people, creating a distinct category of people deserving civil rights and social justice. The journey toward self-actualization and visibility for transgender and transsexual people has been an arduous one, and the emerging transgender *community* is a nascent postmodern phenomena.

People who are called "transgender" within a contemporary context are a people newly coming home to themselves. Self-awareness involves the ability to name oneself (Lev, 2004) and involves the recognition of others who are like oneself. As individuals, transgender people express diverse gender identities and often utilize complex and contrasting language to describe themselves. Additionally, they experience conflicting perspectives within the social matrix of their communities, raising questions of exactly which groups are, or should be, included within the parameters of the transgender community. Communities organized around cross-gendered experience appear to be a recent historical development that is a direct result of certain historical and sociopolitical circumstances.

This chapter provides an overview of transgender community development with special attention to the influence of, and confluence with, the lesbian and gay civil rights movement. Transgender issues have often been seen as the latest issue contending for attention in the national gay media, stealing precious time away from other (supposed more important) issues; transgender issues are often seen as the "stepchild" of the lesbian, gay, bisexual, and transgender (LGBT) community (see Forman, 2004). However, gender variance has been an integral part of lesbian and gay struggles for equality throughout history and within contemporary culture, although it has rarely been acknowledged (see Feinberg, 1998; Katz, 1976; Prosser, 1998; and Vidal-Ortiz, 2002). The question lesbian and gay people need to answer is not, "Why are transgender issues suddenly demanding so much attention?" but rather, "Why have we abandoned transgender people and their concerns in our rush for equality?" The answer to this question will determine the direction of LGBT community development and social policy initiatives for the next few decades.

In order to facilitate an understanding of the rise of transgender communities in the past few decades, a basic overview of gender-variant experience is explored, with a specific focus on the psychological and medical treatment of transsexualism. Additionally, terminology is defined, and the process of identity formation for cross-gendered people is presented (see Korell & Lorah, chap. 11, this volume, for a further discussion). The central role of cyber-communication in the political organizing of transgender and transsexual people is also examined. However, it is first necessary to establish the ubiquitous presence of cross-gender expression throughout human communities in order to dispel assumptions that transgenderism is a new social experience or an emerging psychomedical syndrome.

THE HISTORICAL PRESENCE

Gender-variant and cross-dressing expression has been documented in a diversity of human cultures across all continents and epochs (Blackwood & Wiering, 1999; Bullough & Bullough, 1993; Herdt, 1994; Williams, 1992). However, gender-variant people typically have not created separate cultural communities based on their gender differences, but instead have been socially integrated (although sometimes marginalized) within the cultures and tribes in which they were born (Jacobs, Thomas, & Lang, 1997; Roscoe, 1998; Tafoya & Wirth, 1996). In many American Indian cultures "two-spirit" people (e.g., the Navaho Nádleehí and the Lakota Winkte) have performed distinct roles and achieved unique status (Roscoe, 1998; Williams, 1992). In some African tribes "female-husbands" carried out the economic duties of men, marrying women and becoming the legal and social father to her children (Carrier & Murray, 1998). Ancient legends from the Indian subcontinent, as well as mythologies from the Greco-Roman era, are replete with tales of male gods, gurus, kings, and heroes who transformed themselves into females (Bullough & Bullough, 1993; Nanda, 1994). References to cross-dressing behavior are found in the scriptures of nearly all religious traditions. Leslie Feinberg (1996) has suggested, "The patriarchal fathers wouldn't have felt the need to spell out these edicts [regarding transgender behaviors] if they weren't common practice" (p. 50). Jeanne d'Arc, the martyred Christian saint, was tried by the Inquisition and condemned, in part, because she refused to wear female clothing (Bullough & Bullough, 1993; Feinberg, 1996). She insisted, "For nothing in the world will I swear not to arm myself and put on a man's dress; I must obey the orders of Our Lord" (Evans, 1978, p. 5, quoting T. Douglas Murray).

Modern European history reveals the presence of a tradition of male cross-dressing involving prominent, aristocratic men, who were often flamboyant in their dress and personality, including two members of the French Court, Abbé de Choisy/François de Choisy (1644–1724), and Chevalier d'Éon (1728–1810; Bullough & Bullough, 1993). Female cross-dressing has also been revealed, including soldiers Hanna Snell/James Grey (1723–1792), Flora Sandes (1876–1956), and Emma Edmonds/ Franklin Thompson (1841–1889). Two other well-known cross-dressing females were political figures, including Queen Christina/Count Dohna of Sweden (1626–1689), who abdicated her throne to dress in male attire, and Murray Hall (1831–1901), who was active in New York City politics (Bullough & Bullough, 1993; Cromwell, 1999). However, with the possible exception of the Hijira of India (Nanda, 1994) who lived (and continue to live) within their own separate socioreligious communities, gender-variant people have not historically formed separate organized social communities.

As urbanization developed in Europe, the rudimentary beginnings of social organization for cross-dressing and gender-variant people became increasingly manifest. In the 18th century cross-dressed homosexual males gathered in brothels referred to as Molly houses and enacted mock marriages and childbirth rituals (Trumbach, 1994). Females were less socially organized than males, although the historical record reveals females who clandestinely married women and worked in traditional male trades. It can be assumed that many more females have lived as men throughout history than have been revealed (Bullough & Bullough, 1993; Cromwell, 1999; Feinberg, 1996; Trumbach, 1994), though it is unlikely that they were known to one another and able to socially organize themselves.

During the 19th century, people who expressed variant sexual and gender behaviors became the focal point of researchers and sexologists who were seeking to define and categorize human sexual behavior within a larger cultural discourse of labeling madness and deviance (Foucault, 1965). Social reformers and medically trained social scientists such as Karl Ulrichs, Magnus Hirschfeld, Havelock Ellis, and Richard von Krafft-Ebing began investigating and cataloguing diverse sexual and gender expressions (Hekma, 1994). Their research and analysis became the underpinnings of a psychomedical model that pathologized both homosexual activity and gender-variant behavior. The deconstruction of this theoretical framework that diagnosed diverse sexual and gender expressions as mental illnesses, perversions, and pathologies has been at the center of the LGBT civil rights movements for the past 40 years. It is essential to examine this model, and its contribution to the psychomedical establishment, to fully understand what has hampered the growth of transgender communities and to comprehend the tensions that currently exist within these communities.

THE MEDICAL MODEL AND TERMINOLOGY

Sexologists at the end of the 19th century developed a model to understand homosexuality and what we now call transgenderism, a model that conflated the two into one category called "inversion." Inverts were defined as men or women who pursued same-sex relationships and who dressed and acted like members of the opposite sex. Inverts were identified as a "third sex," and all homosexuality was assumed to be inverted (i.e., cross-gendered; Hekma, 1994). Homosexuality was unknown outside of gender transposition, and all same-sex relationships were assumed to have one member who behaved as a member of the opposite sex. Conversely, all cross-gender appearance was assumed to be related to homosexual behavior. This preserved a heteronormality whereby coupling was assumed to depend on an opposite-gender expression of one partner, even within homosexual pairs (Lev, 2004).

Many of these early sexologists were committed to educating the public about sexual diversity and were social reformers dedicated to removing laws that punished people who transgressed proscribed gender behavior (Hekma, 1994). Nonetheless, the sexologists' primary focus, in their search for a cure, was the development of etiological theories that explained the cause of gender-variant behaviors. Their legacy was the creation of diagnostic systems within the larger rubric of psychomedical theories that pathologized both same-sex relationships and gender-variant expression. As the field has progressed over the last hundred years, the research into sexual identity development, etiology, and treatment has been interdisciplinary, including scientific research of potential biological, genetic, and hormonal factors; psychoanalytic examination of childhood and familial patterns; and cognitive–behavioral and social learning theory's consideration of gender acquisition (see Lev, 2004). However, there has yet to be a unified theory to unequivocally explain the etiology of cross-gendered behavior. Bockting and Coleman (1992) stated, "There is no scientific consensus about a single developmental pathway which leads to gender dysphoria. Determinants of gender dysphoria remain controversial and hypothetical" (p. 113).

The study of gender variance is an immersion in language ambiguity, from the 19th-century use of words like *bisexual* and *hermaphrodite* to mean *cross-gendered* to the modern medical lexicon that includes complex terminology like ~~autogynephilia~~ (Blanchard, 1993), defined as ~~being erotically excited by the thought of being a woman or performing activities that symbolize femininity~~. Despite the limitations inherent in the current nomenclature and the difficulty sorting through the politics of language in a community still struggling with its identity, it is necessary to define, as best as we can, some words for clarity.

The term *transgender* was derived from Virginia Prince's term *transgenderist*, a word Prince originally used to describe heterosexual men who cross-dressed as a lifestyle but did not desire sex reassignment surgery (Bullough & Bullough, 1993; Meyerowitz, 2002). In the 1990s the term *transgender* morphed into a wider, more inclusive concept, what some have referred to as an umbrella term to include *all* gender-variant people (Bornstein, 1994; Green, 2004). Stryker (2004) credits Les Feinberg, transgender author and activist, for first using the term in a politicized manner to create an alliance "between all gender-variant people who do not conform to social norms for typical men and women, and who suffer political oppression as a result."

The term ~~transgender~~ is now often used to include cross-dressers, transsexuals and transgenderists, male-to-female transsexuals (MTFs), female-to-male transsexuals (FTMs), androgynes, feminine gay men, butch lesbians, drag queens, heterosexual as well as gender-bent queers, and two-spirit and intersex people, which should not, of course, imply that all people with those identities include themselves within the larger matrix or consider themselves transgender. The word *transgender* serves as both a political and a linguistic tool that breaks down the historical bipolar divisions between transsexuals and transvestites (Turner, 2004). A number of publications were seminal in the development of a specific transgender identity that rejects previous pathological medical models and encourages a bold, "out of the closet," cross-gender expression that is politically and socially visible (see Bornstein, 1994; Boswell, 1991; Feinberg, 1993; Stone, 1991; Wilchins, 1997). Within a decade, the term became well-established (Valentine, 2000) within the academic lexicon and the media. But perhaps most importantly, it gained status as a self-descriptor of a radical, proud, activist transgender community that currently demands social justice and the right to self-definition and actualization.

Transsexuals are best described as people who believe that their physiological body does not represent their true sex. Although transsexuals, by definition, desire sex reassignment surgery, transsexual people may also be preoperative, postoperative, or nonoperative (i.e., choosing to not have surgical modification; Lev, 2004). Transsexuals generally prefer to simply be called men or women, acknowledging their actual gender identity as it is expressed, regardless of their natal sex or sexual status.

Cross-dressers have been referred to in the clinical literature as transvestites and are people who wear the clothing usually assigned to the opposite sex. Some cross-dress for erotic fulfillment, some for social fun (i.e., doing "drag"), and still others just for comfort (Lev, 2004). Since women have more freedom of dress in American culture, cross-dressers are, by clinical definition, males who dress in women's clothing. Many are heterosexually identified. Drag queens are males, often gay men, who dress as women in an extreme feminine manner for fun or "camp." Drag kings are females who dress as men in an extremely masculine manner, often for entertainment. Female impersonators are men who work in the entertainment industry and who dress as women as part of their job; they may be cross-dressers or be transgender, but not necessarily. Male impersonators are their female counterparts.

Homosexual behavior and transsexualism have been treated with a variety of unsuccessful medical, psychoanalytic, and behavioral modalities. In 1966 endocrinologist Harry Benjamin presented his clinical findings in the groundbreaking book, *The Transsexual Phenomenon*. In it, he suggested that psychotherapeutic interventions aimed at curing transsexuals were futile and that the medical community should focus instead on assisting transsexuals in successful sex transition (Meyerowitz, 2002). It was a radical suggestion that heralded the development of a new psychomedical professional specialty of gender therapists and sex reassignment surgeons.

One of the central concerns for gender specialists has been the ability to recognize "true transsexuals," because of the potential danger to patients who seek transsexual treatments they might come to regret. Medical providers must be certain that the person who is being treated with cross-sex hormones or who is receiving genital surgery is actually transsexual and not

definitions

152   ARLENE ISTAR LEV

a homosexual, a cross-dresser, or a person suffering from a comorbid mental illness. Hence, modern researchers developed classification systems in their attempts to distinguish various kinds of cross-gender behavior and expression. These detailed taxonomies were developed by diverse research teams, each categorizing distinct clinical features and highlighting different salient subtypes, including erotic partner choice (i.e., sexual orientation), presence (or absence) of cross-gender fetishistic cross-dressing, the age of onset of gender dysphoria, comorbid mental health issues, and the intensity of the desire for body modification (Bentler, 1976; Blanchard, 1985, 1989, 1993; Buhrich & McConaghy, 1977; Levine & Lothstein, 1981; Person & Ovesey, 1974a, 1974b). Despite nosological differences, two basic discrete groups were delineated—"true" transsexuals and erotic transvestites.

Transsexuals commonly self-identify and report being born into the "wrong body." Their goal is transitioning to the "opposite sex" through medical and surgical treatments. Transsexuals usually recognize their gender issues from a young age and present with opposite-gender attributes. Cross-dressers are clinically defined as natal males who enjoy dressing up in women's clothing for erotic pleasure. Generally, their desire for feminine clothing starts in puberty, and they tend to be masculine in their appearance and behavior when not cross-dressed (Buhrich & McConaghy, 1977; Person & Ovesey, 1974a, 1974b). Cross-dressers often heterosexually marry and work in traditionally male trades. Their need to cross-dress has been described in the literature as somewhat obsessive–compulsive and fetishistic. Historically, people seeking sexual reassignment were first evaluated to determine if they were "true transsexuals" and not erotic cross-dressers. The function of the psychiatric assessment was to carefully root out all cross-dressers from transsexuals because transsexuals were perceived as the only gender-variant people with a legitimate right to sex reassignment.

People seeking medical treatment have had to fit into the diagnostic classification boxes that have been used to describe them. Those not fitting the classification models have been forced to lie and create false narratives so that they could be approved for the treatments that are essential to their self-actualization (Hausman, 1995; Lev, 2004; Prosser, 1998; Stone, 1991; Walworth, 1997). Therapists who specialize in gender issues were forced to become gatekeepers that assessed if the transsexual narrative fit the prescribed model. Referral for medical treatment rested on this assessment (see Meyer et al., 2001).

This medical model of diagnosis and approval based on psychosocial assessment has come under critical examination in the past decade by clinicians as well as activists (see Bockting & Coleman, 1992; Denny 2004; Lewins, 1995; Rachlin, 1997; Raj, 2002). These clinicians are questioning the accuracy of the classification systems and the necessity to approve or refuse those seeking medical treatments based on rigid diagnostic markers that may not represent the diversity of extant gender expressions. Broader-based models that see gender identity on a continuum and encourage educated consent and advocacy instead of expert

EXHIBIT 6.1
Developmental Stages That Transgender People Experience While Engaging in Conscious Decision Making Regarding Sex Reassignment

Awareness—In this first stage of awareness, gender-variant people are often in great distress; the therapeutic task is the normalization of the experiences involved in emerging as transgendered.

Seeking information/Reaching out—In the second stage, gender-variant people seek to gain education and support about transgenderism; the therapeutic task is to facilitate linkages and encourage outreach.

Disclosure to significant others—The third stage involves the disclosure of transgenderism to significant others—spouses, partners, family members, and friends; the therapeutic task involves supporting the transgendered person's integration in the family system.

Exploration—Identity and self-labeling—The fourth stage involves the exploration of various (transgender) identities, and the therapeutic task is to support the articulation and comfort with one's gendered identity.

Exploration—Transition issues/Possible body modification—The fifth stage involves exploring options for transition regarding identity, presentation, and body modification; the therapeutic task is the resolution of the decisions and advocacy toward their manifestation.

Integration—Acceptance and post-transition issues—In the sixth stage the gender-variant person is able to integrate and synthesize (transgender) identity; the therapeutic task is to support adaptation to transition-related issues.

approval are being promulgated (see Bockting & Coleman, 1992; Cole, Denny, Eyler, & Samons, 2000; Lev, 2004; Rachlin, 1997; Raj, 2002). This author has described a model, called transgender emergence (Lev, 2004), that outlines the developmental stages that transgender people experience while they engage in conscious decision making regarding sex reassignment (see Exhibit 6.1). It is a model based on client empowerment in which the therapist is an advocate, an educator, and a mentor, but minimizes her role as a gatekeeper.

These newer models support clients' unique gender narratives and minimize the clinician's role as gatekeeper for medical treatments. Although it is important to recognize the seriousness and irreversibility of transsexual surgeries, as well as the importance of a mental health evaluation within the dialogic clinical relationship, it is equally necessary to recognize client autonomy and the limits of clinical control. It is important to note that it is rare for those who have been approved for treatment to have postsurgical regrets (Green & Fleming, 1990). This may be a result of the comprehensive evaluative process in place. Yet it might also be that those who seek these services are characteristically and intrinsically prepared for the inherent stress in the process. This possibility may suggest that a more flexible evaluative process would yield similar satisfactory results (Carroll, 1999; Landén, Wålinder, Hembert, & Lundström, 1998; Lawrence, 1991). The Harry Benjamin International Gender Dysphoria Association (HBIGDA), the only professional organization devoted to the understanding and treatment of gender-identity issues, continues to reevaluate the standards of care in light of these evolving paradigms (Meyer et al., 2001).

In sum, the medical model of gender identity as a disorder has been damaging to transgender people's self-esteem and has negatively impacted their social cohesion and their collective sense of identity (Korell & Lorah, chap. 11, this volume; Lev, 2004; Raj, 2002). It is no coincidence that new clinical models based in empowerment and self-identification are developing alongside of the growth of transgender politics and community organizing. This is a familiar trajectory for those knowledgeable about the community building in the early days of the lesbian and gay liberation movement that culminated in the removal of homosexuality from the *Diagnostic and Statistical Manual of Mental Disorders (DSM)*. When homophile groups began organizing in the late 1960s and early 1970s, one of the first political endeavors was to remove homosexuality from the *DSM* (Bayer, 1981). Interestingly enough, the development of a diagnosis for transsexuality coincided with the removal of homosexuality from the *DSM* (Whittle, 1993). Whether this was a "back-door maneuver" is debatable (Zucker, 2005), but it is not debatable that the pathologizing of gender variance in the *DSM* was concurrent with the depathologizing of same-sex sexuality. The current diagnosis of gender identity disorder in the most recent edition of the *DSM* (American Psychiatric Association, 2000) has sometimes been used to mandate young gay children into psychiatric treatment (Scholinski, 1997), raising ethical questions about the continuing psychiatric treatment of homosexuality. It also shows the continuing conflation and confusion within the medical and psychiatric communities of gender identity and sexual orientation.

GENDER IDENTITY AND SEXUAL ORIENTATION

The relationship between gender identity and sexual orientation is undoubtedly complex. The sexologists of the 19th century saw them as entwined, whereas more contemporary gender specialists have tried to sort out their distinct parts. Sexual identity is actually a broad term that includes a biopsychosocial integration of four component parts: biological sex, gender identity, gender role expression, and sexual orientation (Lev, 2004).

Biological, or natal, sex refers to genetic, hormonal, morphological, chromosomal, biochemical, and anatomical determinates that impact the physiology of the body and the sexual differentiation of the brain. Gender identity is defined as the internal experience of gender, a fundamental sense of belonging to one sex or the other. This core identity determines whether one experiences oneself as a "man" or as a "woman." Typically gender identity is consistent with one's natal sex, but for transgender and transsexual people, their gender identity does not simply conform to their biological sex and is often in direct conflict with it. Gender (or sex) role describes one's expression of masculinity or femininity and is the socialized aspect of gender identity. Commonly, people enact their gender identity through the gender role they express; however, someone can present with a gender role that is congruent with one's natal sex in order to hide gender variance or gender dysphoria. People can also express cross-gendered role behavior and not have dysphoria related to their gender identity or natal sex. Finally, sexual orientation is the direction of a person's sexual desire, including their sexual preference and emotional attraction (Lev, 2004).

These component parts interact with one another in numerous and complex ways. For example, researchers have often referred to some male-to-female transsexuals as "homosexual" because they are attracted to natal males (Blanchard, Clemmensen, & Steiner, 1987). However, this assumes that their natal sex is their "true" sex. If they see themselves as women, then their behavior and desire would actually be heterosexual. Mental health practitioners have tended to privilege natal sex over self-perceived gender identity. Due to prevalent homophobic bias, approval for surgical treatment once rested upon a heterosexual identity after sexual reassignment (Denny, 1992).

The relationship between same-sex sexual orientation and gender-variant behavior has been impacted by social and political forces. Homosexuality, long considered a psychopathology, was removed from the *DSM* in 1973 because of the tremendous pressure of the burgeoning gay liberation movement (Bayer, 1981). The emergence of a politically organized lesbian and gay civil rights movement was instrumental in the depathologizing of homosexuality. It is arguable whether the success of this movement would have been possible if homosexuality had remained a diagnosable mental illness. Would gay marriage, child-rearing rights, or employment and job protections be on the public agenda if same-sex sexuality were a psychopathological perversion? Unfortunately, the struggle for civil liberties for lesbian, gay, and bisexual people was established by normalizing same-sex (i.e., natal) sexual desire and downplaying the relevance of gender identity and expression in identity development. Indeed, gender-variant behavior became separated from sexual orientation completely within the clinical discourse *and* among political activists (despite its frequent expression within the LGB community). Additionally, gender identity disorder became a suitable category of mental illness. According to Wilson (1997), "American psychiatric perceptions of transgendered people are remarkably parallel to those for gay and lesbian people before the declassification of homosexuality as a mental disorder in 1973" (p. 15). Furthermore, gender identity disorder has been used to diagnose gender-variant homosexuals, especially youth, continuing the pathologizing of lesbian, gay, and bisexual people under a new diagnostic category (Rottnek, 1999; Scholinski, 1997).

Before the LGBT movement became a collective force impacting social policy change within the mental health establishment, same-sex relationships and gender-variant expression endured within very different social milieus. Although what is currently referred to as transgender community is a recent contemporary development, there is evidence of organized social relationships for cross-gendered people (Herdt, 1994). There are two communities of cross-dressing people that deserve specific recognition as forerunners of the contemporary transgender movement, although they predate contemporary social and political organizing. The roots of progressive transgender organizing are clearly visible in an examination of the cross-dressing social clubs for heterosexual males of the 1950s and 1960s and of female cross-dressing within the butch–femme lesbian communities of the same era, both of which are outlined next.

CROSS-DRESSING CLUBS FOR HETEROSEXUAL MALES

In the 1950s and 1960s, cross-dressers (or transvestites, as they were then known) began to gather in small groups in various parts of the United States. Virginia Prince, who was the founder of the earliest cross-dressing club and magazine (e.g., The Hose and Heels Club and Transvestia magazine), proposed an affirmative approach to heterosexual cross-dressing (Ekins & King, 2005). The Tri-Ess Sorority: The Society for the Second Self developed following the organized gatherings of The Hose and Heels Club and remains a large and active national organization for heterosexual cross-dressers to this day (Bullough & Bullough, 1993; Denny, in press; Meyerowitz, 2002). Tri-Ess groups were the first nationally organized social spaces developed explicitly for cross-dressed men to gather and socialize, and they served to advance Prince's conviction that cross-dressers should accept themselves and their "femmiphilia." Tri-Ess groups allowed cross-dressers to know others like themselves and to learn tips about makeup and self-presentation as a woman, but most important, organized cross-dressing gatherings lessened the stigma and shame of being a cross-dressing man in a rigidly gendered society. Tri-Ess allowed for the socialization of cross-dressers and the early development of a community ethos. It is important to note that Tri-Ess did not embrace all cross-dressers and all cross-gender behavior. Tri-Ess did not, and still does not, welcome gay cross-dressers or drag performers.

Despite the limitations of her vision, Virginia Prince contributed much to the advancement of transgender issues and was instrumental in developing professional interest in the cross-dressing phenomenon. She was committed to normalizing male cross-dressing. Through her magazine Transvestia, she encouraged cross-dressers to participate in research in order to increase accurate knowledge of their lifestyles and experiences. She worked closely with social scientists in promoting and publishing supportive research (Prince & Bentler, 1972). Professionals at the time viewed cross-dressing as a "psychopathological state" that was the "final result of a psychosexual maldevelopment" (Beigel, 1969, p. 121), but research data consistently showed that cross-dressers did not generally exhibit mental health problems (Bentler & Prince, 1970). Stryker notes that Prince is a "superbly well-educated person with medical credentials" (2005, p. xvi), yet because she was openly a cross-dresser, she was not considered an "expert" in her own right and often published cojointly with other professionals. Nonetheless, Prince's research was vital to changing the psychological bias against transgender behavior. Virginia Prince's advocacy for cross-dressers within professional circles, her support of cross-dressers as mentally stable, as well as her role in the development of organized (albeit discreet) social spaces for gender-variant males was instrumental to the early community development of transgender people.

FEMALE MASCULINITY AND BUTCH LESBIANS

At the same time that Tri-Ess was organizing its social clubs, another group of cross-dressers was gathering socially: ~~masculine-identified females within lesbian communities. Butch lesbians~~, whose experience within an organized clandestine social community predates and overlaps with the development of cross-dressing clubs for heterosexual males, have often been ignored within the transgender literature. The butch narrative has been relegated to gay or women's studies as if butch lesbian's cross-gendered nature was superfluous to their identity. Contemporary understanding of masculine females has been occluded by an historical conflation of gender identity and sexual orientation as well as layers of feminist and gay historical revision (Cromwell, 1999). Same-sex desire, as has been noted, was viewed exclusively through a gendered lens throughout most of the 19th century, leaving a legacy well into the 20th (Hekma, 1994; Trumbach, 1994). Not only was lesbianism that did not involve gender inversion inconceivable, but additionally, gender inversion that was not lesbian was equally unimaginable (Crowmwell, 1999).

As gay historians began to uncover lesbian history outside of the theory of gender inversion, cross-dressing expression in females was assumed to be a consequence of women's oppression, enacted either for economic gain within an oppressive social system or to shelter their lesbian relationships from a homophobic culture (Cromwell, 1999). In Kennedy and Davis's (1993) excellent ethnography of pre-Stonewall butch–femme communities, the authors attested to the salience of masculine identity for butches within that cultural context and note that many butches had lived as men at various times in their lives. The authors focused, however, on the distinctions rather than the similarities between butch lesbians and women who passed and lived as men, overlooking the lack of financial or social options for most masculine females, particularly working class butches who might have desired to live as men. Butch–femme communities of the 1950s and 1960s created an emotionally safe haven for masculine females, harboring them and offering a community and identity in which they could belong. However, the lesbian context of butch–femme communities also effectively silenced questions regarding gender identity, a silence that was later reinforced through feminist and queer historical revision.

Females who have lived as men, cross-dressing in male clothing and working in traditional male trades, have been referred to as passing women. They have often remained hidden, passing throughout their entire lives and only being discovered upon their death. Passing women have passed so well that they have, until recently, remained hidden to history. As Cromwell (1999) asserted, even the term passing *women* itself renders these *men* invisible (i.e., it would be more accurate to call them passing *men*), privileging their natal sex over their lifelong identity. Even if most butches were unequivocally lesbian-identified, it is likely that some cross-dressing females and passing women were in reality not women, but rather female-bodied men (i.e., transsexual). Nestle (1998) has acknowledged the need to reexamine the historic role of masculine females within the butch–femme community through the lens of our current understanding of transgenderism. Nestle, a longtime advocate for butch–femme identities, has admitted that she herself might not have understood that some of the passing women she knew might have seen themselves not as masculine lesbians, but rather as men. Devor (1997) has documented a process whereby female-to-male transsexuals attempted to fit into a lesbian social role when other options were not (yet) available.

Deconstructing the meaning of masculine identity is essential to the reclaiming of cross-dressing females and transmen in a historical context. Female-to-male transsexuals, commonly known as transmen, remain invisible socially and marginal within the contemporary professional literature. This may be a result, in part, of a misunderstanding and "misfiling" of the meaning and social context of passing women and female-bodied men within the lesbian communities of the 1950s and 1960s. The challenges and confusions of identity continue to this day as butch-identified lesbians and female-bodied men debate and discuss identity issues. They grapple with the sometimes-ambiguous edge and imprecise perimeters delineating various masculine identities in bodies born female; this has been referred to in the literature as the "Butch/FTM Border Wars" (Halberstam, 1998b; Hale, 1998).

There are, or course, many expressions of female masculinity, and the border-wars of identity (distinguishing butch lesbians from transmen) have produced contemporary emergent narratives that recognize that some masculine women are in actuality female-bodied men (see Cromwell, 1999; Halberstam, 1998b; Prosser, 1998). Butch–femme communities have undoubtedly sheltered and celebrated masculine females who were or are transgender, but the nature of the communities themselves might have disallowed any conversation about gender identity that would have supported a male-identity paradigm. This highlights the need for a careful and conscious use of language when discussing transgender issues, considering that language is often controlled by those who have the power to name, and part of identity development and community identification lies in the ability to name oneself.

TRANSGENDER COMMUNITY DEVELOPMENT

In recent years some gender-variant people have rejected the bipolar choice of being either male or female and have ~~felt their gender encompasses "both" genders~~ (i.e., ~~gender-blended;~~ Bornstein, 1994; Ekins & King, 1996; Wilchins, 1997). Some people feel that they are bigendered or androgynous, simultaneously exhibiting masculine and feminine traits. Others sometimes purposely gender-bend, as a way to celebrate mixed gender or even shock more conventionally minded people. Others feel they are neutral, or without gender (Ekins & King, 1999). This steps outside of a "changing sex" paradigm and allows for more flexibility of gender expression and identity. Within contemporary urban life, ~~bigendered people often refer to themselves as "gender queers," "gender benders," "third sex," and "gender perverts" as terms of pride~~ (Nestle, Wilchins, & Howell, 2002). Within some American Indian cultures, expressing both genders is referred to as being "two-spirited," but this has also been used as a term for lesbians and gay men (Roscoe, 1998; Tafoya & Wirth, 1996).

Having defined the language of gender variance and transgender, it also seems necessary to define what is meant by a *community*. The word *community* derives from the Latin *munus*, which means "gift," and "cum," which means "together, among each other," forming the word *communitas*, or the "sharing of gifts together" (Craig, 2005; Farlex, Inc., 2005). The word *community* describes a group of people, a collectivity, in which the members share something in common, whether interests, values, or characteristics. Being part of a community assumes communication or informal, spontaneous interactions with other like-minded people. There is a presumed trust or camaraderie between members of a community based on shared values or beliefs, in addition to an exclusion of outsiders.

According to Bernd and Klandermans (2001), the development of a collective political identity depends on the ability of a community to meet certain psychological needs. In order for transgender people to begin organizing collectively, they had to develop a sense of belongingness, seeing themselves as part of a group called transgender people, but also a sense of distinctiveness, recognizing the ways that they are different from non-transgender people. Additionally, transgender people had to change their self-perception from one of people with mental health problems to one of individuals deserving respect. They needed to develop a sense of meaning in their community identity and have the experience of agency and empowerment that comes from belonging to a larger group. For a group to have a collective political identity, the members must have an awareness of themselves as marginalized and must attribute their grievances to an outside adversary who can be pressured to change (Bernd & Klandermans, 2001); the transgender community met these criteria in the early 1990s, creating a veritable transgender explosion.

Transgender community identity became public and vocal in the 1980s and early 1990s, although the roots of this activism lay in earlier organizations, such as Prince's Tri-Ess, which can be traced back to cross-dressing clubs in the 1950s, and the Erickson Educational Foundation (EEF; Bullough & Bullough, 1993; Denny, in press; Meyerowitz, 2002). EEF, started in the 1960s by a wealthy philanthropist, provided educational resources and funded numerous projects instrumental to raising public awareness of transsexualism. Grants from EEF supported the original Gender Identity Clinic at John Hopkins University, which was the site of the first sexual reassignment procedure in the United States. These grants also funded conferences on gender dysphoria, which eventually evolved into the HBIGDA, an international organization for professionals who work in the field of transsexualism (Devor, 2000).

Community activism coalesced in San Francisco in the late 1980s and early 1990s and served as a catalyst of national organizing. First, Lou Sullivan began bringing the nascent FTM community in San Francisco together in a support group that later developed into FTM International. In 1992, Transgender Nation formed. Based on the militant, direct-action political style of Queer Nation, this organization insisted on social justice and civil rights for all gender-variant people. This paved the way for other organizations like Transsexual Menace and It's Time, America to work and grow nationally and in other communities (Green, 2004; Stryker, 1999, 2004).

Other organizations, such as the Renaissance Educational Association, the American Educational Gender Information Service (AEGIS; which later became Gender Education & Advocacy), and the International Foundation for Gender Education (IFGE; which grew out of Boston's Tiffany Club), were dedicated to addressing educational issues and providing community resources. AEGIS produced Chrysalis: The Journal of Transgressive Gender Identities; and IFGE still prints Transgender Tapestry, a national magazine for transgender and transsexual people.

National conferences became a focal point for organizing. In the early 1990s, The International Conference on Transgender Law and Employment formed under the leadership of Phyllis Frye to address public policy; discrimination in employment, housing, and marriage; and legislation affecting transgender people. Another important conference was The American Boyz, which met yearly in the 1990s and brought together those who were labeled female at birth but felt that the label was not an accurate or complete description of their identity. This conference celebrated many forms of masculine identity expression. In more recent years, GenderPAC has broadened its focus to work toward ending all forms of gender oppression (i.e., not limiting itself to transgender issues) through lobbying for changes in legislation. The National Transgender Advocacy Coalition also concentrates on changing public policy and perception through education and advocacy, working exclusively in transgender and transsexual politics.

The work of these organizations has garnered public support for transgender issues and has served to transform the mainstream assumption of gender as a rigidly bipolar and immutable identity. Maintaining a consistent political presence in lobby representation, educational efforts, and vocal advocacy has fostered the development of antidiscrimination laws and equality for transgender and transsexual citizens (Denny, in press; Shapiro, 2004; Stryker, 1999).

The emergence of a burgeoning transgender community was the result of the confluence of a number of social, political, and technological occurrences that enabled a pathologized, marginalized, and stigmatized minority to form a collective and politicized community advocating for social activism and legal change. Certainly the success of previous social justice movements, most notably the civil rights movement and the women's liberation movement, proved that a change in status was possible for minority and oppressed groups. These movements also fostered a greater acceptance of diversity, a wider range of potential gender expressions, and direct challenges to traditional sex roles. Additionally, the achievements of the lesbian and gay liberation movement proved that an organized movement of "queer perverts" could successfully challenge large institutions like the American Psychiatric Association and the U.S. Supreme Court. The visible power of community organization gave hope to transgender people and heralded their self-actualization and politicization.

THE ROLE OF THE INTERNET IN TRANSGENDER COMMUNITY DEVELOPMENT

Due to the complexities of shame, isolation, and the stigma of mental illness and perversion, the transgender community would have been unlikely to become collectively organized if not for the rise of modern communication technology. In the past few decades, radio, television, and the wider distribution of newspapers and books gave gender-variant people greater access to information about other transsexuals. They were no longer alone with their gender dysphoria (Califia, 1997; Meyerowitz, 2002). But it was the advent of the Internet that served as the most significant and powerful catalyst in facilitating communication between gender-variant people and in linking disparate communities of people together under the banner of a transgender political community (Hill, 2004; Meyerowitz, 2002; Shapiro, 2004; Whittle, 1998). Communities have commonly been viewed as existing within a geospatial context in which people had to be in physical proximity to one another to be considered part of the same community. However, the growth of the Internet has resulted in virtual online communities, not only spanning geography and national borders, but also creating intimate human connections across those borders (Lev et al., in press; Thomsen, Straubhaar, & Bolyard, 1998). The Internet is not simply a digital tool of communication; it is also a tool that facilitates "webs of personal relationships in cyberspace" (Rheingold, 2000, Introduction, para. 25).

The Internet has played a seminal role in the political and social development of the transgender community. Typing the word *transgender* into any search engine will reveal hundreds of personal Web sites, blogs, live journals, newsgroups, and academic resources. Discussion lists and online chats have spawned relationships between transgender people that have altered their collective consciousness as well as their ability to organize for civil rights (Hegland & Nelson, 2002; Hill, 2004; Shapiro, 2004; Whittle, 1998). In cyber communication, gender is not immediately evident. Therefore, presentation, body image, and assumptions about sex and gender are less restrictive and more fluid. Hill wrote, "On-line, the body is potentially rendered invisible because it lacks boundary, substance, and geographic position" (2004, p. 8). This enables people to express their gender and the internal understanding of their own gender without being confined by the actual body they inhabit or worrying about how well they "pass" within their physical body. Gender, in Internet communication, relies on language and inference as well as honesty, rather than on visual cues or appearance.

Gender may be mystified online, but it nevertheless remains an important variable for communication. Without visual cues, people continually seek information regarding the "real" sex of the person with whom they are talking (Jaffe, Lee, Huang, & Oshagan, 1995; O'Brien, 1999). Gender is, of course, more easily masked online, allowing people to "pretend" to be the opposite sex in a purposeful attempt to "fool" others (Kornbluth, 1994). Sometimes this ability to not be seen visually can allow the expression of a more authentic self. Concurrently, it becomes difficult if not impossible to "prove" your natal sex; sometimes women who have strong personalities are accused of being male on the Internet, especially when they are being sexually assertive with other women (Rodriguez, 2002). Strong sexually assertive lesbians have been accused of "really" being male. The difficulty of discerning sex and gender categories can make it easier for transgender people who are naturally on the border of these categories to express themselves authentically.

The rise of technology has dramatically influenced the lives of many transgender people by facilitating communication with other transgender people. This has influenced their identities, indeed their subjectivities— their very sense of themselves (Hill, 2004; Shapiro, 2004). Whittle (1998) suggested that trans identities can flourish within cyberspace precisely because the virtual self emerges as a more authentic representation of the experienced self than does one's physical self. The anonymous nature of the Internet allows people to reveal personal information, socialize, and develop intimate relationships with others without risking public exposure, job loss, or ostracism (Hegland & Nelson, 2002; Jaffe et al., 1995; Matheson &

Zanna, 1992). Cyber communication creates a neighborhood, a virtual community (Haan, 2002), a "public space" (Shapiro, 2004) existing outside of traditional geospatial boundaries.

In addition to facilitating socialization and communication across national borders, the Internet fosters identity development for transgender individuals outside of the dominant medical model. The Internet has served as a forum for cyber-based support groups for transgender people in all stages of coming out and transition.

Cyber communication cultivated the rise of political activism born of a newly emerging sense of social justice. Most transgender activists use the Internet as a vital tool for organizing (Nangeroni, 2005; Shapiro, 2004; Whittle, 1998). Numerous issues have become the focus of political debate and discussion on the Internet, including, for example, the meaning of sex and gender transgression, the relationship of transgender community to the LGB community, and the relationship between transsexual-identified people and those who see themselves as gender-benders. These political debates often create passionate fervor, which sometimes culminates in political activism.

For example, Denny's (in press) study offers three examples of organized political protest that galvanized the transgender community, all of which were fostered by discussion on the Internet. When Brandon Teena, a young FTM, was murdered, demonstrations were organized around the country, with demonstrators using the Internet as the primary organizing tool. These demonstrations generated significant national media attention. In another example, Tyra Hunter was refused needed medical attention by emergency medical technicians after they realized she was a preoperative transsexual woman. She later died from her injuries. Information about this ghastly event, the political protests, and the subsequent legal battle that followed was disseminated on the Internet, creating a community-wide response. It is unlikely that the mainstream media would have thought this worthy of public attention; but the Internet allowed for wide-scale awareness of the events. Finally, the development of CampTrans, an organized protest in response to the exclusive and biased gender policies of the lesbian/feminist Michigan Womyn's Music Festival, was cultivated and promoted through activism on the Internet. These political actions could not have taken place without the formidable identity politics nurtured by community development on the Internet (Denny, in press).

DISCURSIVE TENSIONS IN COMMUNITY MEMBERSHIP

All communities by their very nature have permeable boundaries and struggle with issues of membership and exclusion. The strength of the growing transgender community rests on its inclusive model that embraces all transgender people and eliminates the divisions between gender-variant people, making the need for stealth and closets anachronistic. Yet, there remains a discursive tension between the older psychiatry-based model of transsexualism as a birth defect needing to be fixed and the more radical, postmodern, and gender-fluid model of transgenderism emerging within the transgender movement (Roen, 2001). The transsexual model may be a "curious brand of identity politics where the purpose is to obscure the question of identity" (Roen, 2001, p. 502), and many transsexuals want to obscure their identity as transsexual (or their previous history as a member of the other sex). For some transsexuals, "passing over" to the "other" side is precisely what they desire to do (Gagné, Tewksbury, & McGaughey, 1997). Often, adherents to the older medical model disavow any relationship to transgender politics and transgender community identity. They embrace a view of their "condition" as biological and repairable by medical and surgical treatment. They resist any attempt at linking their political or legal needs with those of other gender-variant people, whom they often refer to in disparaging terms. Transgender activists may include transsexuals under their umbrella, but some transsexuals clearly do not want to be associated with the diversity of a transgender liberation movement or be affiliated within that community. This raises the question about whether one can still be included as part of a community in which one rejects membership.

Another site of tension that raises questions of inclusion is the relationship between the transgender community and the gay and lesbian community, which has been, in many ways, a historical refuge for gender-variant people (Denny, in press; Fassinger & Arseneau, chap. 1, this volume). The boundary differentiating these groups has often been blurry, as previously described in terms of the butch–femme communities of the 1950s. Additionally, many gender-variant people have been accepted within the entertainment and theater communities, specifically in roles as drag performers and female impersonators (Livingston, 1991; Newton, 1972). They were perceived to be part of the larger gay or trans community, although participation in drag performance does not necessarily imply transgender identity. Namaste (2000) has discussed the invisibility and erasure of the actual lived-lives of transsexuals within the emerging academic field of queer studies, which nonetheless intellectually theorizes about gender-variant experience. This erasure has been most notable in the lack of historical recognition of the vital presence of cross-dressing people in the Stonewall Rebellion, which marked the beginning of the modern lesbian and gay civil rights movement (Feinberg, 1996, 1998; Wilchins, 1997).

Currah (2001) stated that transsexuals and transgender people do not have "a permanent seat on the freedom train" precisely because the term sexual orientation "remains intelligible only if sex and gender remain relatively stable categories" (p. 182). For example, if a heterosexual married man transitions, and her wife remains in the relationship, are they now lesbians and part of the lesbian community? How far into transition does she have to be? What if she chooses to not have sex reassignment surgery (or can't afford it)? Alternatively, if a partner in a lesbian couple transitions, are the two now no longer gay? Do they deserve the services of lesbian legal-aid organizations? Does a transman belong within the confines of the lesbian community (assuming he would want to be there)? Is the couple still welcome in the LGB movement (posttransition), while the two are living as an essentially heterosexual couple? Transgenderism disrupts the boundary of not only gender, but also sexual orientation, creating an upheaval in community inclusion and membership, not to mention ideology and epistemology (see Fassinger & Arseneau, chap. 1, this volume).

In some measure the success of the LGB civil rights movement has been at the expense of transgender people. As LGB people began to reject the pathologizing of their identities, transgender and transsexual people became the focus of clinical diagnosis as well as social condemnation. Lesbian and gay liberation and the celebration of same-sex relationships as "normal" have further marginalized gender-variant people. It has taken nearly 30 years for issues relevant to transgender and transsexual people to take a main stage within the larger LGBT movement. Understanding and incorporating the integral role of cross-gender behavior and gender-variant people within the LGBT community is the necessary next step in building an inclusive community and a civil rights movement that fully embraces all its members.

There have been enormous struggles within national gay politics over transgender issues. Significant anger has been levied at the LGB political leaders because of the way transgender issues have been ignored and minimized. After years of confrontation from the transgender community, the Human Rights Campaign (HRC) finally recognized that "transgender people have always been part of our community. Usually, it is transgender people both transitioning individuals and gender nonconforming gay and lesbian folks who are on the front lines" (Birch, 2003, para. 2). It is no small matter and is the result and sign of enormous political change that the HRC recently came to the legal aid of Sharli'e Vicks, a New Orleans transgender evacuee from Hurricane Katrina who was jailed in Texas for using a women's bathroom (Grey, 2005). Whittle (1998) credits transgender activism on the Internet for forging an organized confrontation of HRC, which brought about a change in its national policy agenda. Despite this progress, there remains tension between the transgender community and the lesbian and gay community (Green, 2004). Perhaps the resistance will increase as gay issues become increasingly mainstreamed (Vidal-Ortiz, 2002). Many transgender individuals are skeptical about whether the "T" in LGBT has a permanent home in national political movements for lesbian and gay rights.

Class and race issues also impact the development and viability of transgender community development (Broad, 2002). Working class and poor gender-variant people, who are often of color and/or young, have less access to cyber communication, as well as less access to medical treatment (Shapiro,

2004; Wakeford, 2000). Black and Latino cross-dressers have often formed their own cross-dressing communities, which have been less documented and studied than their middle-class White counterparts (Livingston, 1991).

Additionally, language, definitions, identity constructs, and relationships to both the gay and trans communities are profoundly impacted by race, ethnic, and class considerations (Rosario, 2004). Gender-variant young people, often homeless and impoverished, have also formed underground communities that are, sadly, too often characterized by drug and alcohol abuse, prostitution, illegal hormone and silicone use, and are vulnerable to HIV and other sexually transmitted diseases (Mallon, 1999). On the other hand, organization on the Internet has created a stronger, more politically aware middle-class transgender youth community, the members of which are advocating for their rights to medical treatment and safer living situations within college environments (Shapiro, 2004). This younger generation is committed to living their lives fully without the emotional shame of previous generations. These youth often identify as "genderqueer," bridging the gulf between the mainstream gay and lesbian community and the transgender and transsexual gender community—creating an out, proud, gender-bending identity that is not easily contained within defined boundaries (Mallon, 1999; Nestle et al., 2002). Genderqueers are not trying to pass or fit, but are demanding their rights to step outside of the rules and roles dictating gender-appropriate behavior.

Finally, it is important to remember that community includes not only gender-variant people themselves, but also their significant others, family members, and loved ones. This includes heterosexual wives, lesbian and gay partners, children, and an array of others whose lives are touched by transgender people (Califia, 1997; Lev, 2004).

CONCLUSION

There is, of course, not one monolithic transgender community (anymore than there is one monolithic gay or lesbian community). As Shapiro pointed out, "There are a number of trans movements which are tied together by identity and issue, and separated by race, class, nationality, goal, surgery status, and other characteristics" (2004, p. 167). Sometimes these communities are only tied together loosely, but like the gay and lesbian community, or the Jewish community, or communities of people of color, the transgender community is learning to develop broad-based coalitions to address issues of mutual concerns.

The transgender community is a recently organized community born of a newly emerging identity. Green (2004) wrote, "Identity has often been a powerful organizing tool, but it should not be mistaken for the ideal model of community" (p. 81). Organizing for social justice and challenging social policy is empowering, but community is about more than marching for change; it is about the comfort of feeling at home with like-minded people. It remains to be seen how transgender communities will develop over the next few decades and the kind of home life it will create and sustain.

Transgender community development is intimately linked to the therapeutic process, given that development of individual authenticity and gender emergence frequently take place within a community setting, online or face-to-face. Stage two (see Exhibit 6.1) of the developmental trajectory of transgender emergence involves assisting clients in developing appropriate linkages to their communities and in developing peer support, consequently enabling them to receive the benefits of witnessing other transgender people living healthy satisfied lives (Lev, 2004). Transgender people are often struggling with familial problems and medical challenges and experience isolation during transition (see Korell & Lorah, chap. 11, this volume). Community involvement can serve as an antidote to loneliness and offer newly coming out transgender people positive role models. Community identification, connection, organization, and advocacy are essential to quality and effective therapeutic engagement.

When the gay community was small, it was enough to be with other gay people (and this is still often true for rural gays who rarely get to be among others like them). This is important to the development of a full sense of self. But as the LGBT community has grown, communities have developed within racial, religious, class, and age boundaries, and these communities may have little in common with one another outside of sharing same-sex attraction and the need for civil rights protections. This is likely to be true for transgender individuals as the community grows and includes a wider spectrum of people, many of whom may not seek out other transgender people for social connections.

Transgender communities will likely continue expanding their sense of identity and inclusion as well as their ability to serve more members through political advocacy and emotional support. For a community in its infancy, it has had a powerful impact on national politics and psychological theory, in part because it stands firmly on the successes of previous civil rights struggles. The transgender community has put pressure on the larger society to "question gender" and is now creating safe spaces, online as well as outside of the virtual world, to express the answers they have found. It seems irrefutable that a burgeoning transgender community exists where none did before—a community that is politically organized to advocate for its own needs, to educate the wider society about its experience, and to support members of the community in living successful lives in diverse ways. The transgender community shares similar historical roots with the LGB community, and the communities' struggles for equality will likely remain entwined as well.

REFERENCES

American Psychiatric Association. (2000). *Diagnostic and statistical manual of mental disorders* (4th ed., text rev.). Washington, DC: Author.

Bayer, R. (1981). *Homosexuality and American psychiatry: The politics of diagnosis.* Princeton, NJ: Princeton University Press.

Beigel, H. G. (1969). A weekend in Alice's wonderland. *The Journal of Sex Research, 5,* 108–122.

Benjamin, H. (1966). *The transsexual phenomenon.* New York: Julian Press.

Bentler, P. M. (1976). A typology of transsexualism: Gender identity: Theory and data. *Archives of Sexual Behavior, 5,* 567–584.

Bentler, P. M., & Prince, C. (1970). Psychiatric symptomatology in transvestites. *Journal of Clinical Psychology, 26,* 434–435.

Bernd, S., & Klandermans, B. (2001). Politicized collective identity. *American Psychologist, 56,* 319–331.

Birch, E. (2003, June 16). *ENDA & the Transgender Community* (press release). Retrieved March 25, 2005, from http://www.genderadvocates.org/News/HRC%20on%20ENDA.html

Blackwood, E., & Wiering, S. E. (Eds.). (1999). *Same-sex relations and female desires: Transgender practices across cultures.* New York: Columbia University Press.

Blanchard, R. (1985). Research methods for the typological study of gender disorders in males. In B. W. Steiner (Ed.), *Gender dysphoria: Development, research, management* (pp. 227–257). New York: Plenum.

Blanchard, R. (1989). The classification and labeling of nonhomosexual gender dysphorias. *Archives of Sexual Behavior, 18,* 315–334.

Blanchard, R. (1993). Varieties of autogynephilia and their relationship to gender dysphoria. *Archives of Sexual Behavior, 22,* 241–251.

Blanchard, R., Clemmensen, L., & Steiner, B. (1987). Heterosexual and homosexual gender dysphoria. *Archives of Sexual Behavior, 16,* 139–152.

Bockting, W. O., & Coleman, E. (1992). A comprehensive approach to the treatment of gender dysphoria. In W. O. Bockting & E. Coleman (Eds.), *Gender dysphoria: Interdisciplinary approaches in clinical management* (pp. 131–155). Binghamton, NY: Haworth Press.

Bornstein, K. (1994). *Gender outlaw: On men, women and the rest of us.* New York: Routledge.

Boswell, H. (1991). The transgender alternative. *Chrysalis: The Journal of Transgressive Gender Identities, 1*(2), 29–31.

Broad, K. L. (2002). Fractering transgender: Intersectional constructions and identization. In P. Gagné & R. Tewksbury (Eds.), *Gendered sexualities* (pp. 235–266). Kidlington, Oxford, England: Elsevier Science.

Bullough, B., & Bullough, V. (1993). *Crossdressing, sex, and gender.* Philadelphia: University of Pennsylvania Press.

Buhrich, N., & McConaghy, N. (1977). The discrete syndromes of transvestism and transsexualism. *Archives of Sexual Behavior, 6,* 483–495.

Califia, P. (1997). *Sex changes: The politics of transgenderism.* San Francisco: Cleis Press.

Carrier, J., & Murray, S. O. (1998). Woman–woman marriage in Africa. In S. O. Murray & W. Roscoe (Eds.), *Boy-wives and female-husbands: Studies of African homosexualities* (pp. 255–266). New York: St. Martin's Press.

Carroll, R. (1999). Outcomes of treatment for gender dysphoria. *Journal of Sex Education and Therapy, 24,* 128–136.

Cole, S. S., Denny, D., Eyler, A. E., & Samons, S. L. (2000). Issues of transgender. In L. T. Szuchman & F. Muscarella (Eds.), *Psychological perspectives of human sexuality* (pp. 149–195). New York: Wiley.

Craig, B. (2005). *Latin roots of "Communication."* Retrieved March 25, 2005, from University of Colorado at Boulder Web site: http://www.colorado.edu/communication/meta-discourses/Theory/latin.htm

Cromwell, J. (1999). *Transmen and FTMs: Identities, bodies, genders, and sexualities.* Champaign: University of Illinois Press.

Currah, P. (2001). Queer theory, lesbian and gay rights, and transsexual marriages. In M. Biasius (Ed.), *Sexual identities—Queer politics* (pp. 178–197). Princeton, NJ: Princeton University Press.

Denny, D. (1992). The politics of diagnosis and a diagnosis of politics: The university-affiliated gender clinics, and how they failed to meet the needs of transsexual people. *Chrysalis: The Journal of Transgressive Gender Identities, 1*(3), 9–20.

Denny, D. (2004). Changing models of transsexualism. *Journal of Gay and Lesbian Psychotherapy, 8*(1/2), 25–40.

Denny, D. (in press). Transgender communities of the United States in the late twentieth century. In P. Currah, R. M. Juang, & S. Minter (Eds.), *Transgender rights: History, politics, and law.* Minneapolis: University of Minnesota Press.

Devor, H. (1997). More than manly women: How female-to-male transsexuals reject lesbian identities. In. B. Bullough, V. L. Bullough, & J. Elias (Eds.), *Gender blending* (pp. 87–102). Amherst, NY: Prometheus Books.

Devor, H. (2000). *Reed Erickson and the beginnings of the Harry Benjamin International Gender Dysphoria Association.* Paper presented at the 16th Harry Benjamin International Gender Dysphoria Association Symposium, August 17–21, 1999, London. Abstract retrieved March 25, 2005, from http://www.symposion.com/ijt/greenpresidental/green11.htm

Ekins, R., & King, D. (1996). *Blending genders: Social aspects of cross-dressing and sex-changing.* New York: Routlege.

Ekins, R., & King, D. (1999). Towards a sociology of transgendered bodies. *Sociological Review, 47,* 580–602.

Ekins, R,. & King, D. (2005). Virginia prince: Transgender pioneer, *International Journal of Transgenderism, 8*(4), 5–16.

Evans, A. (1978). *Witchcraft and the gay counterculture.* Boston: Fag Rag Books.

Farlex, Inc. (2005). *Community*. Retrieved March 25, 2005, from http://encyclopedia.thefreedictionary.com/community

Feinberg, L. (1993). *Stone butch blues*. Ithaca, NY: Firebrand Books.

Feinberg, L. (1996). *Transgendered warriors*. Boston: Beacon Press.

Feinberg, L. (1998). *Trans Liberation: Beyond pink or blue*. Boston: Beacon Press.

Foreman, M. (2004, August). ENDA as we've known it must die. *National Gay and Lesbian Task Force*. Retrieved March 25, 2005, from http://www.thetaskforce.org/downloads/OpEdENDAAug2004.pdf

Foucault, M. (1965). *Madness and civilization: A history of insanity in the age of reason* (R. Howard, Trans.). New York: Pantheon.

Gagné, P., Tewksbury, R., & McGaughey, D. (1997). Coming out and crossing over: Identity formation and proclamation in a transgender community. *Gender & Society, 11*, 478–508.

Green, J. (2004). *Becoming a visible man*. Nashville, TN: Vanderbilt University Press.

Green, R., & Fleming, D. (1990). Transsexual surgery follow-up: Status in the 1990s. *Annual Review of Sex Research, 7*, 351–369.

Grey, L. (2005, September 15). Katrina's aftermath: Transgender evacuee survives all obstacles. *Houston Chronicle*. Retrieved September 16, 2005, from http://www.chron.com/cs/CDA/ssistory.mpl/special/05/katrina/3354399

Haan, W. (2002). Een virtuele mythe? Transgender gemeenschappen op internet [A virtual myth? Transgender communities on the Internet]. *In de Marge, 11*(4), 8–15. Retrieved March 25, 2005, from http://www.bezinningscentrum.nl/virtueel/virtual-myth.htm

Halberstam, J. (1998a). *Female masculinity*. Durham, NC: Duke University Press.

Halberstam, J. (1998b). Transgender butch: Butch/FTM border wars and the masculine continuum. *GLQ, 4*(2), 287–310.

Hale, C. J. (1998). Consuming the living, dis(re)memebering the dead in the butch/ftm borderlands. *GLQ, 4*(2), 311–348.

Hausman, B. L. (1995). *Changing sex: Transsexualism, technology, and idea of gender*. Durham, NC: Duke University Press.

Hegland, J. E, & Nelson, N. J. (2002). Cross-dressers in cyber-space: Exploring the Internet as a tool for expressing gender identity. *International Journal of Sexuality and Gender Studies, 7*(2/3), 139–161.

Hekma, G. (1994). A female soul in a male body: Sexual inversion as gender inversion in nineteenth-century sexology. In G. Herdt (Ed.), *Third sex third gender: Beyond sexual dimorphism in culture and history* (pp. 213–240). New York: Zone Books.

Herdt, G. (1994). *Third sex third gender: Beyond sexual dimorphism in culture and history* (pp. 21–81). New York: Zone Books.

Hill, D. B. (2004, July). *Coming to terms: Using technology to know identity*. Paper presented at the 112th Annual Convention of the American Psychological Association, Honolulu, HI.

Jacobs, S. E., Thomas, W., & Lang, S. (1997). *Two-spirit people: Native American gender identity, sexuality, and spirituality*. Urbana: University of Illinois Press.

Jaffe, J. M., Lee, Y.-E, Huang, L., & Oshagan, H. (1995). *Gender, pseudonyms, and CMC: Masking identities and baring souls*. Paper submitted for presentation at the 45th Annual Conference of the International Communication Association, Albuquerque, NM. Retrieved March 25, 2005, from http://members.iworld.net/yesunny/genderps.html

Katz, J. (1976). *Gay American history: Lesbians and gay men in the USA*. New York: Crowell.

Kennedy, E. J., & Davis, M. D. (1993). *Boots of leather, slippers of gold: The history of a lesbian community*. New York: Penguin Books.

Kornbluth, J. (1994). *You make me feel like a virtual woman*. Retrieved March 25, 2005, from http://www.sherryart.com/newstory/jesse.html

Landén, M., Wålinder, J., Hembert, J., & Lundström, B. (1998). Factors predictive of regret in sex reassignment. *Acta Psychiatrica Scandinavia, 97*(4), 284–289.

Lawrence, A. (2001, November). *SRS without a one year RLE: Still no regrets*. Paper presented at the XVII Harry Benjamin International Symposium on Gender Dysphoria, Galveston, TX.

Lev, A. I. (2004). *Transgender emergence: Therapeutic guidelines for working for gender-variant people and their families*. Binghamton, NY: Haworth Press.

Lev, A. I., Dean, G., De Filippis, L., Evernham, K., McLaughlin, L., & Phillips, P. (in press). Dykes and Tykes: A Virtual Lesbian Parenting Community. *Journal of Lesbian Studies*.

Levine, S., & Lothstein, L. (1981). Transsexualism or the gender dysphoria syndromes. *Journal of Sex and Marital Therapy, 7*, 85–113.

Lewins, F. (1995). *Transsexualism in society: A sociology of male-to-female transsexuals*. South Melbourne, Australia: MacMillian Press.

Livingston, J. (Artist/Author/Producer). (1991). *Paris is burning* [Documentary film]. San Francisco: Off White Productions.

Mallon, G. (1999, October). On the stroll: Helping gay teen prostitutes get off the streets. *In the Family, 5*(2), 8–13.

Matheson, K., & Zanna, M. P. (1992). Computer-mediated communications: The focus is on me. *Social Science Computer Review, 8*, 1–12.

Meyer, W., Bockting, W., Cohen-Kettenis, P., Coleman, E., DiCeglie, D., Devor, H., et al. (2001, February). The standards of care for gender identity disorder—sixth version. *International Journal of Transgenderism, 5*(1). Retrieved June 7, 2006, from http://www.symposion.com/ijt/soc_2001/index.htm

Meyerowitz, J. (2002). *How sex changed: A history of transsexuality in the United States*. Cambridge, MA: Harvard University Press.

Namaste, V. K. (2000). *Invisible lives: The erasure of transsexual and transgendered people*. Chicago: University of Chicago Press.

Nanda, S. (1994). Hijras: An alternative sex and gender role in India. In G. Herdt (Ed.), *Third sex third gender: Beyond sexual dimorphism in culture and history* (pp. 373–417). New York: Zone Books.

Nangeroni, N. R. (2005, March 19). The virtual movement. When the rules change, it pays to notice. *Gendertalk*. Retrieved March 25, 2005, from http://www.gendertalk.com/comment/political/virtual.shtml

Nestle, J. (1998). On rereading "Esther's story." In J. Nestle, *A fragile union* (pp. 107–114). San Francisco: Cleis Press.

Nestle, J., Wilchins, R., & Howell, C. (2002). *GenderQueer: Voices from beyond the sexual binary.* Los Angeles: Alyson.

Newton, E. (1972). *Mother camp: Female impersonators in America.* Chicago: University of Chicago Press.

O'Brien, J. (1999). Writing in the body: Gender (re)production in online interaction. In M. A. Smith & P. Kollock (Eds.), *Communities in cyberspace.* New York: Routledge.

Peck, M. S. (1998). *The different drum: Community-making and peace.* New York: Simon & Schuster.

Person, E., & Ovesey, L. (1974a). The transsexual syndrome in males, I: Primary transsexualism. *American Journal of Psychotherapy, 28,* 4–20.

Person, E., & Ovesey, L. (1974b). The transsexual syndrome in males, II: Secondary transsexuality. *American Journal of Psychotherapy, 28,* 174–193.

Prince, C., & Bentler, P. M. (1972). Survey of 504 cases of transvestism. *Psychological Reports, 31,* 903–917.

Prosser, J. (1998). *Second skins: The body narratives of transsexuality.* New York: Columbia University Press.

Rachlin, K. (1997, June). *Partners in the journey: Psychotherapy and six stages of gender revelation.* Paper presented at the Second Congress on Sex and Gender, King of Prussia, PA.

Raj, R. (2002). Towards a transpositive therapeutic model: Developing clinical sensitivity and cultural competence in the effective support of transsexual and transgendered clients. *The International Journal of Transgenderism, 6*(2). Retrieved March 25, 2005, from http://www.symposion.com/ijt/ijtvo06no02_04.htm

Rheingold, H. (2000). *The virtual community: Homesteading on the electronic frontier.* Retrieved March 25, 2005, from http://www.rheingold.com/vc/book/

Rodriguez, J. M. (2002). *Queer Latinidad: Identity practices, discursive spaces* (Sexual Cultural Series). New York: New York University Press.

Roen, K. (2001). "Either/or and both/neither": Discursive tensions in transgender politics. *Signs: Journal of Women in Culture and Society, 27,* 501–523.

Rosario, V. A. (2004). "Qué joto bonita!": Transgender negotiations of sex and ethnicity. In L. Ubaldo & J. Drescher (Eds.), *Transgender subjectivities: A clinician's guide* (pp. 89–97). New York: Haworth Press.

Roscoe, W. (1998). *Changing ones: Third and fourth genders in native North America.* New York: St. Martin's Press.

Rottnek, M. (Ed.). (1999). *Sissies and tomboys: Gender nonconformity and homosexual childhoods.* New York: New York University Press.

Scholinski, D. (with Adams, J. M.). (1997). *The last time I wore a dress: A memoir.* New York: Riverhead Books.

Shapiro, E. (2004). Transcending barriers: Transgender organizing on the Internet. *Journal of Gay and Lesbian Social Services: Special Issue on Strategies for Gay and Lesbian Rights Organizing, 16*(3/4), 165–179.

Smith, M. A., & Kollock, P. (Eds.). (1999). *Communities in cyberspace*. New York: Routledge.

Stone, S. (1991). The empire strikes back: A posttranssexual manifesto. In J. Epstein & K. Straub (Eds.), *Body guards: The cultural politics of gender ambiguity* (pp. 280-304). New York: Routledge.

Stryker, S. (1999). Portrait of a transfag hag as a young man: The activist career of Louis G. Sullivan. In K. More & S. Whittle (Eds.), *Reclaiming genders: Transsexual grammars at the fin de siècle* (pp. 62–82). London: Cassell.

Stryker, S. (2004). Transgender. *glbtq: An encyclopedia of gay, lesbian, bisexual, transgender, and queer culture*. Retrieved March 3, 2006, from http://www.glbtq.com/social-sciences/transgender.html

Stryker, S. (2005). Foreword. *International Journal of Transgenderism*, 8, xv–xvi.

Tafoya, T., & Wirth, D. A. (1996). Native American two-spirit men. In J. F. Longres (Ed.), *Men of color: A context for service to homosexually active men* (pp. 51–67). New York: Harrington Park Press.

Thomsen, S. R., Straubhaar, J. D., & Bolyard, D. M. (1998). Ethnomethodology and the study of online communities: Exploring the cyber streets. *Information Research*, 4(1). Retrieved March 25, 2005, from http://informationr.net/ir/4–1/paper50.html

Trumbach, R. (1994). London's sapphists: From three sexes to four genders in the making of modern culture. In G. Herdt (Ed.), *Third sex third gender: Beyond sexual dimorphism in culture and history* (pp. 111–136). New York: Zone Books.

Turner, L. (2004). *Gender renaissance: Re-configurations of femininity*. Unpublished doctoral dissertation, Women's Studies Department, Lancaster University, England.

Valentine, D. (2000). *"I know what I am": The category "Transgender" in the construction of contemporary U.S. American conceptions of gender and sexuality*. Unpublished doctoral dissertation, Anthropology Department, New York University.

Vidal-Ortiz, S. (2002). Queering sexuality and doing gender: Transgender men's identification with gender and sexuality. In P. Gagné & R. Tewksbury (Eds.), *Gendered sexualities* (pp. 181–234). Kidlington, Oxford, England: Elsevier Science.

Wakeford, N. (2000). Cyberqueer. In D. Bell & B. M. Kennedy (Eds.), *The cybercultures reader* (pp. 403–315). New York: Routledge.

Walworth, J. (1997). Sex reassignment surgery in male-to-female transsexuals: Client satisfaction in relation to selection criteria. In B. Bullough, V. L. Bullough, & J. Elias (Eds.), *Gender blending* (pp. 352–373). Amherst, NY: Prometheus Books.

Whittle, S. (1993). The history of a psychiatric diagnostic category: Transexualism. *Chrysalis: The Journal of Transgressive Gender Identities*, 1(5).

Whittle, S. (1998). The trans-cyberian mail way. *Social & Legal Studies*, 7, 389–408.

Wilchins, R. A. (1997). *Read my lips: Sexual subversion and the end of gender*. Ithaca, NY: Firebrand Books.

Williams, W. (1992). *The spirit and the flesh: Sexual diversity in American Indian culture*. Boston: Beacon Press.

Wilson, K. (1997, July). *Gender as illness: Issues of psychiatric classification*. Paper presented at 6th annual ICTLEP transgender law and employment policy conference, Houston, TX. Retrieved March 25, 2005, from http://www.transgender.org/gidr/kwictl97.html

Zucker, K. (2005). Was the gender identity disorder of childhood diagnosis introduced into the DSM-III as a backdoor maneuver to replace homosexuality? *Journal of Sex and Marital Therapy, 31*, 31–42.

II

AFFIRMATIVE COUNSELING AND PSYCHOTHERAPY WITH LESBIAN, GAY, BISEXUAL, AND TRANSGENDER CLIENTS

INTRODUCTION: AFFIRMATIVE COUNSELING AND PSYCHOTHERAPY WITH LESBIAN, GAY, BISEXUAL, AND TRANSGENDER CLIENTS

This section is intended to provide readers with guidance about how to take an affirmative approach to counseling and psychotherapy with lesbian, gay, bisexual, and transgender (LGBT) individuals. We strongly believe that affirmation for LGBT individuals is not population-specific. Nor do we believe that affirmation begins once it becomes evident that a client is lesbian, gay, bisexual, or transgender. Rather, we believe LGBT affirmation must be evident throughout every interaction a therapist has with a client. Each of the authors in this section addresses how to infuse affirmation into clinical work. In addition, each chapter reflects a developmental and contextual approach to counseling and psychotherapy with LGBT individuals. Issues specific to transgender clients are not integrated throughout this section. Rather, we devote one chapter (Korell & Lorah, chap. 11, this volume) to providing readers with an overview of counseling and psychotherapy with transgender clients.

This section leads off with a chapter by Greene (chap. 7). She focuses on the ethical concerns often associated with contextual issues (e.g., heterosexism, multiple identities, conversion therapy) for LGB clients. Her thought-provoking chapter asks mental health providers to challenge the heterosexism and homophobia that confront all persons in a heterosexist society. Further, she asks therapists to consider how their personal beliefs and feelings about sexual behavior influence the therapy process. Greene also tackles how counselors and psychotherapists can competently work with LGB clients who have multiple stigmatized identities. Her chapter concludes with an in-depth examination of the ethics of conversion therapy. Greene's comprehensive treatise on this subject is enlightening and challenging.

Matthews's chapter (chap. 8) emphasizes the importance of being affirmative with all clients, even those who may not currently identify or present as lesbian, gay, or bisexual. Her discussion addresses specific therapist behaviors (e.g., heterosexism), but also includes a discussion of affirming organizational environments. She goes on to discuss how to work with clients who may best be described as having a normative coming out experience or who have already come to accept their sexual orientation.

Beckstead and Israel's chapter (chap. 9) addresses how psychotherapists might work with clients who are in acute conflict around sexual orientation issues, particularly in regard to religious or racial identity. Their focus is on those clients who desire to change their sexual orientation to heterosexual or who are unable to adopt an openly positive LGB identity. Beckstead and Israel provide valuable insight into the importance of attending to context when working with clients who present with such conflict. In addition, these authors provide information about what areas in which therapists might seek training as well as what counseling strategies might be adopted to facilitate resolution of such conflicts. Finally, this chapter carefully examines the ethical, cultural, and psychological considerations present in the treatment of sexual minority clients in conflict.

Attending to workplace issues is a concern for the vast majority of LGB clients. Lidderdale, Croteau, Anderson, Tovar-Murray, and Davis (chap. 10) begin with a succinct review of the empirical research focused on LGB vocational psychology that has been published since the first edition of the handbook. They then present a comprehensive and groundbreaking theoretical model of workplace sexual identity management that situates the empirical literature within a social cognitive framework. Lidderdale et al. facilitate the reader's ability to apply this model by providing valuable case illustrations as well as a detailed research agenda.

Korell and Lorah (chap. 11) provide an overview of the basic issues in affirmative counseling for transgender individuals and their family members. Their chapter serves as an effective companion piece to chapter 6 (Lev). These authors focus their attention on five specific areas relevant to transgender clients, including support systems, family, social and emotional stressors, medical needs, and career concerns. The real strength of this chapter lies in the authors' ability to use their considerable combined clinical experience to bring alive the sparse theoretical and empirical literature focused on transgender individuals and clients.

All in all, the chapters presented in this section illustrate the essence of affirmative psychotherapy. That is, affirmative psychotherapy begins with the knowledge and awareness of therapists of their own internalized, socialized biases. Affirmation is key to competent, ethical counseling and psychotherapy in effectively addressing the complex needs of clients and the scope of life issues that they experience.

7

DELIVERING ETHICAL PSYCHOLOGICAL SERVICES TO LESBIAN, GAY, AND BISEXUAL CLIENTS

BEVERLY GREENE

Neither the delivery of psychological services to lesbian, gay, and bisexual (LGB) men and women nor ethical considerations about what those services should be or how they should be delivered is a new phenomenon. Placing those ethical dilemmas in their proper perspective requires understanding the political and historical context in which mental health institutions in the United States once considered persons of lesbian, gay, or bisexual orientation psychologically disordered. Brown (1988, 1996) argues that there is a long-standing connection between the mental health establishment and discrimination against sexual minorities that continues to complicate the delivery of services to this population.

This chapter is not intended to serve as a comprehensive review of all ethical issues that are relevant to the treatment of LGB persons. It focuses on ethical dilemmas that are particularly pertinent to clinical work with this population and discusses dilemmas related to the role of the clinicians' personal beliefs and feelings about sexual behavior in the therapy process, the clinician's competence at treating a diverse group of LGB clients and the diversity of LGB clients, and the ethics of conversion therapies. Overall, this discussion emphasizes the ubiquitous challenge of managing heterosexism and homophobia. These phenomena confront all persons in a heterosexist society, and as such, the effects extend to therapy with LGB clients.

THERAPISTS' PERSONAL BELIEFS AND THE LGB CLIENT: HETEROSEXIST BIAS

An individual's assessments of sexual behavior and relationships are always embedded in a cultural context that defines both what is appropriate and what is not from a range of perspectives while usually reflecting attitudes and values of the dominant group in that individual's culture. Sexuality is generally a provocative issue about which most people have feelings, and mental health professionals are no exception. Both client and clinician develop in a heterosexist culture that affects everyone, regardless of their sexual orientation (Brown, 1988; Haldeman, 2002; see also Matthews, chap. 8, this volume). The antigay attitudes that are formed in that environment are not necessarily mitigated by professional training. Indeed, heterosexist thinking and behavior can be exacerbated by training that either ignores LGB issues or attends to them but reinforces old distortions. Brown (1996) has argued that conducting ethical practice requires that practitioners presume that they themselves harbor heterosexist bias and that they actively work to understand and disengage from it.

In many fundamental ways, lesbians, gay men, and bisexual men and women continue to challenge many clinicians' personal beliefs about sexual behavior and fundamentally about what men and women are even supposed to be (Greene, 2000a). Western culture views gender as a binary and mutually exclusive category, with the expectation that individuals fit within the boundaries of gender as proscribed by their biological sex. This engendered culture embeds the object of erotic attraction in the definition of what makes one a normal man or woman. Being "normal" in this context means more than being a part of the arithmetic average. It speaks to being correct or healthy as opposed to unhealthy, sick, or "wrong" and also speaks to having a sense of belonging in fundamental ways. Kaschak (1992) observed that in patriarchal societies such as ours, gender is an essential component of our identities, and most people have internalized the need to get that component "right" and fit where they are supposed to. For example, Kaschak explained that when individuals are mistaken for the other sex, they experience a sense of personal mortification and shame. They feel not that the person who mistook them for male if they were female or vice versa was simply wrong, but that they are "wrong" themselves if their gender presentation was not absolutely clear. They experience themselves as defective.

Because being a normal man or woman has traditionally been defined by attraction to the other sex, the very person of an LGB man or woman is instantly deemed "wrong," as not simply different but as defective or perverse (Brown, 1996; Greene, 2000a). Despite the fact that such thinking is no longer codified in the professional diagnostic nomenclature, it is embedded in Western cultural attitudes and beliefs to which therapists are not immune (Brown, 1996; Dworkin, 1992; Haldeman, 1994, 2000). It is likely that most LGB persons have at one time or another felt as though something were wrong with them in ways that can be connected to the cultural context in which we all live. That subjective sense of shame associated with this difference represents internalized heterosexism or homophobia (Shidlo & Schroeder, 2002). Therapists share that world with their clients because their own identities are subject to the same judgments. How therapists feel about their own gender and other aspects of their identities will influence the way they view the client as well as influence the way psychological services are rendered. The degree to which those feelings are internalized in the client determines whether the feelings are so problematic that they warrant psychological intervention in and of themselves. Similarly, in the LGB-identified therapist, internalized homophobia distorts the therapists' view of the client and the client's dilemma. Homophobia and internalized homophobia also influence the therapist's choice of interventions with clients.

Heterosexist Bias in Research and Clinical Training

The content of training programs has reflected the prevailing heterosexist status quo (Phillips, 2000). In this author's graduate training in clinical psychology in the mid- to late 1970s, heterosexist bias was presented without awareness and without apology. Clients were presumed to be heterosexual unless they stated otherwise. The presumption of heterosexuality was the same for therapists and trainees as well. When clients who were lesbian or gay were presented at case conferences, either their sexual orientation was viewed as the cause of their problems, or they were at best objects of pity. On one end of the spectrum of heterosexism, a supervisor noted that he did not think that therapies to change sexual orientation were successful and that he would not insist on an LGB client pursuing them. However, he indicated that he would tell a client how sorry he felt for them if they did not wish to pursue options that would attempt to make them heterosexual. Another therapist responded to an adult LGB client's conflict around the struggle to reveal his or her sexual orientation to his or her parents with the notion that one of the characterological flaws of LGB people, based on this therapist's experience with clients, was their insistence on "exposing their homosexuality" to their families instead of leaving well enough alone. Their need to "expose" their families to this perceived "sordid" aspect of their lives was seen as inviting the deserved rejection and punishment the LGB clients often received. Phillips (2000) noted that students in professional training programs continue to report exposure to heterosexual bias in some aspect of their training experience or a lack of any coverage of these issues at all. These trends suggest that practitioners must always be aware of the need for additional training, supervision, and consultation when treating LGB clients.

The omission of LGB issues and the presence of heterosexist bias has been a persistent problem in the mainstream psychological literature as well (Goldfried, 2001). Several researchers have documented the dearth of published research on LGB issues from affirmative perspectives in mainstream psychological literature (Allison, Crawford, Echemendia, Robinson, & Knapp, 1994; Biaggio, Orchard, Larson, Petrino, & Mihara, 2003; Murphy, Rawlings, & Howe, 2002), although there are now a range of specialty journals and publications that focus specifically on LGB research. Goldfried (2001) analyzed the degree to which mainstream psychology continues to ignore much of the clinical and research literature on LGB issues and the effects of doing so. The absence of this material in literature on life span, family, substance abuse, victimization and abuse, and couple relationships renders LGB persons invisible, contributing to their marginalization to the LGB ghetto in the professional literature. The invisibility of LGB persons can support the idea that they are not as worthy of consideration as heterosexual clients. This not only reinforces their marginalization, but also leaves us with an incomplete or distorted picture of the myriad effects of clinical problems being investigated. My belief is that at best, research samples that do not include LGB people as part of their demographic base and that do not examine the effects of the omission of LGB people in research do not constitute representative samples and are methodologically flawed and limited in their generalizability to heterosexual persons.

Although training and research issues are beyond the scope of this chapter, I mention them because they are an important and inextricable piece of the matrix in which practice takes place. Training and research can mitigate or facilitate ethical practice with LGB clients. Many practitioners do not have or are not aware of LGB individuals as family members, friends, or acquaintances. Professional training may represent the first time that there is an opportunity to challenge cherished stereotypes and distortions held about LGB individuals by future psychologists, stereotypes that may be acted on if they are not challenged and supplanted with accurate information.

The Continuing Problem of Biased Practice

Despite changes in the diagnostic nomenclature, policies of professional mental health associations that oppose discrimination against LGB individuals, and empirical evidence challenging the foundation of bias against LGB persons, heterosexist bias continues to be a problem in the delivery of psychological services, training, and research (Bieschke, McClanahan, Tozer, Grzegorek, & Park, 2000). Brown (1996) observed that in the aftermath of changes in the diagnostic nomenclature, bias against LGB clients persisted but went underground, where in some ways it is more insidious. In the immediate aftermath of the removal of LGB sexual orientations as a diagnostic category, clinicians perhaps felt less emboldened to openly admit their heterosexism to their professional peers. For example, several practitioners who responded to a Committee on Lesbian and Gay Concerns (Garnets, Hancock, Cochran, Goodchilds, & Peplau, 1991) survey expressed their disagreement with the changes in the nomenclature and said that they would continue to treat LGB sexual orientations as expressions of psychopathology regardless of what any resolution said. Reports from clients support the contention that some practitioners continued to behave this way (Liddle, 1999; Schroeder & Shidlo, 2000; Youngstrom, 1991). I contend that the current national climate of heightened, overt hostility toward lesbians and gay men may has been prompted by resistance to same-sex marriage initiatives and a higher visibility of LGB persons who are social activists. In such a climate, more of the practitioners who harbored heterosexist beliefs may feel comfortable overtly expressing their bias.

Heterosexist bias remains a persistent problem in psychological research, training, and practice (Biaggio et al., 2003; American Psychological Association [APA], Division 44 / Committee on Lesbian, Gay, and Bisexual Concerns Joint Task Force, 2000). What is considered ethical is always a function of the social context, the maturity of the discipline, and the discipline's willingness to interrogate its own embeddedness in the culture itself and in the social pathology of that culture (Greene, 2004). Ethical practice at this juncture includes a willingness to interrogate the values of a culture when those values are directly linked to discrimination, social inequality, and harm to many members of our society. Hence, ethical practitioners understand that clients' problems and beliefs take place in and are shaped by a wider context than just their individual psyches and behaviors. Because research informs training and training in many ways determines practice, the ethical delivery of services to LGB men and women warrants placing all of those professional activities under ethical scrutiny and requiring the highest performance standards for each (Greene, 2004; Haldeman, 2000).

COMPETENCE OF PRACTITIONERS AND THE DIVERSITY OF LGB CLIENTS

Although the APA's "Ethical Principles of Psychologists and Code of Conduct" (APA, 2002) is not written specifically for LGB clients, it contains standards that are particularly relevant to counseling this population. This discussion focuses on those standards and guidelines that are concerned with the diversity of this population. I draw from the Ethics Code itself (APA,

2002) as well as from the APA "Guidelines for Psychotherapy With Lesbian, Gay, and Bisexual Clients" (APA, Division 44 / Committee on Lesbian, Gay and Bisexual Concerns Joint Task Force, 2000). The following discussion is not exhaustive, but seeks to highlight those standards and guidelines that have particular salience and are often problematic in the delivery of psychological services to diverse groups of LGB clients, such as LGB clients of color, LGB men and women with disabilities, children who may be struggling with having a nontraditional sexual orientation, and those clients struggling with the connection between LGB identities and gender imperatives in patriarchal societies. I begin with a general examination of the issues relevant to LGB clients who have multiple stigmatized identities and then consider a few specific examples of those groups.

One of the overarching principles of the APA Ethics Code is to take care to do no harm and to guard against conflicts of interest that would lead to the misuse of professional influence (APA, 2002). Ethical practice requires putting the needs of the client first. This requires all practitioners to examine their own beliefs for any bias that might lead them to place their own needs or beliefs ahead of the client's needs. Principle D (Justice) urges psychologists to practice in ways that recognize all persons as entitled to professional services of equal quality and also encourages psychologists to take care to ensure that their own limitations in expertise and competence do not lead to or condone unfair practices (APA, 2002). Principle E (Respect for People's Rights and Dignity) specifically challenges psychologists to be aware of cultural distinctions that include sexual orientation and to eliminate from their professional work any behavior based on bias and prejudice about those distinctions.

LGB men and women constitute a special population that warrants specific knowledge and skills in the delivery of services that are not routinely acquired in the training of psychologists (Brown, 1996; Dworkin, 1992; Greene, 1994, 2000a). The pervasiveness of heterosexism in the lives of LGB men and women results in the need to create accepting subculture communities. A socially devalued status and its particulars affect LGB persons' relationships with family members, partners, friends, colleagues and coworkers, and community, and this status informs every aspect of LGB individuals' lives in different ways (Garnets et al., 1991). Ethical practitioners must be able to recognize the impact an LGB sexual orientation has on the entirety of the client's life. Not the least of the challenges involved is the development of a healthy self-esteem in the context of a pervasive environment of hostility, violence, secrecy, and stigma. Stages of LGB identity development have been delineated and have been shown to be associated with fairly predictable developmental tasks and challenges (Reynolds & Hanjorgiris, 2000); however, not everyone progresses through those stages in a linear fashion, and practitioners should be familiar with the stages and their relevance with any given client.

Lesbians and gay men are often presumed to be a part of a mono-lithic community. This presumption obscures the wide range of diversity that is represented in all ethnocultural, racial, sex, gender-presentation, socioeconomic, age, and other groups of LGB persons (Dworkin, 1992; Greene, 1997). Brown (1989) suggested that there is no unitary lesbian or gay reality; rather, there are multiple realities as diverse as lesbians and gay men themselves. LGB clients, just like their heterosexual counterparts, have multiple identities, and the degree to which sexual orientation is experienced as the "master" identity varies from person to person (Greene, 2000a, 2000b). Within those multiple identities, some identities may be socially privileged, and others may be disadvantaged (Greene, 2003). Each identity interacts with others to define the uniqueness of each individual's experience. Though LGB people are often grouped together because of their nontraditional identities (see Fassinger & Arseneau, chap. 1, this volume, for a more thorough discussion of this issue), the clinical imperatives and issues that diverse LGB individuals bring to therapy are quite different.

In a patriarchal society, biological sex matters. Whether you are male or female is a determinant in your access to social opportunity and the way you are seen in all arenas of your life (Kaschak, 1992). Being a lesbian, gay man, or bisexual man or woman will elicit different reactions from heterosexual men and women as well as lesbian women and gay men. Kurdek (1994) suggested that gay men are more like heterosexual men and lesbians are more like heterosexual women than they are necessarily like one another. Hence, the therapist must have an understanding of the role of sex, gender, and gender roles in the lives of LGB persons in a patriarchal society as well as a grasp on how heterosexism interacting with sexism can create very different problems and realities.

The social hierarchy poses an additional challenge for LGB persons of color, who are already stigmatized on the basis of their ethnocultural identities. Guidelines 9, 11, 12, and 13 of the "Guidelines for Psychotherapy With Lesbian, Gay, and Bisexual Clients" (APA, 2003; APA, Division 44/Committee on Lesbian, Gay, and Bisexual Concerns Joint Task Force, 2000) specifically address the issue of the multiplicity of LGB persons' identities and lives. The guidelines encourage clinicians to be familiar with diversity of identities and experiences and to recognize the particular challenges that may be related to multiple risk factors for some LGB persons. Simultaneous membership in one or more other socially disadvantaged groups makes it likely that these clients experience multiple oppressions (Greene, 2000b). I now discuss this phenomenon as it applies to LGB men and women of color and LGB people with disabilities, as examples of LGB men and women who are multiply marginalized.

Just as practitioners are obliged to engage in appropriate training to understand the cultural imperatives of LGB men and women on the basis of sexual orientation, they are similarly obliged to do this with respect to the client's country of origin or ethnocultural group (Greene, 1997, 2000b). Because sexuality is culturally defined and understood, the nuances and rules of the client's culture need to be appreciated for the ways they may interact or be in conflict with the identities of people who are lesbian, gay, or bisexual. LGB ethnoracial-minority group members may be confronted with conflicting norms or values as well as competing demands from ethnoracial peers or family to choose one identity over the other in importance. They may also meet with considerable pressure to altogether reject an LGB identity as something that is of dominant cultural origins (Greene, 1997). LGB people of color come from diverse groups that are often socially marginalized by the dominant heterosexual culture. In addition, they experience similar marginalization by the broader LGB community (Greene, 1997, 2000a). Within their ethnoracial groups, they may receive positive cultural mirroring to counter the effects of racism and discrimination as well as a legacy of ways of to respond to and understand the real nature of their discriminatory treatment. They also develop within the protective racial buffer that their families and communities may offer. They often do not, however, get that positive mirroring from family members about their sexual orientation. Further, revealing sexual orientation may put these individuals at risk for rejection by this crucial source of emotional and tangible support (Greene, 1997).

When pressures on an LGB client, from friends and family, to reject LGB sexual orientations are couched in cultural proscriptions, it can be difficult for the practitioner to appropriately evaluate the client's response without some formal knowledge about the culture itself. Often, demands for cultural loyalties and rigid adherence to select religious proscriptions and prohibitions may conceal the family or cultural group's homophobia, heterosexism, internalized racism, or other issues that are more related to the family's preexisting functioning and dynamics (Greene, 2000b). For most LGB clients who are in the midst of such dilemmas, it may be difficult for the client to appreciate the fact that cultural values are being used selectively and in ways that may depart from the manner in which the family or group generally adheres to them. A therapist can only help the client understand the influence of culture and religion if they are conversant in what those cultural and religious norms are as well as in the variations in their actual practice. The therapist must also appreciate the distinction between the cultural or religious value itself and how and when that value is selectively used. Religious beliefs can be viewed as a cultural tool used to exacerbate the tensions, differences, and discord between family members or as a tool to bring disparate family elements together in harmony. While ethical practice requires practitioners to be sensitive to cultural and religious norms, this does not mean that such norms should be accepted blindly without regard for whether or not they are causing harm (Greene, 2003).

Guideline 13 of the "Guidelines for Psychotherapy With Lesbian, Gay, and Bisexual Clients" (APA, 2003; APA, Division 44/Committee on Lesbian, Gay, and Bisexual Concerns Joint Task Force, 2000) addresses the need for psychologists to appreciate the challenges faced by LGB people with disabilities. If LGB people are a footnote in the psychological literature, LGB men and women with disabilities are less than a footnote. Because the presence of a disability can have a direct impact on the degree to which an individual must depend on others, the homophobia in the individuals on whom a disabled person depends can create major obstacles to accessing LGB communities for those LGB clients with a disability. Familiarity with the literature on disability is essential, despite a paucity of literature on LGB persons with disabilities. As for conflicting aspects of their multiple identities, most persons with disabilities are regarded as asexual, though this is not the case (Fine & Asch, 1988). Conversely, excessive sexual behavior is a stereotype of LGB men and women. How LGB men and women with disabilities negotiate these seeming contradictions and the challenges they bring to developing a healthy sexual identity seems to be a significant aspect of their development. Furthermore, LGB communities as well may fail to make themselves accessible to such individuals because of their own internalized heterosexism and their acceptance of stereotypes about who group members are, compounding the challenges the disabled individuals face (Greene, 2000b). Just as internalized heterosexism may lead LGB individuals to reject their own nontraditional identities in favor of idealized depictions of heterosexuals, it can also negatively influence their regard for other people who have been devalued by the dominant cultural status quo with respect to what people are supposed to look like and how they are supposed to behave.

Social class represents another important aspect of identity that interacts with an LGB sexual orientation and that is rarely examined. At both ends of the economic spectrum, social class can directly influence the degree to which a client can literally afford to be out, if being out can result in the loss of one's job (Greene, 2000b). It also affects the degree to which the client has access to the venues in which LGB people often meet and interact, given that socializing at such venues usually requires some level of disposable income. Because poverty increases an individual's social vulnerability and is associated with higher levels of stress, LGB men and women at the lower end of the economic spectrum may be at heightened risk both for the health sequelae that can come as a result of such stressors and for exploitation under threat of exposure of their sexual orientation (Hall & Greene, 2002).

When we think about sexuality and developmental periods, we tend to think about adolescents and adults, despite knowing that many LGB persons are aware of their sexual orientation very early on in life, as children. In both my clinical and personal experience, significant numbers of LGB persons have reported struggling in childhood with a sense of difference about themselves that they may or may not have concretely identified as sexual attraction to members of their gender by the time they were in latency. These individuals' experiences are, however, invisible in the psychological literature. In fact, most children in therapy are assumed to be heterosexual unless they have an atypical gender presentation. It is as if feelings of sexual attraction do not emerge in people until adolescence. Although such feelings are often heightened during adolescence, they do not always begin during that period. Yet many practitioners view children as if they were asexual. These ~~young people's struggles and attempts to determine what their feelings mean and what to do about them may be an invisible factor in school performance and social skill development as well as in disruptive or depressed behavior and other factors that may have triggered a referral for psychological services~~. In this realm, the therapist's preconceived notions about sexuality may interfere with seeing a child as a burgeoning sexual person for whom sexual orientation should not be presumed. Given that the developmental, clinical, and counseling psychology literature has virtually nothing to say about the developmental challenges of LGB sexual orientation for younger children and how these challenges may have an effect on other developmental imperatives, practitioners would be advised to be particularly sensitive to this possibility. Practitioners who routinely treat children may be limited in their competence to treat LGB children who may be struggling with issues about having a nontraditional sexual orientation well before the adolescent period.

Practitioners must be aware that some LGB individuals confront differential risks to their well-being and mental health as a function of their membership in other social groups that may or may not be accepting of their sexual orientation but may be critical to their survival in other ways (Greene, 1997, 2000). Hence, training for mental health professionals must include an appreciation for the diversity within LGB persons as a group and the ways this diversity may affect the clients' understanding of who they are, as well as affect how the client will be seen by other group members and in different contexts. ~~Diverse LGB individuals often face rejection of nontraditional sexual orientations within their ethnoracial group, but they also experience marginalization in the dominant LGB community because of their ethnoracial identity~~. Such individuals may face multiple marginalizations because they have more than one important aspect of their person stigmatized. This kind of multiple marginalization can leave clients feeling as though they are always under siege and that no one community is completely safe. This ~~heightened marginalization can be a locus of psychological vulnerability and places individuals at heightened risk for mental health problems~~ (Greene, 1997). Although marginalization and social disadvantage can lead some individuals to develop strengths and talents, these factors may just as easily leave individuals vulnerable to erosions in their self-esteem, transform mundane and routine stressors into something greater, and make their healthy psychological survival doubtful. In the assessment realm, a therapist's competence is also reflected in the ability to distinguish between symptoms of mental disorders and symptoms that are a reaction to the extreme stressors that an individual confronts on a daily basis. The ways that multiple identities complicate treatment and the ethical approach to their resolution requires attention in the formal training of clinicians as well as in their continued education if they are to fulfill the ethical mandate to be competent in the delivery of services to this population.

ETHICS OF CONVERSION THERAPY

LGB clients seek psychological services for many of the same reasons that heterosexual clients seek such services. It is common, however, for LGB persons who are distressed about their sexual orientation to seek psychological services for that reason as well (Bieschke, Paul, & Blasko, chap. 12, this volume). The hostile social climate for LGB people makes that distress normative. The treatment of this dilemma raises perhaps one of the most controversial issues in considerations of ethical practice: conversion therapies. Conversion therapies are controversial practices; hence, they raise serious ethical questions. APA commentary on conversion therapies states, "These findings suggest that efforts to repair homosexuals are nothing more than social prejudice garbed in psychological accoutrements" (Welch, 1990, cited in Haldeman, 1991, p. 160). Central to this dilemma are two questions: Is providing therapy to change sexual orientation unethical? And is it unethical to deny therapy to change sexual orientation to those who want the therapy (Lasser & Gottlieb, 2004)? Discussion of these questions revolves around considering why a client wants to change, the client's autonomy and right to demand the kind of treatment he or she wants, and the social milieu in which heterosexism and homophobia are ubiquitous and have been pervasive in our professional paradigms and conduct (Brown, 1996; Haldeman, 1991, 2000).

The belief that LGB sexual orientations are chosen and heterosexual sexual orientations are not (Greene, 2000a) is often a rationale for abuse of LGB persons and represents a critical context in which to examine the ethics of conversion therapies. The psychological literature cannot offer conclusive arguments about the origin of any sexual orientation, and clearly individuals of all sexual orientations can have sexual desire and choose not to act on their feelings. It is also true that some individuals feel that they chose their LGB sexual orientation. Conversion therapies, however, raise a question worthy of consideration. What if LGB men and women *could* choose to change their orientation to heterosexual? Should they be obliged to do so simply to gain fair and equal treatment and to avoid abuse that is based on distortions of who they are? Furthermore, in the context of psychological literature that offers no evidence of impairment on the basis of sexual orientation per se, what kind of message do practitioners who offer conversion therapies send not only to their clients but also to society about the social pathology of heterosexism? Supporting conversion therapies can send a message that the individual, rather than societal attitudes, is the problem (Haldeman, 2000).

Despite changes in the diagnostic nomenclature, efforts to change the sexual orientation of gay and lesbian clients have persisted and are referred to as reparative (Nicolosi, 1991; Socarides, 1995) or conversion therapies (Haldeman, 1991). Reparative therapies are based on the assumption that LGB sexual orientations are a function of pathological development and as such should be corrected (Nicolosi, 1991). These therapies conceptualize minority sexual orientation as a form of pathology that should be therapeutically corrected and view changes in the diagnostic nomenclature as based on gay activism rather than on science. This view is not supported by most professional mental health disciplines (Haldeman, 2000). Conversion therapies state that they do not take a position based on pathology. Rather, their assertions are based on the belief that the decision to convert is one that should be an option available to clients if they want it. APA's resolution on sexual orientation establishes the position of the association. This position states that there is no credible evidence of pathology associated with LGB sexual orientations per se and that therapy should not "treat" minority sexual orientation as something based on pathology (Committee on Lesbian & Gay Concerns, 1986).

Bieschke et al. (chap. 12, this volume), Haldeman (1991, 1994, 1999, 2000), Schroeder and Shidlo (2001), and Shidlo and Schroeder (2002) have conducted extensive reviews of reports from ex-gay ministries and psychological research (Spitzer, 2003; Yarhouse, 1998; Yarhouse & Throckmorton, 2002). A detailed review of these works is beyond the scope of this discussion, but these authors generally reported that sexual orientation can be altered in a select group of highly motivated clients (Bieschke et al., chap. 12, this volume; Shidlo & Schroeder, 2002; Yarhouse & Throckmorton, 2002). Haldeman (1999, 2000) and Shidlo and Schroeder (2002) critiqued this research on a range of methodological grounds and suggested that even therapists advocating these services (excluding ex-gay ministries) claim that roughly only 30% of individuals who desire change are actually successful and that success is defined differently in each study (Brown, 1996; Haldeman 1991, 1994, 1999, 2000; Shidlo & Schroeder, 2002). Moreover, Haldeman (1999) argued that his clinical and anecdotal data indicate that many clients are directly harmed by these therapies; therefore, the therapies do not represent benign undertakings. Haldeman (1999) reported that harmful reactions to conversion therapies ranged in severity depending on the type of conversion treatment utilized. Such therapies have ranged from the introduction of electric shock and vomit-inducing drugs while homoerotic material is presented to more recent religious or prayer-based talk therapies (Haldeman, 1999). Harm to clients ranged from experiencing exacerbated levels of shame and "asexual" outcomes to continued depression about their sexual orientation and concomitant shame about failing to alter it. Some clients, Haldeman (1999) reported, develop severe problems in interpersonal interactions, particularly sexual intimacy. Shidlo and Schroeder (2002) reported similar findings as well as clients' exacerbated alienation and loneliness, spiritual harm, and fears of being a child abuser. In summary, there is no credible empirical evidence to warrant the assumption that therapies aimed at altering sexual orientation are successful at completely changing sexual orientation when sexual orientation is viewed as a complex identity with many components in addition to behavior. If the client wants this kind of treatment, however, does that mean that it is ethical and that practitioners should provide it? Based on APA ethical standards and the consensus of the psychological literature, it is not.

One argument in favor of conversion therapies is that clients' autonomy is infringed upon if they cannot make the choice themselves (Yarhouse, 1998; Yarhouse & Throckmorton, 2002). But although ethical practice warrants the recognition of client autonomy and the right to make choices the therapist might not personally endorse, that position is not synonymous with providing whatever intervention clients want just because they want it, particularly if the therapist understands the risk-versus-benefit and the likelihood of certain adverse outcomes. Furthermore, advocates for conversion therapies do not suggest that if heterosexual clients want to change their sexual orientation, therapists should do so. These treatments are aimed primarily at LGB people, not at all clients. That alone makes the notion of client autonomy as a rationale for these treatments suspicious. Professionals are expected to have special knowledge that the client does not have about the relative risks and benefits of procedures as well as the ability to understand both the procedure and the meaning of the client's wish in the prevailing social context. Therapists always have the responsibility to avoid practices that may cause the client harm. Beyond this, there are serious questions about whether it is even possible to encourage conversion efforts without directly reinforcing heterosexist bias. Furthermore, it is unlikely that people would seek to change their sexual orientation if they were not being punished in some way for that identity or behavior or did not fear the possibility of this. One cannot separate the potential for rejection, ridicule, and violence that is a factor in such decisions. Self-hate and self-loathing expressed by LGB clients do not develop in a vacuum. LGB clients who feel negatively about themselves have learned to do so, whether from religious or secular sources. This does not mean that they cannot unlearn those attitudes.

The clients' feelings that they are morally wrong can reflect their attempt to make emotional sense out of the rejecting behavior of many of the loved and trusted people in their lives, as well as their attempt to hold on to values that they hold dear. Many clients have internalized values that include a condemnation of their sexual orientation, and they have been exposed to only that one negative interpretation of those values; they often have had no exposure to people who may be viewed as faithful but have not internalized heterosexist values. Heterosexist values are often based on a history of unchallenged cultural myth and distortion. The ethical clinician is challenged to critique, not reinforce, the social pathology that created and maintains distortions about LGB people. The offer of conversion therapy in such instances represents collusion with the part of the clients that feels that *they* are the problem. Clinicians are reminded that when clients have internalized distortions about other aspects of themselves, therapy's purpose is to assist the clients in exploring the distortion, not to simply collude with the clients' assumptions about themselves just because the clients *believe* the assumptions are true or because the assumptions are presented as beliefs based on religious faith. In therapy, we accept that the client may absolutely believe a great many things, some of which may be attributed to religious or cultural values. When those beliefs become so intrapunitive that they become psychologically harmful to the client, we seek to explore them so that the client can better understand and critique their harmful effects as well as their origins.

Yarhouse (1998) argued that many clients are insistent that they want to change their sexual orientation as a function of their religious or cultural beliefs and that they will not take no for an answer. Clients' *beliefs* are always a function of many factors and can represent both conscious and unconscious needs to see the world in particular ways. These may include distortions about themselves and about others. In the case of heterosexism, all people in this society are reinforced for having such beliefs and are not generally encouraged to challenge them. Furthermore, there are divergent opinions about LGB sexual orientation within religious and cultural groups; hence, the idea that there is only one way to interpret or understand a cultural or religious proscription is always questionable. Blind acceptance of a client's request is far from the only way to work with clients distressed about their sexual orientation. Doing so may represent the therapist's unwillingness or limitation in his or her ability to engage clients in exploring their beliefs, not with the intent of changing those beliefs, but with the intent of assisting the clients in understanding how they make choices. For many religiously committed LGB clients, choosing between religious participation and LGB sexual orientation is not always the only option available to them although they may *believe* this to be so. Religious congregations that are supportive and affirming exist across all major religious denominations and can represent alternative choices. In the presence of such options, therapists can explore all aspects of the client's belief system in ways that are respectful. The pervasiveness of heterosexism makes it unlikely that most LGB persons would not at some point experience distress about their sexual orientation. In fact such distress may even be considered normative. Distinctions must be made, however, among distress about what they think being LGB makes of them, distress related to internalized heterosexism, and distress about the psychological and physical violence that clients may face if they identify as LGB persons.

Yarhouse's (1998) assertion is that valuative frameworks or religious values of clients influence their feelings about same-sex desire and that clients who wish to change their orientations as a function of those beliefs should be assisted in doing so. Failure to do so in that context is, according to Yarhouse, culturally intolerant of the client's religious values. Yet Yarhouse approached these values as if they have little to do with a homophobic social milieu. It is impossible, however, to separate valuative frameworks, religious or otherwise, from the culture in which those frameworks are embedded. In this case, the homophobia that is a persistent feature of Western culture is a part of the context of the client's values. In that context of patriarchal values and contempt for same-sex relationships that permeate the culture, religious doctrine is selectively used to support the social status quo. Most religious texts have internal inconsistencies that are a part of the mystery of religious faith. It is problematic but has not been unusual at different points in our history for religious teachings and doctrine to be selectively used to support behavior that maintains social hierarchies. For example, in a patriarchal culture, there are many Bible verses that can be used to suggest that women should occupy a status of second-class citizen. Similarly, in a homophobic culture, selective verses can be used against LGB men and women. History, however, has shown us that the Bible and other religious texts have been used to support miscegenation laws, racial segregation, the Holocaust, slavery, genocide among Native Americans, and other debacles that in the 21st century we would find abhorrent. The most potent symbol of racial terrorism and White supremacy in the 20th century was a burning cross. In that context ethical practitioners understood expressions of self-hate among Black American or Jewish clients as a function of a society that taught them to despise themselves and that made them targets of violence. Hence, beliefs about sexual orientation do not occur in a historical or professional vacuum, but in a much broader social context in which some groups are privileged and others are socially disadvantaged. In this context, not all values are benign.

Yarhouse's (1998) statement that the client's values must be respected out of a tolerance for diversity suggests that intolerance for any value is disrespectful of the client, particularly if the client's belief is based on religious belief. But even though ethical practice dictates that practitioners must be tolerant of human diversity and that diversity is reflected in differences in values, it also obliges practitioners to do no harm. It is important to acknowledge that some values, if acted upon, may be damaging to self and others. In effect, such values cause harm. An important question to ask is whether or not the value in question supports or requires the marginalization or estrangement of one group or groups from the others. Does the value in question scapegoat or deem one group less valuable, deserving, or human than others? Essentially, does the valuative framework in question explicitly devalue people and in so doing cause harm? Every group in human history that has practiced social domination or genocide against another group did so out of a valuative framework, and such frameworks were often religiously based. Most had values to support their behavior, which was often explained as a religious mandate and often enjoyed wide popular support. Invariably, the dominant group or groups sought to impose values on subordinate groups and often imposed violence on subordinate group members.

LGB men and women may be seen as a subordinate social group that some valuative frameworks deem inferior, defective, or immoral and that, on that basis, some valuative frameworks justify harming, by denying individuals in the subordinate group equal access to social privileges and opportunities and by directing violence toward them. The harm and the compromised psychological functioning that result from such treatment have been historically minimized or considered a consequence of group membership. To the extent that conversion therapies fail to critique social pathology and support and do not challenge the clients' beliefs that they are defective, such therapies cause harm. Reinforcing rather than challenging homophobia and heterosexism causes LGB people and their families harm.

CONCLUSION

The APA Ethics Code explicitly and implicitly urges therapists to be aware of their own beliefs, predispositions, and worldviews and of how those views and beliefs affect their work. All clinicians have values and beliefs on which they might stake their lives. However, the ethical challenge to therapists is to understand the beliefs and feelings of clients whose worldview may be very different. The capacity to step outside of one's own beliefs is critical to the ability to practice in accordance with ethical professional guidelines that urge respect for the dignity of all clients. Despite this mandate, many therapists may find that they cannot suspend their own moral or religious judgments about clients. Therapists who are unable to see LGB clients as people who are not defective or somehow less deserving because of their sexual orientation should not treat those clients. The most ethical action is to refer the client elsewhere, acknowledging that it is because of the therapist's limitation, not a failure or defect of the client.

Perhaps the most persistent ethical and clinical problem in the treatment of LGB clients is the problem of antigay bias. Professional incompetence and lack of training to provide culturally informed and competent services represent other challenges. Course work and supervised practice are essential to implementing the ethical mandates for service delivery at the highest levels. Another component of ethical practice involves the development of more representative research on LGB populations and their inclusion in mainstream psychological research. Competent treatment of LGB persons inextricably includes an understanding of the pervasive role of heterosexism in LGB persons' lives and in society as a whole and of heterosexism's effects on theoretical paradigms, research, training, and the personal beliefs and attitudes of therapists. Finally, therapists are obliged to be tolerant and accepting of clients' beliefs; however, they are also responsible for helping clients to scrutinize all of their beliefs and behaviors and to identify those that are harmful to themselves and others. That, however, is often easier said than done.

REFERENCES

Allison, K. W., Crawford, I., Echemendia, R., Robinson, L., & Knapp, D. (1994). Human diversity and professional competence: Training in clinical and counseling psychology revisited. *American Psychologist, 49,* 792–796.

American Psychological Association, Division 44/Committee on Lesbian, Gay, and Bisexual Concerns Joint Task Force on Guidelines for Psychotherapy With Lesbian, Gay, and Bisexual Clients. (2000). Guidelines for psychotherapy with lesbian, gay, and bisexual clients. *American Psychologist, 55,* 1440–1451.

American Psychological Association. (2002). Ethical principles of psychologists and code of conduct. *American Psychologist, 57,* 1060–1073.

American Psychological Association. (2003). Guidelines on multicultural education, training, research, practice and organizational change for psychologists. *American Psychologist, 58,* 377–402.

Biaggio, M., Orchard, S., Larson, J., Petrino, K., & Mihara, R. (2003). Guidelines for gay/lesbian/bisexual-affirmative educational practices in graduate psychology programs. *Professional Psychology: Research and Practice, 34,* 548–554.

Bieschke, K., McClanahan, M., Tozer, E., Grzegorek, J. L., & Park, J. (2000). Programmatic research on the treatment of lesbian, gay and bisexual clients: The past, the present, and the course for the future. In R. M. Perez, K. A. DeBord, & K. J. Bieschke (Eds.), *Handbook of counseling and psychotherapy with lesbian, gay, and bisexual clients* (pp. 309–335). Washington, DC: American Psychological Association.

Brown, L. S. (1988). Lesbians, gay men and their families: Common clinical issues. *Journal of Gay and Lesbian Psychotherapy, 1,* 65-77.

Brown, L. S. (1996). Ethical concerns with sexual minority patients. In R. Cabaj & T. Stein (Eds.), *Textbook of homosexuality and mental health* (pp. 897–916). Washington, DC: American Psychiatric Press.

Committee on Lesbian and Gay Concerns. (1986). *APA policy statement on lesbian and gay issues.* Washington, DC: American Psychological Association.

Dworkin, S. (1992). Some ethical considerations when counseling gay, lesbian and bisexual clients. In S. Dworkin & F. Gutierrez (Eds.), *Counseling gay men and lesbians: Journey to the end of the rainbow* (pp. 325–334). Alexandria, VA: American Association of Counseling and Development.

Fine, M., & Asch, A. (1988). Beyond pedestals. In M. Fine & A. Asch (Eds.), *Women with disabilities: Essays in psychology, culture and politics* (pp. 1–37). Philadelphia: Temple University Press.

Garnets, L., Hancock, K. A., Cochran, S. D., Goodchilds, J., & Peplau, L. A. (1991). Issues in psychotherapy with lesbians and gay men: A survey of psychologists. *American Psychologist, 46,* 964–972.

Goldfried, M. R. (2001). Integrating gay, lesbian and bisexual issues in mainstream psychology. *American Psychologist, 56,* 977–988.

Greene, B. (1994). Lesbian and gay sexual orientations: Implications for clinical training, practice, and research. In B. Greene & G. Herek (Eds.), *Psychological perspectives on lesbian and gay issues: Vol. 1. Lesbian and gay psychology: Theory, research and clinical applications* (pp. 1–24). Thousand Oaks, CA: Sage.

Greene, B. (1997). Ethnic minority lesbians and gay men: Mental health and treatment issues. In B. Greene (Ed.), *Ethnic and cultural diversity among lesbians and gay men* (pp. 216–239). Thousand Oaks, CA: Sage.

Greene, B. (2000a). African American lesbian and bisexual women in feminist psychodynamic psychotherapy: Surviving and thriving between a rock and a hard place. In L. C. Jackson & B. Greene (Eds.), *Psychotherapy with African American women: Innovations in psychodynamic perspectives and practice* (pp. 82–125). New York: Guilford Press.

Greene, B. (2000b). Beyond heterosexism and across the cultural divide. In B. Greene & G. L. Croom (Eds.), *Education, research, and practice in lesbian, gay, bisexual, and transgendered psychology: A resource manual* (pp. 1–45). Thousand Oaks, CA: Sage.

Greene, B. (2003). What difference does a difference make? Societal privilege, disadvantage, and discord in human relationships. In J. Robinson & L. James (Eds.), *Diversity in human interactions: The tapestry of America* (pp. 3–20). New York: Oxford University Press.

Greene, B. (2004). African American lesbians and other culturally diverse people in psychodynamic psychotherapies: Useful paradigms or oxymoron? *Journal of Lesbian Studies, 8,* 57–77.

Haldeman, D. (1991). Sexual orientation conversion therapy for gay men and lesbians: A scientific examination. In J. Gonsiorek & J. Weinrich (Eds.), *Homosexuality: Research implications for public policy* (pp. 149–160). Newbury Park, CA: Sage.

Haldeman, D. (1994). The practice and ethics of sexual orientation conversion therapy. *Journal of Consulting and Clinical Psychology, 62,* 221–227.

Haldeman, D. (1999). The pseudo-science of sexual orientation conversion therapy. *Angles: The Policy Journal of the Institute for Gay and Lesbian Strategic Studies, 4,* 1–4.

Haldeman, D. (2000). Therapeutic responses to sexual orientation: Psychology's evolution. In B. Greene & G. L. Croom (Eds.), *Education, research and practice in lesbian, gay, bisexual and transgendered psychology: A resource manual* (pp. 244–262). Thousand Oaks, CA: Sage.

Haldeman, D. (2002). Gay rights, patients rights: The implications of sexual orientation conversion therapy. *Professional Psychology: Research and Practice, 33,* 260–264.

Hall, R. E., & Greene, B. (2002). Not any one thing: The complex legacy of social class on African American lesbian relationships. *Journal of Lesbian Studies, 6,* 65–74.

Kaschak, E. (1992). *Engendered lives: A new psychology of women's experience.* New York: Basic Books.

Kurdek, L. A. (1994). The nature and correlates of relationship quality in gay, lesbian and heterosexual cohabiting couples: A test of the individual, difference, interdependent, and discrepancy models. In B. Greene & G. Herek (Eds.), *Lesbian and gay psychology: Theory, research & clinical applications* (pp. 133–155). Thousand Oaks, CA: Sage.

Lasser, J. S., & Gottlieb, M. C. (2004). Treating patients distressed regarding their sexual orientation: Clinical and ethical alternatives. *Professional Psychology: Research and Practice, 35,* 194–200.

Liddle, B. J. (1999). Gay and lesbian clients' ratings of psychiatrists, psychologists, social workers, & counselors. *Journal of Gay & Lesbian Psychotherapy, 3,* 81–93.

Murphy, J. A., Rawlings, E. I., & Howe, S. R. (2002). A survey of clinical psychologists on treating lesbian, gay, and bisexual clients. *Professional Psychology: Research and Practice, 33,* 183–189.

Nicolosi, J. (1991). *Reparative therapy of male homosexuality.* Northvale, NJ: Jason Aronson.

Phillips, J. (2000). Training issues and considerations. In R. M. Perez, K. A. DeBord, & K. J. Bieschke (Eds.), *Handbook of counseling and psychotherapy with lesbian, gay, and bisexual clients* (pp. 337–358). Washington, DC: American Psychological Association.

Reynolds, A. L., & Hanjorgiris, W. F. (2000). Coming out: Lesbian, gay, and bisexual identity development. In R. M. Perez, K. A. DeBord, & K. J. Bieschke (Eds.), *Handbook of counseling and psychotherapy with lesbian, gay, and bisexual clients* (pp. 35–56). Washington, DC: American Psychological Association.

Schroeder, M., & Shidlo, A. (2001). Ethical issues in sexual orientation conversion therapies: An empirical study of consumers. *Journal of Gay & Lesbian Psychotherapy, 5,* 131–166.

Shidlo, A., & Schroeder, M. (2002). Changing sexual orientation: A consumer's report. *Professional Psychology: Research and Practice, 33,* 249–259.

Socarides, C. W. (1995). *Homosexuality: A freedom too far.* Phoenix, AZ: Adam Margrave Books.

Spitzer, R. L. (2003). Can some gay men and lesbians change their sexual orientation? 200 subjects report a change from homosexual to heterosexual orientation. *Archives of Sexual Behavior, 32,* 403–412.

Throckmorton, W. (2002). Initial empirical and clinical findings concerning the change process for ex-gays. *Professional Psychology: Research and Practice, 33,* 242–248.

Welch, B. (1990, January 26). *Statement on homosexuality.* (Available from American Psychological Association, 750 First Street, NE, Washington, DC 20002-4242.)

Yarhouse, M. A. (1998). When clients seek treatment for same sex attraction: Ethical issues in the "right to choose" debate. *Psychotherapy, 35,* 248–259.

Yarhouse, M. A. (2001). Sexual identity development: The influence of valuative frameworks on identity synthesis. *Psychotherapy, 38,* 331–341.

Yarhouse, M. A., & Throckmorton, W. (2002). Ethical issues in attempt to ban reorientation therapies. *Psychotherapy: Theory/Research/Practice/Training, 39,* 66–75.

Youngstrom, N. (1991, July). Lesbians and gay men still find bias in therapy. *APA Monitor, 22,* 24–25.

8

AFFIRMATIVE LESBIAN, GAY, AND BISEXUAL COUNSELING WITH ALL CLIENTS

CONNIE R. MATTHEWS

In the mid-1990s, when I was doing a presentation at a national conference, a participant who worked as a counselor at a very large university in a major metropolitan area reported that in 17 years she had never had a gay, lesbian, or bisexual client. This is unlikely. The likelihood of one practicing counseling for 17 years without seeing anybody but heterosexual clients is slim. It is, however, quite probable that this counselor had numerous clients whom she did not know were gay, lesbian, or bisexual. Thus, one of the main points of this chapter is that affirmative counseling with gay, lesbian, and bisexual clients begins before we know the client's sexual orientation.

Lesbian, gay, and bisexual (LGB) individuals have been referred to as a "hidden minority" (e.g., Fassinger, 1991; Pope, 1995). This is because, for a long time, they received very little attention in scholarly research or graduate training and because their minority status is not immediately evident. A client's sexual orientation can only be determined when the topic is openly discussed. However, because of the prejudice and discrimination that accompany a nonheterosexual orientation (e.g., see Herek, 1995), lesbians, gay men, and bisexual individuals are often reluctant to offer this information. Furthermore, depending on their process of identity development, clients may not always be sure what information to offer. This means that it is incumbent upon the counselor to create an atmosphere that makes it safe for clients to explore this aspect of their lives.

This chapter begins by addressing the nature of heterosexism and its effect on the therapeutic relationship. Included is a discussion of the work that therapists themselves need to do with respect to attitudes and beliefs about sexual orientation. The chapter also includes discussion of the organizational climate as well as direct work with clients. This section is followed by a brief review of some of the major models of sexual orientation identity development. Finally, a few concerns that are unique to the LGB population are addressed, along with their implications for clinical practice. This chapter focuses on work with LGB clients whose presenting problems are either developmental adjustments or are tangentially related to sexual orientation. For more in-depth discussion of the issues facing clients who are severely conflicted about their sexual orientation, see Beckstead and Israel (chap. 9, this volume).

HETEROSEXISM AND THE THERAPEUTIC RELATIONSHIP

How Heterosexism Works

Heterosexism has been defined as "the ideological system that denies, denigrates, and stigmatizes any nonheterosexual form of behavior, identity, relationship, or community" (Herek, 1995, p. 321). In this 1995 study, Herek explained that there are dual and mutually reinforcing processes operating within heterosexism. First, heterosexuality is considered the norm to such a degree that any alternative perspectives are left invisible. Second, when gay, lesbian, bisexual, queer, or other orientations do become visible, the consequences are prejudice, discrimination, and stigma. It is important to keep in mind, however, that such overt "hatred and persecution" are not necessary for heterosexism to be present (Brown, 1996, p. 900). It is also critical to remember that heterosexual counselors are not the only ones who need to be aware of heterosexism. Because we have all been raised and live in a heterosexist culture, LGB counselors can also be subject to that culture's influence. The psychological literature has begun to address the implications of the assumption of heterosexuality for LGB individuals (e.g., Brown, 1996; Garnets, Hancock, Cochran, Goodchilds, & Peplau, 1991; Ritter & Terndrup, 2002).

Assumption of heterosexuality refers to the premise that all people are heterosexual unless and until they indicate otherwise. As the anecdote at the opening of this chapter points out, therapists frequently operate under this premise, including many therapists who otherwise work to practice affirmatively with clients they know are gay, lesbian, or bisexual. Although the intention is usually not malicious, assuming heterosexuality prior to discussing sexual orientation with a client is a biased and ethically problematic practice (Brown, 1996; Garnets et al., 1991) because it is harmful to clients.

Assuming heterosexuality marginalizes gay, lesbian, and bisexual individuals by forcing them into the role of "other" (Reynolds, 2003). Furthermore, assuming heterosexuality places the burden of disclosing this otherness on the gay, lesbian, or bisexual individual. Given the discrimination and prejudice that exist in society, such disclosure always represents some level of risk for the individual (Reynolds, 2003). When therapists assume heterosexuality, they reinforce the marginality that LGB clients experience and add turmoil to the therapy process by forcing clients to either keep an important secret or take a significant risk in raising the issue of sexual orientation. Thus, it is vital that all counselors remain open to the possibility that any client who walks through the door might identify him- or herself anywhere along a broad continuum with respect to sexual orientation. In addition to recognizing that all clients are not heterosexual, it is important to remember that gay and lesbian are not the only alternatives. Bisexual individuals frequently experience additional invisibility when therapists assume heterosexuality or homosexuality based on the gender of a client's current partner rather than exploring further (Fox, 1996; Ochs, 1996). Potoczniak (chap. 5, this volume) and Firestein (chap. 4, this volume) address bisexuality in greater detail.

It is also important to understand that a client's current identity may not be a fixed point, but rather may be fluid over time (Fox, 1996; Golden, 1987; Reynolds, 2003). In addition, it is important not to make assumptions based on current behavior or marital status (Reynolds, 2003). In her investigation of the reactions of gay, lesbian, and bisexual people to the antigay amendment passed by voters in Colorado in the early 1990s, Russell (2000) found many bisexual individuals who were in mixed-sex relationships reporting that they were not open about their bisexuality because of safety concerns. Therapists must provide opportunity and a safe environment for clients to share such information.

Avoiding Heterosexism

It is important for therapists to be proactive in minimizing heterosexist assumptions and approaches. This means being open-minded with respect to each client's sexual orientation and also communicating this openness to clients, beginning with promotional materials. Literature about a practice or agency that contains a nondiscrimination statement that is inclusive of sexual orientation communicates to prospective clients that the professionals involved are aware that there are a variety of possibilities with respect to sexual orientation and that discrimination is often linked to some of those orientations. Such a statement lets LGB clients know that the agency has considered the possibility that LGB individuals may be clients.

Likewise, agencies can create a climate that communicates affirmation through the policies and practices that are established (Eldridge & Barnett, 1991). Forms that gather personal information about clients should reflect the fact that some clients may be in permanent committed relationships that do not legally qualify as marriages. If reading material is provided in waiting rooms, it should include publications of particular interest to the LGB population. If informational material about different problems (e.g., depression, anxiety, substance abuse) is provided for clients, there should be some materials that address concerns unique to the gay, lesbian, and bisexual population (e.g., coming out, coping with oppression). Agencies should have readily available information about resources in the community that might be helpful for LGB clients. When providing information, counselors should include materials specific to each group (gay, lesbian, bisexual) as well as information that addresses the more general LGB community.

Eldridge and Barnett (1991) provided a useful overview of practices that help to create a climate that is not heterosexist. Bieschke and Matthews (1996, 2003; Matthews & Bieschke, 2003; Matthews, Selvidge, & Fisher, 2005) operationalized some of these practices and others to develop an instrument that assesses the degree to which the climate in counseling agencies is nonheterosexist. They found that the organizational climate in which counselors worked was predictive of the degree to which individual counselors practiced affirmatively (Bieschke & Matthews, 1996, 2003; Matthews et al., 2005). The more that an agency established a nonheterosexist climate, the more likely individual counselors were to be affirmative in their work with clients.

Individual therapists can also help to create such a climate. Just as it is important for counseling agencies to communicate openness and affirmation, so too is it necessary for counselors to convey this affirmation to all clients, regardless of how clients identify themselves. A therapist's office can say a lot to a client. Something as simple as a rainbow button pinned to a bulletin board can tell the client looking for signs of safety that the counselor has made a conscious effort to communicate affirmation. Similarly, the books on a therapist's shelf tell something about areas in which the therapist has sought to educate him or herself. Having this handbook and other books about LGB clients on the shelf indicates to the observant client that the counselor has taken the time to learn something about the client's experience.

Creating a climate reflective of affirmation includes therapists' communicating affirmation within the therapeutic relationship. Again, much of this begins with not making assumptions about clients. It is important to use language that does not assume heterosexuality. If a client is dating, it is appropriate to ask whether she or he dates men, women, both, or people who define themselves in some other way. Asking if a client has a partner is more affirming than asking about a husband or wife. A thorough intake should address sexual orientation, whether the client raises the issue or not. This should be done in a way that allows clients to define themselves, but that also invites clients to discuss the meaning of that definition. For example, a Latino man may identify himself as heterosexual even if his sexual relationships are exclusively with men if his role is always the active or inserter role (Rust, 1996). Likewise, some clients may struggle with identifying themselves with respect to sexual orientation at all because sexuality is not a source of personal identity in some cultures (Rust, 1996). Rust has stressed that this should not be interpreted as denial or lack of maturity, but rather should be examined within a cultural context.

It is also important for both LGB and heterosexual therapists to have enough knowledge of lesbian, gay, and bisexual experience to grasp nuances that clients may use as a way of testing counselors' ability to understand them. There are a number of ways to become familiar. One could begin by reading books or watching movies that are intended for an LGB audience or that seek to educate on this issue. There are also numerous local and national periodicals that target gay men, lesbians, and bisexual individuals. In the end, though, there is no substitute for going into the community. This could involve participating in a local Pride or Unity rally, attending an LGB spiritual event or service, or becoming involved with a local community center or agency serving this population. Many communities have a gay switchboard, which can serve as a resource for identifying groups or organizations.

Overcoming Heterosexism

A critical first step that counselors need to take to avoid perpetuating heterosexism is to perform an honest self-examination of their own attitudes and beliefs regarding sexual orientation (Haldeman & Buhrke, 2003; Pope, 1995). This is consistent with the standards for multicultural competency (American Psychological Association [APA], 2003; Sue, Arredondo, & McDavis, 1992), which explicitly incorporate a commitment to cultural awareness and knowledge of self and others. In addition, these standards call for therapists and counselors to be aware of their own biases. Mental health professionals live in the same heterosexist society as everybody else and are subject to the biases and prejudices that permeate that culture (e.g., Garnets et al., 1991). This is true for therapists who identify as gay, lesbian, or bisexual as well as for those who identify as heterosexual (Brown, 1996).

There are a number of areas to explore. First, to what degree does one consider a range of possibilities as viable? Does one perceive a variety of equally acceptable alternatives with respect to sexual orientation, or is heterosexuality considered preferable, with other identities being acceptable but less preferable (or even unacceptable)? Second, to what extent does one place limits on those who do not identify themselves as heterosexual? These limits might pertain to such factors as career options or parenting or other areas in which gay men, lesbians, and bisexual individuals have historically been discriminated against. Third, to what degree does one fully embrace the professional organizations' removal of homosexuality as mental illness, or does one view LGB orientation as indicative of instability, regardless of the official position of one's association? Finally, one must examine his or her religious beliefs regarding the shamefulness or sinfulness of nonheterosexual orientations. Religion can be a particularly difficult problem for many LGB individuals. This is an issue that often brings them into therapy (Ritter & Terndrup, 2002). Therapists need to be able to help clients address religion and spirituality in ways that are affirmative, not further condemning (see Ritter & Terndrup, 2002).

One related topic that has received recent attention in the literature has been conversion therapy, or treating clients with the goal of changing the clients' sexual orientation from gay, lesbian, or bisexual to heterosexual (see Benedict, VandenBos, & Kenkel, 2002; Shidlo, Schroeder, & Drescher, 2001). Serious ethical concerns have been raised about the appropriateness of therapists' practicing conversion therapy (e.g., Haldeman, 1994; Tozer & McClanahan, 1999). Scholars have, however, also raised the question of respecting religious diversity and have begun addressing the complexities of trying to adhere to sometimes-competing ethical imperatives (e.g., Yarhouse & Burkett, 2002). Many professional associations, including the APA (1998), have taken official positions on the practice of conversion therapy. Therapists need to be familiar with the guidance provided by their professional associations on this topic and with the research regarding the effectiveness of conversion therapy and must be keenly aware of their own attitudes and biases regarding this issue (Beckstead & Israel, chap. 9, this volume, address working with clients conflicted about sexual orientation; Bieschke, Paul, & Blasko, chap. 12, this volume, address the empirical research on conversion therapy).

For therapists who identify as heterosexual, another critical area of self-awareness involves one's own heterosexual identity development. Although inquiry into sexual orientation identity development initially focused on gay men and lesbians and then, to a lesser extent, on bisexual men and women, Worthington and Mohr (2002; Mohr, 2002; Worthington, Savoy, Dillon, & Vernaglia, 2002) have recently proposed models of heterosexual identity development. They argue the importance of examining identity development from a majority-group perspective as well as from a minority-group perspective. Heterosexuality thus becomes not simply an assumption, but a sexual orientation identity that people develop, just as people develop a gay, lesbian, bisexual, or other identity. Heterosexuality is different, however, in that part of that identity involves membership in an oppressive majority group. As lesbians, gay men, and bisexual individuals develop an awareness of the stigma and prejudice associated with their identities, heterosexual individuals who examine their heterosexuality become aware of the privilege that accompanies that identity. This has a number of implications for therapists working with all clients (Bieschke, 2002). It helps to articulate how complicated heterosexuality is, and it provides an additional mechanism for understanding potential bias in the therapeutic relationship, regardless of the client's or the therapist's sexual orientation.

It is critical for counselors and therapists to develop the knowledge and skills necessary for working with this population, along with self-awareness (APA, 2003; Sue et al., 1992). The ethical codes and standards of practice for the APA (2002) and other mental health professional associations (e.g., American Counseling Association, 1995) all address the issue of counselors and therapists practicing only within areas in which they are competent. Since there are unique challenges and concerns facing LGB clients, it is essential that therapists proactively work to develop that competence. The APA has adopted "Guidelines for Psychotherapy With Lesbian, Gay, and Bisexual Clients" (APA Division 44/Committee on Lesbian, Gay, and Bisexual Concerns Joint Task Force, 2000), which addresses issues that competent therapists need to address with respect to working with this population. The Association for Gay, Lesbian, and Bisexual Issues in Counseling (AGLBIC), a division of the American Counseling Association, has developed "Competencies for Counseling Gay, Lesbian, Bisexual, and Transgendered (GLBT) Clients" (n.d.). Since therapists do not always know when they are working with LGB clients, it is essential that they develop competence in this area in order to avoid doing harm unknowingly (Brown, 1996). It is also important to remember that although the gay, lesbian, and bisexual population is often addressed as one population, in reality there are issues that are unique to each group, and competence in one area does not mean competence in all areas.

It is likely that continuing education is and will be necessary for many therapists given that research has repeatedly indicated that graduate training programs are not adequately preparing mental health professionals to work with LGB clients (e.g., Buhrke, 1989; Phillips & Fischer, 1998). Furthermore, since there has been relatively little empirical research on working with this population, and much of that research has been methodologically flawed (Bieschke, McClanahan, Tozer, Grzegorek, & Park, 2000), such continuing education will have to be ongoing as more information becomes available. In addition to educating oneself about the lives of lesbians, gay men, and bisexual individuals, it is also important to examine the assumptions of one's theoretical approach(es) to counseling (Fassinger, 2000; Stein, 1988). Regardless of the perspective from which one practices, counseling theory provides the framework both for understanding a client's situation and for formulating an approach to addressing it. Thus, it is essential to have a clear understanding of how one's theoretical preferences might influence one's conceptualization of and work with gay, lesbian, and bisexual clients.

An additional aspect of educating oneself about the lives of LGB individuals is making an effort to get to know gay, lesbian, and bisexual people (Brown, 1996; Ritter & Terndrup, 2002). Research has shown that people who have had positive associations with gay, lesbian, or bisexual people are more likely to have positive attitudes toward them, whereas those with no such contact are more likely to hold negative attitudes (Herek, 1994). Thus, there is value in interacting with the LGB community as a way of counteracting the heterosexist biases of the dominant culture. Furthermore, although therapists can learn about clients' lives by listening to them, clients should not be made to shoulder the full responsibility of teaching their therapists about LGB culture.

SEXUAL ORIENTATION IDENTITY DEVELOPMENT

It is critical that counselors have at least a working knowledge of sexual orientation identity development (Brown, 1996; Pope, 1995; Reynolds, 2003). Pope (citing Elliot, 1990) stressed that the process of identity development for gay men and lesbians is complicated by the fact that, unlike other minority groups, gay men and lesbians usually do not have families who are able to help them through this developmental process. The same is true for bisexual individuals. Furthermore, the process of identity development for LGB individuals involves not only developing an identity as gay, lesbian, or bisexual, but also moving away from a heterosexual identity. This means transitioning from a majority identity to a minority identity. Matthews and Bieschke (2001) suggested that this process is similar to the acculturation that occurs for transnational immigrants who must adapt to a new culture. Therapists often play a crucial role in helping LGB clients address concerns associated with identity development. It is therefore essential that they be familiar with models of sexual orientation identity development. In addition, this is another area in which assumptions of heterosexuality can be harmful to clients silently struggling with early stages of identity development (Brown, 1996).

There are various models of sexual orientation identity development. The initial work on sexual orientation identity focused on gay men and lesbians. Cass (1979, 1984, 1996) is generally credited with developing an early model that became a foundation for future work in this area. Her model of homosexual [sic] identity formation includes six stages of progression, from initial questioning of assumed heterosexuality to full integration of a homosexual identity, with cognitive, affective, and behavioral components influencing the outcome of the stage. Her model allows for both progression and stagnation, as well as for differentiation between behavior and identity.

A number of stage-type models were built on Cass's early work (e.g., Coleman, 1982; Sophie, 1986; Troiden, 1979). Reynolds and Hanjorgiris (2000) have provided a useful review of sexual orientation identity development models.

McCarn and Fassinger (1996) took the sexual orientation identity literature, literally, to another level when they presented a model that addresses identity development in a manner that incorporates both individual identity and membership in a stigmatized minority group. Drawing from the literature on racial identity development and gender identity development, as well as from the literature on sexual orientation identity development, they separated the processes by which an individual identifies herself individually as a lesbian and as an individual who is part of a minority group. This is an important distinction between McCarn and Fassinger's model and previous models, which tended to incorporate involvement in the community into personal identity development. McCarn and Fassinger have more clearly articulated the social realities that might keep one from more public pronouncements of her sexual orientation despite a sophisticated level of personal understanding and acceptance. They also intentionally use the word "phases" rather than "stages" (p. 521) to describe the components of their model, arguing that "stages" suggests a linear movement that is not reflective of the process as it occurs in people's lives. "Phases" better reflects the lifelong process of identity development. Their model addresses four phases each for individual and group identity development, beginning with awareness and progressing to internalization and synthesis. Fassinger and Miller (1996) tested this model with gay men and found it to be applicable to them as well.

Scholarship on bisexual identity development has been more uneven than that on gay and lesbian identity development. There has been a tendency in the literature, in practice, and in society to discount bisexuality either as a transitional period between heterosexuality and homosexuality or as a homophobic reluctance on the part of some individuals to accept a gay or lesbian identity (Dworkin, 2001). As a result, people who identify as bisexual can experience prejudice and animosity from both the heterosexual community and the gay and lesbian community. This can make development of a bisexual identity more cumbersome than development of a gay or lesbian identity (see Potoczniak, chap. 5, this volume, and Firestein, chap. 4, this volume, for more information regarding bisexuality).

Weinberg, Williams, and Pryor (1994) offered a research-based model that described four stages of identity development, and Brown (2002) built upon that model, suggesting that the process through the stages is likely somewhat different for women and men. Both models describe an identity development process that is tenuous throughout and requires greater effort for long-term maintenance due to society's dichotomous expectation of identification as either heterosexual or gay/lesbian. It is not surprising that some bisexual individuals choose to identify as heterosexual or gay/lesbian, depending on the gender of their partner (Dworkin, 2001).

Knowledge of sexual orientation identity development is essential because it is a process that can influence therapists' interactions with clients. As with racial and ethnic identity development, clients may respond differently to counseling interventions and, indeed, to the counselor, depending on where they are developmentally. It is important for counselors to understand this process because clients, especially those in early phases of development, may be reluctant to raise the issue. Likewise, both heterosexual and nonheterosexual therapists are at varying places with respect to their own sexual orientation identity development, and this likely influences their interactions with both heterosexual and nonheterosexual clients (Brown, 1996; Mohr, 2002). It is also crucial to remember that identity development models are meant to be descriptive—useful as mechanisms for understanding a client's frame of reference, but not as a basis for judging health or pathology.

In addition to developing familiarity with sexual orientation identity models, it is also important for therapists to have an understanding of models of racial and ethnic identity development (APA, 2003). These developmental trajectories overlap in individuals who are gay, lesbian, or bisexual and who are also racial or ethnic minorities, resulting in a complex and dynamic interaction (Greene, 1997). Counselors must have enough familiarity with both processes to help clients move through them in ways that are empowering.

WHEN GAY, LESBIAN, OR BISEXUAL ORIENTATION IS KNOWN

When a client does indicate that she or he is lesbian, gay, or bisexual, it is important not to assume that the presenting problem is related to sexual orientation (Garnets et al., 1991). Such biased assumptions can lead to misdiagnosis and potential harm to the client if the real problem is not addressed because the therapist focuses on sexual orientation instead (Brown, 1996). LGB clients enter therapy for a wide variety of problems. Not all problems are attributable to sexual orientation. At the same time, there are some unique concerns facing LGB clients because of their oppressed status. Likewise, sexual orientation can have an impact on other problems, even when sexual orientation itself is not the problem. It is critical for counselors to be able to help clients distinguish between problems that are or are not influenced by sexual orientation. When presenting problems are influenced by sexual orientation, it is important to help clients to clearly define them in a way that avoids making sexual orientation the problem (Gluth & Kiselica, 1994). The following sections address several concerns that LGB individuals face as a result of their oppressed status and that might bring them to therapy.

Assessment

Effective assessment begins with openness during intake to a wide range of possibilities with respect to sexual orientation. It also includes recognition that sexual orientation is not simple and static, but rather is complex and fluid. The various models of sexual orientation identity development provide a framework for assessing sexual orientation and the concerns that might accompany any aspect of development. Matthews and Bieschke (2001) developed a semistructured interview approach to assessing a gay or lesbian client's status with respect to sexual orientation. Based on Comas-Diaz and Jacobsen's (1987, cited in Matthews & Bieschke, 2001) Ethno-cultural Assessment, this tool examines the movement of a client from a heterosexual identity to a gay or lesbian identity. In exploring sexual orientation identity development during intake, it is important to remember that such information is being elicited in order to better understand the client, not to pathologize the client.

Although not much has been written about assessment with respect to LGB clients, there has been some scholarship that cautions clinicians about potential bias in standard assessment instruments. Such bias might include omission bias when instruments assume heterosexuality, connotation bias when negative concepts are associated with lesbians, gay men, and bisexual individuals, or contiguity bias when scales assessing sexual orientation are intermixed with diagnostic scales (Chernin, Holden, & Chandler, 1997). There is also the potential for bias in the selection and interpretation of tests (Prince, 1997), so therapists must be judicious when using instruments that might not have been normed on this population. Gonsiorek (1991) addressed the importance of interpretation by providing examples in which gays and lesbians were labeled less psychologically healthy because they scored lower than heterosexuals, even when their scores fell within the normal range. Thus, therapists must use caution in both their selection of instruments and their interpretation of results.

Client Concerns Rising From Oppressed Status

Coming Out. Being a hidden minority in a culture that assumes heterosexuality means that LGB people must constantly face the question of when, to whom, and under what circumstances to disclose their sexual orientation. Given that there can be severe consequences for doing so, this process can be distressing. It can also be empowering. There are two different aspects to coming out. The first involves recognition and, eventually (hopefully), acceptance of one's nonheterosexual identity. This is the process generally described in the sexual orientation identity models discussed previously. If one has a high level of internalized homophobia (i.e., negative attitudes about oneself due to identification with societal negative beliefs about homosexuality; Szymanski, Chung, & Balsam, 2001), the process can be fraught with turmoil; however, if the individual is able to connect with supportive people who can help him or her dispel the negative attitudes of society, that state is temporary (Gluth & Kiselica, 1994; Gonsiorek & Rudoph, 1991; Ritter & Terndrup, 2002). This is an area in which counselors can aid in the process. An affirmative counselor can model a positive response that can facilitate the client's movement toward self-acceptance. Conversely, a counselor who reinforces negative social messages can thwart this process or cause additional distress for the client (Brown, 1996). Occasionally, the stress of coming out may trigger more serious underlying psychological problems, unrelated to sexual orientation, problems that can be masked by the ordeal of coming out (Gonsiorek & Rudolph, 1991). It is important for therapists to be able to distinguish between expected developmental adjustment problems related to coming out and pathology that may be unrelated but exacerbated by the coming out process.

The second aspect of coming out involves disclosing one's identity to others. Part of the coming out process involves informing family. Although the initial disclosure is likely to create turmoil, the literature on coming out within families stresses the importance of taking a long-term perspective. Coming out can create permanent breaks in family relationships; however, in most cases families work through the initial disruption to find ways to retain, or even strengthen, family bonds (see Matthews & Lease, 2000, for review). The individual and family processes are likely to have reciprocal effects on each other. In the case of ethnic minority families, there are likely to be additional stresses related to different cultural systems, although there can be additional avenues for resilience as well (Rust, 1996). Affirmative therapists can help LGB individuals and their families to negotiate this process.

The family is only one place where LGB individuals have to address the issue of disclosure of sexual orientation. Coming out is a lifelong process that must occur every time a gay, lesbian, or bisexual individual wants to be truly her- or himself in an interpersonal relationship. These circumstances may include relationships in the workplace for adults and in school for adolescents, friendship networks, dealings with health care providers, or any other situations in which people interact with others. Coming out can be a risky process because of the stigma and discrimination associated with nonheterosexual identities. Indeed, an additional concern for lesbian, gay, and bisexual individuals is accidental or intentional disclosure of their identity when they had not intended to disclose. At the same time, coming out can also be empowering. Affirmative therapists need to be able to help clients navigate the lifelong coming out journey in a way that minimizes the risks and maximizes empowerment.

In addition to being a lifelong process, coming out is also a cultural process. Smith (1997, p. 287) referred to coming out as "a White, Western, middle-class phenomenon" because it is so often portrayed as indicative of more mature development as a gay, lesbian, or bisexual person. Such conceptualization fails to take into account the cultural realities of many ethnic minority gay men, lesbians, and bisexual individuals, who often must confront racism in the LGB community and heterosexism in their racial and ethnic communities (Greene, 1997; Smith, 1997). It thus becomes necessary for these individuals to find ways to balance competing expectations in ways that are life-enhancing. Choices regarding coming out become entwined with such things as loyalty to family and community, respect for cultural prescriptions regarding sexuality of any sort, and cultural expectations regarding gender roles, marriage, and carrying on family and ethnic lineage. Counselors must understand and be sensitive to these complex issues as they work with clients facing multiple levels of oppression.

Finding Community. An element included in virtually all of the sexual orientation identity models is finding and developing some sort of connection to the LGB community. Community is important in helping to break the sense of isolation and despair that can occur from feeling different, which is an early piece of identity development. At the same time, there can be reluctance to associating with a stigmatized minority group (D'Augelli & Garnets, 1995). Although this reluctance tends to ease over time, it does so through positive and empowering experiences with others who are gay, lesbian, and bisexual. Thus, it is vital that counselors be able to facilitate access to positive and healthy elements of the LGB community. There are a variety of options available; however, finding them can sometimes be difficult, another problem of an invisible community (D'Augelli & Garnets, 1995). It is essential that therapists be familiar with the resources available for LGB clients. This may be easier in large metropolitan areas, but it is equally vital in smaller cities and towns. It may also involve becoming familiar with online resources, especially in smaller, more isolated communities.

Locating and learning about the local and regional LGB community can serve other important functions for therapists. It provides an opportunity for getting to know gay, lesbian, and bisexual people, which in turn is helpful in developing more positive attitudes (Herek, 1994). It also provides a mechanism for learning about the diversity within the community, which is necessary for a more accurate understanding of gay, lesbian, and bisexual lives (Haldeman & Buhrke, 2003; Reynolds, 2003). This can be helpful in progressing to higher levels of integration in one's own sexual orientation identity development, which can further facilitate one's competence as a clinician in working with this population. Section 1 of this volume provides additional information about LGBT communities.

Negotiating Life As a Gay, Lesbian, or Bisexual Individual. Research has repeatedly shown that lesbians, gay men, and bisexual individuals are subject to prejudice and discrimination (see Herek, 1998). This contributes to stress, whether or not one is open about a nonheterosexual orientation (DiPlacido, 1998). When one is more open about sexual orientation, there is greater likelihood of overt acts of discrimination, perhaps including violence. Hiding, however, can also have consequences, such as perpetuating internalized homophobia, which can contribute to depression, substance abuse, and suicide (DiPlacido, 1998). Counselors must be aware of the oppression that gay men, lesbians, and bisexual individuals face and recognize that it may play a role in the problems they present. Again, it is important to explore this rather than make assumptions and to clearly articulate to the client that, although the oppression may be related to sexual orientation, sexual orientation is not the problem and did not cause the oppression. Therapists must also be prepared to help clients learn to be resilient in the face of such stress.

CONCLUSION

Affirmative counseling with gay, lesbian, and bisexual clients often begins before counselors know the client's sexual orientation. Indeed, communicating affirmation may determine whether the client discloses a nonheterosexual orientation or risks addressing confusion and uncertainty about sexual orientation. Affirmative counseling likewise requires a therapist who is self-aware with respect to sexual orientation, regardless of how he or she self-identifies. It also requires the knowledge and skills to work competently with this population. Because this is an area that is often neglected in graduate training programs, it may be incumbent on individual therapists to acquire the additional information and training that they need. Such continuing development should include information about sexual orientation identity development and about concerns that are specific to this population, such as coming out, finding community, or living as an oppressed minority, as well as information regarding ways in which sexual orientation may influence more general concerns.

REFERENCES

American Counseling Association. (1995). ACA code of ethics and standards of practice. Alexandria, VA: Author.

American Psychological Association. (1998). Proceedings of the American Psychological Association, Incorporated, for the legislative year, 1997. American Psychologist, 53, 934–935.

American Psychological Association, Division 44/Committee on Lesbian, Gay, and Bisexual Concerns Joint Task Force on Guildlines for Psychotherapy With

Lesbian, Gay, and Bisexual Clients. (2000). Guidelines for psychotherapy with lesbian, gay, and bisexual clients. *American Psychologist, 55,* 1440–1451.

American Psychological Association. (2002). Ethical principles of psychologists and code of conduct. *American Psychologist, 47,* 1597–1611.

American Psychological Association. (2003). Guidelines on multicultural education, training, research, practice, and organizational change for psychologists. *American Psychologist, 58,* 377–402.

Association for Gay, Lesbian, and Bisexual Issues in Counseling. (n.d.). *Competencies for counseling gay, lesbian, bisexual, and transgendered (GLBT) clients.* Retrieved June 25, 2002, from http://www.aglbic.org/resources/competencies.html

Benedict, J. G., VandenBos, G. R., & Kenkel, M. B. (Section Eds.). (2002). Responding to sexual orientation issues [Special section]. *Professional Psychology: Research and Practice, 33*(3).

Bieschke, K. J. (2002). Charting the waters. *The Counseling Psychologist, 30,* 575–581.

Bieschke, K. J., & Matthews, C. R. (1996). Career counselor attitudes and behaviors toward gay, lesbian, and bisexual clients. *Journal of Vocational Behavior, 48,* 243–255.

Bieschke, K. J., & Matthews, C. R. (2003, August). *Non-heterosexist organizational climate and affirmative counselor behavior: Validation of instruments.* Poster presented at the 111th Annual Convention of the American Psychological Association, Toronto, Ontario, Canada.

Bieschke, K. J., McClanahan, M., Tozer, E., Grzegorek, J. L., & Park, J. (2000). Programmatic research on the treatment of lesbian, gay, and bisexual clients: The past, the present, and the course for the future. In R. M. Perez, K. A. DeBord, & K. J. Bieschke (Eds.), *Handbook of counseling and psychotherapy with lesbian, gay, and bisexual clients* (pp. 309–335). Washington, DC: American Psychological Association.

Brown, L. S. (1996). Ethical concerns with sexual minority patients. In R. P. Cabaj (Ed.), *Textbook of homosexuality and mental health* (pp. 897–916). Washington, DC: American Psychiatric Press.

Brown, T. (2002). A proposed model of bisexual identity development that elaborates on experiential differences of women and men. *Journal of Bisexuality, 2*(4), 67–91.

Buhrke, R. A. (1989). Female student perspectives on training in lesbian and gay issues. *The Counseling Psychologist, 17,* 629–636.

Cass, V. (1996). Sexual orientation identity formation: A Western phenomenon. In R. P. Cabaj & T. S. Stein (Eds.), *Textbook of homosexuality and mental health* (pp. 227–251). Washington, DC: American Psychiatric Press.

Cass, V. C. (1979). Homosexual identity formation: A theoretical model. *Journal of Homosexuality, 4,* 219–235.

Cass, V. C. (1984). Homosexual identity formation: Testing a theoretical model. *Journal of Sex Research, 20,* 143–167.

Chernin, J., Holden, J. M., & Chandler, C. (1997). Bias in psychological assessment: Heterosexism. *Measurement and Evaluation in Counseling and Development, 30,* 68–76.

Coleman, E. (1982). Developmental stages of the coming-out process. *American Behavioral Scientist, 25*, 469–482.

D'Augelli, A. R., & Garnets, L. D. (1995). Lesbian, gay, and bisexual communities. In A. R. D'Augelli & C. J. Patterson (Eds.), *Lesbian, gay, and bisexual identities over the lifespan: Psychological perspectives* (pp. 293–320). New York: Oxford University Press.

DiPlacido, J. (1998). Minority stress among lesbians, gay men, and bisexuals: A consequence of heterosexism, homophobia, and stigmatization. In G.M. Herek (Ed.), *Psychological perspectives on lesbian and gay issues: Vol. 4. Stigma and sexual orientation: Understanding prejudice against lesbians, gay men, and bisexuals* (pp. 138–159). Thousand Oaks, CA: Sage.

Dworkin, S. H. (2001). Treating the bisexual client. *Journal of Clinical Psychology, 57*, 671–680.

Eldridge, N. J., & Barnett, D.C. (1991). Counseling gay and lesbian students. In N. J. Evans & V.A. Wall (Eds.), *Beyond tolerance: Gays, lesbians, and bisexuals on campus* (pp. 147–178). Alexandria, VA: American College Personnel Association.

Fassinger, R. E. (1991). The hidden minority: Issues and challenges in working with lesbian women and gay men. *The Counseling Psychologist, 19*, 157–176.

Fassinger, R. E. (2000). Applying counseling theories to lesbian, gay, and bisexual clients: Pitfalls and possibilities. In R. M. Perez, K. A. DeBord, & K. J. Bieschke (Eds.), *Handbook of counseling and psychotherapy with lesbian, gay, and bisexual clients* (pp. 107–131). Washington, DC: American Psychological Association.

Fassinger, R. E., & Miller, B. A. (1996). Validation of an inclusive model of sexual identity formation on a sample of gay men. *Journal of Homosexuality, 32*, 53–78.

Fox, R. C. (1996). Bisexuality in perspective: A review of theory and research. In B. A. Firestein (Ed.), *Bisexuality: The psychology and politics of an invisible minority* (pp. 3–50). Thousand Oaks, CA: Sage.

Garnets, L., Hancock, K. A., Cochran, S. D., Goodchilds, J., & Peplau, L. A. (1991). Issues in psychotherapy with lesbians and gay men: A survey of psychologists. *American Psychologist, 46*, 964–972.

Gluth, D. R., & Kiselica, M. S. (1994). Coming out quickly: A brief counseling approach to dealing with gay and lesbian adjustment issues. *Journal of Mental Health Counseling, 16*, 163–173.

Golden, C. (1987). Diversity and variability in women's sexual identities. In Boston Lesbian Psychologies Collective (Eds.), *Lesbian psychologies: Explorations and challenges* (pp. 19–34). Urbana: University of Illinois Press.

Gonsiorek, J. C. (1991). The empirical basis for the demise of the illness model of homosexuality. In J. C. Gonsiorek & J. D. Weinrich (Eds.), *Homosexuality: Research implications for public policy* (pp. 115–136). Newbury Park, CA: Sage.

Gonsiorek, J. C., & Rudolph, J. R. (1991). Homosexual identity: Coming out and other developmental events. In J. C. Gonsiorek & J. D. Weinrich (Eds.), *Homosexuality: Research implications for public policy* (pp. 161–176). Newbury Park, CA: Sage.

Greene, B. (1997). Ethnic minority lesbians and gay men: Mental health and treatment issues. In B. Greene (Ed.), *Psychological perspectives on lesbian and gay issues: Vol. 3. Ethnic and cultural diversity among lesbians and gay men* (pp. 216–239). Thousand Oaks, CA: Sage.

Haldeman, D.C. (1994). The practice and ethics of sexual orientation conversion therapy. *Journal of Consulting and Clinical Pscyhology, 62,* 221–227.

Haldeman, D.C., & Buhrke, R. A. (2003). Under a rainbow flag. In J. D. Robinson & L. C. James (Eds.), *Diversity in human interactions: The tapestry of America* (pp. 145–156). New York: Oxford University Press.

Herek, G. M. (1994). Assessing heterosexuals' attitudes toward lesbians and gay men. In B. Greene & G. Herek (Eds.), *Psychological perspectives on lesbian and gay issues: Vol. 1. Lesbian and gay psychology: Theory, research, and clinical applications* (pp. 206–228). Thousand Oaks, CA: Sage.

Herek, G. M. (1995). Psychological heterosexism in the United States. In A. R. D'Augelli & C. J. Patterson (Eds.), *Lesbian, gay, and bisexual identities over the lifespan: Psychological perspectives* (pp. 321–346). New York: Oxford University Press.

Herek, G. M. (Ed.). (1998). *Psychological perspectives on lesbian and gay issues: Vol. 4. Stigma and sexual orientation: Understanding prejudice against lesbians, gay men, and bisexuals.* Thousand Oaks, CA: Sage.

Matthews, C. R., & Bieschke, K. J. (2001). Adapting the ethnocultural assessment to gay and lesbian clients: The sexual orientation enculturation assessment. *Journal of Humanistic Education and Development, 40,* 58–73.

Matthews, C. R., & Bieschke, K. J. (2003, August). *Factors influencing psychologists' affirmative attitudes and behaviors with GLB clients.* Poster presented at the 111th Annual Convention of the American Psychological Association, Toronto, Ontario, Canada.

Matthews, C. R., & Lease, S. H. (2000). Focus on lesbian, gay, and bisexual families. In R. M. Perez, K. A. DeBord, & K. J. Bieschke (Eds.), *Handbook of counseling and psychotherapy with lesbian, gay, and bisexual clients* (pp. 249–273). Washington, DC: American Psychological Association.

Matthews, C. R., Selvidge, M. M. D., & Fisher, K. (2005). Addiction counselors' attitudes and behaviors toward lesbian, gay, and bisexual clients. *Journal of Counseling and Development, 83,* 57–65.

McCarn, S. R., & Fassinger, R. E. (1996). Revisioning sexual minority identity formation: A new model of lesbian identity and its implications for counseling and research. *The Counseling Psychologist, 24,* 508–534.

Mohr, J. J. (2002). Heterosexual identity and the heterosexual therapist: An identity perspective on sexual orientation dynamics in psychotherapy. *The Counseling Psychologist, 30,* 532–566.

Ochs, R. (1996). Biphobia: It goes more than two ways. In B. A. Firestein (Ed.), *Bisexuality: The psychology and politics of an invisible minority* (pp. 217–239). Thousand Oaks, CA: Sage.

Phillips, J. C., & Fischer, A. R. (1998). Graduate students' training experiences with lesbian, gay, and bisexual issues. *The Counseling Psychologist, 26,* 712–734.

Pope, M. (1995). The "salad bowl" is big enough for us all: An argument for the inclusion of lesbians and gay men in any definition of multiculturalism. *Journal of Counseling and Development, 73,* 301–304.

Prince, J. P. (1997). Assessment bias affecting lesbian, gay male, and bisexual individuals. *Measurement and Evaluation in Counseling and Development, 30,* 82–87.

Reynolds, A. L. (2003). Counseling issues for lesbian and bisexual women. In M. Kopala & M. Keitel (Eds.), *Handbook of counseling women* (pp. 53–73). Thousand Oaks, CA: Sage.

Reynolds, A. L., & Hanjorgiris, W. F. (2000). Coming out: Lesbian, gay, and bisexual identity development. In R. M. Perez, K. A. DeBord, & K. J. Bieschke (Eds.), *Handbook of counseling and psychotherapy with lesbian, gay, and bisexual clients* (pp. 35–55). Washington, DC: American Psychological Association.

Ritter, K. Y., & Terndrup, A. I. (2002). *Handbook of affirmative psychotherapy with lesbians and gay men.* New York: Guilford.

Russell, G. M. (2000). *Voted out: The psychological consequences of anti-gay politics.* New York: New York University Press.

Rust, P. C. (1996). Managing multiple identities: Diversity among bisexual women and men. In B. A. Firestein (Ed.), *Bisexuality: The psychology and politics of an invisible minority* (pp. 53–83). Thousand Oaks, CA: Sage.

Shidlo, A., Schroeder, M. (Guest Eds.), & Drescher, J. (Ed.). (2001). Sexual conversion therapy: Ethical, clinical, and research perspectives [Special issue]. *Journal of Gay & Lesbian Psychotherapy, 5*(3/4).

Smith, A. (1997). Cultural diversity and the coming-out process: Implications for clinical practice. In B. Greene (Ed.), *Psychological perspectives on lesbian and gay issues: Vol. 3. Ethnic and cultural diversity among lesbians and gay men* (pp. 279–300). Thousand Oaks, CA: Sage.

Sophie, J. (1986). A critical examination of stage theories of lesbian identity development. *Journal of Homosexuality, 12*(2), 39–51.

Stein, T. S. (1988). Theoretical considerations in psychotherapy with gay men and lesbians. *Journal of Homosexuality, 15,* 75–95.

Sue, D. W., Arredondo, P., & McDavis, R. J. (1992). Multicultural competencies and standards: A call to the profession. *Journal of Counseling and Development, 70,* 477–486.

Szymanski, D. M., Chung, Y. B., & Balsam, K. F. (2001). Psychological correlates of internalized homophobia in lesbians. *Measurement and Evaluation in Counseling and Development, 34,* 27–41.

Tozer, E. E., & McClanahan, M. K. (1999). Treating the purple menace: Ethical considerations of conversion therapy and affirmative alternatives. *The Counseling Psychologist, 27,* 722–742.

Troiden, R. R. (1979). Becoming homosexual: A model of gay identity acquisition. *Psychiatry, 42,* 362–373.

Weinberg, M. S., Williams, C. J., & Pryor, D. W. (1994). *Dual attractions: Understanding bisexuality.* New York: Oxford University Press.

Worthington, R. L., & Mohr, J. J. (2002). Theorizing heterosexual identity development. *The Counseling Psychologist, 30,* 491–495.

Worthington, R. L., Savoy, H. B., Dillon, F. R., & Vernaglia, E. R. (2002). Heterosexual identity development: A multidimensional model of individual and social identity. *The Counseling Psychologist, 30,* 496–531.

Yarhouse, M. A., & Burkett, L. A. (2002). An inclusive response to LGB and conservative religious persons: The case of same-sex attraction and behavior. *Professional Psychology: Research and Practice, 33,* 235–241.

9

AFFIRMATIVE COUNSELING AND PSYCHOTHERAPY FOCUSED ON ISSUES RELATED TO SEXUAL ORIENTATION CONFLICTS

LEE BECKSTEAD AND TANIA ISRAEL

Denise, age 24, is an African American college student. She is the oldest child and was raised in a strongly religious family. Denise has believed from a young age that homosexuality is a sin and as a result has always been afraid that someone will find out her secret—that she is attracted to women. To avoid dealing with her feelings, she has kept herself busy by focusing on her academic goals. However, it has become increasingly difficult on campus because of her desires for sexual and emotional connections with women. Denise comes into counseling stating that she cannot be a lesbian because her family, church, and God expect her to marry and have children. She especially fears how her family, friends, and church members would react if they knew she had these attractions. She states that she feels that "homosexuality just isn't right" and that her "homosexual tendencies" are a trial or test from God. She is depressed because she feels she has failed in overcoming her attractions. She asks for help to get rid of her feelings toward women so that she can feel sexually, emotionally, and socially "normal."

Although every individual who identifies as lesbian, gay, or bisexual (LGB) may have initially experienced some degree of conflict regarding sexual orientation, these conflicts may be more pronounced and longer-term for some than for others. This chapter focuses on clients who experience acute conflict about their sexual orientation and describes a variety of affirmative and ethical strategies to facilitate resolution of their distress. In particular, we focus on those clients who desire to change their sexual orientation to heterosexual, who are unable to adopt an openly positive LGB identity, and who experience their sexual orientation at odds with their cultural or social identities. In contrast to Matthews (chap. 8, this volume), who describes issues related to a normative coming out process, we highlight concerns for clients whose conflicts are particularly complex or problematic.

The goals of this chapter are to (a) contextualize the experiences of individuals who present in counseling conflicted about their sexual orientation; (b) prepare clinicians to work effectively with such clients by suggesting areas in which they can increase knowledge, awareness of attitudes, and skills; and (c) provide counseling strategies to facilitate resolution of the conflicts surrounding sexual orientation. Moreover, this chapter seeks to help therapists understand ethical, cultural, and psychological considerations in treating sexual minority clients in conflict.

POTENTIAL SOURCES OF CONFLICT ABOUT SEXUAL ORIENTATION

Heterosexist and Homonegative Society

"Compulsory heterosexuality" can be described as the mechanisms by which society enforces a narrow range of acceptable expressions of sexuality and penalize deviations from the norm (Rich, 1980). Heterosexual attractions and relationships are thus celebrated and reinforced while same-sex ones are marginalized, criminalized, and demonized. Some examples of the mechanisms that enforce heterosexuality are the increased risk of violence that LGB individuals experience (American Psychological Association [APA], Division 44/Committee on Lesbian, Gay, and Bisexual Concerns Joint Task Force on Guidelines for Psychotherapy With Lesbian, Gay, and Bisexual Clients, 2000), the failure of federal law to provide protection from discrimination in jobs and housing based on sexual orientation (Human Rights Campaign Foundation, 2002), and the long-standing state laws criminalizing same-sex sexual behavior that only recently have been deemed unconstitutional (Lambda Legal, 2003). Subtle modes of heterosexism take the form of persistent stereotypes of LGB individuals and language that promotes negative associations with homosexuality (e.g., "that's so gay"). Individuals who discover that they are emotionally or sexually drawn to members of the same sex must find a way to reconcile their attractions with the social, legal, physical, and emotional consequences of openly identifying with and expressing these feelings.

Cultural Conflicts

Although the values of most cultures are heterosexist to some extent, the values of some cultures explicitly and severely condemn same-sex attractions and relationships. Consequently, conflict between same-sex attractions and societal homonegativity may be particularly acute for individuals associated with such cultures. Culture can be defined as the beliefs, values, and behaviors of a social group, which may be associated with a particular ethnicity, nationality, political history, socioeconomic status, geographical region, or religion (Greene, 1997). Cultural conflicts with same-sex attractions may be associated with the values of any one of these sources or a combination of multiple sources.

Various cultures reflect a range of approaches to dealing with sexual orientation. As research suggests, East Asian cultures tend to locate sexuality in a private realm rather than recognize it as a public identity, and sexuality is expressed only indirectly in public (Chan, 1997). For Latino men who engage in same-sex sexual behavior, identity and status may be derived from the role in sex rather than from the sex of the partner (Rodriguez, 1996). Another example of diverse cultural views of sexual orientation is Strickland's (1997) description of White Southerners in the 1950s accommodating "eccentric" individuals, without naming them as lesbian or gay. Conceptualizing same-sex attractions in the context of an LGB identity is a contemporary Western concept not necessarily shared by other cultures or even by subcultures within U.S. society.

Individuals with same-sex attractions who are members of other marginalized cultural groups must learn how to cope with compounded oppression due to their minority statuses. As Miville and Ferguson (2004) emphasized, many oppressed individuals (e.g., women and people of color) are faced daily with making choices between social environments in which only a part of their being can be affirmed or expressed. This daily conflict and compartmentalization may lead to increased stress and self-negation. Consequently, claiming a heterosexual orientation or living heterosexually may be the only source of privilege for some minority individuals (Bing, 2004). Moreover, LGB identities and communities may be viewed as White, and association with them may be seen as a rejection of one's culture of origin (Bohan, 1996). For instance, ethnic minority individuals who view the family as a key defense against a racist society may perceive same-sex orientation as a betrayal of cultural values and heritage (Garnets, 2002). Loyalty may be divided between honoring cultural values, roles, expectations, and communities and valuing one's same-sex attractions and relationships. For example, emphasis on an individual identity may challenge collectivist cultural values (Chan, 1997), and same-sex relationships may be seen as a threat to continuation of family name and traditions. Thus, identifying too strongly with one group risks membership in others, and conflict about sexual orientation may be viewed, in part, as a conflict of allegiance (Morales, 1989). The difficulties of openly identifying as LGB within a heterosexist culture or of trying to exist as a person of color within a racist LGB community may leave ethnic minority same-sex attracted (SSA) individuals fragmented and displaced with little sense of support or community (Bing, 2004; Bohan, 1996).

Religious Conflicts

Same-sex attractions and conservative religions have a long-standing history of incompatibility with each other. Few religions celebrate or even recognize a same-sex orientation as a valid expression of the self, and most support only heterosexual relationships. Conservative religious doctrines also articulate clear negative messages and consequences about disobeying religious laws and acting on same-sex attractions. Such heterosexist and homonegative pressures have the potential to isolate, confuse, and damage same-sex attracted individuals (Haldeman, 1996; Ritter & O'Neill, 1989). In fact, conservative religiosity shows a positive correlation with homonegativity and has a strong role in motivating individuals to seek therapy to change their sexual orientation (Tozer & Hayes, 2004; Worthington, 2004).

Therapists must recognize that, similar to other cultural backgrounds, a client's religious background may be central to her or his identity (Yarhouse & Burkett, 2002). As Haldeman (1996) emphasized, religion may be the only source of solace for some SSA individuals who lack other positive external social supports. Consequently, for some individuals, an LGB identity goes against moral convictions and leads to rejection from family; ostracization from religious communities; considerable shifts in core identity, purpose, and sense of order; and loss of potential afterlife rewards. Options may seem limited for such individuals to integrate their sexual, cultural, and religious identities into one complete sense of self. Therefore, giving up sexuality may seem easier and more honorable than sacrificing a religious or cultural identity.

Other Sources of Conflict

Some of the most identifiable conflicts with sexual orientation are related to religion, culture, and the overall context of a heterosexist society. However, a wide range of less evident individual differences may heighten conflict regarding same-sex attractions. For example, socioeconomic status, ability status, appearance or size, age, and gender identity create multiple layers of oppression and conflicts between sexuality and community.

Personal and political pressures from LGB communities may also exacerbate identity conflicts. For example, individuals who experience same-sex attractions may feel pressure from LGB-identified people to identify openly as LGB. Such pressures can be attributed, in part, to the marginalized experience of LGB individuals and may be analogous to the negative reactions that bisexual individuals have received from lesbians and gay men (see Firestein, chap. 4, this volume; Potoczniak, chap. 5, this volume). Udis-Kessler (1990) explained such binegativity by positing that the very idea of bisexuality may threaten the sense of self and community for individuals who have based their social identity on a lesbian or gay identity because bisexuality may present such individuals with the possibility that the pain of being lesbian or gay in a homophobic society could have been avoided. Similarly, openly LGB individuals may feel invalidated by SSA individuals who choose not to identify as LGB and seemingly represent an "easy way out" that LGB-identified individuals did not take. Thus, some SSA individuals may be conflicted as a result of feeling uncomfortable in and excluded from heterosexual and LGB communities.

Additional conflicts may arise due to other situational and social factors. For example, an individual may come to recognize same-sex attractions within the context of a mixed-sex relationship, such as a marriage. In this situation, an individual may want to express same-sex attractions but may be concerned about the impact on the spouse, children, and self. Such conflicts may lead to secretiveness, liaisons, rationalizations, time away from home, guilt, desires for connection and to be known, and desire for stability with the family (Isay, 1998).

Overall, conflict about same-sex attractions may be expressed both externally and internally. Emotional and behavioral manifestations of conflict may include emotional distress, isolation from self and others, negative self-concept, and suicidal ideation. Because such symptoms of distress may lead an individual to seek counseling, therapists are in a good position to help clients resolve conflicts about sexual orientation. The remainder of this chapter provides suggestions for therapists to apply their knowledge, increase awareness of their attitudes, and implement strategies and skills to assist clients who are in conflict regarding their sexual orientation.

PROVIDING A BROADER-BASED TREATMENT APPROACH

Until the past few decades, the field of psychology reflected the heterosexism in society by labeling same-sex attractions as pathological and typically responded to clients' conflicts by attempting to eradicate such attractions through biological, psychodynamic, behavioral, cognitive, or religiously oriented methods (Drescher, 1998; Haldeman, 1994; Murphy, 1997). Armed with empirical evidence that depathologized homosexuality, LGB activists and allies responded to such practices by advocating for the declassification of homosexuality as a mental disorder and by challenging the use of therapeutic practices designed to "cure" LGB clients (Coleman, 1982). In contrast to earlier heterosexist therapeutic techniques, lesbian- and gay-affirmative approaches have encouraged clients who experience same-sex attractions to adopt an outwardly open LGB identity (e.g., Browning, Reynolds, & Dworkin, 1991; Shannon & Woods, 1991). Therapists may encourage such clients to openly identify as LGB in an attempt to counteract society's invalidation of sexual minorities and help clients overcome internalized homonegativity. In fact, therapists may assume that to be LGB-affirming, they *must* help a client develop an LGB identity. Yet this singular goal may be too narrowly defined and may not fit all conflicted SSA individuals, given religious or cultural considerations (Beckstead, 2001; Fukuyama & Ferguson, 2000).

In support of a more inclusive approach than what historically has been offered, the authors of this chapter advocate a therapy approach that strategically counteracts societal heterosexism and other forms of oppression while maintaining a broad view of acceptable lifestyle and identity choices. This approach goes beyond the dualistic agendas of directing the client toward either an "ex-gay" or "out-gay" outcome; considers all sexual, affectional, spiritual, and value orientations (Beckstead & Morrow, 2004); and seeks to attend to the interrelated aspects of the client's multiple cultural identities and to integrate them into one unique identity (Stanley, 2004). Similarly, Haldeman (2004) described through case examples the importance for practitioners to adhere not to a "one size fits all" approach, but to a person-centered approach, whereby no client who struggles with these issues is left out and practitioners do not invalidate a client's experience or automatically assume what the client needs to resolve conflicts.

Acting Affirmatively and Ethically

Therapists may experience a conflict of ethical principles as they struggle to simultaneously do no harm (Principle A of the APA's "Ethical Principles of Psychologists and Code of Conduct," 2002); promote accuracy, honesty, and truthfulness in their practice (Principle C); and respect clients' cultural, individual, and role differences and right to self-determine in accordance with their values and needs (Principle E). Some professionals (e.g., Rosik, 2003; Throckmorton, 2002) have responded by suggesting that therapists affirm a client's initial treatment goals, even if the initial goal involves a request to change sexual orientation. However, such a relativistic approach ignores the possibility that failure to confront internalized homonegativity will implicitly support heterosexual hegemony. Clients may also be vulnerable as a result of facing high levels of pressure from intra- and interpersonal conflicts. As research (e.g., Beckstead & Morrow, 2004; Tozer & Hayes, 2004) suggests, issues of self-determination are complex with this client population because of the internalization, conformity, and compliance that may occur because of the socialization of cultural norms. Thus, a client's autonomy and choice may be restricted as a result of believing heterosexist ideals and stereotypes of LGB people and being misinformed about sexuality (Green, 2003; Schneider, Brown, & Glassgold, 2002; Shidlo & Schroeder, 2002). Before negotiating treatment goals with such clients, therapists will need to explore their biases about sexuality and what they perceive constitutes a desirable identity and lifestyle for those who experience same-sex attractions.

Being aware that clients could be susceptible to power influences both outside and within the counseling relationship should guide the therapist to focus on correcting or managing any collusion or coercion with anti-LGB sentiments. As Murphy (1997) warned, "Patients may unwittingly absorb the therapist's views on sexual orientation without due reflection" (p. 93). Given these considerations, therapists must recognize how their biases, agendas, and emotional reactions will contribute to clients' fears, hopes, and beliefs—because any negative attitudes and restricted knowledge may affect the counseling process. For example, a therapist's internalized homonegativity may be expressed through negative representations of same-sex relationships. Unexplored binegativity may take the form of dismissing the possibility of a stable bisexual identity and automatically considering a client lesbian or gay if she or he experiences any degree of same-sex attractions (Israel, 2004b). Internalized racism will impede therapists' ability to help ethnic minority clients to affirmatively integrate their conflicted identities. Furthermore, some therapists may have unresolved conflicts concerning religion. Because some religious leaders and communities have manifested heterosexist ideals, LGB and LGB-affirming therapists may view religious values primarily as impediments to a healthy process of identity development. Thus, a referral should be made when the therapist's biases or lack of information significantly hinder the client's potential to reflect fully on the client's feelings, needs, and perspectives, and the effective ways to resolve sexual orientation conflicts (Lasser & Gottlieb, 2004).

Therapists working with this client population must therefore develop the skills to navigate and respect multiple identities simultaneously (Miville & Ferguson, 2004). By expanding his or her viewpoint, the therapist may help the client to explore and embrace complex and conflicting perspectives. Yet as the therapist reflects empathy for the client's struggles and circumstances, the therapist must also develop the skills to confront client's misinformation and the ways in which the client's cultures are oppressive, so as not to recreate a null counseling environment that implicitly supports such biases (Betz, 1989). Thus, balancing how to act both affirmatively and ethically is a constant responsibility for the therapist who works with conflicted SSA clients.

Collaborating on the Goals and Direction for Therapy

As in the example presented at the beginning of this chapter, an SSA client in conflict may present with his or her own agenda about treatment plan and outcome, an agenda that may be at odds with what the therapist would consider reasonable or justified. One option for a middle-ground negotiation of treatment goals may include committing to work consistently within the client's present cultural values and relational circumstances while providing accurate information and exploring realistic outcomes that fit the client. In this way, the client may receive validation, enhance self-understanding, and discover a variety of resolutions. A therapist can facilitate this process by avoiding any initial categorization of sexual orientation and by using less meaning-laden terms, such as "having same-sex attractions" rather than "being LGB." In addition, therapists and clients must avoid simplistic notions about sexuality, including the assumptions that it is always a salient factor in shaping identity and life choices and that sexual orientation is a dichotomous variable (Phillips, 2004). Clients may also be informed regarding what research suggests can be changed regarding sexuality (e.g., attitudes, construction of identity, and deliberate behaviors, such as deciding with whom and in what contexts one acts sexually) and what the literature fails to support can be changed (e.g., the direction of one's underlying sexual orientation and arousal; Beckstead & Morrow, 2004; Diamond, 2003; Rust, 2003; Shidlo & Schroeder, 2002).

Therapist and client may discuss the benefits of taking time to explore the numerous affirmative ways for the client to integrate her or his cultural aspects with being SSA or LGB and distinguish the short- and long-term psychosocial effects of each option. With this approach, goal-setting and treatment-planning become an ongoing dynamic process as therapist and client gain a deeper understanding of the sources of the client's conflicts and as the client hears and gains new perspectives and has more accurate information available to make informed decisions (Haldeman, 2004; Lasser & Gottlieb, 2004). With this broader approach, the client and therapist may reach an agreement that it is unnecessary to decide at the onset what will be the final outcome of therapy but agree on the process of how the client will make his or her decisions about sexual identity congruence.

Responding to a Client's Request to Change Sexual Orientation

Conversion therapy continues to be offered by some counselors—and to be perceived by many clients and their families—as a viable option to treat sexual orientation conflicts (Nicolosi, Byrd, & Potts, 2000a, 2000b). Such therapy tends to define homosexuality as a developmental disorder that results when a child does not receive love through attachment to the same-sex parent, thereby creating a sense of feeling different and inferior toward same-sex others (Moberly, 1983). Accordingly, conversion ideology views clients as heterosexuals who have sexualized same-sex emotional needs. For example, Nicolosi (1993) proposed that for gay and bisexual men, "it is this internal sense of incompleteness in one's own maleness [that] is the foundation for homoerotic attraction" (p. 211). Conversion treatments thus offer "gender lessons" and support groups whereby clients can view others of the same sex as friends rather than sexual partners and construct a traditional gender identity. Conversion treatments also utilize conservative religious ideologies and interventions that rely on the power of prayer and doctrinal prohibitions to strengthen willpower, reduce desire, and limit same-sex sexual behavior (see Besen, 2003; Ritter & O'Neill, 1989).

Therapists working with this client population must be acquainted with professional guidelines regarding conversion therapy. Specifically, the APA has articulated concerns, though not explicitly imposing a ban on such practices (APA, 1998; APA, Division 44/Committee on Lesbian, Gay, and Bisexual Concerns Joint Task Force on Guidelines for Psychotherapy With Lesbian, Gay and Bisexual Clients, 2000). Yet the APA resolution supports the "dissemination of accurate information about sexual orientation, and mental health, and appropriate interventions in order to counteract bias that is based in ignorance or unfounded beliefs about sexual orientation" (p. 934). The resolution also requires a full discussion by the therapist of the client's potential for happiness as an LGB individual and communication that no solid scientific evidence exists that conversion treatments are effective in changing sexual orientation. The American Psychiatric Association (2000) has expressed stronger cautions by warning practitioners against attempting to change a client's sexual orientation until more is known about the risks, benefits, and long-term outcomes of such interventions. Similarly, the Association for Gay, Lesbian, and Bisexual Issues in Counseling (n.d.) stated that competent counselors do not attempt to alter the sexual orientation of LGB clients.

As descriptive data (Beckstead & Morrow, 2004; Shidlo & Schroeder, 2002) and clinical experience (Haldeman, 2001) suggest, clients who undergo conversion therapy may experience initial hope and relief from working within their values framework and being provided with cognitive and behavioral strategies to reduce acting on same-sex attractions and disassociate from an LGB identity. Yet such therapy has the potential to reinforce negative stereotypes of LGB individuals, misinform about realistic outcomes, restrict education of the range of lifestyle options, and mislead clients to internalize treatment failure. These aspects have been known to intensify self-hatred, confusion, hopelessness, discrimination, intimacy difficulties, and suicidal ideation (Beckstead & Morrow, 2004; Bieschke, Paul, & Blasko, chap. 12, this volume; Haldeman, 2001; Shidlo & Schroeder, 2002). Given that the positive aspects found in conversion therapy (such as religious validation, reframing, behavioral strategies, and group work) can be found in most effective therapies, and given that the potential exists for significant harms from conversion ideology and interventions, it is unnecessary and unethical to provide such therapy (Beckstead & Morrow, 2004).

Despite the potentially negative consequences of conversion therapy, Haldeman (2004) emphasized that therapists must neither reflexively agree with nor discourage clients' requests for sexual reorientation. Reflexively supporting a client's request for conversion therapy is problematic for reasons stated earlier. Concerns about the negative impact of reflexively discouraging an acutely conflicted client from seeking out conversion therapy are based on the possibility that if the therapist is unable to join and dialogue with the client in a way that feels affirmative, then distrust and resistance may impede or end the therapeutic relationship. Some clients may believe that the therapist does not respect their interests or understand the complexity of their dilemmas and thus may seek out conversion treatments elsewhere or lose hope altogether and feel increasingly suicidal.

Alternatively, therapists can normalize their clients' desires to change their sexual orientation, given the significant cultural pressures to be heterosexual and not LGB. A therapist might support a client in examining the pros and cons of conversion principles and interventions and then process together this information to help the client sort out his or her feelings and distinguish biases from facts. Such clients may benefit from education that shows that (a) homosexual and bisexual attractions and behaviors are a normal variant of the human experience (Lasser & Gottlieb, 2004); (b) same-sex relationships can be stable and meaningful (Peplau, 1993); (c) the causes of sexual orientation are unknown (Worthington, 2004); (d) evidence supporting the possibility of sexual conversion is lacking (O'Donohue & Plaud, 1994); and (e) theories underlying conversion therapy are misguided and unsubstantiated (Drescher, 1998). Therapists must also be prepared to respond to clients' questions about the well-publicized study in which Spitzer (2003) asserted that some LGB people had changed their sexual orientation. Therapists can enlighten clients about the significant methodological and conceptual flaws in this study and other research that supports the efficacy of conversion therapy (see Haldeman, 1994; Morrow & Beckstead, 2004; Wakefield, 2003).

Some clients, however, may remain determined about trying to change their sexual orientation. A client's request for a referral for conversion therapy may present a challenge for an LGB-affirmative counselor. As with all issues, therapists should refer only to practitioners who they consider ethical, and given the significant ethical concerns related to conversion therapy, such a referral may be inconsistent with a therapist's professional judgment. Moreover, providing a referral may mislead the client into believing that the therapist endorses such interventions. If a client decides to seek out conversion treatments after being given the previously described informed discussions, the therapist may want to develop an interim plan and negotiate transitions or follow-ups. It would also be imperative to advise the client to monitor during the upcoming treatment process any increased feelings of failure, shame, hopelessness, and homonegativity and to ask the client to return if she or he becomes more conflicted.

ASSESSING THE CLIENT'S MOTIVATIONS FOR SEEKING TREATMENT

Davison (1978) initially proposed that, rather than treating the client's sexual orientation, therapy for those in conflict with their sexual orientation should focus on resolving the problems that the client has with his or her sexual orientation. Supporting this approach, the following sections describe areas to assess so that the client and therapist may understand the inter- and intrapersonal reasons the client may be distressed about her or his same-sex attractions.

Assessing the Client's External Motivations

Given the cultural variations on sexual identity and expression described earlier, it is essential to understand clients' struggles within the contexts of race, ethnicity, culture, and national origin. Because a client's experience of his or her culture may depend on a variety of contextual factors (e.g., acculturation, geographical region, generation, and socioeconomics status) and individual differences (e.g., gender, age, ability status, and appearance or size), a therapist should not rely simply on the client's response to an "ethnicity" question on an intake form. Rather, therapists can gain a more complex and accurate understanding of the impact of culture on sexual identity by assessing the interaction of the client's multiple identities. Dworkin (1997), for example, suggested that therapists work with clients to construct a personal ethnic identity lifeline and sexual identity lifeline and examine how such experiences affect each other. A narrative exploration may uncover effects on the client of growing up as different from members of the dominant culture and any history or fears of marginalization from family, peers, coworkers, and other cultural communities. In this way, the therapist may normalize the client's experiences and help the client to understand how his or her social contexts have validated or conflicted with same-sex attractions, allowing the therapist and client to recognize any stereotypes or social pressures that restrict the client's viewpoint and choices. Therapists can further enhance their knowledge by familiarizing themselves with literature that describes the intersections of culture and sexual orientation (e.g., Bing, 2004; Espin, 1993; Israel, 2004a; Loiacano, 1989; Ratti, 1993; Rust, 1996).

In addition to gathering information about the attitudes of the client's cultural community regarding sexual orientation, a therapist may want to inquire about how connected the client is to his or her culture(s) and what social resources are available. Tozer and McClanahan (1999) suggested asking who within the client's surroundings would reject and who would accept the client as SSA or LGB; who the client knows who is happy being SSA or LGB; and who the client knows who has integrated or resolved the conflicts faced by the client. Similarly, Bing (2004) suggested assessing the ability of the client and her or his family to openly discuss issues regarding ethnicity and sexuality and to support an identity that defies or contradicts traditional cultural standards. The therapist should also explore any concerns the client may have about his or her racial or other cultural identity not being validated within the larger LGB community. With this extensive information, the therapist may be able to empathize more fully and explore with the client ways to develop necessary external and internal resources.

To understand the context of a client's religious and sexual conflicts, a therapist can explore the client's definition of religion and spirituality; the role spirituality and religion play in the client's life; the client's attitudes toward her or his deity and religious community; what the client's religious leaders and doctrines say about sexuality, gender roles, homosexuality, and bisexuality; and the client's view of his or her deity's judgment of same-sex attractions and of the client. A respectful assessment is required to understand what it means for that client to live by the normative teachings of her or his religion, what influences a client's choice not to engage in same-sex behavior, and what it means if that client has such feelings or acts on those feelings (Buchanan, Dzelme, Harris, & Hecker, 2001; Yarhouse & Burkett, 2002). Further areas to assess include how religion has affected clients' morals (e.g., perceptions of what is good versus what is bad), how much they rely on authorities for answers, what level of tolerance for differences their religion allows, and how family attachments and racial and other cultural experiences affect the underlying meanings of clients' religious attachments. Similarly, Haldeman (2004) suggested asking clients whether they are attached to their religious institutions out of family tradition, fear, genuine love, or a combination thereof. Many of these suggestions draw on literature that explicitly or implicitly focuses on Judeo-Christian doctrines and practices. Thus, a therapist may need to go beyond available literature and consult with professionals who have expertise in non-Judeo-Christian religions to understand clients who have conflicts with other religions.

A final external motivator to assess will be the clients' history with and current status of romantic and sexual relationships. Counselors will want to understand the range of emotional experiences, needs, difficulties, and joys that clients have gone through within past and present same-sex and mixed-sex relationships. Knowing a client's dreams and expectations for future relationships may identify her or his life goals. Counselors can explore married clients' reasons for marrying, degree of commitment and intimacy toward spouse and family, and conflicts related to divergent roles and needs. Specific cultural pressures that may impact a client's marital decisions may include norms to avoid divorce at all costs, beliefs about the invalidity of same-sex partnerships, and gender role restrictions. Above all, a married client may feel overwhelmed with trying to decide how to keep the family intact while exploring sexuality and identity.

Assessing the Client's Internal Motivations

In addition to exploring the client's cultural pressures and messages regarding same-sex attractions, the therapist and client can work together to understand the degree to which the client has internalized and is affected by these viewpoints. Clients who are conflicted may believe restricted stereotypes that allege being LGB means a lifestyle of promiscuity, disease, gender-variant behaviors, loneliness, and discrimination (Krajeski, Myers, Valgemae, & Pattison, 1981; Rosik, 2003). The social devaluation of LGB people may also contaminate SSA clients' identity development with shame and self-negation (Green, 2003; Malyon, 1982). For example, Beckstead and Morrow (2004) described a variety of labels that conservative religious SSA individuals had adopted growing up. These individuals considered themselves different and unacceptable; lost and alone; perverts; sissies or tomboys (or not male/not female); abominations, evil, and damned; and worthless, inferior, and not good enough. Such self-concepts were described as causing considerable distress and influencing these individuals' motivations to be heterosexual because, for them, not being LGB was the only way to change such negative self-identities. Tozer and McClanahan (1999) proposed several questions to bring into awareness the negative messages about LGB issues that may have become deeply ingrained within clients: What are your beliefs about your chances for happiness if you identify as LGB, how does being LGB not fit and being heterosexual fit more for you, and what do you imagine would be your daily life if you lived within a heterosexual or a same-sex relationship? In addition, some clients may experience negative emotions and hold negative attitudes about sex and sexuality in general. Thus, assessing the client's erotophobia and history of sexual trauma is essential to understanding the layers of conflicts that clients are facing. Overall, it is important to understand clients' associations as to what LGB, SSA, heterosexual, and even sexual would mean to them and what experiences formed their viewpoints.

Once therapist and client understand the negative self-labels adopted by the client from living within the client's social environments, therapy can proceed with understanding the emotional impact of being subjected to and believing these self-labels. Through this multileveled evaluation, the client may decide to reject such labels and consider more affirming and accurate self-concepts. Other specific areas to assess may be clients' ability to deal with conflict, their desires for social acceptance, and their beliefs about locus of control and sense of autonomy.

Assessing the Client's Coping Strategies

A therapist may want to assess how clients have coped with their attractions, conflicts, differentness, and painful emotions, given that mood and personality disorders may have developed as a result of inadequate external support and internal resources. Therapists should be attuned to both maladaptive coping strategies, such as denial, passivity, substance abuse, suicidal ideation, disconnection from emotions, and avoidance of or hatred toward LGB people, as well as adaptive ones, such as obtaining self-worth and identity from sources other than heterosexist or homonegative communities (Beckstead & Morrow, 2004; Troiden, 1993). Some clients may also confuse the distress caused by their maladaptive coping with their desires to change sexual orientation. For example, a male client may focus on trying to change his sexual orientation because he is distressed when he obsessively "cruises" for sex and jeopardizes his values and marital and work commitments. Thus, counselors may need to help clients distinguish between problems arising from dealing with same-sex attractions and behavioral patterns experienced regardless of sexual orientation (e.g., sexual compulsiveness, objectification of others, lack of assertiveness, and intimacy problems).

Additional Aspects of Diagnosis

Last, therapists must be able to identify psychological issues that could contribute to conflicts about sexual orientation. For example, a client with obsessive–compulsive disorder may ruminate on fears of being gay that have no basis in same-sex attractions, or a client who is questioning gender identity may initially present with concerns about sexual orientation. Overall, a counselor's listening to clients' complex underlying needs to change helps both the counselor and the client focus on what is required for the client to maximize the development of a congruent and healthy lifestyle.

THERAPEUTIC CONSIDERATIONS FOR RESOLVING SEXUAL ORIENTATION CONFLICTS

Certain steps seem to help some conservative religious clients in conflict develop self-acceptance and consolidate a positive identity (Beckstead & Morrow, 2004). The variables that facilitate these changes are described in the following sections, with guidance from other research and clinical literature and suggestions on how such variables may relate to other cultural conflicts. Therapists must decide which of the following considerations would be useful for their clients, given the context and evolving perspective of each particular client. For a thorough review, therapists may read the case examples provided in the clinical literature regarding clients conflicted about their sexual orientation (e.g., Bing, 2004, Green, 1998; Haldeman, 2004; Isay, 1998; Lasser & Gottlieb, 2004; Schneider, Brown, & Glassgold, 2002). General goals include broadening clients' perspectives, increasing self-efficacy, and empowering clients through a process of normalization, psychoeducation, exploration, reevaluation, and integration. Research is sorely needed regarding how people of color and other oppressed groups resolve their unique conflicts with sexual orientation.

Rejecting Negative Self-Labels and Finding One's Value

A therapist's task is to correct the harmful effects of antigay socialization on the self-concepts of LGB individuals (Haldeman, 1996, 2002). Confronting racism, sexism, and other oppressive socialization is an additional task for those working with SSA individuals holding multiple minority statuses. Some clients may also benefit from healing their experiences related to gender nonconformity (Landolt, Bartholomew, Saffrey, Oram, & Perlman, 2004). Techniques from diverse theoretical orientations (see Fassinger, 2000) may be used to help the client identify, evaluate, and replace internalized negative beliefs with feelings of worth, acceptance, self-understanding, and belongingness. By focusing on the positive aspects of his or her individuality and diverse cultural identities, the client may begin to accept and internalize his or her self-worth and strengths (Bing, 2004; Tozer & McClanahan, 1999). Yet this work may be difficult for clients who rely on validation from family, community, and the dominant culture to dictate how to feel or act. Thus, exploring with clients the process and effects of such external validation may help clients select more reliable and valid sources of information to describe themselves and their relationships.

Dispelling Myths About LGB People and Meeting Similar Others

A variety of tools are available to help therapists challenge myths and stereotypes and provide clients with accurate information. This may be done by providing clients with LGB-affirming literature and facilitating their involvement with a variety of LGB and SSA community groups. It may be particularly helpful for clients to meet others with similar values, interests, and cultural backgrounds. Conflicted or ambivalent clients may need help managing any disappointments and exclusions experienced in or from LGB communities, for this disillusionment may compel some to foreclose future exploration and engagement (Brzezinski, 2000). Moreover, Haldeman (2004) pointed out that therapists may need to help clients understand how self-loathing becomes projected onto the LGB community, so that clients recognize how negativity toward the LGB community may be a reflection of internalized homonegativity. Haldeman also suggested discussing with clients their fears of exposure or any other consequences if they were to explore LGB venues. This overall process has multiple benefits of helping clients dispel inaccurate fears, expand perspectives of the multiple ways of being LGB and SSA, desensitize anxiety about self-disclosure, gain resources, feel more normal, resolve feelings of being alone, and find a place to belong and fit in.

Accepting and Feeling Congruent With One's Attractions

Essential to developing a positive self-identity is learning how to accept one's attractions as a core part of self. Results from Beckstead and Morrow (2004), for example, suggested that those who stopped trying to reject their attractions and learned ways to reframe them in a positive light were the ones who found the most peace in their lives, regardless of behavioral or identity outcome. This acceptance and affirmation seemed to give these research participants permission to be "who they are" and not hate or fear their sexual feelings. This result was influenced by participants' evaluating the negative messages they internalized about same-sex attractions, evaluating their ability to eliminate these attractions, and hearing alternative perspectives about such attractions. There are a variety of ways to view one's attractions (e.g., as a sin, a burden, an emotional need, a normal impulse, a test, a joy, a gift; as unimportant or essential; or as urges used to create or destroy), and clients may need help in deciding which framework fits best with their values and developing perspectives.

A counselor can also help the client establish an accurate picture of the complexity of the client's sexuality and sexual orientation. This may be done by using multidimensional assessments of the degrees of emotional and erotic attractions and aversions toward men and women; the range of sexual fantasies, behaviors, values, gender roles, and identity preferences; and the duration and changes in intensities of these experiences over time (e.g., Klein, Sepekoff, & Wolf, 1986). This comprehensive assessment is important in determining and accepting the realistic possibilities and shortcomings of various relationship outcomes. Although some clients may, through their developing perspectives, redefine a same-sex relationship as essential and fulfilling, others may not. For example, a client who is primarily attracted to the same sex with little or no erotic opposite-sex attractions may still want to live as a heterosexual; yet hoping to create significant other-sex erotic attractions may prove futile and disappointing. However, this same client may decide to adopt a heterosexual or bisexual identity and enter into or remain in a mixed-sex relationship if she or he is with an other-sex person who does not emphasize the sexual components of the relationship but focuses on emotional intimacy and is comfortable with a partner who is same-sex attracted. Clients who pursue this route will need to take into account the short- and long-term consequences of self-disclosing to those they date or marry. Therapists can help clients attend to integrity with self and others when deciding on the best relationship outcome for the client and any current or potential partners.

After understanding and ceasing to fight against the reality of their attractions, clients can then decide on a personal ethical code of how and with whom they will express their attractions. This process may expand clients' sense of self-control, congruence, and enactment of a healthy sexuality. For clients struggling to limit their sexual behaviors, treatment may focus on developing self-monitoring skills, such as expressing needs in nonsexual ways, acknowledging sexual attractions to same-sex individuals but not following through with continual eroticizing of those individuals, developing relationship boundaries and limits, enhancing emotional intimacy with others, and increasing satisfaction in other life roles. As stated earlier, therapy may focus on replacing a client's maladaptive coping with effective ways of dealing with stress and sexuality.

Consolidating a Self-Identity

When therapists assist clients in identifying, sorting out, examining, and prioritizing the multiple dimensions of their lives, clients may become clearer about who they are and what they want (and do not want). This process of commitment (Troiden, 1993) may also include the client's reevaluation of the appropriateness for her- or himself of the variety of norms within LGB and SSA communities as well as his or her cultural communities. In this manner, clients may construct personal relationships to and affirmation of their specific culture(s) and sexuality without committing to any behaviors or values that do not fit for them (Dworkin, 1997). As research suggests, some conservative, religious individuals may need to undergo a process of disillusionment with and redefining of previous ideologies to reconcile conflicts and construct affirming self-concepts (Beckstead & Morrow, 2004; Goodwill, 2000; Wolkomir, 2001; Yarhouse & Tan, 2004). This may include, for the client, finding acceptable ways to alter religious and cultural beliefs to feel welcome within society and his or her deity's plan, redefining sin and the meaning of being SSA and LGB, believing that his or her deity continues to love the client because of or despite her or his attractions, and feeling spiritual outside the context of religion. Other alternatives include joining an LGB-affirmative religion or remaining faithful within one's religion but self-identifying as being SSA (Perlstein, 1996).

After clients decide which ideologies and behaviors of their diverse identities fit for their developing perspective, the next step may be to adopt and integrate the selected ideologies and behaviors into one unified self-identity. This may correspond to first taking on an LGB, SSA, or heterosexual identity, or no label at all, or to creating one's own label and then deciding how this sexual identity interrelates with the other cultural identities and within which contexts. Because of the potential "either/or" dilemma faced by clients in conflict, many may have focused their energies on developing certain areas of their lives while leaving other areas in the periphery. Clients may decide then to create flexible and integrated ways of expressing their multiple aspects of self in diverse settings and to focus on developing all identities simultaneously or some sequentially (Bing, 2004). Therapists may thus help clients expand their self-categories by showing them how to embrace possible ways to validate "the whole package" and integrate all the aspects of their lives. As clients make such choices, therapists may need to help clients identify the tangible and intangible losses encountered by such decisions so that clients may grieve and find other ways of meeting their needs (Haldeman, 2004). In this way, clients may find individualized and integrative solutions in which benefits are maximized, harms are minimized, and they feel the most comfortable.

Helping a Client Negotiate Her or His Identity With the Outside World

As clients strengthen their worth, security, and identity, more tasks may lie ahead. Specifically, they may need help in enhancing acceptance and honesty within their present support systems and in making decisions to leave, stay in, or redefine their relationships and associations. Counselors can help clients who have started to self-identify as LGB (or who wish to be more open about being SSA) to develop decision-making skills about coming out to others (Matthews, chap. 8, this volume). For some clients, it may be adaptive to selectively conceal an LGB identity to maintain key familial, cultural, and economic support, and counselors can help clients to consider the advantages and disadvantages of disclosure in various settings (Green, 2000; Israel, 2003). With such steps, clients will need to develop internal and external resources to withstand losses, fears, and discrimination often accompanied by being openly SSA or LGB. Connecting the client with community resources and role models who are affirming seems indispensable. Along these lines, it may be necessary to support LGB or SSA ethnic minority individuals in actively finding or forming organizations and support groups that represent their multicultural identities (Loiacano, 1989).

Providing Group Therapy

Given the unique challenges faced by clients in conflict, therapists may want to develop a group therapy modality whereby clients may find a safe, middle-ground perspective to explore their ambivalence and conflicts without participating in an LGB-identified therapy group or conversion therapy program. Recruiting may be difficult, given the outreach limitations and potential clients' fears of "if I go to group, it's admitting I have these attractions." However, group therapy would encompass many of the variables described previously in developing self-acceptance and a positive self-identity. Specifically, a heterogeneous group, with male and female group members from diverse cultural backgrounds with differing perspectives and goals, has the potential to increase exploration of a variety of solutions, provide feedback about misinformation, and enhance respect for diversity. Through a process of being interested in, questioning, dialoguing with, and relating to each other, members may learn to validate their own diverse choices, values, and relationships. Above all, a group setting can desensitize anxiety and provide opportunities to develop authentic relationships and emotional closeness. For those clients who wished to remain "closeted" or keep their same-sex attractions private, group would be at least one place where they could be known and feel accepted.

CONCLUSION

Clients in conflict regarding their sexual orientation face unique challenges. Therapists who work with this client population are reminded to prepare themselves by acquiring accurate information, exploring attitudes, and developing skills regarding clients' complex issues. Ultimately, therapists may need to consider the benefits of broadening their treatment approach to focus on helping clients gain new perspectives about themselves and their options. Given the homonegative, binegative, and heterosexist environments that prevail, therapists can help clients by creating space to affirm and celebrate the variety of ways in which individuals may live out their sexuality and sexual orientation within their social contexts and throughout their life span.

REFERENCES

American Psychiatric Association. (2000). Commission on Psychotherapy by Psychiatrists (COPP): Position statement on therapies focused on attempts to change sexual orientation (reparative or conversion therapies). *American Journal of Psychiatry, 157*, 1719–1721.

American Psychological Association. (1998). Appropriate therapeutic responses to sexual orientation in the proceedings of the American Psychological Association, Incorporated, for the legislative year 1997. *American Psychologist, 53*, 882–939.

American Psychological Association. (2002). Ethical principles of psychologists and code of conduct. *American Psychologist, 57*, 1060–1073.

American Psychological Association, Division 44/Committee on Lesbian, Gay, and Bisexual Concerns Joint Task Force on Guidelines for Psychotherapy With Lesbian, Gay, and Bisexual Clients. (2000). Guidelines for psychotherapy with lesbian, gay, and bisexual clients. *American Psychologist, 55*, 1440–1451.

Association for Gay, Lesbian, and Bisexual Issues in Counseling (n.d.). *Competencies for counseling gay, lesbian, bisexual and transgendered (GLBT) clients.* Retrieved September 12, 2004, from http://www.aglbic.org/resources/competencies.html

Beckstead, A. L. (2001). Cures versus choices: Agendas in sexual reorientation therapy. *Journal of Gay & Lesbian Psychotherapy, 5*(3–4), 87–115.

Beckstead, A. L., & Morrow, S. L. (2004). Mormon clients' experiences of conversion therapy: The need for a new treatment approach. *The Counseling Psychologist, 32*, 651–690.

Besen, W. R. (2003). *Anything but straight: Unmasking the scandals and lies behind the ex-gay myth.* Binghamton, NY: Harrington Park Press.

Betz, N. E. 1989. Implications of the null environment hypothesis for women's career development and for counseling psychology. *The Counseling Psychologist, 17,* 136–144.

Bing, V. M. (2004). Out of the closet but still in hiding: Conflicts and identity issues for a Black-White biracial lesbian. *Women & Therapy, 27,* 185–201.

Bohan, J. S. (1996). *Psychology and sexual orientation: Coming to terms.* New York: Taylor & Francis/Routledge.

Browning, C., Reynolds, A. L., & Dworkin, S. H. (1991). Affirmative psychotherapy for lesbian women. *The Counseling Psychologist, 19,* 177–196.

Brzezinski, L. G. (2000). *Dealing with disparity: Identity development of same-sex attracted/gay men raised in the Church of Jesus Christ of Latter-day Saints.* Unpublished doctoral dissertation, University of Utah, Salt Lake City.

Buchanan, M., Dzelme, K., Harris, D., & Hecker, L. (2001). Challenges of being simultaneously gay or lesbian and spiritual and/or religious: A narrative perspective. *The American Journal of Family Therapy, 29,* 435–449.

Chan, C. S. (1997). Don't ask, don't tell, don't know: The formation of a homosexual identity and sexual expression among Asian American lesbians. In B. Greene (Ed.), *Ethnic and cultural diversity among lesbians and gay men* (pp. 240–248). Thousand Oaks, CA: Sage.

Coleman, E. (1982). Changing approaches to the treatment of homosexuality: A review. In W. Paul, J. D. Weinrich, J. C. Gonsiorek, & M. E. Hotvedt (Eds.), *Homosexuality: Social, psychological, and biological issues* (pp. 81–88). Beverly Hills, CA: Sage.

Davison, G. C. (1978). Not can but ought: The treatment of homosexuality. *Journal of Consulting and Clinical Psychology, 46,* 170–172.

Diamond, L. M. (2003). Was it a phase? Young women's relinquishment of lesbian/bisexual identities over a 5-year period. *Journal of Personality and Social Psychology, 84,* 352–364.

Drescher, J. (1998). I'm your handyman: A history of reparative therapies. *Journal of Homosexuality, 36*(1), 19–42.

Dworkin, S. H. (1997). Female, lesbian, and Jewish: Complex and invisible. In B. Greene (Ed.), *Ethnic and cultural diversity among lesbians and gay men* (pp. 63–87). Thousand Oaks, CA: Sage.

Espin, O. M. (1993). Issues of identity in the psychology of Latina lesbians. In L. D. Garnets & D.C. Kimmel (Eds.), *Psychological perspectives on lesbian and gay male experiences* (pp. 348–363). New York: Columbia University Press.

Fassinger, R. (2000). Applying counseling theories to lesbian, gay, and bisexual clients: Pitfalls and possibilities. In R. M. Perez, K. A. DeBord, & K. J. Bieschke (Eds.), *Handbook of counseling and psychotherapy with lesbian, gay, and bisexual clients* (pp. 107–132). Washington, DC: American Psychological Association.

Fukuyama, M. A., & Ferguson, A. D. (2000). Lesbian, gay, and bisexual people of color: Understanding cultural complexity and managing multiple oppressions. In R. M. Perez, K. A. DeBord, and K. J. Bieschke (Eds.), *Handbook of counseling and psychotherapy with lesbian, gay, and bisexual clients* (pp. 81–105). Washington, DC: American Psychological Association.

Garnets, L. D. (2002). Sexual orientations in perspectives. *Cultural Diversity and Ethnic Minority Psychology, 8,* 115–129.

Goodwill, K. A. (2000). Religion and the spiritual needs of gay men. *Journal of Gay & Lesbian Social Services, 11*(4), 23–37.

Green, B. C. (1998). Thinking about students who do not identify as gay, lesbian, or bisexual, but . . . *Journal of American College Health, 47,* 89–91.

Green, R. J. (2000). Lesbians, gay men, and their parents: A critique of Lasala and the prevailing clinical "wisdom." *Family Process, 39,* 257–266.

Green, R. J. (2003). When therapists do not want their clients to be homosexual: A response to Rosik's article. *Journal of Marital and Family Therapy, 29,* 29–38.

Greene, B. (1997). *Ethnic and cultural diversity among lesbians and gay men.* Thousand Oaks, CA: Sage.

Haldeman, D. C. (1994). The practice and ethics of sexual orientation conversion therapy. *Journal of Consulting and Clinical Psychology, 62,* 221–227.

Haldeman, D. C. (1996). Spirituality and religion in the lives of lesbians and gay men. In R. P. Cabaj & T. S. Stein (Eds.), *Textbook of homosexuality and mental health* (pp. 881–896). Washington, DC: American Psychiatric Press.

Haldeman, D. C. (2001). Therapeutic antidotes: Helping gay and bisexual men recover from conversion therapies. *Journal of Gay & Lesbian Psychotherapy, 5*(3–4), 117–130.

Haldeman, D. C. (2002). Gay rights, patient rights: The implications of sexual orientation conversion therapy. *Professional Psychology: Research and Practice, 33,* 260–264.

Haldeman, D. C. (2004). When sexual and religious orientation collide: Considerations in working with conflicted same-sex attracted male clients. *The Counseling Psychologist, 32,* 691–715.

Human Rights Campaign Foundation. (2002). *The state of the workplace for lesbian, gay, bisexual, and transgender Americans 2002.* Washington, DC: Author.

Isay, R. (1998). Heterosexually married homosexual men: Clinical and developmental issues. *American Journal of Orthopsychiatry, 68*(3), 424–432.

Israel, T. (2003). Integrating gender and sexual orientation into the multicultural counseling competencies. In G. Roysircar, P. Arredondo, J. N. Fuertes, J. G. Ponterotto, & R. L. Toporek (Eds.), *Multicultural counseling competencies 2003: Association for Multicultural Counseling and Development* (pp. 69–77). Alexandria, VA: Association for Multicultural Counseling and Development.

Israel, T. (2004a). Conversations, not categories: The intersection of biracial and bisexual identities. *Women & Therapy, 27,* 173–184.

Israel, T. (2004b). What counselors need to know about working with sexual minority clients. In D. R. Atkinson and G. Hackett (Eds.), *Counseling Diverse Populations* (pp. 347–364). Boston: McGraw-Hill.

Klein, F., Sepekoff, B., & Wolf, T. J. (1986). Sexual orientation: A multivariable dynamic process. *Journal of Homosexuality, 11*(1–2), 35–49.

Krajeski, J. P., Myers, M. F., Valgemae, A., & Pattison, E. M. (1981). "Ex-gays": Religious abuse of psychiatry? *American Journal of Psychiatry, 138*, 852–853.

Lambda Legal. (2003). *Background on Lambda Legal's Supreme Court case challenging Texas's "Homosexual Conduct" law.* Retrieved September 12, 2004, from http://www.lambdalegal.org/cgi-bin/iowa/documents/record?record = 1190

Landolt, M. A., Bartholomew, K., Saffrey, C., Oram, D., & Perlman, D. (2004). Gender nonconformity, childhood rejection, and adult attachment: A study of gay men. *Archives of Sexual Behavior, 33*, 117–128.

Lasser, J. S., & Gottlieb, M. C. (2004). Treating patients distressed regarding their sexual orientation: Clinical and ethical alternatives. *Professional Psychology: Research and Practice, 35*, 194–200.

Loiacano, D. K. (1989). Gay identity issues among Black Americans: Racism, homophobia, and the need for validation. *Journal of Counseling and Development, 68*, 21–25.

Malyon, A. K. (1982). Psychotherapeutic implications of internalized homophobia in gay men. *Journal of Homosexuality, 7*(2–3), 59–69.

Miville, M. L., & Ferguson, A. D. (2004). Impossible "choices": Identity and values at a crossroads. *The Counseling Psychologist, 32*, 760–770.

Moberly, E. (1983). *Homosexuality: A new Christian ethic.* Cambridge, England: James Clark.

Morales, L. (1989). Ethnic minority families and minority gays and lesbians. *Marriage and Family Review, 14*, 217–239.

Morrow, S. L., & Beckstead, A. L. (2004). Conversion therapies for same-sex attracted clients in religious conflict: Context, predisposing factors, experiences, and implications for therapy. *The Counseling Psychologist, 32*, 641–650.

Murphy, T. F. (1997). *Gay science: The ethics of sexual orientation research.* New York: Columbia University Press.

Nicolosi, J. (1993). *Healing homosexuality.* Northvale, NJ: Jason Aronson.

Nicolosi, J., Byrd, A. D., & Potts, R. W. (2000a). Beliefs and practices of therapists who practice sexual reorientation psychotherapy. *Psychological Review, 86*, 689–702.

Nicolosi, J., Byrd, A. D., & Potts, R. W. (2000b). Retrospective self-reports of changes in homosexual orientation: A consumer survey of conversion therapy clients. *Psychological Reports, 86*, 1071–1088.

O'Donohue, W., & Plaud, J. J. (1994). The conditioning of human sexual arousal. *Archives of Sexual Behavior, 23*, 321–344.

Peplau, L. A. (1993). Lesbian and gay relationships. In L. D. Garnets & D. C. Kimmel (Eds.), *Psychological perspectives on lesbian and gay male experiences* (pp. 395–419). New York: Columbia University Press.

Perlstein, M. (1996). Integrating a gay, lesbian, or bisexual person's religious and spiritual needs and choices into psychotherapy. In C. J. Alexander (Ed.), *Gay and lesbian mental health: A sourcebook for practitioners* (pp. 173–188). New York: Harrington Park Press.

Phillips, J. C. (2004). A welcome addition to the literature: Non-polarized approaches to sexual orientation and religiosity. *The Counseling Psychologist, 32,* 771–777.

Ratti, R. (Ed.). (1993). *A lotus of another color: An unfolding of the South Asian gay and lesbian experience.* Boston: Alyson.

Rich, A. (1980). Compulsory heterosexuality and lesbian existence. *Signs: Journal of Women in Culture and Society, 5,* 631–660.

Ritter, K., & O'Neill, C. (1989), Moving through loss: The spiritual journey of gay men and lesbian women. *Journal of Counseling Development, 68,* 9–14.

Rodriguez, R. A. (1996). Clinical issues in identity development in gay Latino men. In C. J. Alexander (Ed.), *Gay and lesbian mental health: A sourcebook for practitioners* (pp. 127–158). New York: Harrington Park Press.

Rosik, C. H. (2003). Motivational, ethical, and epistemological foundations in the treatment of unwanted homoerotic attractions. *Journal of Marital and Family Therapy, 29,* 13–28.

Rust, P. C. (1996). Managing multiple identities: Diversity among bisexual women and men. In B. A. Firestein (Ed.), *Bisexuality: The psychology and politics of an invisible minority* (pp. 53–83). Thousand Oaks, CA: Sage.

Rust, P. C. (2003). Reparative science and social responsibility: The concept of a malleable core as theoretical challenge and psychological comfort. *Archives of Sexual Behavior, 32,* 449–451.

Schneider, M., Brown, L., & Glassgold, J. (2002). Implementing the resolution on appropriate therapeutic responses to sexual orientation: A guide for the perplexed. *Professional Psychology: Research and Practice, 33,* 265–276.

Shannon, J. W., & Woods, W. J. (1991). Affirmative psychotherapy with gay men. *The Counseling Psychologist, 19,* 197–215.

Shidlo, A., & Schroeder, M. (2002). Changing sexual orientation: A consumers' report. *Professional Psychology: Research and Practice, 33,* 249–259.

Spitzer, R. L. (2003). Can some gay men and lesbians change their sexual orientation? 200 subjects reporting a change from homosexual to heterosexual orientation. *Archives of Sexual Behavior, 32,* 403–417.

Stanley, J. L. (2004). Biracial lesbian and bisexual women: Understanding the unique aspects and interactional processes of multiple minority identities. *Women & Therapy, 27,* 159–171.

Strickland, B. R. (1997). Leaving the Confederate closet. In B. Greene (Ed.), *Ethnic and cultural diversity among lesbians and gay men* (pp. 39–62). Thousand Oaks, CA: Sage.

Throckmorton, W. (2002). Initial empirical and clinical findings concerning the change process for ex-gays. *Professional Psychology: Research and Practice, 33,* 242–248.

Tozer, E. E., & Hayes, J. A. (2004). The role of religiosity, internalized homonegativity, and identity development: Why do individuals seek conversion therapy? *The Counseling Psychologist, 32,* 716–740.

Tozer, E. E., & McClanahan, M. K. (1999). Treating the purple menace: Ethical considerations of conversion therapy and affirmative alternatives. *The Counseling Psychologist, 27*, 722–742.

Troiden, R. R. (1993). The formation of homosexual identities. In L. D. Garnets & D. C. Kimmel (Eds.), *Psychological perspectives on lesbian and gay male experiences* (pp. 191–217). New York: Columbia University Press.

Udis-Kessler, A. (1990). Bisexuality in an essentialist world: Toward an understanding of biphobia. In T. Geller (Ed.), *Bisexuality: A reader and sourcebook* (pp. 51–63). Ojai, CA: Times Change Press.

Wakefield, J. C. (2003). Sexual reorientation therapy: Is it ever ethical? Can it ever change sexual orientation? *Archives of Sexual Behavior, 32*, 457–460.

Wolkomir, M. (2001). Wrestling with the angels of meaning: The revisionist ideological work of gay and ex-gay Christian men. *Symbolic Interaction, 24*, 407–424.

Worthington, R. L. (2004). Sexual identity, sexual orientation, religious identity, and change: Is it possible to depolarize the debate? *The Counseling Psychologist, 32*, 741–749.

Yarhouse, M. A., & Burkett, L. A. (2002). An inclusive response to LGB and conservative religious persons: The case of same-sex attraction and behavior. *Professional Psychology: Research and Practice, 33*, 235–241.

Yarhouse, M. A., & Tan, E. S. N. (2004). *Sexual identity synthesis: Attributions, meaning-making and the search for congruence*. Lanham, MD: University Press of America.

10

BUILDING LESBIAN, GAY, AND BISEXUAL VOCATIONAL PSYCHOLOGY: A THEORETICAL MODEL OF WORKPLACE SEXUAL IDENTITY MANAGEMENT

MELISSA A. LIDDERDALE, JAMES M. CROTEAU, MARY Z. ANDERSON, DARRICK TOVAR-MURRAY, AND JULIE M. DAVIS

In the first edition of this handbook, Croteau, Anderson, DiStefano, and Kampa-Kokesch (2000) provided a systematic comprehensive review and analysis of the foundational literature in lesbian, gay, and bisexual (LGB) vocational psychology. They then suggested directions for future scholarship that would allow for the construction of more rigorous research and applied scholarship in this nascent field. The authors summarized the literature from 1980 to 1996 into five primary content areas: LGB identity development; anti-LGB discrimination in the workplace and LGB-related climate for LGB workers; managing sexual identity at work; societal messages and occupational interests, choices, and perceptions; and career practitioners and their interventions. In addition to the summaries of each content area, the authors emphasized that research efforts need to be more rigorous and involve a broader array of methods and that LGB vocational scholarship and practice need to be more grounded in specific theoretical formulations related to the experiences of this population. In the current chapter, we implement the recommendation to develop theoretical formulations related to the experiences of the LGB population. We articulate a theoretical model to guide scholarship and practice concerning one of the five content areas originally explicated: workplace sexual identity management.

NEW LITERATURE IN LGB VOCATIONAL PSYCHOLOGY

Before addressing the primary focus of this chapter, we describe key contributions to the field of LGB vocational psychology since 1996. Our intention is to provide a map that guides readers to the new literature. Instead of providing a thorough review, we focus on simply directing attention to key sources and broadly describing some consistent findings and developments across these sources. We begin by focusing on empirical contributions and then describe recent practice-oriented and theoretical literature.

Most new empirical literature addresses two of the five content areas identified in the original handbook chapter: (a) anti-LGB discrimination and LGB-related climate in the workplace and (b) managing sexual identity at work. There are nine relatively well-designed new studies that focus on one or both of these content areas (Anderson, Croteau, Chung, & DiStefano, 2001; Button, 2001; Chrobot-Mason, Button, & DiClementi, 2001; Day & Schoenrade, 1997; Griffith & Hebl, 2002; Liddle, Luzzo, Hauenstein, & Schuck, 2004; Ragins & Cornwell, 2001; Rostosky & Riggle, 2002; Waldo, 1999). These studies offer several interesting findings that should be employed in designing future research. Although a complete description of the findings is beyond the scope of this brief review, we highlight three important themes.

First, a number of studies found that LGB-affirmative policies were associated with workers being more open about their sexual identity and with workers reporting less discrimination and hostility, more support, or both (Button, 2001; Chrobot-Mason et al., 2001; Day & Schoenrade, 1997; Griffith & Hebl, 2002; Ragins & Cornwell, 2001; Rostosky & Riggle, 2002; Waldo, 1999). For instance, Ragins and Cornwell found that gay employees reported significantly less workplace discrimination when the organization had LG-supportive polices and practices ($r = -.28$); Rostosky and Riggle found, after considering the effects of gender, internalized homophobia, and an organization's nondiscrimination policy, that the nondiscrimination policy accounted for 10.7% of the predicted variance in workplace disclosure. Second, several studies found that an LGB-supportive climate was associated with greater disclosure of sexual orientation by LGB workers (Button, 2001; Day & Schoenrade, 1997; Griffith & Hebl, 2002). For example, Button found that a less supportive, more discriminatory workplace climate was associated with more use of concealing identity management strategies (counterfeiting, ß = .23; avoiding, ß = .19) and less use of revealing identity management strategies (integrating, ß = -.18). As a whole, these studies also offered better conceptual definitions and operational measures of both workplace climate and sexual identity management (Anderson et al., 2001; Chrobot-Mason et al., 2001; Liddle et al., 2004). Finally, also worth noting is a recent book by economist M. V. Lee Badgett (2001) that involves a careful analysis of existing economic data for lesbians and gay men. The results of this analysis support the existence of real economic discrimination toward lesbians and gay men, therein debunking myths of economic privilege among lesbians and gay men.

The remaining content areas identified in the original chapter received cursory attention in the new LGB vocational psychology literature. LGB identity development, one of the other content areas, received only marginal empirical attention, with four of the previously mentioned studies including some indicator of identity development (Button, 2001; Chrobot-Mason et al., 2001; Rostosky & Riggle, 2002; Waldo, 1999). Markers of identity development such as internalized homophobia were related to workers' disclosure of sexual orientation (Button, 2001; Rostosky & Riggle, 2002). For instance, Rostosky and Riggle found that, when considering the effects of gender and internalized homophobia, internalized homophobia accounted for 23.5% of the predicted variance in workplace disclosure. One study (Nauta, Saucier, & Woodard, 2001) was relevant to the content area involving occupational interests, choices, and perceptions. In this study, LGB college students endorsed the importance of having LGB career role models in their academic and career decision-making. Although these LGB students reported having statistically significant more role models, they also perceived statistically significant less support or guidance from others in comparison with their heterosexual counterparts. There were no research studies that focused on the remaining content area of career practitioners and career interventions.

As might be expected, the new practice-oriented literature focused on the content area concerning career counseling. Key literature included overviews of providing LGB-affirmative career services in employee assistance practice (Poverny, 2000) and higher education settings (Pope, Prince, & Mitchell, 2000; Worthington, McCrary, & Howard, 1998). The most significant new development in practice-oriented literature, however, focused uniquely on issues in career assessment with LGB clients. Chernin, Holden, and Chandler (1997) provided an initial examination of heterosexist bias in psychological assessment instruments, including the Strong Interest Inventory. Prince (1997) added significantly to their analysis by also considering assessor and interpretation bias. Chung (2003b) further extended the discussion by proposing a comprehensive framework for addressing the ethical and professional issues in the formal use of career testing as well as other forms of career assessment with LGB persons. He discussed the attitudes, skills, and knowledge necessary for the practice of, research into, and training in LGB career assessment.

Despite the recognition that theory-based research and practice are essential (Chung, 2003a; Croteau, 1996; Croteau et al., 2000; Longborg & Phillips, 1996), Chung's (2001) model of workplace discrimination and coping was the only new theoretical development since 1996. He delineated three dimensions of LGB workplace discrimination and discussed three strategies that LGB workers employ to cope with discrimination. In Chung's (2003a) review of LGB vocational psychology, he identified three approaches to advancing theory. He suggested applying traditional vocational development theories to this population, utilizing avocational LGB-specific theoretical models and developing "special theoretical frameworks" explaining LGB vocational behavior (p. 79). He further argued that the integration of these approaches holds promise for a more holistic and complete understanding of LGB career lives. The theoretical model concerning workplace sexual identity management proposed in this chapter employs Chung's suggested integration.

NEED FOR A COMPREHENSIVE MODEL OF WORKPLACE SEXUAL IDENTITY MANAGEMENT

Reviews of LGB vocational psychology have identified workplace sexual identity management as a core issue in understanding the unique vocational experiences of LGB people (Croteau, 1996; Croteau et al., 2000). According to these reviews, conceptual and empirical literature on how LGB workers deal with their identity at work was initially discussed and examined in terms of the amount of disclosure at work (e.g., who knows, whether one is "out," etc.). This research indicated that there was a great deal of variability in degree of disclosure, but provided little information concerning the process of how and why particular choices about disclosure are made. A more process-oriented understanding of LGB workers' choices came from qualitative studies. Workers in these qualitative studies described a multifaceted process involving numerous daily choices about revealing or concealing sexual identity in the face of potential discrimination and hostility in the workplace.

The most useful extant conceptual framework describing this complex process is the model of identity management that developed from Griffin's 1992 qualitative study (Chung, 2001; Croteau, 1996; Croteau et al., 2000). The model posits four general sexual identity management strategies located along a continuum from totally closeted to publicly out: passing, covering, implicitly out, and explicitly out. The passing strategy involves fabricating information in order to be perceived as heterosexual. The covering strategy involves censoring information in order to avoid being perceived as lesbian or gay. The implicitly out strategy involves being honest about one's life but not explicitly labeling oneself as lesbian or gay. The final strategy, explicitly out, involves being honest about one's life and explicitly identifying to others as lesbian or gay. According to the model, workers develop identity management strategies in response to the tension between fear of negative consequences and the need for self-integrity. Fear leads to passing and covering, whereas the need for integrity leads to being implicitly or explicitly out.

The strength of Griffin's (1992) model lies in its description of a range of strategies employed by workers. The model, however, is quite limited in a number of ways. The single motivation involving the tension between fear and integrity is too simplistic for fully understanding all the motivations that lead workers to choose and implement strategies. Key theoretical questions about how the strategies are learned and how they change over time remain unanswered. The influence of individual and contextual variables is not explained. More complex explanations are needed for questions such as the following:

- Why does a particular individual implement certain strategies in some work contexts and different strategies in other work contexts?
- What explains individual differences in identity managements for two people in the same work context?
- Why does a particular identity management strategy have different effects for various workers in various contexts?
- How does a person come to change his or her workplace identity management strategies over time?

In an effort to address such questions and integrate empirical findings, we present in this chapter a model that offers a more complete and complex explanation for how identity management strategies come to be chosen and implemented by LGB workers.

BACKGROUND TO THE WORKPLACE SEXUAL IDENTITY MANAGEMENT (WSIM) MODEL

Understanding sexual identity and its development is necessary to any consideration of how identity is managed. Initially, identity development models described a sequential process including discovering one's minority sexual orientation, overcoming internalized heterosexism in order to become accepting of one's orientation, and arriving at a proud and open identification as a member of the lesbian or gay social group (e.g., Cass, 1979; Sophie 1985/1986; Troiden, 1989). Although these early notions still have application, recent advances in LGB identity development models have increased the complexity and diversity in how identity is understood, particularly involving the separation of individual from group identity development and the inclusion of bisexuality. For example, McCarn and Fassinger (1996) proposed an identity development model that outlines a dual process in which a personal sexual orientation identity can unfold separately from, and at a different pace than, the development of identity as a member of the gay and lesbian community. Furthermore, discussion of bisexual identity development contradicts simple dichotomous notions of sexual orientation and asserts that orientation is not always static or defined solely on the basis of the gender of one's partner (Fox, 1996; Klein, 1993; Rust, 1997; Weinberg, Williams, & Pryor, 1994).

In addition to these advances in the way that identity is understood, there is increasing recognition that sexual identity and its management develop within cultural contexts and in interaction with multiple social group identities (e.g., Fukuyama & Ferguson, 2000; Greene, 1997, 2000; Lowe & Mascher, 2001; Reynolds & Pope, 1991; Smith, 1997). For example, the Multidimensional Identity Model (MIM) developed by Reynolds and Pope presents various options of how persons can identify with their multiple oppressed statuses (i.e., identify with a single oppressed status, identify with different oppressed statuses in different contexts, or identify with an integration of each oppressed status). Culture also profoundly shapes development and management of sexual identity; for instance, extended family and community may be centralized in how collectivist-oriented individuals construct their identities (Fukuyama & Ferguson, 2000; Greene, 1997; Smith, 1997).

Although limited in scope, rigor, and integration, the growing body of research aimed at identifying correlates of workplace sexual identity disclosure is very useful in pointing to several broad factors that may influence intentions and choices regarding workplace sexual identity management (Badgett, 1996; Chrobot-Mason et al., 2001; Croteau & Lark, 1995; Croteau & von Destinon, 1994; Day & Schoenrade, 1997; Driscoll, Fassinger, & Kelley, 1996; Griffith & Hebl, 2002; Rostosky & Riggle, 2002; Schneider, 1986). The most promising correlates include

- workplace climate factors such as sociability and size of workplace, perceptions of coworkers' level of comfort with disclosure, perceptions of support for LGB workers, discrimination against LGB workers, presence of LGB-affirmative organizational policies;
- nature of the work role, such as level in organization, specific occupation, and perceived risk of job loss; and
- interpersonal factors such as length of romantic partnership, a partner's level of identity development or identity management strategy, and parental status.

The model of workplace sexual identity management (WSIM) proposed in this chapter incorporates the literature reviewed previously into a social cognitive framework. A sociocognitive perspective is particularly useful for understanding how individual differences, such as variation in sexual identity development, and personal cognitions concerning past experiences with sexual identity and sexual identity management, interact with specific social and cultural contexts to influence specific individual behaviors. In articulating how the social cognitive process applies to workplace sexual identity management, we employed Griffin's (1992) description of identity management strategies as described previously, key concepts from LGB identity development scholarship, and key findings from the research on the correlates of workplace identity disclosure. The WSIM model presented also accounts for the influence of more multifaceted, inclusive, and culturally sensitive understandings of sexual identity.

AN SCCT-BASED MODEL OF WORKPLACE SEXUAL IDENTITY MANAGEMENT

According to Bandura (1986, 1997), the acquisition and performance of specific behaviors is influenced by reciprocal interactions among three factors: observed behavior, personal characteristics including cognitions, and situational or environmental variables. From this perspective, individuals continuously learn about alternative behaviors from observing others, using cognitive processes to develop and alter interpretations of experiences, and acting upon the environment in ways that influence future learning opportunities. Bandura's general social cognitive theory has been adapted to focus on understanding specific behaviors, such as the career choice model within Social Cognitive Career Theory (SCCT; Lent, Brown, & Hackett, 1996). The career choice model (Lent et al., 1996) focuses on understanding how personal characteristics, past learning experiences concerning the self and the world of work, and environmental contexts jointly influence occupational interests, specific career goals, and career choices.

The value of the SCCT career choice model is that it considers not only an individual's prior learning experiences and personal characteristics but also the meaning that an individual makes of those experiences and the environmental facilitators or barriers that impact implementation of a specific occupational choice. The heart of the model is the interaction between personal cognitions based on past social learning experiences and environmental supports and barriers. For example, self-efficacy beliefs about academic ability and outcome expectations related to satisfaction in certain careers are expected to interact to form particular career interests. The translation of career interests into specific career goals and choice is expected to be influenced by the interactions between career-related self-efficacy beliefs, outcome expectations, and proximal contextual factors. The occupational choice is then implemented and the outcomes of that implementation are evaluated. Those evaluations, in turn, become new learning experiences that may modify self-efficacy beliefs and outcome expectations, which in turn influence future career-related behaviors.

The WSIM model presented here uses the SCCT career choice model as a conceptual framework to consider how prior learning experiences, self-efficacy beliefs, outcome expectations, and past and present contextual influences interact in shaping the choice and implementation of identity management strategies. Presentation of the model is organized into four segments aimed at illuminating the complexity of these interactions. An overview of the WSIM model is diagrammed in Figure 10.1, with each segment of the model identified by differential shading. The brief descriptions of these four segments that follow provide an introductory overview of our model.

In Segment 1, personal and distal contextual variables and sexual and other group identities interact to shape learning experiences about sexual identity management. The primary components of Segment 2 are the self-efficacy beliefs and outcome expectations about sexual identity management that were shaped by the learning experiences. These cognitive expectations are what determine the range of sexual identity management strategies that an individual finds personally acceptable. Segment 3 explains the movement from those strategies an individual finds acceptable to actual identity management behaviors enacted in the workplace. In this segment, proximal contextual variables are critical influences on the development of

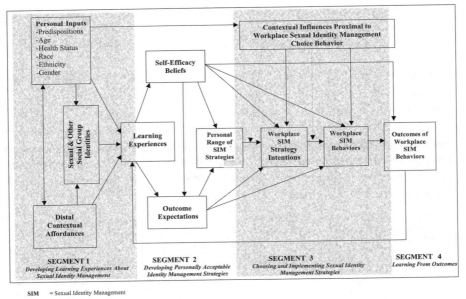

Figure 10.1. SCCT-based model of workplace sexual identity management.

workplace identity management intentions and behaviors. Segment 4, the final segment of the model, represents a feedback loop where the outcomes of identity management behaviors function as new learning experiences that are incorporated into self-efficacy beliefs and outcome expectations for the future. Next we offer more detailed explanations of each segment with illustrations.

Segment 1: Developing Learning Experiences About Sexual Identity Management

Similar to the consideration that the SCCT framework places on previous experiences, the WSIM model incorporates the influence of person inputs, distal contextual affordances, and past learning experiences in examining the career-related choice behaviors involved in sexual identity management. In Segment 1 of the WSIM model, person inputs and distal contextual affordances shape learning about sexual identity management and more generally about sexual and other social group identities. "Person inputs" refers to various individual predispositions such as gender, race and ethnicity, disability status, health status, and particular sexual orientation (lesbian or gay or bisexual). "Distal contextual affordances" is a comprehensive term that refers to a broad range of influential environmental factors such as familial and cultural messages related to understanding sexual orientation; economic and educational opportunities; exposure to LGB people; and community norms concerning tolerance, diversity, and social justice. The interactions between person inputs and distal contextual affordances are illustrated in the following examples. A White man who grew up in an affluent suburban southern setting with little exposure to diversity generally—and to LGB people in particular—might have had very little direct learning in his youth about sexual identity and its management. Being from an affluent family, however, would allow easy economic access to a college education, during which exposure to LGB people and issues would be likely. In contrast, a person who grew up without exposure to LGB people but who lacked enough financial resources to attend college would have less opportunity to learn about sexual orientation and sexual identity.

In the WSIM model, we add sexual identity itself as a cognitive personal variable that influences learning experiences in shaping self-efficacy beliefs and outcome expectations in regard to sexual identity management. Existing theory on sexual identity can be used to conceptualize where a person is with same-sex or both-sex attractions. How an individual cognitively constructs her or his sexual identity helps shape the learning of self-efficacy *
beliefs and outcome expectations in regard to identity management. For instance, a man's identity may incorporate the acknowledgment of a gay orientation, but he may remain negative about that orientation. This man is then unlikely to choose experiences in which he would interact with openly

gay men who are leading successful lives. Further, if such exposure does occur, he is likely to interpret the successful life as an "exception" to the rule. Thus, the individual's sexual identity has a large influence on what that individual may learn about sexual identity management.

Also important to a social cognitive understanding of sexual identity management are an individual's other social and cultural group identities and how those identities interact with sexual orientation. Culture- and gender-sensitive analyses of sexual identity and conceptual understanding of multiple identities provide a means for assessing possible influences on the learning process. For instance, a gay man may identify with his Latino cultural norms involving collectivism and centrality of the family. His future learning experiences about identity management, as well as his cognitive interpretations of learning experiences, will be shaped not only by his personal interpretations but also by his understanding of the meanings relevant to his family and community.

A more extensive example illustrates Segment 1 and the variety of factors that provide a historical influence on a person's learning about sexual identity management. A White woman (person input), who later will come to understand herself as lesbian, grew up in a college town with parents who were financially secure and worked at the university. She received strong, liberal familial messages of acceptance for all persons (distal contextual affordance). A significant early context was the university-influenced church of her family of origin that was socially active and LGB-affirmative (distal contextual affordance). These historical contexts afforded her a breadth of early learning experiences related to sexual identity and its management. For example, while growing up, she was exposed to a gay church leader who was explicitly out, and she observed his struggles with the local and national church on LGB issues. She also experienced the pride this man and the whole congregation took in their LGB-affirmative stance. These early contexts will have a profound influence on her learning experiences and her cognitions about such learning as she later comes to understand herself as a lesbian and begins the task of forming her own sexual identity management strategies.

Segment 2: Developing Personally Acceptable Identity Management Strategies

In Segment 2 of the WSIM model, learning experiences shape self-efficacy beliefs and outcome expectations about sexual identity management that in turn determine the range of sexual identity management strategies that an individual finds personally acceptable. This process of developing a personal range of sexual identity management strategies is analogous to the development of personal career interests described within the SCCT model. Self-efficacy beliefs in relation to sexual identity management refer to the person's beliefs about his or her ability to perform a given identity management behavior. We consider a range of sexual identity management behaviors that have been classified into strategies along the continuum from concealment to openness with sexual identity (see Griffin, 1992). Concealment strategies include passing and covering, and open strategies include being implicitly and explicitly out. For example, a bisexual woman who recently started a relationship with a lesbian believes that she can successfully continue to assert her bisexual identity with her lesbian friends. She has this belief because of having seen an admired friend be successfully open about her bisexuality in the lesbian community; thus, she has a strong source of vicarious learning that contributes to her positive self-efficacy beliefs about being open about her bisexuality in the lesbian community.

Outcome expectations in relation to sexual identity management refer to the person's beliefs about the outcomes of performing particular open or concealing identity management behaviors. The two basic components of outcome expectations are the consequences an individual anticipates resulting from a given activity (instrumentality) and the relative value of these consequences to the individual (valence). Outcomes can be extrinsic, intrinsic, or process-related. For example, a gay man has previously experienced much more intimacy in relationships with people who know that he is gay and finds the greater intimacy quite fulfilling. Thus, from explicitly out identity management behaviors, he anticipates the intrinsic and process-oriented consequences of greater intimacy, which he finds to have positive valence.

Self-efficacy beliefs and outcome expectations about sexual identity management combine to shape the personal range of sexual identity management strategies that are conceivable for an individual or that are experienced as "good fits." Often an individual would consider implementing multiple strategies, but the conceivable strategies for any individual "should cluster around a given point on the identity management continuum" (Anderson et al., 2001, p. 245). A range of personally acceptable sexual identity management strategies is formed through a complex process of evaluating the self-efficacy beliefs and outcome expectations that an individual associates with particular identity management strategies.

A more extensive example of the variables in Segment 2 can help to clarify the cognitive processes involved in developing a personal range of sexual identity management strategies. A lesbian woman most often considers passing as heterosexual and sometimes entertains covering her lesbian identity. How might she have come to find this cluster of passing and covering strategies acceptable? First, she probably thinks she is capable of creating an image of herself that appears to be heterosexual and capable of hiding information related to her being lesbian. Further, she imagines a series of positive outcomes related to passing and covering strategies, such as being more liked or valued if perceived as heterosexual or at least not seen as lesbian. Thus, her consideration of passing or covering as viable strategies was formed from the combination of positive self-efficacy beliefs in regard to passing or covering along with the expectation of positive outcomes from such strategies.

The cognitive processes involved in workplace sexual identity management, however, are often much more complicated than the previous example. For instance, someone may think of him- or herself as capable of passing, covering, or being implicitly out and may also envision both positive and negative outcomes for each strategy. This individual's personal range of identity management strategies would be broader and have more contingencies to reflect that complexity.

Segment 3: Choosing and Implementing Sexual Identity Management Strategies

Segment 3 of the WSIM model involves the movement from a range of personally acceptable identity management strategies to workplace-specific sexual identity management intentions and behaviors. Intentions for workplace sexual identity management represent an individual's plans to implement one or more of the sexual identity management strategies from his or her personal range in a particular situation in the work setting. Workplace sexual identity management behaviors are the particular actions LGB workers take in the workplace in regard to identity management.

Translation of an individual's personal range of sexual identity management strategies into specific intentions regarding workplace sexual identity management strategies and then into specific workplace sexual identity management behaviors is analogous to the movement in the SCCT model from career interests to career choice goals and career choice actions. As in SCCT, the model of sexual identity management incorporates the concept of proximal contextual influences. As noted previously, existing research concerning correlates of workplace sexual identity disclosure can be used to identify three broad categories of contextual influences that may be especially salient impact for LGB workers. We posit two additional categories for a total of five: context of immediate work situation, work climate, nature of work role, interpersonal factors, and community context. Proximal contextual influences can more generally be described as all current social and environmental factors that directly and indirectly influence workplace sexual identity management strategies and behaviors. The influence of any particular context is based on an individual's perceptions and interpretations of that context.

Proximal contextual factors directly or indirectly influence sexual identity management intentions and behaviors by providing, limiting, or shaping the nature of opportunities to implement specific strategies or behaviors. For example, the nature of the work role in some jobs may directly provide opportunities to be out at work because of the availability of work tasks that directly address LGB issues (e.g., university faculty research on LGB issues; business managers who develop policy on LGB issues), whereas other jobs exist in work climates that directly discourage personal disclosures of any form, including disclosures that may reference one's sexual orientation. Proximal contexts can also indirectly influence the formation of workplace sexual identity management intentions and behaviors. For example, a worker may generally intend to use implicitly out strategies, but, in the context of an upcoming anti-LGB city ballot initiative (community context), the worker may make plans to be explicitly out in order to encourage coworkers to vote against the initiative.

Proximal contextual factors may also indirectly influence the translation of intended workplace sexual identity management strategies into actual workplace sexual identity management behaviors. For example, a woman may intend to discuss her plans for a romantic weekend with a close friend at work over lunch break (an explicitly out intention). However, several other colleagues join the pair of friends for lunch (context of immediate situation), so instead she steers the conversation toward nonpersonal topics to avoid disclosing anything that could lead the others to know she is lesbian (a covering behavior).

An elaborated example is given here to portray the complex dynamics involved in this third segment of the model. Consider a gay man who is most comfortable simply being truthful about his life without necessarily labeling himself gay; he also feels able to avoid references to his personal life, covering that he is gay in situations in which he is less sure of the degree of LGB support. In some circumstances, however, he has found it advantageous to be more explicit with others about being gay and feels he can do this, though he is less comfortable with an explicitly out strategy than he is with an implicitly out strategy. Within his small immediate work environment in a large corporation, there are many opportunities to discuss personal lives, thus forcing him to make many daily decisions about identity management in the course of casual conversations. He feels trusting and rather safe with the colleagues in his immediate environment who live in an urban area and who seem to be somewhat familiar with lesbian, gay, and bisexual people. In his immediate work context, he intends to manage his identity in the way he generally prefers, being implicitly out. His behaviors in casual conversations typically follow this intention, and his immediate colleagues have heard much about his home life with his partner during their casual workday conversations. He also occasionally engages in covering by avoiding casual conversation when there are visitors or supervisory personnel whose reactions his being gay are less predictable. At the same time, he is aware that the corporate union plans to survey its membership about negotiating for domestic-partner benefits, and he is considering more explicitly out strategies in order to encourage his colleagues to support the union's efforts to get such benefits. This example shows how a variety of proximal work contexts directly and indirectly influence the translation of a range of personally acceptable identity management strategies into identity management intentions and behaviors.

Segment 4: Learning From Outcomes

As the final segment of the WSIM model, Segment 4 is a feedback loop that highlights the importance of personal assessment of the outcomes of specific workplace sexual identity management behaviors. A few outcomes have been examined in existing LGB vocational psychology literature, including the impact of sexual identity management behaviors on

- workplace rewards such as income and promotion;
- workplace climate factors such as support or hostility;
- interpersonal relationship factors such as intimacy or separation; and
- personal reactions such as satisfaction with level of disclosure, sense of integrity, and sense of personal safety. (Croteau et al., 2000)

Perceptions and interpretation of these outcomes feed back into the model as learning experiences, which in turn shape self-efficacy beliefs and outcome expectations concerning sexual identity management.

A more extensive example can illustrate Segment 4 of the WSIM model. A lesbian woman who typically covers her sexual orientation at work may choose to bring her partner to a work-related social gathering for employees and their families. At the social gathering some coworkers make a point to befriend her partner while others seem uncomfortable and wonder why she brought another woman to the party. After the party the woman feels glad that she took her family (i.e., her partner) to the party and she experiences a stronger sense of integrity in her relationship with some of her coworkers. She is also a bit worried about future interactions with other coworkers who were less welcoming, and she is particularly interested in getting a read on her supervisor's reactions, given that she has an upcoming performance evaluation that some coworkers might try to negatively influence. These outcomes and this woman's assessments of these outcomes now feed back into the model as new learning experiences that shape her self-efficacy beliefs and outcome expectation for future identity management behaviors. She now knows she is able to be implicitly out in a social setting with her coworkers (self-efficacy), and she has experienced potentially positive outcomes (coworker support, sense of integrity) and negative outcomes (awkwardness with coworkers, worry about evaluation) of this sexual identity management strategy. Her choices concerning future identity management strategies and behaviors will be influenced by the relative value she places on these outcomes and how they interact with her prior learning history with respect to other identity management behaviors.

CLINICAL APPLICATIONS OF THE WSIM MODEL

Social cognitive conceptualizations of career behavior, in this case workplace sexual identity management behavior, suggest multiple pathways for facilitating positive development: self-efficacy beliefs, outcome expectations, environmental or contextual assessment, and outcome assessment of specific identity management behaviors. We also recommend explicitly teaching the model to clients in order to increase self-understanding and personal agency with regard to managing future challenges with workplace sexual identity management. We illustrate application of the model more fully with the case of Durrell. This case was designed to highlight the dynamics of the model as applied to assessment, client conceptualization, and career interventions. The authors created the case from a variety of their professional experiences and within the range of their own collective diverse identities and multicultural experiences.

The Case of Durrell

Durrell, a 20-year-old African American man, sought counseling services to discuss and decrease worries about his upcoming summer internship placement. A successful third-year college student at a predominantly White state university in the upper Midwest, Durrell has secured a summer internship with a large civil engineering firm in his hometown, which is a large, urban city in the upper Midwest. Durrell has concerns about doing well and feeling like he "belongs" during the internship. As he grew to trust the counselor, he acknowledged that he identifies as a gay man and that a large portion of his anxiety regarding the internship arises from his concern about "what to do about being gay" at the engineering firm. This anxiety can be understood as stemming from his uncertainty about managing his sexual identity in the internship workplace. We first discuss Segments 1 through 3 of the WSIM model as useful ways to organize information about Durrell's background and career concerns. Finally, we discuss ways to assist him in career counseling including Segment 4 as a focus for intervention.

Segment 1

Durrell's current sexual identity management behaviors have been shaped by his person inputs, distal contextual affordances, and the interactions between his sexual and other social group identities. Durrell is an African American, gay man. He was raised in a predominantly middle-class, African American community, which he considers his "home" community. Durrell's family and community are the center of his social life and a great source of emotional support. His worldview reflects the value of collectivism. He describes most of the people in his home community as having conservative attitudes toward sexuality. Durrell has had limited exposure to other gay men within his home community as well as in the larger community. He currently sees the gay community as largely White, and he is concerned about a lack of inclusion for him as an African American man.

Durrell's racial, sexual, and other social group identities are also key components in shaping learning experiences in regard to sexual identity management. Because of a strong family and community background, Durrell has always had a strong positive sense of himself as an African American. This positive sense of identity has been strengthened by experiences of dealing successfully with racism at his predominantly White university. Durrell is currently in the internalization or integration statuses of Helms's (1995) and other racial identity models.

In terms of his sexual identity, Durrell acknowledged clearly to himself at about age 17 that he had predominantly same-sex attractions. He also has a current yearlong dating relationship with another student whom he considers his partner. This relationship has deepened his growing positive personal identity as gay. However, Durrell has only recently become involved with the LGB student group. With regard to his gay identity development, Durrell can best be described as being in the Deepening/Commitment phase of personal identity development and in the Exploration phase of group identity (McCarn & Fassinger, 1996). Within a Multidimensional Identity Model (Reynolds & Pope, 1991), Durrell seems to identify with multiple aspects of himself in a segmented fashion. His "gay time" is spent with predominantly White LGB people. His "African American time" is spent with African Americans who he presumes are all heterosexual and with whom he avoids discussion of LGB issues. He feels "compartmentalized" and is beginning to want more integration of his identities.

Segment 2

Durrell's current self-efficacy beliefs and outcome expectations have been shaped by past learning experiences. One of his earliest learning experiences about his own sexual identity management occurred after he first identified himself as gay. At age 17, Durrell explicitly came out to a friend in his home community. When that friend stopped associating with him, Durrell began to cover up his identity, and no one seemed to suspect he was gay. Durrell developed positive self-efficacy beliefs for concealing his sexual orientation. In terms of outcome expectations, Durrell reports thinking that being open about being gay in his home community might mean losing some of the special closeness he feels there; he expects "they would be really shocked" to find out he is gay, and he worries that people there might see his family in a negative light if his identity were known.

Durrell has more recent learning experiences that have led to additional self-efficacy beliefs and expanded outcome expectations. In his first year of college, he observed that other gay men at the university were explicitly out in numerous contexts and seemed to have a lot of acceptance "even" from heterosexual people. More recently, he has gained a greater sense of ease and comfort with his sexual identity as a result of being explicitly out with other LGB people at the university. In addition, Durrell recently utilized an implicitly out management strategy with his family by taking his partner to a family event back home. Durrell perceived that he and his partner were "silently" and "wonderfully" accepted and welcomed by his family. Durrell now knows that he is capable of being explicitly out with other LGB people and implicitly out with his family. He also knows that more revealing strategies can lead to acceptance and to feelings of greater comfort with being gay.

Durrell's current personal range of sexual identity management strategies can be described as centering around covering but transitioning toward an expanded range that includes the more revealing or open end of the strategy continuum. He has a long history of successfully covering and expects covering to protect him and his family from social rejection. More recently, he has added the possibility of being implicitly out and feels drawn to the possibility of welcoming outcomes from his family and home community. However, he still feels apprehensive about possible negative reactions from important others toward him individually and toward his family collectively. His actual choices and strategies are contingent upon context, and the workplace context will be a major factor in shaping Durrell's choices concerning sexual identity management strategies during his internship.

Segment 3

Explicit consideration of a breadth of proximal contextual influences provides further insight into how Durrell will translate his range of personally acceptable identity management strategies into intentions and behaviors concerning sexual identity management during his internship. For Durrell, interpersonal factors and community context are interwoven proximal contextual influences. A major interpersonal factor for Durrell is the relationship with his partner, who will be staying at college. Durrell values and is invested in this relationship and anticipates needing support in being in a long-distance relationship. His partner is implicitly out to most people. Durrell's recent success with being implicitly out, his need for relationship support, his partner's sexual identity management strategy, and his desire to integrate his multiple identities pull him toward developing implicitly out workplace sexual identity management intentions. Durrell also feels some pull toward covering because he wants to protect his strong connections to his home community for himself and his family. He continues to have some reservations about people in his home community discovering his identity through his disclosure at the workplace.

The work climate is another important proximal contextual influence in this case. Durrell has tried to assess the climate for LGB people at his internship placement. During his search for an internship site, he deliberately looked for firms with a reputation for diversity and chose the civil engineering firm because it is owned and predominantly staffed by African Americans. Also, the company nondiscrimination statement includes sexual orientation as a protected status. During his interview, Durrell perceived some degree of LGB support in the work environment, some signs of negative LGB attitudes, and a high level of expectation regarding socializing with coworkers. One of the engineers at the firm was friendly in extending an invitation to join the group of guys who "hang out every Friday after work at the sports bar down the street." During the business lunch, another senior engineer told a negative gay joke. However, Durrell immediately liked his project team leader, an African American woman, who commented on the importance of "all types of diversity" in making project teams more creative. This mixture of experiences makes Durrell uncertain about the level of LGB support in the internship workplace and pulls him toward seeking safety by covering his sexual identity. He knows the high degree of sociability at his internship site means that he will need to make many choices about identity management.

The nature of the work role is another relevant contextual factor for Durrell. As an intern, the work experience is designed to be temporary. Durrell thinks this "might be a good time to try out new behaviors" that involve more open strategies. On the other hand, he wonders if his internship evaluation and recommendation letters might be negatively affected if supervisors know he is gay. Once again, these contextual influences pull him in two directions with respect to his intentions for workplace sexual identity management.

In summary, Durrell is experiencing conflict and confusion around the anticipated outcomes of his sexual identity management choices and behaviors while performing his internship. Currently, he does not have clarity on how to prepare himself for managing his sexual identity at his internship workplace. Durrell's anxiety about this appears to be a result of his struggle to make meaning amidst changing cognitions concerning sexual identity management at the same time that he needs to navigate identity management in a new workplace environment.

Directions for Career Counseling

Counselors can use the WSIM model to help clients develop more agency and satisfaction in managing their sexual identity at work by examining potential influences on identity management and exploring the myriad of possible directions for client actions that alter work-related contexts or develop new and desired learning experiences. Application of the model to this case suggests that Durrell can be assisted to make changes through examination of cognitive mediators and his perceptions of contextual influences relevant to sexual identity management. Durrell can also be aided in the process of identifying and selecting new learning experiences related to sexual identity management. These experiences would then provide new feedback that would shape his future sexual identity management and that could increase his sense of personal agency.

Focus on Cognitive Mediators

In SCCT-based counseling, self-efficacy is an important point of intervention. Interventions focused on self-efficacy may include helping with accuracy of self-appraisal and skill development. Individuals may have limiting workplace sexual identity management self-efficacy beliefs because of a lack of opportunity to develop a broad range of identity management behaviors. Durrell's self-efficacy beliefs about managing his sexual identity seem accurately appraised and sufficiently functional; thus, they may not require much attention in counseling. One area that could be explored is self-efficacy concerning sexual identity management that is specific to the workplace. Durrell may need to explicitly envision the translation of past successes with identity management outside of the work environment to the workplace. This envisioning process can assist him in developing an expanded set of self-efficacy beliefs regarding workplace sexual identity management.

Outcome expectations appear to be particularly salient for Durrell as he considers various workplace identity management strategies. The career counselor and Durrell can explore the accuracy of his existing outcome expectations, identify additional salient outcomes he has not yet anticipated, and articulate the valences of particular outcomes, especially those that pull his identity management in different directions. Durrell may benefit from comparing the work performance-related effects of using covering strategies versus open strategies. For example, Durrell can be encouraged to compare the amount of energy it takes to be vigilant enough to cover with the amount of energy it takes to venture the risks involved with more open strategies. In addition, counseling can help him weigh the potential costs of rejection with these colleagues against the potential benefit of integrating his racial and sexual identities. Durrell's exploration of anticipated outcomes and associated valences directly assists him in the process of clarifying his understanding of, and relative values associated with, various workplace sexual identity management strategies and behaviors.

Focus on Contextual Influences

Proximal contextual influences play a key role in sexual identity management, and helping Durrell clarify his personal perceptions and understandings of contextual influences will be important. For example, assessment of the degree of LGB affirmation versus hostility in the work climate may be particularly salient for Durrell, as it is for most LGB workers. Durrell's assessment of the work climate is mixed and has left him uncertain about outcomes. Durrell and the career counselor could focus on implementing additional climate-assessment strategies. For instance, Durrell could ask his LGB friends if they know someone who can provide him information about work climate at the firm. Durrell could also be encouraged to consider a more direct strategy such as approaching the team leader he thinks is supportive and asking her directly about her perceptions of work climate regarding LGB issues. It may also be important for Durrell to explore other contextual influences. For example, in the realm of interpersonal factors, Durrell may need to explore more fully how his family and his partner currently influence his identity management. From his assessment of these and other influences, Durrell can have more personal agency in terms of the meaning and impact contextual factors have on his identity management. From a social cognitive perspective, it is also important to consider how Durrell could exercise personal agency to directly alter contextual influences. As Durrell becomes more involved in the engineering firm, he can also consider how he might act to create more LGB affirmation in the work climate.

Focus on Learning Experiences

From an SCCT perspective, it can be particularly potent for counselors to help clients modify self-efficacy beliefs and outcome expectations in desired ways by creating new learning experiences and reinterpreting old learning experiences. Because Durrell has limited learning experiences in several areas, new learning experiences will be especially valuable in helping him to further develop workplace-specific self-efficacy beliefs and outcome expectations for sexual identity management. Durrell has little previous experience managing his sexual identity in the workplace, no information about other African American gay men and their identity management, little data about how his home African American community might react to his gay identity, and little awareness of the possibility of getting LGB affirmation from heterosexual people.

Possible ways of expanding Durrell's learning base are brainstorming, discussing, and role-playing novel sexual identity management behaviors in order to increase the number of specific behavioral choices that he could make, thus increasing his sense of control. Another way to increase Durrell's relevant learning experiences is for him to connect with the African American LGB community in the larger, urban setting of his hometown; Durrell could explore and learn about how other LGB African American people manage their sexual identities both inside and outside the workplace. Involvement in LGB communities of color could also provide Durrell with direct and vicarious learning experiences related to the possibility of integrating his racial and sexual identities. The counselor could help Durrell then make sense of these new learning experiences and how new options generated by such experiences fit for him given his particular learning history and contexts.

THE WSIM MODEL AND LGB VOCATIONAL PSYCHOLOGY RESEARCH

Although the primary focus of this chapter is the application of the WSIM model to practice, the model also has implications for research and scholarship in LGB vocational psychology. We briefly discuss two important issues in the application of the model to research. First, we highlight the current status of measures for core theoretical variables. Next, we explore the usefulness of the model for organizing and integrating past research in ways that are helpful to planning future research.

Two measures of workplace sexual identity management have recently been proposed (Anderson et al., 2001; Button, 2001). We recommend that future research utilize or improve upon these efforts. Although measurement of contexts and outcomes in identity management research is less fully developed, numerous studies have investigated specific relevant variables that can be used as starting points in future research (Badgett, 1996; Chrobot-Mason et al., 2001; Croteau & Lark, 1995; Croteau & von Destinon, 1994; Day & Schoenrade, 1997; Driscoll et al., 1996; Griffith & Hebl, 2002; Rostosky & Riggle, 2002; Schneider, 1986).

The most urgent current measurement issue is the lack of measures for self-efficacy beliefs and outcome expectations in regard to workplace identity management. Without tools for assessing these core psychological variables, even the most basic mechanisms of the WSIM model cannot be tested. Initial direction for developing such measures could come from existing career-related self-efficacy measures (e.g., Betz & Hackett, 1983; Robbins, 1985; Taylor & Betz, 1983).

The WSIM model is immediately useful in organizing and integrating past research in order to plan future research and build a knowledge base concerning workplace sexual identity management. For example, existing LGB vocational psychology research has examined a number of correlates of workplace sexual identity management, but it has been difficult to integrate findings across studies (Croteau, 1996; Croteau et al., 2000). When viewed from a WSIM perspective, many of these correlates can be described as specific examples of proximal contextual influences. When these individual variables are conceptualized as belonging to the broader categories of proximal influences described in the model, we can integrate findings across studies and broaden our scope of research. Other important and specific variables within the already-studied broad categories can also be identified. In addition, other broad categories of proximal contextual variables may also merit consideration. We suggested two such categories, community context and immediate work situation, in the presentation of the model.

Existing research has also examined correlates that can be conceptualized within the WSIM model as outcomes of workplace identity management. This research has been quite limited in scope, focusing primarily on discrimination and job satisfaction (Croteau, 1996; Croteau et al., 2000). When viewed from a WSIM perspective, discrimination can be conceptualized as an extrinsic outcome, whereas job satisfaction is an intrinsic outcome. Placing these variables within the WSIM conceptual framework aids in interpreting findings and planning future investigations on these variables. The WSIM model also suggests the need for scholarship on additional extrinsic and intrinsic outcomes as well as on process-oriented outcomes and the valence of various outcomes for individual LGB workers.

The model can further be used to generate theory-based understanding of many existing research findings. For example, the findings of past research concerning the relationship between sexual identity disclosure and job satisfaction are mixed (Croteau, 1996; Croteau et al., 2000; Day & Schoenrade, 1997; Griffith & Hebl, 2002). The WSIM model is a theoretical perspective from which to generate hypotheses to account for these and other phenomena in current research. For example, concerning the aforementioned finding, it is likely that some workers place more value on outcomes of disclosure strategies (e.g., feeling of personal integrity or role-modeling for other LGB workers) than on outcomes of concealing strategies (e.g., safety from discrimination).

CONCLUSION

This chapter presents a model of sexual identity management based on a sociocognitive perspective. The model adds to existing literature by explaining how LGB workers come to choose and implement workplace sexual identity management strategies. Personal and distal contextual influences shape the learning of self-efficacy and outcome expectations related to sexual identity management, which in turn, determine the range of sexual identity management strategies that are acceptable to a LGB worker at any given time. Given the range of personally acceptable strategies, proximal contextual influences then affect the actual intentions and behaviors of LGB workers concerning sexual identity management. The outcomes of identity management behaviors then become learning experiences that help reshape self-efficacy and outcome expectations.

This model is applied to the case of Durrell to illustrate the dynamics of the model and to show how such understandings can be applied to assessment, conceptualization, and intervention in career counseling. We have concluded by briefly discussing applications of the model to advance measurement and guide future research on workplace sexual identity management. Overall, the WSIM model is intended to provide a conceptual framework for the dynamic process of sexual identity management with application to career practice as well as to research and scholarship that will further refine understandings of this important aspect of the career lives of LGB people.

REFERENCES

Anderson, M. Z., Croteau, J. M., Chung, Y. B., & DiStefano, T. M. (2001). Developing an assessment of sexual identity management for lesbian and gay workers. *Journal of Career Assessment, 9,* 243–260.

Badgett, M. V. L. (1996). Employment and sexual orientation: Disclosure and discrimination in the workplace. *Journal of Gay & Lesbian Social Services, 4,* 29–30.

Badgett, M. V. L. (2001). *Mercy, myths, and change: The economic lives of lesbians and gay men.* Chicago: University of Chicago Press.

Bandura, A. (1986). *Social foundations of thought and action.* Englewood Cliffs, NJ: Prentice-Hall.

Bandura, A. (1997). *Self-efficacy: The exercise of control.* New York: Freeman.

Betz, N., & Hackett, G. (1983). The relationship of mathematics self-efficacy expectations to the selection of science-based college majors. *Journal of Vocational Behavior, 23,* 329–345.

Button, S. B. (2001). Organizational efforts to affirm sexual diversity: A cross-level examination. *Journal of Applied Psychology, 86,* 17–28.

Cass, V. C. (1979). Homosexual identity formation: A theoretical model. *Journal of Homosexuality, 4*(3), 219–235.

Chernin, J., Holden, J. M., & Chandler, C. (1997). Bias in psychological assessment: Heterosexism. *Measurement and Evaluation in Counseling and Development, 30,* 68–76.

Chrobot-Mason, D., Button, S. B., & DiClementi, J. D. (2002). Sexual identity management strategies: an exploration of antecedents and consequences. *Sex Roles, 45,* 321–336.

Chung, Y. B. (2001). Work discrimination and coping strategies: Conceptual frameworks for counseling lesbian, gay, and bisexual clients. *Career Development Quarterly, 50,* 33–44.

Chung, Y. B. (2003a). Career counseling with lesbian, gay, bisexual, and transgendered persons: The next decade. *Career Development Quarterly, 52,* 78–86.

Chung, Y. B. (2003b). Ethical and professional issues in career assessment with lesbian, gay, and bisexual persons. *Journal of Career Assessment, 11,* 96–112.

Croteau, J. M. (1996). Research on the work experiences of lesbian, gay and bisexual people: An integrative review of methodology and findings. *Journal of Vocational Behavior, 48,* 195–209.

Croteau, J. M., Anderson, M. Z., DiStefano, T. M., & Kampa-Kokesch, S. (2000). Lesbian, gay, and bisexual vocational psychology: Reviewing foundations and planning construction. In R. M. Ruperto, K. A. DeBord, & K. J. Bieschke (Eds.),

Handbook of counseling and psychotherapy with lesbian, gay, and bisexual clients (pp. 383–408). Washington, DC: American Psychological Association.

Croteau, J. M., & Lark, J. S. (1995). On being lesbian, gay or bisexual in student affairs: A national survey of experiences on the job. *NASPA Journal, 32,* 189–197.

Croteau, J. M., & von Destinon, M. (1994). A national survey of job search experiences of lesbian, gay and bisexual student affairs professionals. *Journal of College Student Development, 35,* 40–45.

Day, N. E., & Schoenrade, P. (1997). Staying in the closet versus coming out: Relationships between communication about sexual orientation and work attitudes. *Personnel Psychology, 50,* 147–163.

Driscoll, J. M., Fassinger, R. E., & Kelley, F. A. (1996). Lesbian identity and self-disclosure in the workplace: Relation to occupational stress and satisfaction. *Journal of Vocational Behavior, 48,* 229–242.

Fox, R. C. (1996). Bisexuality: An examination of theory and research. In T. S. Stein (Ed.), *Textbook of homosexuality and mental health* (pp. 147–171). Washington, DC: American Psychiatric Press.

Fukuyama, M. A., & Ferguson, A. D. (2000). Lesbian, gay, and bisexual people of color: Understanding cultural complexity and managing multiple oppressions. In R. M. Ruperto, K. A. DeBord, & K. J. Bieschke (Eds.), *Handbook of counseling and psychotherapy with lesbian, gay, and bisexual clients* (pp. 81–105). Washington, DC: American Psychological Association.

Greene, B. (1997). Ethnic minority lesbians and gay men: Mental health and treatment issues. In B. Greene (Ed.), *Ethnic and cultural diversity among lesbians and gay men* (pp. 216–239). Thousand Oaks, CA: Sage.

Greene, B. (2000). Beyond heterosexism and across the cultural divide: Developing an inclusive lesbian, gay, and bisexual psychology: A look to the future. In B. Greene (Ed.), *Education, research, and practice in lesbian, gay, bisexual, and transgendered psychology* (pp. 1–45). Thousand Oaks, CA: Sage.

Griffin, P. (1992). From hiding out to coming out: Empowering lesbian and gay educators. In K. M. Harbeck (Ed.), *Coming out of the classroom closet* (pp. 167–196). Binghamton, NY: Harrington Park Press.

Griffith, K. H., & Hebl, M. R. (2002). The disclosure dilemma for gay men and lesbians: "Coming out" at work. *Journal of Applied Psychology, 87,* 1191–1199.

Helms, J. E. (1995). An update of Helms' white and people of color racial identity models. In J. G. Ponterotto, J. M. Casas, L. A. Suzuki, & C. M. Alexander (Eds.), *Handbook of multicultural counseling* (pp. 181–198). Thousand Oaks, CA: Sage.

Klein, F. (1993). *The bisexual option* (2nd ed.). New York: Harrington Park Press.

Lent, R., Brown, S., & Hackett, G. (1996). *Career development from a social cognitive perspective* (3rd ed., pp. 373–422). San Francisco: Jossey-Bass.

Liddle, B. J., Luzzo, D. A., Hauenstein, A. L., & Schuck, K. (2004). Construction and validation of the lesbian, gay, bisexual, and transgendered climate inventory. *Journal of Career Assessment, 12,* 33–50.

Longborg, S. D., & Phillips, J. M. (1996). Investigating the career development of gays, lesbians, and bisexuals: Methodological considerations and recommendations. *Journal of Vocational Behavior, 48*, 176–194.

Lowe, S. M., & Mascher, J. (2001). The role of sexual orientation in multicultural counseling: Integrating bodies of knowledge. In J. A. Ponterotto, J. M. Casas, L. A. Suzuki, & C. M. Alexander (Eds.), *Handbook of multicultural counseling* (pp. 755–778). Thousand Oaks, CA: Sage.

McCarn, S. R., & Fassinger, R. E. (1996). Revisioning sexual minority identity development formation: A new model of lesbian identity and its implications for counseling and research. *The Counseling Psychologist, 24*, 508–534.

Nauta, M. M., Saucier, A. M., & Woodard, L. E. (2001). Interpersonal influences on students' academic and career decisions: The impact of sexual orientation. *The Career Development Quarterly, 49*, 352–362.

Pope, M. S., Prince, J. P., & Mitchell, K. (2000). Responsible career counseling with lesbian and gay students. In D. A. Luzzo (Ed.), *Career counseling of college students: An empirical guide to strategies that work* (pp. 267–282). Washington, DC: American Psychological Association.

Poverny, L. M. (2000). Employee assistance practice with sexual minorities. *Administration of Social Work, 23*, 69–91.

Prince, J. P. (1997). Career assessment with lesbian, gay, and bisexual individuals. *Journal of Career Assessment, 5*, 225–238.

Ragins, B. R., & Cornwell, J. M. (2001). Pink triangles: Antecedents and consequences of perceived workplace discrimination against gay and lesbian employees. *Journal of Applied Psychology, 86*, 1244–1261.

Reynolds, A. L., & Pope, R. L. (1991). The complexities of diversity: Exploring multiple oppressions. *Journal of Counseling and Development, 70*, 174–180.

Robbins, S. B. (1985). Validity estimates for the Career Decision-Making Self-Efficacy Scale. *Measurement and Evaluation in Counseling and Development, 18*, 64–71.

Rostosky, S. S., & Riggle, E. D. B. (2002). "Out" at work: The relation of actor and partner workplace policy and internalized homophobia to disclosure status. *Journal of Counseling Psychology, 49*, 411–419.

Rust, P. C. (1997). "Coming out" in the age of social constructionism: Sexual identity formation among lesbian and bisexual women. *Journal of Lesbian Studies, 1*, 25–54.

Schneider, B. E. (1986). Coming out at work: Bridging the private/public gap. *Work and Occupations, 13*, 463–487.

Smith, A. (1997). Cultural diversity and the coming-out process: Implications for clinical practice. In B. Greene (Ed.), *Ethnic and cultural diversity among lesbians and gay men* (pp. 279–300). Thousand Oaks, CA: Sage.

Sophie, J. (1985/1986). A critical examination of stage theories of lesbian identity development. *Journal of Homosexuality, 12*(2), 39–51.

Taylor, K. M., & Betz, N. E. (1983). Applications of self-efficacy theory to the understanding and treatment of career indecision. *Journal of Vocational Behavior, 22*, 63–81.

Troiden, R. R. (1989). The formation of homosexual identities. *Journal of Homosexuality, 17*(1–2), 43–73.

Waldo, C. R. (1999). Working in a majority context: a structural model of heterosexism as minority stress in the workplace. *Journal of Counseling Psychology, 46*, 218–232.

Weinberg, M. S., Williams, C. J., & Pryor, D. W. (1994). *Dual attraction: Understanding bisexuality.* New York: Oxford University Press.

Worthington, R. L., McCrary, S. I., & Howard, K. A. (1998). Becoming an LGBT affirmative career advisor: Guidelines for faculty, staff, and administrators. In R. L. Sanlo (Ed.), *Working with lesbian, gay, bisexual, and transgender college students: A handbook for faculty and administrators* (pp. 135–143). Westport, CT: Greenwood Press.

11

AN OVERVIEW OF AFFIRMATIVE PSYCHOTHERAPY AND COUNSELING WITH TRANSGENDER CLIENTS

SHANNON CHAVEZ KORELL AND PEGGY LORAH

Current training programs for mental health professionals do not typically address counseling concerns that are specific to transgender clients (Carroll & Gilroy, 2002; Israel & Tarver, 1997). Even though the field has come far in work with gay, lesbian, and bisexual clients, transgender individuals have either been ignored or tacked on in ways that do not necessarily meet their therapeutic needs. The goal for this chapter is to introduce mental health professionals to basic issues in affirmative counseling for transgender individuals. We hope to provide mental health professionals with an understanding of the special needs that transgender clients and their families may bring to counseling.

Both authors of this chapter have worked with transgender clients in community settings, and our commitment to providing quality services has come from the trust of many individuals and their willingness to share their stories with us. We believe that there are many reasons that transgender individuals present for counseling, just as there are many reasons that other individuals present for counseling.

In this chapter, we provide general information that will assist mental health professionals in providing affirmative psychotherapy and counseling to transgender clients. First, we articulate the assumptions that underlie this chapter. Next, we provide terms and definitions related to transgender issues and briefly describe transgender identity development. We then identify, using our own experience and the literature, the most salient issues transgender individuals bring to counseling. We discuss five specific areas relevant to transgender clients, including support systems, family, social and emotional stressors, medical issues, and career. We end the chapter by discussing what we see as the most important issues in providing affirmative counseling for transgender clients.

ASSUMPTIONS

As we begin a discussion of affirmative counseling with transgender clients, we believe it is important to articulate the assumptions that underlie this chapter. Although we describe some of these assumptions in greater detail throughout the chapter, the following concepts are the foundation for our beliefs about working with transgender individuals.

- Many therapists will see at least one transgender client during their careers.
- More therapists will work with family members of transgender individuals than with transgender individuals themselves.
- Most practitioners have limited information about transgender clients and how to work with them.
- A transgender identity is not synonymous with pathology.
- Transgender identity is not connected to sexual orientation.
- Transgender clients present for counseling services for the same reasons as the general population.
- Sex (or gender) reassignment surgery is not always of interest to the transgender individual presenting for clinical services.

STANCE OF PROFESSIONAL ORGANIZATIONS

The ethical codes for both the American Psychological Association (APA) and the American Counseling Association (ACA) discuss the importance both of clinicians' not practicing beyond their levels of competence and of their respecting differences among clients (ACA, 1995; APA, 2002), and both organizations have advocacy divisions that address the importance of doing affirming work with lesbian, gay, and bisexual (LGB) populations. APA's Division 44, the Society for the Psychological Study of Lesbian, Gay, and Bisexual Issues, has published guidelines for working with LGB clients.

ACA's advocacy division is the Association for Gay, Lesbian, and Bisexual Issues in Counseling (AGLBIC), and this division has published guidelines for affirmative counseling (AGLBIC, 2003). Neither of these national organizations has yet added the "T" for transgender clients. We encourage readers to become advocates for the inclusion of guidelines for working with transgender clients in the competency recommendations for APA and ACA.

UNDERSTANDING TRANSGENDER ISSUES

Terms and Definitions

There is limited language that describes the transgender experience in affirmative and inclusive ways. This section highlights and defines existing terminology. Additionally, we deal with the subject of appropriate pronouns to use when addressing transgender clients.

- *Gender* "is a social construct that divides people into 'natural' categories of men and women that are thought to derive from their physiological male and female bodies" (Lev, 2004, p. 81).
- *Gender identity* is one's own ideas about one's gender regardless of one's biological sex (Lev, 2004).
- *Gender variance* is an umbrella term that identifies the spectrum of gender expression. As theory has developed, this has been described as gender occurring on a *continuum* (Ellis & Erikson, 2002). As conceptualization of gender has moved beyond being a dichotomy, the continuum is a schema that helps us to visualize the breadth of gender possibilities.
- *Transgender* is an umbrella term that refers to all individuals whose gender expression is not in alignment with the socially prescribed gender norms assigned to their biological sex. Transsexuals and cross-dressers are examples of people with transgender expression. Transgender people can have any sexual orientation (Devor, 2002; Lombardi, 2001).
- *Cross-dresser* refers to someone who dresses in clothing as an expression of masculinity or femininity that is not socially aligned with the individual's biological sex (Ellis & Erikson, 2002).
- *Transsexual* is a term describing "people who believe that their physiological bodies do not represent their true sex" (Lev, 2004, p. 400). Transsexual people make a wide range of choices as they attempt to find alignment between sex and gender. Some individuals choose to do nothing, some individuals choose to express gender with clothing, some individuals choose hormonal treatments, some individuals choose sex reassignment surgery, and some individuals make other choices that we have not identified here.

Sex reassignment surgery (SRS) is a surgical procedure that changes one's primary or secondary sex traits. For *male-to-female* (MTF) transsexuals, SRS could mean genital reconstruction, breast implants, electrolysis, and paring down of the Adam's apple. For *female-to-male* (FTM) transsexuals, this could mean construction of a penis and mastectomy. In order for individuals to be candidates for SRS, they must first undergo hormonal therapy and adhere to further treatment recommendations designed by the Harry Benjamin International Gender Dysphoria Association (HBIGDA). We do not address the HBIGDA recommendations in depth, but we do provide more information throughout the chapter as appropriate.

Pronouns

As the definitions show, talking about transgender issues presents many language dilemmas. Because language has been such a difficulty, some transgender individuals have developed creative, self-affirming pronouns when talking about themselves. Although most transgender individuals still use *he* and *she* as their identifying pronouns, some activists in the transgender community have proposed that alternative pronouns, such as *sie, ze, hir,* and others, be used as ways to indicate the blurring of rigid gender status (Feinberg, 1996).

Transgender Development

Individuals may begin to question their socially assigned gender and biological sex as early as 2 years old (Cohen-Kettenis & Pfafflin, 2003). It is common for these young children to state that they are or will become members of the other sex. Transgender children tend to reveal their gender choice by their actions (Ramsey, 1996). Many parents of transgender children often struggle with this information and turn to blaming themselves for their child's gender-identity "confusion" (Cohen-Kettenis & Pfafflin, 2003).

Experiences of transgender feelings often peak during puberty (Israel & Tarver, 1997). With the emergence of secondary sex characteristics (e.g., development of breasts, deepening of voice, appearance of facial and pubic hair), transgender adolescents often experience a sense of loss and betrayal by their bodies (Gainor, 2000). Feelings of isolation and ostracism are common experiences for transgender youth, often leading to substance abuse, self-abuse, depression, suicide, and attempted suicide. Particular caution should be taken regarding suicide; approximately 50% to 88% of transgender youth have considered or attempted suicide (Israel & Tarver, 1997).

The adult transgender individual may suffer from stress-related medical conditions resulting from social pressures, limited support systems, living in secrecy, and emotional stress. Some transgender individuals experience intense feelings of urgency to openly express their transgender identity, especially if they have been suppressing their transgender identity since early childhood or adolescence (Gainor, 2000).

SALIENT ISSUES FOR COUNSELING

Many transgender individuals with whom we have spoken have described finding themselves in the awkward position of being the first transgender person with whom their counselors have worked. They report frustration at having to educate the person to whom they are turning for help (Carroll & Gilroy, 2002; Gainor, 2000). In addition, in the cases of transsexual individuals who want hormone therapy or sex reassignment surgery, counselors are often in positions of assessing their clients for "appropriateness" for treatment. This has often led to anger and frustration for clients who have understood much more than do the therapists who have power over the clients' access to much-desired procedures (Fontaine, 2002; Israel & Tarver, 1997).

Negative responses may also come from mental health professionals who may misdiagnose clients or pressure clients to "make a decision," whether that decision is to "come out" as one's desired gender, submit to hormone therapy, live as the other gender, or seek sex reassignment surgery (Israel & Tarver, 1997). Mental health professionals sometimes also encourage transgender clients to identify as gay or lesbian, confusing gender identity with sexual orientation.

As previously stated, many transgender clients present for counseling services for reasons that have nothing to do with their transgender status. Practitioners should not assume that transgender status means that counseling is needed or required. When clients do present with issues regarding gender identity, they are often engaged in a natural human process of self-examination and exploration. This process may be evident in such behaviors as dress, language, or physical presentation. We have seen that such presentations often have met with negative responses from family members, friends, coworkers and employers, and the general public. Because of these negative responses, transgender clients may suffer social isolation, emotional anguish, and distorted self-image (Israel & Tarver, 1997).

Support Systems

Support systems are an important component in maintaining basic mental well-being. Unfortunately, a large majority of transsexuals do not have adequate social support systems (Tully, 1992). Some of the important support systems affecting the lives of transgender individuals include family, the transgender community, the medical community, and the mental health community.

The support that transgender individuals experience from their families is often temporarily or permanently strained. Family members go through their own unique process of "coming out" as they come to terms with a loved one's transgender identity; the family process differs from the transgender individual's process (Bockting & Coleman, 1992; Emerson & Rosenfeld, 1996). After becoming aware of the transgender identity of a family member, families go through overlapping stages, depending on their relationship with the transgender individual, stages that include denial, anger, bargaining, depression, and acceptance (Emerson & Rosenfeld, 1996). According to general family-systems theory, each individual member's experience of a process impacts the family system, and in a reciprocal fashion, the family system affects each individual's private experience (Becvar & Becvar, 2000). Mental health professionals working with family members should be familiar with transgender issues in order to educate and support the family as they move through this process toward acceptance. Mental health professionals can be helpful to both the individual and the family by creating a counseling atmosphere that goes beyond dichotomous-gender norms (Bockting & Coleman, 1992), considering that the family's reaction is likely due to the culturally defined dichotomy of gender (Emerson & Rosenfeld, 1996). Because there are many layers of cultural definition, it is particularly important for counselors to be aware of racial, ethnic, faith tradition, and class implications when working with transgender clients. There is little research on transgender individuals, and most research that has been completed has focused primarily on Caucasian individuals (Gainor, 2000; Israel & Tarver, 1997). This topic is beyond the scope of this chapter and merits continued consideration.

Another possible realm of support for the transgender individual is the transgender community. Many transgender individuals become socially involved with the transgender community (Tully, 1992), which consists of a number of social support groups and information-based conferences that focus on transgender issues (Dallas, 2002). Through this involvement, they are able to meet people with identities similar to their own, thus limiting feelings of isolation and enhancing a sense of belonging. In many communities, transgender groups are aligned with the LGB community. Although LGB and transgender identities have historically shared a similar social status, LGB identities have begun to gain an acceptance that transgender identities have yet to achieve (Devor, 2002; Seil, 2002). Through the involvement with a larger LGBT community, the transgender individual can find support, validation, identity, and power (Broad, 2002). On the other hand, the dissonance in social acceptance related to the LGBT community may provoke feelings of alienation and powerlessness among transgender people (Lombardi, 2001). See Lev (chap. 6, this volume) and Fassinger and Arseneau (chap. 1, this volume) for a fuller description of the experience of community within the transgender population.

Another important community for the transgender individual is the medical community. In general, transgender people have two sets of health care providers, those involved with gender transition and those involved with regular health care (Middleton, 1997). Transsexuals rely heavily on the medical community not only for medical services but also for obtaining valuable information on transsexual-specific issues (e.g., SRS, hormone treatments, gender clinics, specific surgical procedures). Unfortunately, many health care programs are not sensitive to the needs of transgender individuals (Bockting, Robinson, & Rosser, 1998; Clements, Wilkinson, Kitano, & Marx, 1999). Transgender individuals are at risk for many health care-related problems, including discrimination within the treatment setting (Dean, Meyer, & Robinson, 2000). Health care service providers have found that it is often difficult to locate important services for transgender clients (e.g., substance use treatment, housing, health care) because other service providers do not want to work with transgender people (Savulescu, Chalmers, & Blunt, 1996). When transgender individuals do locate adequate services, the services are often underutilized because of the insensitivity of health care professionals (Savulescu et al., 1996). Reports of insensitive behavior among health care providers (e.g., referring to transgender women as "he" or "him" and not acknowledging or respecting their identity) suggest that services are severely lacking in terms of provisions of culturally sensitive interventions and health care (Gainor, 2000).

In addition to the medical community, the mental health community is also important to many transgender individuals. Individuals experiencing concerns about gender identity may experience various emotional and psychological stressors, which lead them to seek mental health services (Carroll & Gilroy, 2002). Affirmative counseling formats give the transgender client maximum control in discussing his or her needs (Israel & Tarver, 1997), and the clients can find valuable information and emotional support in either individual or group counseling. Additionally, transsexual clients may seek mental health services to meet the psychological criteria set by the HBIGDA, which requires varying amounts of psychotherapy and the approval of a mental health professional to proceed with particular treatments or procedures (HBIGDA, 2001; 4.6.2, Standard of Care, p. 8; 4.8.1, Standard of Care, p. 9). The dual role of a mental health professional, as both the counselor and the evaluator, creates a paradoxical situation (Feinbloom, 1976) that is likely to compromise the conduciveness of the therapeutic process (Bolin, 1988). However, despite the challenges, transgender individuals can have a positive experience by learning personally relevant information, gaining insight, and finding out about resources (Anderson, 1998). Mental health professionals should possess the experience and information needed to address gender-identity issues and to provide education regarding medical treatment options, if this is of interest to the client (Israel & Tarver, 1997).

It is important to note that not all transgender individuals are interested in SRS or are pursuing psychological services as a means of obtaining medical treatment options (Carroll & Gilroy, 2002). Unfortunately, several barriers exist that may prevent transgender individuals from receiving or accessing the mental health services needed. One such barrier is the general lack of knowledge about transgender identity, gender identity disorder, and SRS issues among practicing mental health professionals (Seil, 2002).

Family Issues

Although mental health professionals are likely to see transgender clients during a lifetime of practice, they are probably more likely to see family members of transgender individuals (Carroll & Gilroy, 2002). Family members who seek mental health services may often be parents who wonder what they did wrong, and thus they may be looking for guidance, affirmation, and acceptance as parents. Parents will typically present for services if their transgender child questions identity as a child, adolescent, or young adult (Cohen-Kettenis & Pfafflin, 2003). Parents of children may also seek services as they notice their child's struggles with gender identity. They may want the mental health professional to "fix" their child, or they may want to learn how to best help their child. Supportive, affirming mental health professionals can greatly facilitate a child's or adolescent's discovery process by assisting parents in understanding and accepting their child's struggles and helping them to deal with teachers, extended family, friends, and community members.

The authors have worked with many transgender individuals who have expressed concern about the impact of their transgender identities on their family systems, and these individuals have made choices they thought worked best for their situations. Some of these individuals have struggled throughout their young lives and have arrived at adulthood trying to convince themselves that they could be "normal." They often have had heterosexual relationships, as members of their identified gender, with members of their desired gender. Some have married and had children, and they have described to us the pain involved in doing this while hoping against hope that their feelings of being trapped in the wrong body would go away if they lived the way they believed they should. Some people have followed this route and have lived their entire lives without openly acknowledging who they really are.

For others, the suppression of feelings becomes impossible, and they find themselves telling their spouses about their true selves. Because gender identity is not about sexual orientation, transgender individuals may deeply love their spouses and may not wish to sever marital ties. Many transgender individuals continue living with their marital partners and raising their children (Lev, 2004). With their spouses, they work out how this will occur. Mental health professionals can provide support, encouragement, and education as the parties make decisions about how their lives will look.

As expected, it can be a great shock when a spouse learns that his or her life partner is struggling with gender identity. For many partners, this happens within the context of finding one's spouse wearing clothing identified with the other gender, and there appear to be more reports of this with biological males who feel trapped in their male bodies (Boylan, 2003; Devor, 2002). Usual responses from a spouse in these circumstances are to wonder whether the partner is gay, to believe that she or he is unappealing as a mate, and to be certain that their marriage has been a lie and so now is over (Boylan, 2003; Lev, 2004). This turmoil may bring either or both of the parties to counseling (Carroll & Gilroy, 2002).

In the sparse literature that exists, there is little written about how to work with family members, and there is little that indicates that there is hope that marital relationships can work when one of the partners is gender-variant. Because most clinicians have not received training to deal with these issues in families wherein a member identifies as transgender, family members, particularly wives, have been pathologized and often blamed for the transgenderness (Lev, 2004). An affirming counselor can offer support and can help to educate about, and normalize, behaviors in a way that leads the individuals or the couple to see that the relationship will be different but that transgender identity does not have to equal a family tragedy. This means helping family members to understand that both the transgender individual and the family move through developmental processes as they come to terms with gender variance as a dynamic in their family system. It further means the clinical work should deal with both individual struggles and the family's discomfort with the transition (Lev, 2004).

For families that include a transgender member, finances can be an issue that needs to be addressed in counseling. Medical interventions are expensive, and when transgender individuals opt for hormone therapy or sex reassignment surgery, the cost can be enormous, typically making medical interventions available only to individuals with extraordinary resources. These occurrences can cause additional stress in families that are already struggling to understand what is happening. An affirmative counselor will directly discuss financial concerns and help the client identify how the client's gender expression needs can be met when financial resources are limited.

Social and Emotional Stressors

There is a pervasive pattern of discrimination and prejudice against transgender people (Lombardi, 2001). As targets of prejudicial treatment, transgender individuals remain largely unprotected and are discriminated against in numerous ways (Green & Brinkin, 1994). Acts that victimize transgender individuals vary from subtle forms of harassment and discrimination to blatant verbal, physical, and sexual assault. There are numerous legal issues that interfere with, control, or inhibit the lives of transgender individuals;

therefore, ~~affirmative mental heath professionals should be aware of state and federal laws that directly pertain to transgender legislation.~~ State laws ~~vary widely and federal laws do not (yet) protect transgender status in regard to sexual harassment and discrimination~~ (Seil, 2002).

Studies are beginning to document ~~violence as a major public-health threat to the transgender community~~ (Bowen, 1995; Wilchins, Lombardi, Priesing, & Malouf, 1997; Xavier, 2000). It has been reported that over half of all transgender individuals will experience some form of discrimination or violence during their lives (Kenagy, 2005; Lombardi, 2001). Additional reports show that 60% of transgender individuals within the United States have experienced some form of harassment or violence and that 37% have experienced some form of economic discrimination (GenderPAC, 1997; Lombardi, 2001; Otis & Skinner, 1996). The National Coalition of Anti-Violence Programs (NCAVP) began to collect data concerning attacks upon trans-people in 1995; they believe that violence against transgender people is pervasive and grossly underreported. NCAVP (2002) found that although transgender people made up only 2% of the population they studied, they constituted approximately 6% of all murder victims studied.

The emotional stress of being transgender in a society that is generally unaccepting of gender-variant behavior can take a very serious toll on the lives of transgender individuals. ~~Emotional stressors may lead to serious issues such as suicide, substance abuse, and eating disorders. Suicidal feelings often develop when individuals feel that there is no support available to meet their needs.~~ Suicide attempts and completed suicides are common in transgender persons (Israel & Tarver, 1997). Studies generally report a pretransition suicide attempt rate of 20% or more, with MTFs relatively more likely to attempt suicide than FTMs, hypothesizing that the awareness of lost male privilege carries an additional burden (Gainor, 2000). There is some evidence that transsexual people are less likely to attempt suicide once they have completed the transition to the other sex (Israel & Tarver, 1997).

Few studies have examined substance abuse within the transgender community. However, the research studies that have been conducted suggest a high prevalence of drug and alcohol abuse. Focus group research conducted in San Francisco showed that ~~among transgender persons, a street lifestyle, lack of education and job opportunities, and low self-esteem all contributed to drug and alcohol abuse,~~ just as they do for the general population (Green & Brinkin, 1994; Lombardi, 2001).

~~Eating disorders may result from attempts to obtain more feminine or masculine body shapes;~~ thus, transgender individuals may be at risk for developing eating disorders (Surgenor & Fear, 1998). In a case study, Surgenor and Fear (1998) identified a close link between transgender issues and eating disorders. By virtue of the emphasis on estrangement from the body, transgender individuals may experience heightened body dissatisfaction and excessive concern with appearance.

Medical Issues

The literature suggests that transgender people experience barriers to health care access (Bockting, Robinson, Forberg, & Scheltema, 2005; Kenagy, 2005; Lombardi, 2001). Transgender people have been denied health care services such as transgender-related care and HIV-prevention services (Bowen, 1995; Reback & Simon, 2001). Lack of knowledgeable providers (JSI Research & Training Institute, 2000), insensitivity or hostility by providers (Xavier, 2000), and lack of health insurance (JSI Research & Training Institute, 2000; Reback & Simon, 2001; Xavier, 2000) were also found to be barriers to obtaining general and transgender-related health care.

It is important for mental health professionals to be aware of medical issues relating to their transgender clients. As mentioned previously, it is also important to note that not all transgender individuals are interested in or want to pursue surgical procedures. Medical procedures that are of primary importance to some transgender individuals include hormone administration, aesthetic surgery, and SRS. It is estimated that since the late 1970s, approximately 10,000 sex reassignment surgeries have been successfully performed worldwide (Israel & Tarver, 1997). Of these surgeries, approximately 4,500 were performed on U.S. residents. By being familiar with these procedures and available resources, the clinician can better meet and support the client's needs.

There is basic information that mental health professionals should understand regarding the medical process involved in SRS. SRS is a medical procedure that assists transgender individuals in bringing the physical body in line with self-identification of gender (Israel & Tarver, 1997). SRS is no longer considered experimental, with access to SRS being regulated by HBIGDA and medical and psychological professionals.

In 1979, the publication of "Standards of Care" by the Harry Benjamin International Gender Dysphoria Association established minimal consensual guidelines for the medical treatment of transsexuals and set the requirement for ongoing involvement from mental health professionals as gatekeepers for access to hormonal therapy and sex reassignment surgery. The standards include a one-year "real-life experience" that requires applicants for SRS to live and work 24 hours a day, 7 days a week, in the new gender. The standards of care are periodically revised, most recently in 1996, and are once again under revision (see http://www.symposium.com for the latest version).

Transgender individuals seeking SRS must meet both legal and psychological criteria prior to being approved for the surgery. Requirements for a "real-life experience" or the establishment of a permanent cross-gender identity prior to SRS vary anywhere from one to four years, depending on the source of the recommendation. In addition, the psychological criteria include attending psychotherapy for a predetermined amount of time, and it is within this context that many mental health professionals see transgender clients (Ellis & Erikson,

2002; Israel & Tarver, 1997). Changes in legal documentation (e.g., driver's license, birth certificate, and passport) are another part of the SRS process.

Career Issues

Employment issues are almost universal concerns for transgender individuals. Transgender individuals who are not "out" at work frequently fear having their transgender identity revealed (Israel & Tarver, 1997). They may be fearful of having their transgender status discovered during inconvenient times or under inappropriate circumstances. They may also be fearful of the disclosure process, repercussions from management, or the negative responses of coworkers. Despite these challenges, some transgender individuals choose to come out at work in various stages. Some individuals disclose their transgender behavior to reduce feelings of isolation and to counteract their fear of being found out (Israel & Tarver, 1997).

Transgender individuals may pursue counseling for a number of career-related reasons. They may enter counseling to pursue information about suitable career options, discuss employment discrimination, get support on coming out at work, or express general employment concerns. Affirming clinicians can help clients to strategize how they will navigate gender-identity concerns in the workplace. Disclosure of one's transgender identity can also be a means of gaining understanding and support; however, such disclosures should be considered in relation to potential risks. The level of tolerance for transgender identity in the work environment should be considered prior to the disclosure process. An intolerant environment may result in hostility, harassment, and potential violence. In addition, one's employment status may become jeopardized. An affirming clinician can help transgender clients to develop safe plans that address these concerns. Some transgender clients will enter counseling in search of support as they pursue new employment situations in which their gender variance will be better tolerated or supported (Israel & Tarver, 1997).

Individuals pursuing sex reassignment surgery may be anxious about on-the-job transitioning. Though many individuals complete on-the-job transitions, other options exist, such as finding new jobs where employment can begin with the individual living in role full-time. It is important that mental health professionals be informed about on-the-job transitions and possible employment risks so that they can meet their transgender clients' career-counseling needs (Carroll & Gilroy, 2002; Gainor, 2000; Israel & Tarver, 1997).

SPECIFIC RECOMMENDATIONS FOR COUNSELORS AND PSYCHOTHERAPISTS

Affirmative counseling for transgender individuals should be as basic as listening to the concerns they bring to sessions and supporting them as they deal with those concerns (Carroll & Gilroy, 2002; Israel & Tarver, 1997). Many transgender clients have told us that this has not been their experience, but rather it has felt to them that helping professionals have not known how to provide support, encouragement, and affirmation. We believe this occurs for two reasons. First, counselors are products of their own socialization, and so they may be uncomfortable working with individuals they see as different from the general population (Carroll & Gilroy, 2002). Second, counselors have not typically received specific training for dealing with transgender clients and so have not felt competent to provide services (Israel & Tarver, 1997).

It is possible for a counselor to work with a transgender person for an extended period of time and never know about the client's transgender status, even though the client may want or need to deal with issues connected to gender status, because the client does not feel safe sharing these concerns. We believe that it is important for counselors to gain skills that enable them to be safe and affirming helpers and for them to understand that transgender identity is not indicative of pathology—that is to say that transgender individuals are not "sick" or "perverted" by virtue of their gender identity. Transgender individuals are typically not mentally disordered, and they do not have a higher incidence of mental disorders than the population in general (Israel & Tarver, 1997).

An issue for many counselors who want to be affirming is how to refer to transgender individuals. They can be confused about whether to refer to a client as "he" or "she." Affirmative counseling begins with the premise that individuals have the right to self-determination, and affirmative counselors refer to individuals in ways that are consistent with the clients' current presentation (Carroll & Gilroy, 2002). As is the case with all affirmative counseling, if the counselor is uncertain, it is important to ask how clients prefer to be identified.

Rather than seeing gender as occurring on a continuum, some transgender individuals and affirmative practitioners describe it as being fluid. This can be a helpful way of detailing the variance that some individuals experience throughout their lifetimes. Lev (2004) made the point that affirmative practitioners assume that "gender variance is as natural as any other expression of gender" (p. 5) and that theories that describe it otherwise add to the isolation that transgender individuals already feel.

Assessment and Diagnostic Issues

There is some controversy over diagnosis of transgender clients. "Whereas gay men and lesbian women are diagnosed for *how they suffer* [e.g., depression], transsexuals are diagnosed for *who they are*" (Wyndzen, 2004, p. 3). A transgender identity does not constitute a mental disorder; however, there are times when transgender individuals may experience psychological distress because of gender confusion or indecision regarding gender expression. This state of distress is recognized in the *Diagnostic and Statistical Manual of Mental Disorders* (American Psychiatric Association, 2000) as "gender identity disorder." Affirmative mental health professionals understand that transgender identity is not reflective of mental health and is not indicative of pathology. However, it is important for clinicians to recognize when a client is experiencing psychological distress as a result of gender-identity confusion or gender-identity indecision because this is a time when suicide may be a risk factor (Israel & Tarver, 1997). It is important to explore what is going on with transgender clients in the same ways we might with any other client. In other words, affirmative therapy is about seeing the person sitting with us and addressing the concerns they bring to sessions.

What Can Mental Health Professionals Do?

It is important that mental health professionals seek out opportunities for special training for working with transgender individuals. They are encouraged to seek and maintain formal membership or affiliation with recognized specialty provider organizations focused on gender-oriented medical and psychotherapeutic practice and consumer education. Such organizations include the American Educational Gender Information Service, the International Foundation for Gender Education, and the Harry Benjamin International Gender Dysphoria Association.

It is also important that mental health professionals familiarize themselves with national, state, and local laws that have impact on transgender individuals. The Transgender Law and Policy Institute (http://www.transgenderlaw.org) does an excellent job of maintaining current information, providing resources, and identifying legal issues. Because counselors function as advocates for transgender clients, it is crucial that they understand the implications of laws that provide protections and laws that serve to take away protections.

To date, there has been little research and scholarly writing about counseling issues specific to transgender individuals. What little information there has been has focused on pathology rather than on affirmative counseling interventions. It is important that mental health professionals become familiar with the available research and writings about this population, and it is important that they seek out information from other sources as well.

Some of the most powerful work has come from individuals who have lived at various places on the transgender continuum, and we recommend several books that describe these experiences. *She's Not There* (Boylan, 2003) details the lived experience of a male-to-female transgender individual who married and had children while struggling with the knowledge that she was a woman trapped in a man's body. Boylan provides an evocative account of the process of sharing one's story with a spouse one loves, of opting for hormone therapy, and of having sex reassignment surgery. *Stone Butch Blues* (Feinberg, 1993) and *Transgender Warriors: Making History From Joan of Arc to Dennis Rodman* (Feinberg, 1996) are accounts written by a female-to-male transgender individual who has strong opinions on hormone therapy, sex reassignment surgery, and affirming ways to express gender. *As Nature Made Him: The Boy Who Was Raised as a Girl* (Colapinto, 2000) details the life of an intersex individual whose genitals were surgically altered and who was assigned female gender as an infant. Colapinto was born with a penis that a doctor determined was too small to allow for a normal boyhood and manhood. *Dress Codes of Three Girlhoods: My Mother's, My Father's, and Mine* (Howey, 2002) describes a daughter's coming to terms with her father's male-to-female transgender status and the journey they take in their relationship. Each of these books provides a firsthand account of the struggles that transgender individuals have, and each has lessons to teach about acceptance and the importance of being true to oneself. Counselors will find the books instructive for their own clinical practices, and they will find them affirming to recommend to transgender clients and their family members who present for services.

It is important that counselors stay current with research and practice issues for transgender individuals. As advocates have stressed the importance of listening to the voices of transgender individuals and as transgender individuals have articulated their therapeutic needs, many clinicians have responded, and best practices have changed. It is anticipated that changes will continue to occur, and it is important to keep abreast of those changes.

CONCLUSION

It is important that mental health professionals have an understanding of the special needs that transgender clients and their families may bring to counseling. Although transgender individuals may present because of gender-identity concerns, we stress that transgender status does not indicate pathology. Like the population in general, most transgender individuals come to counseling because they are dealing with situational stressors, family issues, career concerns, substance abuse, grief and loss, depression, and anxiety, not because they are transgender. In instances wherein transgender individuals do present for counseling because of gender status, it is often in the context of needing a mental health professional to "give approval" for hormone therapy or sex reassignment surgery, and we have discussed the clinical and ethical issues this presents for counselors who strive to be affirming in their practice. Family members of transgender individuals often present for counseling, and it important that counselors understand the dynamics of the anger, grief, and loss issues they may bring to therapy. In short, it is important that mental health professionals be able to see and hear any client who presents for counseling as a unique individual worthy of caring, respect, and culturally competent therapeutic services.

REFERENCES

American Counseling Association. (1995). *ACA code of ethics and standards of practice*. Alexandria, VA: Author.

American Psychiatric Association. (2000). *Diagnostic and statistical manual of mental disorders* (4th ed., text rev.). Washington, DC: Author.

American Psychological Association. (2002). Ethical principles of psychologists and code of conduct. *American Psychologist, 47,* 1597–1611.

Anderson, B. F. (1998). Therapeutic issues in working with transgendered clients. In D. Denny (Ed.), *Current concepts in transgender identity* (pp. 215–226). New York: Garland.

Association for Gay, Lesbian, and Bisexual Issues in Counseling. (2003). *Competencies for counseling gay, lesbian, bisexual and transgendered clients*. Retrieved February 15, 2005, from http://www.aglbic.org/resources/competencies.html

Becvar, D. S., & Becvar, R. J. (2000). *Family therapy: A systemic integration* (4th ed.). Needham Heights, MA: Allyn Bacon.

Bockting, W. O., & Coleman, E. (1992). A comprehensive approach to the treatment of gender dysphoria. In W. O. Bockting & E. Coleman (Eds.), *Gender dysphoria: Interdisciplinary approaches in clinical management* (pp. 131–155). New York: Haworth Press.

Bockting, W. O., Robinson, B., & Rosser, B. (1998). HIV prevention: A qualitative needs assessment. *AIDS Care, 10,* 505–526.

Bockting, W. O., Robinson, B. E., Forberg, J., & Scheltema, K. (2005). Evaluation of a sexual health approach to reducing HIV/STD risk in the transgender community. *AIDS Care, 17,* 289–303.

Bolin, A. (1988). *In search of Eve: Transsexual rites of passage*. South Hadley, MA: Bergin & Garvey.

Bowen, G. (1995). *Violence and health poll*. (Available from The American Boyz, P. O. Box 1118, Elkton, MD 21922-1118.)

Boylan, J. (2003). *She's not there: A life in two genders*. New York: Broadway Books.

Broad, K. L. (2002). GLB+T? Gender/Sexuality movements and transgender collective identity (de)constructions. *International Journal of Sexuality and Gender Studies, 7,* 241–264.

Carroll, L., & Gilroy, P. J. (2002). Transgender issues in counselor preparation. *Counselor Education and Supervision, 41*(3), 233–242.

Clements, K., Wilkinson, W., Kitano, K., & Marx, R. (1999). HIV prevention and health service needs of the transgender community in San Francisco. *International Journal of Transgenderism, 3,* 1–2.

Cohen-Kettenis, P. T., & Pfafflin, F. (2003). *Transgenderism and intersexuality in childhood and adolescence*. Thousand Oaks, CA: Sage.

Colapinto, J. (2000). *As nature made him: The boy who was raised as a girl*. New York: HarperCollins.

Dallas, D. (2002). A selective bibliography of transsexualism. *Journal of Gay & Lesbian Psychotherapy, 6*(2), 35–66.

Dean, L., Meyer, I. H., & Robinson, K. (2000). Lesbian, gay, bisexual, and transgender health: Findings and concerns. *Journal of Gay & Lesbian Medical Association, 4*, 102–151.

Devor, H. (2002). Who are "we"? Where sexual orientation meets gender identity. *Journal of Gay & Lesbian Psychotherapy, 6*(2), 5–21.

Ellis, K. M., & Erikson, K. (2002). Transsexual and transgenderist experiences and treatment options. *The Family Journal: Counseling and Therapy for Couples and Families, 10*, 289–299.

Emerson, S., & Rosenfeld, C. (1996). Stages of adjustment in family members of transgender individuals. *Journal of Family Psychotherapy, 7*(3), 1–12.

Feinberg, L. (1993). *Stone butch blues*. Ithaca, NY: Firebrand Books.

Feinberg, L. (1996). *Transgender warriors: Making history from Joan of Arc to Dennis Rodman*. Boston: Beacon.

Feinbloom, D. H. (1976). *Transvestites and transsexuals: Mixed views*. New York: Dell.

Fontaine, J. H. (2002). Transgender issues in counseling. In L. D. Burlew & D. Capuzzi (Eds.), *Sexuality in counseling* (pp. 177–194). New York: Science Publishers.

Gainor, K. A. (2000). Including transgender issues in lesbian, gay, and bisexual psychology: Implications for clinical practice and training. In B. Greene & G. L. Croom (Eds.), *Education, research, and practice in lesbian, gay, bisexual, and transgendered psychology: A resource manual* (Vol. 5, pp. 131–160). Thousand Oaks, CA: Sage.

GenderPAC. (1997, August 29). Appeals court upholds right to express gender. *National News*. Retrieved March 4, 2005, from http://www.gpac.org/archive/news/index.htmlcmd=view&archive=news&msgnum=0003

Green, J., & Brinkin, L. (1994). *Investigations into discrimination against transgendered people*. San Francisco: San Francisco Human Rights Commission.

Harry Benjamin International Gender Dysphoria Association. (2001). *The Harry Benjamin International Gender Dysphoria Association's standards of care for gender identity disorders* (6th version). Retrieved February 15, 2005, from http://www.hbigda.org/Documents2/socv6.pdf

Howey, N. (2002). *Dress codes of three girlhoods: My mother's, my father's, and mine*. New York: Picador.

JSI Research & Training Institute. (2000). *Access to health care for transgendered persons in greater Boston*. Boston: GLBT Health Access Project.

Israel, G. E., & Tarver, D. E., II. (Eds.). (1997). *Transgender care: Recommended guidelines, practical information, and personal accounts*. Philadelphia: Temple University Press.

Kenagy, G. P. (2005). Transgender health: Findings from two needs assessment studies in Philadelphia. *Health & Social Work, 30*, 19–26.

Lev, A. I. (2004). *Transgender emergence: Therapeutic guidelines for working with gender-variant people and their families*. New York: Haworth Clinical Practice Press.

Lombardi, E. (2001). Enhancing transgender health care. *American Journal of Public Health, 91*, 869–872.

Middleton, L. (1997). Insurance and the reimbursement of transgender health care. In B. Bullough, V. L. Bullough, & J. Ellias (Eds.), *Gender blending* (pp. 455–465). Amherst, MA: Prometheus Books.

National Coalition of Anti-Violence Programs (NCAVP). (2002). *National hate crimes reports*. Retrieved February 15, 2005, from http://www.ncavp.org/publications/NationalPubs.aspx

Otis, M. D., & Skinner, W. F. (1996). The prevalence of victimization and its effect on mental well-being among lesbian and gay people. *Journal of Homosexuality, 30* (3), 93–121.

Ramsey, G. (1996). *Transsexuals: Candid answers to private questions*. Freedom, CA: Crossing Press.

Reback, C. J., & Simon, P. A. (2001). *The Los Angeles transgender health study: Community report*. Los Angeles: Cathy Reback.

Savulescu, J., Chalmers, I., & Blunt, J. (1996). Are research ethics committees behaving unethically? Some suggestions for improving performance and accountability. *BMJ, 3*(13), 1390–1393.

Seil, D. (2002). Discussion of Holly Devor's who are "we"? *Journal of Gay & Lesbian Psychotherapy, 6*(2), 35–66.

Surgenor, L. J., & Fear, J. L. (1998). Eating disorder in a transgender patient. A case report. *International Journal of Eating Disorders, 24,* 449–452.

Tully, B. (1992). *Accounting for transsexualism and transhomosexuality*. London: Whiting & Birch.

Wilchins, R. A., Lombardi, E., Priesing, D., & Malouf, D. (1997). *First national survey of transgender violence*. New York: GenderPAC.

Wyndzen, M. H. (2004, Spring). A personal and scientific look at a mental illness model of transgenderism. *Division 44 Newsletter, 20*(1), 3.

Xavier, J. M. (2000). *The Washington transgender needs assessment survey*. Retrieved November 11, 2005, from http://www.gender.org/vaults/wtnas.html

III

EMERGING ISSUES IN COUNSELING AND PSYCHOTHERAPY

INTRODUCTION: EMERGING ISSUES IN COUNSELING AND PSYCHOTHERAPY

With the second edition of the *Handbook,* we have attempted to include the most recent and salient areas for research and practice in counseling and psychotherapy with lesbian, gay, bisexual, and transgender (LGBT) clients. All in all, the earlier chapters in this book have focused on the important considerations of community, identity development, culture, and ethics in working with LGBT clients as they face issues of sexual prejudice, religious beliefs, and career decisions and as they manage multiple identities. As the field of counseling and psychotherapy with LGBT clients continues to grow, more areas to which therapists are asked to attend are brought to light in the provision of affirmative psychotherapy. The focus and purpose of this section is to explore the burgeoning contemporary issues related to counseling and psychotherapy with lesbian, gay, bisexual, and transgender clients, including an examination of the critical factors for providing affirmative psychotherapy and of the therapist's influence as an agent of social change.

This section begins with Bieschke, Paul, and Blasko (chap. 12), providing a thorough empirical review and critical analysis of the experiences of LGBT clients in therapy. Through their thoughtful analysis, the authors arrive at conclusions that define the core conditions of affirmative psychotherapy with LGBT clients. In addition, their chapter takes a critical look at the validity and implications of research focusing on reparative or conversion therapy.

Chapter 13 examines the potential conflict that arises for psychologists when they are asked to simultaneously affirm sexual diversity and some forms of religious diversity that are not LGB affirming. Fischer and DeBord take an innovative approach in looking at the critical ethical issues in addressing this potential dilemma. Their use of a feminist ethical decision-making model is unique in its analysis of the issues that arise as psychologists and the field struggle with this issue. Their conclusion serves as an illustration of the foundation of affirmative psychotherapy.

The area of affirmative clinical supervision is explored and discussed by Halpert, Reinhardt, and Toohey in chapter 14. The chapter begins with a critique of the major supervision models and an examination of the most germane aspects of each theory that contributes to affirmative supervision. The authors introduce and discuss a proposed model integrating the various theories (Integrative Affirmative Supervision) that weaves the essential and salient aspects of previous supervision theories into a cohesive, unifying theory of affirmative supervision. A case example is provided that illustrates the use of the Integrative Affirmative Supervision model in clinical supervision.

The ever-changing social and political climate has direct implications for the emotional and social welfare of LGBT clients. In chapter 15, Charlotte J. Patterson takes a look at the contemporary issues facing lesbian and gay parents. In her chapter, Patterson examines and discusses the legal and political implications of state laws that impact lesbian and gay families, including laws that relate to issues of same-sex marriage, partner benefits, and adoption. Her thoughtful and thorough examination of these and other issues highlights the critical role of therapists in providing affirmative psychotherapy and in promoting social justice.

The implications of public policy for the mental health of LGBT clients are considered by Michael R. Stevenson in chapter 16. Stevenson takes a critical look at the current and hotly contested social issues influencing current public policy, the ramifications for LGBT persons, and the implications for therapists providing affirmative psychotherapy. In the end, Stevenson's chapter is a call to the important role that therapists can play in promoting and practicing affirmative psychotherapy and to the role that psychologists can have in serving to enhance the quality of life for LGBT persons by promoting social justice through their work.

Chapter 17 concludes the book by revisiting Barón's challenge to the field of psychology "to make homosexuality boring" (Barón, 1991, p. 240). Perez examines the degree to which psychology has succeeded in making homosexuality "boring" by reviewing the core themes of previous chapters and the progress made to date in fully integrating LGBT issues in the practice and scholarship of psychology. Additionally, this chapter discusses the important implications for future practice and research. Through this review, Perez addresses whether or not psychology has succeeded in making homosexuality boring and emphasizes the ever-important role of the therapist in the practice of affirmative psychotherapy in enhancing the lives of LGBT persons.

REFERENCE

Barón, A. (1991). The challenge: To make homosexuality boring. *The Counseling Psychologist, 19*, 239–244.

12

REVIEW OF EMPIRICAL RESEARCH FOCUSED ON THE EXPERIENCE OF LESBIAN, GAY, AND BISEXUAL CLIENTS IN COUNSELING AND PSYCHOTHERAPY

KATHLEEN J. BIESCHKE, PARRISH L. PAUL, AND KELLY A. BLASKO

Bieschke, McClanahan, Tozer, Grzegorek, and Park concluded in 2000 that lesbian, gay, and bisexual (LGB) clients participate in therapy more frequently than heterosexual clients, and evidence indicates that this utilization pattern persists (Cochran, Sullivan, & Mays, 2003; Jones & Gabriel, 1999). Scholars have speculated that this may in part be a result of the distress created by both the social stigma and the stress associated with a minority status sexual orientation (Cochran, 2001; Cochran et al., 2003). These results are particularly meaningful when considered in a larger professional context. The American Psychological Association (APA, n.d.) has issued resolutions and guidelines for treatment that are affirmative of LGB individuals (APA, Division 44/Committee on Lesbian, Gay, and Bisexual Concerns Joint Task Force, 2000), yet the professional literature is resplendent with articles debating the ethics and value of conversion therapy. Even those therapists who profess to be affirmative in their approach demonstrate evidence of subtle heterosexual bias (Bieschke et al., 2000). One can only conclude that LGB individuals often enter into therapeutic situations uncertain of the reception they will receive.

Our goal for this chapter is to provide a succinct, comprehensive summary of what the field has learned about the provision of counseling and psychotherapy to LGB clients since the previous edition of the handbook (Perez, DeBord, & Bieschke, 2000). We have based our summary on empirical research articles published in refereed journal articles that were not reviewed in the last version of this chapter (Bieschke et al., 2000). We begin by reviewing studies focused on clients' experiences in therapy and then move to examining studies that considered therapists' attitudes toward LGB clients. Next, we turn our attention to studies concerning conversion therapy. We conclude the chapter by providing a discussion of the implications of the empirical literature for research, training, and practice.

CLIENT EXPERIENCES OF COUNSELING AND PSYCHOTHERAPY

Since our last chapter (Bieschke et al., 2000), only eight studies (Dorland & Fischer, 2001; Hunt, Matthews, Milsom, & Lammel, in press; Jones & Gabriel, 1999; Lebolt, 1999; Liddle, 1999; Mair & Izzard, 2001; Saulnier, 1999, 2002) have explicitly examined the experiences of gay, lesbian, and bisexual clients in counseling and psychotherapy. Five of these studies were quantitative and three were qualitative. The areas addressed include preferences for therapists, ratings of helpfulness, and factors influencing helpfulness. These studies are largely independent of one another, hence the somewhat diffuse nature of this review. Within each section we first discuss those results that either confirm or extend previous empirical findings. We then discuss those studies that represent relatively new data or findings relative to the implications for affirmative therapy.

LGB Clients' Perceptions of Therapists

There is some evidence that LGB clients prefer therapists who are of the same sex (Jones & Gabriel, 1999; Saulnier, 1999). Saulnier (1999) used convenience and snowball sampling to gather region-specific information about lesbians' experiences, perceptions, and choices regarding mental (and physical) health care, and 106 surveys were completed and returned. The sample was predominately White (80%) and working class. As found in previous studies, most lesbians in this study preferred a female provider (64.4%), and a lower proportion preferred that that individual be a lesbian (38.5%). In Jones and Gabriel's (1999) nationwide study of 600 LGB individuals, participants tended to choose therapists who were of the same sex. Female clients appeared to be more likely to choose female therapists with each successive course of therapy; no such pattern was exhibited for male clients.

The evidence regarding preference for therapist sexual orientation continues to be equivocal. Saulnier (2002) conducted focus groups with 33 lesbian and bisexual women. In sum, Saulnier found that participants believed provider sexual orientation was less important than competence. Jones and Gabriel (1999) found that participants exhibited an increased tendency to choose therapists of the same sexual orientation with each additional episode of therapy. Lebolt's (1999) participants indicated that though therapists who identified as nonheterosexual had particular qualities that increased their effectiveness (e.g., serving as a role model), heterosexual therapists were also described as effective. Less than 10% of the participants in Hunt et al.'s (in press) qualitative study of lesbians with disabilities felt strongly about having a counselor of the same sexual orientation; most reflected flexibility with respect to sexual orientation. Some noted that such a preference may depend on the presenting concern.

With regard to clients' perceptions of mental health care providers, the results from each of the three qualitative studies indicated that therapists are perceived as helpful (Hunt et al., in press; Lebolt, 1999; Mair & Izzard, 2001). In addition, Jones and Gabriel's (1999) results suggest that positive ratings of therapists were positively related to the number of sessions of therapy. Liddle (1999) was the only researcher to investigate client preferences regarding type of mental health care professionals. She distributed 867 surveys to 66 assistants (i.e., faculty and graduate students) across the country who then distributed the survey to gay and lesbian people in their local communities. Of the 339 surveys that were returned, 336 provided data on mental health care that survey participants had received from a professional (i.e., nonstudent) therapist. Social workers, psychologists, and counselors were all judged to be significantly more helpful than psychiatrists. Psychiatrists were five times more likely ✳ than the other groups to be seen as destructive to gay and lesbian clients.

Factors Influencing Helpfulness

The most innovative studies have been those that investigated factors influencing helpfulness. Dorland and Fischer (2001) conducted an analogue study of 126 participants who self-identified as lesbian, gay, or bisexual. They found that using language free of heterosexist bias resulted in more positive counselor ratings, expression of a higher likelihood of returning to see the counselor, expression of a greater willingness to disclose personal information to the counselor, and expression of greater comfort in disclosing sexual orientation to the counselors.

Three qualitative studies investigated factors that influenced therapists' helpfulness: two focused on gay men (Lebolt, 1999; Mair & Izzard, 2001), and one focused on lesbians with disabilities (Hunt et al., in press).

Although all of the participants in these studies found therapy to be helpful in general, the participants in Mair and Izzard's study reported that they felt limited in the extent to which they were comfortable discussing experiences associated with their sexual orientation and that they felt particularly unsafe talking about sexual experiences or practices. Mair and Izzard concluded that once a counselor becomes aware that a client is gay, it is incumbent upon the counselor to engage in discussion about sexual orientation and demonstrate affirmation, either implicitly or explicitly. In contrast, Lebolt (1999) interviewed nine gay men (all of whom saw different therapists) and found that the therapists behaved in ways that were supportive of the client's gay identity (e.g., "[they] appeared comfortable with sexuality in general, and homosexuality in particular," p. 361). Lebolt concluded that these results suggest that therapists can incorporate interventions into therapy that will result in an affirmative and healing experience for gay men.

Hunt et al. (in press) conducted a qualitative study of 25 lesbians with physical disabilities relative to their experiences with counseling. Though these participants found therapy to be helpful in general, these participants also had experiences that compromised the extent to which therapy could be helpful. Participants discussed the importance of therapists' familiarity with lesbian culture. Other clients expressed frustration with counselors who assumed they were heterosexual. Finding a counselor who knew about both disability and lesbian culture was rare. Participants also described incidents of discrimination emanating from either the counselors or the office staff. Participants varied in their decisions to self-disclose either their sexual identity or disability status. Decisions not to self-disclose seemed to be guided by fear of a negative reaction. Participants reported frequently having to advocate for themselves within the counseling relationship as evidenced by educating or prescreening therapists. Accessibility to therapy was also described as problematic, in terms of both physical facilities and funding resources.

Methodological Critique

Almost two thirds of the studies reviewed utilized survey methodology to analyze data from relatively large samples (sample sizes ranged from 106 to 600 participants). With one exception, these relied-upon quantitative studies included bisexual individuals; none of the studies focused exclusively on bisexual individuals. These samples tended to be obtained via snowball sampling and friendship networks, and as a result, the samples were predominantly White and well educated. Saulnier's (1999, 2002) studies were inclusive of working class women, and her 2000 study is noteworthy for specifically targeting groups of lesbians and bisexual women. The generalizability of Saulnier's studies is limited, however, because of their regional focus. An additional problem with the quantitative research studies is the tendency to use "home-grown" measures (i.e., instruments created for a particular study). In general, these instruments had little psychometric support (Liddle's 1999 study is a notable exception), and thus our ability to generalize beyond the individual studies is limited.

Certainly the findings of the qualitative studies are limited in their generalizability to the lesbian and gay population. Further, none of the qualitative studies included bisexual men or women. These studies do, however, provide a comprehensive view of lesbian and gay clients' experiences not found elsewhere in the literature. The Hunt et al. (in press) study may be a notable exception given the size of their sample (25 participants) and the unique characteristics of the population under scrutiny (i.e., lesbians with disabilities). The studies varied considerably in regard to the extent to which the methodology was described, and this also limited the extent to which we utilized those results to inform our conclusions.

Summary

Research has found that LGB clients tend to prefer therapists of the same sex (Jones & Gabriel, 1999; Saulnier, 1999). Focus group data (Saulnier, 2002) and qualitative interview data (Hunt et al., in press; Lebolt, 1999) indicate that therapist competence is very important; Saulnier's findings indicate that it may be more important than therapist sexual orientation. Jones and Gabriel's study indicated that with each subsequent course of treatment, clients tend to choose therapists who are of the same sexual orientation. Other research findings also suggest that reasons for clients' preferences for therapists of a particular sexual orientation go beyond similarity in sexual orientation and include, at minimum, competence by the therapist (e.g., Hunt et al., in press; Lebolt, 1999). There is good evidence to suggest that clients perceive therapists as helpful (e.g., Hunt et al., in press; Lebolt, 1999; Mair & Izzard, 2001). Liddle's (1999) survey found that psychiatrists were judged significantly less helpful than social workers, psychologists, and counselors. These results also suggest that clients are sensitive to heterosexual bias (e.g., Dorland & Fisher, 2001; Hunt et al., in press; Lebolt, 1999; Mair & Izzard, 2001) relative to areas such as heterosexist language, lack of knowledge about sexual orientation issues, and a tendency to avoid certain topics.

THERAPISTS' ATTITUDES TOWARD LESBIAN, GAY, AND BISEXUAL CLIENTS

This section describes the current state of attitudinal research focused on therapists in their work with LGB clients. Eleven of the studies presented addressed therapists' attitudes. One study by Israel, Ketz, Detrie, Burke, and Shulman (2003) extended that focus to establish a set of attitudinal competencies for therapists working with LGB clients. We begin with a review of their study because it provides a useful framework for organizing our discussion.

Israel et al. (2003) used a Delphi technique that utilized a panel of professional experts and LGB-identified experts to rate counselor competencies in the areas of knowledge, attitudes, and skills. Twenty-three attitude components were rated as "helpful" to "very important" in working with LGB clients. The top-ranked attitudes required of counselors were (a) no strong personal convictions that homosexuality is immoral, wrong, or evil or should be changed; (b) a nonhomophobic attitude; and (c) comfort with and acceptance of same-sex intimacy as a healthy lifestyle. The majority of the attitudinal research presented in this section is related to the competency Israel et al. (2003) have labeled as "a non-homophobic attitude."

Studies Focused on Attitudes Toward LGB Clients

Recent research literature confirms a trend identified by Bieschke et al. (2000): Therapists are affirmative of LGB clients. Perhaps the most direct measure of homophobic attitudes toward gay and lesbian clients reviewed for this chapter was in the study by Phillips and Fischer (1998). They reported that 94% of 117 doctoral-level psychology trainees scored in the nonhomophobic range of the Index of Homophobia (Hudson & Ricketts, 1980). Barrett and McWhirter (2002) investigated the relationship between client sexual orientation and counselor trainee homophobia by having 162 counselor trainees read a lesbian, gay male, or heterosexual client case and complete the "unfavorable" and "favorable" subscales of the Adjective Check List (Gough & Heilbrun, 1980). They found that counselor trainees, regardless of their level of homophobia, assigned fewer unfavorable adjectives to gay male and lesbian clients than to heterosexual clients.

A number of investigators have conducted research designed to deepen understanding of therapists' attitudes toward LGB clients. Though therapists report being affirmative of LGB clients, beneath the sheen of affirmation lies complex relationships among attitudes and factors such as LGB-awareness training, therapeutic interactions, and self-efficacy with LGB clients.

Only one study has focused on the effect of training on therapist attitudes toward LGB individuals. Israel and Hackett (2004) found that when a group of affirmative counselor trainees underwent attitude training on LGB issues, they reported more negative cognitive attitudes afterward than did a group of counselor trainees who did not explore their attitudes. The authors hypothesized that counselor trainees reassessed their affirmative attitudes when given more knowledge about LGB issues. The authors speculate that this change in attitudes could be from discomfort the trainees felt in firmly stating what they once labeled affirmative attitudes. We wondered whether participants felt more comfortable being honest about their attitudes after prolonged exposure to the trainers.

Two studies have focused on how attitudes toward LGB clients influence therapist reactions and cognitions. In an analogue study of 425 psychologists that investigated the relationships among therapist homophobia, client sexual orientation, and the source of client HIV infection, Hayes and Erkis (2000) found that therapists were affirmative toward gay male clients. These researchers also found, however, that higher levels of homophobia in therapists were associated with differences in therapeutic reactions, such as less empathy or willingness to accept the client for treatment. Dillon and Worthington (2003) found that the more positive the attitudes of therapists toward LGB clients, the greater their self-efficacy in performing LGB-affirmative counseling.

Gender differences in attitudes toward LGB clients have also been identified. Male therapists have less affirmative attitudes than female therapists when working with LGB clients (Barrett & McWhirter, 2002; Bowers & Bieschke, 2005; Matthews, Selvidge, & Fisher, 2005). Bowers and Bieschke (2005) investigated the attitudes of 303 psychologists by having participants respond to a clinical vignette that described a client experiencing moderate depressive symptoms. The vignette varied by client gender and sexual orientation. Results indicated that male psychologists rated LGB clients as significantly more likely to threaten to harm another person than heterosexual clients; female psychologists' ratings did not differ significantly across the LGB or heterosexual client conditions. Matthews et al. (2005) found similar results when they surveyed 179 addiction counselors to examine factors that predict affirmative attitudes and behaviors toward LGB clients. Female addiction counselors reported significantly more affirmative behavior than their male counterparts. In the Barrett and McWhirter (2002) study, the relationship between homophobia scores on the IHP and the assignment of unfavorable adjectives to gay males and lesbians was stronger for male counselor trainees than for female counselor trainees.

Attitudinal Research Specific to Topic and Population

A recent development in the literature shows that attitudinal research is starting to become more specialized by focusing on topics of interest to LGB clients (i.e., parenting and HIV status) and by targeting specialties within the counseling field (e.g., addiction and substance abuse counseling, school counseling). These studies suggest that even in these specialized contexts, there are still trends toward more affirmative attitudes. Crawford, McLeod, Zamboni, and Jordan (1999) examined attitudes toward gay and lesbian parenting by presenting 388 practicing psychologists with one of six vignettes describing a couple interested in adopting a 5-year-old child. The vignettes were identical except for the couple's sexual orientation. This study suggests that the ~~participants held affirming attitudes toward gay and~~ ~~lesbian parenting and were sensitive to the level of stigmatization and bias~~ ~~that gay and lesbian families encounter in our society.~~ In a study of a small sample of school counselors by Fontaine (1998), the participants reported their current attitudes toward lesbian and gay students as more tolerant than 10 years earlier. Matthews et al. (2005) surveyed 179 addiction counselors to examine factors that predict affirmative attitudes and behaviors toward LGB clients and found that ~~working in a nonheterosexist organizational climate~~ ~~contributed to LGB-affirmative attitud~~es. A study of 242 substance abuse counselors by Eliason (2000) found a fairly high level of tolerance or acceptance of LGBT clients.

Attitudes Toward Bisexual Clients

In the literature, we are beginning to see an emergence of attitudinal research related to bisexual clients. Mohr, Israel, and Sedlacek (2001) conducted one of the first studies to focus exclusively on bisexual issues in counseling. Ninety-seven doctoral- and master's-level counselor trainees participated in an analogue study and responded to an intake vignette of a bisexual woman. ~~Trainees who felt positively about bisexuality were less~~ ~~likely to view a bisexual client as having low levels of psychosocial func-~~ ~~tions and problems in areas related to bisexual stereotypes.~~ Also, ~~trainees~~ ~~who viewed bisexuality as a stable and legitimate sexual orientation were~~ ~~less likely than others to rate the bisexual client as having problems in~~ ~~areas related to bisexual stereotype~~s. Bowers and Bieschke (2005) included a bisexual clinical vignette in their study and found that ~~female psycholo-~~ ~~gists expected greater improvement in depressive symptoms for bisexual~~ ~~clients than for heterosexual clients~~, which is suggestive of supportive attitudes toward bisexuality.

Methodological Critique

Measurement of attitudes toward LGB clients was approached in very different ways in the studies reviewed. All of the studies had a quantitative component to the research design. Almost one-half of the studies had a focus on assessing attitudes using an analogue research design. In two cases, home-grown measures were utilized to assess attitudes (Crawford et al., 1999; Fontaine, 1998). Almost 75% of the studies, rather than relying on only one homophobia measure to assess attitude, linked several measures to establish relationships between attitude and other therapeutic variables (e.g., therapist gender, self-efficacy, clinical reactions). Although one of the studies reviewed measured social desirability (Dillon & Worthington, 2003), researchers for four of the studies (Crawford et al., 1999; Israel & Hackett, 2004; Matthews et al., 2005; Phillips & Fischer, 1998) mentioned social desirability as a limitation in the discussion section. Specifically, these researchers noted that they were uncertain about whether therapists responded based on how they "should" respond. These studies used a mixture of sample pools including trainees and licensed mental health providers. Using diverse samples facilitates our understanding of trends in attitudes for the general therapist population and allows us to draw conclusions about specific therapist specialties.

Summary

In general, the trend of affirmation of LGB clients by therapists continues. Further, there is a more sophisticated understanding of the context in which affirmation occurs. The emergence of studies on therapists' attitudes toward bisexual clients is a step toward recognizing nonheterosexual subgroups other than just gay males or lesbians. More studies inclusive of bisexual clients are necessary. Specialized attitudinal studies with a focus on different sample pools and clinical issues are helping to tease out the differences within the assumed monolithic sample pool of psychologists. Despite the variety of types of studies reviewed, one finding continued to emerge: male therapists appear to be less LGB-affirmative than female therapists.

Thus far in the chapter, we have focused on therapeutic experiences that might loosely be termed "affirmative therapy." That is, participants sampled were not asked to report on any psychotherapy or counseling they had engaged in with the explicit or sole purpose of changing their sexual orientation. Further, therapists in the studies on attitudes were not drawn from a population of conversion therapists. Our next section focuses exclusively on the empirical evidence both in support of and in opposition to conversion therapy.

CONVERSION THERAPY

Relative to the chapter in the first edition of this book (Bieschke et al., 2000), we must admit to being surprised by what appears to be an explosion of literature focused on conversion therapy. In the last version of this chapter in 2000, we primarily reviewed studies focused on conversion therapy to provide a historical context for understanding the delivery of psychotherapy to the LGB population. Although the vast majority of the recent literature is nonempirical (e.g., Haldeman, 2004; Morrow & Beckstead, 2004; Throckmorton, 2002; Yarhouse, Burkett, & Kreeft, 2002), there have been important empirical studies that have examined outcomes of conversion therapy for the LGB population. Three studies have explored paraprofessional conversion therapy (Ponticelli, 1999; Schaeffer, Hyde, Kroencke, McCormick, & Nottebaum, 2000; Schaeffer, Nottebaum, Smith, Dech, & Krawczyk, 1999), four studies have focused on the efficacy of conversion therapy (Beckstead & Morrow, 2004; Nicolosi, Byrd, & Potts, 2000; Shidlo & Schroeder, 2002; Spitzer, 2003), and one study has looked specifically at who seeks conversion therapy (Tozer & Hayes, 2004).

In this section, we provide a definition of the term "conversion therapy" as well as some information about the recipients of this treatment modality. We discuss the empirical findings relative to both paraprofessional and professional conversion therapy. Finally, we conclude with a methodological critique of these studies as well as a summary of the research on conversion therapy thus far.

What Is Conversion Therapy?

In the psychological literature, conversion therapy has also been referred to as "reparative therapy" or "reorientation therapy." We believe that the use of the term reparative therapy implies that LGB persons are in need of some repair. The term reorientation therapy implies that LGB persons were once heterosexual and now simply need to be reoriented to a more socially supported identity. In this chapter, we have intentionally chosen to refer to this treatment modality as "conversion therapy." Shidlo and Schroeder (2002) described conversion therapy as any professional or peer-group attempt to change a homosexual orientation. That is, conversion therapy attempts to change an individual's same-sex sexual orientation (i.e., an enduring emotional, romantic, sexual, or affectional attraction to members of the same sex; Worthington, Savoy, Dillon, & Vernaglia, 2002), not merely an individual's propensity to engage in sexual behaviors with a member of the same sex.

It is important to highlight that conversion therapy is not just an intervention delivered by a professionally trained counselor; the research studies and scholarly material we reviewed substantiate the delivery of conversion therapy by paraprofessionals in groups with a religious affiliation (e.g., Exodus International). Resources are available that outline approaches delivered by professionally trained mental health professionals (e.g., Bright, 2004; Nicolosi, 1993) as well as approaches delivered by those without formal mental health training (e.g., Ponticelli, 1996, 1999; Schaeffer et al., 1999, 2000). In our review we seek to distinguish between approaches delivered by a mental health professional and those delivered by others (e.g., peers, pastors, and so on). Seekers of conversion therapy may participate in conversion therapy offered either by a professionally trained mental health professional or by those affiliated with a religion, or they may participate in both simultaneously.

Who Seeks Conversion Therapy?

In the existing psychological literature, several characteristics of individuals who have participated in research on conversion therapy are apparent. First, a ~~large proportion of conversion therapy participants were individuals who were religious at the time they pursued treatment~~ (Beckstead & Morrow, 2004; Nicolosi et al., 2000; Ponticelli, 1996, 1999; Schaeffer et al., 1999, 2000; Shidlo & Schroeder, 2002; Spitzer, 2003; Tozer & Hayes, 2004). Further, the ~~religious beliefs of these participants were experienced as incongruent with the acceptance of a sexual minority identity~~. A ~~large majority~~ of these participants were ~~White men;~~ a ~~small number of female and ethnically diverse participants were represented in these sample~~s. The empirical literature does not directly address why religious White men seem to be the primary candidates for participation in conversion therapy. Only Tozer and Hayes (2004) have explored the roles of internalized homonegativity, religiosity, and sexual identity development as related to an individual's propensity to seek conversion treatment. These researchers found that ~~individuals who held homonegative beliefs, those whose intrinsic religious identities were central and organizing identities, and those in early phases of lesbian or gay identity development were inclined to view conversion therapy as an option for treatment~~.

What Do Empirical Studies of Conversion Therapy Tell Us?

We have organized our review of empirical studies of conversion therapy into two sections. We begin by reviewing the relatively limited research focused exclusively on conversion therapy offered within Christian ministry organizations. The three studies reviewed in this section include treatment offered in a variety of contexts, but most often, treatment includes a small group experience staffed by volunteers or ministry staff. We then summarize the remaining studies of conversion therapy. We are less certain of exactly what type of conversion therapy experience participants in these studies have had. All of these participants identified as having participated in conversion therapy and, consistent with the definition of conversion therapy presented earlier, may have participated in either or both an individual and a small group conversion therapy experience.

Conversion Therapy Within Christian Ministry Organizations

Many individuals seeking conversion therapy have pursued treatment through Christian ministry organizations (Yarhouse et al., 2002). Though a variety of such programs exist, these ministries generally view ~~only heterosexuality as compatible with Christianity. According to these groups, same-sex attraction is a learned behavior that members can and should change~~. Treatment is generally conducted in a small group format, and interventions often include elements of education, discussion, worship, and prayer. Some of these organizations follow a series of steps similar to the 12-step treatment approach, often used in support groups for recovery from addictions. The literature did not provide information on the existence of paraprofessional conversion treatment groups linked to religions other than Christianity.

We found four research investigations that examined the experiences of individuals who have participated in conversion therapy offered by paraprofessional Christian ministries. Schaeffer and her colleagues (1999, 2000) conducted initial and follow-up survey research in which the researchers quantitatively explored paraprofessional conversion treatment outcomes. These researchers published an initial study (2000) that described their survey of 184 males and 64 females who were attempting to change their sexual orientations because of their religious beliefs. Schaeffer and another set of colleagues followed up with 102 males and 38 females from their original sample (1999; the follow-up study was published in advance of the original study), to explore participants' continued experience of change. In both of these studies, mental health variables such as a sense of happiness and a positive outlook were correlated with the self-report of behavior that was "more heterosexual" at the time of the survey administration than it had been in the past. In addition, self-defined "success" in sexual orientation change was positively correlated with frequent and continuing attendance of religious services. Participants who were described as highly religiously motivated were found to be more likely than other participants to have avoided same-sex intimate behavior over time. Because each of the participants in these studies was an attendee at a Christian paraprofessional conference focused on conversion, however, it could be argued that all participants were somewhat religiously motivated. Also, participants with a history of fewer same-sex intimate partners were more likely to have avoided same-sex intimate behavior. Researchers found, however, that paraprofessional conversion therapy was not effective in helping participants to change sexual orientation.

In a 1996 ethnographic account, Ponticelli attended a national conference for one paraprofessional conversion ministry. She reported that gay or lesbian lifestyles [sic] were pathologized and ridiculed by group members, and conference attendees were approached and repeatedly encouraged to pursue conversion to heterosexuality. A lesbian herself, Ponticelli described the experience as a constant barrage of conversion messages that she found both exhausting and unsettling. Ponticelli noted follow-up contacts and attempts by group members to convince her to leave the lifestyle after she had left the conference.

Ponticelli (1999) also conducted a study that focused on self-described ex-lesbians in one paraprofessional conversion ministry. Employing a field research methodology, Ponticelli conducted eight months of participant observation with one group affiliate of Exodus International. She was also a participant observer at two Exodus conferences. Ponticelli interviewed 15 self-described ex-lesbians, 5 of whom were members of the group she observed and 10 of whom were contacted through conference attendance rosters. She analyzed these interviews and the written materials members received from the Exodus organization to develop themes she presented in her study. Ponticelli observed that individuals in this sample communicated in a common discourse, and the language and behaviors that were presented as appropriate by the conversion group were mirrored in the participants' narratives. For example, participants in this study voiced beliefs that all sexual minority individuals experience tension and anxiety related to their sexualities. They also asserted that lesbian or gay behavior could be viewed only negatively in society.

Methodological Critique. The scope and depth of literature related specifically to paraprofessional conversion therapy is limited. As we wrote this chapter, only survey research and qualitative study methodologies that focused on this population were available. The three studies (Ponticelli, 1999; Schaeffer et al., 1999, 2000) drew samples only from participants who either attended national conferences or were members of Exodus. Therefore, members of other paraprofessional conversion groups may not be represented by these findings. We also noted that participants in these studies were largely White, religious, male, and well-educated. Though of course limited in generalizability, Ponticelli's qualitative study and narrative account provide an experiential view of paraprofessional conversion treatment not otherwise available. The qualitative study directly addressed the experiences of women in these groups, which, as noted previously, has been lacking in most studies related to both professional and paraprofessional conversion treatment.

Other Conversion Therapy Experiences

Participants self-identified as having participated in conversion therapy, and consistent with the definition presented previously, reported a range of conversion therapy treatment experiences. The studies represent both quantitative (Nicolosi et al., 2000; Spitzer, 2003) and qualitative (Beckstead & Morrow, 2004; Shidlo & Schroeder, 2002) methodologies. In this section, we describe participants' reactions to conversion therapy relative to its perceived harmfulness and helpfulness. We also discuss whether there is evidence to support the conclusion that conversion therapy can modify sexual orientation. We conclude by highlighting some of the ethical issues that arise within the context of the provision of conversion therapy.

Conversion Therapy and Harmfulness. All three of the studies that explicitly asked participants about harm support the conclusion that conversion therapy has the potential to be harmful (Beckstead & Morrow, 2004; Nicolosi et al., 2000; Shidlo & Shroeder, 2002). Nicolosi et al. (2000) reported that in their sample of 882 "dissatisfied homosexually oriented people" who engaged in attempts to change their sexual orientation, the well-being of approximately 34 (7.1%) participants deteriorated during participation in conversion therapy.

In Shidlo and Schroeder's (2002) qualitative study, 87% of the 202 consumers of professional and paraprofessional interventions reported failure, and many of the participants found conversion therapy to be harmful. Participants who experienced conversion therapy as harmful described harm in the following ways: (a) increase in depression and suicidal ideation and attempts; (b) loss of self-esteem and an increase in internalized homophobia; (c) attribution of all negative life events to an LGB orientation; (d) intrusive and disturbing mental images formed in conversion treatments; (e) increased concern about cross-gender mannerisms; (f) harm to relationships with family after some conversion treatments faulted parents for the participant's sexual orientation; (g) isolation and alienation after losing relationships with others who had also been seeking conversion; (h) difficulty in forming intimate gay or lesbian relationships; (i) fear of becoming a child abuser after such assertions were made in conversion treatment; (j) a delay of gay or lesbian developmental tasks; and (k) a negative impact on religiosity or spirituality.

In the Beckstead and Morrow (2004) study, of the 42 participants interviewed who had participated in conversion therapy, 22 of the participants were classified as opponents of conversion therapy and described primarily negative outcomes. The participants were negatively affected by the process of conversion therapy and described interventions and promises that potentially increased discrimination, relational difficulties, hopelessness, self-hatred, and for some, suicide attempts or completions. The remaining 20 participants, classified as proponents of conversion therapy, did not discuss harms, though four of these participants had attempted suicide after counseling related to the increased self-hatred that resulted from failure to sexually re-orient. Interestingly, some participants in both of the qualitative studies (Beckstead & Morrow, 2004; Shidlo & Schroeder, 2002) who reported negative effects of conversion treatment also described their conversion therapy experiences as useful. Participants in the Shidlo and Schroeder study (2002) found that participating in conversion therapy was helpful in determining that conversion was not possible. In Beckstead and Morrow (2004), participants reported some short-term relief (e.g., learning that they were not alone, beginning an exploration of self), and some described conversion therapy as necessary because it allowed them to explore being an "ex-gay" as well as the opportunity to move toward self-acceptance.

Conversion Therapy and Sexual Orientation Change. There is conflicting evidence regarding whether conversion therapy can change sexual orientation. Spitzer (2003) and Nicolosi et al. (2000) concluded that complete change is possible for at least some individuals who participate in conversion therapy. Nicolosi et al. acknowledged that complete change is an "often difficult and lengthy process" (p. 1084), and Spitzer concluded that complete change "may be a rare or uncommon occurrence" (p. 413). Shidlo and Schroeder (2002) reported that 8 of their 202 participants viewed conversion therapy as helpful in an actual shifting of sexual orientation (we think it is important to note that of those 8, 7 reported currently serving as conversion counselors). Thus, similar to the results for paraprofessional conversion therapy, there is evidence to suggest that conversion therapy is useful primarily to manage behavior but has little long-lasting influence on sexual orientation (Beckstead & Morrow, 2004; Schaeffer et al., 1999, 2000; Shidlo & Schroeder, 2002). Beckstead and Morrow provided some details about how participants, including those self-identified as now heterosexual, relayed that an internal tendency to be aroused by same-sex individuals remained after treatment, and they did not report a substantial increase in heterosexual arousal. Instead, if participants defined conversion therapy as successful, its success was related to a change in the ways some participants understood and experienced their behavior, their relationships, their sexuality, and their spirituality.

Conversion Therapy and Helpfulness. Interestingly, though the evidence suggests that conversion therapy has the potential to be harmful, all four of the studies also concluded that at least some participants found conversion therapy helpful (Beckstead & Morrow, 2004; Nicolosi et al., 2000; Shidlo & Schroeder, 2002; Spitzer, 2003). Estimates and perceptions of helpfulness ranged widely. We attribute this disparity to both methodology and varying definitions of "helpfulness."

Both Nicolosi et al. (2000) and Spitzer (2003) asked participants to retrospectively consider the extent to which they had engaged in homosexual thoughts, behaviors, and feelings both prior to and after conversion therapy. Both studies concluded that some significant change had occurred in sexual orientation as a result of participating in conversion therapy. Spitzer concluded that complete change occurred for 11% of the males and 37% of the females. Nicolosi et al. concluded that complete change occurred for 17.6% of the sample.

In both the Shidlo and Schroeder (2002) and the Beckstead and Morrow (2004) studies, the vast majority of those who found treatment to be helpful were still "struggling" with or still trying to convert their orientations. Participants who perceived conversion therapy as helpful (Shidlo & Schroeder, 2002) described a change in sexual orientation or behavior and an increase in psychological well-being. These participants viewed cognitive and behavioral strategies as helpful in managing same-sex behavior and impulses. Specific perceived benefits of conversion therapy included an increase in coping abilities, sense of hope, and self-esteem and an improvement in family and social relationships. In the Beckstead and Morrow study (see also Beckstead, 2001), those who experienced conversion therapy as successful described positive aspects of treatment that are present in most effective therapeutic approaches, including "religious validation, reframing, congruent solutions, behavioral strategies, and group work" (p. 686). Individuals who deemed conversion therapy helpful described a process of reframing same-sex impulses as externally motivated and then managing same-sex behaviors.

Ethical Issues. Only one study examined ethical issues: Schroeder and Shidlo (2001) reported on a subset of the 202 participants in the Shidlo and Schroeder (2002) study. These 150 participants received professional rather than paraprofessional conversion therapy, and Schroeder and Shidlo concluded that many professional conversion therapists appeared to be treating clients without full informed consent. Further, these therapists seemed to be presenting misinformation about sexual orientation, efficacy of conversion treatment, and other treatment options such as gay-affirmative psychotherapy. Termination of conversion therapy was also a concern; some participants experienced coercion to remain in treatment when they had decided it was not helpful. Participants also described a failure to explore such termination topics as transition back into gay or lesbian life, the loss of ex-gay or ex-lesbian community, or the process of reintegrating a lesbian or gay identity with other valued identities. In addition, 26% of the participants in the original Shidlo and Schroeder (2002) study initially sought psychotherapy for depression, anxiety, and guilt related to sexuality concerns, but received conversion therapy instead after revealing their sexual orientation to the clinician.

Methodological Critique. All of the studies reviewed were composed largely of European American males. A large number, if not all, of participants in the studies reviewed were religious, which further limits generalizability. The definition of conversion therapy varied widely both between and within studies. Participants were included if they self-identified as having received conversion therapy. With both of the quantitative studies (Spitzer, 2003; Nicolosi et al., 2000), the measures lacked both reliability and validity. Although qualitative studies are limited in their generalizability, both of the qualitative studies reviewed here (Beckstead & Morrow, 2004; Shidlo & Schroeder, 2002) are to be commended for utilizing relatively large samples and multiple methods of collecting data and for their focus on model-building. All of the studies exclusively used retrospective self-reports and exhibited limited use of follow-up techniques (though the 2002 Shidlo and Schroeder study made some use of this technique).

It seems important to note that one study examined experiences of conversion therapy participants an average of 12 years after their participation in that treatment modality. In that study, Shidlo and Schroeder (2002) theorized a developmental model of their participants' reactions to and experiences of conversion treatment. This developmental model suggests that individuals who at one time pursued conversion to heterosexuality found their initial treatment to be helpful. However, this model also posits that the same individuals may later identify as gay or lesbian and come to view their earlier conversion treatment as harmful. It is unclear if participants in other reviewed studies, whose conversion therapy experiences may have been more recent, will come to redefine or maintain their understanding of those experiences over time.

Summary of Empirical Evidence for Paraprofessional and Professional Conversion Therapy

We identified four themes in the reviewed studies. First, when qualitative data were provided, great desire and struggle by individuals in their attempts to change sexual orientation were apparent. Second, religious beliefs appeared to be a motive for and were linked to attempted sexual orientation change for the majority of participants. Third, some type of change appeared to have been experienced by a small number of highly motivated individuals, but this change seemed to be defined differently across studies. Specifically, when change in sexual behavior was differentiated from change in sexual orientation, most individuals in the small group of total participants who reported conversion described a shift in their behavior toward same-sex others rather than a change in their orientation, feelings, or attractions. Though a very small subset of highly motivated individuals contended that a change in orientation occurred, more data are needed to elucidate the process and the experience of change noted by these individuals. Finally, we identified a theme that is related to the harm or helpfulness of conversion treatment. When the potential for harm versus help was addressed in a reviewed study, the majority of participants considered conversion therapy as harmful.

IMPLICATIONS

We have assiduously focused our attention on a comprehensive review of the empirical literature examining the provision of services to LGB clients. Specifically, we have reviewed the research relative to LGB client experiences of counseling and psychotherapy, the attitudes of therapists toward LGB clients, and the provision of conversion therapy to this clientele. Our goal has been to provide a fair and unbiased review of these studies in the hope of being able to provide further direction for research endeavors and present research findings that might guide future interventions. In this section, we first address the research implications of our review and then turn our attention to implications for practice and training.

Implications for Research

Our review of the empirical literature indicates that many questions are left unanswered. Relative to LGB clients' perceptions of therapists, the research evidence suggests that LGB clients tend to perceive therapists as affirmative. Furthermore, LGB clients are generally more concerned with finding a competent therapist than with finding one who is of a particular biological sex or sexual orientation. Our review also suggests that clients are sensitive to more subtle forms of bias; that is, clients are aware of the degree to which therapists are affirmative, and these perceptions guide LGB clients' behavior and participation in therapy. Interestingly, the research focused on therapist attitudes supports LGB clients' perceptions that for some therapists, the importance of affirmation of LGB clients is not a deeply held belief. Our belief is that as the mental health professions have become increasingly affirmative via the provision of guidelines and resolutions, trainees and professionals may profess to be affirmative without delving very deeply into what that means for them and how such attitudes may manifest in therapy. Certainly an affirmative attitude toward LGB clients is one of the basic competencies identified by Israel et al. (2003), yet work on fleshing out the meaning and definition of this construct has only just begun. We believe that understanding affirmation, from the perspectives of clients as well as therapists, is essential and that both quantitative and qualitative studies focused on increasing our understanding of this construct are needed.

We also believe that the focus of inquiry must extend beyond White, relatively affluent, well-educated lesbian and gay clients. Few studies have successfully obtained a diverse sample relative to race and SES (Saulnier, 1999, 2002, is one exception). This is a glaring omission in the literature. While some of the quantitative studies focused on client experiences included bisexual individuals, not one study studied bisexual clients' experiences exclusively. A few studies have thoughtfully examined therapists' attitudes toward bisexual clients (Bowers & Bieschke, 2005; Mohr et al., 2001), and these are important contributions. This type of inquiry lends itself to qualitative methodology, given that individuals representing these groups may be few in number. For example, Hunt et al.'s (in press) examination of lesbians with disabilities provides us with a valuable perspective about this population that we would not otherwise have were we to conduct a quantitative study.

Relative to conversion therapy, we are faced with a perennial dilemma. How does one effectively study a treatment many psychologists consider unethical? We believe that alternative models to working with clients in conflict around their sexual orientation have been identified and that these are worthy of empirical scrutiny (Beckstead & Israel, chap. 9, this volume; Beckstead & Morrow, 2004; Haldeman, 2004). Further, samples used in studies examining conversion therapy are made up of primarily men. This raises questions about gender difference. Are women more sexually fluid? Are women less stigmatized? How might this gender difference interact with the heightened religiosity among people who tend to seek conversion therapy? Future researchers may also wish to focus on length of time between completion of conversion therapy and follow-up. In addition, it would be useful to control for sexual orientation at the time conversion therapy was undertaken. Bisexual people who indicate their sexual orientation has changed might in fact be learning to emphasize a preexisting heterosexual attraction.

Implications for Practice and Training

The studies addressing the experiences of LGB clients in therapy suggest that therapist competence is an important ingredient for effective psychotherapy. Israel et al. (2003) identified a set of competencies essential to working effectively with LGB clients and the three top attitudinal competencies they identified include (a) no strong personal convictions that homosexuality is immoral, wrong, evil, or should be changed, (b) a nonhomophobic attitude, and (c) comfort with and acceptance of same-sex intimacy as a healthy lifestyle. Others suggest that in addition to holding affirmative beliefs, therapists must be explicit in regard to their affirmation of LGB clients (e.g., Lebolt, 1999; Mair & Izzard, 2001). Further, evaluating the extent to which the environment where services are provided is affirmative is also important (e.g., Hunt et al., in press; Matthews et al., 2004).

We believe that in order for mental health professionals to be truly affirmative, more than a superficial understanding of LGB issues is necessary. This clearly has implications for training. We were intrigued by Israel and Hackett's (2004) finding that affirmation for LGB clients decreased as a result of training. This finding is consistent with Bieschke, Croteau, Lark, and Vandiver's (2004) characterization of the affirmative discourse (i.e., the counterdiscourse) around sexual orientation in the counseling professions as too simplistic and superficial. These authors call for a strengthening of the counterdiscourse around such sexual orientation issues such that the counterdiscourse integrates advocacy, incorporates complex and socially constructed views, positions sexual orientation within social and cultural contexts, and calls for engagement in difficult exploration and dialogue. Matthews (chap. 8, this volume) discusses the importance of therapists understanding their own heterosexism when working with LGB clients. Training focused on competence with LGB clients must include self-examination of one's biases as well as one's skills.

Working affirmatively with clients in conflict regarding their sexual orientation is difficult, particularly when clients wish to explore options that may, on the surface, seem unaffirmative. We want to state clearly that our review of the empirical literature indicates that we cannot conclude that it is possible for an individual to change his or her sexual orientation. A very small minority of participants do report that they believe they have made a shift in sexual orientation, but without accurate measurement of sexual orientation prior to intervention and long-term follow-up studies, it is difficult to ascertain the validity of these self-reports. Further, in light of the findings of three studies (Beckstead & Morrow, 2004; Nicolosi et al., 2000; Shidlo & Schroeder, 2002), we conclude that the potential for harm to clients exists in conversion therapy and that this treatment modality should not be offered.

What is also clear, however, is that ~~clients in conflict around their sexual orientation need to explore this conflict thoughtful~~ly (Beckstead, 2001; Beckstead & Morrow, 2004) ~~and have the freedom to explore a wide range of options~~. Beckstead and Morrow suggested that the conceptualization of clients as only out-gay or ex-gay is too narrow and limiting for the complexity and diversity of human experience. They proposed a treatment focus that examines the client's conflicts with same-sex attraction and her or his needs and values. The authors supported the provision of a safe therapeutic relationship, free from judgment or bias, and also suggested providing the client with accurate information on LGB individuals and communities and the social effects of homophobia and heterosexism. Beckstead and Israel (chap. 9, this volume) also detail an approach to working with clients in conflict about their sexual orientation.

CONCLUSION

We began this chapter by asserting that LGB individuals enter into therapeutic situations uncertain of the reception they will receive. Our review of the empirical research confirms such an assertion, considering that the studies reviewed here reflect the range of attitudes and treatments within the profession. Our belief is that clients have the right to expect their therapists to exhibit basic competencies relative to the provision of services to LGB clients. Further, what is clear from our review of these studies is that clients should not ever be offered treatment that has the potential to inflict harm, and thus we are unequivocal in our belief that conversion therapy is not an ethical treatment option. Though we do not believe there is one singular path of coming to terms with sexual identity, we believe it is our responsibility to provide a context of affirmation that honors the difficulty clients often experience when reconciling their sexual identity with complex and competing loyalties to self, others, and society.

REFERENCES

American Psychological Association. (n.d.). *Resolutions related to lesbian, gay, and bisexual issues*. Retrieved March 30, 2005, from http://www.apa.org/pi/reslgbc.html

American Psychological Association, Division 44/Committee on Lesbian, Gay, and Bisexual Concerns Joint Task Force on Guidelines for Psychotherapy With Lesbian, Gay, and Bisexual Clients. (2000). Guidelines for psychotherapy with lesbian, gay, and bisexual clients. *American Psychologist, 55*, 1440–1451.

Barrett, K. A., & McWhirter, B. T. (2002). Counselor trainees' perceptions of clients based on client sexual orientation. *Counselor Education and Supervision, 41*, 219–232.

Beckstead, A. L. (2001). Cures versus choices: Agendas in sexual reorientation therapy. *Journal of Gay & Lesbian Psychotherapy, 5*, 87–115.

Beckstead, A. L., & Morrow, S. L. (2004). Mormon clients' experiences of conversion therapy: The need for a new treatment approach. *The Counseling Psychologist, 32*, 651–691.

Bieschke, K. J., Croteau, J. M., Lark, J. S., & Vandiver, B. J. (2004). Toward a discourse of sexual orientation equity in the counseling professions. In J. M. Croteau, J. S. Lark, M. Lidderdale, & Y. B. Chung (Eds.), *Deconstructing heterosexism in the counseling professions: Multicultural narrative voices*. Thousand Oaks, CA: Sage.

Bieschke, K. J., McClanahan, M., Tozer, E., Grzegorek, J. L., & Park, J. (2000). Programmatic research on the treatment of lesbian, gay, and bisexual clients: The past, the present, and the course for the future. In R. M. Perez, K. A. DeBord, K. J. Bieschke (Eds.), *Handbook of counseling and psychotherapy with lesbian, gay, and bisexual clients* (pp. 309–336). Washington, DC: American Psychological Association.

Bowers, A., & Bieschke, K. (2005). Psychologists' clinical evaluations and attitudes: An examination of the influence of gender and sexual orientation. *Professional Psychology: Research and Practice, 36*, 97–103.

Bright, C. (2004). Deconstructing reparative therapy: An examination of the processes involved when attempting to change sexual orientation. *Clinical Social Work Journal, 32*, 471–481.

Cochran, S. D. (2001). Emerging issues in research on lesbians' and gay men's mental health: Does sexual orientation really matter? *American Psychologist, 56*, 932–947.

Cochran, S. D., Sullivan, J. G., & Mays, V. M. (2003). Prevalence of mental disorders, psychological distress, and mental health services use among lesbian, gay and bisexual adults in the United States. *Journal of Consulting and Clinical Psychology, 71*, 53–61.

Crawford, I., McLeod, A., Zamboni, B. D., & Jordan, M. B. (1999). Psychologists' attitudes toward gay and lesbian parenting. *Professional Psychology: Research and Practice, 4*, 394–401.

Dillon, F. R., & Worthington, R. L. (2003). The lesbian, gay, and bisexual affirmative counseling self-efficacy inventory (LGB-CSI): Development, validation, and training implications. *Journal of Counseling Psychology, 50*, 235–251.

Dorland, J. M., & Fischer, A. R. (2001). Gay, lesbian, and bisexual individuals' perceptions: An analogue study. *The Counseling Psychologist, 29*, 532–547.

Eliason, M. J. (2000). Substance abuse counselors' attitudes regarding lesbian, gay, bisexual, and transgendered clients. *Journal of Substance Abuse, 12*, 311–328.

Fontaine, J. H. (1998). Evidencing a need: School counselors' experiences with gay and lesbian students. *Professional School Counseling, 1*, 8–14.

Gough, H. G., & Heilbrun, A. B., Jr. (1980). *Adjective Check List manual*. Palo Alto, CA: Consulting Psychologists Press.

Haldeman, D. (2004). When sexual and religious orientations collide: Considerations in working with conflicted same-sex attracted male clients. *The Counseling Psychologist, 32,* 691–715.

Hayes, J. A., & Erkis, A. J. (2000). Therapist homophobia, client sexual orientation, and source of client HIV infection as predictors of therapist reactions to clients with HIV. *Journal of Counseling Psychology, 47,* 71–78.

Hudson, W. W., & Ricketts, W. A. (1980). A strategy for the measurement of homophobia. *Journal of Homosexuality, 5,* 357–372.

Hunt, B., Matthews, C., Milsom, A., & Lammel, J. A. (in press). Lesbians with physical disabilities: A qualitative study of their experiences with counseling. *Journal of Counseling and Development.*

Israel, T., & Hackett, G. (2004). Counselor education on lesbian, gay, and bisexual issues: Comparing information and attitude exploration. *Counselor Education & Supervision, 43,* 179–191.

Israel, T., Ketz, K., Detrie, P. M., Burke, M. C., & Shulman, J. L. (2003). Identifying counselor competencies for working with lesbian, gay, and bisexual clients. *Journal of Gay & Lesbian Psychotherapy, 7,* 3–21.

Jones, M. A., & Gabriel, M. A. (1999). Utilization of psychotherapy by lesbians, gay men, and bisexuals: Findings from a nationwide survey. *American Journal of Orthopsychiatry, 69*(2), 209–219.

Lebolt, J. (1999). Gay affirmative psychotherapy: A phenomenological study. *Clinical Social Work Journal, 27,* 355–370.

Liddle, B. J. (1999). Gay and lesbian clients' ratings of psychiatrists, psychologists, social workers, and counselors. *Journal of Gay & Lesbian Psychotherapy, 3,* 81–93.

Mair, D., & Izzard, S. (2001). Grasping the nettle: Gay men's experiences in therapy. *Psychodynamic Counselling, 7*(4), 475–490.

Matthews, C. R., Selvidge, M. M. D., & Fisher, K. (2005). Addiction counselors' attitudes and behaviors toward lesbian, gay, and bisexual clients. *Journal of Counseling and Development, 83,* 57–65.

Mohr, J. J., Israel, T., & Sedlacek, W. E. (2001). Counselors' attitudes regarding bisexuality as predictors of counselors' clinical responses: An analogue study of a female bisexual client. *Journal of Counseling Psychology, 48,* 212–222.

Morrow, S., & Beckstead, A. (2004). Conversion therapies for same-sex attracted clients in religious conflict: Context, predisposing factors, experiences, and implications for therapy. *The Counseling Psychologist, 32,* 641–650.

Nicolosi, J. (1993). *Healing homosexuality: Case stories of reparative therapy.* Northvale, NJ: Jason Aronson.

Nicolosi, J., Byrd, A. D., & Potts, R. W. (2000). Retrospective self-reports of changes in homosexual orientation: A consumer survey of conversion therapy clients. *Psychological Reports, 86,* 1071–1088.

Perez, R. M., DeBord, K. A., & Bieschke, K. J. (Eds.). (2000). *Handbook of counseling and psychotherapy with lesbian, gay, and bisexual clients* (pp. 309–336). Washington, DC: American Psychological Association.

Phillips, J. C., & Fischer, A. R. (1998). Graduate students' training experiences with lesbian, gay, and bisexual issues. *The Counseling Psychologist, 26,* 712–734.

Ponticelli, C. M. (1996). The spiritual warfare of Exodus: A postpositivist research adventure. *Qualitative Inquiry, 2,* 198–219.

Ponticelli, C. M. (1999). Crafting stories of sexual identity reconstruction. *Social Psychology Quarterly, 62*(2), 157–172.

Saulnier, C. F. (1999). Choosing a health care provider: A community survey of what is important to lesbians. *Families in Society, 80,* 254–262.

Saulnier, C. F. (2002). Deciding who to see: Lesbians discuss their preferences in health and mental health care providers. *Social Work, 47,* 355–365.

Schaeffer, K. W., Hyde, R. A., Kroencke, T., McCormick, B., & Nottebaum, L. (2000). Religiously-motivated sexual orientation change. *Journal of Psychology and Christianity, 19,* 61–70.

Schaeffer, K. W., Nottebaum, L., Smith, P., Dech, K., & Krawczyk, J. (1999). Religiously-motivated sexual orientation change: A follow-up study. *Journal of Psychology and Theology, 27,* 329–337.

Schroeder, M., & Shidlo, A. (2001). Ethical issues in sexual orientation conversion therapies: An empirical study of consumers. *Journal of Gay & Lesbian Psychotherapy, 5,* 131–166.

Shidlo, A., & Schroeder, M. (2002). Changing sexual orientation: A consumers' report. *Professional Psychology: Research and Practice, 33,* 249–259.

Spitzer, R. L. (2003). Can some gay men and lesbians change their sexual orientation? 200 participants reporting a change from homosexual to heterosexual orientation. *Archives of Sexual Behavior, 32,* 403–417.

Throckmorton, W. (2002). Initial empirical and clinical findings concerning the change process for ex-gays. *Professional Psychology: Research and Practice, 33,* 242–248.

Tozer, E. E., & Hayes, J. A. (2004). Why do individuals seek conversion therapy? *The Counseling Psychologist, 32,* 716–741.

Worthington, R. L., Savoy, H. B., Dillon, F. R., & Vernaglia, E. R. (2002). Heterosexual identity development: A multidimensional model of individual and social identity. *The Counseling Psychologist, 30,* 496–531.

Yarhouse, M. A., Burkett, L. A., & Kreeft, E. M. (2002). Paraprofessional Christian ministries for sexual behavior and same-sex identity concerns. *Journal of Psychology and Theology, 30*(3), 209–228.

13

PERCEIVED CONFLICTS BETWEEN AFFIRMATION OF RELIGIOUS DIVERSITY AND AFFIRMATION OF SEXUAL DIVERSITY: THAT'S PERCEIVED

ANN R. FISCHER AND KURT A. DeBORD

The purpose of this chapter is to explore and invite further discussion of what we perceive as an ethical dilemma within the field of psychology: How do individuals and organizations proceed when there is a *perceived* conflict between the two important professional values of respect for religious diversity and respect for sexual diversity? In its most basic form, our question is, "What should psychologists do when students or colleagues perceive that their religion tells them it is wrong to be lesbian, gay, or bisexual?" To affirm religious diversity, we ought to be respectful of norms and ideals of religion as people experience it, but to affirm sexual diversity, we ought to emphasize respect for and normalcy of (American Psychological Association [APA], 1998) lesbian, gay, and bisexual (LGB) identities. To approach students or colleagues with one of two assertions—"I respect your religion, but it's wrong" or "I respect LGB orientations, but they're wrong"—may defy the other kind of affirmation. To us, it seems disingenuous and, frankly, to sidestep the conflict to claim in the face of a perceived conflict, "I affirm both LGB identities *and* your religious values that hold that it's wrong to be LGB."

We thank Thomas Meyer for his insightful comments on an earlier draft of this chapter.

We emphasize "perceived" conflict and take this perception as our starting point, rather than attempting to argue about whether such a perception is warranted. Readers interested in perspectives on LGB-affirming and LGB-oppressing aspects of various religious systems may refer to sources such as Ritter and Terndrup (2002) and Davidson (2000). In other words, our domain here is not the concordance between affirmation of sexual diversity and doctrine or sacred texts within any particular religious tradition, but rather is what we in the mental health fields might do when a conflict is perceived. We are not suggesting by any stretch that affirming religious diversity or religiosity necessarily implies either difficulty in affirming sexual diversity or negative attitudes toward sexual minorities. Clearly, some religious people are extremely LGB-affirming, and some nonreligious people are extremely bi- and homophobic.

The "Ethical Principles of Psychologists and Code of Conduct" of the APA (2002) requires us to minimize bias and prejudice regarding both religion and sexual orientation in our work but does not address potential conflicts arising from the sometimes competing demands to affirm both. The language of the code also is vague, understandably. Here we quote relevant portions of Principle E (Respect for People's Rights and Dignity), italicizing key words and phrases germane to our purposes. Psychologists are to

> [be] *aware of and respect* cultural, individual, and role differences, including those based on age, gender, gender identity, race, ethnicity, culture, national origin, *religion, sexual orientation*, disability, language, and socioeconomic status and consider these factors when working with members of such groups. Psychologists try to eliminate the effect on their work of *biases* based on those factors, and they do not knowingly participate in or condone activities of others based upon such *prejudices*. (p. 1063, italics added)

It may be simpler to think of these diversity dimensions one at a time, but to do so is unrealistic. Respecting both religious beliefs and sexual diversity simultaneously does sometimes create a contradiction (i.e., when a religious belief is that being LGB is wrong). Although there have been a few recent attempts to address this conflict (Gonsiorek, 2004; Haldeman, 2004; Mobley & Pearson, 2004), these studies have generally focused on individual clients' perceived conflicts. From a different perspective, we have been concerned about the scant attention in the published literature on perceived conflicts for mental health professionals between avoiding bias based on sexuality and avoiding bias based on religion, particularly in regard to training policies and programs. Therefore, our goal is to stimulate public discussion of how best to address this perceived conflict that sometimes arises in professional, academic, or other training situations.

To us, the critical nature of this question is clear when we think about possible outcomes of avoiding confronting this dilemma directly. Anecdotally, our impression is that avoidance creates unwelcoming environments for many stakeholders. What messages does it send to students, for example, when we steer away from the conflict question, with voices fading into the refrain of how difficult and complex the dilemma is? Perhaps it communicates a shaky affirmation of both sexual and religious diversity, such that LGB students, as well as students who experience conflict between religious doctrine and LGB affirmation, feel unsafe. Thus, in this chapter we address this issue directly by articulating how we attempted to resolve parts of the conflict by working through the steps of an ethical decision-making model (Hill, Glaser, & Harden, 1995).

SYSTEMATIC INQUIRY INTO THE PERCEIVED DILEMMA: ETHICAL DECISION-MAKING MODELS

To begin the process of exploring the perceived conflict in depth, we examined a number of models for ethical decision-making, including Kitchener (2000), Koocher and Keith-Spiegel (1998), and Hill et al. (1995). Of these major models, we chose the Hill et al. model for several reasons. First, it contains the core steps delineated in the other two models and in all major models we have seen. Although the steps are not listed in the same ways across models, the Hill et al. model addresses the common issues in other steps. Second, Hill et al.'s model is very strong in its explicit and integrated attention to power issues. Its feminist underpinnings add a valuable dimension to decision-making in keeping power as a front-and-center consideration. We felt that this was an especially important component of the model given the topics at hand and given the history of psychology's role in pathologizing women, members of racial- and ethnic minority groups, LGB people, people with disabilities, and people from lower social classes. A third and related point is that this model requires attending to "the practitioner's psychology" throughout the decision-making process (p. 23). We appreciated this acknowledgment of the subjectivity of the decision-makers, such that weighing of issues may vary depending not only on one's relative power but also on one's cultural affiliations and values. Fourth, we found this model's use of intuitive questions (e.g., "What am I worried about?") to be very helpful in identifying layers and nuances of the primary issues as we worked our way through this dilemma.

Because the power-and-diversity–attentive focus of this model was paramount in our choosing it as a template, we elaborate a bit further on Hill et al.'s (1995) thinking. The authors assert that interpretation of ethical principles and codes "varies according to where one is located within a context of power (race, gender, class, etc.)" and that "one's position in the culture, particularly in relation to power, deeply affects how one defines each of these principles and thus is at the very heart of one's ethical decision making" (p. 21). Given this assertion, we would like to state at the outset that we, the authors, consider our LGB affirmation to form a critical piece of each our identities. Fischer identifies as a heterosexual ally, and DeBord identifies as a gay man. Further, neither of us could be considered religious in a traditional sense. We acknowledge that our worldviews therefore place us in just a few of many possible positions from which to consider the perceived conflict we address in this chapter. Please note that we are inviting discussion of these issues, rather than attempting to impose one correct answer. Because this distinction is so critical to our goals, we reiterate it at several points throughout the chapter.

Despite the fact that most decision-making models, including Hill et al.'s (1995), depict the decision-making process in a linear fashion, real decision-making is messier and typically nonlinear, with steps in the process being repeated over time. However, as further introduction to the model, we list the steps as follows, with more description forthcoming as we address each step in turn: (a) recognizing a problem, (b) defining the problem, (c) developing solutions, (d) choosing a solution, (e) reviewing the process, (f) implementing and evaluating the decision, and (g) continuing reflection. Many readers will recognize in these steps the foundational elements of other major models. But unlike other models, we have followed Hill et al.'s recommendation of devoting significant consideration to the feeling-intuitive processes that influenced our discussions, as we engaged in rational evaluation during each step of the model. Next, we attempt to apply the steps of this model to the dilemma identified previously. Please note that we are inviting readers to take part in all steps of the model. We acknowledge and appreciate that we are in no position to choose and implement a specific course of action. Our primary goal is to stimulate discussion about this topic.

DECISION MAKING: APPLYING HILL ET AL.'S (1995) MODEL TO THE STATED DILEMMA

Step 1: Recognizing a Problem

Hill et al. (1995) suggest that the experience of discomfort or uncertainty may be among the first hints that there is a problem to be addressed. Thus, it is no accident that many of the thoughts included in this step end in question marks. Both of us (the authors) have been experiencing discomfort for a period of years about the lack of clarity in the field regarding how to handle perceived conflicts between religious- and sexual diversity affirmation. Uncertainty also has informed our decision to address this issue publicly, given that we have wished for guidance from the field as a collective and have found little.

More specifically, Fischer has been troubled by issues that have arisen occasionally over the years she has been a student, taught graduate-level diversity courses, supervised student counselors, and otherwise participated in training of future therapists. One recurring issue has been that of trainees stating that, because of their religious beliefs that homosexuality is wrong (bisexuality typically receives far less attention in such discussions), they would not be able to work with LGB clients. Particularly in diversity courses covering a variety of diversity issues, including both sexual orientation and religion, it has been difficult to resolve this productively with no clear guidance from policy statements either at the local level or—importantly, we think—the national level. (We hope programs that do have policy statements will make their processes and resulting statements public.) We see many layers to a problem such as this one. One element is that allowing students or colleagues to remain incompetent in any domain, simply because they wish to for whatever reasons, seems dangerous. In a discussion about this danger, one colleague astutely asked, "Why would you want to remain incompetent?"(B. Medler, personal communication, April 9, 2003). Another component that makes resolving our dilemma difficult, however, is that anecdotally, many training programs seem to allow students to avoid developing competence to work with clients who trigger students' own trauma histories (e.g., not requiring survivors of childhood sexual abuse to work with known perpetrators). So what, if anything, makes these two issues different? We think there probably are important differences related to topics we discuss subsequently, but we wanted to acknowledge this genuine question that surfaced as we attempted to sort through our feelings and concerns as recommended by this step in Hill et al.'s ethical decision-making model.

Another concerning aspect of the primary problem is that to succumb to therapists' desire to avoid working with LGB clients is to condone the withholding of service to members of a population based solely on their group membership, which sounds very much like approving of a prejudice and, behaviorally, of discrimination. Further, if we condone what therapists *think* is avoidance of working with LGB clients, we open ourselves to the risk that such therapists will have LGB clients who do not come out to their therapists. In that case, it is likely that subtle prejudices will still emerge from the therapist. At another level, simply having a therapist tell an LGB client, in effect, "We need to find you a therapist who can be LGB-affirming" sends a powerfully negative message (i.e., "I'm an expert in human behavior, and I disapprove of you"). Here, one's expert role is conflated with his or her personal beliefs and system of values. Although it may be impossible to entirely tease the two apart, keeping them interlinked in this situation institutionalizes a prejudiced worldview that inevitably results in harm to therapy clients. We have heard many counselors (professionals and students) argue that we can soften the blow of a referral by toning it down to refer more benignly to lack of competence on the part of the therapist. Still, this leads again to the question of condoning incompetence, if we do not require such therapists to be moving toward competence with LGB clients.

In the next section, we define the problem more clearly, but we hope that we have illustrated with these examples some of the ways we have recognized that a problem exists.

During this stage of decision-making, we are required by the Hill et al. (1995) model to explore personal reactions and "identify any aspects of [our] feelings that stand in the way of understanding and sorting through the problem" (p. 28). Given the coauthors' long-standing (i.e., 20-year) friendship, we felt relatively confident in our ability to push each other to "own" our reactions in this step, without the fear of damaging our relationship, an issue we have seen occasionally interfere with coauthored writing projects. Among the feelings we identified as possibly obstructing our honest, ethical decision making were the following:

1. We identified strong, preexisting desires to be as LGB-affirming as possible.
2. We recognized a lack of strong desire to empower religious justifications for not being LGB-affirming. Taking this a step further, to be true to the Hill et al. (1995) model, we must admit with trepidation (due to concerns about political backlash) that we also identified feelings of anger at *some* religious institutions for what we saw as destructive and oppressive anti-LGB doctrines; again, our goal in this chapter is not to debate whether various religious institutions are or are not LGB-affirming or LGB-oppressing but is instead to take as our starting point situations in which psychologists or psychologists-in-training perceive that their religion prohibits their LGB affirmation.
3. We acknowledged a tendency to revert to already-decided stances; in other words, we both bring to the table preconceptions about resolving this dilemma. It is precisely because we have these preconceptions (and are fairly certain other people have developed their own) that we see a public discussion and careful consideration of the dilemma as so crucial; otherwise, we fear the discussion may remain argumentative, defensive, and reactive rather than reflective.
4. We noticed subtle devaluation of the feeling-intuitive, over the rational-evaluative, aspects of ethical decision-making.

In identifying these possible interferences, we hoped to minimize any disproportionate or undue effects of them upon our decision-making. We also agreed that over the course of our many discussions, we would play devil's advocate with each other and try to consciously seek opposing arguments. Further, we sought and incorporated feedback from several other scholars, both within and outside of psychology.

Step 2: Defining the Problem

Thus far, our working problem definition has been "How do we proceed when psychologists or trainees perceive conflict between their religious values and APA's LGB-affirming stance?" By defining the problem in this way, we were able to follow Hill et al.'s (1995) recommendation that we name the ethical principles that may be at odds with regard to the dilemma at hand. Because of space limitations and our extensive consideration of these principles in choosing possible solutions, we only briefly identify here the principles that were of most relevance to our dilemma. Additionally, at this stage, Hill et al. urge those who implement their model to recognize the people and institutions that are stakeholders in the resolution of proposed dilemmas.

Clients potentially suffer when they are faced with limited access to high-quality services and with subtly or overtly hostile therapy environments due to the nonaffirming attitudes that some therapists maintain because of their religious beliefs. Thus, in considering the "Ethical Principles of Psychologists and Code of Conduct" (APA, 2002), the principles of Beneficence/Nonmaleficence (Principle A), Justice (Principle D), and Respect for People's Rights and Dignity (Principle E) are of utmost concern in this dilemma. Alternately, therapists who are forced to work affirmatively with LGB clients of whom they disapprove face the possibility that their autonomy rights (a component of Principle E) would be abridged. If therapists were compelled to work affirmatively with LGB clients or risk being excluded from psychology, questions of justice and autonomy would have to be considered.

Feminist ethics also informed our analysis of and feelings about the struggles involved with this dilemma. One basic principle we identified in the literature is an explicit rejection of ethical relativism (e.g., Vasquez & de las Fuentes, 2000). Although we certainly appreciate the APA's (2002) mandates to "respect" both religious and sexual diversity, it should be apparent by now that the fuzziness inherent in this mandate contributes to the creation of the dilemma we have stated. When the field does not want to risk disrespecting either set of values when they are perceived to be in conflict, it seems to us that the field—publicly, at least—is in something of an impasse. Rejecting ethical relativism is not solely a feminist value (e.g., see Fowers & Richardson, 1996), but the idea that not every value must be equally appreciated or condoned is a powerful one. Acknowledging this has the potential to pull us from what might otherwise be doomed as a quicksand of contradictions, empowering us to weigh our judgments carefully and to make, not avoid, them. It is with this in mind that we recall multiculturalism's original emphasis on protecting the rights of minorities in the face of institutional oppression. The valuing of justice, not relativism as it is sometimes assumed, is a core principle at the root of the multicultural movement (Okin, Cohen, Howard, & Nussbaum, 1999) that has so richly and recently informed psychological practice and theory.

A second principle of relevance, articulated by philosopher Andrea Jaggar (1992), is feminist ethicists' commitment to understanding "individual actions in the context of broader social practices, evaluating the symbolic and cumulative implications of action as well as its immediately observable consequences" (p. 366). From this perspective, appeals to ethical codes and principles must be situated in a broad context, including clear attention to power and both historical and current societal hierarchies. Regarding our dilemma, this principle encourages us to be mindful of contextual factors such as the fact that non–LGB-affirming attitudes and behaviors are directed at a group that has been pathologized officially (in previous editions of the *Diagnostic and Statistical Manual of Mental Disorders*) and that continues to be discriminated against legally. Further, religion has traditionally been privileged to have "enormous social and institutional power behind it" (Haldeman, 2004, p. 712). Given these realities, there are likely to be substantial and continued "symbolic and cumulative implications" (Jaggar, 1992, p. 366) for how we as a field eventually resolve our dilemma. Specifically, privileging religious values over LGB affirmation would be (or would continue to be) an extension of existing and historical marginalization of LGB people.

The Hill et al. (1995) model asks that as we determine the definition of the problem, we identify personal reactions and consider answers to the questions "What do my feelings tell me about the situation?" and "What am I worried about?" (p. 29). Beyond the issues identified previously, we discovered that we continued to be worried about such issues as the following: whether this dilemma is "solvable" on such a large scale (i.e., concern that someone will be left out in the cold and that a balance of justice, respect, and autonomy is out of reach), how people in our profession will react to the decision to write this chapter, how easy it will be for someone to quote us out of context and misrepresent what we are attempting to do here, and how ongoing apprehension about the meaning of the disparity in legal protections for religious versus sexual diversity will affect matters. Further, given our privileges and biases as politically liberal, middle-class, White faculty members in university settings, we regularly asked ourselves what we might be missing. One concern repeatedly emerged: that we might not be fully empathizing with or understanding the hardships this dilemma poses for psychologists who perceive a conflict between their religious values and LGB affirmation. During the conceptualizing and writing process we reminded ourselves regularly of the felt immutability of some religious stances and of the subsequent distress our stated dilemma may arouse in many psychologists. This is so important that it bears reiteration. We acknowledge that this conflict is a painful, difficult struggle for many students, faculty, and counselors. Our respect for this fact has provided partial impetus for writing this chapter and attempting to generate possible solutions.

Step 3: Developing Solutions

In keeping with the ethical decision-making model, we brainstormed 19 solutions to our stated dilemma that ranged from "do nothing" to "change the APA code of ethics." As we discussed the potential solutions, some converged, others evolved, and many developed into dualistic solutions, reflecting either a "support LGB affirmation" or a "support religions that are non–LGB-affirming" nature. At this point in the decision-making process, Hill et al. (1995) recommended assessing the costs and benefits of each solution while prioritizing the ethical principles of nonmaleficence (minimizing harm) and beneficence (doing good). In further accord with Hill et al., we evaluated the practicality and prudence of the solutions and considered our own intuitive-feeling responses to them. We then attempted to give an overall evaluation of each possible solution, weighing possible maleficence considerations against ones of beneficence. We acknowledge that our solutions and judgments certainly differ substantially from those of other professionals and readers. In keeping with our desire to be direct and concise, we briefly present two solutions that merit discussion. Subsequently, we present a third solution and provide commentary as to why we concluded that it deserved full elaboration in the text. Again, our primary goal is to stimulate discussion and consideration of this dilemma, not to solve the problem once and for all.

Solution 1: Integrative Solutions

One potential course that we considered in response to this dilemma has been identified collectively as "integrative solutions" (Beckstead & Morrow, 2004; Haldeman, 2004; Lasser & Gottlieb, 2004). Haldeman's proposed integrative approach is exemplary of this group of therapeutic alternatives. His approach challenges counselors to thoroughly immerse themselves in the nondirective aspect of the person-centered approach in order to truly respect clients' abilities to make well-informed and carefully weighed choices. Though Haldeman presented his practice considerations as a way of ethically working with clients who may be torn with regard to their own conflicts regarding religion and sexual orientation, we considered the value his approach might hold for training counselors who have a similar conflict. If counselor-training programs were to require all trainees to adopt his approach when values conflicts arise between clients and counselors, the "polarized" sides (e.g., LGB-affirming and non–LGB-affirming) involved in the current dilemma might become less polarized.

Haldeman's interpretation of the person-centered approach asks therapists to avoid utilizing both LGB-affirmative and religion-affirmative interventions when doing therapy with clients who have conflicts between values originating from these aspects of their lives. In our stated dilemma, counselors, not clients, are confronted with a conflict between the ethical principle to respect sexual diversity and their own religiously based anti-LGB attitudes and values. In this potential solution, these counselors would be supported in their willingness to engage clients in nondirective exploration of client values, without having to explicitly affirm clients' LGB status, thus providing the counselors with an "out" with regard to their lack of LGB affirmation.

The problem with this solution is that it does not solve or greatly diminish the dilemma. Granted, it has the appeal of being consistent with the part of Principle E of APA's Ethics Code (2002) that plainly states that psychologists should avoid participating in activities based on prejudice and that they should respect both religious and sexual diversity. But what happens when non–LGB-affirming counselors complete the exploration process with their clients only to find themselves with a happily "out" client whose identity they don't respect or affirm? The potential for client harm in this case seems great. Additionally, trusting psychologists, or anyone for that matter, to be genuinely neutral and to honestly communicate neutrality in cases such as this where deeply held values are involved is not "desirable or ethical" (Morrow, Beckstead, Hayes, & Haldeman, 2004, p. 780). Further, recent research on automatic processes involved in prejudicial attitudes indicates that successfully faking such neutrality may be nearly impossible (Kawakami, Young, & Dovidio, 2002).

When evaluating this solution, we concluded that the nonmaleficence and beneficence factors related to it were less relevant than the practicality factors. Though the solution initially appeared to us to offer a way to bridge the opposing values in this debate, in the long run it failed to provide resolution for the current dilemma. Nonetheless, one should bear in mind that the integrative counseling approaches were designed for clients in conflict, not counselors in conflict. We are simply concluding that they are less appropriate for helping with the latter than with the former.

Solution 2: A Two-Track Training System

A second possible solution we considered would require radical reorganization of counselor training, certification, and licensing institutions and processes. Two professional tracks of preparation could be established such that counselors-in-training could select to be trained, licensed, and identified as (a) counselors who prioritize an affirmation of spiritual or religious diversity over LGB diversity or (b) counselors who do not. For this solution to work effectively, training programs would have to identify which kind of track their graduates would be provided. Although the two–training-track solution would require training programs to be accredited and their graduates to be identified according to their affiliation with one of the two professional tracks, there are some public policies already in place that may make this option feasible and possibly, desirable, to some. We turn, briefly, to a discussion of these policies.

Currently, it is illegal in the United States to discriminate against people based on their religion, as the U.S. Department of Education reminded the APA by letter. The Education Deputy Secretary sent the letter (Hansen, 2001; available at http://www.ed.gov/policy/highered/guid/secletter/010906.html) in September of 2001 in response to the APA Committee on Accreditation's request for public comment on Footnote 4 of the *Accreditation Guidelines and Principles*. This footnote ~~permits religiously affiliated doctoral programs to be exempt from some of the diversity requirements that all other (nonreligious) programs must fulfill~~, allowing in admissions and hiring "a preference for persons adhering to the religious purpose or affiliation of the program" and indicating rights to "permit religious policies as to admission, retention, and employment only to the extent that they are protected by the U.S. Constitution." Both the request for comment and the full text of Footnote 4 are available at http://www.apa.org/ed/reqstforcmnt1.html (APA, 2004).

In its request for public comment, the Committee on Accreditation stated, "Legal interpretation indicates that Footnote 4 . . . does not allow [religious] institutions to refuse to hire faculty or staff or to admit students on the basis of their religious affiliation, sexual orientation, race, or any of the other criteria identified in Domain A [of the accreditation guidelines]." However, particularly given some religious programs' requirements for students and faculty to conform to specific standards of behavior, many were concerned that the exemption could, in effect, discriminate against LGB people.

For example, students and faculty in the APA-accredited clinical-psychology PsyD program at Wheaton College are expected to uphold the "Community Covenant" and "Statement of Faith" (available at http://www.wheaton.edu/welcome/cov/comcov.html), which includes a commitment to "uphold chastity among the unmarried (1 Cor. 6:18) and the sanctity of marriage between a man and woman (Heb. 13:4)." As another example, Fuller Theological Seminary, housing two APA-accredited clinical psychology programs (both PhD and PsyD), also requires students and faculty to abide by their community standards (available at http://www.fuller.edu/catalog2/10_Appendices/3_Community_Standards.html), holding "homosexual forms of explicit sexual conduct to be inconsistent with the teaching of Scripture." One could argue that because the same is stated about premarital and extramarital activity, there is no discrimination. However, the marriage and divorce section of the standards defines marriage as being between a woman and a man, a policy that precludes same-sex marriage. Therefore, no same-sex sexual activity is allowed. In effect, celibacy is required of lesbian and gay students and faculty but not of those who are heterosexual.

Beyond possible discrimination, many have also worried about the chilling effect that this exemption has had for LGB members' confidence in the APA as a professional organization (Gonsiorek, 2004). In other words, what message about LGB affirmation is being communicated when attention to that aspect of diversity for accreditation is not *really* required, unlike every other dimension of diversity?

The letter to the APA from the Department of Education contained a polite but thinly veiled threat that if the APA were to eliminate Footnote 4 (i.e., not allow exemptions to the diversity requirements for religious schools), the department would possibly be forced to revoke the APA's authority to accredit psychology programs. Ultimately, the Committee on Accreditation decided to keep the footnote, briefly citing "recent Supreme Court decisions that show an increased deference to First Amendment [i.e., freedom of religion] interests over anti-discrimination statutes" (as outlined in the Education Department's letter). Vaguely, the committee also noted that in making the decision, they "considered . . . the Committee's role as an accrediting body recognized by the U.S. Department of Education." Therefore, APA policy appears to be one of conditional requirements for LGB affirmation, with religiously affiliated graduate psychology programs free to create and enforce "religious policies . . . to the extent that they are protected by the U.S. Constitution" (from Footnote 4; http://www.apa.org/ed/requestforcmnt1.html).

Given these public statements, it is clear that this "separate-but-equal" standard of professional training proposed by our second solution already exists to some extent, but developing standardized and consistent requirements for program and counselor self-representation based on the affirmation differentiation seems exceptionally complicated and labor intensive. Further, when we examined the nonmaleficence versus beneficence considerations in regard to this solution, we agreed with Gonsiorek's (2004) concern that such an approach could set a precedent and ultimately legitimize "religiously based discrimination against women, nonbelievers, or whatever other group for which a particular faith community felt it had a theological imperative requiring such discrimination" (p. 758). The potential damage that could be done to so many by this solution's implementation does not seem justified by its goal of protecting the autonomy rights of a small number of psychologists or psychologists-in-training.

Initially, we were satisfied with the above analysis of the second solution based on Hill et al.'s (1995) recommendations for evaluation. However, when we reviewed the solution again, we were struck by the way the solution's wording had been influenced by practicality and the status quo. We had failed to attend fully to the dynamics of power. As Katz (1985) stated, one characteristic of institutional power is its ability to make itself seem invisible. The solution we originally generated stated that one training track would allow some religious values to trump LGB affirmation, but the solution did not allow for a training track in which LGB affirmation would trump some religious values. Why? Because in our estimation, the latter training track could never gain support of the state, the church, or the majority of psychologists and, thus, exist. That is the nature of institutionalized power. In attempting to reformulate the solution, we recognized that we did not want to propose or support a training-track option that perpetuated the status quo of allowing some psychologists to marginalize LGB people, identities, and behavior because of the psychologists' religious beliefs. Our decision to reject this solution is consistent with our initial analysis. However, combining that analysis with the current one, which more explicitly emphasizes power, is consistent with our goal to fully assess our solutions using Hill et al.'s model.

Solution 3: Prioritize Nonmaleficence

The third major solution that we brainstormed came only after we wrestled for months with many of the complexities inherent in the dilemma. We think that it best addresses the majority of concerns raised by the dilemma. Thus, we focus on this "solution" throughout the rest of this section's text.

For us, the heart of our stated dilemma is the untenability of uniformly applying Principle E of the "Ethical Principles of Psychologists and Code of Conduct" (APA, 2002), requiring respect for differences stemming from, among other things, religion, culture, and sexual orientation. How can we honestly respect sexual diversity while also honestly respecting religiously justified beliefs that any sexuality besides heterosexuality is wrong, immoral, sinful, maladaptive, or unhealthy? A part of this conundrum is related to the definition of the word "respect." We agreed that our everyday use of the term implies the following sentiments: "to allow space for, to consider, to avoid 'messing with' a person or group." In more formal terms, *Merriam-Webster's Third New International Dictionary of the English Language Unabridged* (1971) used the following phrases to explicate the term: "consider," "to consider worthy of esteem," "to refrain from obtruding upon or interfering with" (p. 1934). Although there are subtle differences among these definitions, each of them is relevant to the issue at hand. As psychologists, we would not freely give esteem and power to White supremacist counselors or those openly supporting racial discrimination who wish to practice according to their beliefs, which may be religiously justified (see, for example, http://www.kingidentity.com/doctrine.htm and http://www.kingidentity.com/seedline.htm). In fact, we often try to interfere with racially discriminatory counselor behaviors, in keeping with the ethical principle of nonmaleficence. In other words, we already regularly make decisions about what beliefs, worldviews, and behaviors are worthy of space, consideration, and esteem, often in the name of nonmaleficence. Thus, we are faced with the realization that giving respect is not always consistent with nonmaleficence.

One problem with enacting Principle E is that it mandates both nonmaleficence and respect. The first three sentences of Principle E refer to awareness of and "respect" for "cultural, individual and role differences" (see p. 318, para 3). In contrast, the last sentence of Principle E indicates that psychologists should work to "eliminate the effect on their work of biases based on those factors, and they do not knowingly participate in or condone activities of others based upon such prejudices" (APA, 2002, p. 1063). Respect for diversity dimensions and avoiding prejudice based on those diversity dimensions do not equate. "Respect" is described previously. Avoiding prejudice and bias, as we see it, aligns closely with nonmaleficence. APA's (2002) Principle A, Beneficence and Nonmaleficence, prioritizes nonmaleficence above other considerations: "When conflicts occur among psychologists' obligations or concerns, they attempt to resolve these conflicts in a responsible fashion that avoids or minimizes harm" (p. 1062).

Our big question, in this light, is this: How can we say we respect sexual diversity when we simultaneously allow prejudice (maleficently) against orientations other than heterosexuality? Perhaps an even more pertinent question than "How can we respect both religious and sexual diversity?" is "How can we minimize harm to each within our quest to respect each?" To address that question, we first need to assess the extent of the harm that may be done by one to the other in the name of respect. In order to do that, we must respond to the following three questions: (a) To what extent might respect for religious diversity cause harm to LGB people? (b) To what extent might respect for sexual diversity cause harm to religious people? and (c) How are responses to questions about harm influenced by a consideration of power?

To What Extent Might "Respect" for Religious Diversity Cause Harm to LGB People? Within the counseling fields, claiming "respect" for culture and religion often is used to signify either esteem of associated values and beliefs or, minimally, the implicit taboo of challenging those values and beliefs. In this light, we think respect for religion sometimes causes harm (even unintentionally) to LGB people, when "respect" means accepting without serious question religiously justified attitudes that orientations other than heterosexuality are wrong. We emphasize the "sometimes" qualification in this conclusion. To reiterate, we are very aware that many religious traditions and beliefs are LGB-affirming. Figure 13.1 illustrates our focus not on religion per se but on anti-LGB attitudes and behaviors, some of which are justified using religious beliefs.

As we have touched on throughout this chapter, religiously justified homonegative attitudes may manifest in such psychologists' claims as (a) "I can't work with LGB people; I'd have to refer LGB clients to someone else for services" and (b) "I could only work with LGB clients if they wanted to change, to become heterosexual" (i.e., if they wanted conversion therapy; see Bieschke, Paul, & Blasko, chap. 12, this volume, for a discussion of recent research on conversion therapy). Anti-LGB attitudes also may take subtler

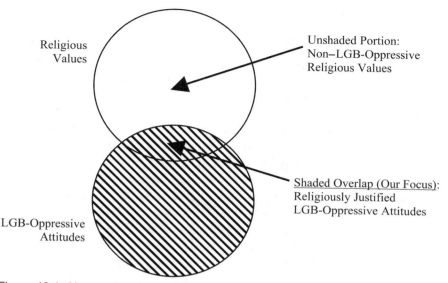

Religious Values

LGB-Oppressive
Attitudes

Unshaded Portion:
Non–LGB-Oppressive
Religious Values

Shaded Overlap (Our Focus):
Religiously Justified
LGB-Oppressive Attitudes

Figure 13.1. Narrow focus on LGB-oppressive attitudes that are religiously justified versus broad focus on religious values.

forms, such as (c) the "love the sinner (an LGB person), hate the sin (sexual engagement with members of the same sex)" argument. This seems to reflect an attempt to be affirming (respectful) while maintaining the prejudice (maleficence) at the same time. However, behavior and identity are usually not so neatly separated. What does it mean to suggest that one loves or affirms an LGB person but just not some of the key features that lead the person to identify as LGB? A bit more legalistic version of that argument may be (d) "Although I think they're wrong choices, I respect LGB people's right to make choices." As a final example, (e) APA allows religiously affiliated, accredited PhD-granting programs, in effect (even if not in letter), to opt out of Principle E's mandate for diversity affirmation with Footnote 4 of the accreditation guidelines.

All of these expressions of attitudes reflect judgments from mental health professionals—who are assumed to be experts in human behavior and mental health—that it is "wrong" to be an LGB person, that a wide range of human behaviors (partially) defining a group is unacceptable. Even without overt discrimination such as denial of services to LGB people, psychologists can contribute to a culture of disrespect and oppression in these ways. Living as a stigmatized minority in such an environment can result in chronic stress or what Root (1992) calls "insidious trauma," the psychological violence that is done by being devalued for one's group membership, even without overt denial of civil rights. This insidious trauma could be exacerbated by the power of mental health professionals relative to those we serve. When the devaluation is justified on religious grounds, unquestioning "respect" for religion likely does psychological harm to LGB people.

To What Extent Might "Respect" for Sexual Diversity Cause Harm to Religious People? One type of harm that psychologists who religiously justify anti-LGB attitudes may experience is feeling oppressed within psychology, feeling that their religiosity is unwelcome. Another kind of harm may be infringement on religious psychologists' rights to enact their vision of "the good" in their professional work (Christopher, 1996), when good is perceived to require heterosexuality (or celibacy) as part of deference to a higher power. We acknowledge the pain that may accompany these experiences of finding an important piece of one's identity disparaged within a helping profession. At the same time, in consideration of nonmaleficence, we posit that the emotional and psychological harm done to religious psychologists by requiring that all psychologists be LGB-affirmative is, on the whole, probably less, both in actuality and in potential, than the harm that results from prioritizing religious values over LGB affirmation. We base this assertion on several ideas.

The first of these ideas is that respect for sexual diversity only sometimes clashes with respect for religion. In fact, our experience within academic and professional psychology has been that many people identifying as religious are very affirming of sexual diversity. Referring again to Figure 13.1, our concern is with non–LGB-affirming attitudes that are religiously justified, not with religion per se. The potential for harm to religious people by LGB affirmation, therefore, may be as small as the proportion of the person's religious identity that is nonaffirming of LGB people.

Another part of our argument rests on the fact that though it is true that requiring LGB affirmation within the field indeed may limit psychologists' ability to enact their personal and religious values, this limitation applies *only* in their roles as psychologists, not generally in their roles as people or as members of nonpsychology communities. They still are free to believe and value anything they choose in their personal lives as private citizens. If psychologists were required to be LGB-affirming, these psychologists would be required to make a concession regarding their personal beliefs. On the other hand, if psychologists were required to respect anti-LGB attitudes, entire personal identities of many therapy clients might be compromised. We appreciate here Nussbaum's (1999) distinction between "comprehensive liberalism" and "political liberalism" in her discussion of multiculturalism and the rights of women; "liberalism" in this context refers to the ranking of autonomy and dignity as core values. The comprehensive version of this philosophy emphasizes metaphysical values, but the political version—such as we propose here—more narrowly describes an endorsement of values applicable only to people's roles as citizens of a polity, which in our case refers to the peopled discipline of psychology. In other words, we have no aspiration to decide these questions of how to rank respect for religious and sexual diversity in general, metaphysically, but instead only in terms of our profession.

How Are Responses to Questions About Harm Influenced by a Consideration of Power? We contend that, in general, religion carries more power to frame public discourse and to guide beliefs and behaviors than does the narrower movement for LGB affirmation. Religiosity is much more far-reaching in its scope of values and proscriptions, is more commonly incorporated into people's lives, and is protected by government in the United States. LGB-affirmative organizations and political movements do not have the same institutional and traditional power.

Psychologists who justify anti-LGB attitudes with religion automatically carry two group identities having power: (a) as professionals, they typically are assumed to be experts in human behavior and mental health; and (b) as people situated within the authority of religious tradition, they also have institutional power that allows their worldview to shape beliefs and hand down judgments (including anti-LGB judgments), whether the individuals intentionally use that power or not. Even if they do not individually feel powerful, they enjoy the privilege of having their worldview as believers function as a frequently unquestioned norm (cf. McIntosh, 1988). Even a counselor within a minority religion in the United States, such as Islam, still has the privilege—again, regardless of whether it is used consciously or intentionally—of being able to invoke the prerogative of "you must respect my religion" as a way to justify oppressive attitudes and to stifle debate. In addition to the symbolic power of "religion," the federal and state governments in the United States protect rights of religious people as a class but typically not of LGB people as a class. Finally, in the middle of an assumed eight-year presidency, the power of religion has been repeatedly invoked as a basis for U.S. public policy by the second-term president of the United States (e.g., Lears, 2003; Niebuhr, 2000; "Transcript of debate," 2004).

Another consideration is that therapists who are LGB-affirming are unlikely, we believe, to use their power to try to change clients' religion (Haldeman, 2004). We were unable to find professional psychotherapy literature that advocated psychologists' right to engage in religious conversion therapy. Further, we were unable to find data identifying the frequency with which clients sought therapy in order to change their religion. Nonetheless, we would guess that clients typically do not seek services from mental health professionals (other than clergy or pastoral counselors) when doubting whether it is appropriate for them to hold certain religious beliefs or ask for the counselor's help with and opinion on their religion. On the flip side, however, clients do sometimes seek services from mental health professionals when they are questioning their sexuality (see Greene, chap. 7, this volume), sometimes struggling to create positive LGB identities within cultures, communities, and families that devalue nonheterosexual orientations. Even if a client's presenting concern is not questioning sexual orientation, this may well be a salient and ongoing issue, given that LGB people are continually faced with choices about coming out in new situations: to whom, when, how much.

When LGB clients recognize that their therapists are non–LGB-affirming (Liddle, 1996), this creates a potential set of interpersonal problems to deal with on top of whatever presenting concern originally brought them to therapy. Empirical data suggest that LGB people perceive counselors more negatively, are less willing to self-disclose, and are less likely to want to return when the counselors make heterosexist assumptions about clients' sexual orientations (even while controlling for LGB people's levels of outness; Dorland & Fischer, 2001). These additional burdens of needing to screen therapists and of needing to censor therapeutic concerns that are imposed on the class of people with nonheterosexual orientations interfere with non–LGB-affirming psychologists' ability to provide efficient and effective service.

Another issue regarding power involves the symbolic meaning of anti-LGB prejudice. Not all prejudices carry equal weight in terms of potential for harm. How threatening is it to religious people *as a group* to disallow religiously justified anti-LGB attitudes within mental health professions, and how threatening is it to LGB people as a group to allow religiously justified anti-LGB attitudes? Jaggar (1992), Vasquez and de las Fuentes (2000), and others have asserted that the effect of prejudices cannot be evaluated as if they occurred in a vacuum where "all else is equal" but instead must be considered in light of their layered meanings and cumulative effects. Relevant to this case, nonaffirmation of LGB people and orientations not only perpetuates a broader cultural prejudice but also continues a powerful history within psychology of pathologizing sexualities other than heterosexuality. It was only about 30 years ago (1973) that homosexuality per se was removed from the *Diagnostic and Statistical Manual of Mental Disorders* (American Psychiatric Association, 1968). The power of mental health professionals to "diagnose" lesbian and gay people as "sick" remains, despite the official omission of homosexuality as an identifiable disorder. How easy it is for a psychologist to remark casually to friends or acquaintances outside of professional settings that she or he thinks homosexuality is wrong. Does a psychologist's judgment of human behavior at a dinner party not carry more weight, on average, than an attorney's, a machinist's, or a dentist's?

We also must consider the differential power of the roles of counselor and client as they overlap with those of a non–LGB-affirming person and LGB person, respectively. Specifically, as counselors, we are enacting our professional selves, not necessarily our total selves and identities. We have the privilege of stepping outside of this professional role and into "real life" at the end of the day, where we are free to do and believe as we choose. Clients' experiences are not so separable, to the extent that they seek help with problems in their real lives. The work they do in session is about their lived experience and does not stay isolated in the therapy room. Therefore, a psychologist's judgment about a client's sexuality is not abstract, not just part of the job, but instead acts as part of the explicit and implicit assessment of the mental health of the client as a person. Our questions again become, "What is the cost to a religious person of not being permitted to carry [and intentionally or unintentionally transmit] anti-LGB attitudes in the role of a psychologist?" versus "What is the cost to an LGB person of having a non-LGB-affirming psychologist, professor, or supervisor?" In the context of counseling, the costs in the latter question involve not only the central psychological cost of being subtly or blatantly shamed, but also the practical costs of wasting time and money having to debate sexuality and having to search for an LGB-affirming therapist.

Further, we encourage readers to consider the fact that professional codes of ethics were devised primarily to safeguard the welfare of the public whom we serve. Psychologists and other mental health professionals, in their roles of power, bear the onus of responsibility to use their power judiciously. Disavowing anti-LGB prejudice within the professions may feel like an infringement on personal, individual liberty of the anti-LGB therapist, but ethical codes are not primarily about our personal liberties; they are at base about safeguarding the public from harm that can be done with our power.

A final issue of power we considered involves the way issues of diversity and multiculturalism have come to be framed within psychology. Multiculturalism and respect for diversity no longer seem to be geared exclusively toward preventing encroachment of rights of political or numerical minority groups. Instead, majority groups also sometimes demand specific, unique doses of "respect" based on majority-group membership. If respect translates into unquestioning acceptance of values and beliefs, then we have lost sight of the mission of multiculturalism to redress societal power imbalances. For example, members of some men's rights groups sometimes claim that men—the political majority—are oppressed. We also have heard religious people and White people claim that they—the political majority—are oppressed. There is no question that these claims are expressions of suffering, which we do not dispute, but suffering is not the same as being oppressed (Frye, 1983). If oppression is about a system by which a more powerful group constrains a less powerful group (and has privilege to control valued resources), then which specific class or category of more powerful people is oppressing these majorities specifically for their membership in the majority group? In general, we wonder whether claiming oppression has become a tool available to majority members to reclaim the bit of power, including power to enact prejudice, they perceive to have been taken away by multiculturalism's demand for the rights of minority groups.

In sum, one issue we ask our communities to consider is whether we sometimes have lost sight of prioritizing nonmaleficence over respect, as required by superordinate Principle A of APA's 2002 "Ethical Principles of Psychologists and Code of Conduct." We acknowledge the positive, aspirational quality of the "respect" injunction but also believe that—for whatever reasons and whether intentionally or not—it sometimes is used as a way around avoiding prejudice. Therefore, we suggest increasing our vigilance and recommitting ourselves to the primacy of nonmaleficence as we also strive toward respecting others.

A final comment on this proposed solution (i.e., vigilantly prioritizing nonmaleficence) is that in comparison with all of our other brainstormed solutions, it appears to run the smallest risk of doing harm to the public. Additionally, we agreed that the public, and particularly members of oppressed groups, would benefit from a stance that directly condemns oppression.

The Final Steps: Choosing a Solution, Reviewing the Process, Implementing and Evaluating the Decision, and Continuing Reflection

The process of jointly composing this chapter has been dynamic, interactive, enlightening, and surprising. We, as authors, made every effort to approach the dilemma and the Hill et al. (1995) model with openness and a willingness to engage in introspection, empathy, reflection, and deliberation. Although it may or may not be obvious, we spent well over a year debating our points of view as we reminded ourselves that our goal was not to choose a single solution, but to stimulate public discussion and thoughtful examination of the issues involved in the present dilemma. The last three steps of the Hill et al. (1995) model, reflected in the subtitle of this section, ask us to proceed in ways that are beyond our control. It was not our intent or desire or within our means to choose for the profession what solution(s) may best resolve the dilemma we have framed. Although it is likely clear that we prefer our third solution (which, at the outset of writing this manuscript, we never expected to articulate), we want to reaffirm our goals to spark public discourse and to encourage open reflection about this difficult and divisive issue facing psychologists. We hope that by posing possible solutions and identifying relevant quandaries, we have worked, in part, to do this.

We eagerly anticipate the participation of many of our professional peers and colleagues in this public dialogue. Perhaps professional organizations within the field (e.g., the American Counseling Association and the APA) will create task forces to draft policy statements with regard to this issue. As with the multicultural counseling competencies, working drafts of such policy statements could be circulated for input and commentary from organizational members. Additionally, graduate training programs could adopt similar measures in responding to this dilemma. We were excited to discover—but only by chance—that during the period in which we were composing this chapter, a semipublic electronic mailing list discussion about this issue spontaneously erupted among a number of counseling psychology graduate-training directors (on the Council of Counseling Psychology Training Programs electronic discussion list). The Association of Counseling Center Training Agencies also has been grappling with these issues for a number of years. We support such deliberation, hope that it continues, and especially challenge readers to make their thoughts and reactions public (e.g., by submitting pieces for consideration at conferences, in journals, and in other professional publications such as APA's *Monitor on Psychology*).

CONCLUSION

In writing this chapter, we addressed the question "What should we do as psychologists when we perceive a conflict between simultaneous affirmation of sexual diversity and affirmation of religious diversity?" Adopting Hill et al.'s (1995) model of ethical decision-making, we considered how we knew a problem existed, who is most affected by the problem, what ethical principles are related to the problem, what reasonable and ethical solutions can be generated in response to the problem, how those solutions could be implemented, and how the primary stakeholders in this dilemma would be affected by the implementation of various solutions. As we began outlining this chapter two years before this book went to press, we had no idea that in wrestling with this problem we would so arduously scrutinize, evaluate, and rely on the wisdom embedded in the APA's "Ethical Principles of Psychologists and Code of Conduct" (2002). Essentially, we concluded that in working with clients, training psychologists, and dealing with the public, psychologists' first priority must continue to be avoidance of harm. We suggest that psychology professionals and students join us in increasing our vigilance and recommitting ourselves to the primacy of non-maleficence as we also strive toward respect, which translates into psychologists' taking responsibility for not only their biases but also their privileges.

Our primary goal with this chapter has been to create a springboard for meaningful dialogue within and among the mental health professions. We know that not everyone will agree with or be happy about the translation of the ethical code we offer here as a starting point. Recognizing the inevitability that every conceivable solution to the dilemma will generate opposition from some, we think it is critical nonetheless to make honest constructive attempts at resolution. This dilemma has not gone away and will not go away of its own accord. We exhort members of our profession to focus collective energies on our common goal: serving the public well.

REFERENCES

American Psychiatric Association. (1968). *Diagnostic and statistical manual of mental disorders* (2nd ed.). Washington, DC: Author.

American Psychological Association. (1998). Appropriate therapeutic responses to sexual orientation in the proceedings of the American Psychological Association, Incorporated, for legislative year 1997. *American Psychologist, 53,* 882–939.

American Psychological Association. (2002). Ethical principles of psychologists and code of conduct. *American Psychologist, 57,* 1060–1073.

American Psychological Association. (2004). *Proposed elimination of footnote 4 to domain D of Accreditation Guidelines and Principles.* Retrieved June 28, 2004, from http://www.apa.org/ ed/reqstforcmnt1.html

Beckstead, A. L., & Morrow, S. L. (2004). The need for a new treatment approach. *The Counseling Psychologist, 32,* 651–690.

Christopher, J. C. (1996). Counseling's inescapable moral vision. *Journal of Counseling and Development, 75,* 17–25.

Davidson, M. G. (2000). Religion and spirituality. In R. M. Perez, K. A. DeBord, & K. J. Bieschke (Eds.), *Handbook of counseling and psychotherapy with lesbian, gay, and bisexual clients* (pp. 409–433). Washington, DC: American Psychological Association.

Dorland, J. M., & Fischer, A. R. (2001). Gay, lesbian, and bisexual individuals' perceptions: An analogue study. *The Counseling Psychologist, 29,* 532–547.

Fowers, B. J., & Richardson, F. C. (1996). Why is multiculturalism good? *American Psychologist, 51,* 609–621.

Frye, M. (1983). Oppression. In M. Frye, *The politics of reality: Essays in feminist theory* (pp. 1–16). Trumansburg, NY: The Crossing Press.

Gonsiorek, J. C. (2004). Reflections from the conversion therapy battlefield. *The Counseling Psychologist, 32,* 750–759.

Gove, P. B. (Ed.). (1971). *Merriam-Webster's third new international dictionary of the English language unabridged.* Springfield, MA: Merriam-Webster.

Haldeman, D. C. (2004). Considerations in working with conflicted same-sex-attracted male clients. *The Counseling Psychologist, 32,* 691–715.

Hansen, W. D. (2001). *Key policy letters signed by the education secretary or deputy secretary.* Retrieved June 28, 2004, from http://www.ed.gov/policy/highered/guid/secletter/ 010906.html

Hill, M., Glaser, K., & Harden, J. (1995). A feminist model for ethical decision-making. In E. J. Rave & C. C. Larsen (Eds.), *Ethical decision-making in therapy: Feminist perspectives* (pp. 18–37). New York: Guilford Press.

Jaggar, A. M. (1992). Feminist ethics. In L. C. Becker & C. B. Becker (Eds.), *Encyclopedia of ethics* (Vol. 1, pp. 361–370). New York: Garland.

Katz, J. H. (1985). The sociopolitical nature of counseling. *The Counseling Psychologist, 13,* 615–624.

Kawakami, K., Young, H., & Dovidio, J. F. (2002). Automatic stereotyping: Category, trait, and behavioral activations. *Personality and Social Psychology Bulletin, 28*, 3–15.

Kitchener, K. S. (2000). *Foundations of ethical practice, research, and teaching in psychology*. Mahwah, NJ: Erlbaum.

Koocher, G. P., & Keith-Spiegel, P. (1998). *Ethics in psychology: Professional standards and cases* (2nd ed.). New York: Oxford University Press.

Lasser, J. S., & Gottlieb, M. C. (2004). Treating patients distressed regarding their sexual orientation: Clinical and ethical alternatives. *Professional Psychology: Research and Practice, 35*, 194–200.

Lears, J. (2003, March 11). How a war became a crusade. *The New York Times*, p. A25.

Liddle, B. J. (1996). Therapist sexual orientation gender, and counseling practices as they relate to ratings of helpfulness by gay and lesbian clients. *Journal of Counseling Psychology, 43*, 394–401.

McIntosh, P. E. (1988). *White privilege and male privilege: A personal account of coming to see correspondences through work in women's studies*. Wellesley, MA: Wellesley College, Center for Research on Women.

Mobley, M., & Pearson, S. M. (2004). Blessed be the ties that bind. In J. M. Croteau, J. S. Lark, M. Lidderdale, & Y. B. Chung (Eds.), *Deconstructing heterosexism in the counseling professions: Multicultural narrative voices*. Thousand Oaks, CA: Sage.

Morrow, S. L., Beckstead, A. L., Hayes, J. A., & Haldeman, D. C. (2004). Impossible dreams, impossible choices, and thoughts about depolarizing the debate. *The Counseling Psychologist, 32*, 778–785.

Niebuhr, G. (2000, August 29). The 2000 campaign: The religion issue. *The New York Times*, p. A19.

Nussbaum, M. C. (1999). A plea for difficulty. In S. M. Okin, J. Cohen, M. Howard, & M. C. Nussbaum (Eds.), *Is multiculturalism bad for women?* (pp. 104–114). Princeton, NJ: Princeton University Press.

Okin, S. M., Cohen, J., Howard, M., & Nussbaum, M. C. (1999). *Is multiculturalism bad for women?* Princeton, NJ: Princeton University Press.

Ritter, K. Y., & Terndrup, A. I. (2002). *Handbook of affirmative psychotherapy with lesbians and gay men*. New York: Guilford Press.

Root, M. P. P. (1992). Reconstructing the impact of trauma on personality. In L. S. Brown & M. Ballou (Eds.), *Personality and psychopathology: Feminist reappraisals* (pp. 229–265). New York: Guilford Press.

Transcript of debate between Bush and Kerry, with domestic policy the topic. (2004, October 14). *The New York Times*, p. A22.

Vasquez, M. J. T, & de las Fuentes, C. (2000). Hate speech or freedom of expression? Balancing autonomy and feminist ethics in a pluralistic society. In M. M. Brabeck (Ed.), *Practicing feminist ethics in psychology* (pp. 225–247). Washington, DC: American Psychological Association.

14

AFFIRMATIVE CLINICAL SUPERVISION

STEPHEN C. HALPERT, BRIAN REINHARDT, AND MICHAEL J. TOOHEY

Affirmative supervision is an important aspect in all supervisory relationships that encompasses the broad spectrum of individual and cultural diversities and should be present in all interactions with a supervisee; however, for lesbian, gay, bisexual, or transgender (LGBT) persons, that may not always be the case.

> Historically those approaches to psychology and therapeutic practice that have pathologised homosexuality have brought the same constrictions to supervision. In supervision literature homosexuality and bisexuality appeared only as evidence of the client's pathology and were treated as such. In most cases there was no question of the supervisor being lesbian, gay or bisexual because these were barred from training in many training institutions (O'Connor & Ryan 1993; Ellis 1994), and even if they did train they found difficulty in advancement. (Pett, 2000, p. 54)

Affirmative supervision is an atheoretical framework that is intended to augment and to be used consistently with the supervisor's existing theoretical model (Davies, 1996). The cornerstone of an LGBT-affirmative approach to supervision is the belief that all gender identities and sexual orientations are equally valid. Hitchings (1999) suggested that "such a stance needs to be evidently congruent with beliefs, attitudes and behaviours of the practitioner in both their professional and private lives" (p. 56). Pett (2000) defined affirmative supervision as

> a mutually agreed and boundaried interpersonal working relationship between a supervisor and supervisee/s which provides support to the latter to assure competent and increasingly good quality counseling for the benefit of clients. This relationship is further characterized by interpersonal, social, developmental and process dimensions, which include respect for, and an acceptance and understanding of, lesbian, gay and bisexual sexuality, culture, and lifestyle. (p. 63)

This chapter briefly reviews selected models of supervision that contribute to an integrative affirmative model that can be applied to any theoretical orientation. Four supervision models (Buhrke, 1989; Holloway, 1995; Pett, 2000; Stoltenberg & Delworth, 1987) were selected to provide the essential elements required for a comprehensive affirmative supervision model. Each makes a unique contribution or expands the contribution of another model (see Table 14.1). In light of existing models of supervision, the authors propose a model of supervision that we are calling the Integrative Affirmative Supervision (IAS) Model.

TABLE 14.1
Contributions to Integrative Affirmative Supervision

Contributing factors	Buhrke (1989)	Holloway (1995)	Pettt (2000)	Stoltenberg & Delworth (1987)
Core values		X	X	
Internal factors		X	X	X
External factors		X	X	
Skill & knowledge		X	X	X
Institutional issues		X		
Dyadic typologies	X			
Assessment/ Evaluation		X		X

CURRENT MODELS OF TRAINING AND
SUPERVISION FOR AFFIRMATIVE PSYCHOTHERAPY

Pett's Gay-Affirmative Model (2000)

Drawing heavily on the work of Davies (1996) and Clark (1987), Pett proposed an atheoretical model of supervision founded on Davies's principles of affirmative therapy, which were, in turn, informed by the "Twelve Guidelines for Retraining" and Clark's (1987) "Ground Rules for Helping." The "Guidelines" and "Ground Rules" were presented in the final section of Clark's (1987) book, *The New Loving Someone Gay*, as a means of informing the helping professionals who work with LGBT individuals. He suggested that affirmative supervision differs little from general good supervision, just as affirmative therapy differs little from general good therapy.

The first characteristic of affirmative supervision as proposed by Pett (2000) is that it accepts gay, lesbian, bisexual, and heterosexual orientations as equally valid expressions of human sexuality. This characteristic is the cornerstone of affirmative supervision because it both defines and permeates supervision. Davies (1996) has referred to this as respect for the client's sexual orientation. We believe that this respect must also extend to the supervisor and supervisee.

Second, supervisors have a duty to explore themselves for attitudes, beliefs, and feelings that may cause difficulties before beginning to work with LGBT clients or supervisees and supervisors (Pett, 2000). According to Davies (1996), this means having respectful attitudes and beliefs. Supervisors have a duty to perform honest self-exploration that will enable them to be aware of strengths and limitations and help supervisees explore their own thoughts and feelings. Pett (2000) stated that for supervisors to develop this openness, sexual orientation issues need to be a part of the curriculum of supervisor training.

According to Pett, the third characteristic of affirmative supervision is that supervisees are respected for their sexuality and choices. If supervisees do not feel safe, or if they feel they must hide parts of their work or themselves, they will not be able to function at their highest levels. Supervisors need to demonstrate respect by being willing to listen and acknowledge that the supervisee may know more about some of these issues than the supervisor; however, it is the supervisor's responsibility, not the supervisee's, to educate him- or herself.

Fourth, supervisors should understand how homophobia operates and be aware of the unique aspects of the lives of LGBT people, such as the coming out process, heterosexism, and the components of an LGBT identity (Pett, 2000). Davies (1996) discussed these issues under the heading of "training and retraining." The purpose of retraining is to simultaneously explore one's attitudes toward homosexuality from a personal and professional perspective while gaining knowledge regarding aspects of the lives of sexual minority persons. Finally, supervisors may use supervision in a didactic way that may include challenging negative stereotypes and giving information. This is intended to meet the dual criteria of education and raising awareness (Davies, 1996).

In sum, Pett's (2000) model of affirmative supervision is grounded in a four-dimensional proposition that characterizes affirmative supervision as (a) accepting of the continuum of sexual orientations and gender identities, (b) including a process in which supervisors engage in an exploration of their own biases that may impede the supervision process, (c) affirming of the sexuality and identity of supervisees, and (d) encompassing an awareness of the impact of homophobia and other biases on the lives of LGBT individuals. Although the strength of Pett's model is the emphasis on affirmation of sexual orientation and the continual need for awareness of homophobia and heterosexism as it impacts the supervision process and the lives of LGBT people, what is lacking is an acknowledgment and integration of the developmental aspects of the supervision relationship and process. One model of affirmative supervision that integrates developmental processes is proposed by Bruss, Brack, Brack, Glickauf-Hughes, and O'Leary (1997).

Affirmative Developmental Model of Supervision

Bruss et al. (1997) have successfully adapted Stoltenberg and Delworth's (1987) developmental model of supervision for supervising clinicians working with LGBT clients. This affirmative supervision model emphasizes assessment of the supervisee's current level of functioning, clarification of expectations, supervisor self-awareness, and provision of appropriate supervisory functions. Three developmental levels and eight specific dimensions using three structures (awareness of self and others, motivation, and autonomy) are specified to trace the supervisee's progression through the levels on each dimension. Supervisory tasks that incorporate awareness and knowledge of LGBT issues are described for each developmental level.

The first developmental level is characterized by self-focus, difficulty in empathizing with clients, and a high degree of dependency on the supervisor. Supervisory tasks at this level include educating the supervisee about LGBT issues (e.g., creating an atmosphere of acceptance and sensitivity to language and its impact on the session). The second developmental level is characterized by focus on the client, overly empathizing with his or her worldview, and a conflict between dependency on the supervisor and autonomy of the therapist-supervisee. The supervisor's task now becomes more confrontational than supportive with the supervisee. At this level, supervisees must begin to deal with their own homophobia, transphobia, and heterosexism in order to become increasingly autonomous.

The third developmental level is characterized by the ideal balance of self/other-focus, empathy/confrontation with the client, and dependence/autonomy in the supervisory relationship. At this advanced level, therapists-in-training are able to see clients both as individuals and as members of a larger LGBT culture. and the supervisor's task becomes assessment of the therapist's strengths and weaknesses, confrontation of discrepancies, and encouragement of integration and exploration on the supervisee's part (Stoltenberg & Delworth, 1987).

The Bruss et al. (1997) study specifies eight domains (intervention skills, assessment techniques, interpersonal assessment, client conceptualization, individual differences, theoretical orientation, treatment goals and plans, and professional ethics) within this developmental supervision model that focus on working with sexual minority clients. Of the eight specific domains, the most important areas are client conceptualization and individual differences (Bruss et al., 1997). Novice therapists may rely excessively on their own perceptions of differences (e.g., cultural, sexual, racial) between clients (Stoltenberg & Delworth, 1987) and may conceptualize symptoms displayed during the coming out process, for example, incorrectly pathologizing clients (Bruss et al., 1997).

With a basis on this model of Bruss et al., we contend that the developmental level of a supervisee is important to address in order to determine whether she or he is ready to work with LGBT clients. The supervisor must conduct an initial assessment of the supervisee's strengths and weaknesses. With undeveloped skills and the influences of heterosexism, transphobia, and homophobia, the supervisee may be likely to pathologize LGBT clients and may be blind to the contextual developmental factors (e.g., LGBT identity) that may define how LGBT clients cope with or respond to social or internal stressors (Buhrke & Douce, 1991, p. 223). Although the Bruss et al. model integrates a developmental component into affirmative supervision, it currently does not address how supervision addresses the issue of homophobia and transphobia in supervision. In order to attend to this important aspect of affirmative supervision, we turn to Buhrke's (1989) model of supervision.

Buhrke's Conflictual Situation Model (1989)

Buhrke (1989) described various situations in working with homophobia in supervision. Two of these situations result in conflictual situations in the supervisory relationship, and two situations are deemed to be nonconflictual. The most productive situation is when neither supervisee nor supervisor is excessively homophobic or heterosexist, and the worst possible situation was judged to be when both are predominantly homophobic. One should note that all supervisors, supervisees, and clients have some degree of homophobia, transphobia, and heterosexism, no matter how accepting or how much training they have had. Buhrke's model looks at the extremes of the homophobia–LGBT-affirmation spectrum, with a high degree of homophobia and heterosexism on one end and a high degree of LGBT affirmation (e.g., having respect, admiration, and positive regard for LGBT individuals) on the other. Buhrke focused on two main issues within the supervisory relationship: coming out and transference/countertransference.

If supervisors communicate an inability or unwillingness to deal with same-sex attraction, the issue will likely be ignored and may be acted out destructively within the clinical session. For example, attraction may "develop into a 'crush' through denial, directly repressed as inappropriate, or communicated as confusing flirtation by the counselor toward the client" (Buhrke & Douce, 1991, p. 227). LGBT supervisees are particularly likely to need a supportive environment to work through issues surrounding overidentification with clients, fear of stereotypes, negative reactions toward homophobic or heterosexist clients, and unresolved issues within themselves; however, non-LGBT supervisees also need support in dealing with these difficult situations.

If a supervisee is excessively homophobic or heterosexist, but the supervisor is LGBT-affirming, a positive resolution is often possible (Buhrke, 1989). The supervisor works with the supervisee in order to overcome his or her biases in a manner similar to the process of overcoming any other prejudicial beliefs the supervisee may have (e.g., racist or sexist beliefs). If the supervisor is a sexual minority, self-disclosure to the supervisee can be useful in dispelling myths associated with homosexuality or bisexuality and may be an invaluable source of learning and information for the therapist-in-training. The supervisor will likely be the individual who raises issues of transference/countertransference, given that a supervisee may have difficulty in acknowledging or recognizing these issues.

We believe that one of the most difficult situations occurs when the supervisor is excessively homophobic. Supervisors with homophobic, transphobic, or heterosexist values may interpret supervisee actions as pathological, covertly reinforcing the supervisee's avoidance of raising sexual orientation issues, attempting to teach "proper" homophobic and heterosexists attitudes, and discouraging confrontation by the supervisee regarding the supervisor's irrational beliefs. In the event that the supervisor is both homophobic and LGBT, there may be a desire on the part of the supervisor to be secretive about his or her sexual orientation or gender identity, and such a position is likely to send a message that sexual orientation is shameful and should remain hidden. The effects of unresolved issues of internalized homophobia can be damaging to the supervisor–supervisee relationship and ultimately to the therapist–client relationship.

In what we consider an ideal situation, wherein both supervisor and supervisee are LGBT-affirming, therapeutic and supervisory issues can be addressed with less bias. Supervision can focus on increasing the supervisee's knowledge base, examining his or her emotional responses to LGBT and non-LGBT clients, and accurately conceptualizing cases and creating substantive, comprehensive treatment plans. An atmosphere of acceptance and respect will facilitate self-disclosure of sexual orientation and gender identity for supervisors, supervisees, and clients. If, however, both supervisor and supervisee are excessively homophobic, this creates a situation that endangers the client (Buhrke, 1989; Buhrke & Douce, 1991; Davies, 1996). The supervisee's homophobic attitudes and beliefs may be exacerbated by a homophobic supervisor, resulting in three possible outcomes: First, both parties may collude in labeling the client's sexual orientation as pathological and inappropriately direct treatment toward changing it. Second, the therapist may communicate to clients that sexual orientation issues are inappropriate for discussion, and the clients' issues in that area will thereby be avoided. Third, both supervisor and supervisee may ignore references to same-sex attraction, depriving the client of ethical or therapeutic services.

Overall, the Conflictual Situation Model (Buhrke, 1989) emphasizes three important areas of supervision: homophobia of both supervisor and supervisee, transference and countertransference, and "coming out." Both supervisor and supervisee are expected to address personal issues of potential same-sex attraction and gender identity that may arise during clinical work. If a supervisor is lesbian, gay, or transgender, the supervisor will seek acceptance of his or her own sexual orientation in addition to seeking it for the orientation of the client. In addition, the sexual minority supervisor may choose to disclose his or her sexual orientation or gender identity as a means of honest communication and building trust.

House and Holloway's Supervisee Empowerment Model (1992)

Holloway's (1995) model of supervision was described by Bernard and Goodyear (1998) as "the most comprehensive of the available models" (p. 32). Holloway suggested seven dimensions—the supervisory relationship itself; characteristics of the supervisor, institution, client, and supervisee; and both functions and tasks of supervision—that interact and influence one another. A preliminary version of this model was applied to LGBT supervision issues by House and Holloway (1992), who emphasized the empowerment of the supervisee within the supervision relationship by means of two primary factors: First, the therapist-in-training must develop both a skill base and knowledge base relevant to the counseling profession. Second, the supervisee must experience a sense of self-efficacy within the supervision and counseling sessions. In light of the experiences of disempowerment reported by many LGBT persons, the supervisory relationship must foster the development of support and empowerment for LGBT supervisees and clients.

The model described by House and Holloway (1992) emphasizes individual characteristics and cultural values of both supervisor and supervisee, goals for professional counselors, the supervisory process, evaluation, and institutional constraints. Supervisor and supervisee bring their own interpersonal characteristics, abilities, knowledge, and cultural values (including attitudes and beliefs about homosexuality) to the supervisory relationship. Thus, the supervisory relationship is based in large part on the individual characteristics and values of both supervisor and supervisee. It is therefore important that supervisors address their own homophobic, transphobic, and heterosexist attitudes and assist the supervisee to do likewise. House and Holloway (1992) suggested that this could be done by having the supervisor acknowledge her or his own issues of heterosexism to the supervisee. The supervisor may also engage the supervisee in a discussion of cultural and personal homophobia and its influence on the supervisory relationship. Both supervisor and supervisee have goals that relate to the supervisee's training and client care. Supervisors must ensure that supervisees possess both knowledge and skills for working with LGBT clients.

Within their model, House and Holloway (1992) described the supervisory process as composed of the interaction between the supervisor and supervisee with regard to objectives and strategies. This interaction represents the reciprocity between the shared goals and learning alliance of both supervisor and supervisee. The learning alliance functions as a vehicle in which learning and teaching objectives are established relative to the supervisee's developmental level and client needs. It is the nature of the client's needs and issues that influences the supervision objectives. Supervisors evaluate the supervisee as part of their professional role, and the evaluation aids the supervisee in discovering how attitudes, values, and beliefs affect clients in therapy. When issues of homophobia, transphobia, and heterosexism become part of the evaluation criteria, supervisees begin to understand the need to practice from an LGBT-affirming stance. Beliefs and attitudes of both supervisor and supervisee become part of the evaluation process. Finally, the institution, as the foundation of every supervisory relationship, is considered. Institutional practices, guidelines, policies, and regulations (both formal and informal) may reflect support or barriers for LGBT clients.

In sum, the Supervisee Empowerment Model outlined by House and Holloway (1992) espouses empowerment of the supervisee by allowing him or her to develop relevant skills and knowledge before working with particular clients. The model also addresses the evaluation of the supervisee by the supervisor. The supervisee needs to understand how one's attitudes, values, and beliefs affect one's clients in therapy. The supervisor must understand the need for affirmative clinical supervision and model appropriate behaviors for the trainee. Supervisor and supervisee must understand institutional policies and procedures affecting work with sexual minority clients.

CONTRIBUTIONS OF EACH MODEL

Each of the supervision models that we have examined has contributed salient aspects to a more integrative model of affirmative supervision. Holloway's (1995) model provides the most contributions to the integrative affirmative supervision model. Core values and principles such as empowerment provide the infrastructure to the model. Pett's (2000) model also highlights the value of respect as a foundation in the supervisor–supervisee, therapist–client relationships.

Three of the selected models (Bruss et al., 1997; Holloway, 1995; Pett, 2000) stress the importance of internal factors of supervisors and supervisees such as self-exploration of strengths and weaknesses and self-awareness of internalized homophobia and heterosexism. These internal factors are important because they inform and direct the behaviors of supervisors and supervisees. In addition, Pett (2000) and Holloway (1995) discussed how external factors such as cultural homophobia impact supervision and counseling. Holloway (1995) further explored how institutional policies and procedures can positively or negatively affect the provision of affirmative supervision and counseling. Most of the models reviewed (Bruss et al., 1997; Holloway, 1995; Pett, 2000) highlight the need for supervisors, and ultimately supervisees, to be knowledgeable about basic processes for LGBT individuals, such as coming out or identity development.

Buhrke's (2000) model contributes the unique factor of dyadic typologies that describe four outcomes of pairing homophobic and LGBT-affirming supervisors and supervisees. Although this model has heuristic value, it uses the extreme endpoints on the homophobic–LGBT-affirming continuum that do not take into account the in-between gray areas where most individuals reside (i.e., most supervisors and supervisees usually can be described somewhere between homophobic and LGBT-affirming). An evaluation or assessment component may help in the creation of a more complex and comprehensive model of supervisor and supervisee pairings related to levels of homophobia, transphobia, and heterosexism.

Assessment and evaluation are vital components of any supervision model. The adapted Stoltenberg and Delworth (1987) model by Bruss et al. (1997) provides a developmental framework that can be used in broadly assessing where supervisees are in their skills and training and in determining what supervisory tasks are most important in supervision. Holloway (1995) included evaluation as an essential part of her model and suggested that issues that can affect clients in therapy, such as the level of homophobia or heterosexism of therapists, can be included as part of the supervisee evaluation criteria.

However, although each of the reviewed supervision models contribute some unique perspectives and assumptions regarding affirmative supervision, they each lack an integrative quality that may prove to be ultimately beneficial in providing affirmative supervision.

With the overview of each of the selected models of supervision and the discussion of how each can contribute to a more comprehensive and integrative affirmative supervision model, the next section presents the IAS model and gives an example of how the model can be applied in supervision.

INTEGRATIVE AFFIRMATIVE SUPERVISION MODEL

We have developed the IAS model that provides for sensitive, supportive, and substantive supervision to LGBT and non-LGBT supervisees that in turn helps them to provide the best possible informed, ethical therapeutic care to their LGBT and non-LGBT clients. The main goal of the IAS model is to provide a comprehensive, inclusive approach to

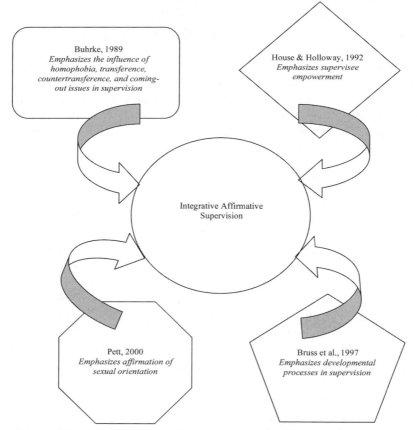

Figure 14.1. Integrative Affirmative Supervision Model.

EXHIBIT 14.1
Tasks for Supervisors in Constructing Integrative Affirmative Supervision

Presupervision	Supervision	Advanced and continuing tasks
1. Obtain necessary training and skills to work competently with LGB clients and supervisees and update with continuing education.	1. Help create a safe, respectful, and empowering supervision environment. Openly discuss their own respect for all sexual identities and encourage discussion of LGB-relevant issues in supervision.	1. Support appropriate discussion of transference and countertransference issues including internalized homophobia and heterosexism, issues of same-sex attraction in counselor–client dyad, and other issues impacting the relationships.
2. Examine their own internalized homophobia and heterosexism. Work toward creating or enhancing an LGB-affirmative stance. Challenge negative stereotypes and beliefs about LGB people.	2. Thoroughly assess supervisees' clinical competence and knowledge, including their developmental stage (Stoltenberg & Delworth, 1987), knowledge and understanding of LGB issues, sensitivity to diversity and differences, and level of homophobia or heterosexism.	2. Assist supervisee with supportive termination processes, appropriate referrals to LGB-sensitive therapists and group and community support, and follow up to ensure ongoing bridging with resources and support.
3. Learn and understand impact of individual and institutional homophobia/heterosexism on LGB individuals and advocate for training and supervision environments supportive of LGB people.	3. Focus on appropriate diagnosis, clinical assessment, conceptualization, treatment-planning, and selection of appropriate interventions in working with diverse clients, including LGB individuals.	3. Conduct ongoing and summative evaluation of supervisees regarding working with diverse individuals and encourage further training and experience in expanding this area of expertise.

providing clinical supervision that can be applied to any supervision style or theoretical orientation. As illustrated in Figure 14.1, the IAS model brings together the best elements of a collection of the selected supervision models (Bruss et al., 1997; Buhrke, 1989; House & Holloway, 1992; Pett, 2000) discussed previously. Exhibit 14.1 also outlines the key features contributed to the IAS model by each of the supervision models.

IAS embraces the fundamental belief that all gender identities and sexual orientations are equally valid and equally respected. IAS gives special attention to the relationship between supervisor and supervisee in terms of transference and countertransference issues, eliciting clarity of values, confronting heterosexist and homophobic collusion, showing sensitivity to power issues, facilitating openness within the supervisory relationship, avoiding minimizing or exaggerating the significance of sexual orientation or gender identity, and maintaining an awareness of wider cultural contexts. Three core conditions help to solidify the success and usefulness of IAS: safety, respect, and empowerment.

In order to effectively take risks and grow through clinical supervision experiences, supervisees must feel professionally and emotionally safe in both individual and group supervision situations. The open, supportive, facilitative stance of the supervisor (regardless of sexual orientation or gender identity) regarding exploring and discussing issues related to sexual orientation and gender identity is key to creating safety. When supervisors demonstrate and model respect for all supervisees and clients, regardless of sexual orientation, gender, race, ethnicity, or presenting concerns and issues, the supervision climate is optimized.

With a sense of safety and a foundation of respect, supervisees can begin to feel empowered to work effectively with a broad range of clients who may or may not be sexual minority members. Feelings of empowerment in supervisees can help them to make courageous interventions within the clinical hour with clients, enhanced by substantive supervision sessions that allow for safety in exploring relevant topics, from internalized homophobia to same-sex attraction in the counselor–client dyad to appropriate referrals for LGBT clients.

Steps in Constructing Integrative Affirmative Supervision

Affirmative supervision provides the opportunity for safe examination of attitudes and biases by supervisees. As Exhibit 14.1 shows, the model begins with a series of tasks for supervisors to master prior to coming to the first supervision session. These tasks involve education, self-exploration, and a thorough understanding of LGBT issues and barriers. These presupervision tasks may be accomplished through graduate coursework, continuing education workshops, personal therapy, independent study and research, or collaboration and consultation with colleagues or through other useful methods. Leading by example is a crucial element in fostering an open, affirmative stance in supervisees. A supervisor's openness about his or her own exploration and understanding of affirmative therapy allows a supervisee to confront his or her own homophobia, heterosexism, and privilege. Supervisors can continually encourage supervisees' ongoing understanding of how homophobia, transphobia, and heterosexism operate in our society. This process parallels the development of being culturally competent: It involves self-examination, training, and skill development that address inequities and biases suffered by marginalized people (e.g., APA, 2003).

An essential initial task for the supervisor who is applying IAS is to use the three core conditions of safety, respect, and empowerment to create an open, working supervisor–supervisee relationship. When a supervisor is informed and affirmative about LGBT issues, she or he can act as a model and teacher of useful information. A supervisor need not wait until a supervisee discloses sexual orientation or identity issues or until the supervisee begins working with a LGBT client. Broaching the subject, the supervisor implies an affirmative stance, thereby releasing the supervisee from the burden of training or educating the supervisor about LGBT issues. Being open and proactive also helps dispel fears of repercussions that a supervisee may have about disclosing his or her sexual orientation or sexual identity. This fosters a relationship between supervisor and supervisee that is open, safe, respectful, and accepting.

Assessment

An element of supervision that is often minimized or left out is the initial assessment and evaluation of the supervisee's skill and competence level in working with diverse clients, followed by the creation of a plan to address any deficits or needed areas of growth. The plan can be tailored to address the specific needs of the supervisee. For example, one supervision goal could be to provide substantive empathy for a client just coming out, rather than minimizing the process. Supervisors can evaluate competency by examining and confronting therapeutic interventions that may reflect heterosexual bias and by determining whether the supervisee is integrating affirmative discussions and techniques into his or her therapeutic relationship with sexual minority clients. Assessment devices, such as scales or measurements of homonegativity and internalized homophobia, may be useful for the supervisee to complete as part of this process. The *Handbook of Sexuality-Related Measures* (Davis, Yarber, Bauserman, Schreer, & Davis, 1998) offers several tools to aid supervisors, supervisees, and clients as well. With this information, the dyadic comparisons of supervisor–supervisee can be explored to consider what interventions may best address the differing or similar levels of internalized homophobia.

Researchers have noted an absence of psychometrically sound assessment instruments specific to the supervision context (e.g., Ellis & Ladany, 1997). The Lesbian, Gay, and Bisexual Affirmative Counseling Self-Efficacy Inventory (LGB-CSI) is one instrument that addresses this situation (Dillon & Worthington, 2003). The LGB-CSI is useful in the supervision and training of therapists to develop self-efficacy skills in working with LGBT clients and allows supervisors to implement and assess a social cognitive model of LGBT-affirmative counselor training. The new scale yields five separate but interrelated factors of counselor self-efficacy in working from an LGBT-affirmative stance (application of knowledge, advocacy skills, self-awareness, relationship, and assessment skills) and has demonstrated high internal consistency along with good convergent, discriminant, and construct validity. The instrument did, however, show low test–retest reliability over a two-week period.

Using the IAS Model

Integrative Affirmative Supervision encourages ongoing learning and discussion about countertransference issues that may impact the clinical relationship. The model provides for ongoing assessment and evaluation coupled with up-to-date training as new information is made available about working effectively with sexual minority clients. As another form of providing affirmative supervision, group supervision presents an opportunity to introduce affirmative topics and to set the tone for the supervisees toward LGBT issues and therapy. The group setting also allows LGBT supervisees the chance to witness colleagues' reactions to this topic, which may facilitate feelings of safety in their treatment setting. Introducing affirmative therapy during group supervision offers supervisees an opportunity to discuss their own sexual orientation and gender identity and transference and countertransference issues with their individual supervisors and other staff clinicians and therapists-in-training who are LGBT-identified or LGBT-affirmative. When a safe and trustworthy relationship is established, supervisees can begin exploring their own experiences and beliefs about homophobia.

Embedded in the foundations of safety, respect, and empowerment, IAS encourages supervisees and supervisors to provide sensitive and affirmative clinical services. Effective knowledge of working with LGBT clients can be applied to all stages of the counseling process: diagnosis, assessment, conceptualization, treatment planning, clinical interventions, and later, termination, referral, and follow-up (APA, Division 44/Committee on Lesbian, Gay, and Bisexual Concerns Joint Task Force, 2000). As the supervisee develops an awareness of the mechanics of homophobia and transphobia, the supervisor can introduce awareness of forms of heterosexism, such as only validating traditional, heterosexual relationships. The affirmative supervisor integrates discussions on how heterosexism, homophobia, transphobia, and oppression can manifest in the therapeutic relationship. Just as culturally competent therapists work to sensitively acknowledge the impact of racism and classism on marginalized populations, LGBT-affirmative therapists have a respectful knowledge and understanding of the impact of homophobia, transphobia, and heterosexism on the sexual minority community (APA, Division 44/Committee on Lesbian, Gay, and Bisexual Concerns Joint Task Force, 2000). Although the steps described in Exhibit 14.1 emphasize the tasks required for supervisors using IAS, supervisees also must be open to the process of learning and providing affirmative therapy. The following case example is used to illustrate how the IAS model may be implemented.

SUPERVISION CASE EXAMPLE USING IAS

Sean is a 23-year-old master's practicum student placed at a university community-based counseling center. He is assigned to Mick, a 31-year-old doctoral student in counseling psychology, as his primary supervisor for the semester-long practicum. Mick is taking his first course in clinical supervision, has extensive experience in working with LGBT clients and issues, and happens to be an openly gay man.

Prior to the first scheduled supervision session with Mick, Sean discovers that Mick is an openly gay man. Given Sean's conservative religious background, he calls the supervisor of supervisors, Dr. D, who assigned the supervision pairs. She attentively listens to his request to change supervisors, but does not honor the request that is based solely on the discomfort Sean feels about working with an openly gay supervisor. Dr. D cites the policies on diversity established by the program and the university and highlights ethical standards addressing diversity. Sean agrees to meet with Mick one time, but he is not pleased that his request was not granted. Before the first supervision session, the supervisor of supervisors consults with Mick so that he is knowledgeable about the potential dynamic he is about to enter into with Sean.

By using the IAS model, the supervisor and the supervisor-of-supervisors begin to address the presupervision tasks. Both Dr. D and Mick have extensive knowledge and experience in working with LGBT individuals and have done their own personal work in addressing internalized homophobia and heterosexism. Dr. D is knowledgeable about the institutional and program policies that fortunately support diversity. From Buhrke's (1989) supervisor–supervisee dyadic typologies, Dr. D and Mick know that the combination of an LGBT-affirming supervisor and a more homophobic and heterosexist supervisee can have a positive outcome.

During the first supervision session, Sean presents as closed and defensive, keeping his hands tightly folded on his lap. Mick begins the session by discussing his supervision approach and clinical background, including his experience in working with LGBT clients, expectations and roles of supervision, meeting times, clinical tape-review schedule, supervision goals, and the evaluation process (which includes competence in working with diversity issues). Although the first session is fairly business-like, it is not confrontational. Mick shows respect for Sean and tries to create an open, safe space for exploration, growth, and the sharing of Sean's experience, goals, and background.

Over time, respect and trust increase between Mick and Sean. When appropriate, Mick interjects important diversity considerations regarding the clinical work and provides readings and articles to support the work. In later sessions, Sean even voices his admiration for Mick's guidance as a supervisor, which comes as a surprise to Mick. Sean discloses that he initially had much hesitation and fear in working with an openly gay supervisor, but now finds the experience to be very positive.

During the first several supervision sessions, Mick has accomplished many of the initial tasks outlined in IAS. He has established a safe, respectful environment in which the supervisee can explore feelings, thoughts, and behaviors that impact his clinical work. He has established the framework for supervision, including the development of supervision goals and ongoing evaluation that address diversity competence. Mick integrates appropriate information and considerations for diversity issues throughout the counseling process.

> After working successfully with a number of clients in supervision, Sean is assigned to work with a 21-year-old male who in the first counseling session discloses his attraction to other men and tells Sean about how he is just beginning to come out to others. Because of the trust developed between Mick and Sean, Sean quickly consults with Mick regarding this client. Mick reviews the intake tape of the session and gives supportive feedback about what Sean did well and more challenging feedback about what he missed (e.g., not giving client enough support and encouragement when he first came out to the therapist-in-training).
>
> In the next supervision session, Mick brings additional readings regarding coming out and working with clients in the beginning stages of coming out. The process of coming out is discussed, and appropriate diagnosis, assessment, and treatment-planning occur. Mick makes sure that Sean has done a complete mental-status exam to rule out depression and suicide, which may be a risk in younger men first coming out without adequate support.
>
> Mick takes time to give support to Sean in working with this client, allowing for processing of countertransference. Although Sean says that his church does not support homosexuality and that he himself is not homosexual, he has great empathy for his client and supports his choices in being more openly gay. Sean also tells Mick that he has consulted with an openly gay student colleague about resources in the community that may help his client.

Sean continues to work with the gay male client for the remainder of the semester and then refers him to another appropriate therapist. He gets the client connected with a coming out support group at the student counseling center, which helps him tremendously. Mick and Sean were able to address the more advanced tasks of IAS given the foundation that had been created in earlier supervision sessions. Open discussions about countertransference issues coupled with substantive knowledge of working with LGBT clients helped to equip Sean with the skills and information he needed to give the best possible services to his client. Obviously, not all situations turn out like this true-life example, and other complex issues exist within the supervision process that may influence affirmative supervision. However, when therapists and therapists-in-training use the IAS model, there may be an increased chance that comprehensive, respectful, empowering, safe, affirmative supervision, and therapy can be realized.

CONCLUSION

Affirmative supervision plays a key role in preparing therapists to become culturally competent with the LGBT population (APA, Division 44/Committee on Lesbian, Gay, and Bisexual Concerns Joint Task Force, 2000). Previous models of supervision (Bruss et al., 1997; Buhrke, 1989; House & Holloway, 1992) all contribute essential elements needed for a comprehensive and integrative approach to providing affirmative supervision. The IAS model connects the best features of these models into a step-by-step blueprint for creating affirmative supervision. These components include the following: (a) professional development and training that focus on working clinically with LGBT individuals; (b) supervisors' and supervisees' examination of their own internalized homophobia, transphobia, and heterosexism; (c) focus on core values and the creation of safe, empowering, and respectful supervision and clinical environments; (d) comprehensive assessment of supervisee's competencies in providing affirmative therapy; and (e) application of the affirmative principles throughout the process of therapy (i.e., from initial assessment to termination and referral).

Effective affirmative supervision is a precursor to successful, supportive affirmative therapy. All clients deserve to receive ethical, competent, and useful clinical services. Supervisors who are serious about providing inclusive, comprehensive supervision to LGBT therapists-in-training and non-LGBT supervisees can systematically prepare themselves by obtaining the necessary skills and training needed to work with a diverse population and by exploring their own biases and internalized "isms." Supervision in the context of a safe, respectful, empowering environment allows supervisees to provide competent mental health services at all stages of the counseling process and to explore their own reactions and impact on the counseling relationship. Ongoing and summative evaluation is a key element to effective affirmative supervision. These elements together make up the essential components of the IAS model. Further research is needed to consider the efficacy of the IAS model.

REFERENCES

American Psychological Association, Division 44/Committee on Lesbian, Gay, and Bisexual Concerns Joint Task Force on Guidelines for Psychotherapy With Lesbian, Gay, and Bisexual Clients. (2000). Guidelines for psychotherapy with lesbian, gay, and bisexual clients. *American Psychologist, 55,* 1440–1451.

American Psychological Association. (2003). Guidelines on multicultural education, training, research, practice, and organizational change for psychologists. *American Psychologist, 58*, 377–402.

Bernard, J. M., & Goodyear, R. K. (1998). *Fundamentals of clinical supervision* (2nd ed.). Boston: Allyn & Bacon.

Bruss, K. V., Brack, C. J., Brack, G., Glickauf-Hughes, C., & O'Leary, M. (1997). A developmental model for supervising therapists treating gay, lesbian, and bisexual clients. *The Clinical Supervisor, 15*, 61–73.

Buhrke, R. A. (1989). Lesbian-related issues in counseling supervision. *Women & Therapy, 8*, 195–206.

Buhrke, R. A., & Douce, L. A. (1991). Training issues for counseling psychologists in working with lesbian women and gay men. *The Counseling Psychologist, 19*, 216–234.

Clark, D. (1987). *The new loving someone gay.* Berkeley, CA: Celestial Arts.

Davies, D. (1996). Towards a model of gay affirmative therapy. In D. Davies & C. Neal (Eds.), *Pink therapy: A guide for counselors and therapists working with lesbian, gay and bisexual clients* (pp. 24–40). Philadelphia: Open University Press.

Davis, C. M., Yarber, W. L., Bauserman, R., Schreer, G., & Davis, S. L. (Eds.). (1998). *Handbook of sexuality-related measures.* Thousand Oaks, CA: Sage.

Dillon, F. R., & Worthington, R. L. (2003). The lesbian, gay, and bisexual affirmative counseling self-efficacy inventory (LGB-CSI): Development, validation, and training implications. *Journal of Counseling Psychology, 50*, 235–251.

Ellis, M. L. (1994). Lesbians, gay men and psychoanalytic training. *Free Associations, 4*, 501–517.

Ellis, M. V., & Ladany, N. (1997). Inferences concerning supervisees and clients in clinical supervision: An integrative review. In C. E. Watkins (Ed.), *Handbook of psychotherapy supervision* (pp. 447–507). New York: Wiley.

Hitchings, P. (1999). Sexual orientation and supervision. In M. Carroll & E. Holloway (Eds.), *Counselling supervision in context* (pp. 54–82). Thousand Oaks, CA: Sage.

Holloway, E. L. (1995). *Clinical supervision: A systems approach.* Thousand Oaks, CA: Sage.

House, R. M., & Holloway, E. L. (1992). Empowering the counseling professional to work with gay and lesbian issues. In S. H. Dworkin & F. J. Gutierrez (Eds.), *Counseling gay men & lesbians: Journey to the end of the rainbow* (pp. 307–323). Alexandria, VA: American Counseling Association.

O'Connor, N., & Ryan, J. (1993). *Wild desires and mistaken identities: Lesbianism and psychoanalysis.* London: Virago.

Pett, J. (2000). Gay, lesbian, and bisexual therapy and its supervision. In D. Davies & C. Neal (Eds.), *Therapeutic perspectives on working with lesbian, gay and bisexual clients* (pp. 54–72). Philadelphia: Open University Press.

Stoltenberg, C., & Delworth, U. (1987). *Supervising counselors and therapists: A developmental approach.* San Francisco: Jossey-Bass.

15

LESBIAN AND GAY FAMILY ISSUES IN THE CONTEXT OF CHANGING LEGAL AND SOCIAL POLICY ENVIRONMENTS

CHARLOTTE J. PATTERSON

How does the legal and social policy context in which lesbian and gay Americans live influence their day-to-day experience? The current historical moment is an intriguing time to consider this question. At the time of this writing, many important legal and policy changes that affect sexual minorities are occurring in the United States. After many years of lesbian and gay Americans' enduring hostility from the legal system (Maggiore, 1992; Murdoch & Price, 2001; Rubinstein, 1996), their struggle for equal rights under the law seems to be gathering momentum in some jurisdictions, even as it suffers setbacks in others. As a result, lesbian and gay lives are changing, and an unusual opportunity to observe the impact of legal and policy change upon human behavior is before us (Patterson, 2004).

This chapter begins with an overview of the legal and policy contexts in which lesbian and gay Americans live today and then explores some of the ways in which issues of couples, parents, and families are influenced by these contexts. Throughout the chapter, the primary focus is on lesbian and gay couples and families in the contemporary United States, and the main concern will be to take note of the ways in which changing legal and policy environments may affect their experiences. At this time, there is a tremendous amount of variability in both environments and experiences, and so the key theme here is diversity.

LEGAL AND SOCIAL POLICY CONTEXTS OF LESBIAN AND GAY FAMILY ISSUES

The legal and ideological landscapes in which lesbian and gay Americans live are shifting in many significant ways. It is helpful to recognize that legal changes have occurred together with major shifts in public attitudes about homosexuality during recent years. In the early 1980s—only 20 years ago—a minority (34%) of Americans surveyed in Gallup polls said that homosexuality should be considered an acceptable alternative lifestyle. By 2003, most Americans (54%) considered homosexuality to be acceptable (Herek, 2003). The trend toward greater tolerance is also evident in public opinion about employment discrimination. In the late 1970s, 56% of Americans favored equal rights in job opportunities, but by 2001, a full 85% favored such equal rights (Herek, 2003). Whether changes in public opinion have caused policy changes or vice versa, these shifts in public opinion have certainly occurred over the same time period as recent legal and policy changes.

After many years of legal hostility toward lesbian and gay Americans, a number of important inroads have been made in recent years (Murdoch & Price, 2001). Some of these have occurred at the federal level and affect all Americans. Others have occurred at state or local levels and have a direct impact only upon those living in a particular jurisdiction. Other policy changes have been made in business or educational settings and affect different numbers of people, depending upon the size of the organizations in question. The result is a patchwork of legal and policy environments that vary dramatically from one part of the country to another (National Gay and Lesbian Task Force, 2005b).

Most important among recent legal changes is the U.S. Supreme Court ruling *Lawrence v. Texas* (2003), which struck down laws criminalizing oral or anal sexual practices between consenting adults (i.e., the so-called sodomy laws). Although sodomy laws were rarely enforced, their enforcement was often targeted specifically at gay men, and the laws were also used to justify various kinds of discrimination against both lesbians and gay men. For example, sodomy laws have been invoked to justify job discrimination (Badgett, 2001, 2003) and to justify discrimination against lesbian and gay parents in the context of child-custody proceedings (Swisher & Cook, 2001). With the Court's decision to strike down these laws, consensual sexual behavior of lesbian and gay couples is now accorded the same fundamental privacy status as that of other Americans, and the criminalization of such behavior has finally ended. The demise of sodomy laws across the country represents an important step toward recognition of lesbian and gay Americans as equal citizens.

Another significant group of changes that has occurred in some states involves legal recognition for the relationships of same-sex couples. Today, mainstream news sources are full of discussion about marriage, civil unions, and domestic partnerships for same-sex couples (e.g., Sullivan, 1997). As a result, it can be difficult to remember that, as recently as 10 years ago, no state offered legal recognition of any kind for the couple relationships of lesbian and gay Americans. Even in the current climate, however, most lesbian and gay Americans do not live in jurisdictions that provide any form of legal recognition for same-sex couples. At the same time, many changes are taking place, and the legal landscape across the country is in flux (Patterson, Fulcher, & Wainright, 2002).

Notable among recent legal changes involving recognition of same-sex couples is a decision by the Supreme Judicial Court of Massachusetts, which found that same-sex couples must be allowed to marry (Goodridge v. Department of Public Health, 2003). The decision was issued in November 2003, and legalization of same-sex civil marriages occurred for the first time when the ruling went into effect in May 2004 (Belluck, 2004). The degree to which same-sex marriages undertaken in Massachusetts will or will not be recognized in other states is not yet known.

A different approach to legal recognition for same-sex couples can be found in Vermont, which as of 2000, began to offer same-sex couples the right to obtain civil unions (Baker v. State, 1999; Goldberg, 2000a, 2000b; Moats, 2004). Civil unions allow couples who enter into them to obtain the same rights and responsibilities under state law as marriages; they do not, however, carry any federal rights or responsibilities. Thus, although civil unions represent an extremely important form of legal recognition for same-sex couples, and although they carry many important rights and protections, they are not identical in these respects to civil marriage. Nevertheless, many same-sex couples have undertaken civil unions in Vermont and have been accorded various forms of legal recognition for their relationships as a result (Solomon, Rothblum, & Balsam, 2004). Vermont thus became the first state in the United States to recognize same-sex couples under state law (Baker v. State, 1999; Goldberg, 2000a, 2000b).

Yet another approach to provision of certain legal rights and responsibilities for same-sex couples is to allow legal and other recognition of domestic partnerships. In September 2003, when former Governor Gray Davis signed a sweeping domestic-partnership bill, California became the second state to eliminate most forms of discrimination against same-sex couples under state law (Jones & Vogel, 2003). When the law went into effect in January 2005, it conferred nearly all the rights, benefits, and responsibilities accorded to married spouses under state law (Jones & Vogel, 2003). These include health-related rights and protections (e.g., access to employer-provided health and retirement benefits for partner and children), increased financial and emotional security (e.g., exemption from taxation of gifts, inheritance rights), and many protections for children (e.g., streamlined second-parent adoption and couple adoption processes). A similar bill was passed in New Jersey, in January 2004 (Mansnerus, 2004), and went into effect there in July 2004. The implementation of these domestic-partner laws is no doubt already transforming the experiences of same-sex couples in these states in many ways.

These and other kinds of recognition for same-sex couples form the leading edge of legal and policy change in the United States today. In addition to these alterations in state and federal law, there have been many changes in local laws and in employment settings that are relevant to lesbian and gay couples. For instance, 16 states and the District of Columbia now have in place laws, and 11 more states have executive orders, that prohibit workplace discrimination based on sexual orientation (National Gay and Lesbian Task Force, 2005b). In addition, many cities and counties have instituted non-discrimination policies that include sexual orientation. Numerous employers have adopted nondiscrimination policies and offer domestic-partner benefits, including 228 of the Forbes 500 companies and 280 colleges and universities in the United States (Human Rights Campaign, 2005b, 2005c). Such changes vary dramatically in their nature, with some proving to be more meaningful than others, but the trend for increasing recognition of equal employment rights is clear (Badgett, 2001).

One result of recent changes is that what was once a unitary experience of discrimination and oppression for same-sex couples in the United States has now been transformed into many very different experiences. A same-sex couple in Vermont who have undertaken a civil union—and are recognized as a couple for purposes of health insurance, homeowners insurance, and automobile insurance coverage—are likely to be open about their couple status and to be recognized as a couple by friends, neighbors, and family members. Same-sex couples in Wyoming, on the other hand, do not have the option of a marriage, civil union, or domestic partnership, do not receive the legal or economic benefits that accompany marriage or domestic partnership, may feel the need to hide their sexual identity and relationship status from many if not most of the important people in their environment, and hence may also encounter various problems with friends, neighbors, and family members. In short, given the uneven pace of change in different parts of the country, lesbian and gay couples who live in different jurisdictions are likely to live in very different circumstances.

The legal and policy situation with regard to the issues of lesbian and gay parents is also highly variable across the United States today, with some states providing more favorable environments than others (Patterson,

Fulcher, & Wainwright, 2002). Automatic legal recognition of parent–child bonds for all children born into a union—taken for granted by married heterosexual couples and their children—may be available to same-sex couples and their children in Massachusetts, but such inherent recognition is not yet available in any other state. In some states, lesbian and gay parents can use second-parent adoptions to create legal ties between their children and both parents in a same-sex couple (Connolly, 2001; Patterson, 1995a). In other states (e.g., Florida), nonheterosexual adults are explicitly barred from adoptive parenthood under the law (Patterson et al., 2002).

Looking at law and policy relevant to adoption and foster care, most states do not discriminate against prospective adoptive or foster parents on the basis of sexual orientation (Patterson et al., 2002). Only four states have laws or administrative policies that restrict or prohibit foster or adoptive parenting by lesbian and gay adults (National Gay and Lesbian Task Force, 2005a, 2005c). In the other 46 states and in the District of Columbia, state laws do not discriminate against lesbian or gay individuals who wish to become foster or adoptive parents. Results of a recent survey of adoption agencies across the country revealed that many are open to working with lesbian and gay prospective adoptive parents (Brodzinsky, Patterson, & Vaziri, 2002).

Second-parent adoption is a legal procedure that allows a same-sex coparent to adopt his or her partner's child, so as to create legal ties between the child and both parents (Patterson et al., 2002; Patterson & Redding, 1996). As of this writing, 8 states and the District of Columbia have appellate-level decisions on the books that allow second-parent adoptions, and at least 15 more states have seen favorable rulings on second-parent adoptions from lower courts (Human Rights Campaign, 2005a). Only four states— Colorado, Nebraska, Ohio, and Wisconsin—have appellate rulings that do not allow second-parent adoptions (National Gay and Lesbian Task Force, 2005c). Almost half of the states have reported no rulings on this issue, with the result being that in most jurisdictions, children of lesbian and gay parents are without the legal ties to both parents that are taken for granted in other families.

Another important area of family law concerns custody and visitation arrangements, especially after the separation or divorce of parenting couples. Opposite-sex couples who divorce after one person declares a nonheterosexual identity may turn to the courts to adjudicate custody and visitation plans for their minor children. For many years, courts across the country were hostile to the interests of lesbian and gay parents and their children, even going so far in some cases as to hold them unfit as parents as a result of their sexual orientation (Maggiore, 1992; Swisher & Cook, 2001). In recent years, such blatant discrimination has become less common, although egregious decisions do still occur (Howard, 2002). Most common now is the so-called nexus standard, holding that a parent's sexual orientation should be presumed irrelevant to custody proceedings unless it can be shown to have had a negative effect upon the children (Patterson et al., 2002).

Overall, though undeniably improved over recent years, the legal and policy landscape for lesbian and gay parents and their children still varies widely from one jurisdiction to another. For example, in Vermont, a same-sex couple in a civil union with children may also complete a second-parent adoption and in this way achieve many of the benefits and protections afforded to married heterosexual couples and their children. In Colorado, however, and in a number of other states, neither civil unions nor second-parent adoptions are available to same-sex couples and their children, and hence their family relationships go without protection from the law.

These issues are highlighted by a still-ongoing case involving child custody and visitation. Janet Miller-Jenkins and Lisa Miller-Jenkins, a lesbian couple who had lived together in Virginia since 1998, traveled to Vermont in 2000 to enter into a civil union. After they returned to Virginia, Lisa conceived and gave birth to a baby, Isabella, whom the couple began raising as their daughter. Taking Isabella with them, Lisa and Janet moved to Vermont in 2002. In 2003, Lisa filed to dissolve the civil union in Vermont. Janet successfully petitioned the Vermont court for full visitation rights with Isabella. Not wishing to comply with the Vermont court ruling, Lisa moved with Isabella back to Virginia. Now calling herself a "former lesbian," Lisa successfully petitioned a Virginia court to overturn the Vermont visitation decision. Calling Janet "no more than a friend" to Lisa and to Isabella, the Virginia judge disallowed visitation rights that had been stipulated by the Vermont court (Kalita, 2004). The case is currently on appeal in both states. Meanwhile, the case highlights the very different situations of lesbian and gay parents and their children in different jurisdictions.

LESBIAN AND GAY INDIVIDUALS AND THEIR FAMILIES OF ORIGIN

Against this backdrop of stigma and discrimination, lesbian and gay people's issues as members of extended families are likely to be complex (D'Augelli & Patterson, 2001; Patterson & D'Augelli, 1998). In addition to the usual issues of young adults that involve renegotiation of family roles as they transition into adult work, couple relationships, and parenthood, lesbian and gay young adults often face additional concerns. The establishment of work and career patterns, the creation of sexual and romantic connections, and the transition to parenthood—all normative tasks of early adulthood—may well pose special concerns for lesbian and gay young adults, particularly in their relationships with members of their extended families.

Consider first the young adult's employment concerns (Badgett, 2001, 2003). One issue is the existence of specific discriminatory policies, such as the U.S. military's infamous "don't ask, don't tell" policy (Herek, Jobe, & Carney, 1996). Considering that the military services are the nation's largest single employer, this policy alone places significant limitations upon the employment options available to openly lesbian or gay adults. Antigay prejudice and discrimination are believed to be particularly common in some lines of work (e.g., professional sports), so openly lesbian or gay adults may see their options in these areas as limited by attitudes toward sexual orientation (Badgett, 2001, 2003). Consider also the fact that family businesses may be controlled by relatives whose attitudes about homosexuality can vary across the spectrum of opinion. Other things being equal, lesbian women and gay men are unlikely to seek out work situations in which they will work for people with negative attitudes about homosexuality.

How will these issues be discussed with members of an extended family? Depending upon the extent of disclosure of nonheterosexual identities, these discussions may be open and clear, on the one hand, or limited and difficult, on the other. Those who do not feel safe disclosing their identities to members of their extended families are also going to experience difficulty explaining why their career choices are more limited than those of their heterosexual siblings. One result may often be an emotional distancing of lesbian and gay young adults from members of the extended family to whom they have not disclosed their nonheterosexual identities (Savin-Williams, 2003).

If a lesbian or gay man has kept her or his sexual identity secret from some or all members of her or his extended family, then this will almost certainly decrease the degree to which it is possible to share information about sexual and romantic dimensions of her or his life (D'Augelli & Patterson, 2001; Savin-Williams, 2003). Even if lesbian and gay family members have disclosed their sexual identities to members of their extended families, they still may encounter reluctance on the part of family members to entertain any real discussion of sexual or even romantic interests. Older family members or those who harbor especially negative attitudes may find it particularly difficult to acknowledge same-sex couple relationships. Again, one result may be the emotional distancing of lesbian and gay young adults from members of the extended family who feel unable to acknowledge the sexual or romantic interests in their lives (Savin-Williams, 2003).

Another process that necessitates renegotiation of roles in families involves the young adult's transition to parenthood, and this process may be especially challenging for lesbian and gay individuals and couples (Patterson, 1994, 1996). If nonheterosexual identities remain undisclosed in the context of transitions to parenthood, problems in family communication are almost certain to arise. Even when nonheterosexual identities are acknowledged by all members of an extended family, however, heterosexual family members may express surprise or disapproval at the thought of a lesbian or gay family member wishing to become a parent (Patterson, 1996). Especially since the legal and policy contexts in most jurisdictions fail to provide legal recognition for same-sex parents' relationships with each other and with children, members of the extended family may find themselves entertaining many questions that would not be raised for heterosexual siblings. Indeed, in many situations, prospective grandparents may be puzzled about the extent to which they should view themselves as grandparents at all (Patterson, 1996). All these and many related issues are likely to provide challenges as families seek to renegotiate roles and relationships upon the birth of a child.

Depending upon the family's response, challenges of these kinds can bring widely different outcomes (Patterson, 1996). The failure to acknowledge and tolerate a family member's homosexuality can result in distancing and other failures of communication and can in this way work against family cohesion. On the other hand, when families successfully respond to such challenges by acknowledging and including nonheterosexual family members, their partners, and children, families may become more cohesive. When a family is flexible enough to meet these kinds of challenges, real benefits may ensue for the entire family (Martin, 1998; Patterson, 1996).

These processes are deeply affected by the legal and policy contexts in which they take place. In jurisdictions where it is possible to do so, family members may have attended (and may become aware of the legal force of) a couple's marriage or civil union. The members of a couple's extended family may also recognize the impact of second-parent adoptions that legalize the bonds between children and both of their same-sex parents. In a state such as Vermont, these and other legal and policy conditions may aid in the extended family's ability to acknowledge and even embrace the nonheterosexual family member and his or her partner and children. In other states, where none of these options is open to same-sex couples, families have fewer supports as they seek to accommodate nonheterosexual family members. Thus, to the extent that legal and policy environments are influential, the experiences of lesbian and gay couples and families in different jurisdictions are likely to diverge.

PSYCHOSOCIAL ISSUES FOR COUPLES

In the context of an extremely diverse and rapidly changing patchwork of law and policy, lesbian and gay couples must somehow negotiate the various issues posed by their daily lives. Of course, all couples, whether same-sex or opposite-sex, must navigate issues of work, sexuality, and power, and all must decide how to build and maintain their social networks of friends and family members. In addition, however, special issues arise for same-sex couples (Patterson, 2000; Peplau & Spalding, 2003), and it is on these issues that the subsequent discussion focuses. Instead of attempting an exhaustive treatment, the discussion focuses on selected issues that exemplify differences in the experience of same-sex and opposite-sex couples, as well as the differences among same-sex couples living in different jurisdictions.

A central issue for lesbian and gay couples concerns the question of how open to be with regard to sexual identities. How safe is it, in various settings, for members of a couple to be open about their lesbian or gay identities as individuals or as members of a couple? Different environments may provide objectively different kinds of incentives and disincentives for disclosure. Individuals in some employment settings may be subject to job discrimination or even loss of employment if they are open about their sexual orientation (Badgett, 2001, 2003). In other employment settings, it may feel much safer to disclose nonheterosexual identities. Likewise, family, neighborhood, and community environments vary widely in their treatment of lesbian or gay individuals (D'Augelli & Garnets, 1995). The costs and benefits of disclosure may therefore differ markedly from one setting to the next.

If members of a couple see costs and benefits of disclosure in the same terms, and if their respective work and social environments afford the same patterns of incentives and disincentives for openness, then they are likely to reach similar decisions about disclosure (Patterson, 2000; Patterson et al., 2002). It is, however, often the case that members of a couple experience different environments in this respect. For instance, one person's parents may be tolerant whereas the other's parents cannot accept nonheterosexual identities. One person's employment setting may welcome diversity whereas the other's work environment may reject those with nonheterosexual identities. In such cases, partners may disagree about the appropriate degree of openness with regard to their sexual identities and their couple status.

When there is disagreement within a couple, negotiation of issues surrounding disclosure of lesbian or gay identities is likely to be a difficult and anxiety-provoking issue (Martin, 1993, 1998; Patterson, 1994). Particularly if existing child-custody or visitation arrangements are placed at risk if a parent decides to disclose his or her nonheterosexual identity (e.g., in locales where lesbian and gay parents are disadvantaged by discriminatory legal precedents), then this can be an especially emotion-laden issue. As more and more environments become safer, and as more and more lesbian and gay individuals opt for full disclosure, problems of this sort are likely to decrease in importance. Until that time, however, many couples must grapple with issues about when, where, and whether to come out.

Another issue worth highlighting is that of division of labor (Patterson, 2000; Peplau & Spalding, 2003). How does a couple divide the paid and unpaid labor involved in their lives? And how does this differ for same-sex and opposite-sex couples? It is well-known that most opposite-sex couples tend to adopt specialized divisions of labor, in which husbands devote themselves more to paid employment and wives spend more time in unpaid household labor and child care. In dual-earner families, the pattern is often less pronounced, but even among two-career heterosexual couples, patterns of specialization can generally be observed. The divisions of labor adopted by same-sex couples, however, appear to be quite different (Patterson, Sutfin, & Fulcher, 2004).

Same-sex couples are much more likely than heterosexual couples to adopt egalitarian patterns, with both members of the couple participating equally in both paid and unpaid labor (Chan, Brooks, Raboy, & Patterson, 1998; Kurdek, 1995; Patterson, 1995b; Patterson et al., 2004). For example, in a recent study of lesbian and heterosexual couples, all of whom were rearing young children, lesbian mothers each spent about 35 hours per week, on average, in paid employment, and they reported sharing childcare evenly (Patterson et al., 2004). In contrast, heterosexual husbands averaged 45 or more hours per week in paid employment, and heterosexual wives averaged about 15 hours per week in paid employment but were primarily responsible for childcare (Patterson et al., 2004). A striking aspect of the results was that, when hours of paid employment for the two members of a couple were summed, they reached about 70 hours per week for both family types; family incomes were likewise similar across family type. In other words, given about the same amount of overall labor to divide, lesbian couples were more likely than heterosexual couples to do so in an egalitarian fashion. This result is consistent with a wide array of data from studies conducted both in the United States and abroad, and similar findings have been reported for gay as well as lesbian couples (Kurdek, 1995; Patterson, 2000, 2002a; Peplau & Spalding, 2003).

Why do same-sex couples seem so much more likely than opposite-sex couples to adopt egalitarian divisions of labor? At least one possible factor may be the legal and policy environments in which the couples live (Patterson et al., 2004). Given their relative lack of access to legal protections, health insurance, and other financial benefits for a nonemployed partner, same-sex couples may favor egalitarian divisions of labor because these help to protect both partners in the event that they someday terminate their relationship. Due to lack of protections, same-sex partners who forego paid employment in order to devote themselves to the unpaid labor involved in home and family maintenance become more vulnerable economically than do heterosexual partners who divide labor in a similar way.

If the economic vulnerabilities of same-sex couples are an important factor in determining their division of labor, then the practice might be expected to shift when law and policies change (Patterson, 2004). For instance, if marriages and civil unions become generally available and domestic-partner benefits become widespread, then some of the economic vulnerabilities of a stay-at-home partner might be reduced. Will the opportunity for same-sex couples to undertake civil marriages result in their adoption of more "traditional" (i.e., specialized) divisions of labor? Or will other factors such as ideological commitments dominate such decision-making processes? There can be little doubt that legal and policy contexts, just as they do for opposite-sex couples, provide the background against which decisions about division of labor are made by same-sex couples. We do not know, however, how decisive these factors have been for decision-making about division of labor among lesbian and gay couples (Patterson, 2004; Patterson et al., 2004).

PSYCHOSOCIAL ISSUES FOR PARENTS

Just as legal and policy contexts affect decisions made by couples, so they also provide the background against which lesbian and gay parents make decisions relevant to their children. Issues that couples must grapple with about whether, when, and how to become parents are resolved in the context of existing law and policy (Patterson, 1994; Patterson et al., 2002). Lesbian couples who are expecting to give birth have been known to rush across state lines during labor in order for the child to be born in a state with favorable legal precedents. Lesbian couples have been known to move their home across county or state lines in order to complete a second-parent adoption. Lesbian and gay couples routinely seek out neighborhoods and schools that they believe will provide safe environments in which to rear and educate their children (Casper & Schultz, 1999). On the other hand, in matters that concern adoption, foster care, custody, and visitation, lesbian and gay parents have many times run afoul of discriminatory legal policies and precedents (Patterson et al., 2002; Patterson & Redding, 1996). As parents, lesbian and gay individuals and couples must take law and policy into account as they attempt to create, maintain, and protect their families.

One important area in which law and policy must be considered concerns becoming a parent (Buell, 2001; Patterson, 1994). In addition to all the usual concerns of prospective parents (e.g., will we able to support a child? will we be good parents?), lesbian and gay prospective parents must consider many additional questions that focus on legal and policy questions. For example, lesbian couples who wish to have a child via donor insemination may discover that not every clinic or sperm bank is willing to work with them, though many are (Chan, Raboy, & Patterson, 1998; Patterson, 1994). A recent study of the screening practices of assisted reproductive technology programs in the United States (Gurmankin, Caplan, & Braverman, 2005) found that 82% were willing to work with lesbian couples seeking donor insemination and 44% were willing to work with gay couples seeking to make surrogacy arrangements.

In a similar vein, gay couples who wish to adopt a child may discover that not every adoption agency is willing to work with gay men, though many are (Patterson, 1995). In a national survey of agencies in the United States (Brodzinsky, Patterson, & Vaziri, 2002), 63% of respondents indicated willingness to work with lesbian and gay applicants, and more than a third reported having completed a recent adoption placement with a lesbian or gay adult. On the other hand, in Florida, lesbian and gay adults are barred from becoming adoptive parents (Buell, 2001). Thus, in adoption, as in other pathways to parenthood, decisions are framed by specific aspects of the varied legal and policy environments in which lesbian and gay couples live (Patterson, 1994, 2000).

Even after becoming parents, lesbian and gay couples may find many of their choices constrained in unwelcome ways by the legal and policy situation in the area where they live (Patterson, 1994). In making decisions about parental employment options, for example, couples may find that health insurance coverage for children is available through one but not another partner's employer and may thus be forced to make decisions about division of labor that are different than those that they would make on other grounds. Even though children may in fact live with two same-sex parents, the case may be in some areas that only one of the adults is accorded parental status in law. In many jurisdictions, the possibility of a second-parent adoption may be more of a remote hope than a realistic possibility (Connolly, 2001). The parent who has been excluded from legal standing may also be barred from decision-making about medical or educational matters for children, and the family's decisions about allocation of many tasks may be constrained by these and other forms of legal and policy discrimination. Especially in jurisdictions that grant little or no recognition to family relationships in families headed by same-sex couples, these and related problems can generate considerable stress in otherwise well-functioning families (Martin, 1998).

One specific form that such challenges can take, especially in jurisdictions that do not allow second-parent adoptions, involves boundary issues (Martin, 1993, 1998; Patterson, 1996, 2000). When one parent does and the other parent does not have parental rights and responsibilities in the eyes of the law, it can also raise questions in the minds of school and medical personnel, friends, neighbors, and members of the extended family about whether both partners are "real" parents. For example, taking up the law's failure to legitimize familial links, extended family members can find themselves questioning the depth and extent of parent–child bonds or may fail to recognize them altogether. When this happens, couples may have to exert remarkable efforts to clarify the situation and demand recognition for important family relationships (Johnson & O'Connor, 2001; Martin, 1998).

CONCLUSION

The legal and social policy contexts of lesbian and gay Americans' lives vary enormously from one jurisdiction to another. Real progress against many forms of discrimination has occurred in recent years. At the national level, decriminalization of private consensual sexual behavior between same-sex partners—that is, the demise of the sodomy laws—is an important development. In states such as Vermont, Massachusetts, California, and New Jersey, significant changes in the degree of legal recognition for same-sex couples have occurred. On the other hand, it is still true that most lesbian and gay Americans live in jurisdictions that do not recognize their couple relationships, that may not recognize their parent–child relationships, and that do not protect them from employment discrimination based on sexual orientation. True equality under the law still eludes lesbian and gay citizens in every corner of the United States.

The contexts of legalized discrimination that most lesbian and gay individuals inhabit result in many special challenges. Issues arise for young adults negotiating relationships with members of extended families, for couples, and for parents. Considered as a group, these issues suggest important directions for research, advocacy, and practice.

RESEARCH DIRECTIONS

Research on the lives of lesbian and gay adults is needed to document the many ways in which experiences are affected by institutionalized legal discrimination. The study of gay-related stress is already well underway (e.g., Meyer, 2003; Smith & Ingram, 2004). Research should also explore subjective experiences and symptoms in relation to characteristics of diverse legal and policy environments. Some efforts have been made to link experiences of discrimination with important behavioral and mental health outcomes, but more such research is needed (Diaz & Ayala, 2001; Meyer, 2003).

In view of rapid changes in legal and social policy environments that are occurring in some jurisdictions, social scientists are also faced with unusual opportunities to study the impact of such change upon human behavior. For example, how are relationships affected when legal recognition for them becomes available? There are first-person descriptions about the impact of second parent adoptions, and a few researchers have begun to study same-sex couples who have undertaken civil unions in Vermont (Solomon et al., 2004), but there is much still to do in this area.

DIRECTIONS FOR ADVOCACY

It is clear that many changes in law and policy are needed before lesbian and gay Americans can achieve equality under the law. There is a tremendous opportunity for advocacy in this area, and the agenda is a lengthy one. In the limited space available here, it is possible to focus briefly on only a few specific issues.

One important recommendation is the legalization of same-sex marriage throughout the United States (Patterson, 2002a, 2002b). Legal marriages for same-sex couples would offer many benefits, both for society at large and for the individuals, couples, and families involved. For partners and children, improved access to health insurance through two places of employment instead of only one would be an immediate benefit. Beyond this, many other tangible and intangible benefits would ensue. These would involve Social Security and inheritance benefits on the one hand and feelings of security and protection from stigma and discrimination on the other. Some of the benefits of marriage could also be achieved through legal recognition of domestic-partnership agreements or civil unions for same-sex couples, as in California or Vermont.

Another direction for advocacy is the legalization of adoption and foster care by lesbian and gay adults, including second-parent adoption, in all the states. In some states (e.g., Florida), this would involve repeal of existing antigay statutes. In other states, necessary changes would be less dramatic. Children and their families would benefit from legal and policy environments that do not discriminate on the basis of sexual orientation (Patterson et al., 2002).

Another important legal protection needed by lesbian and gay Americans is the assurance of equal employment rights (Badgett, 2003). Passage of the federal Employment Non-Discrimination Act (ENDA) would protect lesbian and gay Americans from employment discrimination based on sexual orientation (Human Rights Campaign, 2005a). Although ENDA makes exceptions for military and religious groups, as well as for small businesses, it nevertheless would provide far greater protection than is currently available, and its effects would be felt nationwide.

DIRECTIONS FOR CLINICAL PRACTICE

A number of recommendations can also be offered from the standpoint of clinical practice. Many important points are contained in the American Psychological Association's "Guidelines for Psychotherapy With Lesbian, Gay, and Bisexual Clients" (Division 44/Committee on Lesbian, Gay, and Bisexual Concerns Joint Task Force, 2000), and practitioners should begin by becoming familiar with this document. In addition to these guidelines, a few more ideas can be offered.

First, it is essential to be aware of the diversity that characterizes experiences of lesbian and gay individuals, as a function of the fit between their identities and their legal environments. Even if they live in the same neighborhood, a lesbian woman who is parenting children in the context of a long-term couple relationship is likely to have very different issues than a young gay man who has no children and who is not currently involved in a romantic relationship. The very same people may have different experiences if they move from one jurisdiction to another, or if laws and policies in their jurisdiction change. Each person's individual experiences should be examined in light of the relevant legal and policy contexts, and these are likely to show considerable diversity.

It is worth considering also that class and ethnicity are likely to interact with legal and policy concerns. For example, a recent analysis of data from the 2000 U.S. Census suggests that same-sex couples who are Black are much more likely than those who are White to be parents of minor children (Dang & Frazer, 2004). In fact, 61% of Black female couples and 46% of Black male couples reported children under 18 years of age living in their households, whereas only 38% of White female couples and only 24% of White male couples reported this (Dang & Frazer, 2004). Thus, variations in law that disadvantage parents and their children can be expected to have more impact on Black than on White lesbian and gay parented families.

Second, as is evident from the first point, it is valuable for clinicians to become aware of legal and policy realities in their own area, insofar as these circumstances may be relevant to clients' experiences. Do local laws provide for domestic-partner registration, civil unions, or legal marriage? Do laws and policies permit adoption, foster care, and second-parent adoption by nonheterosexual prospective parents? Does the state or locality have laws prohibiting employment discrimination on the basis of sexual orientation? Lesbian and gay clients' struggles with financial and emotional issues associated with couple relationships, parenting, and the like will be understood properly only if their legal and policy contexts are considered.

Third, it can also be useful to assess clients' own levels of knowledge about relevant legal and policy issues. If clients are not well informed about a particular issue, practitioners can help by offering accurate information. In this way, practitioners can serve educational functions by directing clients' attention to relevant aspects of their environments. Clients are likely to feel more comfortable with practitioners who can demonstrate knowledge of laws and policies that are important to them.

Researchers, advocates, and practitioners can all play a role in creating a supportive environment for all Americans, regardless of sexual orientation (Kuehl, 2003). By studying the consequences of legalized discrimination, researchers can expose injustice when it occurs, and in this way, help to bring about its demise. By helping clients to adapt and by supporting them in their efforts to create needed changes, practitioners can assist their lesbian and gay clients' efforts to live meaningful lives against a backdrop of legalized discrimination. By pushing for better laws and policies, advocates can create a better environment for all. Working together, we can look forward to a day when lesbian and gay Americans will be equal citizens under the law.

REFERENCES

American Psychological Association, Division 44/Committee on Lesbian, Gay, and Bisexual Concerns Joint Task Force on Guidelines for Psychotherapy With Lesbian, Gay, and Bisexual Clients. (2000). Guidelines for psychotherapy with lesbian, gay, and bisexual clients. *American Psychologist, 55*, 1440–1451.

Badgett, M. V. L. (2001). *Money, myths, and change: The economic lives of lesbians and gay men.* Chicago: University of Chicago Press.

Badgett, M. V. L. (2003). Employment and sexual orientation: Disclosure and discrimination in the workplace. In L. D. Garnets & D. C. Kimmel (Eds.), *Psychological perspectives on lesbian, gay and bisexual experiences* (2nd ed.). New York: Columbia University Press.

Baker v. State, 170 Vt. 194, 242 (1999).

Belluck, P. (2004, February 5). Massachusetts gives new push to gay marriage. *The New York Times*, p. A1, col. 6.

Brodzinsky, D. M., Patterson, C. J., & Vaziri, M. (2002). Adoption agency perspectives on lesbian and gay prospective parents: A national study. *Adoption Quarterly, 5*, 5–23.

Buell, C. (2001). Legal issues affecting alternative families: A therapist's primer. *Journal of Gay & Lesbian Psychotherapy, 4*, 75–90.

Casper, V., & Schultz, S. B. (1999). *Gay parents, straight schools.* New York: Columbia University Teacher's College Press.

Chan, R. W., Brooks, R. C., Raboy, B., & Patterson, C. J. (1998). Division of labor among lesbian and heterosexual parents: Associations with children's adjustment. *Journal of Family Psychology, 12*, 402–419.

Chan, R. W., Raboy, B., & Patterson, C. J. (1998). Psychosocial adjustment among children conceived via donor insemination by lesbian and heterosexual mothers. *Child Development, 69*, 443–457.

Connolly, C. (2001). The description of gay and lesbian families in second-parent adoption cases. In J. M. Lehmann (Ed.), *The gay and lesbian marriage and family reader.* Lincoln: University of Nebraska Press.

Dang, A., & Frazer, S. (2004). *Black same-sex households in the United States.* Washington, DC: National Gay and Lesbian Task Force.

D'Augelli, A. R., & Garnets, L. D. (1995). Lesbian, gay and bisexual communities. In A. R. D'Augelli & C. J. Patterson (Eds.), *Lesbian, gay and bisexual identities over the lifespan: Psychological perspectives.* New York: Oxford University Press.

D'Augelli, A. R., & Patterson, C. J. (Eds.). (2001). *Lesbian, gay and bisexual identities among youth: Psychological perspectives.* New York: Oxford University Press.

Diaz, R. M., & Ayala, G. (2001). *Social discrimination and health: The case of Latino gay men and HIV risk.* New York: Policy Institute of the National Gay and Lesbian Task Force.

Goldberg, C. (2000a, April 25). Vermont gives final approval to same-sex unions. *The New York Times*, p. A14, col. 1.

Goldberg, C. (2000b, July 2). In Vermont, gay couples head for the almost altar. *The New York Times*, sec. 1, p. 10, col. 3.

Goodridge v. Department of Public Health, 440 Mass. 309 SJC-08860 (2003).

Gurmankin, A. D., Caplan, A. L., & Braverman, A. M. (2005). Screening practices and beliefs of assisted reproductive technology programs. *Fertility and Sterility, 83*, 61–67.

Herek, G. W. (2003). *Sexual prejudice: Prevalence.* Retrieved January 28, 2004, from http://psychology.ucdavis.edu/rainbow/html/prej_prev.html

Herek, G. W., Jobe, J. B., & Carney, R. M. (1996). *Out in force: Sexual orientation and the military.* Chicago: University of Chicago Press.

Howard, J. (2002, July 14). Gay father's custody battle touches a nerve in Idaho. *Idaho Statesman.*

Human Rights Campaign. (2005a). *Documenting discrimination.* Retrieved February 10, 2005, from http://www.hrc.org

Human Rights Campaign. (2005b). *Domestic partner benefits.* Retrieved February 10, 2005, from http://www.hrc.org

Human Rights Campaign. (2005c). *Nondiscrimination laws.* Retrieved February 10, 2005, from http://www.hrc.org

Johnson, S. M., & O'Connor, E. (2001). *For lesbian parents: Your guide to helping your family grow up happy, healthy, and proud.* New York: Guilford Press.

Jones, G., & Vogel, N. (2003, September 20). Domestic partners law expands gay rights. *The Los Angeles Times*, p. A1.

Kalita, S. (2004, August 25). Vt. same-sex unions null in Va., judge says—Case seen as test of parent rights. *The Washington Post*, p. B01.

Kuehl, S. (2003). Seeing is believing: Research on women's sexual orientation and public policy. In L. D. Garnets & D. C. Kimmel (Eds.), *Psychological perspectives on lesbian, gay and bisexual experiences* (2nd ed., pp. 786–795). New York: Columbia University Press.

Kurdek, L. A. (1995). Lesbian and gay couples. In A. R. D'Augelli & C. J. Patterson (Eds.), *Lesbian, gay and bisexual identities over the lifespan: Psychological perspectives* (pp. 243–261). New York: Oxford University Press.

Lawrence v. Texas, 123 S. Ct. 2472, 2480 (2003).

Maggiore, D. J. (Ed.). (1992). *Lesbians and child custody: A casebook.* New York: Garland.

Mansnerus, L. (2004, January 9). New Jersey to recognize gay couples. *The New York Times*, sec. B, p. 1, col. 5.

Martin, A. (1993). *The lesbian and gay parenting handbook.* New York: HarperCollins.

Martin, A. (1998). Clinical issues in psychotherapy with lesbian-, gay-, and bisexual-parented families. In C. J. Patterson & A. R. D'Augelli (Eds.), *Lesbian, gay and bisexual identities in families: Psychological perspectives*. New York: Oxford University Press.

Meyer, I. H. (2003). Prejudice, stress, and mental health in lesbian, gay, and bisexual populations: Conceptual issues and research evidence. *Psychological Bulletin, 129*, 674–697.

Moats, D. (2004). *Civil wars: A battle for gay marriage*. Orlando, FL: Harcourt.

Murdoch, J., & Price, D. (2001). *Courting justice: Gay men and lesbians v. the Supreme Court*. New York: Basic Books.

National Gay and Lesbian Task Force. (2005a). *Adoption/foster care laws in the United States*. Retrieved February 10, 2005, from http://www.ngltf.org/downloads/adoptionmap.pdf

National Gay and Lesbian Task Force. (2005b). *GLBT civil rights laws in the United States*. Retrieved February 10, 2005, from http://www.ngltf.org/downloads/civilrightsmap.pdf

National Gay and Lesbian Task Force (2005c). *Second-parent/Stepparent adoption in the United States (map)*. Retrieved February 10, 2005, from http://www.ngltf.org/downloads/secondparentadoptionmap.pdf

Patterson, C. J. (1994). Lesbian and gay couples considering parenthood: An agenda for research, service, and advocacy. *Journal of Gay & Lesbian Social Services, 1*, 33–55.

Patterson, C. J. (1995a). Adoption of minor children by lesbian and gay adults: A social science perspective. *Duke Journal of Gender Law and Policy, 2*, 191–205.

Patterson, C. J. (1995b). Families of the lesbian baby boom: Parents' division of labor and children's adjustment. *Developmental Psychology, 31*, 115–123.

Patterson, C. J. (1996). Contributions of lesbian and gay parents and their children to the prevention of heterosexism. In E. D. Rothblum & L. A. Bond (Eds.), *Preventing heterosexism and homophobia* (pp. 184–201). Thousand Oaks, CA: Sage.

Patterson, C. J. (2000). Sexual orientation and family life: A decade review. *Journal of Marriage and the Family, 62*, 1052–1069.

Patterson, C. J. (2002a). Lesbian and gay parenthood. In M. H. Bornstein (Ed.), *Handbook of parenting* (2nd ed.). Hillsdale, NJ: Erlbaum.

Patterson, C. J. (2002b). Same-sex marriage and the interests of children: Comments on Michael Wald's "Same-sex couple marriage: A family policy perspective." *Virginia Journal of Social Policy and the Law, 9*, 345–351.

Patterson, C. J. (2004). What difference does a civil union make? Changing public policies and the experiences of same-sex couples: Commentary on Solomon, Rothblum and Balsam (2004). *Journal of Family Psychology, 18*, 287–289.

Patterson, C. J., & D'Augelli, A. R. (Eds.). (1998). *Lesbian, gay and bisexual identities in families: Psychological perspectives*. New York: Oxford University Press.

Patterson, C. J., Fulcher, M., & Wainright, J. (2002). Children of lesbian and gay parents: Research, law, and policy. In B. L. Bottoms, M. B. Kovera, & B. D. McAuliff (Eds.), *Children, social science and the law* (pp. 176–199). New York: Cambridge University Press.

Patterson, C. J., & Redding, R. (1996). Lesbian and gay families with children: Public policy implications of social science research. *Journal of Social Issues, 52,* 29–50.

Patterson, C. J., Sutfin, E. L., & Fulcher, M. (2004). Division of labor among lesbian and heterosexual parenting couples: Correlates of specialized versus shared patterns. *Journal of Adult Development, 11,* 179–189.

Peplau, L. A., & Spalding, L. R. (2003). The close relationships of lesbians, gay men, and bisexuals. In L. D. Garnets & D. C. Kimmel (Eds.), *Psychological perspectives on lesbian, gay and bisexual experiences* (2nd ed., pp. 449–474). New York: Columbia University Press.

Rouse, M. (2004, January 14). One gay family's Iowa adventure. *Advocate.com* [online exclusive]. Retrieved December 14, 2005, from http://wwww.advocate.com/exclusive_detail_ektid17778.asp

Rubenstein, W. B. (1996). Lesbians, gay men, and the law. In R. C. Savin-Williams & K. M. Cohen (Eds.), *The lives of lesbians, gays, and bisexuals: Children to adults* (pp. 331–344). New York: Harcourt Brace.

Savin-Williams, R. C. (2003). Lesbian, gay and bisexual youths' relationships with their parents. In L. D. Garnets & D. C. Kimmel (Eds.), *Psychological perspectives on lesbian, gay and bisexual experiences* (2nd ed., pp. 299–326). New York: Columbia University Press.

Smith, N. G., & Ingram, K. M. (2004). Workplace heterosexism and adjustment among lesbian, gay, and bisexual individuals: The role of unsupportive social interactions. *Journal of Counseling Psychology, 51,* 57–67.

Solomon, S. E., Rothblum, E. D., & Balsam, K. F. (2004). Pioneers in partnership: Lesbian and gay male couples in civil unions compared with those not in civil unions, and married heterosexual siblings. *Journal of Family Psychology, 18,* 275–286.

Sullivan, A. (Ed.). (1997). *Same-sex marriage: Pro and con.* New York: Vintage Books.

Swisher, P. N., & Cook, N. D. (2001). Bottoms v. Bottoms: In whose best interest? Analysis of a lesbian mother–child custody dispute. In J. M. Lehmann (Ed.), *The gay and lesbian marriage and family reader* (pp. 251–299). Lincoln: University of Nebraska Press.

16

PUBLIC POLICY, MENTAL HEALTH, AND LESBIAN, GAY, BISEXUAL, AND TRANSGENDER CLIENTS

MICHAEL R. STEVENSON

THE POLICY LANDSCAPE

The policy landscape changed dramatically in June 2003 when the U.S. Supreme Court decided in *Lawrence v. Texas* to overturn all remaining sodomy laws as well as an earlier Supreme Court decision, *Bowers v. Hardwick* (1986). Although rarely enforced, state courts had used those laws to justify anti-LGB discrimination. With laws and policies based on the idea that same-sex relationships are either immoral or in other ways less legitimate than other-sex relationships, heterosexism underlies cases that privilege heterosexuals in custody, visitation, and adoption as well as those concerning same-sex marriage and employment or housing discrimination (American Civil Liberties Union [ACLU], 1999, 2004).

Recent changes in the makeup of the U.S. Supreme Court make it even more difficult to predict the likely outcome of future cases. None

I wish to thank Clinton Anderson, Kathryn N. Black, Laura Brown, and Glenda Russell for their assistance and insight. Excerpts from an earlier version of this chapter were presented as part of the 2005 Presidential Address of the Society for the Psychological Study of Lesbian, Gay, and Bisexual Issues: A Division of the American Psychological Association at the annual convention on August 20, 2005, in Washington, DC.

the less, *Lawrence v. Texas* may yet provide the basis for a wide variety of changes in public policy. By confirming that persons in homosexual relationships have the right to define their own concepts "of existence, of meaning, of the universe, and of the mystery of human life," the Court affirmed that LGB people have the same rights as non-LGB people to build relationships and to decide what is important in life (ACLU, 2004). In effect, this decision provides a basis for making schools safe for lesbian, gay, bisexual, and transgender (LGBT)[1] students, it could change the way heterosexist courts decide custody cases, and it might provide the basis for building a LGBT-affirming body of employment and housing policy. At least, courts can no longer uphold anti-LGBT discrimination on the grounds that same-sex sexual behavior is illegal in some states.

In addition to *Lawrence v. Texas*, Massachusetts took the next step in legitimizing same-sex relationships when the Massachusetts Supreme Judicial Court ruled that the state "failed to identify any constitutionally adequate reason for denying civil marriage to same-sex couples" (Douglas-Brown, 2004). Legislators then began to debate whether the courts would support a "separate but equal" compromise and allow the legalization of civil unions for same-sex couples while leaving "marriage" a purely heterosexual (and therefore heterosexist) contract. In an advisory opinion released in February 2004, the court declared that "the history of our nation has demonstrated that separate is seldom, if ever, equal" and that legislation that would legalize same-sex civil unions but ban gay marriage creates "unconstitutional, inferior, and discriminatory status for same-sex couples" (Bean, 2004).

Given these historic court victories (as well as other developments summarized in Patterson, chap. 15, this volume), advocates who work toward LGBT-sensitive public policy may be tempted to take a well-deserved vacation. However, attempts to pass affirming legislation in the United States often lead to backlash, mostly from religious conservatives (Biaggio, Orchard, Larson, Petrino, & Mihara, 2003), and these particular advances have not gone unnoticed. In response to the court decisions, support for a Federal Marriage Amendment to the U.S. Constitution increased. President George W. Bush made explicit his support for a constitutional ban on same-sex marriage in his 2004 State of the Union address while announcing a $1.5 billion initiative to support "healthy" heterosexual marriages (Pear & Kirkpatrick, 2004). Some Massachusetts legislators who supported same-sex civil unions but opposed gay marriage chose to support amending the state constitution after hearing from the Massachusetts court. Campaigns supporting antigay

---

[1] Unfortunately, empirical research on transgender samples is still limited. As a result, I have included the "T" in "LGBT" when it is justified. However, when generalizing to other groups is inappropriate, I refer to LGB persons or only to lesbian and gay persons.

marriage measures, amendments to state constitutions, and broad measures that could also ban domestic partnerships and civil unions have swept the country, state by state. Furthermore, after years of increasing tolerance, a July 2003 Gallup Poll provided further evidence of the backlash in the attitudes of the general public (Newport, 2003).

Despite significant progress, LGBT people seeking support from the courts will need patience and stamina as judges continue to find justifications for discrimination. For example, only months after *Lawrence v. Texas*, the U.S. Circuit Court of Appeals ruled against four gay men who challenged a Florida law that bans lesbian and gay people from adopting children. The three-judge panel argued that this issue should be resolved by the legislature rather than the courts. Despite the weight of psychological evidence (see King, 2003; Patterson, chap. 15, this volume), the state argued (apparently successfully) that Florida has a right to "legislate its 'moral disapproval of homosexuality' and its belief that children need married parents for healthy development" (Wilson, 2004).

Similarly, in 2000, a Kansas appeals court upheld a prison sentence of 17 *years* for Matt Limon, who had been convicted of having consensual sex with a 15-year-old male when Matt had just turned 18. Had his sexual partner been female, the sentence would have been only 15 *months*. Ignoring the Lawrence decision, the court approved the disparity based on the belief that it reflects Kansas's moral judgment about gay youth. The court also indicated the lighter sentence for heterosexual youth was intended to encourage pregnancy and marriage and to get the perpetrator out of jail so that he could support the child! In 2003 the U.S. Supreme Court vacated the original decision, remanding the case to the Kansas court. Subsequently, that court upheld Limon's conviction. As a result, he is set to be released when he is 35 years old (ACLU, 2003; Kansas court, 2004; Seelly, 2004).

Regardless of the public's apparent ambivalence, the absence of explicit, governmentally enforced protections leads to continuing discrimination in employment and housing, as well as harassment, ostracism, assault, and hate crimes against LGBT persons (Biaggio et al., 2003). Therefore, it is more important than ever for mental health professionals to contribute to efforts to advance LGBT-positive public policy.

This chapter attempts to address a variety of interrelated issues concerning the involvement of counselors and therapists in LGBT-affirming advocacy. It begins by reminding readers of the fallacies in antigay rhetoric and the potential consequences of antigay campaigns. It then explores the positive consequences of involvement in advocacy for both clinicians and clients.

The Fallacies of Anti-LGBT Arguments

LGBT people are often portrayed as living a destructive "lifestyle." For example, Paul Cameron and his colleagues (e.g., Cameron & Cameron,

1996, 1998) have argued that lesbian and gay lives are defective and disease-ridden. They have also touted conversion therapies, including medication, as appropriate forms of treatment (see Haldeman, 1994; Herek, 1998). In addition to these misconceptions, anti-LGB advocates often attempt to use data on the high rates of suicide attempts and alcohol use among LGB youth as indicative of individual psychopathology rather than as consequences of oppression. There is little doubt that living in a homophobic and heterosexist society causes emotional stress. However, it is equally clear that the overwhelming majority of LGB people do not attempt suicide or abuse alcohol. In addition to articulating accurately the consequences of oppression, it is important to emphasize the resilience that members of LGBT communities exhibit in the face of prejudice.

For over half of the 20th century, homosexuality and bisexuality were assumed to be mental illnesses (Bieschke, McClanahan, Tozer, Grzegorek, & Park, 2000; Greene & Croom, 2000). However, when Evelyn Hooker first challenged this assumption in 1957 with a rigorous research methodology, she found no difference between nonclinical samples of heterosexual and homosexual men (Hooker, 1957). Subsequent research has demonstrated that comparable samples of gay, bisexual, and straight people do not differ with regard to variables such as cognitive abilities, psychological well-being, and self-esteem (American Psychological Association [APA], Division 44/ Committee on Lesbian, Gay, and Bisexual Concerns Joint Task Force, 2000). In short, an extensive body of research supports the conclusion that there are few significant or meaningful differences between people of different sexual orientations on a wide range of variables associated with overall psychological functioning. It is equally important to note that when differences between gay and straight people are found, such differences are appropriately attributed to the stress associated with stigmatization based on sexual orientation rather than to sexual orientation per se (APA, 2004a). This social stress may lead to increased risk for suicide attempts, substance abuse, and emotional distress (Morris & Hart, 2003).

It is not surprising that LGBT-affirming advocates do not always agree on the best means to achieve policy goals. Concerns about studies of suicide rates in LGBT youth and alcohol and tobacco use throughout LGBT communities are good examples. Highlighting differences between comparable LGBT and straight samples on such variables may be useful in emphasizing the effects of anti-LGBT prejudice and heightening the awareness of health professionals and mental health professionals regarding the specific concerns of these communities. However, anti-LGBT advocates use (and sometimes generate) such information to support their arguments that LGBT people are mentally unstable and lead unhealthy "lifestyles" (e.g., Family Research Institute, 1992). As a result, LGBT-affirming researchers may be hesitant to publish research that demonstrates significant differences between comparable LGBT and straight samples on measures of mental and physical health out of fear that such findings could be used to defeat LGBT-positive advocacy efforts. Given this tension, it is of utmost importance that researchers remain aware of the potential uses of research findings, political as well as scientific. Researchers should not hesitate to publish the results of sound research. However, they need to employ research designs that allow them to present data in ways that minimize misattribution and overgeneralization while accurately depicting the samples they study (Stevenson, 2002).

Despite claims of antigay advocates, health-related organizations across the country have taken an overwhelming and consistent stance affirming diversity in sexual expression. The American Psychiatric Association removed homosexuality from its list of mental disorders in 1973. In 1975 the American Psychological Association adopted a resolution stating, "Homosexuality *per se* implies no impairment in judgment, stability, reliability, or general social or vocational capabilities" (see http://www.apa.org/pi/lgbc/policies.html; Greene & Croom, 2000; Morris & Hart, 2003, pp. 60–61). Since then, other professional organizations have adopted similar positions, including the American Academy of Pediatrics (1993), the National Association of Social Workers (2002), and the American Psychoanalytic Association (n.d.). Similarly, the U.S. Surgeon General has proclaimed that health care and counseling should be free of stigmatization based on sexual orientation (Unites States Department of Health and Human Services, 2001).

Regardless of how many so-called ex-gay people testify before policymakers or appear in ad campaigns, sound research (see Morris & Hart, 2003) in peer-reviewed journals shows that LGB people are both resilient and as mentally healthy as any comparable group and that therapies intended to cure homosexuality are both ineffective and potentially damaging (Morrow & Beckstead, 2004). Moreover, as the following discussion suggests, evidence of the ill-effects of anti-LGB campaigns is growing.

Consequences of Anti-LGB Campaigns

Glenda Russell's *Voted Out* (2000) describes groundbreaking research on Colorado's Amendment 2 and illuminates the damaging effects of anti-LGB political campaigns and the rhetoric they spawn. Had it been implemented successfully, Amendment 2 would have excluded LGB sexual orientation from the protection of antidiscrimination laws anywhere in Colorado. To Colorado for Family Values (CFV), the amendment's primary advocate, that meant denying LGB people "special rights." To LGB Coloradoans and their allies, the amendment meant legalizing anti-LGB discrimination. An injunction by a district judge and subsequent rulings in the district court, the Colorado Supreme Court, and the U.S. Supreme Court prevented the amendment from ever going into effect. However, these court decisions could not undo the harm CFV's campaign had already wrought.

From the time the campaign began to after the passage of Amendment 2, Russell's informants reported significant increases in symptoms associated with generalized anxiety, depression, and posttraumatic stress. In fact, the number of diagnosable cases of these syndromes increased more than tenfold by the end of the campaign. Most participants in the study considered the experience traumatic in one way or another and reported physical and psychological symptoms associated with trauma. To describe their experience, they used words like *devastated, discouraged, weakened,* and *demoralized.* For some, the campaign revived memories of past physical assaults and other incidences of discrimination. Moreover, the fact that the majority of Colorado voters were willing to permit anti-LGB discrimination forced LGB Coloradoans to acknowledge the pervasiveness of anti-LGB prejudice (Russell, 2000).

This important work clearly documents the stress that anti-LGBT campaigns cause and can be seen as a call to action for mental health practitioners. The next section outlines how mental health professionals can use their clinical, pedagogical, and research skills to become better advocates.

ADVOCATING LGBT-POSITIVE POLICY

Making the reasonable assumption that public policy reflects the perspectives of those who make it (i.e., primarily male, European American, temporarily able-bodied, Christian, middle- or upper-class heterosexuals), how would public policy change if LGBT experience were taken as "core and central to definitions of reality" (Brown, 1989, p. 445) rather than as the experience of an "interest group" whose concerns are often disrespectfully caricatured as "special rights"? How would policymakers change their understanding of issues concerning parenting, education, and the workplace if they made assumptions based in the LGBT experience?

Few would advocate basing public policy solely on this view. Such an approach would be just as prejudicial as current policy. However, exploring this perspective might lead policymakers to potentially provocative insights. Take marriage as an example. Except for couples who seek only civil marriage (e.g., visit a justice of the peace), *marriage* is a conflation of two different processes. One is claimed by religion. The other is a civil contract. To the extent that marriage is a religious institution, one could consider the not-so-radical notion that governments have no specific interest in marriage. One solution to "gay marriage" then is to give marriage to the church. Religious institutions could choose for themselves what kinds of relationships they wished to recognize, whose marriages they wished to encourage, and whether or under what circumstances religious unions could be dissolved. The government, on the other hand, could develop its own rules without regard to belief systems that are imbedded in religious institutions. Legal recognition of such unions (e.g., civil unions) could therefore be sought by adult couples regardless of their genders or sexual orientations, whereas marriage would be constructed in purely religious terms. Clarifying the role of the church and the government in this way would certainly not prevent religious LGB people and other advocates from agitating for recognition from their respective churches. It would, however, allow the government to act in accordance with the secular nature of the U.S. Constitution (Jacoby, 2004) by providing all U.S. adults the opportunity to benefit from legal recognition of their relationships.

Moving beyond marriage, consider, for example, the consequences of applying this perspective to the legal meaning of *family*, to the "special rights" rhetoric of the radical right, to the "don't ask, don't tell" policy in the U.S. military, or to the federal government's exclusive endorsement of "abstinence only" approaches to sexuality education. In contrast to current assertions and perspectives, consider the possibility that successful parenting need have little to do with a potential parent's biological capacity to bear or sire the children, and consider the assertions that ensuring its vested interest in the welfare of children does not require the government to privilege one family form over others; that effective military policy governing sexual behavior need not vary with sexual orientation; or that every youth, LGBT or otherwise, deserves to attend a school that is safe, effective, and inclusive.

Applying a perspective centered in LGBT experience in the arena of public policy is a worthwhile exercise. It could lead to a variety of advances that would benefit U.S. citizens regardless of their sexual orientations. It could also lead to changes in policy that would bring government-endorsed discrimination to an end as it creates additional opportunities for greater equality. In the final analysis, neither a person's sexual orientation nor his or her private consensual sexual behavior should be a basis for denying equal legal treatment. As the next section suggests, LGBT-affirming counselors and therapists have important roles to play in this process of spreading that understanding.

Mental Health Professionals as Advocates

Mental health professionals can advocate as content experts, role models, and witnesses. We can help diminish the influence of heterosexist norms and influence the educational development of all health and mental health professionals. We can be affirming in our own work with clients, students, and research participants while supporting the work of LGBT-affirming professional organizations.

At a community level, we can redefine heterosexist social norms by creating institutional protections and safe climates so that LGBT people can be open about their identities (D'Augelli & Garnets, 1995). We can also facilitate public and organizational policies that provide equal status

EXHIBIT 16.1
URLs for Health-Related Organizations That Focus on LGBT Issues

American Psychological Association	http://www.apa.org
Society for the Psychological Study of Lesbian, Gay, and Bisexual Issues	http://www.apa.org/divisions/div44
National Association of Lesbian and Gay Addiction Professionals	http://www.nalgap.org
Gay and Lesbian Medical Association	http://www.glma.org
National Association of Lesbian, Gay, Bisexual, and Transgender Community Centers	http://www.lgbtcenters.org
Association of Gay and Lesbian Psychiatrists	http://www.aglp.org
National Coalition for LGBT Health	http://www.lgbthealth.net

and legal protection against discrimination through political advocacy, community organizing, and legislative lobbying.

In the educational context, we can develop curricula that prepare students to serve LGBT clients regardless of the students' own orientations while we contribute to learning environments that affirm diversity, broadly defined. LGBT students see relevant connections between their own sexual orientation and their identities as mental health professionals, but they may need guidance on how to negotiate these intersecting roles (Biaggio et al., 2003).

Mental health professionals can also be effective advocates by supporting and working within their disciplinary associations. By supporting LGBT-affirming organizations and coalitions (see Exhibit 16.1), practitioners can participate in efforts to improve health and mental health policy.

Actively supporting such organizations is important because not all health associations are affirming. For example, the Catholic Medical Association published a position paper entitled *Homosexuality and Hope* (2003). Rather than provide helpful advice based on scientific data, the paper revisited outdated theories and misrepresented the extant research while conflating science, morality, and theology (Georgemiller & Stevenson, 2003).

These brief examples show how mental health professionals can advocate through their local, educational, and professional communities. The next section demonstrates the importance of the advocacy work done by member organizations.

Advocacy Through Professional Associations

Our professional organizations also provide a variety of mechanisms that can be used to effect change. For example, the APA's Public Policy Office has been working to bring psychology's contributions to bear on issues related to sexual orientation for some time (see http://www.apa.org/ppo.html). In addition, the APA's Public Interest Directorate supports the Office of Lesbian, Gay, and Bisexual Concerns, which works to eliminate the stigma of mental illness historically associated with same-sex sexual orientation and to reduce prejudice, discrimination, and violence against LGB people. State and local advocacy on LGB concerns has been handled through the office in collaboration with the APA's Public Policy Office and the Practice Office on State Associations. The office has also facilitated the production of a wide variety of amicus briefs, reports, and policy statements that have had a dramatic impact in legal and policy contexts (e.g., APA, 2005; see also http://www.apa.org/pi/lgbc/publications/pubsreports.html).

The LGB Concerns office also supports the APA's Committee on Lesbian, Gay, and Bisexual Concerns (CLGBC). The CLGBC's charge includes the ongoing evaluation of issues that concern LGB psychologists, support of LGB-relevant research and LGB-affirming practice, and facilitation of the integration of these issues into the APA's advocacy work. The Office of LGB Concerns and the committee often collaborate with APA's Division 44 (The Society for the Psychological Study of Lesbian, Gay, and Bisexual Issues) in drafting policy statements and other significant documents supportive of advocacy efforts. APA's *Resolution on Appropriate Therapeutic Responses to Sexual Orientation* (1997), its "Guidelines for Psychotherapy With Lesbian, Gay, and Bisexual Clients" (2000), its *Resolution on Sexual Orientation and Marriage* (2004a), and its *Resolution on Sexual Orientation, Parents, and Children* (2004b) are especially important examples.

Advocacy coalitions are one of the most effective ways to affect policy debates (Cogan, 2003). The APA supports the Coalition to Protect Research (http://www.cossa.org/CPR/cpr.html), which lobbies against efforts to restrict funding for peer-reviewed research, including that focused on sexual behavior, and the National LGBT Health Coalition (http://www.lgbthealth.net), which convenes national meetings, sponsors the National LGBT Health Awareness Week, and briefs policymakers on LGBT health issues.

Psychologists contribute to these efforts by being members of APA and Division 44 and by serving on the boards and committees directly involved in this work. Similarly, the professional organizations listed in Exhibit 16.2 have passed resolutions concerning appropriate approaches to treatment for LGB clients (Morris & Hart, 2003; see also Bieschke, Paul, & Blasko, chap. 12, this volume).

In sum, mental health professionals already possess many relevant skills and much knowledge, and professional associations provide useful mechanisms for professionals to become effective advocates. A discussion of whether mental health professionals are morally obligated to support such efforts is beyond the scope of this chapter. However, it is important to consider the therapeutic value such advocacy might have for clients. This topic is addressed in the next section.

EXHIBIT 16.2
Excerpts From Mental Health Organization Resolutions Concerning
the Treatment of LGB Clients

Mental health organization	Excerpt
The American Academy of Pediatrics	*Therapy directed at specifically changing sexual orientation is contraindicated, since it can provoke guilt and anxiety while having little or no potential for achieving changes in orientation.*
The American Counseling Association	*The ACA . . . supports the dissemination of accurate information about sexual orientation, mental health, and appropriate interventions in order to counteract bias that is based in ignorance or unfounded beliefs about same-gender sexual orientation.*
The American Psychiatric Association	*The APA opposes any psychiatric treatment, such as "reparative" or "conversion" therapy, which is based upon the assumption that homosexuality per se is a mental disorder or based upon the a priori assumption that the patient should change his/her homosexual orientation.*
The American Psychoanalytic Association	*Psychoanalytic technique does not encompass efforts to "convert" or "repair" an individual's sexual orientation. Such directed efforts are against fundamental purposeful principles of psychoanalytic treatment and often result in substantial psychological pain by reinforcing damaging internalized homophobic attitudes.*
The National Association of Social Workers	*Increased media campaigns, often coupled with coercive messages from family and community members, has created an environment in which lesbians and gay men often are pressured to seek reparative or conversion therapies, which* **cannot and will not change sexual orientation.**

Note. The information in this table is based on Box 3.1, "Official Statements About Psychotherapy and Sexual Orientation" (pp. 60–61), in Morris and Hart (2003).

OUTNESS, ACTIVISM, AND THE MENTAL HEALTH OF CLIENTS

On a practical level, being involved in policy advocacy may be necessary in order to gain political support and funding for LGB-specific treatment programs or facilities (McDaniel, Cabaj, & Purcell, 1996). Without strong advocates, such programs may be very difficult to start and defend, especially in a climate of budget cuts and program reductions. Clearly, it is advantageous for service providers in LGB communities to be savvy advocates as well.

Empirical data concerning the influence of the therapist's sexual orientation are rare (Cabaj, 1996), and LGB psychologists have not reached consensus on the benefits or consequences of therapist's self-disclosure (see Coleman, 1989; Hancock, 2000; Morrow, 2000). However, the available data suggest that LGB people may be more likely to seek counseling from providers who have been trained to work with LGB clients or who identify as LGB themselves (Liddle, 1997; Murphy, Rawlings, & Howe, 2002), and clients who investigate their potential counselors' sexual orientation or attitudes about sexual orientation may be more satisfied with the services they receive (Liddle, 1997). Although coming out has been synonymous with LGBT-affirmative advocacy, at least for many European Americans (Smith, 1997), it is important to note that effective advocacy need not be related to one's sexual orientation.

Role Models and Witnesses

Involvement in advocacy not only enhances a practitioner's visibility and success in the community. It also creates opportunities to model healthy behavior and to act as a witness to oppression for potential clients and other members of LGBT communities.

The mental health professions are among the most receptive to LGB people and their allies. As a result, LGB-affirming therapists can be out and active in their professions and serve as pillars of LGB communities (Brown, 1996). Furthermore, therapists and counselors can serve as role models for their clients regardless of their sexual orientations (Cabaj, 1996; Rochlin, 1985).

Significant visibility in the community is not without cost. Heterosexual therapists who are allies may become suspected of being LGB themselves. Disapproving colleagues may question their LGB-affirmative advocacy. And they may struggle with how open to be about their role in the community (Morrow, 2000). Regardless of sexual orientation, such visibility can also create significant role overlap in which therapists and clients encounter each other in social or political settings as well as during service provision (Lynn, 1994). This situation can create ethical dilemmas for service providers (Brown, 1996), but it may also provide opportunities to model LGB pride and community involvement. As DeBord and Perez (2000) argued, such modeling can be "a powerful and facilitative therapeutic force" (p. 194).

In addition to being role models, counselors and therapists can act as effective witnesses to oppression. In the context of any stigma, whether resulting from racism, religious bigotry, or anti-LGB prejudice, in addition to a victim and a perpetrator, there is often a witness who can highlight the reactions of others to the victimization. In the best of situations, the witness validates that stigma or discrimination has occurred and offers support and a moral alternative to the perpetration (Russell, 2000).

Successful witnessing can take many forms. In November 2003, National Public Radio aired a report that described the work of a South African group called the Treatment Action Campaign. After neighbors murdered an activist for publicly announcing her HIV status, members of the campaign started wearing T-shirts emblazoned with "HIV$^+$" in large block letters. When they first began using this tactic, the T-shirts functioned like a scarlet letter, eliciting insults and name calling. Observers assumed that the wearers were infected as well. Later, people clamored for shirts of their own and asked where they could find treatment and assistance. People wearing the shirt, and thus bearing witness, forced the government and the society to notice that people were dying for no good reason. The shirt created a way to start a conversation that went well beyond knowledge of the facts.

Successful witnessing, whether at the close interpersonal level, at the political level, or at the judicial level, can be a source of resilience for people facing trauma. Successful witnessing by heterosexual allies, family members, or even public figures helps victims of anti-LGB prejudice feel supported, less outnumbered, and less vulnerable (Russell, 2000). As Russell and Richards (2003) have observed, "successful witnessing seems to reduce the isolation and powerlessness experienced by many LGB people facing political attack" (p. 325). Mental health service providers can be successful as witnesses as they help clients develop a sociopolitical (rather than personal) understanding of the trauma.

In contrast, when witnesses fail to acknowledge the existence of a perpetration, or they fail to intervene on the victim's behalf, a victim's level of stress increases (Russell & Richards, 2003). Failed witnessing in the form of upsetting or hurtful responses from social network members can have a negative impact on psychological and physical well-being (Ingram, Betz, Mindes, Schmitt, & Smith, 2001; Ingram, Jones, Fass, Neidig, & Song, 1999; Ingram, Jones, & Smith, 2001; Lakey, Tardiff, & Drew, 1994). This may be especially true for responses that blame the victim for experiencing heterosexism. Moreover, as Smith and Ingram (2004) suggest, failing to actively affirm the experiences of LGBT clients is to collude with the heterosexist society in which most LGB clients reside.

Involvement in Community Action

In addition to being personally involved in advocacy work as an individual or through a professional organization, it is also important to consider the impact of LGBT clients' community involvement on their mental health. Although psychological engagement with LGB communities has a variety of positive mental health benefits (D'Augelli & Garnets, 1995), a considerable body of work has demonstrated that prejudice and discrimination have substantial negative social, economic, political, and psychological consequences for members of oppressed groups (Crocker & Major, 1989). Reinforced by legal and policy consequences, heterosexism and anti-LGBT prejudice also contribute to psychological alienation by stifling individuals' connections to LGBT communities (D'Augelli & Garnets, 1995).

Although prejudice and discrimination can be psychologically damaging and socially alienating, the coping literature clearly shows that active coping is a healthier response to oppression than passive acceptance. Integration into the gay community has been shown to be associated with various indices of mental health for LGB individuals (e.g., Adam, 1992; Crocker & Major, 1989; Dworkin & Kaufer, 1995; Kurdek, 1988; Paul, Hays, & Coates, 1995). In contrast, withdrawal from the community may exacerbate feelings of isolation, increase internalized homophobia, and diminish support networks (Russell, 2000). Furthermore, as Russell and Richards (2003) demonstrated, LGBT communities can function as sources of resilience for people facing anti-LGBT campaigns because the communities provide access to sources of information and support while functioning as mechanisms through which LGBT people can feel efficacious. LGB people need not be passive victims; they can actively protect or buffer their self-esteem (Crocker & Major, 1989) and enhance feelings of efficacy despite rampant heterosexism and homophobia (Russell, 2000).

Support for the hypothesis that involvement in political advocacy may be therapeutic in itself can be inferred from Russell's (2000) finding that having contact with an LGB community and the act of coming out were seen as direct antidotes to the depression and sadness felt by many LGB Coloradoans during the campaigns surrounding Amendment 2. Although Russell's survey was itself a positive intervention for some of the participants, her data provide clear evidence that observing other LGB people come out and become politically active can be empowering. The same can be said for an LGB person's own steps in becoming more open as an advocate.

Political involvement has been used as a measure of engagement with the LGB community. For example, in a survey of 101 self-identified lesbians, Morgan and Eliason (1996) showed that the vast majority of their respondents thought that therapy and politics were related. In addition, well over half of the sample believed that therapy had made them more aware of how political issues affect them personally and that therapy had helped them to see how being oppressed as a lesbian had affected them. Such a sociopolitical analysis is useful in protecting against the harmful consequences of oppression and can provide a basis for action (Russell, 2000). Russell's data also show that several factors stimulated an activist response, including seeing the struggle for equal rights in terms of a long-term movement, feeling a sense of community with other LGB people, and feeling witnessed by heterosexual allies. Clearly, involvement in an LGBT community increases the likelihood of exposure to these factors.

Similarly, Crocker and Major (1989) argued that stigmatized individuals protect their self-esteem by attributing negative feedback to prejudice (rather than taking it personally), by selectively comparing their outcomes with those of members of their own group (rather than with members of privileged groups), and by selectively devaluing qualities in which their group is perceived to be lacking while valuing those in which their group excels relative to other groups. Again, these outcomes are more likely for people who are engaged in a community than for those who are not.

It may also be useful to note that data from studies of how people make attributions suggests that evaluations by people known to hold prejudiced beliefs have lesser impact on LGB self-esteem than evaluations by those who are not perceived to be prejudiced (Crocker & Major, 1989). In-group comparisons are particularly likely to protect the self-esteem of the stigmatized because they are generally disadvantaged in the larger culture or society. Involvement in an LGB community would provide greater opportunity for such in-group comparisons. Moreover, those who feel they successfully "pass" as straight cannot attribute negative evaluations to group membership and thus cannot experience the feelings of freedom and empowerment described by those who come out.

Taken together, the results of this research suggest that mental health practitioners can be effective advocates. These findings also suggest that active involvement in advocacy efforts can have positive consequences for many clients.

CONCLUSION

This chapter has focused on the importance of the involvement of counselors and therapists in the development of LGBT-affirming advocacy. It has also considered the positive consequences of such involvement, including the potential therapeutic value of a client's involvement in such pursuits. It is reasonable to infer from this discussion that practitioners who assist affected individuals are in a critical position to educate policymakers about the range of experience in LGBT communities.

Counselors and therapists also have special expertise that they can bring to bear in the development of LGB-affirming policy. Despite its value, a discussion of these areas of public policy is beyond the scope of this chapter. Patterson (chap. 15, this volume) provides considerable insight into policy implications of research on lesbian and gay families. In-depth analysis of these and other relevant policy debates can also be found in Stevenson and Cogan (2003).

In sum, the legal and political landscape for LGBT people continues to evolve. The U.S. Supreme Court has ruled that laws prohibiting private, consensual same-sex sexual behavior are unconstitutional. Marriage licenses have been issued to same-sex couples in scattered jurisdictions in a handful of states. The majority of U.S. Americans support equal rights for LGB people in employment contexts (Sobelsohn, 2003). However, state governments across the United States have restricted recognition of same-sex relationships. So these victories may be short-lived without more effective advocacy. As a result, the primary conclusion is this: Engaged practitioners can be effective service providers, educators, and scholars as well as savvy advocates.

REFERENCES

Adam, B. D. (1992). Sociology and people living with AIDS. In J. Huber & B. E. Schneider (Eds.), *The social context of AIDS* (pp. 3–18). Thousand Oaks, CA: Sage.

American Academy of Pediatrics. (1993, October). Policy statement: Homosexuality and adolescence (RE 9332). *Pediatrics, 92*, 631–634.

American Civil Liberties Union. (1999). *Status of U.S. sodomy laws*. Retrieved January 8, 2004, from http://www.aclu.org/issues/gay/sodomy.html

American Civil Liberties Union. (2003). *Kansas v. Matthew Limon case background*. Retrieved September 17, 2004, from http://www.aclu.org/LesbianGayRights/LesbianGayRights.cfm?ID=14476&c=41

American Civil Liberties Union. (2004). *Why the Supreme Court decision striking down sodomy laws is so important*. Retrieved June 9, 2004, from http://www.aclu.org/LesbianGayRights/LesbianGayRightsMain.cfm

American Psychoanalytic Association. (n.d.). *Position statement on the treatment of homosexual patients*. Retrieved September 30, 2005, from http://www.apsa.org/pubinfo/homosexuality.htm

American Psychological Association. (1997). *Resolution on appropriate therapeutic responses to sexual orientation*. Retrieved January 8, 2004, from http://www.apa.org/pi/lgbc/policy/statements.html#10

American Psychological Association. (2004a). *Resolution on sexual orientation and marriage*. Retrieved September 17, 2004, from http://www.apa.org/pi/lgbc/policy/marriage.pdf

American Psychological Association. (2004b). *Resolution on sexual orientation, parents, and children*. Retrieved September 17, 2004, from http://www.apa.org/pi/lgbc/policy/parentschildren.pdf

American Psychological Association. (2005). *APA policy statements on lesbian, gay, & bisexual concerns*. Washington, DC: Author.

American Psychological Association, Division 44/Committee on Lesbian, Gay, and Bisexual Concerns Joint Task Force on Guidelines for Psychotherapy With Lesbian, Gay, and Bisexual Clients. (2000). Guidelines for psychotherapy with lesbian, gay, and bisexual clients. *American Psychologist, 55*, 1440–1451.

Bean, L. (2004). *Mass. Court upholds gay marriage, rejects civil unions*. Retrieved February 4, 2004, from http://www.DiversityInc.com

Biaggio, M., Orchard, S., Larson, J., Petrino, K., & Mihara, R. (2003). Guidelines for gay/lesbian/bisexual-affirmative educational practices in graduate psychology programs. *Professional Psychology: Research and Practice, 34*, 548–554.

Bieschke, K. J., McClanahan, M., Tozer, E., Grzegorek, J. L., & Park, J. (2000). Programmatic research on the treatment of lesbian, gay, and bisexual clients: The past, the present, and the course for the future. In R. M. Perez, K. A. DeBord, & K. J. Bieschke (Eds.), *Handbook of counseling and psychotherapy with lesbian, gay, and bisexual clients* (pp. 309–335). Washington, DC: American Psychological Association.

Bowers v. Hardwick, 478 U.S. 186, 106 S. Ct. 2841, 92 L.Ed.2d 140 (1986).

Brown, L. S. (1989). New voices, new visions: Toward a lesbian/gay paradigm for psychology. *Psychology of Women Quarterly, 13*, 445–458.

Brown, L. S. (1996). Ethical concerns with sexual minority patients. In R. P. Cabaj & T. S. Stein (Eds.), *Textbook of homosexuality and mental health* (pp. 897–916). Washington, DC: American Psychiatric Press.

Cabaj, R. P. (1996). Sexual orientation of the therapist. In R. P. Cabaj & T. S. Stein (Eds.), *Textbook of homosexuality and mental health* (pp. 513–524). Washington, DC: American Psychiatric Press.

Cameron, P., & Cameron, K. (1996). Do homosexual teachers pose a risk to pupils? *Journal of Psychology, 130*, 603–613.

Cameron, P., & Cameron, K. (1998). What proportion of newspaper stories about child molestation involve homosexuality? *Psychological Reports, 82*, 863–871.

Catholic Medical Association. (2003). *Homosexuality and hope.* Retrieved June 1, 2004, from http://www.cathmed.org/publications/homosexuality.html

Cogan, J. C. (2003). Influencing public policy. In M. R. Stevenson & J. C. Cogan (Eds.), *Everyday activism: A handbook for lesbian, gay, and bisexual people and their allies* (pp. 19–38). New York: Routledge.

Coleman, E. (1989). The married lesbian. *Marriage and Family Review, 14*(3/4), 119–135.

Crocker, J., & Major, B. (1989). Social stigma and self-esteem: The self-protective properties of stigma. *Psychological Review, 96*, 608–630.

D'Augelli, A. R., & Garnets, L. D. (1995). Lesbian, gay, and bisexual communities. In A. R. D'Augelli & C. J. Patterson (Eds.), *Lesbian, gay, and bisexual identities over the lifespan: Psychological perspectives* (pp. 293–320). New York: Oxford University Press.

DeBord, K. A., & Perez, R. M. (2000). Group counseling theory and practice with lesbian, gay, and bisexual clients. In R. M. Perez, K. A. DeBord, & K. J. Bieschke (Eds.), *Handbook of counseling and psychotherapy with lesbian, gay, and bisexual clients* (pp. 183–206). Washington, DC: American Psychological Association.

Douglas-Brown, L. (2004). "Unprecedented" court victories mark 2003: Backlash builds support for constitutional ban on gay marriage. *The Washington Blade Online.* Retrieved January 8, 2004, from http://www.washblade.com/2004/1–2/news/national/victories.cfm

Dworkin, J., & Kaufer, D. (1995). Social services and bereavement in the lesbian and gay community. In G. A. Lloyd & M. A. Kuszelewicz (Eds.), *HIV disease: Lesbians, gays and the social services* (pp. 41–60). New York: Harrington Park/Haworth Press.

Family Research Institute. (1992). *Medical consequences of what homosexuals do.* Washington, DC: Author.

Georgemiller, R., & Stevenson, M. R. (2003, Summer). "Homosexuality and hope" revisited. *The Journal, 35*(3), 11–12.

Greene, B., & Croom, G. L. (2000). *Education, research, and practice in lesbian, gay, bisexual, and transgendered psychology: A resource manual.* Thousand Oaks, CA: Sage.

Haldeman, D. C. (1994). The practice and ethics of sexual orientation conversion therapy. *Journal of Consulting and Clinical Psychology, 62,* 221–227.

Hancock, K. A. (2000). Lesbian, gay, and bisexual lives: Basic issues in psychotherapy training and practice. In B. Greene & G. L. Croom (Eds.), *Education, research, and practice in lesbian, gay, bisexual, and transgendered psychology: A resource manual* (pp. 91–130). Thousand Oaks, CA: Sage.

Herek, G. M. (1998). Bad science in the service of stigma: A critique of the Cameron group's survey studies. In G. M. Herek (Ed.), *Stigma and sexual orientation: Understanding prejudice against lesbians, gay men, and bisexuals* (pp. 223–255). Thousand Oaks, CA: Sage.

Hooker, E. (1957). The adjustment of the male overt homosexual. *Journal of Projective Techniques, 21,* 18–31.

Ingram, K. M., Betz, N. E., Mindes, E. J., Schmitt, M. M., & Smith, N. G. (2001). Unsupportive responses from others concerning a stressful life event: Development of the unsupportive social interactions inventory. *Journal of Social and Clinical Psychology, 20,* 173–207.

Ingram, K. M., Jones, D. A., Fass, R. J., Neidig, J. L., & Song, Y. S. (1999). Social support and unsupportive social interactions: Their association with depression among people living with HIV. *AIDS Care, 11,* 313–329.

Ingram, K. M., Jones, D. A., & Smith, N. G. (2001). Adjustment among people who have experienced ADIS-related multiple loss: The role of unsupportive social interactions, social support, and coping. *Omega: Journal of Death and Dying, 43,* 287–309.

Jacoby, S. (2004, January 8). One nation, under secularism. *The New York Times.* Retrieved January 8, 2004, from http://www.nytimes.com/2004/01/08/opinion/08JACO.html?th

Kansas court to hear appeal of gay teen sentenced to 17 years. (2004, June 4). *The Washington Blade,* p. 18.

King, B. R. (2003). Recognizing and legitimizing families. In M. R. Stevenson & J. C. Cogan (Eds.), *Everyday activism: A handbook for lesbian, gay, and bisexual people and their allies* (pp. 193–210). New York: Routledge.

Kurdek, L. A. (1988). Perceived social support in lesbians and gays in cohabiting relationships. *Journal of Personality and Social Psychology, 54,* 504–509.

Lakey, B., Tardiff, T. A., & Drew, J. B. (1994). Negative social interactions: Assessment and relations to social support, cognition, and psychological distress. *Journal of Social and Clinical Psychology, 13*, 42–62.

Lawrence v. Texas, 41 S.W.3d 349 (2002).

Liddle, B. J. (1997). Gay and lesbian clients' selection of therapists and utilization of therapy. *Psychotherapy, 34*, 11–18.

Lynn, L. (1994). Lesbian, gay, and bisexual therapists' social and sexual interactions with clients. In J. C. Gonsiorek (Ed.), *Breach of trust* (pp. 193–212). Newbury Park, CA: Sage.

McDaniel, J. S., Cabaj, R. P., & Purcell, D. W. (1996). Care across the spectrum of mental health settings: Working with gay, lesbian, and bisexual patients in consultation-liaison services, inpatient treatment facilities, and community outpatient mental health centers. In R. P. Cabaj & T. S. Stein (Eds.), *Textbook of homosexuality and mental health* (pp. 687–704). Washington, DC: American Psychiatric Press.

Morgan, K. S., & Eliason, M. J. (1996). The relationship between therapy usage and political activity in lesbians. *Women & Therapy, 19*(2), 31–45.

Morris, J. F., & Hart, S. (2003). Defending claims about mental health. In M. R. Stevenson & J. C. Cogan (Eds.), *Everyday activism: A handbook for lesbian, gay, and bisexual people and their allies* (pp. 57–78). New York: Routledge.

Morrow, S. L. (2000). First do no harm: Therapist issues in psychotherapy with lesbian, gay, and bisexual clients. In R. M. Perez, K. A. DeBord, & K. J. Bieschke (Eds.), *Handbook of counseling and psychotherapy with lesbian, gay, and bisexual clients* (pp. 137–156). Washington, DC: American Psychological Association.

Morrow, S. L., & Beckstead, A. L. (2004). Conversion therapies for same-sex attracted clients in religious conflict: Context, predisposing factors, experiences, and implications for therapy. *Counseling Psychologist, 32*, 641–650.

Murphy, J. A., Rawlings, E. I., & Howe, S. R. (2002). A survey of clinical psychologists on treating lesbian, gay, and bisexual clients. *Professional Psychology: Research and Practice, 33*, 183–189.

National Association of Social Workers. (2002). *"Reparative" and "conversion" therapies for lesbians and gay men.* Retrieved September 30, 2005, from http://www.socialworkers.org/diversity/lgb/reparative.asp

Newport, F. (2003). Public shifts to more conservative stance on gay rights: Change comes in aftermath of Supreme Court decision. *The Gallup Organization.* Retrieved January 14, 2004, from http://www.gallup.com/content/defaut.asp? ci = 8956&pg = 1

Paul, J. P., Hays, R. B., & Coates, T. J. (1995). The impact of the HIV epidemic on U.S. gay male communities. In A. R. D'Augelli & C. J. Patterson (Eds.), *Lesbian, gay, and bisexual identities over the lifespan: Psychological perspectives* (pp. 347–397). London: Oxford University Press.

Pear, R., & Kirkpatrick, D. D. (2004, January 14). Bush plans $1.5 billion drive for promotion of marriage. *The New York Times.* Retrieved January 14, 2004, from http://www.nytimes.com/2004/01/14/politics/campaigns/14MARR.html?ex=107 5085399&ei=1&en=c325elbfd4347d9d

Rochlin, M. (1985). Sexual orientation of the therapist and therapeutic effectiveness with gay clients. In J. C. Gonsiorek (Ed.), *A guide to psychotherapy with gay and lesbian clients* (pp. 21–29). New York: Harrington Park Press.

Russell, G. M. (2000). *Voted out: The psychological consequences of antigay politics.* New York: New York University Press.

Russell, G. M., & Richards, J. A. (2003). Stressor and resilience factors for lesbians, gay men, and bisexuals confronting antigay politics. *American Journal of Community Psychology, 31,* 313–328.

Seelly, C. (2004, February 6). Landmark sodomy ruling dismissed by lower courts: Gay Kansas man faces prison sentence 13 times longer than straight counterparts. *Washington Blade Online.* Retrieved February 6, 2004, from http://www.washblade.com/2004/2-6/news/national/landmark.cfm

Smith, A. (1997). Cultural diversity and the coming-out process: Implications for clinical practice. In B. Greene (Ed.), *Psychological perspectives on lesbian and gay issues: Vol. 3. Ethnic and cultural diversity among lesbians and gay men* (pp. 279–300). Thousand Oaks, CA: Sage.

Smith, N. G., & Ingram, K. M. (2004). Workplace heterosexism and adjustment among lesbian, gay, and bisexual individuals: The role of unsupportive social interactions. *Journal of Counseling Psychology, 51,* 57–67.

Sobelsohn, D. C. (2003). Ending employment discrimination. In M. R. Stevenson & J. C. Cogan (Eds.), *Everyday activism: A handbook for lesbian, gay, and bisexual people and their allies* (pp. 105–122). New York: Routledge.

Stevenson, M. R. (2002). Conceptualizing diversity in sexuality research. In M. W. Wiederman & B. E. Whitley Jr. (Eds.), *Handbook for conducting research on human sexuality* (pp. 455–478). Mahwah, NJ: Erlbaum.

Stevenson, M. R., & Cogan, J. C. (2003). *Everyday activism: A handbook for lesbian, gay, and bisexual people and their allies.* New York: Routlege.

United States Department of Health and Human Services. (2001). *Surgeon General's call to action to promote sexual health and responsible sexual behavior.* Retrieved September 30, 2005, from http://www.surgeongeneral.gov/library/sexualhealth/call.htm

Wilson, C. (2004, January 28). Gay men lose challenge to Florida gay adoption ban. *The Miami Herald.* Retrieved June 10, 2004, from http://www.miami.com/mld/miamiherald/news/state/7818470.htm

17

THE "BORING" STATE OF RESEARCH AND PSYCHOTHERAPY WITH LESBIAN, GAY, BISEXUAL, AND TRANSGENDER CLIENTS: REVISITING BARÓN (1991)

RUPERTO M. PEREZ

In 1991, Barón wrote that the challenge to the field of psychology is to make research and practice with lesbian, gay, and bisexual (LGB) persons "boring." By this, Barón was not suggesting that scholarship and practice issues in LGB psychology should become uninteresting or unexciting. Rather, Barón hoped that that LGB issues could become so well-integrated into mainstream psychology and mental health education, training, and practice that researchers and practitioners would no longer have to provide an explanation or rationale for including the issues of LGB clients as a routine practice in counseling and psychotherapy. Barón further envisioned that, if this integration could be achieved, neither psychologists nor counselors would have to hope for tolerance and acceptance from others for choosing to develop a research interest or practice area in LGB psychology. In short, Barón called for the issues of LGB people to become a routine and integrated aspect of research, education, and practice in psychology and mental health training. As such, Barón's challenge to psychology as a profession (and society as a whole) is to "move toward a time when . . . being gay and lesbian will be considered 'a mundane, inconsequential part of everyday life, requiring no explanation, justification, or pleading for acceptance' " (Barón, 1991, p. 240).

So, after more than a dozen years after Barón's challenge, has psychology met Barón's challenge in making LGB issues "boring"? Additionally, to what extent has psychology met the challenge of making routine the inclusion of the psychological concerns of transgender people in research, training, and practice? This final chapter attempts to answer these questions by exploring the major themes and concepts found in this second edition of the handbook and by seeking to define future courses for scholarship and critical areas for practice in psychotherapy with lesbian, gay, bisexual, and transgender (LGBT) clients.

ARE YOU BORED YET?

In the first edition of this handbook (Perez, DeBord, & Bieschke, 2000), we noted that research in the area of LGB psychology was in its infancy. Since that time, others have maintained that the full integration of LGB issues in psychology still remains a challenge to the profession. Goldfried (2001) addressed this issue by stating that although mental health professionals have demonstrated increased support for the issues that affect LGB people, LGB scholarship has not permeated the mainstream psychological literature. In addition, there still exists a lack of full integration of LGB issues within psychology graduate training curricula (Biaggio, Orchard, Larson, Petrino, & Mihara, 2003; Murphy, Rawlings, & Howe, 2002). Still, others have noted that the study of LGB issues has progressed to some degree (Bieschke, Croteau, Lark, & Vandiver, 2005; Douce, 2004) and has moved "beyond pioneering" (Croteau, Bieschke, Phillips, & Lark, 1998). However, the phrase "beyond pioneering" also acknowledges that LGB psychology remains a relatively young discipline in psychology and that its full incorporation and acceptance within the mainstream of scholarship in psychology is still in the early stages. In fact, the psychological and mental health issues that affect LGB individuals throughout the life span have continued to remain an invisible area within the dominant psychological literature (Goldfried, 2001), just as LGB persons have been an invisible minority within society (Fassinger, 1991).

If conventional psychology has failed to fully integrate LGB issues into the mainstream of its professional scholarship, education, and practice, then attention to issues regarding transgender persons has been sorely lacking. A PsycINFO search conducted at the time of this writing, using the search term *transgender*, yielded a total of only 214 peer-reviewed journal articles and 14 books published within the 15 years from 1990 through

2005. Clearly, important areas of scholarship and psychotherapy regarding transgender issues remain to be explored (Bullough, 2000). In this regard, the field of psychology has yet to also make transgender issues "boring."

In order to further examine the extent to which LGBT issues in psychology have become fully integrated within the areas of theory, research, and practice, this chapter explores the key issues presented in the various chapters of this book that reflect the salient areas for psychologists and therapists to be aware and knowledgeable of when working with LGBT clients. The three major themes that emerged include (a) the role of a diverse LGBT community in identity development and social connection for LGBT persons, (b) the growing sociopolitical clout of the LGBT community, and (c) the definition and practice of affirmative psychotherapy with LGBT clients. The remainder of this chapter reflects on these three important themes as discussed in the various chapters. Additionally, this final chapter discusses the important future implications for areas of practice, research, and education in light of the central ideas and themes in this book.

LGBT COMMUNITY: IDENTITY, DIVERSITY, AND CONNECTION

Community and Identity: Providing Connection and Belonging

Community and identity—these are two distinct yet interwoven facets in the lives of LGBT persons. For LGBT persons, a sense of belonging to LGBT communities can serve as a source of social support, a source of historical belonging, and a source of psychological support and identity. The critical impact of belonging to a community is evident in the developmental process of establishing identity for LGBT persons (this volume, Fassinger & Arseneau, chap. 1; Liddle, chap. 2; Haldeman, chap. 3; Firestein, chap. 4; Potoczniak, chap. 5; Lev, chap. 6). For therapists, it is important to have knowledge of the history of LGBT communities in order to gain an understanding of LGBT clients within the context of community and group identity. History gives smaller communities a sense of tradition and "rootedness" within a larger community or society (Haldeman, chap. 3, this volume).

In the process of identity formation for gay men, identification with and socialization within the gay community can be a therapeutic experience in "reparenting" gay men so that they can be more accepting and affirming in their sense of identity. This community experience can bring two realizations: realization of heterosexism's role and influence in impeding the development of a positive gay identity and realization of a commonality of values and beliefs when identifying with gay-centric culture (Haldeman, chap. 3, this volume). Similarly, individual lesbian identity development is also affected by affiliation and belonging to lesbian culture (Liddle, chap. 2, this volume). Affiliation and involvement with a lesbian community offers lesbian clients support for a number of life span issues, including identity development and coming out, and can also significantly contribute to their psychological health (Morris, Waldo, & Rothblum, 2001). Therefore, it is essential for therapists to understand the importance of the lesbian community to lesbian clients in developing a positive identity and the importance of social affiliation across the life span.

Community also plays an important role in identity formation for bisexual persons (this volume, Firestein, chap. 4; Potoczniak, chap. 5). Indeed, it is ironic that as bisexual persons strive for more visibility as a community, the existence of the bisexual community is, at times, questioned, oftentimes overshadowed and marginalized by the lesbian and gay communities, making a bisexual community difficult to find (Firestein, 1996; Fox, 1996; Ochs, 1996). Both bisexual women and bisexual men have had to struggle to define themselves to other communities and persons. In addition, bisexual men and women have also had to define the fluidity of sexual orientation, the fluidity of group identity, and the validity of bisexuality as a valid aspect of sexual orientation and identity (this volume, Firestein, chap. 4; Potoczniak, chap. 5). Because of this, therapists working with bisexual clients face distinct challenges in confronting issues of biphobia and heterosexism in order to affirm the fluidity of sexuality and to validate the varied ways in which relationships are constructed and expressed for bisexual persons within bisexual communities.

If the bisexual community has been overshadowed by lesbian and gay communities, then transgender persons and the transgender community may be the most marginalized among the sexual minorities (Lev, chap. 6, this volume; Namaste, 2000), making it more difficult for transgender clients to find a community. The existence of transgender persons and community within society and throughout history is evident (Bullough & Bullough, 1993; Carroll, Gilroy, & Ryan, 2002; Lev, chap. 6, this volume). The Internet has allowed transgender individuals to find greater connection to and validation from the transgender community (Lev, chap. 6, this volume). But though the transgender community has made some social gains through identity and has attained greater visibility, the community still suffers from social stigmatization and discrimination (Bullough, 2000; Monro, 2000). Given the marginalization and social discrimination that transgender persons experience and the invisibility that the transgender community experiences, it becomes even more imperative for psychologists and counselors to continue to explore and address the social and psychological constructions of gender and sexual identity in order to gain an understanding of the issues faced by transgender persons.

Impact of Technology in Connecting a Global LGBT Community

The role of technology in facilitating communication and connection within the LGBT community has been a theme echoed throughout the earlier chapters of this book. Because of the widespread impact of the Internet on global communication and interpersonal relationships (Jerome et al., 2000), the use of technology in creating and facilitating connections for LGBT persons has also facilitated the growth of a global LGBT community. Perhaps the diverse nature of LGBT communities has necessitated, in part, reliance on Internet technology to facilitate connections among LGBT individuals and the greater LGBT communities.

The ever-advancing Internet-based communications technology has played an important role in the growth of a more global LGBT community, one in which LGBT individuals can find various connections within communities (this volume, Fassinger & Arseneau, chap. 1; Liddle, chap. 2; Haldeman, chap. 3; Firestein, chap. 4; Potoczniak, chap. 5; Lev, chap. 6). For LGBT individuals, connecting with communities in this way provides an alternative in facilitating networking, gathering resources, and finding support in situations where individuals may be geographically isolated (i.e., rural settings) from substantially sized LGBT communities. On the other hand, the overreliance on such technology may also lead to neglecting efforts to engage in meaningful "in person" interactions and relationships (Haldeman, chap. 3, this volume). As a result, the influence of the Internet on the LGBT community, its efficacy in enhancing and facilitating community connection for LGBT individuals, and its role in enhancing identity formation remains an area for continued exploration and evaluation.

Diversity Within Community

Within LGBT communities there are multifaceted dimensions of individual differences and diversity, multiple layers of identity, and multiple layers of oppression (Fukuyama & Ferguson, 2000; Garnets, 2002). Identity formation for LGBT persons is therefore a complex phenomenon, requiring an integration of a number of individual, social, cultural, and historical variables. In this light, formation of a healthy LGBT identity also involves more than just conceptualizing identity development along linear, discrete, individual stage processes (e.g., Cass, 1979). LGBT identity development must be considered as a fluid process that is intimately influenced by affiliation and identification with community (this volume, Fassinger & Arseneau, chap. 1; Liddle, chap. 2; Haldeman, chap., 3; Firestein, chap. 4; Potoczniak, chap. 5; Lev, chap. 6). Stage-based, linear models of LGBT identity development lack the complexity and the attention to sociohistorical contexts that are reflected in the more comprehensive identity theories and models that affirm the influence of community affiliation in identity development. Thus, the influence of community affiliation on identity formation for LGBT persons is an important factor to consider in working with LGBT clients. Until now, the role that community affiliation or group identity played in influencing individual identity formation for LGBT clients was relatively unclear and unexplored.

To date, few theories of LGBT identity development have directly examined or integrated the influence of LGBT community affiliation on the development of individual LGBT identity. Gonsiorek and Rudolph (1991), Fassinger and Miller (1996), and McCarn and Fassinger (1996) have provided recent theories of gay and lesbian identity development that examine and integrate the role of community as significant caregiver and self-object (Gonsiorek & Rudolph, 1991) and the importance of group affiliation and identity (Fassinger & Miller, 1996; McCarn & Fassinger, 1996) on lesbian and gay identity formation. In chapter 1, by Fassinger and Arseneau (this volume), one of the most comprehensive, integrative theoretical models of LGBT identity development, or "identity enactment," is presented. This model affirms the role of individual and social constructions of identity, the interaction of multiple layers of community affiliation on individual identity, and the effects of multiple layers of oppression on individual identity. Through a deconstruction and a re-construction of community, culture, and identity, Fassinger and Arseneau have set forth a comprehensive theory of LGBT identity formation that challenges therapists to question existing notions of identity construction and to begin considering the multiple constructions, layers, and methods through which LGBT identities (and even non-LGBT identities) are enacted.

As illustrated throughout this volume, the role of the LGBT community is an important one in terms of fostering identity development, offering social support, and supporting resilience in the face of social and political oppression. Given the effect that community identification can have on LGBT identity formation and psychological well-being, research and scholarship are needed to continue to explore the role and impact of community affiliation in LGBT identity formation and mental health. For example, previous literature has illustrated the importance of LGBT community affiliation and supportive social interactions on moderating psychological distress (Morris et al., 2001), promoting healthy workplace environments (Smith & Ingram, 2004), and providing a sense of solidarity in the face of prejudice and multiple sources of oppression (Garnets, 2002). Empirical research is needed to test those identity models that incorporate community identity variables and to determine the unique contribution of community identity to overall LGBT identity development and mental health. Research should attend to the various cultural, historical, and social variables that comprise community, to the degree to which these variables influence community affiliation, and to the ways in which they contribute to individual identity development. In addition, there is a need to develop accurate measures to assess how community affiliation and identity fluidity influence LGBT identity development in order to assist therapists in better understanding the multifaceted nature of identity for LGBT clients.

It is also important to consider the nature of community affiliation in the coming out process, especially with regard to the integration and assessment of diverse facets of identity. These facets are sometimes visible (e.g., race, ethnicity, physical ability; Rosario, Schrimshaw, & Hunter, 2004) and sometimes not readily visible (e.g., social class, political, physical ability, religion/spirituality). Nonetheless, the less visible facets are still important in the formation of a cohesive sense of self. This is particularly salient in the provision of psychotherapy to LGBT clients in conflict with their religious identity.

Beckstead and Israel (chap. 9, this volume) provide thoughtful examination of the issues facing LGB clients, particularly the issues that may be in conflict with the multiple facets of LGB identity (e.g., race, ethnicity, socioeconomic status, physical ability). A main focus of the authors is on clients whose LGB identity conflicts with their religious beliefs. Just as LGB clients of color must manage their identities of sexual orientation and of race or ethnicity, LGB clients in religious conflict must also manage their religious identity. Psychotherapy that affirms a client's lesbian, gay, bisexual, or transgender identity *and also* affirms a client's religious identity can provide LGBT clients a supportive context in which to address, manage, and integrate their LGBT identity and their religious identity (Davidson, 2000; Haldeman, 2004). Thus, for an LGBT client in conflict with his or her religious identity, psychotherapy is focused then not on having to choose one identity over the other (i.e., letting go of individual LGBT identity in favor of individual religious identity), but rather on how to best manage, integrate, and affirm the multiple identities as an LGBT individual and as a religious and spiritual being. In this way, the therapist serves to explore and support healthy and appropriate ways in which an LGBT client's multiple identities can best be expressed and validated.

This approach to therapy, however, may raise ethical dilemmas for therapists who themselves hold a strong religious identity and maintain fundamental religious beliefs that negate and disavow LGBT persons. Fischer and DeBord (chap. 13, this volume) explore how best to resolve the ethical concerns for therapists. In their thoughtful discourse and implementation of a model of ethical decision-making, Fischer and DeBord confront this exceptionally difficult and polarizing professional issue in counseling and psychotherapy. Through examination of their personal and professional struggles in this area, Fischer and DeBord identify the ethical struggles and echo what Barón (1991) identified as professional ethics being "the cutting-edge challenge" for therapists working with sexual minority clients. As a result, there remains a need for ongoing and open dialogue among mental health professionals in examining the considerations of providing ethical, affirmative psychotherapy to LGBT clients. Further, ethical issues at the crossroads of differing religious values and professional values at both individual and systemic levels must be carefully managed. In sum, there is an ongoing challenge to the mental health profession to carefully examine biases, knowledge bases, and practices that serve as barriers to providing affirmative, effective, and ethical counseling and psychotherapy to LGBT clients.

The important themes of the role of the LGBT community in identity development and connection, the diverse nature of LGBT communities, and the growing political power of the LGBT community have been raised by a number of chapter authors. What is evident throughout is the important role that the LGBT community has played in the identity formation and socialization for LGBT clients. Although attention to the role of community has been identified as significant in understanding identity development for LGBT clients, scholarship and practice have just begun to examine the role of community in the formation of multiple identities and the tasks of managing those various facets of identity in the lives of LGBT clients. Future research and scholarship needs to look at specific issues that continue to impact the diversity of LGBT persons, relationships, and communities. The following must be examined: the effects of multiple identities and oppressions on the quality of life for LGBT people (Harper, Jernewall, & Zea, 2004; Parks, Hughes, & Matthews, 2004), issues of domestic violence and abuse (Potoczniak, Mourot, Crosbie-Burnett, & Potoczniak, 2003), health and aging issues, and the needs of LGBT persons with disabilities (Yali & Revenson, 2004). These are but some of the areas that hold promise for continued exploration for practitioners and researchers alike. In the end, pursuing these and a plethora of other possible areas can only lead to increased knowledge for mental health professionals and lead to major contributions to the area of psychology and mental health.

THE POLITICAL CLOUT OF COMMUNITY

The history of LGBT communities is characterized by the defiance of social oppression and injustice. It is also characterized by expressions of hope and desire for social equity, advocacy, and freedom. Over the years and through steady growth and visibility, LGBT communities have gained increased political and economic influence (Bailey, 2000; Currah & Minter, 2000). This growing political voice, or "political clout," represents both a unity and diversity among the LGBT community in their efforts to raise awareness for social and political equality within society. As a marginalized community within society, the increased political activism of the LGBT community may be reflective of the community's maturation in its own identity development. The strong social identity of the LGBT community offers individuals within the community an idealized community and identity pride that can be influential in overall individual identity formation (Gonsiorek & Rudolph, 1991).

In chapter 3 of this volume, Haldeman highlights concerns regarding the advantages and threats of assimilation into or liberation from the larger society by the LGBT community. The outcomes of confronting this dilemma have yet to be foreseen or determined. Nevertheless, it is also important to keep in mind that the growing political clout of the LGBT community has resulted in a sense of pride for LGBT community members, increased sociopolitical power to successfully confront and resist sociopolitical oppression, and a greater sense of community and connection with others.

Various aspects of the LGBT community can serve to assist in the development of a cohesive self-identity for LGBT persons. It is through this lens that both Patterson (chap. 15) and Stevenson (chap. 16) examine the legal and political issues that influence family and public policy issues in LGBT mental health. What can be culled from both chapters is that the role of the therapist can be crucial in advocating for LGBT clients (e.g., by becoming actively engaged in influencing public policy for the betterment of LGBT people and by serving as an agent of prosocial change). Thus, the work of the therapist is carried outside the confines of the "therapy office space" and into the larger community and personal spheres of influence. As such, the therapist's role becomes integrated within the larger sociopolitical context of society, with therapists serving as agents to promote social justice.

Patterson (chap. 15, this volume) challenges therapists to act as change agents to advocate for the social welfare and equity of LGBT individuals, families, and couples in society. The role of the therapist is also clearly examined in this light in Stevenson's chapter (chap. 16, this volume), when the author explores the roles of counselors and therapists as agents of prosocial change in advocating for affirmation of LGBT persons in a heterosexually biased society. Stevenson powerfully describes the ever-evolving current backdrop of social, cultural, political, and legal issues that affect the lives of LGBT people. His chapter serves as a call to action for mental health professionals to become active social and political voices by using their expertise in practice and science to advocate for the welfare of LGBT persons in our society.

The growing role of the therapist as agent for social change in the LGBT literature is a relatively new phenomenon brought about by the current political climate, contrasting political ideologies, and social values that bear directly on the quality of life for LGBT persons. Few theories to date have defined the role of the therapist within a sociopolitical context (e.g., Brown, 2002). However, there has been a growing recognition of the role of the therapist in working to address issues of social justice and equality for all persons in society (Goodman et al., 2004; Greene, chap. 7, this volume). As a result, an area for continued exploration and scholarship is the influence on the therapeutic process of the therapist's role as an agent of social change. From this perspective, some interesting questions could be asked. One question that could be examined is, "How does the role of the therapist influence the delivery of counseling and psychotherapy and public policy?" (see, for example, Riggle, Rostosky, Prather, & Hamrin, 2005). In a related manner, how does the role of the supervisor (in promoting social justice) influence the supervisory relationship and the development and growth of supervisees? How can various religious values and beliefs also be integrated into the ethical and effective practice of counseling and psychotherapy? Although there are currently no clear answers to these questions, continued research and scholarship may lend additional insights into the role of mental health professionals as agents of social change. In the end, therapists are called to social action in the practice of affirmative psychotherapy with LGBT clients. In maintaining the ethical principles of nonmaleficence and beneficence, mental health professionals as social change agents serve as advocates for their clients by taking an active part to establish a culture grounded in a higher good and by striving for the welfare, equity, and affirmation of all people.

THE ESSENCE OF AFFIRMATIVE PSYCHOTHERAPY AND SUPERVISION

In attempting to define the nature and central elements of affirmative psychotherapy, various chapters in this book have considered the fundamental assumptions and necessary conditions for providing affirmative psychotherapy to LGBT clients (this volume, Greene, chap. 7; Matthews, chap. 8; Korell & Lorah, chap. 11); for addressing developmental life span concerns and examining affirmative therapy's utility in exploring conflicts of identity (Beckstead & Israel, chap. 9, this volume); and for addressing unique career and workplace issues (Lidderdale, Croteau, Anderson, Tovar-Murray, & Davis, chap. 10, this volume). From the collection of chapters that examine the nature of affirmative psychotherapy for LGB clients, we arrive at the essence of its definition—affirmative psychotherapy is the integration of knowledge and awareness by the therapist of the unique developmental and cultural aspects of LGBT individuals, the therapist's own self-knowledge, and the translation of this knowledge and awareness into effective and helpful therapy skills at all stages of the therapeutic process. Affirmative psychotherapy is practiced regardless of the therapist's a priori knowledge of the client's sexual orientation. It involves the therapist's effective use of psychological theory and techniques to address the psychological needs of LGBT clients in effectively coping with distress, in addressing salient developmental life span concerns, in managing various aspects of the developmental processes of identity formation, and in successfully coping with the deleterious effects of social oppression and discrimination. Affirmative psychotherapy is ethical therapy that requires therapists (a) to assume an affirming stance at the outset of psychotherapy, (b) to gain knowledge and awareness of the unique developmental and cultural aspects of LGBT individuals, (c) to develop effective therapy skills that assist clients in coping with psychological distress, fostering positive identity development and integration (American Psychological Association [APA], 2002; APA, Division 44/Committee on Lesbian, Gay, and Bisexual Concerns Joint Task Force, 2000; Gainor, 2000; Perez, 2001), and (d) to address internal biases and assumptions regarding the fluidity of gender and the construction of gender and sexual identities. When these tenets of affirmative psychotherapy are present, the therapist also assumes a proactive, social role in striving to empower LGBT persons in the face of the damaging and harmful effects of individual, social, and cultural oppressions and in striving to work toward social justice and advocacy. With this description of affirmative psychotherapy in mind, a number of considerations emerge, including (a) definition of the core conditions for affirmative psychotherapy, (b) the practice of affirmative psychotherapy and supervision, and (c) potential areas of affirmative psychotherapy research.

Core Conditions of Affirmative Psychotherapy

Previous literature (e.g., APA, Division 44/Committee on Lesbian, Gay, and Bisexual Concerns Joint Task Force, 2000; Pachankis & Goldfried, 2004) and Beckstead and Israel (chap. 8, this volume) focus on important areas in providing counseling and psychotherapy to LGB clients, but few areas of scholarship have consolidated these areas and defined them in a coherent, heuristic manner. Similarly, the significant areas to consider in working with transgender clients in psychotherapy have garnered attention and have recently become clearer (Gainor, 2000; Lev, chap. 6, this volume). Now we have even more insight into what constitutes the core conditions of affirmative psychotherapy for LGBT clients based on the chapters of Matthews (chap. 8), Korell and Lorah (chap.11), and Bieschke, Paul, and Blasko (chap. 12). What can be gleaned from the comprehensive information and review of the existing literature contained in these chapters? They are the factors that can be regarded as the necessary, core conditions for affirmative psychotherapy: (a) therapist competence, (b) therapist affirmation of LGBT culture, and (c) therapist openness in attending to sexual orientation and identity issues.

In affirmative psychotherapy, therapist competence can be best described as the therapist's capability to integrate awareness and knowledge of psychological theory and techniques to effectively address the therapeutic needs of LGBT clients. In addition, affirmative psychotherapy for transgender clients requires the therapist to have comprehensive knowledge regarding transgender identity development, ethics, and specified standards of care (Harry Benjamin International Gender Dysphoria Association [HBIGDA], 2001a, 2001b; Israel & Tarver, 1997). Affirmation of LGBT culture includes a constellation of therapist attitudes and beliefs that positively acknowledge and avow the history, culture, and identities of LGBT clients, as opposed to therapist attitudes and beliefs that reflect heterosexist values and phobic beliefs regarding LGBT persons. Finally, therapist openness in attending to sexual orientation and identity issues reflects the therapist's willingness to candidly engage in acknowledgment of a client's sexual orientation or identity as a routine part of therapy. That is, affirmative psychotherapy is provided at all stages of counseling and therapy regardless of the therapist's a priori knowledge of the client's sexual orientation (Matthews, chap. 8; Bieschke, Paul, & Blasko, chap. 12) or gender identity (Korell & Lorah, chap. 11).

Affirmative Psychotherapy in Practice

Affirmative psychotherapy provides a wealth of directions for practice and research. The "Guidelines for Psychotherapy With Lesbian, Gay, and Bisexual Clients" (APA, Division 44/Committee on Lesbian, Gay, and Bisexual Concerns Joint Task Force, 2000) provide therapists with a standard of excellence in all aspects of therapeutic work with LGB clients. The set of core conditions of affirmative psychotherapy with LGBT clients serves as a benchmark in providing ethical and effective psychotherapy to LGBT clients. Affirmative psychotherapy provides a valuable means to assist LGBT clients when addressing life span concerns, in coping with psychological distress, and in integrating and managing various aspects of individual identity. Of prime importance in providing affirmative psychotherapy is the therapist's knowledge of professional ethics, of their own competency to practice, and of the biases and prejudices that obstruct the provision of affirmative psychotherapy. In chapter 7, Greene (this volume) examines ethical quandaries that therapists may face in working with LGB clients. The chapter is a unique analysis of professional ethics and of the ways in which sociocultural and personal biases color the lenses through which therapists view LGB clients. Throughout her analysis, what is clear are the insidious effects of sociocultural and personal prejudices (e.g., homophobia, heterosexism, biphobia) that inhibit the practice of affirmative psychotherapy and the detrimental impact of these prejudicial attitudes on client welfare.

In practice, affirmative psychotherapy can be particularly useful in addressing a number of life span and unique issues for LGBT clients, including issues involving career and workplace concerns. In their chapter, Lidderdale, Croteau, Anderson, Tovar-Murray, and Davis provide an enlightening theory of sexual identity management through their Workplace Sexual Identity Management (WSIM) model (chap. 10, this volume). Affirmative psychotherapy incorporating an understanding of the WSIM model may assist counselors and therapists in gaining insights into the variables that influence how LGBT clients manage their sexual identity in their careers. It may also help therapists understand the ways in which they can assist clients in integrating their career identity and sexual orientation. Therefore, integration of the WSIM model within affirmative psychotherapy provides therapists with a thorough and thoughtful look at the personal and contextual factors that influence LGB identity management in the world of work.

Affirmative psychotherapy can also be an important approach to take when working with clients who are in conflict regarding their sexual orientation or sexual identity (Beckstead & Israel, chap. 9, this volume). In providing affirmative counseling and therapy to LGBT clients, most therapists strive to provide appropriate and ethical service (APA, Division 44/Committee on Lesbian, Gay, and Bisexual Concerns Joint Task Force, 2000; APA, 2002; Greene, chap. 7, this volume). Nevertheless, despite the ethical and practice guidelines that outline the principles of appropriate and affirmative psychotherapy for LGBT clients (Greene, chap. 7, this volume; Morrow, 2000), some therapists continue to maintain that homosexuality is a pathology (Nicolosi, Byrd, & Potts, 2000) and to advocate for the benefits of reparative or conversion therapy for LGB clients who wish to adopt a non-LGB identity (Beckstead & Israel, chap. 9, this volume; Beckstead & Morrow, 2004).

Though the subject of conversion therapy as an effective therapeutic approach for achieving its ends is debatable, the ethical use of conversion therapy is not (Greene, chap. 7, this volume). Nor is the quality of the research that claims the efficacy of conversion therapy debatable (Bieschke et al., chap. 12, this volume). More importantly, it is clear that there are negative and injurious sequelae of conversion therapy on LGB clients who experience distress and conflict in managing multiple aspects of their identity (Haldeman, 2004; Shidlo & Schroeder, 2002). In light of the damaging effects of conversion therapy and the less-than-conclusive evidence as to its therapeutic benefits, conversion therapy cannot be regarded as an ethical, viable therapeutic approach for LGBT clients experiencing distress in coping with conflicts in managing multiple aspects of their identity (Bieschke et al., chap. 12, this volume). As such, in no circumstance is reparative or conversion therapy an option when providing affirmative counseling and psychotherapy to LGBT clients in conflict with their religious identity or in any other instance.

In cases in which LGBT clients are in conflict regarding their religious beliefs and identity, the effective practice of affirmative psychotherapy establishes the core conditions in the therapeutic relationship. This allows therapists to best assist clients who are conflicted in managing multiple identity issues in which sexual orientation or sexual identity clashes with religious beliefs and identity. Therefore, alternative approaches to psychotherapy in which the core conditions are not present (e.g., conversion therapies) are neither appropriate nor ethical applications of psychotherapy with LGBT clients and should not be considered in addressing the mental health and life span needs of LGBT clients and individuals.

Affirmative Supervision

The core conditions for providing affirmative psychotherapy can also be extended to providing affirmative supervision. In chapter 14, Halpert, Reinhardt, and Toohey define affirmative supervision and provide an integrated model for its implementation, the Integrative Affirmative Supervision (IAS) model. In the IAS model of supervision, the core conditions for providing affirmative psychotherapy are reflected. Drawing from previous supervision models, the IAS model emphasizes the integration of the core conditions of competence, LGBT affirmation, and openness to attending to sexual orientation issues in establishing and maintaining an effective and affirming supervisory working alliance.

With a more integrative model of affirmative supervision, it is now possible for supervisors and supervisees to attend to the elements of the supervisory working alliance in the same way as it is now possible to attend to the core conditions of providing affirmative psychotherapy. Additionally, with a heuristic for affirmative supervision, it is also possible to design research that examines aspects of the supervisory working alliance and the influence of the core conditions of affirmative supervision on the supervision process (e.g., Efstation, Patton, & Kardash, 1990). The IAS model of supervision also provides interesting implications for the use of affirmative supervision in relation to the effective practice of affirmative psychotherapy (e.g., Patton & Kivlighan, 1997) and its integration within psychology and mental health graduate programs and training curricula (e.g., Phillips, 2000).

Research in Affirmative Psychotherapy

Future practice and research directions in affirmative psychotherapy can have a significant impact on creating timely and effective therapeutic techniques in the provision of affirmative psychotherapy, especially by exploring a number of different areas of research and practice. One such future direction should be an examination of the effectiveness of the core conditions of both affirmative psychotherapy and supervision and of the ways in which they influence the therapeutic and supervisory processes. Process-outcome research is well-suited to examine the variables that may play an important part in influencing the therapeutic and supervisory working alliance and to lend insight into how best to provide and enhance affirmative psychotherapy for LGBT clients.

Another area of research could investigate process-outcome variables of affirmative psychotherapy. This area of exploration could define the salient features of affirmative psychotherapy that have the most significant effect on client outcomes. Process-outcome research that examines the success of a variety of theoretical orientations in providing affirmative psychotherapy can be useful in both practice and training. It may prove particularly useful to examine the working alliance and its role in affirmative psychotherapy. The importance of establishing a strong working alliance has been long held to be significant in determining clients' successful experience in psychotherapy (Bordin, 1979; Gelso & Carter, 1985, 1994). Specifically, in working with LGBT clients, the working alliance is at the core of the therapeutic relationship (Gelso & Mohr, 2001). Establishing a strong working alliance may require unique efforts on the part of the therapist in order to provide affirmative counseling and psychotherapy.

Future research that examines the process-outcome variables for affirmative group therapy with LGBT clients is also needed. The benefits of group therapy for LGB clients are many (DeBord & Perez, 2000), yet the research informing affirmative group therapy has been lacking. Research in this area may help to distinguish the roles of various group therapeutic factors and their impact on client change and group process. For example, examining critical incidents in an LGBT group can lend qualitative data to the attainment of a clearer and richer picture of the group therapeutic process, which may lead to innovative group theories and effective group therapy for LGBT clients.

Last, developing evidence-based guidelines for practice with LGBT clients can be useful for therapists in determining the most effective and efficient means of providing affirmative therapy. Examining the role of theory-based techniques, their application in affirmative psychotherapy, and the efficacy of their application to the unique developmental and situational issues of LGBT clients can be valuable in determining the utility of various approaches in affirmative psychotherapy and in providing a baseline standard of care and practice.

All in all, LGBT-affirmative counseling and psychotherapy require an adherence by therapists to the ethical principles and guidelines that outline appropriate and effective therapy for LGBT clients (APA, Division 44/ Committee on Lesbian, Gay, and Bisexual Concerns Joint Task Force, 2000; HBIGDA, 2001a, 2001b). Perhaps even more importantly, in affirmative psychotherapy, the therapist is an agent of social change. By advocating for the needs of LGBT people and the LGBT community, therapists provide an invaluable contribution to LGBT communities by striving to dismantle the harmful effects of oppression and discrimination toward LGBT persons and by striving toward the goals of social parity and justice.

CONCLUSION: HAS PSYCHOLOGY SUCCEEDED IN MAKING LGBT ISSUES BORING?

I would like to conclude this chapter by revisiting Barón's challenge and question: "Has psychology reached its goal in making LGB issues 'boring'?" Without question, the answer is—no. Although the amount of scholarly and research literature in LGBT psychology has seen an increase since the first edition of the handbook, there are still gains to be made in incorporating LGBT issues within the mainstream of psychological scholarship and practice. This is particularly true for transgender issues. It is also true that the scholarly literature in transgender psychology is still in need of exploration, expansion, integration and acceptance. With this answer comes a continued challenge for the profession of counseling and psychology to truly make LGBT issues boring.

Throughout this second edition, we have attempted to provide practitioners and scholars with something more than an update of the core areas for theory, practice, and research. Our attempts have focused on bringing to light the myriad identities that LGBT individuals possess, the importance that community and culture play in identity formation and development, and the need to explore evidence-based practices of affirmative psychotherapy. We have highlighted the tensions that sometimes exist when LGBT-affirmative psychotherapy intersects with religious beliefs. In doing so, we maintain our belief that affirmative psychotherapy can only exist within the ethical and practice guidelines outlined in a number of chapters in this book and in the "Guidelines for Psychotherapy With Lesbian, Gay, and Bisexual Clients" (APA, Division 44/Committee on Lesbian, Gay, and Bisexual Concerns Joint Task Force, 2000). Finally, we have attempted to examine the role of public policy and the growing ramifications of legal and political influences in the lives of LGBT persons, the role of the therapist in working to understand the complexity of these issues, and these issues' influence on the therapeutic process. Although we recognize the importance of these areas in working effectively with LGBT clients, perhaps no one role for therapists providing affirmative psychology is more important than their role as agents of social change.

As persons striving toward prosocial change, mental health professionals assume the tenets of affirmative psychotherapy and its core conditions. As agents of prosocial change, mental health professionals must be aware of their responsibility and duty to abide by ethical guidelines of practice and to promote the ethical practice of others. As agents of prosocial change, mental health professionals should be aware of their role within society and the influence of their own personal power and influence in initiating and supporting social change that strives for the affirmation and equity for all.

Perhaps, though, in addressing the needs of LGBT clients, it is also the responsibility of counselors and psychologists to advocate for the needs of LGBT individuals in society, to provide a voice for those LGBT individuals who have been silenced, and to work toward social justice and equity for LGBT communities. In the end, our belief is that the most effective practice of affirmative psychotherapy is undertaken by the therapist who is fully cognizant of the social and personal effects of homophobia, biphobia, and transphobia on LGBT persons, who is willing to accept the responsibility to disarm the powerful ramifications of unawareness and prejudice toward LGBT persons in society, and who assumes the role as an agent of prosocial change in counteracting the deleterious consequences of ignorance and oppression that continue to exist in our society.

REFERENCES

American Psychological Association. (2002). Ethical principles of psychologists and code of conduct. *American Psychologist, 47,* 1597–1611.

American Psychological Association, Division 44/Committee on Lesbian, Gay, and Bisexual Concerns Joint Task Force on Guidelines for Psychotherapy With Lesbian, Gay, and Bisexual Clients. (2000). Guidelines for psychotherapy with lesbian, gay, and bisexual clients. *American Psychologist, 55,* 1440–1451.

Bailey, R. W. (2000, February). *Out and voting, II: The gay, lesbian, and bisexual vote in congressional elections, 1990–1998.* (Available from the National Gay and Lesbian Task Force, 1325 Massachusetts Avenue NW, Suite 600, Washington, DC 20005.)

Barón, A. (1991). The challenge: To make homosexuality boring. *The Counseling Psychologist, 19,* 239–244.

Beckstead, A. L., & Morrow, S. L. (2004). Mormon clients' experiences of conversion therapy: The need for a new treatment approach. *The Counseling Psychologist, 32,* 651–690.

Biaggio, M., Orchard, S., Larson, J., Petrino, K., & Mihara, R. (2003). Guidelines for gay/lesbian/bisexual-affirmative educational practices in graduate psychology programs. *Professional Psychology: Research and Practice, 34,* 548–554.

Bieschke, K. J., Croteau, J. M., Lark, J. S., & Vandiver, B. J. (2005). Toward a discourse of sexual orientation equity in the counseling professions. In J. M. Croteau, J. S. Lark, M. A. Lidderdale, & Y. B. Chung (Eds.), *Deconstructing heterosexism in the counseling professions: A narrative approach* (pp. 189–209). Thousand Oaks, CA: Sage.

Bordin, E. S. (1979). The generalizability of the psychoanalytic concept of the working alliance. *Psychotherapy: Theory, Research, and Practice, 16,* 252–260.

Brown, T. (2002). A proposed model of bisexual identity development that elaborates on experiential differences of women and men. *Journal of Bisexuality, 2*(4), 67–91.

Bullough, B., & Bullough, V. (1993). *Crossdressing, sex, and gender.* Philadelphia: University of Pennsylvania Press.

Bullough, V. L. (2000, July–September). Transgenderism and the concept of gender. *International Journal of Transgenderism, 3,* article 3. Retrieved April 29, 2005, from http://www.symposion.com/ijt/gilbert/bullough.htm

Carroll, L., Gilroy, P. J., & Ryan, J. (2002). Counseling transgendered, transsexual, and gender-variant clients. *Journal of Counseling and Development, 80,* 131–139.

Cass, V. C. (1979). Homosexual identity formation: A theoretical model. *Journal of Homosexuality, 4*(3), 219–235.

Croteau, J. M., Bieschke, K. J., Phillips, J. C., & Lark, J. S. (1998). Moving beyond pioneering: Empirical and theoretical perspectives on lesbian, gay, and affirmative training. *The Counseling Psychologist, 26,* 707–711.

Currah, P., & Minter, S. (2000, June). *Transgender equality: A handbook for activists and policymakers.* (Available from the National Gay and Lesbian Task Force, 1325 Massachusetts Avenue NW, Suite 600, Washington, DC 20005.)

Davidson, M. G. (2000). Religion and spirituality. In R. M. Perez, K. A. DeBord, & K. J. Bieschke (Eds.), *Handbook of counseling and psychotherapy with lesbian, gay, and bisexual clients* (pp. 409–433). Washington, DC: American Psychological Association.

DeBord, K. A., & Perez, R. M. (2000). Group counseling theory and practice with lesbian, gay, and bisexual clients. In R. M. Perez, K. A. DeBord, & K. J. Bieschke (Eds.), *Handbook of counseling and psychotherapy with lesbian, gay, and bisexual clients* (pp. 183–206). Washington, DC: American Psychological Association.

Douce, L. A. (2004). Society of Counseling Psychology Division 17 of APA Presidential Address 2003: Globalization of counseling psychology. *The Counseling Psychologist, 32*, 142–152.

Efstation, J. F., Patton, M. J., & Kardash, C. M. (1990). Measuring the working alliance in counselor supervision. *Journal of Counseling Psychology, 37*, 322–329.

Fassinger, R. E. (1991). The hidden minority: Issues and challenges in working with lesbian women and gay men. *The Counseling Psychologist, 19*, 157–176.

Fassinger, R. E., & Miller, B. A. (1996). Validation of an inclusive model of homosexual identity formation on a sample of gay men. *Journal of Homosexuality, 32*(2), 53–78.

Firestein, B. A. (1996). *Bisexuality: The psychology and politics of an invisible minority.* Thousand Oaks, CA: Sage.

Fox, R. C. (1996). Bisexuality in perspective: A review of theory and research. In B. A. Firestein (Ed.), *Bisexuality: The psychology and politics of an invisible minority* (pp. 3–50). Thousand Oaks, CA: Sage.

Fukuyama, M. A., & Ferguson, A. D. (2000). Lesbian, gay, and bisexual people of color: Understanding cultural complexity and managing multiple oppressions. In R. M. Perez, K. A. DeBord, & K. J. Bieschke (Eds.), *Handbook of counseling and psychotherapy with lesbian, gay, and bisexual clients* (pp. 81–105). Washington, DC: American Psychological Association.

Gainor, K. A. (2000). Including transgender issues in lesbian, gay, and bisexual psychology: Implications for clinical practice and training. In B. Greene & G. L. Croom (Eds.), *Education, research, and practice in lesbian, gay, bisexual, and transgendered psychology: A resource manual* (Vol. 5, pp. 131–160). Thousand Oaks, CA: Sage.

Garnets, L. D. (2002). Sexual orientation in perspective. *Cultural Diversity and Ethnic Minority Psychology, 8*, 115–129.

Gelso, C. J., & Carter, J. A. (1985). The relationship in counseling and psychotherapy: Components, consequences, and theoretical antecedents. *The Counseling Psychologist, 13*, 155–244.

Gelso, C. J., & Carter, J. A. (1994). Components of the psychotherapy relationship: Their interaction and unfolding during treatment. *Journal of Counseling Psychology, 41*, 296–306.

Gelso, C. J., & Mohr, J. J. (2001). The working alliance and the transference/countertransference relationship: Their manifestation with racial/ethnic and sexual orientation minority clients and therapists. *Applied & Preventive Psychology, 10*, 51–68.

Goldfried, M. R. (2001). Integrating gay, lesbian, bisexual issues into mainstream psychology. *American Psychologist, 56*, 977–988.

Gonsiorek, J. C., & Rudolph, J. R. (1991). Homosexual identity: Coming out and other developmental events. In J. C. Gonsiorek & J. D. Weinrich (Eds.), *Homosexuality: Research implications for public policy* (pp. 161–176). Thousand Oaks, CA: Sage.

Goodman, L. A., Liang, B., Helms, J. E., Latta, R. E., Sparks, E., & Weintraub, S. R. (2004). Training counseling psychologists as social justice agents: Feminist and multicultural principles in action. *The Counseling Psychologist, 32,* 793–837.

Haldeman, D. C. (2004). When sexual and religious orientations collide: Considerations in working with conflicted same-sex attracted male clients. *The Counseling Psychologist, 32,* 691–715.

Harper, G. W., Jerenwall, N., & Zea, M. C. (2004). Giving voice to emerging science and theory for lesbian, gay, and bisexual people of color. *Cultural Diversity and Ethnic Minority Psychology, 10,* 187–199.

Harry Benjamin International Gender Dysphoria Association. (2001a). *Ethical guidelines for members of the Harry Benjamin International Gender Dysphoria Association, Inc.* Retrieved April 9, 2005, from http://www.hbigda.org/ethics.cfm

Harry Benjamin International Gender Dysphoria Association. (2001b). *The Harry Benjamin International Gender Dysphoria Association's standards of care for gender identity disorders, sixth version.* Retrieved April 9, 2005, from http://www.hbigda.org/pdf/socv6.pdf

Israel, G. E., & Tarver, D. E. (Eds.). (1997). *Transgender care: Recommended guidelines, practical information, and personal accounts.* Philadelphia: Temple University Press.

Jerome, L. W., DeLeon, P. H., James, L. C., Folen, R., Earles, J., & Gedney, J. J. (2000). The coming of age of telecommunications in psychological research and practice. *American Psychologist, 55,* 407–421.

McCarn, S. R., & Fassinger, R. E. (1996). Revisioning sexual minority identity formation: A new model of lesbian identity and its implications for counseling and research. *The Counseling Psychologist, 24,* 508–534.

Monro, S. (2000). Theorizing transgender diversity: Towards a social model of health. *Sexual and Relationship Therapy, 15,* 33–45.

Morris., J. F., Waldo, C. R., & Rothblum, E. D. (2001). A model of predictors and outcomes of outness among lesbian and bisexual women. *American Journal of Orthopsychiatry, 71,* 61–71.

Morrow, S. L. (2000). First do no harm: Therapist issues in psychotherapy with lesbian, gay, and bisexual clients. In R. M. Perez, K. A. DeBord, & K. J. Bieschke (Eds.), *Handbook of counseling and psychotherapy with lesbian, gay, and bisexual clients* (pp. 137–156). Washington, DC: American Psychological Association.

Murphy, J. A., Rawlings, E. I., & Howe, S. R. (2002). A survey of clinical psychologists on treating lesbian, gay, and bisexual clients. *Professional Psychology: Research and Practice, 33,* 183–189.

Namaste, V. K. (2000). *Invisible lives: The erasure of transsexual and transgendered people.* Chicago: University of Chicago Press.

Nicolosi, J., Byrd, A. D., & Potts, R. W. (2000). Beliefs and practices of therapists who practice sexual reorientation psychotherapy. *Psychological Reports, 86,* 689–702.

Ochs, R. (1996). Biphobia: It goes more than two ways. In B. A. Firestein (Ed.), *Bisexuality: The psychology and politics of an invisible minority* (pp. 217–239). Thousand Oaks, CA: Sage.

Pachankis, J. E., & Goldfried, M. R. (2004). Clinical issues in working with lesbian, gay, and bisexual clients. *Psychotherapy: Theory, Research, Practice, Training, 41,* 227–246.

Parks, C. A., Hughes, T. L., & Matthews, A. K. (2004). Race/ethnicity and sexual orientation: Intersecting identities. *Cultural Diversity and Ethnic Minority Psychology, 10,* 241–254.

Patton, M. J., & Kivlighan, D. M. (1997). Relevance of the supervisory alliance to the counseling alliance and to treatment adherence in counselor training. *Journal of Counseling Psychology, 44,* 108–115.

Perez, R. M. (2001, November). Issues in counseling and psychotherapy with lesbian, gay, and bisexual clients. *Clinician's Research Digest, 1.*

Perez, R. M., DeBord, K. A., & Bieschke, K. J. (Eds.). (2000). *Handbook of counseling and psychotherapy with lesbian, gay, and bisexual clients.* Washington, DC: American Psychological Association.

Phillips, J. C. (2000). Training issues and considerations. In R. M. Perez, K. A. DeBord, & K. J. Bieschke (Eds.), *Handbook of counseling and psychotherapy with lesbian, gay, and bisexual clients* (pp. 337–358). Washington, DC: American Psychological Association.

Potoczniak, M. J., Mourot, J. E., Crosbie-Burnett, M., & Potoczniak, D. J. (2003). Legal and psychological perspectives on same-sex domestic violence: A multisystemic approach. *Journal of Family Psychology, 17,* 252–259.

Riggle, E. D. B., Rostosky, S. S., Prather, R. A., & Hamrin, R. (2005). The execution of legal documents by sexual minority individuals. *Psychology, Public Policy, and Law, 11,* 138–163.

Rosario, M., Schrimshaw, E. W., & Hunter, J. (2004). Ethnic/racial differences in the coming-out process of lesbian, gay, and bisexual youths: A comparison of sexual identity development over time. *Cultural Diversity and Ethnic Minority Psychology, 10,* 215–228.

Shidlo, A., & Schroeder, M. (2002). Changing sexual orientation: A consumer's report. *Professional Psychology: Research and Practice, 33,* 249–259.

Smith, N. G., & Ingram, K. M. (2004). Workplace heterosexism and adjustment among lesbian, gay, and bisexual individuals: The role of unsupportive social interactions. *Journal of Counseling Psychology, 51,* 57–67.

Yali, A. M., & Revenson, T. W. (2004). How changes in population demographics will impact health psychology: Incorporating a broader notion of cultural competence into the field. *Health Psychology, 23,* 147–155.

AUTHOR INDEX

Numbers in italics refer to listings in the reference sections.

Gonsiorek, J. C., 21, *46*, 73, 80, 81, 88,
    211, 212, *216*, 318, 328, *338*, 404,
    406, *416*
Goodchilds, J., 186, *197*, 202, 203, 205, *216*
Goodenow, C., 92, *116*
Goodman, L. A., 407, *416*
Goodridge v. Department of Public Health,
    361, *375*
Goodwill, K. A., 237, *241*
Goodyear, R. K., 347, *358*
Gordon, N., 36, *46*
Gottlieb, M. C., 191, *199*, 227, 228, 230,
    234, *242*, 325, *339*
Gough, H. G., 298, *314*
Gove, P. B., *338*
Green, B. C., 95, *112*, 234, *241*
Green, J., 151, 161, 167, *171*, 279, 280, *287*
Green, R. J., 154, *171*, 226, 233, 238, *241*
Greenberg, D. F., 20, 25, *46*
Greene, B., 32, 33, *46*, 56, 59, 60, 61, 64,
    67, 94, 95, 96, 98, *113*, *114*, 182,
    183, 185, 186, 187, 188, 189, 190,
    191, *197*, *198*, 210, 213, *217*, 223,
    241, 250, *268*, 382, 383, *395*
Grey, L., 166, *171*
Griffin, P., 249, 251, 255, *268*
Griffith, K. H., 246, 250, 265, 266, *268*
Grossman, A., 76, 88
Gruskin, E. P., 36, *46*
Grzegorek, J. L., 185, *197*, 207, *215*, 293,
    294, 310, *313*, 382, *394*
Gurevich, M., 30, *44*, 93, 96, *112*
Gurmankin, A. D., 369, *375*
Guzman, R., 26, *47*
Gwadz, M., 52, 68

Haan, W., 164, *171*
Hack, T., 92, *116*
Hackett, G., 251, 265, *267*, *268*, 298, 300,
    311, *314*
Halberstam, J., 159, *171*
Haldeman, D. C., 33, *46*, 83, 88, 182, 183,
    185, 191, 192, *198*, 205, 206, 213,
    217, 224, 225, 226, 228, 229, 230,
    232, 235, 238, *241*, 301, 310, *314*,
    318, 323, 324, 325, 326, *338*, *339*,
    382, *395*, 405, 411, *417*
Hale, C. J., 159, *171*
Hale, K., 92, *116*
Hall, R. E., 189, *198*
Hamilton, J., 53, 64, *67*

Hamrin, R., 407, *418*
Hancock, K. A., 186, *197*, 202, 203, 205,
    216, 389, *395*
Hanjorgiris, W. F., 80, 89, 186, *199*, 209,
    218
Hansen, W. D., 327, *338*
Harden, J., 319, 320, 322, 323, 324, 325,
    328, 336, 337, *338*
Harper, G. W., 406, *417*
Harris, D., 72, 86, 88, 232, *240*
Harris, E. L., 135, *142*
Harry Benjamin International Gender
    Dysphoria Association, 277, *287*,
    409, 413, *417*
Harry, J., 55, *67*
Hart, S., 36, *46*, 382, 383, 387, *396*
Hauenstein, A. L., 246, 247, *268*
Hausman, B. L., 147, 153, *171*
Hayes, J. A., 224, 226, *243*, 299, 302, 303,
    314, *315*, 326, *339*
Hays, R. B., 26, 35, *48*, 391, *396*
Hebl, M. R., 246, 250, 265, 266, *268*
Hecker, L., 232, *240*
Hegland, J. E., 163, *171*
Heilbrun, A. B., Jr., 298, *314*
Hekma, G., 150, 151, 158, *171*
Helms, J. E., 260, *268*, 407, *416*
Hembert, J., 154, *172*
Hemmings, C., 121, *142*
Hequembourg, A. L., 53, *67*
Herdt, G., 43, *46*, 149, 156, *171*
Herek, G. M., 30, *46*, 55, 56, *67*, 85, 88,
    98, *114*, 201, 202, 208, 213, 214,
    217, 382, *395*
Herek, G. W., 360, 365, *375*
Herman, D., 79, 88
Hershberger, S. L., 26, *46*
Hertz, R., 120, 129, 131, *142*
Hill, D. B., 162, 163, *171*
Hill, M., 319, 320, 322, 323, 324, 325,
    328, 336, 337, *338*
Hirschfeld, M., 150
Hitchings, P., 342, *358*
Hoburg, R., 130, *142*
Holden, J. M., 211, *215*, 247, *267*
Holloway, E. L., 342, 347, 348, 349, 351,
    357, *358*
Honnold, J. A., 36, *44*
Hooker, E., 24, 382, *395*
Horowitz, S. M., 104, 105, *114*, 127, *142*
House, R. M., 347, 348, 349, 351, 357, *358*
Howard, J., 363, *375*

Mattison, A. M., 26, *48*

Mays, V. M., 36, *44*, 135, *143*, 293, *313*

McAnulty, R., 41, *48*

McCarn, S. R., 52, 55, 68, 80, 88, 209, *217*, 250, 260, 269, 404, *417*

McClanahan, M. K., 7, *11*, 185, *197*, 206, 207, *215*, 218, 231, 233, *244*, 293, 294, 310, *313*, 382, *394*

McConaghy, N., 153, *170*

McCormick, B., 301, 302, 303, 304, *315*

McCourt, F., 76, 86, 88

McCrary, S. I., 247, *270*

McDaniel, J. S., 388, *396*

McDavis, R. J., 205, *218*

McDonald, G. J., 52, 68

McGaughey, D., 165, *171*

McIntosh, P. E., 333, *339*

McKenna, W., 28, *46*

McKirnan, D. J., 133, *144*

McLaughlin, L., 155, 156, 162, *172*

McLean, K., 107, *115*

McLeod, A., 299, 300, *313*

McWhirter, B. T., 298, 299, *313*

Meezan, W., 91, 104, *115*

Meyer, I. H., 35, *47*, 57, 68, 277, 287, 371, *376*

Meyer, W., 153, 154, *172*

Meyerowitz, J., 147, 151, 152, 157, 161, 162, *172*

Middleton, L., 277, *288*

Mihara, R., 184, 185, *197*, 380, 381, 386, *394*, 400, *415*

Milk, H., 78

Miller, B. A., 404, *416*

Miller, M., 98, *117*, 123, 126, *143*

Miller, N., 73, 89

Miller, R. L., 126, 133, 134, *144*

Mills, T. C., 34, *47*

Milsom, A., 294, 295, 296, 297, 311, *314*

Mindes, E. J., 390, *395*

Minter, S., 406, *415*

Mitchell, K., 247, *269*

Miville, M. L., 223, 227, *242*

Moats, D., 361, *376*

Moberley, E., 228, *242*

Mobley, M., 318, *339*

Mohr, J. J., 106, *114*, 206, 210, *217*, *219*, 300, 310, *314*, 412, *416*

Monro, S., 402, *417*

Moon, L., 81, 89

Morales, E. S., 56, 68, 95, *115*

Morales, L., 223, *242*

Morgan, K. S., 391, *396*

Morris, J. F., 382, 383, 387, *396*, 402, 404, *417*

Morrow, S. L., 33, *47*, 226, 228, 229, 230, 233, 234, 235, *239*, *242*, 301, 302, 303, 305, 306, 307, 308, 310, 312, *313*, *314*, 325, 326, 338, 339, 383, 389, *396*, 411, *415*, *417*

Moscone, G., 78

Moss, J. F., 105, *115*

Mourot, J. E., 406, *418*

Mulick, P. S., 30, *48*, 106, *115*

Mundhenk, R., 126, 133, 134, *144*

Murdoch, J., 359, 360, *376*

Murphy, J. A., 184, *199*, 389, *396*, 400, *417*

Murphy, T. F., 225, 227, *242*

Murray, S. O., 73, 75, 89, 149, *170*

Myers, M. F., 233, *241*

Namaste, V. K., 165, *172*, 402, *417*

Nanda, S., 149, *172*

Nangeroni, N. R., 164, *173*

National Association of Social Workers, 383, *396*

National Coalition of Anti-Violence Programs, 280, *288*

National Gay and Lesbian Task Force, 360, 362, 363, *376*

Nauta, M. M., 247, *269*

Nearing, R., 102, *115*

Neidig, J. L., 390, *395*

Nelson, N. J., 163, *171*

Nestle, J., 159, 160, 167, *173*

New York Times, 333, *339*

Newport, F., 381, *396*

Newton, E., 165, *173*

Nichols, M., 94, *115*

Nicolosi, J., 191, 192, *199*, 228, *242*, 302, 303, 305, 306, 307, 308, 312, *314*, 411, *417*

Niebuhr, G., 333, *339*

Nordheimer, J., 123, *143*

North, G., 123, 126, *143*

Nottebaum, L., 301, 302, 303, 304, 305, 307, *315*

Nussbaum, M. C., 323, 332, *339*

O'Brien, J., 163, *173*

SUBJECT INDEX

"Default heterosexual identity," 80
Diagnostic and Statistical Manual on Mental Disorders (DSM), 324
    Gender Identity Disorder in, 35, 155–156, 284
    homosexuality as mental disorder in, 35, 155, 383
    Transvestic Fetishism in, 35
Disabilities, physical
    cultural orientation and, 33–34
    among gay males, 76
    lesbians with, 64
Discrimination
    Amendment 2, 79
    against bisexual females, 94–95
    after "coming out," 56
    "double," against bisexuals, 107, 124–125
    under ENDA, 127
    against lesbians, 40
    sexual orientation, legal regulations against, 42
    in workplace, for LGBT, 39–41
Diversity
    in LGBT community, 403
    LGBT counseling and, influence on, 185–190
Domestic partner benefits, 40, 361–362
Donor insemination, 53
"Don't ask, don't tell," 365, 385
"Down Low," 135
Drag kings, 152
Drag queens, 152
Dress Codes of Three Girlhoods: My Mother's, My Father's and Mine (N. Howey), 285
DSM. *See Diagnostic and Statistical Manual on Mental Disorders*

Eating disorders, among transgender individuals, 280
Educational systems, gay-straight alliances in, 62
EEF. *See* Erickson Educational Foundation
Employment. *See also* Vocational psychology; WSIM
    bisexuals and, 40–41
    "coming out" and, 56
    discrimination against LGBT in, 39–41
    for transgender individuals, 41, 282
    WSIM model for, 180

Employment Non-Discrimination Act (ENDA), 127, 372
Erickson Educational Foundation (EEF), 161
Essentialism
    sexual orientation and, 20–21
    social-constructionism v., 20–21
Ethics
    APA code, 185–186, 196, 207, 272, 318, 337
    of conversion therapy, 191–193, 308
    for counselors, 323
    decision-making models for, 319–337
    problem definitions, 323–324
    solution development, 325
Ethnicity
    "coming out" influenced by, 59–61
    community development influenced by, 60–61
    in cultural orientation, 32–33
Ethnocultural Assessment, 211
Exodus International, conversion therapy by, 304

"Family of choice"
    adoption as, 363
    for lesbians, 64–65
Family support
    "Coming out" and, 212
    "families of choice," for lesbians, 64–65
    for LGBT individuals, 364–366
    for transgender individuals, 278–279
Fatherhood, for gay males, 38
Females. *See also* Bisexuals, female
    African American, 34
    bisexual, 21, 91–93
    sexual orientation changes for, 54
Female-to-males (FTMs), 39
"Friendship circles," 58
Frye, Phyllis, 161

Gay-Affirmative Model, 343–344
Gay and Lesbian Alliance Against Defamation (GLAAD), 84
Gay and Lesbian Public Awareness Project, 84
Gay bars, 74, 82
Gay males, 21
    African American female views on, 34
    bisexual males and, 125–126

of color, 75–76
"coming out" for, 77
community development among, 72–80
cultural backlash against, 78
fatherhood as goal for, 38
health issues for, 35
HIV/AIDS and, 35
identity development for, 80–81
MSMs v., 23
"passing" among, 74–75
physical disabilities among, 76
self-labeling among, 23
sexual expression among, 38
SSA v., 72, 75
subcultural communities among, 73
in urban areas, 82
Gay Pride celebrations, 74, 82–84
Gay-Straight alliances, in educational
    systems, 62
Gender, 273
    counselor attitudes by, for LGBT
        clients, 299
"Gender fundamentalism," 29
Gender identity disorder, 35, 155–156, 284
Gender orientation, 27–29
    for bisexuals, 29
    for transgender individuals, 28
Gender reorientation surgery (SRS). See
    Sex reassignment surgery
Gender variance, 273
    history of, 149–150
    language ambiguity as part of, 151
GLAAD. See Gay and Lesbian Alliance
    Against Defamation
"Great Gay Migration," 57–58
Group counseling. See Counseling, group
"Guidelines for Psychotherapy With Lesbian,
    Gay, and Bisexual Clients" (Ameri-
    can Psychological Association), 24,
    187–188, 207, 372, 410, 414

The Handbook of Sexuality-Related Mea-
    sures, 353
Harry Benjamin International Gen-
    der Dysphoria Association
    (HBIGDA), 154, 161, 274, 284
Hate crimes, 42
    LGBT visibility as factor in, 83
HBIGDA. See Harry Benjamin Interna-
    tional Gender Dysphoria Associa-
    tion

health care standards of, 281
Health care
    HBIGDA standards, 281
    for transgender individuals, 281–282
Health issues. See also HIV/AIDS
    for bisexuals, 36
    for gay males, 35
    for lesbians, 36
    for transgender individuals, 36
Heterocentrism, 71
    "default heterosexual identity" and, 80
Heteronormative culture, 98
Heterosexism, 98
    bisexual females and, 94, 97–99
    in clinical research, 183–184
    conversion therapy and, 193–194
    in counseling, 182–185, 202–208
    sexual orientation and, influenced by,
        222
    in therapeutic practice, 184–185
Heterosexuality. See also Heterosexual males
    bisexual females and, 97–99, 101–102
    Identity development for, 206
Heterosexual males
    bisexual males and, 126
    cross-dressing among, 149, 157–158
    same-sex experiences of, 120–121 (See
        also Gay males)
HIV/AIDS. See Human immunodeficiency
    virus/Acquired immune deficiency
    syndrome
Homophobia, in Conflictional Situation
    Model, 346
Homosexuality. See also Gay males;
    Lesbians
    American Psychological Association
        designation of, 24
    as destructive lifestyle, 382
    in DSM, as mental disorder, 35, 155,
        383
    as "inversion," 150
    stereotyping for, 189
Homosexuality and Hope, 386
"Homosexual pollution," 86
The Hose and Heels Club, 157
Human immunodeficiency virus/Acquired
    immune deficiency syndrome
    (HIV/AIDS)
    bisexual males and, influence on, 123
    community development influenced
        by, 79
    among gay males, 35

ABOUT THE EDITORS

Kathleen J. Bieschke, PhD, is an associate professor of counseling psychology at Pennsylvania State University, a licensed psychologist, and director of Clinical Training for Penn State's counseling psychology PhD program, which is accredited by the American Psychological Association. Dr. Bieschke has published over 40 professional journal articles, chapters, and edited books and has delivered approximately 100 professional presentations. In addition to working with gay, lesbian, and bisexual individuals in both a college counseling and a private practice setting, Dr. Bieschke has written about and conducted research pertaining to the delivery of affirmative counseling and psychotherapy to gay, lesbian, and bisexual clients. She is a fellow of the American Psychological Association (Division 17, Society of Counseling Psychology) and currently serves as the vice president for Education and Training for Division 17.

Ruperto M. Perez, PhD, is director of the Counseling Center at the Georgia Institute of Technology. He previously served as assistant director for clinical services and clinical assistant professor in the Counseling Center at the University of Florida and as counseling services coordinator and training director in the Counseling and Testing Center at the University of Georgia. He has authored various publications; presented a number of programs; and provided consultation in the areas of diversity, multiculturalism, and cunseling lesbian, gay, bisexual, and transgender clients. He is a fellow of the American Psychological Association (Division 17, Society of Counseling Psychology) and member of the American College Personnel Association, Commission for Counseling and Psychological Services.

Kurt A. DeBord, PhD, is an associate professor of psychology at Lincoln University, a historically Black university in Jefferson City, Missouri. His highest professional priority is quality teaching. He has published and presented research on the teaching of psychology. He is an active member of the American Psychological Association Division 51 (the Society for the Psychological Study of Men and Masculinity). He is a licensed psychologist in the state of Missouri and provides consultation and training at the University of Missouri's Counseling Center.